Field G

Be

of Great Britain and Ireland

Bloomsbury Wildlife Guides

Field Guide to the Bees

of Great Britain and Ireland

Steven Falk
Illustrated by **Richard Lewington**

B L O O M S B U R Y

Bloomsbury Natural History
An imprint of Bloomsbury Publishing Plc

50 Bedford Square   1385 Broadway
London   New York
WC1B 3DP   NY 10018
UK   USA

www.bloomsbury.com

BLOOMSBURY and the Diana logo are trademarks
of Bloomsbury Publishing Plc

First published 2015
Reprinted with corrections 2016,2017

HB: ISBN 978-1-9103-8902-7
PB: ISBN 978-1-9103-8903-4

4 6 8 10 9 7 5

Cartography by Martin Brown

Edited and designed by D & N Publishing, Baydon,
Wiltshire

Printed in China by C&C Offset Printing Co., Ltd.

AUTHOR'S DEDICATION AND ACKNOWLEDGEMENTS
To Annie and Louis, for their love and support.

Many people and institutions have helped me to become
familiar with British and Irish bees over a period of some forty
years. I am particularly grateful to David Notton of the
Natural History Museum, London, and the entomological
staff of Oxford University Museum (notably Darren Mann and
James Hogan) for allowing me to examine their collections
on various occasions and loaning key specimens to allow
closer scrutiny. Many entomologists provided support,
information and images specifically for the book, the key
ones being Geoff Allen, Dr Michael Archer, David Baldock,
Ian Beavis, Paul Brock, Bex Cartwright, Ian Cheeseborough,
Phill Clayton, Carl Clee, Ian Cross, Jeremy Early, Rosie
Earwaker, Mike Edwards, George Else, Rebecca Evans, Bryan
Formstone, Nikki Gammans, Professor Dave Goulson, Henrik
Gyurkovics, Iain Hamlin, Kara Hardy, Martin Harvey, Louise
Hislop, Cathy Horsley, Bernhard Jacobi, Martin Jenner, Gus
Jones, Nigel Jones, Andy Jukes, Adrian Knowles, Murdo
Macdonald, Kevin McGee, Penny Metal, John Oates, Nick
Owens, Professor Rob Paxton, Ash Perkins, Ed Phillips, Sandy
Rae, Tim Ransom, Ray Reeves, Stuart Roberts, Judith and Elva
Robinson, Paddy Saunders, Gill Smart, Bo Söderström, Alan
Stubbs, Ian Tew, Mark Tunmore, Jaco Visser, John Walters,
Dr Paul Williams, Robin Williams, Tom Wood.

Other organisations that have provided support include
Buglife (my former colleagues who do so much to conserve
British pollinators), the Bumblebee Conservation Trust, the
Centre for Ecology and Hydrology (particular thanks to
Richard Pywell, Ben Woodcock, Claire Carvell and Helen
Roy), the Irish National Biodiversity Data Centre (Una
Fitzpatrick and Tom Murray), the National Trust (Andy Foster
and various reserve and area managers), Natural England
(Jon Curson, Jon Webb and various reserve managers), the
Jersey Government Department of Environment, the Jersey
National Trust, the Royal Society for the Protection of Birds
(assorted conservation officers and reserve staff) and
Warwickshire Museum (Jon Radley).

I would also like to thank Richard Lewington for his
patience and understanding – many more illustrations were
required than was initially anticipated, and working from
often old and distorted or discoloured specimens is
especially challenging.

Steven Falk

ARTIST'S DEDICATION AND ACKNOWLEDGEMENTS
To Georgina and Alexandra.

I would like to thank the Golden Bottle Trust (Tony Hoare),
Kate Lampard, Buglife (Matt Shardlow), and the Oxford
University Museum of Natural History (Darren Mann and
Amoret Spooner).

Richard Lewington

The author and artist would also like to express thanks to
Andrew and Anne Branson, and Katy Roper, for their
patience and enthusiasm during the preparation of this
challenging book, and to the production team at
D & N Publishing, including David Price-Goodfellow and
Shane O'Dwyer for their superb design input, and Hugh
Brazier for meticulous copy-editing.

CONTENTS

PREFACE

Most people are amazed to discover that we have over 270 species of bee in Britain and Ireland, and that bumblebees and the Honey Bee account for only about one-tenth of that figure. They are also surprised to learn that over a quarter of our bee species do not collect pollen or make nests but are 'cuckoos' of other bee species, or that some of our so-called 'solitary' species are actually social, or that some bees look more like wasps. Yet bees are all around us, and even in a flowery urban garden you stand a chance of seeing a variety of species from several genera, including some of those cuckoos. The increasing popularity of wildlife gardening and 'bee hotels' means that gardens are now one of the few habitats where bee numbers might actually be increasing – and it is a sobering fact that today bees often do better in suburban areas than in the intensively farmed landscapes that surround them.

Why record bees? First of all, it is a fascinating activity that will help you to understand the countryside better and potentially take you to some stunning wildlife sites. And we also know that many bees (and not just the Honey Bee) are important pollinators of our crops, especially fruit trees, Oil-seed Rape and cultivated legumes like Broad Bean and Pea. They also help pollinate our wild flowers and garden flowers. But we know that many bees are declining, and that data are often patchy and out of date. We need more amateur recorders to provide us with better distributional information and better data on changes in abundance. The various monitoring schemes for birds, butterflies and moths and, more recently, bumblebees, are models of what we need for bees as a whole.

The national pollinator strategies that are emerging for the individual UK countries place a big emphasis on monitoring abundance and change. They also recognise that amateur recorders need to be involved in this process, and that those recorders need more support and resources to do this. But the lack of user-friendly resources for identifying British and Irish bees other than bumblebees has hampered the study and recording of bees. The last comprehensive treatment was *The Hymenoptera Aculeata of the British Islands*, written by Edward Saunders in 1896!

The need for an up-to-date guide to all British bees is thus an urgent one, and we feel an immense sense of privilege to have been provided with this opportunity. Do not be put off by the dichotomous keys. You do not need to use them to enjoy this book, but if you do buy a microscope and start trying to use them, you may be surprised how quickly you will learn to master them and the hidden world of beauty and fascination that is revealed within magnified bees.

Steven Falk and Richard Lewington

Andrena cineraria, one of the most important pollinators of Oil-seed Rape.

This book follows in the footsteps of several very popular *British Wildlife* field guides covering moths, butterflies, dragonflies and garden wildlife in which a 'match your insect to the picture' approach has tended to prevail. This can work well for large insects identifiable to species level using the naked eye or a hand lens. But whilst it is possible to identify some bees this way, the vast majority are too small or look too similar to one another to rely on this. Many can only be identified under a microscope, and a few species additionally require key parts of the body to be fully exposed, such as the mandibles, mouthparts or male genitalia.

Inevitably, this necessitates a different approach from that adopted in previous guides, and there is a greater reliance on dichotomous keys and diagrams. The objective is to facilitate the identification of all British and Irish bee species in the most user-friendly way possible without compromising rigour or accuracy. For the identification of some species it will be helpful to use the book in conjunction with a museum collection, or with reference to the author's photo-sharing web feature (see p.59). This provides a 'virtual collection' of pinned bees, photographed under magnification, that is as extensive in coverage as the collection of British and Irish bees found in London's Natural History Museum. It also provides photographs of most of our bees in the living state and in many cases photographs of the habitats they require. Even with these resources, however, some of the most difficult species may need verification by an expert.

The term 'field guide' thus needs qualifying. You stand a very good chance of quickly learning some species and many of the bee genera in the field using the colour plates provided here. The more you use the book, the more species and genera you will come to recognise – but you will also become more aware of where the limits of field determination lie.

This book is designed to serve a diverse audience, from the casual observer and keen wildlife photographer through to the serious bee recorder or researcher. You do not need to purchase a microscope or refer to the dichotomous keys to use and enjoy this book at a basic level, but to realise its full potential does mean having access to a microscope and collecting equipment, and developing a collection of reliably identified pinned specimens. This will increase your chances of accurately identifying all the bees you encounter and submitting reliable data to the national recording scheme run by the **Bees, Wasps and Ants Recording Society (BWARS)**. It will also assist in the monitoring and conservation of bees in the area where you live or the places you visit, and there has never been a greater imperative to do this.

We hope that this book will help you to identify all of the bees in Britain, Ireland and the Channel Islands. It provides the latest information on ecology, status and distribution, and furnishes colour illustrations and photographs that cover an impressive proportion of the species.

WHAT IS A BEE?

Bees belong to the great insect order **Hymenoptera**, which is dominated by various sorts of parasitic wasps, gall wasps, hunting wasps, ants and sawflies. About 150,000 Hymenoptera species have been described globally, though the true figure may exceed a million. Within the Hymenoptera, bees initially fall within the suborder **Apocrita**, containing the various 'wasp-waisted' forms which have the abdomen joined to the thorax by a narrow petiole and have grub-like larvae that develop within hosts, galls or nests. The other suborder is the **Symphyta**, containing sawflies and their relatives, which lack a wasp waist and tend to have free-living, caterpillar-like larvae.

The Apocrita is divided into two sections, the **Parasitica** and **Aculeata**. The former contains mostly parasitic species such as ichneumons, chalcids and braconids in which the female ovipositor is used to inject eggs into a host that is usually another insect but can be a plant in the case of cynipid (gall) wasps. Bees belong within the Aculeata, along with ants, hunting wasps and various other parasitic wasps (e.g. chrysidids, sapygids, mutillids and tiphiids). Most aculeates have the ovipositor developed into a sting designed to inject venom, which is used both to paralyse or kill prey and to provide protection.

The classification of the Aculeata is complex and reveals that both ants and bees are essentially specialised wasps. Indeed, it shows that hunting wasps of the families Crabronidae (e.g. digger wasps) and Sphecidae (sand wasps) are more closely related to bees than to other wasps such as social wasps (Vespidae) and spider wasps (Pompilidae). So if you look at the listing of families within the superfamily Apoidea, you will find the various bee families alongside several hunting wasp families, all with a similar basic body plan and a series of unique shared characteristics that are missing from other aculeates and suggestive of a common ancestry. There is little doubt that within the Apoidea, the hunting wasps came first and provided an ancestor that gave rise to bees. Many hunting wasp species visit flowers for nectar, so this is less of a leap than one might imagine.

So bees are basically hunting wasps that have switched from a predatory and carnivorous lifestyle to one that involves collecting pollen and nectar from flowers, or evolving beyond that state to become cuckoos (cleptoparasites) of other bees. As a result, many bees are hairy and all bees (even the virtually hairless ones) have microscopically branched hairs to grip pollen. The proboscis of most bees is modified to allow nectar to be sucked up more efficiently, and pollen brushes (scopae) designed to carry a large pollen load can be present on various parts of the body. Internally, many bees have enlarged crops to allow transportation and processing of

Examples of Hymenoptera: a sawfly *Tenthredo* sp. (top left), an ichneumon wasp (top right), a wood ant *Formica rufa* (centre left), a bumblebee *Bombus hortorum* (bottom left) and a hunting wasp *Crabro cribrarius* (bottom right).

nectar, and various glands in the body have been modified to produce substances that help with processing of food, feeding of young, waterproofing of nests and so on. In a number of bee genera, eusocial behaviour involving the use of female 'workers' has developed.

About 20,000 species of bee have been described to date, but it is likely that the true number is several times this figure. The oldest known fossil bee comes from amber 83 million years old.

CLASSIFICATION OF BEES

The classification of bees is not particularly stable. Whilst there is broad agreement over the major groupings, there is disagreement over how those groups should be ranked at family, subfamily and tribe level, and similar disagreement affects the limits of individual genera, especially as ongoing molecular studies modify assumptions based on external morphology. At one extreme, all bees are placed in one family (Apidae), whilst at the other, up to nine separate families are recognised. In this book, the classification of British species is based on that used by BWARS. Our species fall within the following six families (see also *At-a-glance guide* overleaf):

- **Colletidae** A cosmopolitan group with over 2,000 species of rather diverse form, particularly well-represented in the southern hemisphere. These are short-tongued bees, usually with a bilobed tip to the tongue, that characteristically line their nest cells with a waterproof, cellophane-like substance from the Dufour's gland. The cells are filled with a liquid or semi-liquid pollen mass. No eusocial or cleptoparasitic species are present in our fauna, though some Hawaiian *Hylaeus* are cuckoos of other *Hylaeus*. Regarded as a primitive bee family. Represented here by *Colletes* (9 species) and *Hylaeus* (12 species).

- **Andrenidae** A large group of short-tongued bees with about 2,700 species found in all regions except Australasia. Characterised by having two subantennal sutures on the face below each antennal socket. Several genera have facial foveae, and the hind legs often have pollen brushes on the trochanters and femora as well as the tibiae and basitarsi. This family lacks any cleptoparasitic or eusocial species. Represented here by *Andrena* (67 species) and *Panurgus* (2 species).

- **Halictidae** A cosmopolitan group of about 3,500 species of mostly small to medium-sized, short-tongued bees of diverse form and habits. Many are metallic in colour. Several genera are cleptoparasitic, and halictids also show a fascinating range of sociality, including some subsocial and primitively eusocial species. Often termed 'sweat bees' because of the attraction to sweat by many tropical species. Represented here by *Halictus* (8 species), *Lasioglossum* (34 species) and *Sphecodes* (17 species) within the subfamily Halictinae; also *Dufourea* (2 species) and *Rophites* (1 species) within the subfamily Rophitinae, which are characterised by a very short clypeus.

- **Melittidae** A small but diverse group of about 160 short-tongued bees found in most regions except the Neotropics and with only a single Australian species. Sometimes split into three families. The family includes no social or cleptoparasitic species, though some have unusually modified legs and highly specialised foraging habits (particularly certain foreign species). Floral oil rather than pollen is sometimes used as larval food. Represented here by *Dasypoda* (1 species), which is sometimes placed in the family Dasypodaidae, *Macropis* (1 species) and *Melitta* (4 species).

- **Megachilidae** A cosmopolitan group of long-tongued bees with over 3,000 species, including the world's largest bee *Megachile pluto*. Nearly all species have two submarginal wing cells and a rectangular labrum that is longer than wide (but often obscured by the folded mandibles). The non-cleptoparasitic species have a pollen brush on the underside of the abdomen rather than on the hind legs. Their mandibles are often very broad and powerful for masticating plant material, cutting leaves, shaving plant hairs and sometimes excavating holes in decaying wood. This results in some very 'big-headed' forms. Males often have the sternites and the tip of the abdomen modified by projections, lobes and emarginations. A number of genera are cleptoparasitic but no species are social. Represented here by *Anthidium* (1 species), *Chelostoma* (2 species), *Coelioxys* (8 species), *Heriades* (1 resident species), *Hoplitis* (2 species), *Osmia* (12 species), *Megachile* (10 species) and *Stelis* (4 species).

These pages provide a quick reference to the bee genera in Britain and Ireland, illustrating a representative bee (usually a female) from each genus in each family. They give a brief overview of the variety of bees found in the region, and introduce the main forms and features.

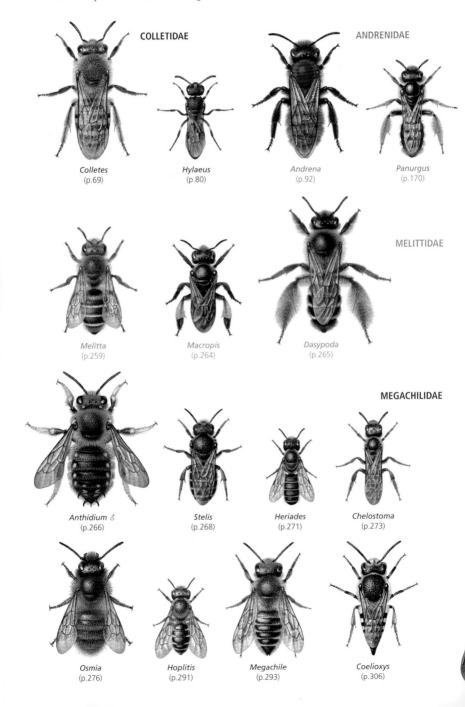

COLLETIDAE

Colletes
(p.69)

Hylaeus
(p.80)

ANDRENIDAE

Andrena
(p.92)

Panurgus
(p.170)

Melitta
(p.259)

Macropis
(p.264)

Dasypoda
(p.265)

MELITTIDAE

MEGACHILIDAE

Anthidium ♂
(p.266)

Stelis
(p.268)

Heriades
(p.271)

Chelostoma
(p.273)

Osmia
(p.276)

Hoplitis
(p.291)

Megachile
(p.293)

Coelioxys
(p.306)

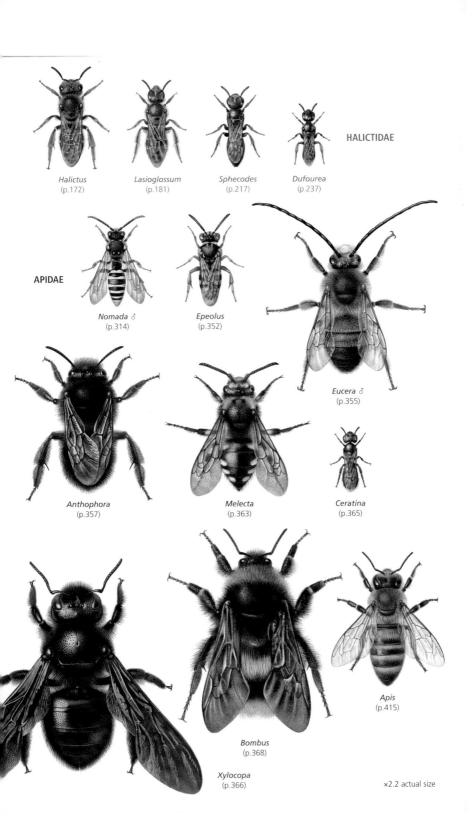

HALICTIDAE

Halictus
(p.172)

Lasioglossum
(p.181)

Sphecodes
(p.217)

Dufourea
(p.237)

APIDAE

Nomada ♂
(p.314)

Epeolus
(p.352)

Eucera ♂
(p.355)

Anthophora
(p.357)

Melecta
(p.363)

Ceratina
(p.365)

Bombus
(p.368)

Xylocopa
(p.366)

Apis
(p.415)

×2.2 actual size

■ **Apidae** A huge cosmopolitan group of long-tongued bees with over 6,000 species now that the former Xylocopidae (carpenter bees) and Anthophoridae (flower bees, long-horned bees, nomad bees etc.) are included. Diverse in form and habits with numerous cleptoparasitic genera. The tongue is often exceptionally long, and many species display superb hovering abilities. The Apidae contains many solitary species plus a range of sociality that includes the most complex eusocial behaviour found in any bees (that of *Apis* honey bees). A number of social genera have 'corbiculate' hind legs, where the hind tibiae are flattened and formed into hair-fringed 'pollen baskets'. Represented here by *Ceratina* (1 species) and *Xylocopa* (2 non-resident species) from the subfamily Xylocopinae, *Epeolus* (2 species) and *Nomada* (34 species) from the subfamily Nomadinae and *Apis* (1 naturalised/cultivated species), *Anthophora* (5 species), *Bombus* (27 species), *Eucera* (2 species) and *Melecta* (2 species) from the subfamily Apinae.

SPECIES, RACES, FORMS AND VARIATIONS

At its simplest level, a species is a series of freely interbreeding populations that all resemble one another and behave in a similar fashion. Reality is often far more complex than this, as some species can exhibit much variation and local adaptation whilst others are very constant; there are also species that can barely be distinguished from each other without DNA analysis. Understanding variation within a species makes identification much easier and can highlight many fascinating aspects of bees such as the effects of voltinism (the number of generations in a year), geographic isolation, environmental pressures, mimicry and genetics. The main forms of variation are described here.

Sexual dimorphism and caste variation Most bees show sexual dimorphism (i.e. males and females look different), and this is particularly extreme in *Andrena* and *Lasioglossum* species, *Osmia bicolor*, *Anthophora plumipes* and bumblebees such as *Bombus lapidarius*. Females are usually larger than males, and often more colourful and distinctive. In eusocial species, workers tend to be smaller than queens. This is called caste variation, and it is very noticeable in bumblebees but more subtle in *Halictus* and *Lasioglossum*. Bees infected by stylopids (see *Parasitoids and parasites*, p.27) are intersexes that often look intermediate between male and female.

Andrena fulva female (left) and male (right) showing the strong sexual dimorphism of many bees.

Polymorphism This is where a gene or some other factor can create two or more 'forms' of a bee within a single population without (or with few) intermediates between those appearances. Examples include female *Anthophora plumipes*, which are usually black but occasionally buff; also male *Bombus ruderatus*, which can be banded with a white tail or entirely black. Polymorphism can also manifest itself in seasonal variation (see below).

Anthophora plumipes females showing the typical black form (left) and uncommon buff form (right).

Continuous variation This is variation that occurs in a more continuous fashion and affects many bee species to varying extents. Examples include queens and workers of *Bombus ruderatus*, which grade from banded with a white tail to entirely black with a full range of intermediates, females of *Andrena marginata*, where the abdomen varies from substantially red to all-dark, and *Nomada* species such as *N. panzeri* and *N. zonata*, where the yellow abdominal markings can vary in size and shape. As well as affecting pattern and colour, variation can also involve size. This can bring about the phenomenon of **allometry**, where variation in size is linked to the physical proportions of a bee. Good examples are the males of *Andrena bucephala*, *A. ferox* and *Panurgus* species. Here, larger males have proportionately bigger heads in relation to the rest of the body.

Seasonal variation This occurs in a number of bivoltine (double-brooded) bees and can involve colour, pattern and physical structure. Examples include several bivoltine species of *Andrena*, e.g. *A. minutula* and *A. alfkenella*, where spring males tend to have extensively black-haired faces (pale-haired in summer males) and much weaker punctures on the scutum, scutellum and tergites than summer males. Females are seemingly unaffected. In *Andrena trimmerana* and *A. rosae* spring males have a long downward-pointing spine on the cheeks just before the

Andrena trimmerana spring male (left) showing cheek spine and longer body hairs and a summer male (right).

mandibles, but summer ones do not, and spring males of *A. trimmerana* also have long mandibles without an apical tooth whilst summer ones have shorter mandibles with an apical tooth. The mechanisms that bring about this seasonal variation are far from clear. The summer generation of bivoltine bees also tend to be shorter-haired and, in *Nomada* species, tend to have more extensive yellow markings.

Geographic variation The variation described above has a relatively trivial genetic or environmental basis. However, some variation can have a deeper genetic basis due to a long period of genetic isolation brought about by physical barriers (e.g. the sea between islands) or the isolating effects of past ice ages. Several of our bees look different from those typically found on the continent. For example, British queens of *Bombus terrestris* (usually termed ssp. *audax*) have a buff-haired tail, whilst continental and Channel Islands queens (usually termed ssp. *terrestris*) have a white-haired one and are therefore not really Buff-tailed Bumblebees at all. The British mainland form of *Anthidium manicatum* (usually termed ssp. *nigrithorax*) is usually darker than the continental and Channel Islands form (ssp. *manicatum*), and our mainland form of *Osmia bicornis* lacks the partially black-haired abdomen of most continental (and Channel Islands) populations. Other species showing geographic variation within Britain and Ireland include *Bombus muscorum*, *B. jonellus*, *Megachile versicolor* and *M. willughbiella* (see species accounts).

Bombus terrestris queens showing buff-tailed British form ssp. *audax* (top) and white-tailed Channel Islands form ssp. *terrestris* (bottom).

Host-induced variation If a cleptoparasitic bee attacks more than one host, differences in size and appearance can arise that result in host-specific forms. For example, certain species of *Sphecodes* and *Coelioxys* that attack two or more host species can vary in size according to which host they have used. Where a single cleptoparasite population is genuinely able to utilise two or more hosts, there will probably be no genetic basis to this size variation. However, if different host forms of a cleptoparasitic species occupy different habitats or places, or fly at different times of the year, or are very loyal to a single host species, genetic isolation of great age may exist between those host forms. DNA analysis is starting to show that some cleptoparasitic 'species' are probably species complexes. The treatment of *Nomada subcornuta* as a full species in this book is an example of this, because DNA analysis has shown that its genetic distance from *N. fulvicornis* is several times too great for it to be considered a form or subspecies. More of this splitting is anticipated as DNA studies of cleptoparasites continue.

Fading/ageing This can have a profound effect on the appearance of a bee. Furry bees can become denuded and look much slimmer and darker than normal. Brightly coloured hairs can become sun-bleached and turn greyish or whitish, and black hair can bleach brownish. It is not unusual to find *Bombus lapidarius* workers and males with brownish bodies and whitish tails in late summer. Solitary bees with pale hair bands on the tergites can lose those bands – old specimens of *Andrena flavipes* and female *Colletes* frequently have an entirely black abdomen. Very tatty wing margins are a good indication of an old bee and of the need to account for wear and fading. It can be tempting to discard specimens of old, worn bees, and many will not be easy to key out. However, if you are building up a collection of pinned bees, it is recommended that you retain such specimens, as there are usually enough structural features to eventually allow determination, by comparing them with less worn examples of named bees.

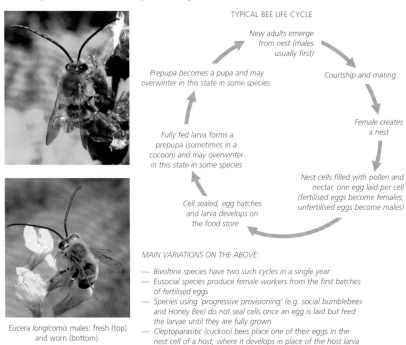

TYPICAL BEE LIFE CYCLE

New adults emerge from nest (males usually first)

Prepupa becomes a pupa and may overwinter in this state in some species

Courtship and mating

Fully fed larva forms a prepupa (sometimes in a cocoon) and may overwinter in this state in some species

Female creates a nest

Cell sealed, egg hatches and larva develops on the food store

Nest cells filled with pollen and nectar, one egg laid per cell (fertilised eggs become females, unfertilised eggs become males)

MAIN VARIATIONS ON THE ABOVE:

— *Bivoltine species have two such cycles in a single year*
— *Eusocial species produce female workers from the first batches of fertilised eggs*
— *Species using 'progressive provisioning' (e.g. social bumblebees and Honey Bee) do not seal cells once an egg is laid but feed the larvae until they are fully grown*
— *Cleptoparasitic (cuckoo) bees place one of their eggs in the nest cell of a host, where it develops in place of the host larva*

Eucera longicornis males: fresh (top) and worn (bottom).

THE LIFE CYCLE OF BEES

Bees are **holometabolous**, i.e. they exhibit complete metamorphosis like moths, butterflies, flies, beetles and several other insect orders. Such insects have true larvae (as opposed to nymphs) which look very different from the adults and pass through a pupal stage to attain the adult body form. The larvae of bees (also called **grubs**) are maggot-like without eyes or obvious appendages. They moult several times as they grow (each stage being called an **instar**) and only defecate when they get to the **prepupa** stage, at which point some species spin a cocoon. Metamorphosis then occurs within the pupa, and adults emerge after a period that varies according to species, location and various other factors. Where bees and many other aculeates depart from most other holometabolous insects is in the use of nests for larval development and the provisioning of nest cells with food, as opposed to simply laying eggs and buzzing off.

Nesting

Bee nesting can be categorised in a number of ways. In terms of physical location of nests, our bees tend to fall into two broad groups, **ground-nesters** and **aerial nesters**. The majority are ground-nesters, and this category is exemplified by *Andrena*, *Colletes* and *Lasioglossum*. Nesting can occur in flat ground, slopes or even vertical faces (some species happily using all three options), though the ground normally has to be dry and exposed to the sun so that it can warm up quickly. Some bees will tolerate a range of soil types, whilst others prefer sandy ground or clay. Nests typically consist of a long tunnel with side branches terminating in one or several cells. The nest entrances often have surrounding mounds of spoil (called a **tumulus**), resembling tiny volcanoes. Nests are usually less than 30cm deep, but a few species will go deeper than

Nest of *Andrena trimmerana*, a ground nester using light, sandy soil (left), and of *Osmia bicornis*, an aerial nester here using a bee hotel (right).

this. Cell walls are usually waterproofed, either with a waxy secretion from the Dufour's gland or, in the case of *Hylaeus* and *Colletes*, with a cellophane-like substance. This helps keep the food store fresh and protects the cells against rain.

Nesting can also be categorised as **dispersed/solitary**, with nest entrances far apart, or **communal**, with nest entrances concentrated into aggregations. The latter sometimes involves thousands of nest entrances concentrated within a few square metres of ground or a short stretch of a bank or cliff face (particularly in species such as *Andrena cineraria*, *A. flavipes*, *Anthophora bimaculata*, *Colletes hederae*, *Dasypoda hirtipes* and *Lasioglossum malachurum*). In the majority of ground-nesting bee species one female controls a single nest. However, in the case of eusocial *Halictus* and *Lasioglossum* species, or in *Andrena bucephala* and *A. ferox* (non-social communal nesters) more than one female can share a single nest entrance. This often results in more complicated nest architecture, sometimes involving subterranean chambers with clusters of cells.

Aerial nesters are those species that typically nest above the ground using hollow plant stems, holes in dead wood and timber, holes or soft mortar in walls, and bee hotels. This category is exemplified by megachilids such as *Anthidium*, *Chelostoma*, *Heriades*, most *Osmia* species and most *Megachile* species, as well as a few members of other families such as most *Hylaeus* species, *Anthophora furcata* and *Ceratina cyanea*. Such bees typically arrange nest cells in a linear sequence, with female cells nearer the end and male ones (which are vacated first) nearer the entrance. The walls and partitions between the cells can be constructed variously of leaf sections (*Megachile*), mud (*Osmia bicornis* and *O. xanthomelana*), mud mixed with nectar (*Chelostoma*), chewed-up leaf mastic (various *Osmia* species), plant hairs (*Anthidium manicatum*)

Nest of a *Megachile* leafcutter showing the nest cells wrapped in leaf sections.

and plant or tree resin (*Heriades truncorum*). The division between ground-nesting and aerial nesting is not always sharp. *Anthophora plumipes* and *Osmia bicornis* will use cliff faces and even the entrances of rabbit burrows as well as walls and structural timbers, and some ground-nesting *Andrena* and *Colletes* species will use the soft mortar of walls as if they were a cliff face.

A further nesting category comprises three *Osmia* species that nest in empty snail shells: *Osmia aurulenta*, *O. bicolor* and *O. spinulosa*. A number of cells may be fitted into one shell. *O. bicolor* is the most interesting of the three in that females hide their shells with grass stems and other plant fragments. Both *O. bicolor* and *O. aurulenta* paste leaf mastic onto the outside of the shell, for reasons that are not entirely clear. *Osmia inermis*, which is

Osmia bicolor nesting in an empty snail shell, which it will conceal with grass stems once its nest is completed.

closely related to aerial-nesting species, has evolved to nest under stones because suitable aerial-nesting opportunities do not exist at the high altitudes it frequents.

Bumblebees can be categorised loosely according to whether they like to nest underground (e.g. *Bombus terrestris*, *B. lucorum* and *B. hortorum*), on the surface amongst dense herbage (the various carder bumblebees) or above ground (*B. hypnorum*, and to a lesser extent species such as *B. pratorum* and *B. jonellus*). Most species seem to require an old rodent nest or bird nest containing moss or other bedding material, and it is now known that using mouse-scented bedding in artificial bumblebee nests dramatically increases the occupancy rates of these. Both bumblebees and the Honey Bee create nest cells from wax secreted by the abdomen. The nest-cell arrangement of bumblebees is rather untidy, but in the Honey Bee it is incredibly neat, with hexagonal wax combs used for both larval development and food storage.

Social behaviour

Within the insect world this is almost entirely confined to certain, bees, wasps and ants (all Hymenoptera) and termites (Isoptera). In British bees it is restricted to the Honey Bee, all but six of our bumblebees, and some of our *Halictus* and *Lasioglossum* species. There are different levels of social behaviour, but the most clear-cut one is **eusocial** behaviour. In a eusocial bee colony, a mated, fertile female (the queen) uses her daughters (workers), which are virgins with poorly developed ovaries, to do much of the nest building, brood care, foraging and nest defence. The queen can lay both fertile eggs (destined to become workers or queens) and unfertilised ones (destined to become males). Workers may occasionally lay unfertilised eggs too, supplementing the production of males, but they never produce females.

The form of eusocial behaviour found in some of our *Halictus* and *Lasioglossum* species is relatively primitive, with workers only slightly smaller than queens, and it can be facultative, with some species social in the south but becoming solitary in the north. Social bumblebees take it to a higher level, with stronger physical and behavioural differences between queens and workers and more complex nesting habits, which even include the queen incubating cells containing developing eggs and grubs. The most complex eusocial behaviour is that seen in the Honey Bee, where the queen is even more reliant on the workers (queens do no foraging or nest building, unlike queen bumblebees). Workers take on a greater variety of roles and have more sophisticated ways of communicating and relaying information to one another, such as the 'waggle dance' which relays information on where to forage.

In eusocial bees, the production of new queens is brought about either by rearing female grubs in larger cells with more food than worker grubs, or by providing better-quality food to a

Apis mellifera comb with worker bees.

BELOW: *Apis mellifera* swarm.

queen grub (royal jelly in the case of Honey Bees). In Honey Bee colonies, the queen produces a pheromone to inhibit the production of new queens. The production of new queens only happens when the colony gets too large (diluting the effect of the pheromone) or the existing queen is becoming old and weak. If the existing queen is still fit, she will leave the colony a few days before new queens are due to emerge and take several thousand of her workers with her, resulting in a **prime swarm**. The first new queen to emerge will attempt to kill off other new or developing queens, though workers will prevent her fully achieving this if the colony is still too big, forcing her to leave with a **post swarm**. Once a new queen is finally established and no rival queens are left, she will undertake a nuptial flight and mate with several males (**drones**). She is then initially served by workers that are her sisters or half-sisters, but these eventually get replaced by her daughters as her fertilised eggs are reared through.

Bumblebees also use queen pheromones in a similar way, and when the queen eventually weakens (usually when she starts to lay infertile eggs destined to become males), the workers rear her final fertilised eggs as queens rather than workers. The different types of bee in a social colony (queen, worker and male) are called **castes**.

Foraging

Bees require flowers as a source of protein-rich pollen, sugar-rich nectar and sometimes floral oils. The shape and size of the body and the length and structure of the tongue can dictate which flowers are used, and many flowers are shaped to favour certain bees over others. Bees also have colour preferences and physiological needs that narrow down the choice of flowers available to a particular bee species. This results in three categories of foraging:

- **Polylectic**, where pollen is obtained from a variety of plant species in numerous genera and families representing varied flower types and colour. The majority of British bees fall into this category.

- **Oligolectic**, where pollen is gathered from a narrower range of plants such as a single genus or a group of closely related and very similar-looking genera. Examples of oligolectic bees include *Andrena humilis*, *A. fulvago* and *Panurgus* species, which all use yellow hawkish Asteraceae such as Cat's-ear, hawkbits and hawk's-beards; also *Andrena hattorfiana* and *A. marginata*, which only use scabiouses, the various *Andrena* species that only use willows, and *Chelostoma campanularum* and *Melitta haemorrhoidalis*, which use bellflowers and their closest relatives.

- **Monolectic**, where pollen is obtained from a single plant species. In a British context, this includes *Andrena florea* (White Bryony), *Macropis europaea* (Yellow Loosestrife) and *Melitta dimidiata* (Sainfoin), though in Europe, where a more diverse flora is present, all these species are actually oligolectic. Species with restricted pollen needs usually still visit a variety of other flowers for nectar.

Andrena hattorfiana (oligolectic) on Field Scabious (left) and *Andrena florea* (monolectic) on White Bryony (right).

The branched body hairs of bees are an adaptation for gathering pollen. When a bee flies, it builds up an electrostatic charge which causes pollen to stick to the body hairs as it forages. The legs then push the pollen grains onto a pollen brush which is usually located on each of the hind legs or, in the case of megachilids, beneath the abdomen. *Andrena* and *Colletes* species additionally use the sides of the propodeum and can collect impressive quantities of pollen in a single foraging session. *Hylaeus* species lack pollen brushes and typically collect pollen in their crops.

Most bees collect **dry pollen** (which can be naturally sticky) but bumblebees, the Honey Bee, *Eucera*, *Macropis* and *Melitta* species moisten pollen with regurgitated nectar to create **wet pollen** which is stickier, allowing larger quantities to be carried. Bumblebees also employ **buzz pollination** (by vibrating their bodies), which is vital to dislodge the pollen of certain flowers including Potato, Tomato, Borage, Blueberry and Cranberry in a manner that other bees cannot achieve. Bees suck up nectar through the mouthparts and store it in the crop. Some short-tongued bumblebees bite holes in the bases of flower corollas to obtain nectar that their

Bombus pratorum male nectar-robbing from Russian Comfrey.

tongues cannot reach using legitimate techniques. This is called **nectar-robbing** and is best observed in plants such as comfreys, Honeysuckle, Red Campion and fuchsias.

Most bees deposit their pollen load directly into a nest cell, sometimes mixing it with nectar (depending on the species), then lay an egg on it and seal the cell. This is called **mass provisioning**. Bumblebees and the Honey Bee by contrast place food initially into separate storage pots or cells and the workers then feed a pollen and nectar mix to the grubs as they grow. This is called **progressive provisioning**. They also convert nectar into **honey** through a process of regurgitation and evaporation. The honey has higher calorific value and more resistance to bacterial degradation than pure nectar. As well as being part of the larval diet, it is vital for sustaining the adult bees through spells of poor weather and helping them to maintain a high body temperature. The Honey Bee and, to a lesser extent, bumblebees also collect water from dew or puddles, especially in hot spells, and use it to cool overheating nests through evaporation. Sugar-rich honeydew from foliage supporting aphids is another food source for the Honey Bee and bumblebees and is the reason why you can sometimes see bees preoccupied with the foliage of non-blossoming shrubs and trees, including conifers.

Seasonality and flight periods

In Britain and Ireland, only one wild bee species (*Bombus terrestris*) can forage in all months of the year, and it only does this to a limited extent where urban microclimates and the presence of non-native winter-flowering shrubs allow it to. All other wild bees have restricted flight periods of varying duration. **Univoltine** species have just one generation/nesting cycle per year, but certain bumblebee, *Andrena* and *Nomada* species have two and are termed **bivoltine**.

Flight periods are typically timed to allow exploitation of particular flowers in particular habitats. A long flight period or bivoltine strategy will often force a bee to be a generalist,

Anthophora plumipes male – one of the first bees to appear in spring.

polylectic species. A shorter flight period can allow better exploitation of a more limited range of flowers and is often a feature of the oligolectic bees noted above. Eusocial *Halictus* and *Lasioglossum* species are often termed bivoltine but their life cycle differs from that of bivoltine *Andrena* in that the first generation produced is mostly female workers whilst the second generation is males and future queens, all of this taking place in one nest and with one long-lived queen, i.e. one nesting cycle. In bivoltine *Andrena* there is wholesale replacement of individuals from one generation to the next and new nests for each. This is also the case with bivoltine bumblebees.

In southern Britain, queen *Bombus terrestris*, male *Anthophora plumipes* and males of *Andrena clarkella* and *A. thoracica* can be flying by late February or early March, especially if temperatures surpass 10°C and there are some sunny spells. The main spring peak is from mid-March as Goat Willow, Cherry Plum, Gorse, Coltsfoot and Red Dead-nettle start to flower. By April, Blackthorn, other willow species, dandelions, White Dead-nettle and Ground-ivy become important. This blossoming sequence is critically important for our bees, with many species only flying for a

Colletes hederae – an autumn-flying bee.

4–6-week period during spring. Even summer bumblebee populations are affected by spring, because newly emerged queens cannot establish new nesting colonies unless they have plentiful spring food supplies plus the weather that allows them to forage. The same is true of bivoltine *Andrena* species, which need success in both generations to survive.

Much bee activity takes place over summer months, with habitats such as heathland, brownfield land and saltmarsh still holding interest well into September as late flowers such as Ling, Fleabane, Michaelmas Daisy, Bristly Oxtongue and Sea Aster peak. Two *Colletes* species, *C. halophilus* and *C. hederae*, have exceptionally late flight periods to allow exploitation of Sea Aster and Ivy respectively. Mild days in October are usually your last chance to see flying wild bees, especially late-flying *Bombus pascuorum* and *Lasioglossum calceatum*.

In northern and upland Britain the foraging season for bees can be greatly compressed. Spring typically starts much later (4–6 weeks later in the Scottish Highlands than in parts of southern England) and autumn can start several weeks earlier too. It can be hard to find bees once the Ling has gone over in September. Short flight seasons can result in bivoltine species switching to a univoltine strategy (e.g. *Bombus pratorum*), eusocial species becoming solitary (e.g. *Halictus rubicundus* and *Lasioglossum calceatum*) and at least one species (*Lasioglossum fratellum*) nesting across two years, a phenomenon known as **iteroparity**.

Where males appear before females this is called **protandry**, and it is particularly noticeable in *Andrena*, *Anthophora*, *Colletes* and *Eucera* species. In bumblebees, *Halictus*, *Lasioglossum* and most *Sphecodes*, females appear in spring well before males. This may appear to be the opposite of protandry, though these are actually hibernated females that initially emerged alongside males the previous summer and mated before overwintering. The males of these genera do not overwinter, except for *Sphecodes spinulosus* and *S. rubicundus*, where males appear alongside females in spring.

Cleptoparasitism

Seventy-three of our bee species exploit the nests of other bees. This is called **cleptoparasitism**, and the bees that do it are termed **cuckoo bees**. Cleptoparasitism has evolved in bees on several occasions, and it is used by all species of *Coelioxys*, *Epeolus*, *Melecta*, *Nomada*, *Sphecodes*, *Stelis* plus six of our bumblebees (**cuckoo bumblebees**). In *Nomada* and *Epeolus*, females are able to detect nest cells that are still being provisioned. Whilst the owner is foraging, the cuckoo enters a nest and places an egg inside a cell embedded in the cell wall. The owner eventually finishes stocking the cell, lays her own egg in it and then seals it. When the cuckoo grub hatches it eats the egg or young grub of the host and then uses the food provisions for its own development. The story is similar in *Coelioxys* and *Melecta* except that these use cells that have already been sealed. *Coelioxys* females use the sharp tip of the abdomen to create a groove in the cell cap and then insert an egg. *Melecta* females break the cap of a cell, insert an egg and then reseal the cap. *Sphecodes* females are more confrontational and will force their way into a host nest

Examples of cuckoo bees: *Coelioxys elongata* (top left), *Nomada goodeniana* (top right), *Epeolus cruciger* (bottom left), *Sphecodes pellucidus* (bottom centre), *Melecta albifrons* (bottom right).

even if the owner is present, sometimes killing it. They then open up a sealed cell, destroy the host egg or grub, deposit their egg and reseal the cell.

In cuckoo bumblebees, the story is more complex still. The large, queen-like female enters a host nest, replaces the host queen (variously by killing or subduing her) and then occupies the nest for the rest of its cycle. The worker bumblebees become slaves, nurturing the cuckoo bumblebee grubs and keeping their new 'queen' fed. The female cuckoo does not collect pollen or produce workers of her own.

Cleptoparasitism has led to some very distinctive forms of bee such as *Nomada*, *Coelioxys* and *Epeolus*. Typically the cuckoos become heavily armoured, lose their pollen-collecting features and sometimes become strongly patterned and even wasp-like in the case of some *Nomada* species. The behaviour of cuckoo bees changes profoundly too – they become stalkers and opportunistic burglars, presumably with the various sensory facilities required to do this effectively with the strict timing that is required. Cuckoo bees still visit flowers, but only for their own needs, and they do not display parental care. Most cuckoo bee species use one host species or a small number of related hosts, though the situation is often confused by the past publication of unreliable records. It is not just cuckoo bees that act as cleptoparasites. The females of many foraging species will sometimes steal a nest belonging to another female of their own species.

Courtship and mating

Competition between male bees to mate with a female and the need for sexes to physically find each other in the landscape results in a variety of behaviours. Bees don't go big on courtship

A mating pair of *Anthidium manicatum* with the larger male above the female (left) and a *Colletes hederae* mating ball with many males surrounding one newly emerged female (right).

compared with some invertebrates, but males of many protandrous species will mass and swarm (often termed **lekking**) around nesting areas waiting for new females to emerge. Swarming can also occur around trees and bushes or along linear features such as banks and cliff tops. Pheromones seem to be important during swarming and can sometimes be detectable, notably the distinctive scent trails left by male *Bombus sylvestris* in and around woods. Various parts of the body can produce pheromones, but it is usually the antennae that detect them.

Some males defend territories, notably *Anthidium manicatum* around a patch of flowers used by females. This is the only British bee in which males average larger than females and intruders are dealt with brutally (see species account). Mating itself can involve mass wrestling matches (e.g. the mating balls of certain *Colletes* species) or high-speed chases (drone Honey Bees chasing a new queen). As well as the genitalia, certain external body parts seem to be designed specifically for the mating process. The expanded tarsi or tarsal hair fringes of some male megachilids are used to cover the female's eyes, and the modified sternites and apical tergites of various male megachilids seem to be devices to help grip females during mating and prevent other males from separating them. In many species, males appear able to mate more than once, but in the Honey Bee, mating involves explosive ejaculation, which means a successful drone dies rapidly after the act.

A final word on mating in bees. They don't always attempt to mate just with female bees. A number of flowers are sexually attractive to male bees, and this is best exemplified by the attraction of *Eucera* males to the flowers of *Ophrys* orchids. The false mating is called **pseudocopulation**. Even more bizarre is the attraction of male *Colletes hederae* to clusters of triungulin larvae of the meloid beetle *Stenoria analis*, which then latch on to the bee. This also seems to have a sexual basis and is presumably based on pheromones, as the clusters look nothing like a female bee.

Haplodiploidy This is where males develop from unfertilised eggs and therefore only have half the normal number of chromosomes (like the sperm or unfertilised eggs of most other organisms, including humans). It is a phenomenon only seen in Hymenoptera and a few other insects. Female bees on the other hand have a full set of chromosomes. This means that male bees produce sperm by the process of **mitosis** (the normal form of non-sexual cell division) rather than **meiosis** (the usual way in which sex cells are produced, which involves a halving of the chromosomes). The results might seem almost identical to normal gamete production, in that the male bee's sperm ends up with half a set of chromosomes like normal sperm and can then combine with the half-set of chromosomes of an unfertilised female egg to create a new full set of chromosomes containing genetic information from both father and mother. But there are some interesting implications of this strategy. It means that male bees have no father, but do

23

have a grandfather, and the workers of a eusocial bee colony (which are mostly sisters mothered by the queen) show 75% relatedness as opposed to the 50% of normal siblings. This impacts heredity in a number of subtle ways and has been considered one of the driving forces behind social behaviour.

Overwintering

Britain and Ireland are highly seasonal, with cool, often freezing winters and warm summers. This results in flowers being scarce or absent for several winter months and temperatures often much too low for adult activity. Bees have several ways of dealing with this. The Honey Bee builds up food reserves that can be used over winter months to ensure that many workers survive to the following season. This means sufficient workers are available to keep the nest/hive warm (by shivering) and to undertake winter forays on mild winter days. It also allows colonies to persist for several years with a single queen and to more fully exploit the first spring blossoms. Most of our other bees only have colonies lasting a few months. The only other winter-active bee is the occasional *Bombus terrestris* population, a phenomenon that makes this a facultatively **trivoltine** bee, with two summer generations followed by a winter one. Each generation has a separate queen.

The most common forms of overwintering in non-active bees involve either a prepupa or a fully developed, non-emerged adult within the birth cell. Eventually, rising temperature or some other physiological cue will trigger the bee to emerge. Bumblebees are different in that the new queens produced in late summer feed up on flowers and then depart their birth nest, find an old rodent hole or some other pre-existing cavity (including compost heaps) and hibernate in this. This is why you can sometimes find 'sleeping' bumblebees in winter when breaking up rotting timber or digging up ground. Unlike nesting sites, which are often in warm, sunny places, bumblebee hibernation sites tend to be in shady or north-facing spots where the temperature stays cool and constant.

ENEMIES AND ASSOCIATES OF BEES

Bees are exploited by a variety of organisms, including viruses, bacteria, fungi, single-celled protists, nematodes and other invertebrates. Trying to record and understand these relationships can add a fascinating dimension to the study of bees and is increasingly important as we try to conserve them. A number of different types of association are involved.

Cleptoparasites (cuckoos) These are organisms that take over the nest or a nest cell of a foraging bee for the development of their own offspring. Such cuckoos are mostly other types of bee (see *Cleptoparasitism*, pp.21–2). If you keep bee hotels supporting *Osmia* bees there is a good chance that you will see small greyish flies walking about the nest entrances. These are the drosophilid *Cacoxenus indagator*. The fly lays several eggs onto the pollen ball of a nest cell that has not yet been sealed. The fly larvae will then devour the host provisions, usually resulting in starvation for the bee larva. *Gasteruption* wasps can also be present around bee hotels and old walls. These have an external ovipositor designed to inject an egg into the sealed nest cell, and they will attack bees such as *Osmia* and *Hylaeus* as well as certain aerial-nesting wasps. Despite being part of the great Parasitica section of the Hymenoptera, they are classic cleptoparasites rather than parasitoids, with a life cycle resembling that of cuckoo bees. Anthomyiid flies of the genus *Leucophora* also appear to be cleptoparasites rather than parasitoids, and some species can be numerous at *Andrena* nesting colonies in spring.

The relationship of *Meloe* oil beetles (Meloidae) with bees probably best qualifies as cleptoparasitism, and it is fascinating. Several species of these large black beetles occur in Britain, with adults that can be active from autumn to early summer (including the depths of winter) depending on species. Eggs are laid in a burrow, and when these hatch, tiny active triungulin larvae emerge and climb up to flowers. As bees visit these flowers, the triungulins latch on to them and hitch a ride back to the nest. Ground-nesting bees of the genera *Andrena*,

Bee cleptoparasites: the drosophilid fly *Cacoxenus indagator* (top left), the anthomyiid fly *Leucophora obtusa* (top right), the gasteruptiid wasp *Gasteruption jaculator* (centre), an adult oil beetle *Meloe proscarabaeus* (bottom left) and its orange triungulin larvae on a *Melitta dimidiata* (bottom right).

Melitta and *Panurgus* seem to be most favoured, and it is possible to identify most triungulins on these bees to species by their shape, size and colour. *Meloe violaceus* seems to target spring-flying *Andrena* species (the triungulins usually waiting on flowers of dandelions and Lesser Celandine in April), whilst *M. proscarabaeus* prefers summer-flying *Andrena*, *Melitta* and *Panurgus* species. Once in a bee nest the *Meloe* larvae proceed to devour the contents of the cells, including any bee grubs and eggs, and it is thought that many cells are required given the size of the adult, though larvae are rarely found and not well studied. Two further meloid beetles that attack bees here are *Sitara muralis* (a very rare species associated with *Anthophora plumipes*) and *Stenoria analis* (associated with *Colletes hederae* on the Channel Islands).

25

Inquilines These are species that can live in a bee nest without necessarily killing the occupant(s). An example is the hoverfly *Volucella bombylans*. Its larvae develop as scavengers in the nests of both bumblebees and social wasps. They do little harm, though they are not especially beneficial either. This relationship is called **commensalism**. Larvae of the Lesser Housefly *Fannia cunicularius*, a generalist that will also breed in your rubbish, regularly turn up in bumblebees' nests. The situation with the Bee Moth *Aphomia sociella*, which uses the nests of bumblebees, social wasps and sometimes Honey Bee, is not quite so innocuous. Its larvae produce dense silken webs that clog up the bee combs, and bore through combs as they devour the food stores, nest material, waste products and eventually bee larvae and pupae. Strong bee colonies will withstand an infestation, but weak ones can collapse prematurely. Two other moths associated with the Honey Bee are the Lesser Wax Moth *Achroia grisella* and the Greater Wax Moth or Honeycomb Moth *Galleria mellonella*. Other commensals of the Honey Bee include the 'Bee Louse' *Braula coeca* (actually a wingless fly of the family Braulidae). The tiny adults will congregate around the mouthparts of a bee (especially a queen) and feed on honey as it is regurgitated. The *Braula* larvae live within the honeycomb, usually under the wax cappings, which they can disfigure by tunnelling. They are not regarded as a serious pest.

The bee-like hoverfly *Volucella bombylans* has larvae that develop inside bumblebee nests.

A mite-infested *Osmia bicornis*.

Numerous species of non-parasitic mite can live inside bee nests, especially those of bumblebees and megachilids such as *Osmia* and *Megachile*. It is the juveniles of these that often occur in large numbers on adult bees, as they try to disperse. Again, they are relatively harmless, though heavily infested bees can struggle to fly and become weakened by an inability to feed properly. Heavy infestations of nests are thought to be a major cause of undersized adults of some bee species. The hitching of a lift on a bee by mite juveniles (as also displayed by meloid larvae) is called **phoresis**.

Parasitoids and parasites of adult bees
Parasitoids are specialised predators rather than true parasites, because they eventually kill their host. The majority of British thick-headed flies (Conopidae) are parasitoids of adult bees. The female conopid ambushes an adult bee and injects an egg into the abdomen. The conopid larva then develops inside the bee for some time before killing it, and it can change the behaviour of the host. It is quite hard to find bees parasitised by conopids, and it is thought that parasitised bees may bury themselves prior to death. However, by

The conopid fly *Myopa vicaria* has larvae that develop inside adult *Andrena* bees.

observing adult conopids on flowers and around bee nesting areas you can sometimes observe ambushing and see which bees are being attacked by particular conopid species. *Myopa* species primarily attack *Andrena* bees, *Thecophora* and *Zodion* species attack *Halictus* and *Lasioglossum* bees, *Physocephala* and *Sicus* species attack bumblebees, and *Conops* species seem to attack several bee genera including bumblebees and *Osmia* species.

Stylopids (members of the order Strepsiptera) are a strange and mysterious group of insects typically associated with bees of the genera *Andrena* and *Lasioglossum*. They develop inside a bee grub and eventually pupate in such a fashion that their heads end up protruding from between two tergites when the adult bee emerges. Infected bees are sterile intersexes with characteristics of both male and female, and it is not unusual to have several stylopids in one bee. The very active male stylopid emerges from the pupae with well-developed hindwings, eyes, mouthparts and antennae and flies off to find another infected bee. Females remain *in situ* as a pupa, and mating occurs by a male jumping onto a stylopised bee and injecting sperm into the female's neck region. Her eggs hatch inside her body to give rise to tiny triungulin larvae which end up on flowers where they wait to find a suitable bee that can take them back to a nest. Here they eventually enter a well-grown grub and the cycle starts again. Very few entomologists have seen male stylopids, but if you collect some living stylopised bees, which can be fairly easily spotted, and keep them in a container for a few days, you may strike lucky and get a male to emerge. *Andrena scotica* and *A. chrysosceles* are the two most frequently stylopised bees.

Stylopised abdomen of *Andrena bucephala* (left) with a male *Stylops* pupa ready to hatch on the left and a female pupa on the right; male *Stylops melittae* (right) showing the large hind wings.

Parasitoids of bee larvae Flies from an assortment of families seem to fall into this category. The life cycle is not unlike that of cuckoo bees, though the fly larva eats the growing bee larva rather than the cell provisions. Some of the most conspicuous examples are long-snouted *Bombylius* bee-flies. *Bombylius major* attacks a variety of *Andrena* species in a range of habitats in spring. The female *Bombylius* hovers over a host nesting area and flicks eggs onto the ground close to a nest entrance. The young larvae then seek out and enter a host cell. *Bombylius discolor* is more restricted and tends to exploit large nesting aggregations of *Andrena flavipes* and *A. cineraria* in open settings. Two smaller *Bombylius* species fly later in summer: *B. canescens* seems to specialise on *Halictus* and *Lasioglossum* species, whilst the very rare *B. minor* uses *Colletes*.

A number of satellite flies (Sarcophagidae) also attack bees, though it is not always clear whether they do this as cleptoparasites or parasitoids. *Miltogramma punctata* uses ground-nesting bees primarily of the genera *Colletes* and *Dasypoda* but may use some ground-nesting solitary wasps too. The much scarcer *M. germari* seems to prefer *Anthophora bimaculata* and *Megachile* species. The larvae of *Brachicoma devia* live in bumblebee and social wasp nests, feeding externally on the larvae and pupae.

Bee larvae parasitoids: the sapygid wasp *Sapyga quinquepunctata* (top left), the bee-fly *Bombylius major* (top right), the velvet ant *Mutilla europea* (middle left), the sarcophagid fly *Miltogramma punctata* (middle right) and the ruby-tailed wasp *Chrysura radians* (bottom).

A number of aculeate wasps also fall into this category. Ruby-tailed wasps (Chrysididae) of the genus *Chrysura* attack certain *Osmia* species, and *Trichrysis cyanea* attacks various aerial-nesting aculeates including bees of the genera *Chelostoma*, *Hylaeus* and *Heriades*. Of our three velvet ants (Mutillidae), *Mutilla europea* typically attacks bumblebees (but occasionally the Honey Bee) whilst the smaller *Smicromyrme rufipes* and *Myrmosa atra* use a range of ground-nesting aculeates including halictid bees. The males of these three species are winged but the females are wingless and rather ant-like. Our two sapygid wasps specialise on megachilids, *Sapyga quinquepunctata* attacking assorted *Osmia* species whilst *Monosapyga clavicornis* specialises on *Chelostoma florisomne*.

External parasites The best-known external parasite of bees is the mite *Varroa destructor*. It attacks the Honey Bee, feeding on the bodily fluids of adults, pupae and larvae. It is known to spread assorted viruses that affect wing development and contribute to colony collapse disorder. *Varroa* is regarded as the biggest threat to the Honey Bee industry.

Internal parasites Bees are susceptible to a large number of internal parasites including viruses, bacteria, nematodes, single-celled microsporidians and tiny mites, though these are poorly studied in bees other than the Honey Bee and bumblebees. A few of the better-known ones are described here. The mite *Acarapis woodi* lives in the breathing tubes of the Honey Bee, and another species, *Locustacarus buchneri*, has a similar biology in bumblebees. Examples of microsporidians that attack bees are *Nosema apis*, which gives the Honey Bee a form of dysentery, and *N. bombi*, which does the same to bumblebees and is thought to be a major cause of death in overwintering queens. A variety of nematodes have been reported from bees, including *Sphaerularia bombi*, which occupies the body cavities and intestines of bumblebee queens causing sterilisation and modified behaviour. It is likely that queens of early-emerging bumblebees still flying several weeks too late and attempting to dig into the ground are infected with *S. bombi*. *Crithidia bombi*, a protozoan related to *Trypanosoma* (the vector of sleeping sickness in humans) also lives in the intestines of bumblebees.

Predators Birds, mammals, spiders and predatory insects will all catch and eat bees in spite of their stings. Honey Bees are one of the commonest prey items on the webs of the Garden-cross Spider *Araneus diadematus*. Strong Badger populations can have a significant impact on the number of bumblebee nests in a district, and even rodents such as wood mice will attack nests and eat the brood. The main insect predators of bees are wasps and dragonflies. Three of our crabronid 'digger wasps' specialise on bees, the 'Bee-wolf' *Philanthus triangulum*, *Cerceris rybyensis* and the long-extinct *C. sabulosa*. The Hornet *Vespa crabro* will often patrol beehives in search of workers or take Honey Bees from flowers. The spider beetle *Ptinus sexpunctatus* lives in the nests of larger cavity-nesting bees such as *Osmia* and *Megachile* species and will eat larvae and pupae.

A 'bee-wolf' hunting wasp *Philanthus triangulum* carrying a Honey Bee back to its nest.

HABITATS OF BEES

Bees interact with the landscape in a far more complex manner than most insects. Within one site or district, each bee species might have very specific nesting locations plus an array of foraging areas that shift during the flight season as different flowers and blossoms wax and wane. Bee species with long flight periods such as bumblebees and bivoltine mining bees make especially heavy demands of the landscape, as they may be foraging in completely different areas between spring and summer and can face local extinction if any one of their foraging requirements disappears.

Relatively few bees are confined to one habitat type, yet different habitats can have fairly distinct bee assemblages and some bees may have an obligate requirement for a certain habitat (or a specific plant within it) as part of a bigger demand on the landscape. A good example is *Bombus monticola*, which appears to have a strict need for Bilberry in late spring even though it will forage on other species in a variety of habitats before and after Bilberry has flowered. The following describes the broad habitats used by bees and some of the characteristics of the bee assemblages you will find in these.

Chalk grassland at Castle Hill, Sussex – a good place to see rarities like *Andrena hattorfiana* and *Halictus eurygnathus*. The bare track is valuable for ground-nesting bees.

Grassland The majority of Britain's bees have evolved to exploit natural grasslands and most species can be recorded in this habitat, though they sometimes show a strong preference for a particular grassland type or require it in conjunction with other habitats. Calcareous grassland that has developed over chalk and limestone tends to be especially diverse floristically and can also be very warm when on a south-facing escarpment in southern downland areas. Bee assemblages here can be large, with over 80 species at the best sites. Bees strongly associated with southern calcareous grassland include *Andrena hattorfiana* (and its cuckoo *Nomada armata*), *A. marginata* (and its cuckoo *N. argentata*), *A. minutuloides*, *Halictus eurygnathus*, *Hylaeus dilatatus*, *Lasioglossum laevigatum*, *L. fulvicorne*, *Melitta dimidiata*, *M. haemorrhoidalis* (often favouring Clustered Bellflower in calcareous settings), *M. tricincta*, *Osmia bicolor* and *O. spinulosa*.

The acid grassland of heathland districts can also be rich when still associated with heathland and other habitats such as sandpits. It can provide an abundance of flowers such as Cat's-ear, Tormentil, Common Ragwort, Wood Sage and Rosebay Willowherb supporting much bee foraging before the blossoming of Ling. Bees characteristic of acid grasslands include *Andrena humilis* (plus its cuckoo *Nomada integra*), *Dasypoda hirtipes*, *Melitta haemorrhoidalis* (this time using Harebell) and *Panurgus* species. In the north and west, species such as *Andrena coitana*,

Base-poor grassland at the Mossy, Grantown-on-Spey, featuring plentiful Devil's-bit Scabious that attracts bees such as *Andrena marginata* and *Bombus soroeensis*.

A. tarsata, *Lasioglossum fratellum* and *Bombus soroeensis* can become characteristic, the latter especially where late-flowering Devil's-bit Scabious is abundant.

Floristically rich hay meadow can provide a valuable foraging habitat up to the point it is cut, and less improved floodplain pasture is also good providing it is not overgrazed. Legume-loving species such as bumblebees, *Andrena labialis*, *A. wilkella*, *Melitta leporina* and occasionally *Eucera longicornis* will take advantage of any clovers, bird's-foot-trefoils, vetches and vetchlings. Coastal grazing marsh, which has much in common with floodplain pasture, is covered in the Coastal section below.

Heathland and moorland Dry lowland heathland is one of the best habitats for bees, especially where sites are large and varied with sandy areas, varied heather stands, some wet heath and mire, acid grassland, some scrub and woodland, and flowery 'verge habitat' supporting flowers such as umbellifers, thistles, ragworts, Knapweed, Rosebay Willowherb and brambles plus blossoming shrubs such as Blackthorn and Hawthorn. Heathland offering little beyond heathers can be pretty poor by comparison. Heathland also tends to be better where historic disturbance has resulted in pits, mounds, sandy banks, cuttings and other erosion features. These can provide superb nesting conditions for ground-nesting bees when in warm, sheltered locations.

Bees heavily reliant upon lowland heathland include *Andrena fuscipes* (and its cuckoo *Nomada rufipes*), *A. argentata* (and its cuckoo *N. baccata*), *Colletes succinctus* (and its cuckoo *Epeolus cruciger*), *Lasioglossum brevicorne*, *L. prasinum*, *L. quadrinotatum* and *Halictus confusus*. Other characteristic species include *Andrena bimaculata*, *A. barbilabris* (and its cuckoo *Sphecodes pellucidus*), *A. dorsata*, *A. ovatula*, *Anthophora bimaculata*, *Bombus jonellus*, *Colletes fodiens* and *Panurgus* species. The best southern heathland sites can support over 120 bee species. This includes some of the chalk heath of the East Anglian Brecks where heather-dominated areas occur in an intimate mosaic with chalk-influenced sandy grassland creating very flowery conditions that feature a unique mix of heathland-loving, chalk grassland-loving and coastal dune-loving bees.

Dry lowland heathland in the Suffolk Sandlings – one of the richest bee habitats, especially when heathers are flowering.

Moorland (a loose concept that best equates with upland dry heath) supports a rather meagre bee fauna by comparison, sometimes containing some of the species listed above such as *Colletes succinctus*, but usually with a greater abundance of northern-biased bumblebees such as *Bombus bohemicus*, *B. cryptarum*, *B. jonellus*, *B. magnus* and *B. monticola*. *Andrena lapponica*, *A. tarsata* and *Lasioglossum fratellum* also seem to prefer cooler upland heathland and have declined substantially in southern and eastern Britain. Many old records of *Andrena rosae* come from moorland edge locations on Dartmoor, and important populations of *Bombus muscorum* can still be found in the high Pennines and Scottish Highlands.

Upland heathland and moorland in the Cairngorms – a good place to see various northern-biased bumblebees but poor for solitary species.

Coastal This encompasses a variety of rather different habitats, each with their own distinct bee assemblages. The main habitats of interest are coastal dune, soft rock cliff, cliff-top grassland and scrub, coastal grazing marsh, vegetated shingle and saltmarsh. Exploring a varied stretch of coastline containing several of the above habitats can result in an impressive day list of bees.

Coastal dune suits the many bees that like sparsely vegetated sandy ground with a hot microclimate. It shares many of its species with lowland heathland, though it should be noted that some ground-nesting bee species dislike the looser 'blown sands' of dunes. Characteristic species include *Colletes cunicularius*, *C. floralis* (in the north), *C. fodiens*, *C. marginatus*, *Dasypoda hirtipes*, *Megachile leachella* (and its cuckoos *Coelioxys mandibularis* and *C. brevis*), *M. maritima* (and its cuckoo *C. conoidea*), *M. circumcincta* (in the north) and *Osmia aurulenta*. Scarcer bumblebees such as *Bombus humilis* and *B. muscorum* can also be present. The value of coastal dune for bees usually depends upon the variety of dune conditions present, and it can become much reduced as sandier areas are lost through succession (a widespread problem on dunes today) or where the floristically rich grassland of stabilised hind dunes is lost to development or golf courses. Bee assemblages of dunes are often richer when other habitats such as coastal grazing marsh, soft rock cliff, saltmarsh and coastal heathland are located nearby.

Les Blanches Banques dunes, Jersey – coastal dunes can support superb bee assemblages and this site supports Channel Islands specialities such as *Coelioxys brevis*, *Halictus scabiosae* and *Sphecodes marginatus*.

Soft rock cliffs can be exceptionally good for bees, especially where south-facing and not too affected by cliff stabilisation or rapid erosion (the latter a frequent consequence of installing groynes to stabilise beaches nearby). The best sites have a sufficient rate of erosion to promote varied successional stages that include patches of flowery grassland and tall herb, bare or sparsely vegetated ground, seepages and small wetlands plus limited scrub. Geology can also be influential, with some species preferring clay cliffs and others sandy ones. Soft rock cliff systems are better where the undercliffs are complemented by flowery cliff-top grassland, heathland or scrub. This is where much foraging takes place. Blackthorn, gorses, Wild Carrot, Hogweed, bird's-foot-trefoils, Viper's-bugloss, thistles, ragworts, hawkish composites, crucifers, Thrift and heathers are particularly important cliff-top flowers.

Bees seemingly confined to soft rock cliffs include *Osmia xanthomelana*, *Lasioglossum angusticeps*, *L. laticeps* and, in Jersey, *L. mediterraneum* (though they will use a wider range of habitats in continental Europe). The only surviving population of *Nomada sexfasciata* is on a stretch of soft rock cliff, though it used a greater variety of habitats in the past. Other characteristic cliff species include *Andrena alfkenella*, *A. flavipes* (and its cuckoo *Nomada fucata*), *A. ovatula*, *A. pilipes*, *A. thoracica*, *A. trimmerana*, *Anthophora bimaculata*, *A. plumipes* (and its cuckoo *Melecta albifrons*), *Eucera longicornis*, plus various *Lasioglossum* and *Sphecodes*

Flowery cliff-top grassland on the Hampshire coast – an important foraging habitat for bees nesting on the undercliff.

Soft rock cliffs at Eype, Dorset – one of the best places to see rare coastal cliff specialists such as *Lasioglossum angusticeps* and *L. laticeps*. South-facing cliffs are best for bees.

species. On the Channel Islands, *Andrena agilissima*, *Halictus scabiosae* and *Lasioglossum limbellum* seem to rely heavily on soft rock cliffs for nesting.

Coastal grazing marsh (coastal levels) is a very different habitat that can easily be dismissed as a monotonous expanse of improved pasture, though it is often surprisingly good for bees. The pasture can be very rich in legumes such as clovers and Common Bird's-foot-trefoil. The sea walls that enclose such levels can support an abundance of composites and umbellifers as well as furnishing south-facing slopes for ground-nesting species. Grazing marsh ditches can also be very flowery with plants such as Hemlock Water-dropwort, Yellow Iris, Lesser Spearwort, forget-me-nots and Yellow Loosestrife.

Coastal grazing marshes of southeast England are amongst the best places to see scarcer bumblebees such as *Bombus humilis*, *B. muscorum*, *B. sylvarum* and *B. ruderatus*. Other characteristic species include *Andrena wilkella*, *A. labialis* and *Melitta leporina*, all of which require legumes. Ditches can support our two wetland bees *Macropis europaea* and *Hylaeus pectoralis* (see Wetland section below). Good stands of Hemlock Water-dropwort can draw in large numbers of bees from surrounding habitats such as downland and farmland, including rarities such as *Andrena proxima*, *A. nitidiuscula* and *Anthophora retusa*. This can result in much regional variation in the bee assemblages of coastal grazing marsh, with those of Sussex influenced by adjacent chalk downland whilst those of west Hampshire are influenced by the New Forest.

Coastal shingle is a challenging habitat for bees, as few can nest in shingle itself. It is best where it contains patches of sandy ground and more stabilised vegetation. Important flowers for bees include Sea-kale, Sea Mayweed, Sea Spurge, Viper's-bugloss, Common Bird's-foot-trefoil, Common Ragwort, thistles, Red Valerian and brambles. Characteristic bees include *Hylaeus annularis* (almost confined to this habitat), *Osmia aurulenta*, *O. spinulosa*, *Megachile leachella* and *M. maritima*. Shingle in conjunction with coastal grazing marsh is also extremely good bumblebee habitat.

Saltmarsh deserves mention as the key habitat for *Colletes halophilus*, which has a significant proportion of its world population on the British coastline between Dorset and Lincolnshire. It forages primarily on Sea Aster and will often nest in the low cliff faces and silty slopes along the landward edge of the saltmarsh below the spring tide mark. Here, remarkably, it can survive occasional seawater inundation. Bumblebees, including the scarce *Bombus muscorum*, will also forage on saltmarsh, using Sea Aster, Golden-samphire and Sea Lavender. Freshwater seepages flowing into saltmarsh often support stands of Hemlock Water-dropwort, which can attract large numbers of bees.

Coastal grazing marsh at Pevensey Levels, Sussex – one of the best habitats to see scarce bumblebees such as *Bombus humilis*, *B. muscorum* and *B. sylvarum*.

Coastal shingle at Rye Harbour Nature Reserve, Sussex – a good place to see species such as *Bombus humilis*, *B. muscorum*, *Hoplitis claviventris*, *Hylaeus annularis* and *Osmia aurulenta*.

Saltmarsh at Christchurch Harbour, Dorset – the special habitat for *Colletes halophilus*, though flowery saltmarsh edge can attract many types of bee.

Woodland The value of woodland for bees depends to a large extent on the open spaces it contains. However, in early spring, before trees have come into leaf, flowers such as Bluebell, Lesser Celandine, Wood Anemone and Bilberry may allow foraging within the depths of a wood. Spring-blossoming shrubs and trees such as willows, Blackthorn, Cherry and Rowan can be a strong feature of woodland and are often much more sheltered here. The bee assemblages associated with these can be much as described for scrub, below, and many bees will visit woodland for its spring blossom even if nesting occurs elsewhere.

A number of bees are more strongly attached to woodland than this. *Osmia pilicornis* obtains its pollen largely from Bugle in older woods and needs woods with good ride systems or active coppicing. Other characteristic species include *Andrena angustior* and *A. bicolor* (and their cuckoo *Nomada fabriciana*), *A. helvola* (and its cuckoo *N. panzeri*), *A. lapponica* (also a host for *N. panzeri* but specifically requiring Bilberry) and *A. subopaca* (and its cuckoo *N. flavoguttata*). The very rare *A. ferox* has most of its populations in the New Forest and collects pollen primarily from English Oak in what can best be described as dense pasture woodland with heathy

Ancient coppice woodland in Sussex – an important habitat for the rare *Osmia pilicornis* but also supporting a good variety of *Andrena* and *Nomada* species.

Native pine woodland in the Cairngorms – the special habitat of *Osmia uncinata*. Carpets of flowering Bilberry attract large numbers of bumblebee queens in spring, including *Bombus monticola*.

clearings that provide nesting areas. Damper woods on base-poor soils of the north and west featuring plentiful Tormentil are good places to search for *Andrena tarsata* (and its cuckoo *Nomada roberjeotiana*), as well as for *A. coitana* (and its cuckoo *N. obtusifrons*). *Bombus bohemicus* can also be frequent in such woods.

In the Scottish Highlands, open-structured Caledonian pine forest is the special habitat for *Osmia uncinata*, which nests in dead wood and forages mainly on Common Bird's-foot-trefoil. Such woodland typically has a carpet of Bilberry and scattered willows, Broom and Rowan. It can be an excellent habitat in spring, attracting large numbers of northern-biased bumblebees such as *Bombus bohemicus*, *B. cryptarum*, *B. jonellus*, *B. magnus* and *B. monticola*. Smaller bees here include *Andrena lapponica* (and its cuckoo *Nomada panzeri*), *A. subopaca* and *Lasioglossum fratellum*. Coniferous plantations can also be interesting sites if they have good ride systems. In fact the longest modern bee list for any wooded site is from Elveden Forest in the Suffolk Brecks, which is essentially a diversified block of pine plantation.

Scrub This is often considered a transitional habitat, subsidiary or even threatening to other habitats. Yet for many bees it is every bit as important. Scrub can comprise various shrub species and young trees, some of which produce valuable spring blossoms. Willows of various sorts are amongst the first to flower, and their catkins are used by virtually all spring-flying bees, notably bumblebee queens, *Andrena* species (and their *Nomada* cuckoos), *Anthophora plumipes* and early-emerging *Lasioglossum* and their *Sphecodes* cuckoos. No fewer than six bee species depend on willows as their primary source of pollen: *Andrena apicata*, *A. clarkella*, *A. praecox*, *A. ruficrus*, *A. vaga* and *Colletes cunicularius*. *Nomada ferruginata* and *N. leucophthalma*, as the special cuckoos of some of these *Andrena* species, are also indirectly reliant on willows. Rosaceous plants such as Blackthorn, Hawthorn, Rowan and Crab Apple are also heavily exploited in spring, with species such as *Andrena varians* and *A. synadelpha* particularly dependent on them. Common Gorse is often in flower by late winter, and *Andrena bimaculata* and *A. ovatula* are rarely found at sites that lack it, even though they are bivoltine and forage on a much broader range of flowers.

Scrub is important for bees in other ways too. It is a source of hollow twigs and dead wood for various aerial nesters such as *Ceratina cyanea*, *Hoplitis claviventris* and species of *Chelostoma*, *Hylaeus*, *Megachile* and *Osmia*. It can provide a valuable windbreak that allows some parts of a site to attain higher temperatures than would otherwise be possible. A few degrees of extra warmth can make a lot of difference to insects such as bees that are often close to their climatic limits here in Britain and Ireland. Scrub is also an important habitat for lekking male bees, notably *Andrena* species. Finally, scrub can be important for bees that visit flowering climbers – e.g. *Andrena florea*, which obtains its pollen from White Bryony – or bees that forage on Honeysuckle, brambles and Ivy.

Blossoming Blackthorn on the South Downs – spring-blossoming shrubs can attract large numbers of bees, especially *Andrena* species and queen bumblebees.

Wetland This can be a very flowery habitat, with abundant blossoming willows in spring and many bee-friendly flowers over the summer months. This includes Marsh Woundwort, Greater Bird's-foot-trefoil, Water Mint, Fleabane, Hemp-agrimony, Wild Angelica, Great Willowherb, Meadowsweet, Purple Loosestrife and Yellow Loosestrife. Many bee species will forage in wetlands, though compared with habitats such as heathland and grassland, the assemblages tend to have a greater proportion of aerial nesters such as *Anthophora furcata* and species of *Hylaeus*, *Megachile* and *Osmia*. Two of our bees are strongly associated with wetlands. *Macropis europaea* likes fen and watersides, and can nest in soils that experience occasional inundation by waterproofing its nests with floral oils obtained from Yellow Loosestrife. *Hylaeus pectoralis* is associated with reedbeds, nesting in old 'cigar galls' of the fly *Lipara lucens* at the tips of Common Reed stems and possibly ungalled hollow reed stems too. *Bombus muscorum* also favours wetlands in many parts of its range, especially expansive and exposed ones.

Brownfield land In many parts of Britain and Ireland, brownfield sites now support the richest bee assemblages with the largest number of rare species. Brownfield land is a broad category that includes quarries, gravel workings, old industrial sites, and railway sidings – typically sites where the original land surface has been radically altered through excavation, dumping,

The Norfolk Broads, one of the best places to see wetland specialists such as *Hylaeus pectoralis* and *Macropis europaea*; this is also a good habitat for aerial nesting bees in general.

demolition and vehicle usage. Once heavy disturbance ceases such sites can develop grassland, wetland, scrub, heathland, even brackish wetlands, often in an intimate mosaic featuring much early successional habitat.

Much of the flora of brownfield sites consists of alien plants rather than natives, yet bees can abound and often do better than in equivalent semi-natural situations. Limestone quarries, for example, often have better bee assemblages than old limestone grassland, probably in part because key flowers such as Great Knapweed, Kidney Vetch and Wild Parsnip can grow at much higher densities in the first few decades following disturbance. Brownfield land can also be much warmer than other habitats, with sheltered south-facing slopes and faces that produce good nesting conditions for ground-nesting species. Brambles, roses, old walls and timbers can also encourage good assemblages of aerial nesters, and if reedbeds are present it is even possible to encounter *Hylaeus pectoralis*.

Bee species heavily dependent upon brownfield sites over substantial parts of their range include *Bombus humilis*, *B. ruderatus*, *Ceratina cyanea*, *Colletes similis*, *Hoplitis claviventris*, *Hylaeus cornutus*, *H. signatus*, *Lasioglossum xanthopus*, *Osmia bicolor*, *O. spinulosa*, *Andrena apicata*, *A. praecox* and *A. tibialis*. *Colletes cunicularius* seems to have used sandy brownfield sites such as old sandpits as stepping stones in its recent expansion across southern Britain.

Canvey Wick, Essex – flowery brownfield land supports some of our finest bee assemblages and is important for rare species such as *Bombus sylvarum*.

Urban The longest modern list of bees from a single site anywhere in Britain (133 species) comes from the Surrey garden featured in the photograph below. It has a good variety of flowers but is for the most part a formal rather than wildlife garden, though it doubtless benefits from a being located near to heathland and woodland. Gardens are important habitats for bees, and several species are easier to encounter here than anywhere else, including *Anthidium manicatum* (and its cuckoo *Stelis punctulatissima*), *Anthophora plumipes* (and its cuckoo *Melecta albifrons*), *A. quadrimaculata*, *Chelostoma campanularum*, *Heriades truncorum* (and its cuckoo *Stelis breviuscula*), *Megachile centuncularis* (and its cuckoo *Coelioxys inermis*), *Osmia bicornis* and *Bombus hypnorum*. These are all aerial nesters capable of using old walls and timbers, and many readily take to bee hotels. Ground-nesting *Andrena*, *Lasioglossum* and *Halictus* species can sometimes take advantage of dry bits of lawn and the soil of rockeries and flowerbeds. Many other species are 'tramps', foraging on the great variety of flowers that gardens provide over many months of the year but nesting in other habitats nearby.

Other urban or semi-formalised habitats of value for bees include churchyards and cemeteries, public parks (especially where these have good flowerbeds and a range of blossoming shrubs and trees), allotments, school grounds, landscaped business parks, village greens and orchards. The growing popularity of wildlife gardening and bee hotels could substantially boost the

This Surrey garden has produced the longest list of bees for any site in the British Isles.

Bee hotels come in many shapes and sizes. You can make them yourself or buy them, but place them somewhere warm and sunny.

abundance of bees in towns and cities over the course of the twenty-first century, and much information and advice is available on the web.

Arable farmland Modern farming practices are widely blamed for the long-term reduction in bee numbers and the dramatic declines of some individual species. Loss of old grasslands, grubbing out of hedges, heavy use of herbicides and pesticides are all thought to have contributed. Yet some sectors of the farming industry have continually striven to promote bee-friendly habitat through the use of flowery arable margins, flowery set-aside, flowery headlands, tolerance of 'weeds' such as ragworts and thistles and the planting of blossoming trees and shrubs. As a consequence, arable farmland can still sometimes be a good place to see a variety of bees, even rarities, and it can interact strongly with surrounding habitat such as chalk grassland, heathland or coastal habitats.

In some districts, Oil-seed Rape can attract about 30 species of bee and complement blossoming shrub species or early umbellifers such as Cow Parsley. Cultivated Pea, Broad Bean, Borage and Potato all produce flowers attractive to bees. But even where crops offer little in the way of forage, arable margins, rested land and field hedges can be important.

In spring, blossoming farm hedges are exploited in much the same way as flowering shrubs are in other habitats, and adjacent field margins may provide dandelions, dead-nettles, Cow Parsley and, in some coastal districts, Alexanders. Over summer months, margins can generate good shows of thistles, umbellifers, poppies, mayweeds, hawk's-beards, wild clovers, spurges, speedwells, mignonettes, pansies and fumitories, attracting dozens of bee species. Arable margins on lighter chalk and limestone soils can be exceptionally good with calcicoles such as Field Scabious, Greater Knapweed, Musk Thistle, Wild Basil and Marjoram – all excellent plants for bees.

Two rare bee species now have significant proportions of their surviving populations at arable sites. *Andrena nigrospina* requires very sandy conditions with abundant crucifers such as Wild Radish, a combination provided by some arable districts of the West Midlands and East Anglia. *Andrena niveata* prefers yellow crucifers such as Charlock, Hedge Mustard and brassicas in the farmland of southern downland districts. The introduction of clovers at field margins in counties such as Warwickshire has resulted in substantial increases in bumblebees, including the severely declined *Bombus ruderatus*, which is now often locally common having once been considered extinct in such areas.

Upper Blackstone Farm, Worcestershire – one of the few places where you can still see *Andrena nigrospina* and its cuckoo *Nomada subcornuta*, the former foraging mainly on Wild Radish and poppies.

Montane Bees are essentially warmth-loving, and very few species can exploit the cool, exposed and flower-poor conditions associated with high altitude. But montane areas are not necessarily bee-free zones. *Osmia inermis* is the closest we have to a montane specialist. Strictly speaking it is a bee of hills up to 550 metres where base-rich soils can support plants such as Common Bird's-foot-trefoil. Conditions can be so challenging that its life cycle can take 2–4 years. On warm, sunny days bees from lower altitudes will also forage surprisingly high. Bumblebees such as *Bombus magnus*, *B. cryptarum*, *B. monticola* and *B. jonellus* can all regularly be found at over 600 metres in the Scottish Highlands foraging on dwarf willows, heathers and *Vaccinium* species. The mining bee *Andrena lapponica* has also been observed at these altitudes. However, these bees are opportunists rather than specialists and cannot normally complete a life cycle this high.

Montane habitat in the Cairngorms – few bees can cope with high altitudes other than *Osmia inermis* and a few bumblebee species.

Distributional biases and anomalies Aside from any habitat requirements, many bee species only use a proportion of the apparently suitable area available. In most instances it seems to be climatic factors at play – perhaps the summers are not quite hot enough north of a certain point, or the climate is too damp and maritime in the west or too dry in the southeast. The vast majority of our bees are warmth-loving, southern-biased species with the natural edge of their range within the British Isles. The strongest evidence that climate is the limiting factor is the recent northern expansion of some once-restricted species as mean temperatures have risen and made the Midlands and northern Britain warmer. Examples include *Andrena flavipes* (and its cuckoo *Nomada fucata*), *Bombus rupestris*, *Lasioglossum malachurum* and *L. pauxillum*.

A select group of species have a strong northern and western bias: *Andrena ruficrus*, *Bombus magnus*, *B. monticola*, *Colletes floralis*, *Osmia inermis*, *O. parietina* and *O. uncinata*. A further group of species were once fairly widespread but have largely or entirely retreated to the north and/or west, including *Andrena coitana* (and its cuckoo *Nomada obtusifrons*), *A. tarsata* (and its cuckoo *N. roberjeotiana*), *Bombus bohemicus*, *B. distinguendus*, *B. muscorum*, *B. soroeensis* and *Megachile circumcincta*.

Cleptoparasitic bees can sometimes be far more restricted than their hosts. For example, *Bombus rupestris* does not extend as far north as *B. lapidarius*, *B. vestalis* does not extend as far north as *B. terrestris*, and *Nomada armata* has never been recorded in the East Anglia Brecks despite this being one of the strongholds for its host *Andrena hattorfiana*.

FIELD TECHNIQUES FOR FINDING AND RECORDING BEES

With experience, you can learn to recognise many bees in the field without needing to collect or kill them. However, if you wish to record everything you see, including those challenging *Andrena*, *Hylaeus*, *Lasioglossum* and *Sphecodes* species that are virtually indistinguishable in the field, you will need to collect and kill a sample of what you find. Bear in mind that what you see in the field is usually a tiny proportion of what actually exists, so it is unlikely you will make any significant dent in a population by taking the odd sample (but you might help conserve it with the data you generate). The main equipment you require to collect bees is a net, pooters, killing tubes and a killing agent.

Remember that bees are most active in warm, sunny weather, and on overcast days you may only see bumblebees and the Honey Bee. Bumblebees and the Honey Bee can be active from early morning until dusk, but most bees tend to emerge from about 10am and often stop foraging by mid to late afternoon. If it is a breezy day, try to find parts of a site that are sheltered from the wind. Most sites have varied topography and microclimate, and bees will generally select the warmest areas for foraging and nesting. Check OS maps, aerial site photographs (using the internet) and weather reports when planning your day, and remember that the position of the sun changes during the day, so if you wish to record an east-facing hillside or cliff, you need to do it in the morning before it gets shaded. If the weather forecast indicates a westerly breeze, you are best to avoid a west-facing hillside or stretch of coast.

Nets Insect nets come in many shapes and sizes. Short-handled kite nets can suffice for gardens, but a more effective and adaptable set-up is a 40cm diameter net frame with a white nylon net on an extendible metal pole (such as the landing-net poles that are sold by fishing shops). A white bag is better than a black one because you can see the bees more easily. The extendible pole can be kept short (typically 1.5 metres) when in a confined space or extended 2–3 metres further (depending on the type of pole) if you want to catch bees high up on shrub blossom, flying around a cliff face or on flowers across a fence line. The other advantage of a long pole is that it allows you to sweep flowers and nesting areas very effectively without your body movements scaring off the bees. After a series of sweeps you can examine the bees in your net bag, and pooter up or tube the ones you wish to retain. Always remember to keep your net bag

Sweeping an undercliff with a long-handled insect net – short handled nets are much less efficient.

facing the sun and as high as possible when you search it, otherwise the bees will fly out past your head before you get a chance to check them. Always keep spare net bags and a small sewing kit so that a ripped net does not prematurely end your recording session. Also, wear a hat so that bees do not get tangled in your hair. Most bees will not sting you, but a trapped bumblebee or Honey Bee might.

Pooters, tubes and killing jars Pooters are the most efficient way of collecting samples of smaller bees. A good southern site might have 12 species of *Lasioglossum* and 8 species of *Sphecodes* on the wing simultaneously. They often have slightly different sizes, shapes and patterns. By pootering up a sample of small, big, dark and pale specimens, you may be able to record a good proportion of the species present. The best pooters are the perspex ones with barrels 15cm long. Glass ones are prone to shattering and smaller pooters have limited capacity and are more prone to getting damp inside and ruining your material. It is wise to keep 2–3 pooters to hand, filling each one with perhaps 50 specimens before moving on to a fresh pooter. Whilst using a pooter, keep your finger over the mouth of the entrance tube between uses, because bees are good at escaping. To kill the catch, carefully insert a small wad of tissue (about the size of a grapefruit pip but slimmer) dosed with ethyl acetate into the barrel via the entrance tube using a short sharp suck (a long suck will fumigate you too!). Then place a sliver of leaf in the mouth of the entrance tube to stop anything escaping and keep the fumes in the barrel.

Larger bees that cannot fit into pooters can be placed individually into tubes such as old 35mm film canisters (lined with paper to stop condensation) or larger killing jars that have been predosed with ethyl acetate on some tissue or crushed Cherry-laurel leaves (which produce cyanide). Bees will become inactive within a minute or so of exposure to fumes, but it can take a few hours to fully kill one. It is important that your container does not get damp as this happens, so it is best to transfer inactive specimens to a fresh container with fresh, dry tissue and fresh killing agent. You can also kill bees by placing them in a freezer overnight. Remember that female bees are often covered in pollen, and it is possible to identify this later to see what flowers a bee has been utilising. We still have much to learn about bee foraging.

Some of the equipment you will need to study bees: a microscope (with lighting source), pinning trays, a pooter, a killing jar, specimen tubes and fine forceps.

Handling bees Some bees can be identified with a hand lens, thereby avoiding the need to kill them. Many bumblebee recorders use tubes with plungers to examine living bumblebees humanely (e.g. checking face length to separate *Bombus hortorum* from *B. jonellus*) and then release them. It is also worth noting that not all bees can sting you. Males lack stings altogether, but you might also be surprised to know that *Andrena* and *Panurgus* females struggle to sting humans. Bumblebees and the

Handling – not all bees can sting you.

Honey Bee certainly have very painful stings, and *Megachile*, *Halictus* and *Colletes* are also fairly painful. If you are allergic to bee stings or at all nervous, do not handle them.

Trapping bees An alternative to active sampling is passive sampling using traps. These can generate good species lists if set up carefully, and they are often favoured over active sampling where standardised monitoring is being carried out. This is because they avoid the problems that can arise with varied competence or different sampling styles of human recorders. The two main trap types suited to bees are water traps (pan traps) and Malaise traps. Water traps are shallow bowls filled with shallow water, a few drops of detergent and a tablespoon of salt. Yellow bowls are often regarded as best, but some bees prefer other colours and some recent studies have used groups of yellow, blue and white bowls. Traps can be placed on the ground or raised on stands. The traps can be left for a few days at a time and the collected material transferred to alcohol. Be careful to avoid the evaporating effects of very hot weather or the impact of heavy rain.

Malaise traps resemble small tents constructed of nylon mesh. Insects fly into them and get channelled into a collecting container containing preservative or a killing agent. This technique

Water-filled pan traps – one of the most effective passive sampling techniques and ideal for long-term monitoring.

has also generated some very impressive site lists. The main drawback of passive sampling is that you do not get the useful observational data that can be gleaned from active sampling, such as seeing first-hand where a bee is foraging or nesting and which cuckoo bees and other parasites might be attacking it. But the numerical data produced, and the replicable nature of such sampling, make it a valuable approach for monitoring bee abundance.

Pinning and storing dead bees You will need a microscope, pins, pinning trays (a shallow container with a layer of polyethylene foam (Plastazote) at the bottom), fine entomological forceps and entomological storeboxes (or an equivalent) to do this properly. The ideal microscope is a stereo zoom model with magnification of 7–45× and 10× eyepieces. Once your bee is dead, it needs to be pinned. This needs to be done fairly quickly, as the specimen will either soon dry out and become brittle and impossible to manipulate or start to rot and become smelly or mouldy. There are several different pinning styles. The simplest involves placing a long pin through the thorax (just to one side of the midline) so that the specimen ends up about halfway up the pin. Labels can then be placed on the pin below the specimen. However, the bee cannot be easily 'set' using this approach, and it is also unsuitable for very small bees.

A better approach is to pin the specimen onto Plastazote using a shorter micropin (these come in assorted lengths and diameters). This allows you to set a specimen, using further micropins to ensure that its legs, wings and mouthparts (mandibles and proboscis) dry in a position that allows easier future examination. The male genitalia and female sting can also be extracted from the tip of the abdomen with a sharp pin and forced to dry in an exposed position so that they are always easily checked. Setting is best done under a microscope. Once dry (usually 1–4 weeks later, depending on the size of the bee), the micropinned specimen can be 'staged'. This involves placing the pinned specimen on one end of a short strip of Plastazote with a long pin inserted through the other end. Labels are placed onto the long pin. This has the advantage that the specimens are less likely to get damaged during handling, and very small bees can be pinned with tiny micropins rather than large pins that destroy valuable thoracic features.

It is critically important that you record the date and locality of each bee specimen you capture, and avoid any mixing up. Every specimen will require a label that gives the date of capture, site of capture, the county of that site, the national grid reference to at least six figures (e.g. SP123789) and the name of the recorder. Determination labels are best kept separate from locality labels and should note the species, determiner, and the date of the determination. It is very important that you are able to see which specimens in your collection have been accurately determined (especially if by an expert), as these will provide reference points that help you to navigate the keys in this book.

The best containers to store a collection of pinned bees are wooden entomological storeboxes with very tight-fitting sections. These can be purchased from various suppliers and are usually lined with Plastazote foam with white paper around the sides. It is also possible to use less appropriate storage containers such as Tupperware-style plastic food boxes with storebox dimensions, placing a layer of foam at the bottom. However, these do not always have airtight lids, and if they do, they are more prone to a build-up of dampness and mould than storeboxes, where the wood buffers against dampness.

Pinned insects of all sorts are very perishable and need careful curation. Attack by *Anthrenus* carpet (museum) beetles, dust mites and mould are the main problems. A tight-fitting lid can

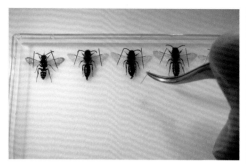

Pinning bees in a pinning tray using fine forceps and micropins (above). One micropin is placed through the thorax and other pins are used to hold the wings, legs and open mandibles in position as the specimen dries. Once dried, the specimen can be staged and labelled (right). Notice how the male genitalia have been extracted to allow easy checking (vital for male *Sphecodes*).

help to protect your specimens from pests, and you can also use mothballs or cedar oil as deterrents. Mould is a regular problem if you have a cool, damp house. Silica gel can help keep dampness at bay. As a rule of thumb, never leave a container containing pinned bees on the floor or touching a wall, and never leave specimens out in the open for long periods between examinations, as they may have attracted carpet beetles during this time and could

Part of the author's bee collection, which is kept in purpose-built entomological storeboxes that are checked regularly for pest attack.

introduce these to the rest of your collection when you return them to their storage box.

An alternative approach to pinning bees is to store them in 70% alcohol. Temporary storage in alcohol is often an inevitable consequence of using traps. However, identifying alcohol-soaked bees is very difficult, as many of the characters used in the keys – such as colour, microsculpture and hair-based characters – are obscured.

Rearing bees This has become increasingly popular in recent years. 'Trap nests' are essentially bee hotels in which the contents of the individual tubes are reared out to see what emerges. Trap nests often reveal the presence of species you have failed to see, such as cuckoo bees including *Coelioxys* and *Stelis* species. Some trap nests can be opened to see and extract nest cells, and some even have glass tubes so that you can see the bee larvae feeding on their provisions. You can also try rearing bees such as *Ceratina cyanea* by collecting hollow bramble and Elder twigs, or *Hylaeus pectoralis* from the old cigar galls of the chloropid fly *Lipara lucens* on Common Reed. This is a great way of filling the winter gap.

Purchasing equipment There are too many entomological equipment suppliers to list here, and the market is very dynamic, with suppliers constantly increasing the range of products they can supply. A simple web search will quickly reveal what is available and allow you to compare prices and specifications of individual items.

Submitting data If you are confident of your determinations, you can send records to BWARS (www.bwars.com). It is also recommended that you send data to county biological records centres, nature reserve owners or National Trust regional managers, as appropriate. If the record is Irish, send it to the Irish Pollinator Initiative (http://pollinators.biodiversityireland.ie). If you are uncertain of a specimen or photograph, it is recommended that you contact BWARS through their online discussion group. You can also get opinions on photographs and submit records through iSpot (www.ispotnature.org).

CONSERVING BEES

The publication of this book coincides with renewed commitment by UK national governments to promote pollinators and undo some of the losses of the past. However, bee conservation has been taking place in Britain and Ireland for many years in a variety of ways.

Conserving species A review of scarce and threatened bee, wasp and ant species (Falk, 1991) provided rarity gradings (Nationally Scarce and assorted Red Data Book levels) for 126 bee species. Shortly afterwards, some of the most rapidly declining and threatened species, including 17 bees, were listed as priority species in the UK Biodiversity Action Plan (BAP) process and became the subjects of species action plans, which resulted in numerous funded and unfunded projects. The BAP process has since been devolved to individual UK countries, and each of the four countries has its own lists of what are now termed Species of Principal Importance. Studies of these have included targeted surveys, monitoring and autecological research, particularly by BWARS members, the Bumblebee Conservation Trust (BBCT) and the charity Hymettus. Amateur bee recorders have played a huge role in this process, and it is hoped that this book will increase capacity for this in the future. The Nationally Scarce and Red Data Book grades in Falk (1991) are now badly out of date, but any new list of rarity grades will be obtainable through the website of the Joint Nature Conservation Committee (JNCC: http://jncc.defra.gov.uk). Conservation gradings for Irish bees can be obtained from the species accounts of the Irish Biodiversity Data Centre (http://www.biodiversityireland.ie).

SPECIES OF PRINCIPAL IMPORTANCE IN ENGLAND (E), WALES (W), SCOTLAND (S) AND NORTHERN IRELAND (NI)

Andrena cineraria (S), *A. coitana* (NI), *A. denticulata* (NI), *A. ferox* (E), *A. fuscipes* (NI), *A. helvola* (S), *A. marginata* (S), *A. nigroaenea* (NI), *A. nitida* (S), *A. praecox* (NI), *A. ruficrus* (S), *A. semilaevis* (NI), *A. tarsata* (E, W), *Anthophora retusa* (E), *Bombus barbutellus* (NI), *B. campestris* (NI), *B. distinguendus* (S), *B. humilis* (E, W), *B. monticola* (S), *B. muscorum* (E, W, S, NI), *B. ruderarius* (E, W, S), *B. ruderatus* (E, W), *B. rupestris* (NI), *B. subterraneus* (E), *B. sylvarum* (E, W), *Colletes daviesanus* (S), *C. floralis* (E, S, NI), *C. fodiens* (S), *C. halophilus* (E), *Epeolus variegatus* (S), *Eucera longicornis* (E, W), *Hylaeus brevicornis* (S, NI), *H. hyalinatus* (NI), *Lasioglossum angusticeps* (E), *L. fulvicorne* (S), *L. nitidiusculum* (NI), *L. rufitarse* (NI), *L. smeathmanellum* (S), *L. villosulum* (S), *Nomada armata* (E), *N. errans* (E), *N. fabriciana* (S), *N. goodeniana* (NI), *N. leucophthalma* (S), *N. obtusifrons* (S), *N. roberjeotiana* (S), *N. striata* (NI), *Osmia aurulenta* (S), *O. bicornis* (S), *O. caerulescens* (S), *O. inermis* (S), *O. parietina* (E, W, S), *O. uncinata* (S), *O. xanthomelana* (E, W), *Sphecodes ferruginatus* (NI), *S. gibbus* (S, NI), *S. pellucidus* (NI), *Stelis punctulatissima* (S)

Examples of the practical conservation that has taken place for individual bee species include much habitat creation and enhancement for our scarcer bumblebees, the reintroduction of *Bombus subterraneus*, and some small-scale works to improve nesting habitat for *Colletes floralis* and *C. halophilus*. Conservation organisations are far more aware of the presence of these species on their land now, and their needs are increasingly accounted for in site management planning.

Conserving bee habitats and key sites Bees can easily be encouraged in your back garden, in a pocket nature reserve, along road verges and field margins, in country parks, wildlife trust reserves or worked-out quarries. At the landscape scale National Parks, Areas of Outstanding Natural Beauty and natural character areas provide huge opportunities. In any of these scenarios it is important to encourage both foraging and nesting areas and to promote varied conditions and habitat mosaics. Bees need a constant supply of suitable flowers throughout their flight period(s), plus suitable nesting habitat.

Bee hotels for aerial nesters are easy to purchase or build, and it is also very easy to create bee banks and other places suited to ground-nesters. As an amateur enthusiast, you can encourage bees in your garden, or help your local wildlife trust, any allotment association you belong to, a local country park or a local National Trust property. Try to undertake a survey first, because the resultant species list, cross-referenced with the information in this book, will help you to formulate a package of recommendations and ensure that key forage plants are recognised.

Protecting the best bee sites (usually those with several rare species or unusually large species assemblages) also means designating them. Many sites of county or district value – Local Wildlife Sites (LWSs) or Sites of Importance for Nature Conservation (SINCs) – have been designated partly on the presence of rare bees, and even some nationally important Sites of Special Scientific Interest (SSSIs) such as Highgate Common in Staffordshire. Whilst the actual process of designation is a technical one usually involving professionals, the data underpinning the process often come entirely from amateur recorders.

Ask your local wildlife trust or biological records centre how you can go about recording bees in a way that will help them identify potential new LWSs or monitor those that already exist. Remember that it is not just pristine meadows and attractive woods that need attention. Some of the best bee sites are brownfield ones, and these receive a disproportionate level of threat compared with other habitats. Always make sure you get permission before you collect bees on somebody's land.

Extinct species Twenty-five bee species appear to have become extinct in these islands during recorded history, though some caution needs to be exercised when making such decrees as two species (*Andrena vaga* and *Halictus eurygnathus*) have recently been rediscovered following long periods without any records. Some of these extinct species may not have been permanent residents, and the validity of a couple is questionable. Nevertheless, these losses, added to recorded losses of plants and other wildlife, reflect the staggering extent to which the British and Irish countryside has changed over the past two hundred years or so. What makes this sadder is the fact that some of these extinct bees were described as new to science on the basis of English specimens: *Andrena nana*, *Bombus cullumanus*, *Lasioglossum laeve* and *Hoplitis leucomelana* are all British bees that are no longer British.

EXTINCT BRITISH AND IRISH BEES (WITH DATE OF LAST RECORD)

Andrena floricola (1939)	*Bombus subterraneus*	*Hylaeus punctulatissimus* (1827)
Andrena lathyri (1990)	(late 1980s, but currently	*Lasioglossum laeve* (pre-1802)
Andrena lepida (1952)	subject of reintroduction)	*Megachile ericetorum* (1844)
Andrena nana (1930)	*Coelioxys afra* (1956)	*Megachile lapponica* (1847)
Andrena nanula	*Dufourea halictula* (1953)	*Megachile parietina*
(period 1875–77)	*Dufourea minuta* (1956)	(mid-nineteenth century)
Andrena polita (1934)	*Eucera nigrescens* (1970)	*Melecta luctuosa* (1912)
Andrena tridentata (1944)	*Halictus maculatus* (1930)	*Nomada errans* (1982)
Bombus cullumanus (1941)	*Halictus subauratus* (pre-1900)	*Rophites quinquespinosus*
Bombus pomorum (1864)	*Hoplitis leucomelana* (pre-1802)	(1878)

SOCIETIES AND RECORDING GROUPS

Here are some of the organisations that you can join if you wish to become more heavily involved in recording and conserving bees:

- **Bees, Wasps and Ants Recording Society (BWARS)** The official recording scheme covering bees. It produces a regular newsletter and holds an annual indoor meeting and runs regular workshops. The website (www.bwars.com) provides maps and species accounts for virtually all species and many useful downloads including the very useful 'Bees in Britain'.

- **Bumblebee Conservation Trust (BBCT)** A conservation charity for bumblebees which undertakes habitat creation and enhancement projects, research and awareness-raising. It runs a national monitoring initiative called BeeWalk that is easy to join. The website (bumblebeeconservation.org) provides much information to help you enjoy and conserve bumblebees.

- **Buglife** A conservation charity that covers all invertebrates and has done much work on bees, especially the species associated with brownfield sites and farmland. They have a number of projects aimed at promoting bees and other pollinators including B-lines, various 'Get Britain Buzzing' initiatives and the South West Bees Project. Much useful information is provided by their website (www.buglife.org.uk).

A number of counties and regions have entomological or invertebrate study groups that will enable you to meet more experienced entomologists who can provide support and advice, notably: Buckinghamshire, Derbyshire & Nottinghamshire, Lancashire & Cheshire, Leicestershire, Shropshire, Staffordshire, Worcestershire and Scotland (through Buglife, Stirling). The Kent Field Club, Essex Field Club and Highland Biological Recording Group provide similar opportunities. Most of these groups have websites with contact details and event programmes.

BEES BEYOND BRITAIN AND IRELAND

The study and recording of bees is increasingly an international affair, and there are a number of reasons for this:

- **Potential for new British and Irish species** Familiarity with bees in adjacent Europe is one of the best ways of discovering new British species. Many additional species occur as soon as you cross the English Channel, and some of these are very similar to British ones. It should also be noted that many European species are expanding their ranges northwards and some of these can be expected to arrive in Britain, either naturally or through human assistance.

- **Conserving bees internationally** The threats to bees and strategies for conserving them are often common across national boundaries. Research into the impacts of pesticides or habitat fragmentation in one country could be equally relevant to numerous other countries. Many bees have shown simultaneous declines in various countries, e.g. *Bombus cullumanus* and *B. pomorum*, suggesting that common factors are at play. The IUCN (International Union for Conservation of Nature) produced a European Red List of bees in 2015 which affords rarity gradings to several British species: *Andrena tridentata* and *Bombus cullumanus* (both Critically Endangered), *Lasioglossum laeve* (Endangered) and *Bombus distinguendus*, *B. muscorum*, *B. pomorum*, *Colletes floralis* and *C. fodiens* (Vulnerable). The last species is threatened in most European countries despite being relatively frequent and secure in Britain.

- **Placing our bees in context** Whilst many of our bees are commonplace in Europe and on the edge of their ranges here, species such as *Colletes halophilus* and *C. floralis* have a significant proportion of their global populations within Britain and Ireland. As noted earlier, we also have some colour forms and perhaps subspecies that are unique to us or unusual abroad, e.g. *Bombus terrestris* ssp. *audax*.

Fortunately, the resources available for understanding the European bee fauna, especially web-based, have increased substantially in recent years (see opposite).

FURTHER READING

BOOKS AND ARTICLES

Archer, M (ed.) 2004 *BWARS Member's Handbook*. Centre for Ecology and Hydrology, St Ives. 157 pp.

Benton, T 2006 *British Bumblebees*. New Naturalist No. 98. Collins, London. 580 pp.

Bogusch, P & Straka, J 2012 Review and identification of the cuckoo bees of central Europe (Hymenoptera: Halictidae: *Sphecodes*). *Zootaxa* 3311: 1–41 (available online)

Edwards, M & Jenner, M 2005 *Field Guide to the Bumblebees of Great Britain & Ireland* (revised edition). Ocelli, Eastbourne. 108 pp.

Falk, S J 1991 *A Review of the Scarce and Threatened Bees, Wasps and Ants of Great Britain*. Research and Survey in Nature Conservation No. 35. Nature Conservancy Council, Peterborough. 344 pp (downloadable from JNCC Publications).

Goulson, D 2009 *Bumblebees: Behaviour, Ecology, and Conservation*. Oxford University Press, Oxford. 336 pp.

Michener, C D 2007 *The Bees of the World* (2nd edition). Johns Hopkins University Press, Baltimore. 953 pp.

O'Toole, C 2013 *Bees: A Natural History*. Firefly Books, Ontario. 240 pp.

Prys-Jones, O E & Corbert, S A 2011 *Bumblebees* (3rd edition). Naturalists' Handbooks No. 6. Pelagic Publishing, Exeter. 144 pp.

Sladen, F W L 1912 (1989 reprint) *The Humble-Bee: Its Life History and How to Domesticate it*. Logaston Press, Little Logaston. 273 pp.

Useful European keys include volumes of *Illustrierte Bestimmungstabellen der Wildbienen Deutschlands und Österreichs* (covering Germany and Austria) and *Fauna Helvetica* (covering Switzerland).

COUNTY OR REGIONAL ATLASES AND CHECKLISTS

Allen, G 2009 *Bees, Wasps and Ants of Kent*. Kent Field Club. 117 pp.

Baldock, D W 2008 *Bees of Surrey*. Surrey Wildlife Trust. 303 pp.

Benton, T 2000 *The Bumblebees of Essex*. Lopinga Books, Wimbish. 180 pp.

Gammans, N & Allen G 2014 *The Bumblebees of Kent*. Kent Field Club. 164 pp.

Jones, N & Cheeseborough, I 2014 *A Provisional Atlas of the Bees, Wasps and Ants of Shropshire*. Field Studies Council. 120 pp.

MacDonald, M & Nisbet, G 2006 *Highland Bumblebees: Distribution, Ecology and Conservation*. Highland Biological Recording Group, Inverness. 51 pp.

Owens, N 2012 *Bumblebees of Norfolk*. Norfolk & Norwich Naturalist's Society Occasional Publication No. 14. 73 pp.

Webb, J, Bloxham, M & Slawson, C 2014 *A Provisional Atlas of the Bees and Wasps (Hymenoptera) of Staffordshire*. Viewable online through Staffordshire Ecological Records: www.staffs-ecology.org.uk.

WEBSITES

Steven Falk Flickr: http://tinyurl.com/nrywslu (see *Author's web feature* p.59)
Atlas Hymenoptera: http://zoologie.umh.ac.be/hymenoptera
Bees, Wasps and Ants Recording Society (BWARS): http://www.bwars.com
Buglife: http://www.buglife.org.uk
Bumblebee Conservation Trust: http://bumblebeeconservation.org
Bumblebees of the World: http://www.nhm.ac.uk/bombus
Checklist of the Western Palaearctic bees (Hymenoptera: Apoidea: Anthophila):
    http://westpalbees.myspecies.info
Discover Life: http://www.discoverlife.org
Dutch bee survey: http://www.wildebijen.nl/beeguide.html
Hymettus: http://www.hymettus.org.uk
iSpot: http://www.ispotnature.org
National Biodiversity Data Centre (Ireland): http://www.biodiversityireland.ie
Palaearctic Osmiine Bees: http://blogs.ethz.ch/osmiini
The Wild Bees and Wasps of Europe (Flickr): http://www.flickr.com/groups/wild_bees

HOW TO USE THIS GUIDE

Some bees are very distinctive, and the plates and photographs will provide a quick indication of their identity. But for the majority you will require either a good photograph showing the crucial diagnostic features or a pinned specimen which can be 'keyed out' using the dichotomous keys in this book, with the help of a microscope. The keys start on p.60 with two keys to genera (one for females and another for males) which direct you to the keys dealing with the species within each genus. Recognising whether you have a female or male is critical to using the keys (see *Male or female?* on p.52), and there is a high probability that you will misidentify a species if you take the wrong sex through a key. It is even more fundamental that you are not trying to key out a bee-like hoverfly! – see *Is it a bee?* on p.53.

Having used a key and arrived at a determination, you can then use the illustrations, photographs, species accounts, the author's photo-sharing web feature (see p.59) or a reliably identified museum collection to double-check. If you think you have found a rare Scottish species in Sussex or a coastal specialist in Warwickshire, or a species not seen for over 100 years, the chances are you will have made a mistake. Do not be put off. The more you practise, the easier the keys will become, and every mistake is a step up the learning curve. The keys and species accounts inevitably use terminology that might appear intimidating at first, though we have tried to use the most user-friendly terms possible without compromising accuracy. It will not take long to learn the few dozen body-part names referred to, or the adjectives that accompany these, and the diagrams and *Glossary* (pp.55–59) will help you.

DICHOTOMOUS KEYS

These are identification keys consisting of a series of numbered steps, with each step presenting a pair of options (a couplet) that take you to other couplets, and eventually to the determination of a species. It is a little like snakes and ladders, but instead of rolling a dice, you check the features on your bee to see whether these match the first option in a couplet or the second. Some bee genera or species groups are inherently difficult, and the couplets for these will be difficult to interpret without having comparative material or good images to hand. This is why we encourage you to build up a collection of pinned specimens if you want to accurately record as many bees as possible. The author's web feature (p.59) provides many additional photographs of key characters taken down a microscope, with accompanying notes. The keys for large genera such as *Andrena*, *Lasioglossum*, *Nomada* and *Bombus* have been subdivided into smaller bite-size keys to make them less intimidating. These approaches will make the keys easier and faster to use as you become familiar with them. Keys to males and females are usually kept separate, and some variable species are keyed out more than once in a key.

FORMAT OF THE SPECIES ACCOUNTS

Every British, Irish and Channel Island species (275 species) is the subject of a species account containing the following information:

- **Scientific name** These follow those used by BWARS at the point of text completion in May 2015.

- **Common name** The majority of English names presented here are new, but we have adopted well-used existing names where possible, and have also given alternative names that might still be in common use (e.g. Hill Cuckoo Bee for *Bombus rupestris*). The names attempt both to establish the type of bee (e.g. mining bee or leafcutter bee) and to supplement this with a single attribute that helps to make that species distinctive. This might be a physical character (e.g. Violet-winged Mining Bee *Andrena agilissima*), a foraging preference (e.g. Ivy Bee *Colletes hederae*), a habitat preference (e.g. Pinewood Mason Bee *Osmia uncinata*) or a geographic bias (e.g. Northern Colletes *Colletes floralis*). Previously published English names have been replaced where they are deemed poor (e.g. Early Mining Bee for *Andrena haemorrhoa*, which flies no earlier than various other mining bees but has other more distinctive attributes).

■ **Description & similar species** This initially gives the forewing (FW) length, as measured from the base of the tegula to the tip, for each sex, giving any standard range in size. The remainder of the section briefly describes the most obvious characteristics of that species (females first, as they are usually the more distinctive sex) and compares it to those other species with which it is most likely to be confused. This section variously supplements, amplifies and contextualises information given in the keys.

■ **Variation** This describes any standard variation that might be present in a bee species, such as colour forms and seasonal variation. It also covers the effects of wear, where this might interfere with identification.

■ **Flight season** The main periods during which a species is likely to be observed flying and foraging, noting any peaks, geographical variation or voltinism. Freakish records or records based on hibernating adults are ignored.

■ **Habitat** The main habitat(s) used by a species, both as a broad category and with supplementary detail where this helps to better understand how to find a species, e.g. 'wetlands and watersides with plentiful Yellow Loosestrife' for the Yellow Loosestrife Bee *Macropis europaea*.

■ **Flowers visited** The main flowers visited by a bee species, variously at species, genus or family level, noting key pollen sources where known. Vernacular names of plants are mostly based on C. A. Stace, *New Flora of the British Isles*, 3rd edition (Cambridge University Press, 2010), though we have used alternative names in two cases, Buddleia (Butterfly-bush) and Amelanchier (Juneberry).

■ **Nesting habits** The typical nesting location of a species, e.g. sandy ground, dead wood, cliff faces, walls or hollow twigs. If a species nests in aggregations or exhibits eusocial behaviour this is also noted here.

■ **Status & distribution** The known geographic range, usually mentioning any northern limits for southern-biased species and usually stating whether a species is recorded or unrecorded in Wales, Scotland, Ireland and the Channel Islands. Individual sites, islands and counties are only cited for the rarest species. The status of a species within its range is also noted, i.e. whether it is common, local, rare or especially frequent, also if it is declining or increasing/spreading. Rarity gradings and conservation statuses are not given in the species accounts (the British ones are badly out of date at the point of publication) and are best obtained by checking for updates on the JNCC and Irish Biodiversity Data Centre websites (see *Conserving bees*, p.46).

■ **Parasites & associates** The main species known to exploit a given bee species, with an emphasis on cleptoparasitic bees and wasps, plus parasitic flies of better-known families such as the Bombyliidae (bee-flies), Sarcophagidae (satellite flies) and Conopidae (thick-headed flies). Species prone to stylopisation are also noted. This is not an exhaustive list, and groups such as microbes, nematodes and mites have largely been ignored. For bees that are cleptoparasites this section is replaced with **Host(s)**, and the host species are detailed.

■ **Maps** Simple maps provide a basic impression of current distribution based on data from BWARS and the Irish Biodiversity Centre. These are based on records from 2000 onwards, and hence have only been produced for species with post-2000 records. It should be noted that some bees have shown a decline of more than 90% over the past 100 years, which makes historic data almost useless in predicting where they now occur (notably for *Bombus distinguendus*). The Channel Islands have been omitted as it is not currently possible to separate out post-2000 records. To see more detailed maps showing historic distributions too, visit the BWARS website and click on 'Species Accounts'.

■ **Photographs** Most species accounts are accompanied by photographs of live individuals (and in some cases pinned), including a female, male and examples of any significant variation that the recorder needs to know about (note they are not shown to scale). These complement the artwork, which typically features top views. This two-pronged approach substantially increases your chances of learning to recognise individual bee species.

The genera are arranged in a taxonomic sequence based on Michener (2007) to keep related genera close together. Taxonomy at the species level is relatively unstable, and species descriptions have therefore been arranged alphabetically within genera, for ease of navigation. Species illustrations in the colour plate section have been arranged to allow maximum comparison.

THE COLOUR PLATES

A high proportion of the British and Irish species are covered by the colour artwork. This usually includes a female and male, plus examples of any common variation (e.g. several of the bumblebees, plus species such as *Andrena hattorfiana* and *A. marginata*), although for some particularly variable species it has not been practicable to represent the entire range. Most of the colour figures represent a top view, but a few side views and also faces have been featured where these assist with identification. All colour figures are printed at ×2.5 the actual size of the bee except for *Xylocopa*, *Bombus* and *Apis* which are at ×1.5. Where a number of species look almost identical (e.g. within genera such as *Lasioglossum* and *Sphecodes* or the small *Andrena* 'mini-miners'), only representative examples are provided in the plates. Use the colour plates in conjunction with the photographs in the species accounts, because the appearance of a species can alter depending on angle of view, play of light and its posture and behaviour.

MALE OR FEMALE?

Most of the keys in this book treat females and males separately, because they tend to have their own unique character sets. This is how you separate the sexes:

Females

- Antennae shorter and with 12 segments (the flagellum with 10)

- Abdomen usually with 6 visible tergites

- A sting is present, often hidden inside the body but easily teased out of a freshly killed specimen with a pin

- A densely haired pollen brush or basket is present either on the hind legs or under the abdomen, except in *Hylaeus* and the various cleptoparasitic species

- Often larger, more robust and more colourful (notably in *Andrena* and *Osmia*)

Males

- Antennae with 13 segments (the flagellum with 11) and usually visibly longer than those of the female

- Abdomen usually with 7 visible tergites (the apical ones sometimes obscured) and usually more elongate

- A genital capsule with an apical pair of claspers (gonostyli) is present, often hidden inside the body but easily teased out of a freshly killed specimen with a pin

- No obvious pollen brushes are present

- Surface of face yellow or whitish in certain genera or species where it is black in the female (notably within *Ceratina*, *Eucera*, *Macropis* and some *Andrena*) or more extensively yellow or white than in the female (*Hylaeus*). Mandibles often slimmer or longer

shorter antennae (12 segments)

female

abdomen usually broader, often furrier, typically with 6 visible tergites

pollen brushes on hind legs or under abdomen (except cuckoo bees and *Hylaeus* species)

longer antennae (13 segments)

mandibles often much longer (especially *Andrena*)

male

abdomen usually slimmer, typically with 7 visible tergites

Andrena fulva female and male.

IS IT A BEE?

Distinguishing bees from flies

Many bees can sting or are distasteful to predators such as birds, which learn to avoid eating them. A number of unrelated insects, notably certain hoverflies (Syrphidae) have come to resemble (mimic) bees – presumably to trick predators into thinking that they too are not worth eating. These hoverflies are often shaped and patterned like bees, and fly like them too. But put a pinned bee and bee-like hoverfly together and they have a multitude of differences. Flies have only a single pair of wings, and these have a very different venation from bees. The eyes are much larger than those of a bee (except for a drone Honey Bee) and the mouthparts and antennae have a very different structure.

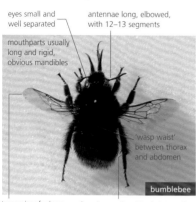

eyes small and well separated

antennae long, elbowed, with 12–13 segments

mouthparts usually long and rigid, obvious mandibles

'wasp waist' between thorax and abdomen

bumblebee

two pairs of wings, wing cells stopping well short of wing tips

female usually with obvious pollen brushes on hind legs or under abdomen (except cuckoo bees and *Hylaeus* species)

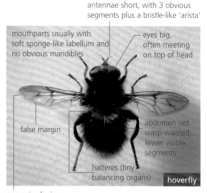

antennae short, with 3 obvious segments plus a bristle-like 'arista'

mouthparts usually with soft sponge-like labellum and no obvious mandibles

eyes big, often meeting on top of head

false margin

abdomen not wasp-waisted, fewer visible segments

halteres (tiny balancing organs)

hoverfly

one pair of wings, usually with a false margin

The most frequent bumblebee-mimicking hoverflies are *Eristalis intricarius*, *Merodon equestris* and *Volucella bombylans*, though the most convincing ones are scarcer species such as *Criorhina berberina*, *Arctophila superbiens* and particularly *Pocota personata*. A good Honey Bee mimic is *Eristalis tenax*, which even lands with its somewhat swollen hind legs hanging down in the same manner. The best mimics of solitary bees include the brown-furred *Cheilosia grossa*, which resembles certain *Andrena* species, and the golden-furred *Cheilosia chrysocoma*, which specifically resembles *Andrena fulva*. Small hoverflies such as *Eumerus* species can resemble *Lasioglossum* bees when they fly. Bee mimics in other families include some bumblebee-like warble flies (Oestridae) such as *Hypoderma bovis* and *Cephenemyia auribarbis*. In the Scottish Caledonian pinewoods the large yellow- and black-haired robberfly *Laphria flava* (Asilidae) can resemble a bumblebee when it flies.

Bombus hypnorum (far left) and hoverfly *Criorhina berberina* (left).

Bombus muscorum (left) and hoverfly *Arctophila superbiens* (right).

Andrena nigroaenea (left) and hoverfly *Cheilosia grossa* (right).

Distinguishing bees from wasps

Separating wasp-like bees such as *Nomada* species from wasps is more tricky, as they are structurally very similar. The main difference is the presence of branched body hairs on bees. This is most obvious in furry bees and can be difficult to see in species of *Hylaeus*, *Epeolus* and the shortest-haired *Nomada* species, though it is still there. Some wasps can have a quite hairy body but the hairs are never branched. Bees also have the hind basitarsi laterally flattened and with very dense, bristly hairs on the inner surface. In wasps the basitarsi are fairly cylindrical, with any hairs shorter and finer. With practice you soon come to distinguish the rather different body shapes of wasp-like bees from various types of real wasp.

A wasp-like nomad bee *Nomada succincta* (left) and a real hunting wasp *Cerceris arenaria* (right).

BEE ANATOMY

Bee anatomy is fairly typical for an insect, with a head, thorax, abdomen and the usual limbs and other appendages associated with these. Note that the propodeum, which appears to be the back of the thorax, is actually the base of the abdomen, but we have continued to use the term thorax for simplicity. The keys in this book make great use of body-part terminology, so these terms are described and figured here.

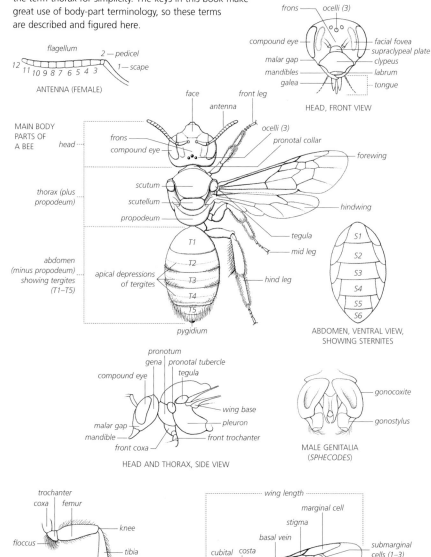

ANTENNA (FEMALE)

HEAD, FRONT VIEW

MAIN BODY PARTS OF A BEE

ABDOMEN, VENTRAL VIEW, SHOWING STERNITES

HEAD AND THORAX, SIDE VIEW

MALE GENITALIA (SPHECODES)

RIGHT HIND LEG SHOWING TARSI

WING DETAILS

GLOSSARY

Abdomen the most posterior of the three major body divisions, strictly speaking consisting of the propodeum (fused to the hind part of the thorax) and the gaster, which is connected to the propodeum by a narrow petiole ('wasp waist') and is the abdomen referred to in the text here

Aculeate a species belonging to the section Aculeata of the insect order Hymenoptera

Adpressed describing hairs that lie flat against the body surface

Aggregation (of nests) a concentration of nests, usually in relation to the entrance holes of ground-nesting species

Allometry the relationship between overall size and the physical proportions of a bee, best exhibited in some *Andrena* species where larger males are proportionally 'bigger-headed' than smaller ones

Antenna the segmented sensory appendages arising from the head of a bee where the face meets the frons

Anterior at the front, e.g. the face of the antennae or the legs that would face you if they were stretched outwards perpendicular to the body when you were looking at the bee directly from the front; also the front (foremost) part of the thorax, abdomen, a tergite etc.

Apex the tip

Apical depression (of the tergites) the hind margin of the tergites where this is slightly lower than the anterior section and usually demarked by a shallow step or change of texture, especially in *Andrena*

Arolium the pad-like lobe projecting between the tarsal claws

Axilla(e) the plate located on either side of the scutellum, most noticeable in *Coelioxys* and *Epeolus* species

Basal at the base, i.e. nearer to the centre of the body or the initial point of articulation in the case of an appendage such as a limb

Basitarsus (basitarsi) the first and usually longest of the five tarsal segments, joined to the tibia

Bifid ending in a pair of similar-sized points, e.g. the mandibles of *Nomada ruficornis*

Bivoltine having two generations, and therefore two flight periods, in a year; or **facultatively bivoltine**, i.e. bivoltine under some circumstances but univoltine in others

Bloom(ed) where the body surface has a greyish, waxy covering like that of damsons or blueberries, e.g. tergites of *Lasioglossum albipes*

Bristle a relatively large, thickened and rigid hair (usually a modified hair)

Calcicolous preferring habitats featuring calcareous rocks and soils

Carinate bearing ridges (carinae), used here to describe the hind face of the propodeum of some *Lasioglossum* species (carinate species) where ridges separate this face from the side faces

Caste(s) the different forms of a social insect, i.e. queen, worker and male (drone)

Clavate hooked, usually in relation to the abdomen when it is strongly downcurved in side view

Cleptoparasite a species that robs or usurps the nest and food provisions of another species, replacing the host egg or larva with its own, e.g. the cuckoo bees in this book

Clypeus usually the main part of the face, between the antennae and the labrum

Cocoon the silk case spun by a fully grown grub of some

bees to protect the prepupa and pupa inside the nest cell

Collar the pale hair band at the front of the thorax immediately behind the head of many bumblebee species

Comb spines the small spines at the tip of the hind tibiae dorsally of most *Nomada* species, which can be arranged like a teeth of a comb

Compound eye(s) the pair of large eyes on the sides of the head comprising many ommatidia

Corbicula(e) the concave, shiny, hair-fringed 'pollen basket' of the hind tibiae of honey bees and social bumblebees (corbiculate bees)

Coxa(e) the first segment of the leg, which in bees has rather limited movement but has a more flexible articulation with the trochanter

Crenulate where the edge (of tergite 6 of male bees here) is very unevenly serrated, with projections of different sizes, e.g. in leafcutter bees

Cuckoo see Cleptoparasite

Dimorphism the phenomena whereby one species has two rather different appearances which may be related to gender (sexual dimorphism), generation (brood dimorphism) or some other genetic or environmental factor

Dorsal at the top, e.g. the sides of the antennae or the legs that would face you if they were fully stretched outwards perpendicular to the body when you were looking at the bee directly from above; also the top of the body

Drone the male of a social bee, wasp or ant

Dufour's gland a gland located off the vagina that can produce a variety of substances such as waterproof nest-cell lining, pheromones and larval food supplements

Emarginated where a margin has a shallow notch or concavity, e.g. the lower margin of the clypeus of many bees or the margin of tergite 6 in some male bees

Eusocial insects that use non-fertilised and often sterile females to help serve one or more reproducing queens, through assorted duties such as foraging, care of grubs, nest defence, nest building etc.

Extant not extinct

Extinct no longer present within a given area, e.g. Britain, England or a county

Face here used in a general sense to denote the front of the head below the level of the antennal insertion points, including the entire clypeus (other definitions include the top of the head as well)

Facial fovea(e) the strips of short, felt-like hairs that run alongside the inner eye margins of bees such as *Andrena* species

Facial suture(s) the grooves of the face that define the edge of the clypeus and some other parts of the face

Femur (femora) the third segment of the leg, functionally equivalent to our thigh or upper arm and usually relatively long and thick compared with other segments

Flagellum (flagella) the long, articulated part of the antenna, comprising the final 10 segments of the female antenna and the final 11 segments of the male antenna

Floccus (flocci) a tuft of curled hairs on the hind trochanters, notably in female *Andrena* species, where they help to form a larger pollen basket/pollen brush

Frons the top of the head between the ocelli and the antennal insertion points, which can bear features such as the bristles of female *Rophites*

Galea(e) lateral appendages of the mouthparts which can provide valuable identification features in some *Colletes* and *Andrena* species

Gena(e) the area on the side of the head behind and below the eyes

Genitalia the sex organs, which in males are normally folded inside the tip of the abdomen but can be easily hooked out in fresh specimens and often contain valuable identification features

Gonocoxite(s) a pair of structures that usually form the greater part of the male genital capsule and give rise to a pair of claspers, the gonostyli

Gonostylus (gonostyli) see Gonocoxite

Gradulus the transverse groove that runs across a tergite, notably in *Coelioxys* species

Hawkish composites flowers of the family *Asteraceae* that resemble hawkweeds, hawkbits, hawk's-beards, cat's-ears etc.

Impunctate lacking punctures

Inquiline a species that lives in the home/nest of another species, often as a relatively harmless scavenger or small-time thief, usually without preventing larval development in the way a cleptoparasite does

Instar one of the several stages of larval development

Integument the hard external skeleton, composed of the cuticle, i.e. the hard areas of body surface

Intersex a bee that has both male and female characteristics, especially stylopised bees

Knee(s) the junction of the femur and tibia

Labrum the lowest part of the face, a flap-like, articulating appendage immediately below the clypeus, the shape and

colour of which can be important in identification

Lekking sexual swarming by males

Malar gap the gap between the bottom of the eyes and the base of the mandibles

Mandible(s) the pair of articulating 'jaws' that flank the mouthparts at the bottom of the head

Marginal cell the last cell along the front part of the forewing, immediately after the stigma

Median located on, or running down, the midline

Melanic a black form of a species that is not usually black, most often seen in certain bumblebees

Mesonotum see Scutum

Mesopleuron (mesopleura) the main plate forming the sides of the thorax beneath the wings

Microsculpture the minute grooves, ridges or other texturing of the integument of many bees that can create a dull appearance

Midriff band a pale (usually yellow) hair band that takes in both the scutellum and the first tergite of a bumblebee e.g. *Bombus hortorum* and *B. jonellus*

Monolectic obtaining pollen from just one plant species

Ocellus (ocelli) the three 'simple' eyes arranged in a triangle on the top of the head between the two main compound eyes

Oligolectic obtaining pollen from a limited range of flowers such as plants belonging to just one genus or a series of closely related genera

Parapsidal lines the pair of short or longer lines on the scutum about halfway between base of the wings and the midline

Parasitoid an animal that lives on or within a host

animal, obtaining its food from the tissues or fluids of the host, eventually killing it

Parthenogenesis reproduction without sex, the normal form of male production in all bees but apparently sometimes used for the production of females too in some *Ceratina* species

Pile dense, more or less upright hairs (much longer than pubescence)

Pollen basket see Corbicula

Pollen brush (also termed a scopa) the dense hairs, usually either on the hind legs or on the underside of the abdomen, that are designed to carry pollen whilst a female bee is foraging

Polylectic obtaining pollen from a varied assortment of flowers, representing assorted plant genera, plant families and often varied flower structure

Posterior at the rear, e.g. the face of the antennae or the legs that would face you if they were stretched outwards perpendicular to the body when you were looking at the bee directly from behind; also the hind part of the thorax or the abdomen (or a tergite of the abdomen)

Postscutellum the narrow section of the thorax between the scutellum and propodeum, also known as the metathorax

Prepupa the final, fully fed, inert larval stage prior to pupation (often the overwintering stage)

Pronotal collar the top part of the pronotum, which usually manifests itself as a narrow 'collar' at the front of the scutum and immediately behind the head

Pronotal tubercle a rearward extension of the pronotum that takes the form of a large circular tubercle (often white or yellow) on the side of the thorax in front of the wing bases

Pronotum the most anterior section of the thorax

Propodeum the rear section of the thorax, technically the base of the abdomen but separated from the rest of the abdomen by the petiole (the 'wasp waist')

Pubescence short but fairly upright hairs (much shorter than pile)

Punctate bearing punctures

Punctures small to minute pits on the body integument, but not on soft, membranous areas

Pustulose in the sense used here, where punctures have raised rims, like minute volcanoes, to create a form of roughened surface, e.g. tergite 1 of *Andrena humilis*

Pygidium a rigid, narrow projection at the tip of the abdomen of many bees, both male and female, often used by females for lining the nest cell with waxy secretions

Queen the mated, egg-laying female of a eusocial species, served by her worker daughters

Rima the bare or microscopically hairy groove or furrow running down the centre of tergite 5 in *Halictus* and *Lasioglossum* females

Rugose a surface roughened by a coarse network of ridges rather than punctures or bumps

Scape the first segment of the antenna, usually elongate but highly swollen in the males of some *Hylaeus* species

Scopa(e) see Pollen brush

Scutellum the section of the top of the thorax immediately behind the scutum, usually semicircular in shape

Scutum the main part of the top of thorax, located between the wings, with the pronotal collar to the front and scutellum to the rear; also known as the mesoscutum or mesonotum

Sensoria external sensory organs, which in bees often take the form of patches of pubescence on the segments of the antennal flagella, e.g. *Melecta albifrons*

Social parasite a parasite that takes advantage of the social behaviour of another species, e.g. a cuckoo bumblebee

Solitary bee a bee that does not use workers and is therefore not eusocial, though it may still be communal and nest in dense aggregations

Spine a slim, elongate, often pointed projection such as those at the tip of the abdomen of male *Anthidium manicatum* or *Coelioxys species*, which are part of the integument and not modified hairs

Spur the term used for some large, rigid spines, notably those at the tips of the tibiae

s.s. a species as defined in the strict sense (*sensu stricto*) e.g. the true *Bombus lucorum* as opposed to *B. lucorum* s.l. (*sensu lato*), which equates to *B. lucorum*, *B. magnus* and *B. cryptarum*

Sternite(s) the series of overlapping hard plates (one per segment) that form the lower surface of the abdomen and also contribute to parts of the genitalia

Stigma the thickened and darkened section along the anterior edge of the forewing immediately before the marginal cell

Stylopised a bee containing one or more stylopid parasites (see *Enemies and associates of bees*, p24)

Submarginal cell(s) the two or three cells in the apical part of the wing behind the marginal cell

Subspecies (ssp.) variation within a species that represents significant and consistent genetic differences (genetic distance) but not quite enough to justify a split into more than one species

Supraclypeal plate the small plate of the face above the clypeus

Tarsus (tarsi) the final five segments of each leg, representing the functional equivalent of our hands or feet

Tegula(e) the pair of semicircular plates that protect the base of each pair of wings on top

Tergite(s) the series of overlapping hard plates (one per segment) that form the upper surface and sides of the abdomen and also contribute to parts of the genitalia

Thorax the middle of the three major body divisions, between the head and the abdomen, giving rise to the legs and wings, though in bees the hind part of thorax (the propodeum) is technically the base of the abdomen

Tibia (tibiae) the fourth segment of the leg, between the femur and the tarsus, functionally equivalent to our shin or forearm

Tomentum/tomentose woolly-looking patches of tiny, adpressed, flattened hairs, best featured on the tergites of various *Lasioglossum* species

Transverse situated or extending from side to side across a body part perpendicular to the axis, e.g. a band of hairs, punctures or colour on a tergite

Triungulin the newly hatched (first-instar) larvae of parasitic meloid beetles (oil beetles and blister beetles) and stylopids

Trivoltine having three generations, and therefore three flight periods, in a year, e.g. winter-active *Bombus terrestris* populations

Trochanter the second segment (but first freely articulating segment) of the legs, between the coxa and the femur

Truncate square-ended, as if abruptly cut off, as opposed to pointed, rounded or bifid, e.g. the mandibles of *Nomada striata*

Type specimen the specimen (holotype) or further specimens (paratypes) on the basis of which a species was originally described as new to science

Tumulus (tumuli) the small mound of sand or soil that surrounds the nest entrance of many ground-nesting bees

Univoltine having one generation, and therefore one flight period, in a year

Variety (var.) variation within a species that has a more trivial genetic basis than found in a subspecies; often variation that exists within a population or even a single nest

Ventral at the bottom, e.g. the sides of the antennae or the legs that would face you if they were fully stretched outwards perpendicular to the body when you were looking at the bee directly from below; also the underside of the body

Voltinism the number of broods or generations within a year

Worker an unmated, often sterile female with poorly developed ovaries that carries out assorted duties in support of her queen and nesting colony, as seen in eusocial species

AUTHOR'S WEB FEATURE (STEVEN FALK FLICKR)

Steven Falk http://tinyurl.com/nrywslu

This Flickr web feature provides ever-growing albums of high-quality photographs of every British and Irish bee species (arranged by genera). This includes living bees, pinned specimens and microscopic photos showing key parts of the body, often with accompanying notes. The photos reinforce and sometimes expand upon the images and information provided in this guide. The web feature also provides photos of key sites and key habitats for many of the rarer bees, associated parasites or hosts, and further sections of the site cover groups such as hoverflies, which contain various bee mimics.

KEY TO BEE GENERA

GENERIC KEY TO FEMALES

1   Forewings with two submarginal cells (Fig. 1) 2

—   Forewings with three submarginal cells (Fig. 2) (check both wings in case one
wing has dropped a cell) 16

2   Underside of abdomen with a dense, usually continuous pollen brush of dense hairs
consisting mostly of hairs that are longer then the length of a sternite (Fig. 3).
Hind tibiae without a pollen brush, any hairs shorter than the greatest width
of the tibia and usually sparse 3

—   Underside of abdomen without a dense pollen brush, with most if not all the hairs
shorter than the length of a sternite and in some species minute. Some species
with a distinct pollen brush on the hind leg (Figs 4 & 5) 8

3   Tarsi with an arolium between the claws (Fig. 6) 4

—   Tarsi without an arolium between the claws (Fig. 7) 7

Fig. 1   Fig. 2   Fig. 4   Fig. 5   Fig. 6   Fig. 7

Fig. 3

4   Tergite 1 with a strong curved ridge across the top, separating the
vertical anterior face from the top and sides (Fig. 8) .... *Heriades* p.271

—   Tergite 1 without a strong transverse ridge, the anterior face merging
more smoothly into the top and sides 5

5   Mandibles more than twice as long as wide and narrowing towards their
tips, never fitting tightly against the clypeus when folded; labrum at least
twice as long as wide and visible even when the mandibles are folded
(Fig. 9). Body very slim, the thorax in top view almost twice as long
as wide (Fig. 10) .... *Chelostoma* p.273

—   Mandibles no more than 1.5 times as long as wide, either parallel-sided or
broadening towards their tips, fitting tightly against the clypeus when folded;
the labrum shorter, largely hidden by the mandibles when these are folded
(Fig. 11). Body broader, the thorax about as wide as long in top view
(a little more elongate in *Hoplitis leucomelana*) (Fig. 12) 6

6   Pollen brush beneath abdomen black or orange. Parapsidal lines
very short except in *Osmia spinulosus* (Fig. 13) .... *Osmia* p.276

—   Pollen brush beneath abdomen creamy-white. Parapsidal lines
elongate (Fig. 14) .... *Hoplitis* p.291

Fig. 8   Fig. 9   Fig. 10   Fig. 11   Fig. 12   Fig. 13   Fig. 14

Fig. 15   Fig. 17    Fig. 18    Fig. 20 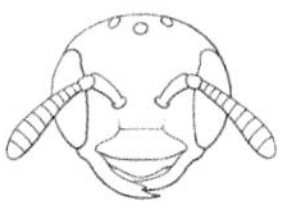   Fig. 21
Fig. 16   Fig. 19

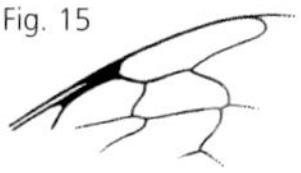

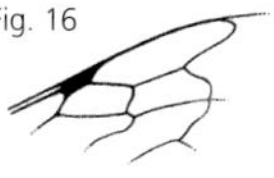

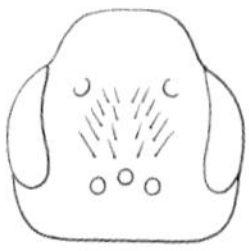

7   Surface of tergites, legs and face (beneath any hairs) entirely dark. Forewings with vein 2m-cu entering the second marginal cell before the end (Fig. 15) .... *Megachile* p.293

—   Surface of tergites, legs and face (beneath any hairs) with yellow marks. Forewings with vein 2m-cu meeting basal vein at or beyond the end of the second submarginal cell (Fig. 16) .... *Anthidium* p.266

8   Hind tibiae and basitarsi usually with an obvious dense pollen brush (Figs 4 & 5). If this is not so long and dense (*Dufourea*), the sternites are obviously hairy with semi-upright hair fringes along the hind margins **9**

—   Hind legs without a pollen brush, the hairs short or sparse. Sternites either with tiny inconspicuous hairs or (*Coelioxys*) with dense patches of adpressed white hairs **14**

9   Hind legs with particularly dense, orange and pantaloon-like pollen brushes comprising hairs that are longer than the greatest width of the hind tibia (Fig. 4) **10**

—   Hind legs with the pollen brush less dense and not so bright, comprising hairs that are no longer than the greatest width of the hind tibia (Fig. 17) **11**

10   Thorax with a conspicuous brownish pile, the underlying surface dull. Tergites 2–4 with white hair bands across the apical depressions. Tip of pygidium notched (Fig. 18) .... *Dasypoda* p.265

—   Body shiny black with an inconspicuous pile of mostly black hairs except for denser orange hairs at the tip of the abdomen. Tip of pygidium bluntly rounded (Fig. 19) .... *Panurgus* p.170

11   Antennae inserted at a point level with the midpoint of the eyes, the flagella clearly longer than the length of an eye with most flagellar segments much longer than wide. Clypeus not especially short and transverse, much longer than the labrum **12**

—   Antennae inserted at a point below the midpoint of the eyes, the flagella about the length of an eye and with most flagellar segments wider than long; the clypeus short and transverse, not much longer than the labrum (Fig. 20) **13**

12   Pollen brush of hind legs with dense white hairs on the tibia contrasting with black hairs on the basitarsus, the basitarsi very broad in side view (Fig. 5). Tergite 1 shiny, virtually impunctate and hairless. Top of the thorax semi-shining with an inconspicuous pile. Smaller and slimmer (wing length 7–8mm) .... *Macropis* p.264

—   Pollen brush of hind legs mostly buff-haired, the basitarsi not expanded (Fig. 17). Tergite 1 dulled by dense punctures and with long hairs. Top of the thorax dull with a conspicuous orange-brown pile. Large and robust (wing length typically 10mm) .... *Eucera* p.355

13   Tergites densely punctate with whitish hair bands across the apical depressions. Thorax very dull with a dense brownish pile. Frons with bristle-like hairs (Fig. 21). Larger and more robust (wing length 6mm) .... *Rophites* p.236

—   Tergites more sparsely punctate and without hair bands. Thorax shinier with sparse hairs. Frons without bristle-like hairs. Smaller and slimmer (wing length up to 4.5mm) .... *Dufourea* p.237

Fig. 22 Fig. 23 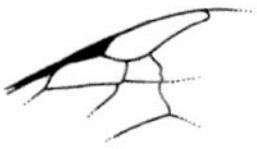 Fig. 24  Fig. 25 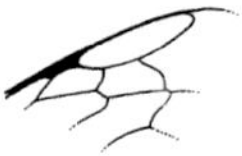 Fig. 26  Fig. 27 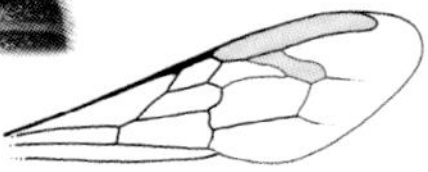 Fig. 28  Fig. 29

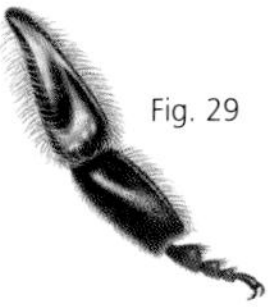

14 Eyes hairy. Abdomen progressively narrowing towards apex with a
     pointed tip and with white hair patches on most tergites and sternites
     (Fig. 22). Large, pointed axillae present on either side of the scutellum .... *Coelioxys* p.306

—   Eyes bare. Abdomen parallel-sided or oval with a blunter tip and without
     conspicuous white hair patches. Axillae inconspicuous **15**

15 Forewings with vein 2m-cu entering the end of the second marginal cell
     (Fig. 23). Face virtually bare and typically with two yellow or whitish markings
     (except *cornutus*) (Plate 2). Pronotal collar fully visible behind the head;
     the postscutellum and top of propodeum visible behind the scutellum when
     viewed from above (Fig. 24) .... *Hylaeus* p.80

—   Forewings with vein 2m-cu meeting basal vein beyond the end of the second
     marginal cell (Fig. 25). Face hairy, without markings. Pronotal collar hidden by
     back of head; postscutellum and top of propodeum hidden below scutellum when
     viewed from above (Fig. 26) .... *Stelis* p.268

16 Eyes hairy. Forewings with marginal cell very long and third submarginal cell strongly
     slanted (Fig. 27). Workers (but not queens) with hind tibiae 'corbiculate', i.e. with a
     flattish, shiny, hairless outer face fringed by long hairs (Fig. 28). Honey Bee-like .... *Apis* p.415

—   Eyes bare. Forewings with marginal cell shorter and third submarginal cell not
     strongly slanted. Mostly not Honey Bee-like **17**

17 Hind tibiae 'corbiculate', i.e. with a flattish, shiny, hairless outer
     face fringed by long hairs (Fig. 29). Plump, furry 'bumblebees'
     with a long tongue and often an elongate face .... *Bombus* (social species) p.368

—   Hind tibiae more cylindrical without a bare, shiny outer face,
     this face often with a dense pollen brush **18**

18 Third submarginal cell of forewings with an internal area that is clearly greater
     than that of the second submarginal cell (Figs 30–32) **19**

—   Third submarginal cell of forewings with an internal area that is about equal to
     or less than that of the second submarginal cell (Figs 33–35) **26**

19 Basal vein of forewings strongly curved, especially basally, meeting the longitudinal
     vein at more or less a right angle (Fig. 30) **20**

—   Basal vein of forewings either straight (Fig. 31) or if gently curved (*Ceratina* and
     some *Andrena*) meeting the longitudinal vein at rather less than a right angle **22**

Fig. 30 Fig. 31 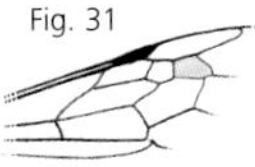 Fig. 32 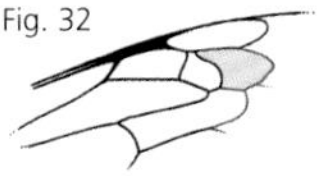 Fig. 33 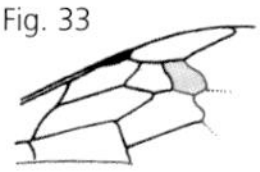 Fig. 34 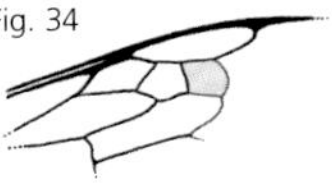 Fig. 35

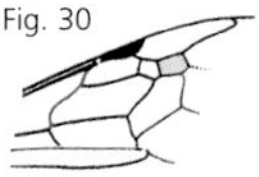

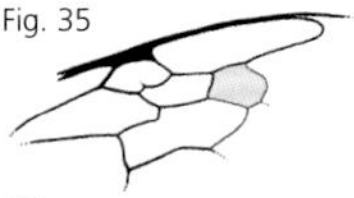

20 Tergite 5 without a bare-looking furrow ('rima'). Hind leg without a dense pollen
   brush. Abdomen red and black. Body inconspicuously haired .... **Sphecodes** p.217

— Tergite 5 with a rima running down the midline (Fig. 36). Hind leg with a dense
  pollen brush. Abdomen ground colour dark, at most with translucent brownish or
  dull orange apical depressions or pale hair bands/streaks. Thorax and head more
  conspicuously haired **21**

21 Tergites with bands or lateral streaks of adpressed whitish hairs located along the
   hind margin (Fig. 37), sometimes with a further band of such hairs across the base
   (but never just the latter). Forewings with outer cross veins of similar thickness and
   colour to the other typical wing veins .... **Halictus** p.172

— Tergites with any bands or lateral patches of adpressed whitish hairs located
  at the base only (Fig. 38), except for *sexstrigatum*, which has tergite 1
  shiny and impunctate unlike any *Halictus*. Forewings with outer cross
  veins thinner and often paler than the other typical wing veins .... **Lasioglossum** p.181

22 Body metallic-blue and inconspicuously haired. Forewings with basal vein
   gently curved (small, wing length to 5mm) .... **Ceratina** p.365

— Body not usually metallic blue, but if slightly so (e.g. *Andrena cineraria*),
  the size is much larger and the body has obvious hairs. Forewings with
  basal vein straight or barely curved **23**

23 Forewings with vein 2m-cu entering the third submarginal cell well
   beyond the middle of that cell (Fig. 31) **24**

— Forewings with vein 2m-cu entering the third submarginal cell near
  the middle of that cell (Figs 32 & 39) **25**

Fig. 36    Fig. 37 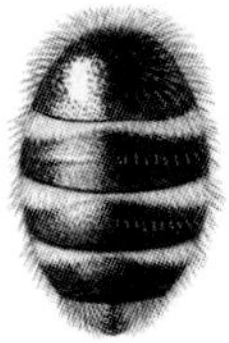   Fig. 38    Fig. 39    Fig. 40    Fig. 41

Fig. 42    Fig. 43    Fig. 44

24 Antennae with tips pointed (beware broken antennal tips – there should be
   12 segments) (Fig. 40). Sides of face alongside the eyes with a broad strip
   of short, velvety hairs (the 'facial foveae') which are often paler than
   the rest of the facial hairs when viewed from certain angles (Fig. 41).
   Last segment of tarsi long and slim (Fig. 42) .... **Andrena** p.92

— Antennae with tips blunt (Fig. 43). Sides of face without facial foveae. Last segment
  of tarsi relatively short and broader than other tarsal segments (Fig. 44) .... **Melitta** p.259

25 Medium-sized (wing length to 11.5mm) without darkened wings. Lower face
   inflated. Hind legs without a pollen brush. Forewings with marginal cell short,
   not or barely extending beyond the end of the third submarginal cell (Fig. 32).
   Body usually with a pattern of white and grey hairs .... **Melecta** p.363

— Extremely large (wing length at least 18mm) with darkened, iridescent wings.
  Hind legs with a pollen brush. Forewings with marginal cell extending well
  beyond the end of the third submarginal cell (Fig. 39). Body either entirely
  black or black with thorax and base of abdomen yellow-haired .... **Xylocopa** p.366

26   Vein 2m-cu bulging outwards at its far lower corner but bending towards
     the wing base where it meets the third submarginal cell (Fig. 33) .... ***Colletes*** p.69

—   Vein 2m-cu not bulging outwards below and furthest from the wing base
     where it meets the third submarginal cell (Figs 34 & 35) **27**

27   Legs extensively red or yellow or if black, abdomen ground colour mostly red. Inconspicuously
     haired, rather wasp-like bees without pollen brushes **28**

—   Legs entirely dark beneath any coloured hairs. Furrier bees with abdomen ground colour
     entirely black **29**

28   Axillae small and inconspicuous (Fig. 45). Tergites without whitish patches
     of tiny hairs, any markings resulting from pigmented integument (usually
     red, yellow, black or a combination of these colours) .... ***Nomada*** p.314

—   Thorax with large and projecting axillae on either side of the scutellum (Fig. 46).
     Tergites with paired whitish spots composed of tiny adpressed hairs .... ***Epeolus*** p.352

29   Hind legs with outer face of tibia and basitarsus with short black hairs and no
     pollen brush (Fig. 47). Forewings with vein 2m-cu entering the third submarginal
     cell before the end of that cell (Fig. 35). Queen-sized 'bumblebees'
     often with a white or red tail and yellowish bands .... ***Bombus* (cuckoo species)** p.408

—   Hind legs with outer face of tibia and basitarsus with an orange or buff-coloured
     pollen brush. Forewings with vein 2m-cu entering the third submarginal cell at
     the lower outer corner of that cell (Fig. 34). Smaller and less bumblebee-like .... ***Anthophora*** p.357

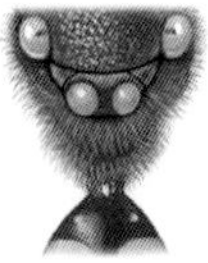

Fig. 45 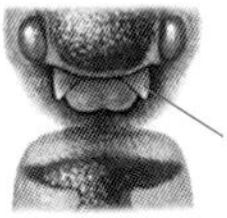   Fig. 46 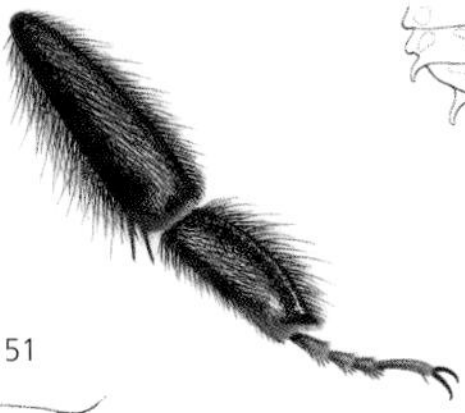   Fig. 47 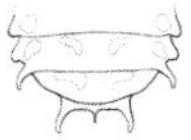   Fig. 48 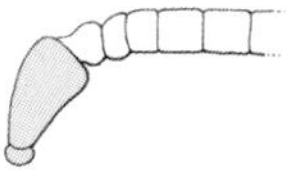   Fig. 49

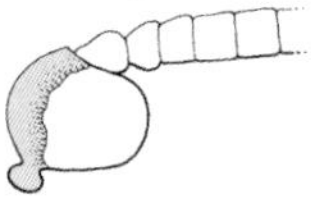

Fig. 50    Fig. 51 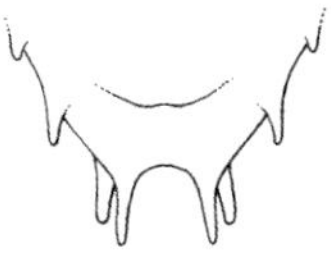   Fig. 52

GENERIC KEY TO MALES

1   Forewings with two submarginal cells (Fig. 1) **2**

—   Forewings with three submarginal cells (Fig. 2) (check both wings in case one
     wing has dropped a cell) **16**

2   Face surface and/or legs with yellow or whitish markings. Fore tarsi never expanded **3**

—   Ground colour of face and legs entirely dark (there may be a covering of paler hairs)
     except for the front legs of three *Megachile* species with expanded fore tarsi **6**

3   Antennae much longer than the wings (large, furry bees) .... ***Eucera*** p.355

—   Antennae much shorter than the wings **4**

4   Tergites with yellow markings at the sides, and often the middle of the
     apical segments. Tip of abdomen with a series of spines arising
     from tergites 6 and 7 (Fig. 48) .... ***Anthidium*** p.266

—   Tergites entirely dark. No spines at the tip of the abdomen, at most
     a projecting pygidium centrally **5**

Fig. 53   Fig. 54 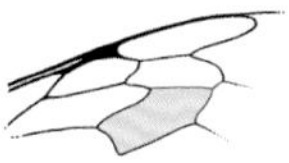   Fig. 55 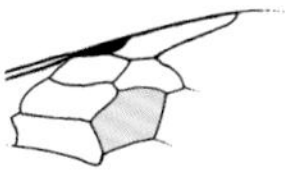   Fig. 56    Fig. 57 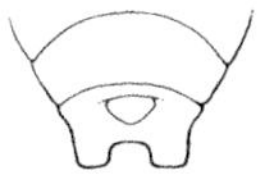   Fig. 58

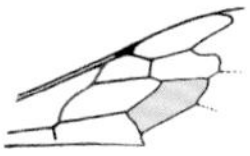

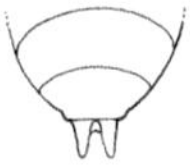

Fig. 59

5 Legs slim and usually yellow- or white-marked. Tip of abdomen without a pygidium. Antennal scapes usually expanded to varying extent (Figs 49 & 50). Small, slim, black and inconspicuously haired (wing length to 5.5mm) .... *Hylaeus* p.80

— Legs robust, the hind legs especially swollen. Tip of abdomen with a prominent pygidium (Fig. 51). Antennal scapes not swollen. Medium-sized (typical wing length 7–8mm), robust with an obviously hairy thorax and white hair fringes on tergites 3–5 .... *Macropis* p.264

6 Eyes hairy. Abdomen (tergites and sternites) with conspicuous patches of adpressed white hairs and with a series of spines arising from tergite 6 (Fig. 52) .... *Coelioxys* p.306

— Eyes bare. Abdomen not as above **7**

7 Second medial cell at least 1.5 times as long as wide (Figs 53 & 54) **8**

— Second medial cell at most slightly longer than wide (Fig. 55). Clypeus short and transverse (not much longer than the labrum) (Fig. 20) **15**

8 Tarsi without an arolium between the claws (Fig. 7). Robust bees with swollen front tarsi in some species .... *Megachile* p.293

— Tarsi with an arolium between the claws (Fig. 6) **9**

9 Either sternite 2 with a large, protruding welt (p.291, Fig. 4) *and* tergite 7 lacking a pair of square-ended lobes, or apical antennal segment strongly hooked (p.291, Fig. 5) .... *Hoplitis* p.291

— Sternite 2 lacking a large projecting welt (except *Chelostoma florisomne* where tergite 7 bears a pair of square-ended lobes apically, see p.273, Fig. 3) and apical antennal segment never strongly hooked **10**

10 Vein 2m-cu meeting basal vein just beyond the end of the second submarginal cell (Fig. 25) .... *Stelis* p.268

— Vein 2m-cu entering the second submarginal cell (Fig. 54) **11**

11 Tergite 1 with a strong, curved, transverse ridge across the top which separates the vertical anterior face from the top and sides (Fig. 8). Abdomen in side view strongly clavate .... *Heriades* p.271

— Tergite 1 without a strong transverse ridge, the anterior face merging more smoothly into the top and sides. Abdomen in side view not strongly clavate **12**

12 Body very slim, the thorax in top view almost twice as long as wide (Fig. 10). Labrum at least twice as long as wide and projecting well beyond the mandibles when these are folded. Tergite 7 produced into a pair of downward-pointing projections that protrude well beyond tergite 6 (Figs 57 & 58) .... *Chelostoma* p.273

— Body broader, the thorax about as wide as long in top view (Fig. 12). Labrum either wider than long, or if longer than wide (*Osmia*) barely protruding beyond the folded mandibles. If tergite 7 has a pair of projections (*Osmia*) these do not, or barely, protrude beyond tergite 6 (Fig. 59) **13**

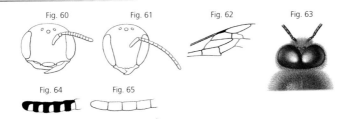

Fig. 60   Fig. 61   Fig. 62   Fig. 63

Fig. 64   Fig. 65

13   Mandibles longer than the length of an eye and sickle-shaped, face in
front view wider than high; antennae short with most flagellar segments
wider than long (Fig. 60). Shiny black species with body hairs mostly black .... *Panurgus* p.170

—   Mandibles shorter than the length of an eye, face in front view roundish or higher
than wide; antennae longer with most flagellar segments longer than wide.
(Fig. 61). Body hairs mostly pale **14**

14   Vein 2m-cu entering the second submarginal cell close to the end of that cell (Fig. 54).
Mandibles broad, up to twice as long as wide. Labrum (when visible) longer than wide .... *Osmia* p.276

—   Vein 2m-cu entering the second submarginal cell close to the middle of that
cell (Fig. 62). Mandibles smaller and about 4 times as long as wide.
Labrum (when visible) much wider than long .... *Dasypoda* p.265

15   Small, slim, shiny-black and inconspicuously haired bees (wing length to 4.5mm).
Sternite 6 simple .... *Dufourea* p.237

—   Larger (wing length 6mm), more robust and dull-looking, with a densely hairy
thorax. Tergites densely punctate with whitish hair bands across the apical
depressions. Sternite 6 with a median ridge and lateral spines .... *Rophites* p.236

16   Eyes hairy, large and meeting on top (Fig. 63). Forewings with marginal cell very
long and the third submarginal cell strongly slanted (Fig. 27). Mouthparts vestigial .... *Apis* p.415

—   Eyes bare, not meeting on top. Forewings with marginal cell very short and the
third submarginal cell not strongly slanted. Mouthparts fully formed **17**

17   Third submarginal cell of forewings with an internal area that is clearly greater
than that of the second submarginal cell (Figs 30–32) **18**

—   Third submarginal cell of forewings with an internal area that is about equal to
or less than that of the second submarginal cell (Figs 33–35) **25**

18   Basal vein of forewings strongly curved, especially basally, meeting the longitudinal
vein at more or less a right angle (Fig. 30) **19**

—   Basal vein of forewings either straight (Fig. 31) or if gently curved (*Ceratina* and
some *Andrena*) meeting the longitudinal vein at less than a right angle **21**

19   Tergites usually red-marked, never with patches of adpressed whitish hairs.
Antennal flagella distinctly knobbly along front, often with discrete zones of
minute hairs on the individual segments that are conspicuous from certain
angles (Fig. 64). Legs black, at most with the tarsi and knees brownish .... *Sphecodes* p.217

—   Tergites usually black, but if red-marked, also with patches of adpressed whitish
hairs and with the legs, lower clypeus and often labrum yellow-marked. Antennal
flagella not knobbly, the segments more cylindrical and lacking discrete zones of
minute hairs (Fig. 65). Some species metallic **20**

20 Tergites with any zones of adpressed whitish hairs located along the hind margin, sometimes with a further band of such hairs across the base (but never just the latter). If no hair bands, the body is metallic-green and the hind tibiae entirely yellow. Forewings with the outer cross veins of similar thickness and colour to the other typical wing veins .... *Halictus* p.172

— Tergites with any bands or lateral patches of adpressed whitish hairs located at the base only, except for *sexstrigatum*, which has tergite 1 shiny and impunctate unlike any *Halictus*. If no hair bands, the species are non-metallic or the hind tibiae are partially darkened. Forewings with the outer cross veins thinner and often paler then the other typical wing veins .... *Lasioglossum* p.181

21 Body metallic blue and inconspicuously haired. Abdomen rather club-shaped, broadest at tergites 4 and 5. Mandibles short and narrowing towards apex (Fig. 66). A small species (wing length 5mm) with clypeus and labrum whitish .... *Ceratina* p.365

— Body not metallic blue, if slight blue reflections (*Andrena cineraria*) then a larger and obviously hairy species. Abdomen usually oval. Mandibles usually longer and sickle-shaped **22**

22 Forewings with vein 2m-cu entering the third submarginal cell well beyond the middle of that cell (Fig. 31) **23**

— Forewings with vein 2m-cu entering the third submarginal cell near the middle of that cell (Figs 32 & 39) **24**

23 Antennae with tips pointed (beware broken tips, there should be 13 segments) (Fig. 40). Last segment of tarsi long and slim (Fig. 42). Hindwings with jugal lobe long, extending to the end of the cubital cell (Fig. 67) .... *Andrena* p.92

— Antennae with tips blunt (Fig. 43). Last segment of tarsi relatively short and broader than other tarsal segments (Fig. 44). Hindwings with jugal lobe short, extending to about the midpoint of the cubital cell (Fig. 68) .... *Melitta* p.259

Fig. 66	Fig. 67	Fig. 68	Fig. 69

24 Medium-sized (wing length to 11.5mm) without darkened wings. Forewings with marginal cell short, not or barely extending beyond the end of the third submarginal cell (Fig. 32). Body usually with a pattern of white and grey hairs .... *Melecta* p.363

— Extremely large (wing length at least 18mm) with darkened, iridescent wings. Forewings with marginal cell longer, extending well beyond the end of the third submarginal cell (Fig. 39). Body either entirely black or black with thorax and base of abdomen yellow-haired .... *Xylocopa* p.366

25 Vein 2m-cu bulging outwards at its far lower corner but bending towards the wing base where it meets the third submarginal cell (Fig. 33) .... *Colletes* p.69

— Vein 2m-cu not bulging outwards below and furthest from the wing base where it meets the third submarginal cell (Figs 34 & 35) **26**

26 Tip of abdomen with a prominent pygidium (Fig. 69). Legs usually marked with red, orange or yellow but occasionally dark. Inconspicuously haired, rather wasp-like bees **27**

— Tip of abdomen without a prominent pygidium. Legs entirely dark beneath any coloured hairs. Furrier bees **28**

27 Axillae small and inconspicuous (Fig. 45). Tergites without whitish patches
    composed of tiny hairs, any markings resulting from pigmented integument
    (usually red, yellow, black or a combination of these colours) .... *Nomada* p.314

— Thorax with large and projecting axillae on either side of the scutellum (Fig. 46).
    Tergites with paired whitish spots composed of tiny adpressed hairs .... *Epeolus* p.352

28 Surface of face black (overlying hairs may be pale). Forewings with vein
    2m-cu entering the third submarginal cell before the end of that cell
    (Fig. 35). 'Bumblebees', often with a white or red tail and yellow bands .... *Bombus* p.368

— Surface of face extensively yellow below any hairs. Forewings with vein 2m-cu
    entering the third submarginal cell at the lower outer corner of that
    cell (Fig. 34). Less bumblebee-like .... *Anthophora* p.357

FAMILY COLLETIDAE

COLLETES – PLASTERER BEES

Medium-sized, variably furry solitary bees with short, bilobed tongues. All but one of the British species have banded abdomens. Pollen is collected on the femora, tibiae and basitarsi of the hind legs, and also the sides of the propodeum, in impressive quantities. Most species nest in light soil, with some species forming very large nesting aggregations. The tongue is used to line the nest cells with a

Colletes hederae *Colletes cunicularis* *Colletes daviesanus*

cellophane-like substance which is waterproof and fungus-resistant. The cells are filled with a semi-liquid mixture of pollen and nectar, with the egg attached to the upper cell wall. Foraging habits vary, with some species being broadly polylectic whilst others concentrate on a single family (especially Asteraceae) or even single species of plant in the cases of *C. halophilus* and *C. hederae*. Males usually appear a week or so before females.

The shape and shininess of the galeae on either side of the mouthparts can greatly assist in separating various species, so the mouthparts should be fully pulled out when pinning specimens. The identification of many males requires close examination of the underside of the abdomen, notably the pits, projection and hairs of sternite 6.

This is a near-cosmopolitan genus, with about 500 described species. Nine are known from Britain, one of which (*C. hederae*) is a recent colonist. A number of additional species are found on the near-continent. Members of the genus are variously parasitised by cleptoparasitic bees of the genus *Epeolus*, sarcophagid flies such as *Miltogramma punctata*, the bee-fly *Bombylius minor* and the blister beetle *Stenoria analis*.

ASSOCIATED SPECIES

Bee-fly *Bombylius minor* (left), sarcophagid fly *Miltogramma punctata* (top right) and blister beetle *Stenoria analis* (bottom right).

COLLETES FEMALES

1   A large, brownish, furry species (typical wing length 10mm) with black-haired tergites that lack conspicuous bands .... *cunicularius*

—   Tergites conspicuously banded and abdomen not furry. Mostly smaller species **2**

2   Dorsal fringe of hind tibiae dark-haired. Hind margin of tergite 1 conspicuously translucent orange-brown (Figs 1–3). No long outstanding hairs on upper surface of tergite 1. Larger (wing length at least 8mm) **3**

—   Dorsal fringe of hind tibiae whitish, pale grey or buff. Hind margin of tergite 1 dark or, if somewhat brownish, tergite 1 has long and outstanding hairs across the upper surface. Smaller (wing length up to 7mm) **5**

Fig. 1 *C. hederae*

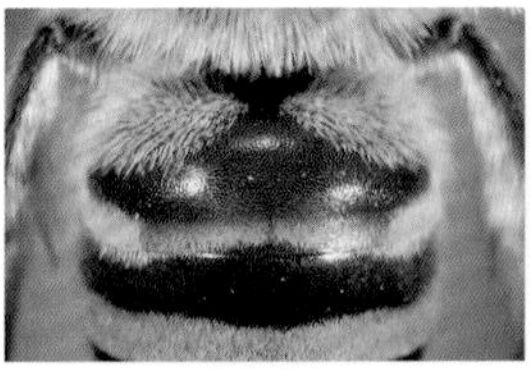

Fig. 2 *C. halophilus*

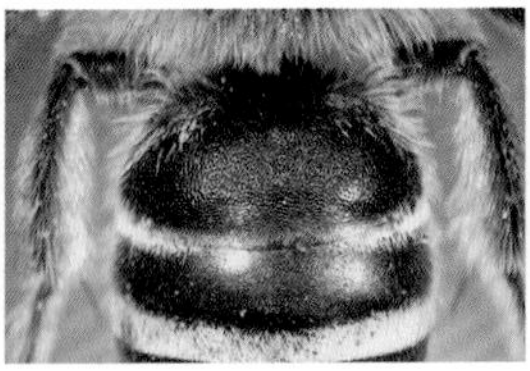

Fig. 3 *C. succinctus*

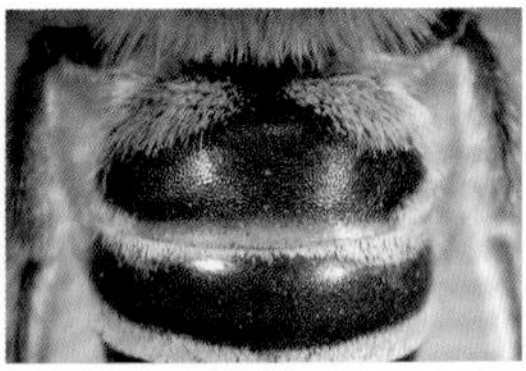

Fig. 4 *C. daviesanus*

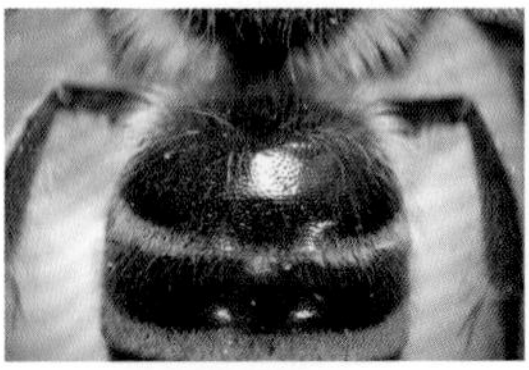

Fig. 5 *C. floralis*

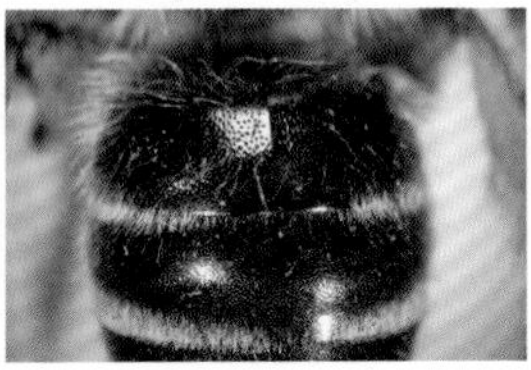

Fig. 6 *C. marginatus*

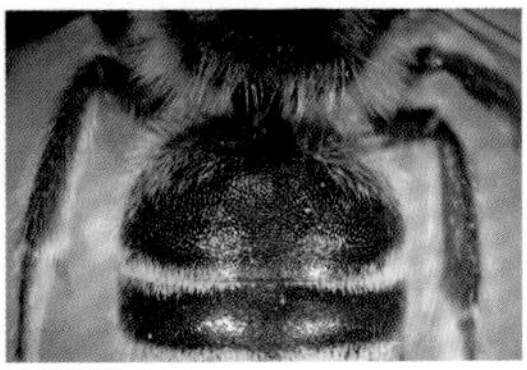

Fig. 7 *C. similis*

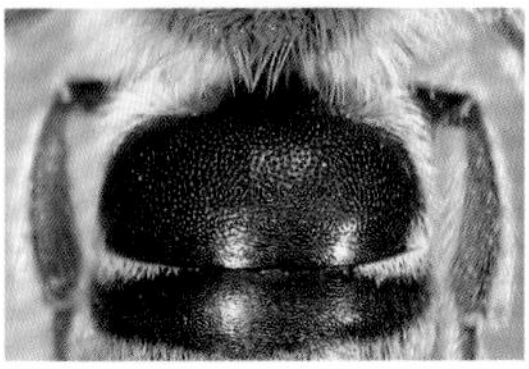

Fig. 8 *C. fodiens*

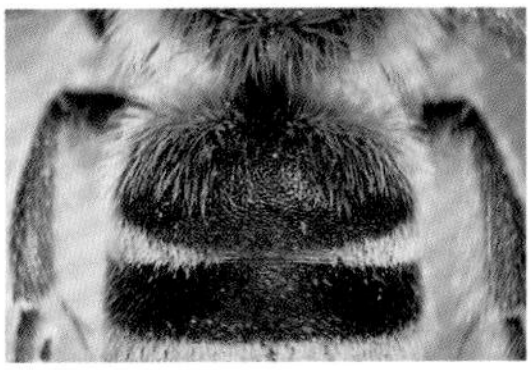

Base of abdomen of banded female *Colletes*.

3   Bands of tergites 2–4 relatively wide and bright buff in fresh individuals. Tergite 1 with conspicuous and extensive patches of orange-buff hairs at sides. Lower clypeus with ridges forming concentric rings when illuminated from certain angles. Galeae semi-shining with shallow microsculpture (Fig. 9). Larger (typical wing length 10mm) .... *hederae*

—   Bands of tergites narrower and whiter. Tergite 1 with less conspicuous patches of pale hairs at the sides. Clypeus with ridges not forming such obvious rings. Smaller (wing length rarely exceeding 9mm) **4**

4   Galeae dulled by dense microsculpture (Fig. 10). Bands of tergites 2–4 and hair patches at sides of tergite 1 whiter. Tergite 1 with relatively coarse punctures and some microsculpture. Wing length usually more than 8.5mm .... *halophilus*

—   Galeae shining without microsculpture (Fig. 11). Bands of tergites 2–4 and hair patches at sides of tergite 1 usually buffish-white. Tergite 1 with fine punctures and no microsculpture. Wing length usually less than 8.5mm .... *succinctus*

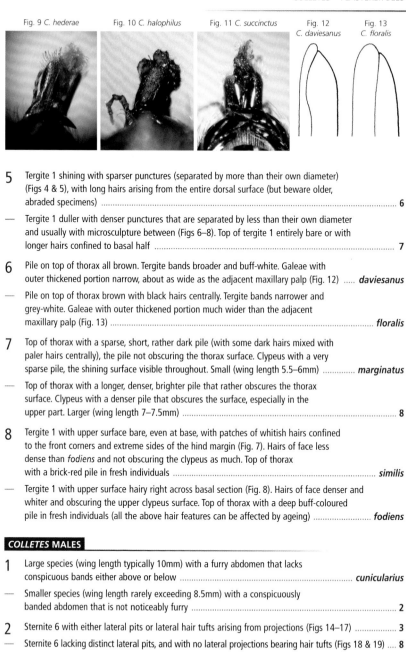

Fig. 9 *C. hederae*   Fig. 10 *C. halophilus*   Fig. 11 *C. succinctus*   Fig. 12 *C. daviesanus*   Fig. 13 *C. floralis*

5 Tergite 1 shining with sparser punctures (separated by more than their own diameter) (Figs 4 & 5), with long hairs arising from the entire dorsal surface (but beware older, abraded specimens) **6**

— Tergite 1 duller with denser punctures that are separated by less than their own diameter and usually with microsculpture between (Figs 6–8). Top of tergite 1 entirely bare or with longer hairs confined to basal half **7**

6 Pile on top of thorax all brown. Tergite bands broader and buff-white. Galeae with outer thickened portion narrow, about as wide as the adjacent maxillary palp (Fig. 12) ..... ***daviesanus***

— Pile on top of thorax brown with black hairs centrally. Tergite bands narrower and grey-white. Galeae with outer thickened portion much wider than the adjacent maxillary palp (Fig. 13) .... ***floralis***

7 Top of thorax with a sparse, short, rather dark pile (with some dark hairs mixed with paler hairs centrally), the pile not obscuring the thorax surface. Clypeus with a very sparse pile, the shining surface visible throughout. Small (wing length 5.5–6mm) .... ***marginatus***

— Top of thorax with a longer, denser, brighter pile that rather obscures the thorax surface. Clypeus with a denser pile that obscures the surface, especially in the upper part. Larger (wing length 7–7.5mm) **8**

8 Tergite 1 with upper surface bare, even at base, with patches of whitish hairs confined to the front corners and extreme sides of the hind margin (Fig. 7). Hairs of face less dense than *fodiens* and not obscuring the clypeus as much. Top of thorax with a brick-red pile in fresh individuals .... ***similis***

— Tergite 1 with upper surface hairy right across basal section (Fig. 8). Hairs of face denser and whiter and obscuring the upper clypeus surface. Top of thorax with a deep buff-coloured pile in fresh individuals (all the above hair features can be affected by ageing) .... ***fodiens***

COLLETES MALES

1 Large species (wing length typically 10mm) with a furry abdomen that lacks conspicuous bands either above or below .... ***cunicularius***

— Smaller species (wing length rarely exceeding 8.5mm) with a conspicuously banded abdomen that is not noticeably furry **2**

2 Sternite 6 with either lateral pits or lateral hair tufts arising from projections (Figs 14–17) **3**

— Sternite 6 lacking distinct lateral pits, and with no lateral projections bearing hair tufts (Figs 18 & 19) **8**

Fig. 14   Fig. 15   Fig. 16   Fig. 17   Fig. 18   Fig. 19

C. daviesanus   *C. fodiens*   *C. hederae*   *C. similis*   *C. marginatus*   *C. floralis*

Sternite 6 of banded male *Colletes* (*halophilus* and *succinctus* resemble *hederae*).

3 Sternite 6 with lateral pits but no lateral hair tufts (Fig. 16) **4**

— Sternite 6 with lateral prominences giving rise to hair tufts and shallow depressions
on each side of the midline (Figs 14, 15 & 17) **6**

4 Galeae shining (Fig. 11). Abdominal bands relatively narrow. Averaging small
(typical wing length 7mm) .... *succinctus*

— Galeae dulled by microsculpture (Figs 9 & 10). Abdominal bands wider. Typically larger **5**

5 Galeae with light microsculpture, semi-shining (Fig. 9). Abdominal bands broad
and buff when fresh. Scutum and scutellum sparsely punctate and extensively
shining. Punctures of tergites relatively fine .... *hederae*

— Galeae dull with dense microsculpture (Fig. 10). Abdominal bands narrower and
whitish. Scutum and scutellum densely punctate throughout, duller. Punctures
of tergites coarser .... *halophilus*

6 Sternite 6 with lateral tufts of long hairs (Fig. 14). Sternites 4–6 with marked
lateral bumps. Tergite 1 shining with sparser punctures that are separated by
more than their own diameter .... *daviesanus*

— Sternite 6 with lateral tufts of short hairs (Figs 15 & 17). Sternites 4–6 without lateral
bumps. Tergite 1 duller with denser punctures that are separated by less than their
own diameter **7**

Fig. 20   Fig. 21    Fig. 22

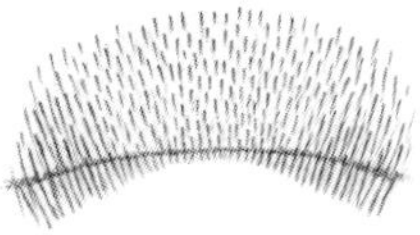

Fig. 23

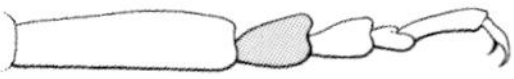

7 Sternite 3 with hairs of apical margin arranged in a 'chrysanthemum' pattern (Fig. 20).
Second segment of hind tarsus only slightly longer than wide in side view, and about
as wide as the preceding basitarsus (Fig. 21) .... *similis*

— Sternite 3 without such a pattern of hairs (Fig. 22). Second segment of hind tarsus
about 1.5 times as long as wide in side view, and narrower than the preceding
basitarsus (Fig. 23) .... *fodiens*

8 Sternites 2–4 with dense apical bands of long white hairs that arise on the margins
and project some way beyond. Sternite 6 with a general covering of adpressed hairs
and no pronounced lateral tufts (Fig. 18). Smaller (typical wing length 5.5mm) .... *marginatus*

— Sternites 2–4 with less conspicuous apical bands consisting of short hairs that do
not extend far beyond the apical margins. Sternite 6 with pronounced lateral hair
tufts (Fig. 19). Larger (typical wing length 7mm) .... *floralis*

Colletes cunicularius (Linnaeus, 1761)   **Early Colletes**

Plate 1

Description & similar species FW 10–11mm female, 9.5–10.5mm male. Our largest *Colletes*, and the only one with an unbanded, furry abdomen, this being mostly black-haired and contrasting with the brown-haired thorax. It most resembles an oversized *Andrena scotica*, with an early flight period that compounds this potential for confusion. However, the antennae are much shorter than in an *Andrena* and no facial foveae are present. Males are smaller, slimmer and paler-haired than females and the abdomen can give the impression of hair bands from some angles, though these consist of long hairs, not the dense adpressed whitish hairs of other male *Colletes*. They also look more like a large *Andrena* or *Melitta* in the field. **Variation** Minor size variation and fading with age. **Flight season** Early March to early May, peaking with the blossoming of willows, females occasionally lingering into June. **Habitat** Until recently, confined to western coastal dunes. Since about 2010 it has started to colonise sandy sites well inland, particularly heaths, sandpits and quarries. **Flowers visited** Strongly associated with Creeping Willow at its dune sites. Inland, Goat Willow and Grey Willow are the main pollen sources, though it will use other spring-blossoming shrubs such as Blackthorn and cherries and take nectar from dandelions and Alexanders. **Nesting habits** Nesting occurs in bare or sparsely vegetated sandy ground, especially south-facing slopes, with very loose, non-compacted sand preferred. It can form large, dense and surprisingly noisy nesting aggregations. Mating balls can occur as new females emerge. **Status & distribution** Formerly regarded as a rare and restricted species of western dunes between south Wales and Cumbria. It has recently turned up at numerous sites across southern England from the Hampshire and Essex coast as far north as Shropshire and Nottinghamshire. It has also turned up at new sites in Wales, both coastal and a short distance inland. It is not clear if this increase represents an expansion from established British colonies, or the arrival of continental bees from the south, though its recent discovery on Jersey suggests that the latter could be partly responsible. Not recorded from Scotland or Ireland. **Parasites & associates** None known in Britain but attacked by the cleptoparasitic bee *Sphecodes albilabris* abroad (a species much larger and redder than any British *Sphecodes*).

female

male

Colletes daviesanus Smith, 1846   **Davies' Colletes**

Plate 1

Description & similar species FW 6.5–7mm female, 5.5–6.5mm male. The shiny, relatively sparsely punctured, hairy tergite 1 of both sexes distinguishes it from all species except *C. floralis*, females of which have narrower, grey-white abdominal bands and black hairs on the top of the thorax. Males are readily distinguished from all other *Colletes* under magnification by checking sternite 6, which has tufts of long hairs arising from a small prominence in each basal corner. **Variation** Some size variation and fading through wear. **Flight season** Late May to early September. **Habitat** Able to exploit a wide range of flowery habitats in both coastal and inland areas. It is the main *Colletes* found in gardens, along arable margins, on brownfield sites and within districts featuring heavier clay soils.

Flowers visited Pollen seems to be obtained entirely from composites such as mayweeds, chamomiles, Oxeye Daisy, ragworts, Tansy, Yarrow and Common Fleabane, though it will visit a wider range of flowers for nectar.

Nesting habits Large nesting aggregations can form in bare or sparsely vegetated dry soils, especially on south-facing slopes and faces. It is the only *Colletes* that regularly nests in walls, typically using weathered sandstone or soft mortar.

Status & distribution Locally common throughout much of England but scarce in Wales and Scotland. Very rare in Ireland. Recorded from several of the Channel Islands. **Parasites & associates** The cleptoparasitic bee *Epeolus variegatus*; also an important host for the sarcophagid fly *Miltogramma punctata* and possibly a subsidiary host for the rare Heath Bee-fly *Bombylius minor*.

Colletes floralis Eversmann, 1852   **Northern Colletes**

not illustrated

Description & similar species FW 7mm female, 6–7mm male. Females resemble *C. daviesanus* in having a shiny abdomen with relatively sparse punctures on tergite 1, but the pile on top of the thorax is brighter in fresh individuals, has black hairs centrally, and contrasts more strongly with the pale hairs on the sides of the thorax. The bands on the abdomen are also narrower and greyer. Under magnification, the galeae have a much broader thickened edge. Males have sternite 6 flat and lacking lateral pits or projections but with numerous long hairs along the side margins. In the field, they also have narrow and greyish abdominal bands. *C. marginatus* is the only other species with a flat sternite 6, but it has much more conspicuous white hair fringes along the hind margins of sternites 2–4. **Variation** Little noted. **Flight season** Mid-June to late August. **Habitat** Almost entirely confined to coastal dunes and machair grassland. **Flowers visited** Flowers from a variety of families are used, including umbellifers such as Hemlock Water-dropwort, Common Hogweed, Giant Hogweed and Wild Carrot; also Wild Thyme, White Clover, Knotted Pearlwort, Lady's Bedstraw, buttercups, brambles, crucifers, composites and legumes. Preferences can vary widely between sites.

Nesting habits Nesting occurs in non-compacted sand, especially sheltered south-facing slopes and banks of mid and fore dunes, and typically in aggregations. It has also been recorded nesting in masonry. **Status & distribution** A very restricted species, almost entirely confined to coastal districts of Ireland (where widespread) and western Scotland (mostly within the Uists of the Outer Hebrides, Mull, Coll, Tiree, Islay and Ayrshire). It has also been recorded from two sites in Cumbria. **Parasites & associates** None known.

Colletes fodiens (Geoffroy, 1785)   **Hairy-saddled Colletes**
not illustrated

Description & similar species FW 5.5–6.5mm (sexes similar). Females most resemble *C. similis* in the field but have more densely white-haired faces, and the top of the thorax never has the reddish-brown pile of fresh *C. similis*. Under magnification, tergite 1 will be seen to have hairs across the top (top bare in *C. similis* except at sides). Males are not easily distinguished in the field, but the sternite characters in the key allow easy confirmation under the microscope. **Variation** Some size variation and fading through wear. In females loss of hairs of the face and the top of tergite 1 can result in easy confusion with *C. similis*.
Flight season Late June to early September. **Habitat** Strongly associated with sandy habitats, primarily lowland heathland, acid grassland, sandpits and coastal dunes but also some soft rock cliffs, vegetated shingle sites and saltmarsh edge. **Flowers visited** Composites such as Common Ragwort, Common Fleabane, Tansy and mayweeds are the main pollen sources, but nectar is obtained from a wide variety of plants. **Nesting habits** Nesting occurs in sandy ground, but it does not seem to form dense nesting aggregations. **Status & distribution** Locally common in southern heathland districts, becoming more restricted to the coast elsewhere and extending north to southwest Scotland. Not recorded from Ireland. Recorded from several of the Channel Islands. **Parasites & associates** The cleptoparasitic bee *Epeolus variegatus*, and possibly *E. cruciger* too.

Colletes halophilus Verhoeff, 1944   **Sea Aster Bee**
not illustrated

Description & similar species FW 8.5–9mm female, 7–8.5mm male. One of a group of three closely related species (together with *C. hederae* and *C. succinctus*). Females are intermediate in size between the other two, with the abdominal bands of tergites 2–4 and hair patches at the sides of tergite 1 paler (when all species are fresh). The bands of tergites 2–4 are narrower than in *C. hederae* but broader than in *C. succinctus*. Tergite 1 has somewhat larger, coarser punctures than the other two species and is dulled by microsculpture centrally. The galeae, which are much duller than in the other two, are the most reliable character in both sexes, and the strong association with Sea Aster can be a good field clue, though *C. hederae* will occasionally forage on this plant alongside *C. halophilus*. **Variation** Giant males that resemble *C. hederae* (but with whiter, narrower abdominal bands) can occur. Old females can have the abdominal bands much abraded. **Flight season** Males appear in early August, females a little later to peak with the flowering of Sea Aster in September. In some years it will persist as late as November. **Habitat** Associated with Sea Aster on upper saltmarsh and other brackish coastal habitats. Nesting can occur nearby in a variety of drier habitats including sea banks, sandhills, coastal brownfield land (including quarries) and eroding clifflets at saltmarsh edge. **Flowers visited** Sea Aster is the main pollen and nectar source. Other flowers may also be visited, e.g. Bristly Oxtongue, ragworts and Weld. **Nesting habits** Large and dense nesting aggregations can be formed in bare or sparsely vegetated light soils, especially south-facing slopes and clifflets, and along paths and tracks. Mating balls can occur as new females emerge. The nests are sometimes below the high spring tide mark, which it seems perfectly capable of surviving. **Status & distribution** This bee is almost entirely confined to sites around the southern North Sea, the English Channel and the east coast of France to the Spanish border. Hence, a significant proportion of its world population is centred on the coastline of southeast England between Christchurch Harbour and Spurn Point. The Thames Gateway and the East Anglian coast hold the bulk of the British population, and it can be common at some sites, though it is vulnerable to coastal development and rising sea levels. It has also been found well inland in the East Anglian Brecks but is not thought to be established here. **Parasites & associates** A large form of the cleptoparasitic bee *Epeolus variegatus*; also the sarcophagid fly *Miltogramma punctata*. On the near-continent it is also a host for the non-British *Epeolus tarsalis*.

female

male

Colletes hederae Schmidt & Westrich, 1993 — Ivy Bee

Plate 1

Description & similar species FW 9.5–10mm female, 8–8.5mm male. The largest of our banded *Colletes*. Fresh females are unmistakable, with broad buff abdominal bands, bright orange-buff hairs on the top of the thorax and similar-coloured hair patches on the sides of tergite 1. *C. halophilus* and *C. succinctus* are similar but smaller with paler, narrower abdominal bands. With the right angle of lighting, the ridges of the clypeus form concentric rings to an extent not seen in the other two species. Fresh males have buff abdominal bands which are also slightly broader than in the other two species. In older, faded individuals of both sexes, the best character are the galeae, which are shinier than in *C. halophilus* but not polished as in *C. succinctus*. The late flight period and association with Ivy can also support identification. **Variation** The abdominal bands of older specimens become paler and abraded and the thoracic hairs duller. Small males can occur that overlap in size with *C. halophilus*. **Flight season** The last solitary bee to emerge each year and Britain's only true autumn bee. Males appear in late August, females typically in mid-September to peak with the Ivy blossom in October, and they can persist into November. **Habitat** A great variety of habitats are used, including urban locations and farmland with minimal semi-natural habitat. It can occur alongside *C. halophilus* at coastal sites, or alongside *C. succinctus* in heathland districts. **Flowers visited** Ivy is the main pollen and nectar source, and the flowers can attract large numbers. Females will also gather pollen from other late flowers before Ivy is in flower (e.g. Bristly Oxtongue and Perennial Wall-rocket) and both sexes take nectar from other plants (even Sea Aster at *C. halophilus* sites). **Nesting habits** Large and dense nesting aggregations can form in bare or sparsely vegetated light soils, especially south-facing slopes and paths. It has even been reported nesting in allotment plots and the lawns of gardens and public parks. Mating balls can occur as new females emerge. **Status & distribution** Only described as new to science in 1993, since when it has been recorded over much of Europe. It has been present on the Channel

female

male

Islands since at least the 1970s (originally considered to be *C. halophilus*) but was not discovered on the mainland until 2001 (Dorset). It is now spreading northwards and westwards and had reached Pembrokeshire, Shropshire and the north Norfolk coast by 2014. The spread is being monitored by BWARS, and the latest distribution can be seen on their website. **Parasites & associates** On the Channel Islands it the host of the meloid beetle *Stenoria analis*. Large numbers of first-instar *Stenoria* larvae (triungulins) cluster on vegetation and release a pheromone that acts as a sexual attractant to *C. hederae* males. This allows the triungulins to latch on to the bees, which carry them to the female nesting aggregations where they undergo the rest of their development as cleptoparasites. The cleptoparasitic bees *Epeolus cruciger* and the non-British *E. fallax* attack *C. hederae* abroad.

Colletes marginatus Smith, 1846   Margined Colletes
not illustrated

Description & similar species FW 5–6mm female, 4.5–5.5mm male. Our smallest *Colletes*, with squat and dark-looking females that have a particularly short and sparse pile on the face and on top of the thorax. Tergite 1 is densely punctate with a band of sparse hairs across the base. The small size of the males is a good field clue, and they can be quickly confirmed under magnification through the combination of an unmodified sternite 6 and strong white hair bands across sternites 2–4. In both sexes, the thickened outer portion of the galeae is very broad, being equal in width to the shiny inner portion (outer section much

female

narrower in species such as *C. fodiens* and *C. similis*). **Variation** Some size variation, and fading through wear. **Flight season** Late June until late August. **Habitat** Strongly associated with loose sands, primarily coastal dunes, but also vegetated shingle and sandy, rabbit-disturbed areas of the East Anglian Brecks. **Flowers visited** A variety of plant types appear to be visited for both pollen and nectar, though legumes, brambles and mignonettes seem to be especially important pollen sources, and it visits umbellifers more than most *Colletes*. There is no special association with composites, in contrast to most of the smaller *Colletes*. **Nesting habits** Rarely observed but can involve small aggregations in non-compacted sandy ground. **Status & distribution** A very restricted species, recorded mostly from larger dunes or shingle areas of Lancashire, south Wales, Cornwall, the Solent area, Kent and East Anglia, plus a cluster of inland sites in the East Anglian Brecks. Recorded from the Channel Islands (Jersey). Not recorded from Scotland or Ireland. **Parasites & associates** A small form of the cleptoparasitic bee *Epeolus cruciger*.

Colletes similis Schenck, 1853   **Bare-saddled Colletes**

not illustrated

Description & similar species FW 6–7mm female, 5.5–7mm male. Females most resemble *C. fodiens* (worn females of the two species can be especially challenging), but the pile on top of the thorax is reddish-brown in fresh *C. similis* (bright orange-brown in fresh *C. fodiens*), tergite 1 is entirely bare over most of its surface (even basally) and the face is never densely haired. Males are not easily distinguished in the field, but under magnification the 'chrysanthemum' pattern of hairs on sternite 3 allows easy separation from all other *Colletes*. **Variation** Some size variation, and fading through wear. **Flight season** Mid-June to early September. **Habitat** Various dry, flowery habitats are used including soft rock cliffs, coastal dunes and shingle, chalk grassland and heathland. Particularly reliant on brownfield sites in some parts of its range, e.g. the Midlands. Not as strongly attached to sandy sites as *C. fodiens* and *C. marginatus*, and not as tolerant of clay soils as *C. daviesanus*.

female

male

Flowers visited Composites such as ragworts, Oxeye Daisy, mayweeds, chamomiles and Tansy are the main pollen sources, but nectar is gathered from a wider variety of plants. **Nesting habits** Nesting occurs in light soil, but it does not seem to form dense nesting aggregations. **Status & distribution** Widespread but rather localised in southern England; scarce in Wales and the Midlands, with mainland records extending north to Lancashire. Present along the eastern coast of Ireland alongside *C. floralis* and with an old record for the Isle of Man. Not recorded from Scotland. Recorded from several of the Channel Islands. **Parasites & associates** The cleptoparasitic bee *Epeolus variegatus*.

Colletes succinctus (Linnaeus, 1758)

Heather Colletes

Plate 1

Girdled Colletes

Description & similar species FW 8–8.5mm female, 6.5–8mm male. Resembling *C. halophilus* and *C. hederae* but averaging smaller with narrower abdominal bands. It is the darkest-looking of the three in the field and the only one with polished galeae that lack microsculpture. The strong association with heathers can support identification. **Variation** Moderate size variation and occasional oversized males. The abdominal bands and hairs of the thorax can become paler in old specimens. **Flight season** Males appear in July, females a little later, peaking with the flowering of Heather (Ling) in August and often persisting into October. **Habitat** A dry heathland specialist over most of the British Isles, using both lowland and upland heathland (rarely moorland), though occasionally recorded well away from these habitats. Strongly associated with dune heath in northern Scotland.

Flowers visited Ling is the main pollen and nectar source, and the flowers can attract large numbers of the bee. It will also visit other heathers and occasionally ragworts, thistles, brambles, Yarrow, Ivy, melilots, even Sea Aster at some Scottish sites where dune heath occurs alongside saltmarsh. **Nesting habits** Large and dense nesting aggregations can form in bare or sparsely vegetated sandy ground, especially south-facing slopes and faces. **Status & distribution** Largely confined to heathland districts, and abundant on many English heaths in the south and Midlands, though much scarcer in Wales and southwest England. In Scotland it is largely confined to coastal districts. Scarce but widespread in Ireland. Present on several of the Channel Islands. **Parasites & associates** The cleptoparasitic bee *Epeolus cruciger* is usually much in evidence at southern *C. succinctus* colonies. The rare Heath Bee-fly *Bombylius minor* seems to use *C. succinctus* as its main host at its few southern heathland sites.

female

male

HYLAEUS – YELLOW-FACE BEES

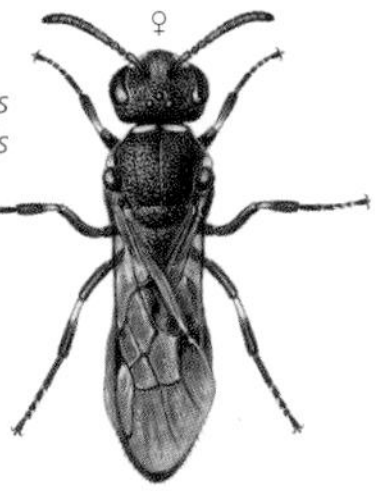

Mostly small to very small, predominantly black solitary
bees that are inconspicuously haired and lack pollen brushes.
Yellow or white markings are usually present on the face,
antennae, legs and thorax. Females usually have a pair of yellow
or white spots on each side of the face whilst males usually have
the face predominantly white or yellow, allowing easy sexing in the
field. The tongue is short and bilobed. Some foreign species have
partially red abdomens, and a few are even metallic.

Hylaeus communis

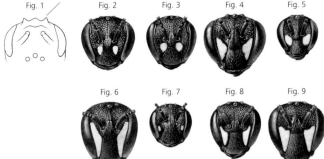

Unusually for bees, pollen is carried back to the nest in the
crop and regurgitated into the nest cell. The exception is *H. cornutus*, which carries a pollen
ball in its facial depression. As in the related genus *Colletes*, the nest cells are lined with a
waterproof cellophane-like substance, applied with the tongue, and filled with a semi-liquid
mix of pollen and nectar. Nesting occurs variously in hollow plant stems and pre-existing holes
(including old nests of other aculeates) in wood, walls and vertical earth banks. Foraging habits
vary, with some species polylectic whilst others (e.g. *H. signatus*) restrict pollen collecting to a
single plant genus. A number of Hawaiian species have become cleptoparasites of other *Hylaeus*.

This is a near-cosmopolitan genus with over 500 described species. Twelve are known in the
British Isles, though several further ones occur on the near-continent and should be looked out
for. Parasitic wasps of the genus *Gasteruption* seem to be the main parasites of *Hylaeus*,
injecting an egg into the bee cell which then develops as a cleptoparasite.

In the following key, beware that a small proportion of females can have the yellow facial
markings poorly formed and may not key out easily. Always retain such specimens, as they
can usually be determined with reference to comparative material of typical specimens, using
features such as head shape, punctures on the tergites and propodeal sculpturing.

HYLAEUS FEMALES

1   Face black with two triangular projections, one on either side (Fig. 1) .... *cornutus*

—   Face with a pair of yellow markings (occasionally reduced or absent) and
never with projections **2**

Fig. 1   Fig. 2   Fig. 3   Fig. 4   Fig. 5

Fig. 6   Fig. 7   Fig. 8   Fig. 9

Female facial
characteristics
(see Plate 2 for
full set).

2   Face with a pair of yellow or whitish markings that are well separated from the
eye margins and tend to be circular or irregular and not triangular (Figs 2 & 3).
Tergite 1 never with a fringe of short white hairs on hind margins at sides **3**

—   Face with a pair of yellow or whitish markings that hug the eye margins on their
longest side, these spots usually triangular and never circular (e.g. Figs 4 & 5).
Tergite 1 often with a fringe of short white hairs on the hind margins at the sides **4**

3 Tergite 1 sparsely punctate on basal two-thirds, with a more distinct band of punctures and microsculpture across the apical third. Tergite 2 with fine punctures and microsculpture throughout. Top of propodeum with distinct longitudinal striae. Pale body markings creamy-yellow .... *dilatatus*

— Tergites 1 and 2 densely punctate throughout, without microsculpture. Top of propodeum reticulate without striae. Pale body markings bright yellow .... *annularis*

4 Yellow facial markings extending well above the antennal insertion points (Fig. 6). Pronotal collar very broad throughout (twice the width of an antennal flagellum), creating a tight-fitting cushion between the scutum and back of the head (Fig. 10) .... *punctulatissimus*

— Yellow facial markings rarely extending as high as the antennal insertion points. Pronotal collar much narrower (less than the width of an antennal flagellum) and not tightly hugging the back of the head 5

Fig. 10   Fig. 11 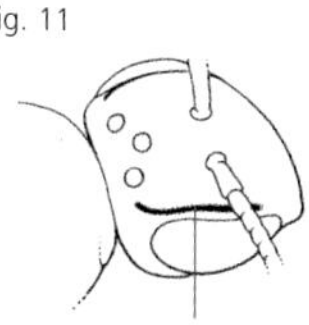   Fig. 12 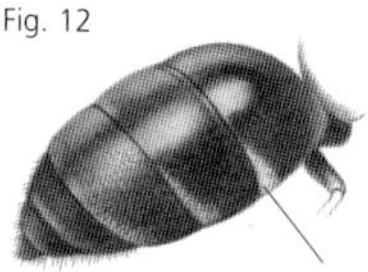   Fig. 13

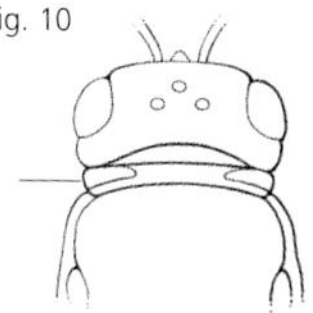

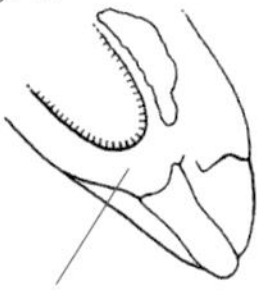

5 Groove alongside each inner eye margin extending above and behind the top of the eye and curving inwards towards the lateral ocellus (Fig. 11). Facial spots trapezoidal and rather oblique, broadly contacting both the eye margins and the facial sutures (Fig. 5) .... *pictipes*

— Groove alongside inner eye margin not extending so high or curving towards the lateral ocellus. Facial markings typically triangular, not oblique or trapezoidal and sometimes not reaching the facial sutures.. 6

6 Tergite 1 without a pronounced fringe of short white hairs along the hind margin at sides (though sparse hairs can be present). Pronotal collar always black 7

— Tergite 1 with a pronounced fringe of short white hairs along hind margin at sides (can be hard to discern in worn individuals or specimens that have been exposed to damp) (Fig. 12). Pronotal collar often marked with yellow or white................................... 8

7 Tergite 1 with a band of sparse punctures across apical third. Sternites without apical bands of short white hairs (viewed obliquely from behind). Top of thorax shinier. Smaller and more compact (wing length typically 4.5mm, body length 5mm) .... *communis*

— Tergite 1 impunctate across apical third. Sternites with apical bands of short white hairs (viewed obliquely from behind). Top of thorax duller. Larger and slimmer (wing length typically 5mm, body 7.5mm)..*pectoralis*

8 Hind tibiae black, at most obscurely pale on basal eighth. Tergite 1 punctured throughout. Usually relatively large and robust (wing length usually over 5mm) .... *signatus*

— Hind tibiae clearly yellow on basal quarter or more. If tergite 1 punctured throughout, wing length 4mm or less. Smaller (wing length up to 5mm) 9

9 Head in front view roundish (Fig. 7), the facial spots typically narrow and well separated from facial sutures except sometimes at bottom. Antennae unusually short with the basal flagellar segments much wider than long. Small species (wing length only 3.5–4mm, body length 5mm) .... *brevicornis*

— Head in front view clearly longer than wide and rather oval. Antennae of typical length, the basal flagellar segments only slightly wider than long. Larger species (wing length 4–5mm, body at least 6mm).. 10

10 Face noticeably elongate with a wide malar gap (Fig. 13). Tergite 1 densely punctate at sides. Underside of antennal flagellum always obviously orange .... *hyalinatus*

— Face shorter with a much narrower gap between the eyes and the mandibles. Underside of antennal flagellum often dark or obscurely orange **11**

11 Face broader with black central section relatively broad, the yellow facial marks smaller and usually not extending as high as the antennal insertion points, and well separated from these insertion points (Fig. 8). No distinct semi-shining, impunctate area on frons immediately above the antennal insertion points. .... *confusus*

— Face longer with black central section relatively long and narrow, the yellow facial marks larger, extending as high as the antennal insertion points and extending relatively close to those insertion points (Fig. 9). Distinct semi-shining, impunctate areas on frons immediately above the antennal insertion points .... *incongruus*

HYLAEUS MALES

1 Face entirely black (Fig. 14). Antennae mostly yellow, only narrowly darkened on the dorsal face of the flagellum and scape (which is often oriented downwards with the yellow side more conspicuous). Abdomen elongate .... *cornutus*

— Face extensively yellow or white. Antennae dark, at most reddish beneath flagellum or with partially yellow scape. Abdomen less elongate **2**

Fig. 14 Fig. 15 Fig. 16 Fig. 17 Fig. 18

Male facial characteristics (see Plate 2 for full set).

Fig. 19 Fig. 20 Fig. 21 Fig. 22 Fig. 23

Fig. 24 Fig. 25

2 Antennal scapes as wide as long and extensively yellow (Figs 24 & 25) **3**
— Antennal scapes obviously longer than wide, at most narrowly yellow beneath (Figs 27–29)............... **4**

3 Mandibles black (Fig. 15). Mid and hind tibiae entirely yellow. Sternite 3 without a welt .... *annularis*
— Mandibles marked with white (Fig. 16). Mid and hind tibiae with black marks or rings. Sternite 3 with a small welt .... *dilatatus*

4 Mandibles marked with white or yellow **5**
— Mandibles black **7**

5 Labrum white (Fig. 18) .... *incongruus*
— Labrum black **6**

6   Mid and hind basitarsi mainly pale. Pale facial markings not extending above
     the antennal insertion points (Fig. 17). Tergites more finely punctate .... *confusus*

—   Mid and hind basitarsi dark. Yellow facial markings extending well above the
     antennal insertion points (Fig. 19). Tergites densely and strongly punctate.................*punctulatissimus*

7   Face yellow with a distinct black pattern that is much more obvious than the
     facial sutures, and with the yellow markings curling around the top of antennal
     insertion points (Fig. 20) (a small, shining species with no fringe of white hairs
     along the hind margin of tergite 1 at sides) .... *communis*

—   Face with just the facial sutures narrowly black and the yellow not extending
     so high. Most species with a fringe of white hairs along the hind margin of
     tergite 1 at sides **8**

8   Legs almost entirely black, just extreme base of tibiae and base of hind basitarsi
     pale. A large, densely punctate species (wing length usually over 5mm) .... *signatus*

—   Legs extensively yellow. Smaller species (wing length usually less than 5mm) **9**

9   Face with obvious long hairs that are as long as the width of an antennal
     flagellum (Fig. 26). Thorax with a long whitish pile (underside of flagellum
     conspicuously orange).. *hyalinatus*

—   Facial hairs much shorter than the width of an antennal flagellum or microscopic.
     Thorax with a less conspicuous pile **10**

Fig. 26   Fig. 27 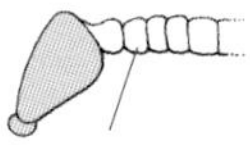   Fig. 28 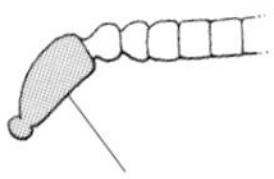   Fig. 29

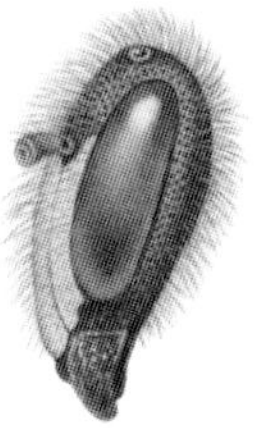

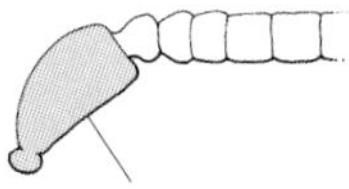

10   Head in front view roundish (Fig. 21). Antennae short, segments 3–5 about
     twice as wide as long (Fig. 27) (small, wing length 3.5–4mm) .... *brevicornis*

—   Head in front view longer than wide (Figs 22 & 23. Antennae longer, segments
     4 and 5 about as wide as long (Figs 28 & 29) **11**

11   Antennal scapes narrow, only 1.5 times the width of the flagellum (Fig. 28).
     Tergite 1 punctate throughout. Sternites without obvious hair fringes along
     hind margins. Small (wing length 3.5mm) .... *pictipes*

—   Antennal scapes about twice as wide as flagellum (Fig. 29). Tergite 1 shining,
     smooth and scarcely punctate. Sternites with dense hair bands along hind
     margins. Larger (wing length typically 5mm) .... *pectoralis*

Hylaeus annularis (Kirby, 1802)   Shingle Yellow-face Bee

Plate 2

Description & similar species FW 4–4.5mm female, 3.5–4.5mm male. The scarcer of a pair of very similar, medium-sized *Hylaeus* species. Like *H. dilatatus*, females have a pair of roundish or irregular spots on the face that are well separated from the eye margins, whilst males have highly expanded black and yellow antennal scapes. Females can only be reliably separated from *H. dilatatus* (alongside which it often flies) under the microscope by checking the surface punctures and microsculpture of tergites 1 and 2, though the presence of yellowish rather than whitish markings on the body is a good clue. Males are more easily separated, by their entirely yellow mid and hind tibiae and black mandibles. **Variation** The facial spots of females can vary somewhat in shape and size, and where they are particularly large they can almost touch the eye margins. **Flight season** Mid-June to late August. **Habitat** Coastal vegetated shingle and to a lesser extent coastal dunes. **Flowers visited** Sea-kale (one of the best flowers on which to find it), Wild Carrot, Wild Parsnip, Fennel, Sea Spurge, Sea Mayweed, Yarrow,

Creeping Thistle, ragworts, mallows, Biting Stonecrop and brambles. **Nesting habits** Nesting has been reported both in hollow plant stems and in sandy ground. **Status & distribution** Mostly known from scattered sites along the south coast of England between Dorset and Kent; also outlying records from Suffolk and the Avon side of the Severn Estuary. Occasionally recorded a short distance inland. It can be common at larger shingle sites, e.g. Dungeness, Kent, and Hurst Spit, Hampshire.

female

Not recorded from Wales, Scotland or Ireland. On the Channel Islands recorded from Jersey and Guernsey. Note that this species has been known as *H. euryscapus* or *H. spilotus* previously, with the commoner *H. dilatatus* being called *H. annularis* until recently. **Parasites & associates** None noted in Britain.

Hylaeus brevicornis Nylander, 1852   Short-horned Yellow-face Bee

Plate 2

Description & similar species FW 3.5–4mm (sexes similar). One of two very small *Hylaeus* species (*H. pictipes* is the other). Both sexes have a roundish face (slightly wider than long in the male) and particularly short antennae with the basal flagellar segments much wider than long. In females, the yellow facial spots are generally narrow, hugging the eye margins and well separated from the mid-facial sutures. Males have a particularly dull abdomen and thorax, with much microsculpture between the punctures. **Variation** Some variation in the shape of the female facial spots and the leg markings of both sexes. Occasionally the female facial spots can be poorly formed. **Flight season** Late May to mid-September, possibly as two generations in the south. **Habitat** Found in a wide variety of lowland habitats, especially where flowery early successional habitat is present alongside scrub and bramble patches, e.g. soft rock cliffs, vegetated shingle, heathland, chalk grassland, quarries, brownfield sites and open areas in woodland. **Flowers visited** Various, including brambles, umbellifers of

various sorts, mignonettes, thistles, ragworts, hawk's-beards, Sea Spurge, thymes, Sheep's-bit and stonecrops. **Nesting habits** Hollow bramble twigs and pithy stems appear to be the normal nesting sites. **Status & distribution** Widespread and common in many parts of lowland Britain, extending north to southwest Scotland. Widely recorded in Ireland but seemingly much declined here. Recorded from several of the Channel Islands. **Parasites & associates** Parasitic ichneumonid and eurytomid wasps have been reared from the nests.

Hylaeus communis Nylander, 1852   Common Yellow-face Bee
Plates 1 & 2

Description & similar species FW 4.5–5mm female, 4–4.5mm male. Females of this species and *H. pectoralis* have the unique combination of triangular facial spots that hug the eye margins and the complete lack of any white hair fringes on the hind margin of tergite 1 at the sides. *H. communis* is smaller than *H. pectoralis* with a more compact build, and under magnification will be seen to have a band of sparse punctures occupying the apical third of tergite 1. Males are easily distinguished from all other *Hylaeus* species by the facial pattern. **Variation** Some females can have the facial spots substantially reduced, and these also tend to have less yellow on the pronotal tubercles, tegulae and legs. The markings on the male face also vary somewhat. Moderate size variation is present, and the smallest males are no larger than those of *H. brevicornis* and *H. pictipes*. **Flight season** Late May to mid-September. It may be bivoltine in the south. **Habitat** Found in a wide variety of lowland habitats, with no obvious biases, and the most frequent *Hylaeus* in gardens. **Flowers visited** Many sorts of flower are visited, with umbellifers, composites and mignonettes especially favoured. **Nesting habits** Nesting occurs in a variety of holes and cavities, including hollow twigs and stems, holes in dead wood, timber, walls and soil. This is the main *Hylaeus* to utilise garden bee hotels. **Status & distribution** Widespread and common in many parts of southern Britain north to Cumbria and Yorkshire. Also known from Perthshire in Scotland and few sites in eastern Ireland. Recorded from Guernsey and Sark in the Channel Islands. **Parasites & associates** The parasitic sapygid wasp *Sapyga quinquepunctata* has been reported as attacking this species (it more typically uses *Osmia* species, which can sometimes nest alongside *H. communis*); also *Gasteruption* wasps.

Hylaeus confusus Nylander, 1852   White-jawed Yellow-face Bee
Plate 2

Description & similar species FW 4.5–5mm (sexes similar). The more frequent of a pair of similar, medium-sized *Hylaeus* species, the other being *H. incongruus*. Separation of female *H. confusus* from *H. incongruus* is only possible under the microscope, using the characters outlined in the key. Males of this species pair have white-marked mandibles (only otherwise seen in *H. dilatatus* and *H. punctulatissimus*). They are easily separable from each other by checking the labrum (black in *H. confusus*, white in *H. incongruus*). **Variation** Some variation in the size of the female facial spots and the extent of pale markings on the pronotal collar, pronotal tubercles and legs. **Flight**

female

season May to September. **Habitat** Found in a variety of habitats both coastal and inland, and one of the more frequent *Hylaeus* species in wooded settings. **Flowers visited** Females visit a variety of flowers but are most frequently found on umbellifers and brambles. **Nesting habits** Nesting typically occurs in dead twigs, pithy stems and holes in dead wood, and it will also use garden bee hotels. It has also been seen burrowing into the ground. **Status & distribution** Widespread and locally common in southern England, (except the southwest) scarcer in Wales and northern England and with a few highly scattered Scottish records. Widespread in Ireland, where it is the commonest *Hylaeus*. Not recorded from the Channel Islands. **Parasites & associates** None known.

Hylaeus cornutus Curtis, 1831   Spined Hylaeus
Plate 2

Description & similar species FW 4.5–5mm female, 4.5mm male. Our most easily recognised yellow-face, because it has a black face! Females have a pair of projections on the sides of the face that help form a circular depression in the centre of the face (used to carry a pollen ball) and very short antennae. Occasional black-faced variants of other species never have these projections. Males have the unique combination of a black face and predominantly yellow antennae, and have a more elongated build than other *Hylaeus* species. **Variation** Very little. **Flight season** Early June to late August. **Habitat** Occurs in a variety of umbellifer-rich habitats, especially sites where Wild Carrot is abundant, including chalk grassland, chalk heath, soft rock cliffs, vegetated shingle, chalk and limestone quarries and brownfield sites. Heavily dependent upon brownfields in some parts of its range, e.g. the Midlands. **Flowers visited** Much foraging occurs on umbellifers such as Wild Carrot and Wild Parsnip, but it has also been noted on Wild Mignonette, Lesser Stitchwort, Field Scabious, Yarrow and Oxeye Daisy. **Nesting habits** Nesting typically occurs in hollow plant stems, e.g. docks and umbellifers. **Status & distribution** Widespread though rather localised in southeast England west to Avon and north to Warwickshire and Norfolk. Not recorded from

Wales, Scotland, Ireland or the Channel Islands. There is some evidence of an increase and spread of this species in recent decades. **Parasites & associates** None noted in Britain.

female

male

Hylaeus dilatatus (Kirby, 1802)   Chalk Yellow-face Bee
Plate 2

Description & similar species FW 4–4.5mm female, 3.5–4.5mm male. The more frequent of a pair of very similar, medium-sized *Hylaeus* species in which the females have a pair of roundish or irregular spots on the face that are well separated from the eye margins, whilst the males have highly expanded black and yellow antennal scapes. Females can only be reliably separated from the rare *H. annularis* under the microscope by checking the surface punctures and microsculpture of tergites 1 and 2, though the presence of whitish rather than yellowish markings on the body is a good clue. Males are more easily separated owing to their black-marked tibiae and white-marked mandibles. **Variation** The extent of the facial spots, pale marks on the pronotal collar, and dark areas of the legs can vary somewhat; also moderate size variation. **Flight season** Early June to early September, peaking in June and July. **Habitat** Found in a variety of calcareous habitats including chalk grassland, chalk and limestone quarries, chalk heath, brownfield sites, soft rock cliffs, vegetated shingle (sometimes alongside *H. annularis*), woodland clearings and occasionally wetlands. **Flowers visited** A wide variety of flowers are used, though it can be especially common on umbellifers, thistles and brambles. **Nesting habits** Nesting occurs in hollow stems and twigs of plants such as brambles, roses, docks and Mugwort; also holes in wood. **Status & distribution** Widely recorded and locally common in calcareous districts of southern England north to Warwickshire, Lincolnshire and Norfolk (but absent from extreme southwest England); also a few sites in south Wales. Not recorded from Scotland, Ireland or the Channel Islands. This species was known as *H. annularis* until recently. **Parasites & associates** None known in Britain, though a species of *Gasteruption* wasp is recorded attacking it abroad.

female

male

Hylaeus hyalinatus Smith, 1842   **Hairy Yellow-face Bee**
Plate 2

Description & similar species FW 4–4.5mm female, 3.5–4.5mm male. A medium-sized *Hylaeus* with females that resemble *H. confusus* and *H. incongruus*. Easily separable by the much longer face (the longest of any *Hylaeus*) with a relatively large malar gap. The dense punctures at the sides of tergite 1 are also a useful distinction. In the field, females appear strongly marked, with the tibial bases, pronotal tubercles, front of the tegulae and pronotal collar extensively white-marked. Males are easily distinguished from all other *Hylaeus* species by the long hairs on the face. Both sexes have the underside of antennal flagella conspicuously orange. **Variation** Females occasionally have the facial spots absent, and these usually also lack pale markings on the pronotum and tegulae but remain distinguishable by the very long face and dense punctures on the sides of tergite 1. Old males can have the facial hairs largely abraded. **Flight season** May to September. **Habitat** Found in a variety of habitats both coastal and inland, especially where sparsely vegetated light soils are present. It can be particularly frequent at brownfield sites, on vegetated shingle and along soft rock cliffs. **Flowers visited** A wide variety of flowers are visited, but it can be especially frequent on umbellifers and thistles. **Nesting habits** Nesting occurs in light soils, the soft mortar of walls, cliff faces and possibly beetle holes in dead wood. **Status & distribution** Widespread and locally common over much of southern Britain, extending north to southwest Scotland. Scarce in Ireland, with most records from the southeast coastal zone. Recorded from most of the larger Channel Islands. **Parasites & associates** Parasitic *Gasteruption* wasps.

female

male

Hylaeus incongruus Förster, 1871   **White-lipped Yellow-face Bee**
Plate 2

Description & similar species FW 5mm (sexes similar). Females are extremely similar to *H. confusus* but the yellow facial spots are larger, extending as high as the antennal insertion points and relatively closer to those insertion points. The frons immediately above the antennal insertion points lacks punctures and is shinier than the surrounding frons (no such differentiation in *H. confusus*). The face is also longer, with the black central section relatively long and narrow. In males, the labrum is white (black in *H. confusus*) and, in the limited number of specimens seen, the antennae are darker and the legs, pronotal tubercles and tegulae much more extensively yellow. Both sexes average a little larger than *H. confusus*. **Variation** Little noted. **Flight season** June to August. **Habitat** Usually recorded in flowery scrubby areas and woodland edge of heathland areas; also found in the rides and clearings of broadleaved woodland elsewhere. **Flowers visited** British records include brambles, thistles, dandelion, Hogweed, Tormentil, Wild Angelica and Wild Parsnip. **Nesting habits** Nesting occurs in old hollow plant stems and dead wood. **Status & distribution** A rare species, with records concentrated within the Dorset heaths, New Forest and heathland districts of West Sussex and the west of Surrey. More isolated records from Kent and east Hampshire. Not recorded in Wales, Scotland, Ireland or the Channel Islands. This species was known as *H. gibbus* until recently. **Parasites & associates** None known.

Hylaeus pectoralis Förster, 1871   **Reed Yellow-face Bee**
Plate 2

Description & similar species FW 4.5–5mm (sexes similar). Females of this species and *H. communis* have the unique combination of triangular facial spots that hug the eye margins and a lack of any white hair fringes on the hind margin of tergite 1 at the sides. *H. pectoralis* is noticeably larger and slimmer than *H. communis* and tergite 1 is virtually impunctate. Males have a bright yellow face, a very shiny tergite 1 and conspicuous hair bands across the apical margins of the sternites. The hind margin of tergite 1 at the sides lacks the dense fringes of some *Hylaeus* species but can have a sparser hair fringe. **Variation** Very little apart from moderate size variation. **Flight season** Early June to late September. **Habitat** A specialist of reedbeds, using these in a variety of locations including fens, boggy valley mire, coastal marsh, ditches, flooded quarries and brownfield sites. **Flowers visited** Most frequently observed on umbellifers, brambles and thistles; also recorded on hawkbits and sowthistles. Males sometimes carry orchid pollinia. **Nesting habits** Nesting typically occurs in the 'cigar galls' created by the chloropid fly *Lipara lucens* at the growth tips of Common Reed. Up to eight cells are arranged linearly within a single gall, sealed with a plug of leaf fragments. It will also nest in non-galled hollow reed stems and can occur at sites where *L. lucens* seems to be absent. **Status & distribution** A localised species of southern England, with the majority of records for southern Hampshire, East Anglia

and the Cambridgeshire Fens. More isolated populations occur north to Warwickshire. Not recorded in Wales, Scotland, Ireland or the Channel Islands. Almost certainly under-recorded, and has a clear ability to colonise new, often very isolated reedbeds. Sweeping reeds in summer with a long-handled net is a good way of finding it; also collecting *Lipara* galls and rearing out the contents (which can contain various other inquilines and parasites as well as the distinctive fly that created them). **Parasites & associates** Two species of *Gasteruption* wasps have been reared from it in Britain.

Hylaeus pictipes Nylander, 1852   Little Yellow-face Bee
Plate 2

Description & similar species FW 3.5mm (sexes similar). One of two very small *Hylaeus* species (*H. brevicornis* is the other). The female has a more elongate face and longer antennae than *H. brevicornis*. The facial spots have a very distinct trapezoidal, slanting shape and usually make broad contact with both the eye margins and the facial sutures. The most unique character is the grooves that run alongside the inner eye margins, which extend higher than in other *Hylaeus* species and curve inwards towards the lateral ocelli. Males are easily confirmed by the narrow antennal scapes but can look like males of *H. brevicornis* in the field. **Variation** Some variation in the shape of the female facial spots and the extent of yellow on the tegulae, pronotal collar and legs. **Flight season** Mid-June to late August. **Habitat** Found in a variety of lowland habitats including chalk grassland, chalk heath, woodland rides and clearings, vegetated shingle, coastal dunes and occasionally gardens. **Flowers visited** Various, but with a particular liking for mignonettes and umbellifers. **Nesting habits** Nesting occurs in old hollow twigs and pithy stems of plants such as roses and brambles. It will also use the holes of wood-boring *Anobium* beetles in old gorse stems. **Status & distribution** A scarce species mostly recorded from southeast England west to the Solent. More isolated records extend north to Shropshire and the East Anglian Brecks. Recorded from the Channel Islands (Jersey and Alderney). Not recorded in Wales, Scotland or Ireland. **Parasites & associates** A chalcid wasp has been reared from a nest.

female

male

Hylaeus punctulatissimus Smith, 1842   Onion Yellow-face Bee
Plate 2

Description & similar species FW 6mm female, 5mm male. A relatively large, heavily punctured and dull-looking species that most resembles *H. signatus*, though the facial markings are yellow rather than white and extend well above the antennal insertion points in both sexes. The female pronotal collar viewed from above is larger than in other *Hylaeus* and forms a conspicuous 'cushion' behind the back of the head, creating a solid and cylindrical appearance. The male mandibles have a whitish streak as in *H. confusus*, *H. incongruus* and *H. dilatatus*, but the much darker legs, heavily punctured body and facial markings allow easy separation. **Variation** None noted. **Flight season** May to August on the continent. **Habitat** Grassland and other habitats with onions. **Flowers visited** Pollen seems to be obtained exclusively from onion species, though it will visit other flowers such as melilots and elders, possibly just for nectar. **Nesting habits** Nesting can occur in dead wood and also in artificial trap nests (notably in a Swiss study of foraging behaviour). **Status & distribution** The only certain British record is a male taken from Onion flowers at Chelsea, Middlesex (1827). There is also a very old female specimen labelled 'Ham' which might refer to a British locality such as Hampstead Heath or Ham in Surrey, but conceivably a foreign location. Several other old records appear to be dubious and lack supporting specimens.

female

Hylaeus signatus (Panzer, 1798)

Large Yellow-face Bee

Plate 2

Description & similar species FW 4.5–5.5mm female, 4–6mm male. Averaging our largest *Hylaeus* and one of the few British bees where large males exceed the size of large females. Readily distinguishable in both sexes from all species except some *H. punctulatissimus* by the mainly black legs (tibiae usually with only the extreme bases pale) and, when large, through size and build. The white hair bands on the sides of tergite 1 are usually particularly conspicuous. Males have a white rather than yellow face and the body densely punctate all over and much dulled by microsculpture between the punctures. They have a particularly robust and 'small-headed' build. Both sexes of *H. punctulatissimus* can look similar, but they have the facial markings extending well above the antennal insertion points plus various other differences discussed under that species. **Variation** Dwarf individuals that overlap in size with other medium-sized *Hylaeus* species are not uncommon and are less easy to distinguish in the field. Some females have the facial spots very reduced, and these tend to have the bases of the tibiae very dark. **Flight season** Late May to early September, peaking in June and July. **Habitat** Typically associated with mignonette-rich calcareous habitats such as chalk grassland, chalk and limestone quarries, chalk heath, calcareous brownfield sites and disturbed coastal sites. In some urban and industrialised areas it can occur on non-calcareous brownfield land where Weld is abundant. **Flowers visited** Strongly associated with Weld and Wild Mignonette (the pollen sources), though it will sometimes visit other flowers such as umbellifers, crucifers, thistles and bramble for nectar. **Nesting habits** Quite varied, with nesting locations including hollow twigs, vertical earth faces (often using old nests of *Colletes daviesanus*) and walls. Dense nesting aggregations have sometimes been observed. **Status & distribution** Widespread but patchily distributed in England north to Yorkshire (but not southwest England), also a few records in south Wales. It can be locally common in some districts, e.g. the West Midlands, East Anglian Brecks and southern downland districts. Not recorded from Scotland or Ireland, but known from Jersey. **Parasites & associates** *Gasteruption* wasps.

female

male

FAMILY ANDRENIDAE

ANDRENA – MINING BEES

The largest bee genus in Britain and Ireland, with 67 species (*A. agilissima* only from the Channel Islands). Size varies from small (the 'mini-miners' of the subgenus *Micrandrena*) to rather larger than a Honey Bee (*A. hattorfiana*). Most have black integument but a few feature a red-marked abdomen. They vary from densely 'furry' (e.g. *A. fulva*) to inconspicuously hairy. Some species are strongly banded (e.g. *A. flavipes*), others have 'flecked' abdomens with discrete patches of adpressed white hair on the sides of some tergites (e.g. *A. dorsata*, *A. wilkella* and their close relatives). The tip of the abdomen is golden-haired in a number of species.

♀

Andrena fulva

♀

Andrena labiata

♂

♀

Andrena haemorrhoa

♀

Andrena dorsata

♀

Andrena cineraria

Andrena nitidiuscula

Andrena bees can be readily distinguished from superficially similar genera such as *Melitta* or *Colletes* by the broad strips of velvety pile (the facial foveae) alongside the inner eye margins, these being most obvious in females. They also have more extensive pollen-collecting apparatus than most other bees, involving most parts of the hind legs plus the sides of the propodeum, which have hairs arranged to form a 'propodeal pollen basket'. The mouthparts are short and the tongue pointed. The basal vein of the forewing is straight (strongly curved in *Halictus* and *Lasioglossum*). The antennal tips are pointed (blunt in *Melitta*).

Nesting typically occurs in light soils on ground ranging from level to vertical. Some species will also use the soft mortar of walls or the muddy root plates of wind-blown trees. Species such as *A. barbilabris* and *A. argentata* require almost pure sand. Nesting can be solitary or in aggregations, the latter sometimes involving thousands of densely arranged nests (notably species such as *A. cineraria* and *A. flavipes*). In *A. bucephala* and *A. ferox*, many females can use a common nest entrance, giving the impression of social behaviour, though all *Andrena* species are technically solitary, with no evidence of cooperative worker behaviour.

The majority of species are univoltine, with flight periods that can vary from early spring to late summer depending on species. A smaller number of species are regularly bivoltine, typically peaking in April and July, and a few are partially or irregularly bivoltine, usually in the south of their range. Bivoltine species can display brood dimorphism, especially the males of species such as *A. trimmerana*, *A. rosae*, *A. minutula* and *A. alfkenella* (see species accounts for details). Males always appear before females and generally disappear well before the end of the female flight period. They will swarm or lek, sometimes in very specific places such as around the nesting areas, or around blossoming shrubs, or by flying up tree trunks and telegraph poles. Giant males are common in some species and allometry in male *Andrena* is widespread, with larger individuals often proportionately bigger-headed and more robustly built than small individuals of the same population (notably in *A. bucephala* and *A. ferox*).

Most mining bees are polylectic, but a small number are oligolectic (e.g. our five willow and two scabious specialists) and one species (*A. florea*) only uses White Bryony in Britain. Nectar may be obtained from a variety of flowers that are not pollen sources.

Mining bees are attacked by a variety of cleptoparasites and parasitoids, including bees of the genera *Nomada* and *Sphecodes*, *Bombylius* bee-flies (Bombyliidae), *Myopa* flies (Conopidae), *Leucophora* flies (Anthomyiidae) and *Stylops* (Strepsiptera). Stylopised examples of *A. scotica* and *A. chrysosceles* are particularly frequent in spring and are always infertile intersexes. Mining bees seem to be important hosts for *Meloe* oil beetles (Meloidae) and often carry the beetles' tiny first-instar triungulin larvae.

This is a near-cosmopolitan genus with about 1,500 described species. The European fauna contains some 600 species, and a number of these occur on the near-continent and should be watched out for. To make identification less daunting the genus has been subdivided into smaller keys. These are designed for relatively fresh and well-preserved material and may not work for worn, faded or badly preserved specimens that have lost much of their body hair. However, such specimens can still be identified by comparing them carefully against fresher, named material. Group A species (mini-miners) are particularly difficult, and the keys to these species are best used in conjunction with the author's web feature (see p.59), which furnishes the microscopic photos given here at much higher resolution.

ANDRENA CLEPTOPARASITES AND PARASITOIDS

Clockwise from above: bee-fly *Bombylius discolor*, *Myopa testacea*, *Leucophora obtusa*, stylopised *Andrena scotica* and female *Andrena hattorfiana* carrying *Meloe proscarabaeus* triungulins.

ANDRENA FEMALE GROUPS

1   Very small, dark species, wing length no greater than 6.5mm (typically 5.5mm or less). Tergites 1–3 hairless except for lateral fringes of white hairs along the hind margins of most species. Hind tibiae always with a pale pollen brush and facial foveae conspicuously pale from some angles (Fig. 1) .... female group A

—   Larger, sometimes very furry species, some with broad abdominal hair bands or a partially red abdomen. If tergites hairless with white lateral hair fringes as in previous couplet, then hind tibiae with dark hairs dorsally, or facial foveae dark, or wing length over 6.5mm (usually well over this) 2

2   Top of propodeum with a well-defined zone of very coarse reticulation that contrasts markedly with the smoother sides and rear of the propodeum (Fig. 4). Wing length at least 8mm .... female group B

—   Top of propodeum relatively smooth with a texture similar to the sides and rear (Fig. 5). If the top is rough (*proxima*), this continues down the sides and hind face and the wing length is less than 8mm 3

3   Surface of tergites extensively or partially red, the red markings forming a complete band across tergite 2 .... female group C

—   Tergites either entirely black or with red markings confined to the sides of tergites 1 and 2 4

4   Flocci with black or sooty-grey hairs. Rest of hind leg usually entirely dark-haired ...... female group D

—   Flocci with whitish or pale buffish hairs. Hind femora pale-haired on at least front face, the hind tibiae often entirely or extensively pale-haired 5

5   Hind tibiae clear orange beneath hairs, at most somewhat darkened at base .... female group E

—   Hind tibiae dark beneath hairs, at most slightly paler at extreme apex 6

6   Upper side of abdomen virtually hairless with discrete fringes of dense, adpressed white hairs along the hind margins of tergites 2–4 (visible with the naked eye), at least laterally, though these never filling the entire apical depression (Fig. 2) .... female group F

—   Tergites either without conspicuous fringes of dense, adpressed white hairs along the hind margins (though looser fringes of white hairs may be present), or, if such zones are present, either these take the form of broad bands filling the entire apical depression (Fig. 3), or there is a dense semi-upright pile on the remainder of the tergites (view from side) 7

Fig. 1

Fig. 2

Fig. 3

Fig. 4

Fig. 5

Fig. 6

Fig. 7

7   Dorsal fringe of hind tibiae pale-haired, hairs whitish, straw-coloured, orange or
orange-brown, sometimes darker-haired at base .... **female group G**

—   Dorsal fringe of hind tibiae mid-brown, dark brown or black along its entire length, but
beware of pale pollen trapped amongst the hairs which can make the pollen brush appear paler **8**

8   Tergite 1 polished between punctures and shining, any microsculpture very weak ...... **female group H**

—   Tergite 1 with obvious microsculpture between any punctures and duller **9**

9   Flocci small and sparse (Fig. 6) .... **female group I**

—   Flocci very large and dense (Fig. 7) .... **female group J**

ANDRENA FEMALE GROUP A (MINI-MINERS PLUS SMALLER *A. NITIDIUSCULA*)

1   Tergite 1 with microsculpture over most of the surface, even if weak, any punctures
fine and inconspicuous. Basal sections of tergites 2 and 3 dull with any punctures set
within dense microsculpture (Figs 8 & 9) **2**

—   Tergite 1 with dense and distinct punctures, microsculpture weak or absent except
along hind margin. Basal sections of tergites 2 and 3 with dense and conspicuous
punctures, microsculpture weak or absent (Fig. 17) **9**

2   Tergite 1 shining with rather weak microsculpture and sparse fine punctures, a little
shinier than tergite 2. Undersides of antennal flagella mostly orange-red, this spreading
onto the top side of the last few segments .... *nanula*

—   Tergite 1 (except the hind margins of some species) with dense microsculpture and
as dull as tergite 2 (Figs 8 & 9). Antennal flagella usually dark or obscurely brownish
below, rarely as reddish as above **3**

3   Anterior part of tergites 2 and 3 with obvious punctures amongst the microsculpture
(Fig. 8), and if rather faint (*falsifica*) then hind margin of tergite 1 broadly shining **4**

—   Anterior part of tergites 2 and 3 with no obvious punctures amongst the microsculpture,
tergites 1–3 having an almost uniform texture over their entire surfaces (Figs 9, 14 & 15) **7**

4   Apical depressed area of tergites 2–4 strongly shining with only faint microsculpture,
the apical depressions strongly defined from the basal area of those tergites by a
deep transverse rim (Fig. 8). Top part of propodeum with coarse ridges confined to
base and contrasting with the more granular area beyond .... *semilaevis*

—   Apical depressed area of tergites 2–4 with obvious microsculpture, the apical
depressions of tergites 3 and 4 not so strongly defined from the basal area by the
rim, the rim often becoming very weak in the middle of tergite 3 (Figs 10–12). Top part
of propodeum with coarse ridges covering the entire area **5**

5   Hind margin of tergite 1 broadly shining (with very weak microsculpture) and strongly
convex so as to appear thickened (Fig. 10). Apical depressions of tergites 2 and 3
relatively shiny (but microsculpture much more obvious than *semilaevis*) .... *falsifica*

—   Hind margin of tergite 1 and apical depressions of tergites 2 and 3 with dense
microsculpture and as dull as the anterior part of those tergites **6**

6   Bands of white hairs across tergite 4 and the sides of tergites 2 and 3 dense and
occupying the full depth of the apical depressions and obscuring the underlying
integument, the bands mostly consisting of hairs as long as the depth of an apical
depression (Fig. 11). Build slimmer .... *niveata*

—   Bands of white hairs across tergite 4 and the sides of tergites 2 and 3 only dense
along the extreme hind margins and not obscuring the majority of the apical depression,
the hairs of these fringes mostly much shorter than the depth of an apical depressed area
(Fig. 12). Build broader .... *alfkenella*

FEMALE ABDOMENS

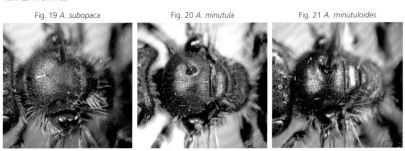

Fig. 8 *A. semilaevis*

Fig. 9 *A. minutula*

Fig. 10 *A. falsifica*

Fig. 11 *A. niveata*

Fig. 12 *A. alfkenella*

Fig. 13 *A. subopaca*

Fig. 14 *A. minutula*

Fig. 15 *A. minutuloides*

Fig. 16 *A. nitidiuscula*

Fig. 17 *A. nana*

Fig. 18 *A. floricola*

FEMALE THORAXES

Fig. 19 *A. subopaca*

Fig. 20 *A. minutula*

Fig. 21 *A. minutuloides*

7   Scutum very dull with small, barely discernible punctures (Fig. 19). Head and thorax
     longer-haired .... *subopaca*

—   Scutum shinier with obvious punctures (Figs 20 & 21). Head and thorax shorter-haired 8

8   Scutum with denser punctures (Fig. 20). Front of scutellum with obvious microsculpture
     between punctures, much like adjacent scutum. Hind margin of tergites 2 and 3 with
     conspicuous white lateral hair fringes (these can get rubbed off) (Fig. 14).
     Propodeum more transverse in dorsal view .... *minutula*

—   Scutum with sparser punctures (Fig. 21). Front of scutellum shiny between punctures
     and shinier than adjacent scutum. Hind margin of tergites 2 and 3 at sides without
     conspicuous white hair fringes even in fresh specimens (Fig. 15). A more narrowly
     built species with propodeum less transverse in top view .... *minutuloides*

9   Hind margin of tergites 2–4 with dense, snow-white hair fringes which form a complete
     band on tergite 4 (Fig. 16). Apical depression of tergite 2 shining and without obvious
     microsculpture. Scutellum evenly dulled by microsculpture with rather few, unevenly
     distributed punctures. Sides of propodeum with rather sharply defined hair fringes.
     Clypeus shining with distinct punctures throughout but little microsculpture .... smaller *nitidiuscula*

—   Hind margin of tergites 2–4 without dense, snow-white hair fringes. Apical
     depression of tergite 2 dulled by microsculpture. Scutellum semi-shining with
     dense and even punctures. Sides of propodeum without sharply defined hair
     fringes. Clypeus distinctly dulled by microsculpture at least on top 10

10   Apical depression of tergites 2–4 of normal width (not extending more than halfway
     towards the base of the tergite) (Fig. 17). Basal section of tergite 2 shining between
     the punctures and without microsculpture. Clypeus very dull with dense microsculpture
     and weak punctures. Pollen brush of hind tibiae and tip of abdomen greyish-white
     haired. Top of thorax with a rather inconspicuous brownish pile. Stigma blackish .... *nana*

—   Apical depression of tergites 2–4 unusually wide (extending more than halfway towards
     the base of the tergite) (Fig. 18). Basal section of tergite 2 with weak microsculpture
     between the punctures. Clypeus rather shiny on lower part with obvious punctures.
     Pollen brush of hind tibiae and tip of abdomen buff-haired. Top of thorax with a
     rather conspicuous buff pile. Stigma brown or orange .... *floricola*

ANDRENA FEMALE GROUP B

1   Head, thorax and abdomen entirely, or almost entirely, black-haired 2

—   Head and thorax partially pale haired, those hairs either brown, reddish or white 3

2   Whitish hairs on the outer face of hind tibiae more extensive and mixing with the
     black hairs of the dorsal fringe. Wings usually paler .... *pilipes*

—   Whitish hairs on the outer face of hind tibiae less extensive leaving the hairs of the
     dorsal fringe entirely black. Wings often darkened .... *nigrospina*

3   Wings darkened and iridescent. Body black with conspicuous white hairs on sides
     of face, back of head, sides of propodeum, sides of tergites 5 and 6 plus hind legs
     (Channel Islands) .... *agilissima*

—   Wings not darkened. Body not patterned as above 4

4   Abdomen inconspicuously hairy except for bright golden hairs at the tip. Top of
     thorax with a very even-lengthed, reddish pile. Facial foveae whitish and conspicuous.
     Hind tibiae and tarsi clear orange .... *haemorrhoa*

—   Abdomen more obviously hairy with hairs at the tip blackish. Top of thorax with a
     less even-lengthed, brown pile. Hind tibiae and tarsi orange or dark 5

5   Hind tibiae and tarsi orange (sometimes rather obscurely so), the pollen brush of the hind legs mostly orange-haired. Face white-haired. Tergites entirely black with a greyish pile that contrasts with the brown-haired thorax. Typically larger (wing length up to 12mm) .... *tibialis*

—   Hind tibiae and tarsi dark, the pollen brush of the hind legs with cream and brown hairs. Face black- or brown-haired. Tergites with a brownish pile that does not contrast strongly with the brown hairs of the thorax, tergites 1 and 2 often reddish at the sides. Typically smaller (wing length up to 10.5mm) .... *bimaculata*

ANDRENA FEMALE GROUP C

1   Tergites 2–4 densely punctate (punctures separated by their own width or less) 2

—   Tergites 2–4 with much sparser punctures 4

2   Hind basitarsi black-haired ventrally. Scutum dull with obvious microsculpture between the punctures. Tergite 3 always predominantly dark, the reddish abdominal markings usually confined to tergite 2 and the hind margin of tergite 1. Larger (typical wing length 9mm) .... *florea* (redder examples)

—   Hind basitarsi pale-haired ventrally. Scutum shining between punctures. Tergite 3 can be entirely red. Smaller species (wing length to 7mm) 3

3   Abdomen with a conspicuous bright-red band that extends from the hind margin of tergite 1 to the anterior corners of tergite 4 and contrasts strongly with the black tip. Pile on top of thorax short and inconspicuous .... *labiata*

—   Abdomen dull orange-red to varying extent (often entirely from the hind margin of tergite 1 onwards) and never with a strongly demarked black tip. Top of thorax with a more conspicuous brownish pile .... *marginata* (redder examples)

4   Hind tibiae with entirely pale hairs. Tip of abdomen with bright orange hairs and a conspicuous black pygidium. Scutum shining with obvious punctures. Wings darkened. Hind margins of tergites with narrow white hair fringes. Very large (typical wing length 12mm) .... *hattorfiana* (red-banded form)

—   Hind tibiae dark-haired dorsally. Tip of abdomen dark-haired. Scutum dull with very shallow punctures. Wings clear. Hind margins of tergites without white hair fringes. Smaller (typical wing length 9mm) .... *rosae* (red-banded form)

ANDRENA FEMALE GROUP D

1   Tergites with a dense pile that obscures the underlying integument 2

—   Tergites shiny black with an inconspicuous pile 3

2   Tergites with a bright orange pile, contrasting with a dark red pile on top of the thorax. Sides of propodeum black-haired .... *fulva*

—   Tergites buff-haired with black hairs at the anterior corners of tergites 2–4. Top of thorax with a paler red-brown pile. Sides of propodeum buff-haired .... *nigriceps*

3   Top of thorax with a reddish-brown pile .... *thoracica*

—   Top of thorax extensively grey-haired with a band of black hairs between the wings .... *cineraria*

ANDRENA FEMALE GROUP E

1   Scutum mostly shining with distinct punctures, at most slightly dulled by microsculpture (Fig. 22) 2

—   Scutum distinctly dulled by microsculpture between the punctures or entirely dull and lacking punctures (Fig. 23) 3

Fig. 22   Fig. 23   Fig. 24   Fig. 25

Fig. 26   Fig. 27

2   Top of scutum with black hairs centrally. Propodeum in top view with sharply defined fringes of pale grey hairs at sides. Hind tibiae in side view with dorsal fringe less than half the greatest width of the tibia (Fig. 24). Tip of abdomen with greyish hairs .... *tarsata*

—   Top of scutum mostly brown-haired. Propodeum without such dense lateral fringes. Hind tibiae with dorsal fringe longer than the greatest width of the tibia (Fig. 25). Tip of abdomen conspicuously orange-haired .... *fulvago*

3   Tergites 2–4 with dense white hair fringes along hind margins – often just laterally, tergites 1–4 otherwise virtually bare (Figs 28–30) **4**

—   Tergites without dense white hair fringes along hind margins. Tergites with long hairs, at least on sides of tergite 1 .... **8**

4   Tergite 1 shining with distinct punctures. Facial foveae conspicuously pale from some angles. Build slimmer .... *chrysosceles*

—   Tergite 1 dulled by microsculpture, the punctures less conspicuous. Facial foveae darker and less conspicuous. Build more robust **5**

5   Tip of pygidium with a deep semicircular incision (Fig. 26). Punctures of tergites very faint. Top of thorax with a relatively longer pile. Larger (wing length usually at least 9mm) .... *lathyri*

—   Tip of pygidium rounded (Fig. 27). Tergites with more obvious punctures. Top of thorax with a shorter pile. Smaller (wing length to 8.5mm) **6**

6   White hair fringes of tergites 2 and 3 separated by at least twice their width, that of tergite 4 usually broken in the middle (Fig. 28). Top of thorax with a reddish pile that is particularly dense around the margins of the scutellum. Tip of abdomen orange-haired .... *similis*

—   White lateral hair fringes of tergites 2 and 3 less widely separated, that of tergite 4 usually complete (Figs 29 & 30). Top of thorax with a less conspicuous brownish pile. Tip of abdomen orange- or brown-haired **7**

Fig. 28 *A. similis*   Fig. 29 *A. wilkella*   Fig. 30 *A. ovatula*

7 Hairs at tip of abdomen orange, the white hair fringe of tergite 3 usually broken in the middle (Fig. 29). Hairs on top of thorax paler brown. Dorsal fringe of hind tibia with at most a few darker hairs at the extreme base. A slightly larger, broader species .... *wilkella*

— Hairs at tip of abdomen brown, the white hair fringe of tergite 3 usually complete (Fig. 30). Hairs on top of thorax darker brown. Dorsal fringe of hind tibia often darker-haired for basal fifth or so. A slightly smaller, narrower, duskier-looking species .... **typical** *ovatula*

8 A large species with abdomen typically densely black-furred and contrasting with the reddish pile of the thorax (the red hairs sometimes spreading onto the base of the abdomen) .... *clarkella*

— Abdomen not densely furry, thorax brown- or greyish-haired 9

9 Antennal segments 4 and 5 much longer than wide (Fig. 31). Top of abdomen with a sparse but obvious pile of long brown hairs that form weak bands along the hind margins of tergites 2–4. Face (including eye margins), genae and sides of thorax buff-haired. Larger (typical wing length 10mm) .... *ferox*

— Antennal segments 4 and 5 no longer than wide (Fig. 32). Top of abdomen almost bare but with some longer white hairs at sides. Sides of thorax, face and genae white-haired, with some black hairs alongside the inner eye margins. Smaller (typical wing length 8mm) .... *ruficrus*

ANDRENA FEMALE GROUP F

1 Hind tibiae relatively broad, the length of the dorsal fringe at most one-third the greatest width of the tibia (Figs 33 & 34). Top of thorax with a rather conspicuous reddish pile 2

— Hind tibiae narrower, the length of the dorsal fringe at least half the greatest width of the tibia (Fig. 35). Top of thorax with a duller or less conspicuous pile (except *congruens*) 3

2 Length of dorsal fringe of hind tibiae about one-fifth the greatest width of the tibia (Fig. 33). Scutum dulled by obvious microsculpture, the punctures less conspicuous. Hair fringes of tergites 2–4 narrow and well separated from the basal ridge of the apical depression (Fig. 36) .... *dorsata*

— Length of dorsal fringe of hind tibiae about one-third the greatest width of the tibia (Fig. 34). Scutum shiny with obvious punctures and only weak microsculpture. Hair fringes of tergites 2–4 broader and reaching the basal ridge of the apical depression at the sides (Fig. 37) .... *lepida*

3 Dorsal fringe of hind tibiae sooty-grey .... *coitana*

— Dorsal fringe of hind tibiae white, buff or pale grey 4

4 Tergite 1 shining, with scattered fine punctures and barely any microsculpture 5

— Tergite 1 dulled by microsculpture, either with dense punctures or (*proxima*) virtually puncture-free 6

Fig. 31   Fig. 32 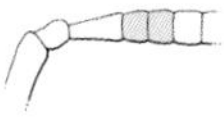   Fig. 33 *A. dorsata*    Fig. 34 *A. lepida*    Fig. 35 *A. congruens*

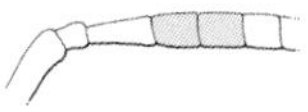

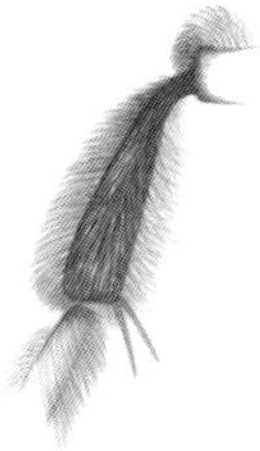

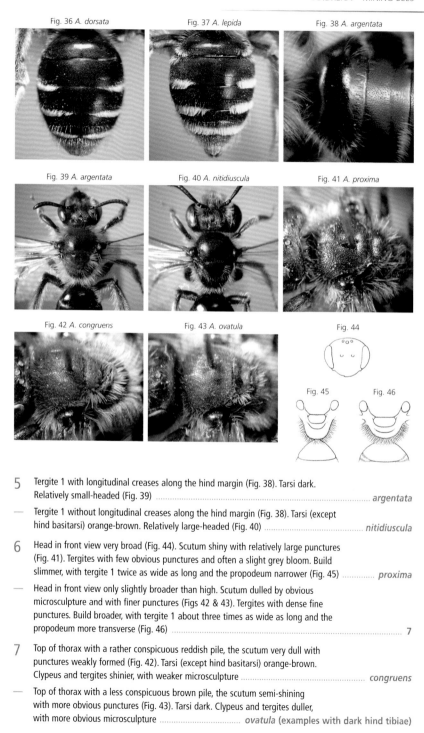

Fig. 36 *A. dorsata*

Fig. 37 *A. lepida*

Fig. 38 *A. argentata*

Fig. 39 *A. argentata*

Fig. 40 *A. nitidiuscula*

Fig. 41 *A. proxima*

Fig. 42 *A. congruens*

Fig. 43 *A. ovatula*

Fig. 44

Fig. 45

Fig. 46

5   Tergite 1 with longitudinal creases along the hind margin (Fig. 38). Tarsi dark.
    Relatively small-headed (Fig. 39) .... *argentata*

—   Tergite 1 without longitudinal creases along the hind margin (Fig. 38). Tarsi (except
    hind basitarsi) orange-brown. Relatively large-headed (Fig. 40) .... *nitidiuscula*

6   Head in front view very broad (Fig. 44). Scutum shiny with relatively large punctures
    (Fig. 41). Tergites with few obvious punctures and often a slight grey bloom. Build
    slimmer, with tergite 1 twice as wide as long and the propodeum narrower (Fig. 45) .... *proxima*

—   Head in front view only slightly broader than high. Scutum dulled by obvious
    microsculpture and with finer punctures (Figs 42 & 43). Tergites with dense fine
    punctures. Build broader, with tergite 1 about three times as wide as long and the
    propodeum more transverse (Fig. 46) 7

7   Top of thorax with a rather conspicuous reddish pile, the scutum very dull with
    punctures weakly formed (Fig. 42). Tarsi (except hind basitarsi) orange-brown.
    Clypeus and tergites shinier, with weaker microsculpture .... *congruens*

—   Top of thorax with a less conspicuous brown pile, the scutum semi-shining
    with more obvious punctures (Fig. 43). Tarsi dark. Clypeus and tergites duller,
    with more obvious microsculpture .... *ovatula* (examples with dark hind tibiae)

ANDRENA FEMALE GROUP G

1   Facial hairs entirely or predominantly black or dark brown 2

—   Facial hairs entirely or almost entirely whitish or pale brown 4

2   Tergites 1–4 with a dense buff pile that contrasts with the black hairs of tergite 5.
Hind tibiae with a dense, even-lengthed, orange pollen brush. Hind basitarsi in side
view relatively broad, the dorsal edge curved and with a short, dark dorsal fringe
(Fig. 47). Larger (typical wing length 10mm) .... *nigroaenea*

—   Tergites 1–4 with a sparser pile that forms weak bands. Hind tibiae with a sparser,
yellowish pollen brush. Hind basitarsi in side view narrow and parallel-sided with a
longer, paler dorsal fringe (Fig. 48). Smaller (wing length to 8mm) 3

3   Clypeus without a longitudinal groove. Apical depressions of tergites 2–4 narrower,
not extending into the basal half of the tergites. Femora and sides of thorax often
partially black-haired (especially spring generation). Flocci usually greyish-brown .... *bicolor*

—   Clypeus with a longitudinal groove in upper part (Fig. 49) (angle of light critical to
see this). Apical depressions of tergites 2–4 broader, extending well into the basal
half of the tergites in the middle. Femora and sides of thorax always pale-haired.
Flocci whitish .... *angustior* (black-faced examples)

4   Tip of abdomen yellow- or orange-haired with a conspicuous dark pygidium 5

—   Tip of abdomen black- or brownish-haired, the pygidium inconspicuous amongst these hairs 7

5   Abdomen very dull and uniformly dark except for orange-buff hairs at tip. Tergite 1
with a band of pustulose punctures across the middle (Fig. 50). Upper part of
facial foveae dark brown and inconspicuous .... *humilis*

—   Hind margins of tergites 2–4 with narrow white hair fringes (these can get rubbed
off with age). Tergite 1 with normal punctures. Upper part of facial foveae very
pale and conspicuous from some angles 6

Fig. 47

Fig. 49

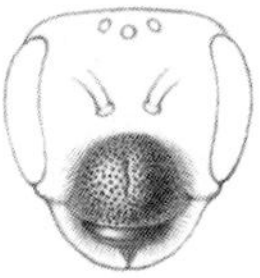

Fig. 50 *A. humilis*

Fig. 48

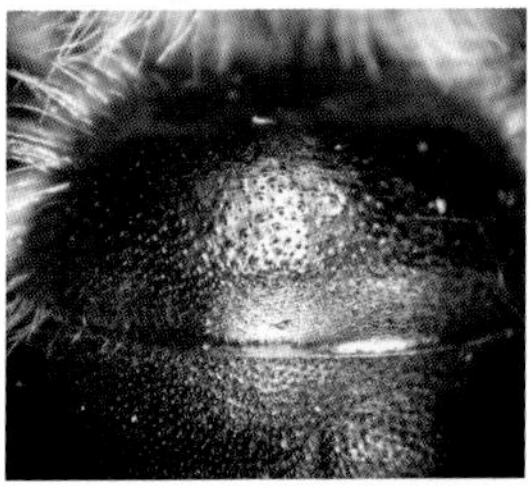

Fig. 51 *A. labialis*

Fig. 52 *A. bucephala*

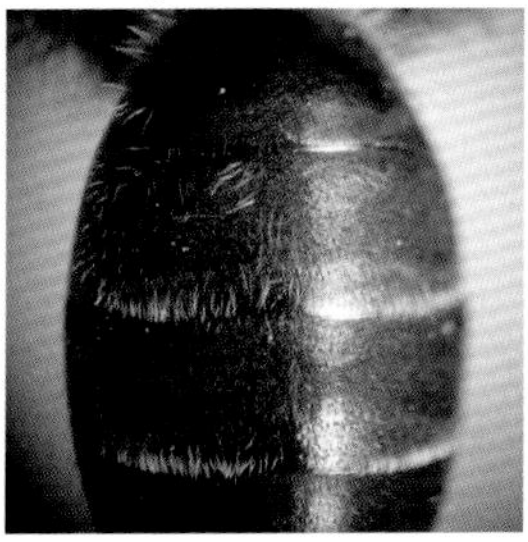

Fig. 53 *A. flavipes*

6   Top of thorax shining with little microsculpture between the punctures, the hairs here and on the propodeum inconspicuous. Tergites sparsely punctate. Upper part of facial foveae grey-brown. Large (typical wing length 12mm) .... *hattorfiana* (black form)

—   Top of thorax dulled by microsculpture between the punctures and with a longer, more conspicuous brown pile here and on the propodeum. Tergites densely punctate. Facial foveae whitish. Smaller (typical wing length 9.5mm) .... *polita*

7   Tergites 1–4 and scutum with dense and obvious punctures throughout (Fig. 51) 8

—   Tergites and scutum with any punctures weak and inconspicuous (Fig. 52) 10

8   Hind margins of tergites 2–4 with pale hair fringes that are much narrower than the apical depressions, the fringes of tergites 2 and 3 widely broken centrally (Fig. 51). Facial foveae very pale from some angles. Tip of abdomen brown-haired .... *labialis*

—   Hind margins of tergites 2–4 with conspicuous pale hair bands that fully occupy the apical depressions, with black hairs occupying the basal part of the tergites (Fig. 53). Facial foveae dark. Tip of abdomen black-haired 9

9   Pile on top of the thorax relatively short and dull brown, not contrasting strongly with the buffish pile on the sides of the thorax, face, femora and flocci. Pale hair bands of the tergites narrower and consisting of shorter hairs (buffish when fresh). Underside of hind femora with a longitudinal groove separating the lower surface and the hind face (Fig. 54) .... *flavipes*

—   Pile on top of the thorax longer and orange-brown, contrasting strongly with the whitish pile on the sides of the thorax, face, femora and flocci. Pale hair bands of tergites broader and consisting of longer hairs (always white). Underside of hind femora without a longitudinal groove below .... *gravida*

10   Flocci very large, dense and white-haired (Fig. 7). Tergite 1 with hairs much longer and denser than those of subsequent tergites 11

—   Flocci smaller, sparser and buffish-haired (Fig. 6). Tergite 1 with hairs not significantly longer than those of subsequent tergites 12

11   Abdomen with rather dense orange-brown hairs on tergite 1 and the base of tergite 2, with tergites 3, 4 and the base of tergite 2 white-haired to create a greyish appearance. Hind tibiae broader in side view, with the dorsal fringe somewhat shorter than the greatest width of the tibia (Fig. 55) .... *helvola*

—   Abdomen with much sparser, duller hairs on tergite 1 and the base of 2, the rest of the tergites mainly dark-haired. Hind tibia narrower in side view, with the dorsal fringe as long as the greatest width of the tibia (Fig. 56) .... some *fucata*

12   Antennal segments 4–12 obviously longer than wide (Fig. 57). Clypeus without a longitudinal groove centrally. Tergites very inconspicuously haired. Larger and slimmer (typical wing length 10mm) .... *bucephala*

—   Antennal segments 4–12 slightly wider than long (Fig. 58). Clypeus with a longitudinal groove centrally (Fig. 49). Abdomen more obviously hairy. Smaller and dumpier (typical wing length 7.5mm) .... typical *angustior*

Fig. 54   Fig. 55 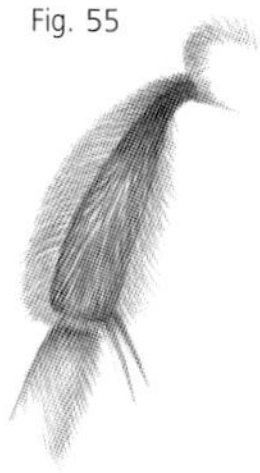   Fig. 56    Fig. 57

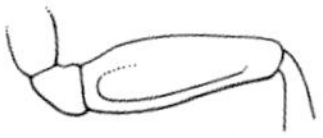

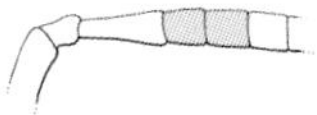

Fig. 58

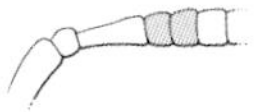

ANDRENA FEMALE GROUP H

1   Hind basitarsi dark-haired ventrally 2

—   Hind basitarsi pale-haired ventrally 4

2   Thorax entirely grey-haired, contrasting with a shiny black abdomen .... *vaga*

—   Thorax brown or orange-haired on top 3

3   Top of thorax with a dense brick-red pile. Abdomen shining-black and inconspicuously
    haired except for patches of white hairs at the sides of tergites 1–3. Facial hairs mostly
    white, black at sides .... *nitida*

—   Top of thorax with a less conspicuous brown pile. Abdomen with a more general
    covering of brownish hairs and usually with reddish markings at the sides and
    rear margins of tergites 1 and 2. Face entirely brown-haired .... *florea* (darker examples)

4   Head in front view wider than long. Top of thorax with a dense, reddish-brown pile,
    the underlying integument very dull with inconspicuous punctures. Tergites 2–4
    with narrow whitish hair fringes along hind margins. Tip of abdomen black-haired .... *barbilabris*

—   Head in front view longer than wide. Top of thorax with a less conspicuous, duller pile,
    the underlying integument shiny with obvious punctures. Tergites either
    dark or partially red but without obvious white hair fringes.
    Tip of abdomen brown-haired .... *marginata* (darker examples)

ANDRENA FEMALE GROUP I

1   Tergites and sternites completely dark, no red at sides of tergites 1 or 2 .... *scotica*

—   Sides of tergites 1 and 2, and the underside of the abdomen at its base,
    reddish to varying extent 2

2   Dorsal surface of abdomen viewed from side with a distinct pile of upright
    brownish hairs above (Fig. 59) (longer in spring generation). Hairs on top
    of thorax longer (especially in spring generation) .... *trimmerana*

—   A less hairy species, tergites 2–4 mostly with extremely short dark
    hairs (Fig. 60). Hairs on top of thorax relatively short .... *rosae* (darker examples)

ANDRENA FEMALE GROUP J

1   Face entirely black-haired, also tergites 3–5 and the hind margin of 2 2

—   Face partly or entirely pale-haired, or if black-haired then tergites 3 and 4 at least
    partly pale-haired, or apical depressions of tergite 3 and 4 very extensive (Fig. 68) 3

Fig. 59

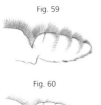

Fig. 60

Fig. 61 *A. varians*

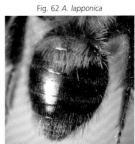

Fig. 62 *A. lapponica*

2   Apical depressions of tergites 3 and 4 as dull as the basal parts of the tergites, creating a duller overall appearance (Fig. 61). Tergite 1 and base of tergite 2 with a denser, more conspicuous pile of long orange-brown hairs. Tergite 1 with denser punctures (best seen at base). Build slightly slimmer .... typical *varians*

—   Apical depressions of tergites 3 and 4 shinier than the basal parts of the tergites, creating a shinier appearance (Fig. 62). Tergite 1 and base of tergite 2 with a sparser, less conspicuous pile of longer hairs. Tergite 1 with sparser punctures (best seen at base). Build slightly broader .... *lapponica*

3   Hind tibiae in side view (ignoring the hairs) broader and more triangular, becoming progressively broader virtually to the tip, the length of the dorsal hair fringe never more than half the greatest width of the tibia (Fig. 63). Apical depressions of tergites 2–4 with dense adpressed hairs that are paler and more conspicuous than those of the base, producing a banded appearance to varying extents 4

—   Hind tibiae in side view slimmer and less triangular, becoming more parallel-sided in apical quarter, the length of the apical hair fringe at least half the greatest width of the tibia (Figs 64 & 65). Apical depressions of tergites 2–4 with hairs no denser or more conspicuous than those of the base of those tergites, indeed sometimes less so 7

4   Top of thorax extensively black-haired. Sides of thorax whitish-haired. Tergites 2–4 with well-formed whitish bands occupying the apical depressions, with short black hairs on the basal parts of those tergites .... *denticulata*

—   Top of thorax entirely brownish- or reddish-haired. Sides of thorax buff-haired. No black hairs across the basal sections of tergites 2–4 5

5   Tergite 5 with pale hairs .... *tridentata*

—   Tergite 5 with brown or blackish hairs 6

6   Flocci and hair fringes of femora yellowish. Pale hair bands of tergites 2–4 better-differentiated. Scutum shinier with more obvious punctures and a browner pile. Galeae of mouthparts shining (Fig. 66). Smaller and less densely furry (typical wing length 7.5mm) .... *fuscipes*

—   Flocci and hair fringes of femora white. Bands of tergites 2–4 poorly differentiated. Scutum duller with less obvious punctures and a redder pile. Galeae of mouthparts dulled by microsculpture (Fig. 67). Larger and more densely furry (typical wing length 8mm) .... *simillima*

7   Flocci and fringes of femora buff or buffish-white. Abdomen with a long, uniform, buff pile which only becomes darker at the tip 8

—   Flocci and fringes of femora pure white. Tergites 1 and 2 with longer buff or golden hairs that contrast with the shorter whitish, greyish or black hairs of tergites 3 and 4 9

8   Apical depression of tergite 4 with hairs much darker than the anterior part of that tergite. Tergite 5 mainly black-haired. Larger (typical wing length 11mm) .... *apicata*

—   Apical depression of tergite 4 with pale buff hairs, like the anterior part of that tergite and paler than those of tergite 5, which are brownish. Smaller (typical wing length 9mm) ...... *praecox*

Fig. 63   Fig. 64    Fig. 65    Fig. 66 *A. fuscipes*    Fig. 67 *A. simillima*

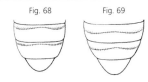

Fig. 68   Fig. 69

9   Apical depressions of tergites 3 and 4 very extensive, so that they usually occupy all of
    the visible tergite centrally and have their defining ridges visible only at the base (Fig. 68).
    Tergite 1 and base of tergite 2 with a long buff or golden pile that obscures the
    underlying surface, tergites 3 and 4 usually with shorter greyish hairs (but occasionally
    black hairs) .... *synadelpha*

—   Apical depressions of tergites 3 and 4 less extensive, the transverse defining ridges
    running across the middle of the tergites (Fig. 69) 10

10 Tergite 1 and base of tergite 2 with long but sparse pale hairs; tergites 3 and
    4 for the most part with short black hairs (only pale at the sides) and with
    rather shiny apical depressions with faint microsculpture. Darker and shinier .... some *fucata*

—   Tergite 1 and base of tergite 2 with dense buff hairs; tergites 3 and 4 with
    short greyish hairs, the apical depressions duller than *fucata*. Paler and duller
    looking (closely resembling typical *synadelpha*) .... *varians* form *mixta*

ANDRENA MALE GROUPS

1   Surface of face extensively white or yellow (Fig. 70) .... male group A
—   Surface of face entirely dark 2

2   Very small species, wing length no greater than 5mm. Mandibles much shorter
    than the length of an eye, when folded barely extending beyond the midline
    of the face. Tergites 1–4 hairless except for lateral fringes of white hairs along
    the hind margins of most species. Distance between outer edges of the tegulae
    about equal to the width of the head .... male group B

—   Wing length usually greater than 5.5mm, but if shorter the mandibles are at
    least as long as the length of an eye, or the distance between the outer edges
    of the tegulae is distinctly less than the width of the head, or the hind edge of
    the genae has a distinct flange (Fig. 71). Tergites often with long hairs throughout 3

3   Top of propodeum with a sharply defined zone of coarse reticulation that
    contrasts markedly with the smoother sides and rear of the propodeum (Fig. 4) .... male group C

—   Top of propodeum relatively smooth with a texture similar to the sides and rear
    (Fig. 5). If the top is rough (*proxima*) this continues down the sides and hind face 4

4   Base of mandibles with a distinct ventral projection (Fig. 72) (not to be confused
    with the genal spine or projection of some species as shown in Fig. 123) .... male group D
—   Base of mandibles without such a projection 5

5   Antennal segment 4 about twice as long as segment 3 (Fig. 73) .... male group E
—   Antennal segment 4 at most about 1.5 times as long as segment 3, often shorter 6

6   Face either entirely black-haired or dark brown-haired, or at least with the lower
    clypeus dark-haired across its full width .... male group F
—   Face white- or buff-haired, at most with black hairs alongside the inner eye margins 7

7   Face with black or brown hairs alongside the inner eye margins (Fig. 74)
    (sometimes just a single row of hairs) .... male group G
—   Face entirely pale-haired, including the area adjacent to the inner eye margins 8

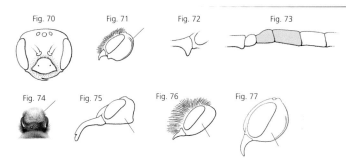

Fig. 70   Fig. 71   Fig. 72   Fig. 73

Fig. 74   Fig. 75   Fig. 76   Fig. 77

8   Head in strict side view with gena clearly wider than the greatest width of an
eye (Figs 71 & 75) .... male group H

—   Head in strict side view with gena at most slightly wider than the greatest width
of an eye (Figs 76 & 77) .... male group I

ANDRENA MALE GROUP A

1   Abdomen with a broad red band occupying tergites 2, 3 and the base of tergite 4.
Wing length up to 6.5mm .... *labiata*

—   Abdomen black or, if with limited red markings (*hattorfiana*), wing length
at least 10mm 2

2   Pale facial markings confined to the clypeus (Figs 78–80) 3

—   Pale facial markings spreading to sides of the face outside of the clypeus (Figs 81 & 82) 7

3   Scutum shining between the punctures 4

—   Scutum dulled by microsculpture 6

4   Head in front view wider than high, the lower margin of the clypeus only slightly
lower than the bottom of the eyes (Fig. 78). A small species (wing length to 6.5mm) .... *tarsata*

—   Head about as wide as high, the lower margin of the clypeus much lower than
the bottom of the eyes 5

5   A large species (wing length at least 10mm) with darkened wings. Lower margin
of the clypeus not drawn into acute lateral points (Fig. 80). No ridge along the
hind margin of the genae, the hind margin of the head only moderately concave
in top view .... *hattorfiana*

—   A smaller species (wing length 6mm) with clear wings. Lower margin of the
clypeus drawn into acute, outcurved lateral points (Fig. 79). Hind margin of
the genae with a ridge (Fig. 83), the hind margin of the head strongly
concave in top view .... *marginata*

Fig. 78 *A. tarsata*   Fig. 80 *A. hattorfiana*   Fig. 81 *A. labialis*   Fig. 82 *A. coitana*   Fig. 83

Fig. 79 *A. marginata*

6   Tergite 1 polished with fine but distinct punctures. Hind tarsi and at least apex of hind tibiae orange. Tergites 2–4 with narrow white hair fringes along hind margins .... *chryscoceles*

—   Tergite 1 dull with punctures set amongst a rough, pustulose surface. Hind tibiae and all tarsi dark. No white hair fringes on tergites 2–4 .... *humilis*

7   Pale markings of the face more extensive (Fig. 81). Top of thorax dulled by microsculpture between the punctures and with a conspicuous orange-brown pile (when fresh). Tergites densely punctate with short buff hairs throughout and buff fringes along the hind margins of tergites 2–4. Larger (wing length at least 7.5mm) .... *labialis*

—   Pale markings of the face less extensive (Fig. 82). Top of thorax polished between the punctures. Tergites shining, sparsely punctate and inconspicuously haired except for narrow white hair fringes along the hind margins of tergites 2–4. Smaller (wing length to 6.5mm) .... *coitana*

ANDRENA MALE GROUP B (MINI-MINERS)

1   Head usually with substantial black hair, at least some black hairs around the bases of the antennae (Fig. 84) (no spring material of *A. floricola* has been seen, but it would fall out here) 2

—   Head entirely pale-haired 5

2   Tergites 1–4 dulled by dense microsculpture except along hind margins, with any punctures exceedingly faint (Fig. 85) 3

—   Tergites 1–4 clearly punctate (Figs 86 & 87) 4

3   Scutum very dull with any punctures usually difficult to discern, but when detectable they are more numerous and denser (Fig. 95). Scutellum dulled by microsculpture, at most semi-shining. Tergites 2 and 3 with stronger lateral hair fringes. Build broader, especially across the thorax .... *minutula* (spring generation)

—   Scutum shinier than in *minutula*, the punctures more obvious but few and sparse (Fig. 96). Scutellum strongly shining between punctures. Tergites 2 and 3 with relatively weak lateral hair fringes. Build narrower, especially across the thorax .... *minutuloides* (spring generation)

4   Tergite 1 with fine and sparse punctures which peter out well before the hind margin; tergites 2 and 3 finely punctate basally, the apical depressions shining, with only weak microsculpture (Fig. 86). Scutum with sparse punctures (like *minutuloides*) .... *alfkenella* (spring generation)

—   Tergite 1 with denser punctures which extend to the hind margin; tergites 2 and 3 densely and coarsely punctate basally, the apical depressions dulled by obvious microsculpture (Fig. 87). Scutum with denser punctures separated by about their own width .... *nana* (spring generation)

5   Tergite 1 and the basal part of tergites 2–4 with obvious punctures and little if any microsculpture between the punctures (Figs 88–90) 6

—   Tergite 1 with obvious microsculpture and any punctures weak or sparse (Figs 93 & 94). Basal part of tergites 2–4 much dulled by microsculpture, without obvious punctures (except *niveata* and *semilaevis*) 8

6   Scutum shining with little microsculpture, the punctures separated by about twice their own width (Fig. 97). Tergite 1 more sparsely punctate, the punctures separated by about twice their own width (Fig. 88), the punctures petering out well before

MALE ABDOMENS

Fig. 84 *A. alfkenella*

Fig. 85 *A. minutula* spring

Fig. 86 *A. alfkenella* spring

Fig. 87 *A. nana* spring

Fig. 88 *A. alfkenella* summer

Fig. 89 *A. nana* summer

Fig. 90 *A. floricola* summer

Fig. 91 *A. semilaevis*

Fig. 92 *A. niveata*

Fig. 93 *A. falsifica*

Fig. 94 *A. minutula* summer

the hind margin (apical depression of tergites 2 and 3 shining
and without punctures, wing stigmas orange-buff) .... *alfkenella* (summer generation)

— Scutum either with punctures separated by about their own width or with
obvious microsculpture (Fig. 98). Tergite 1 more densely punctate (punctures
separated by about their own width), the punctures extending almost to the hind margin 7

7   Tergites and scutum very densely and coarsely punctate, the
     punctures separated by less than their own width, those of tergite 1
     extending fully to the hind margin (Fig. 89). Apical depression of
     tergite 2 clearly punctate. Wing stigmas dark brown. Antennal
     segment 4 about half as long as wide in front view (Fig. 102) .... *nana* (summer generation)

—   Tergites and scutum less densely punctate, the punctures separated
     by about their own width, those of tergite 1 not quite reaching the
     hind margin (Fig. 90). Apical depression of tergite 2 shining and
     barely punctate. Wing stigmas orange-buff. Antennal segment 4
     about 0.75 times as long as wide in front view (Fig. 103) .... *floricola* (summer generation)

8   Apical depressed area of tergites 2–4 polished and strongly defined
     from the basal area of those tergites by a deep transverse rim (Fig. 91).
     Scutum dull with sparse and shallow punctures (facial hairs particularly
     long and whitish) .... *semilaevis*

—   Apical depressed area of tergites 2–4 usually obviously dulled by microsculpture,
     but if shinier, then not defined by such a deep rim 9

9   Hind margin of tergites 1–4 with a dense microsculpture that is as dull as the
     anterior parts of those tergites. Anterior part of tergites 2 and 3 with very dense
     and obvious punctures amongst the microsculpture. White hair fringes at sides
     of tergites 2 and 3 and across hind margin of tergite 4 dense and long (Fig. 92).
     Hairs of face and underside of antennal scapes long, dense and very white
     (those of the scape longer than the width of an eye) .... *niveata*

—   Hind margin of tergites 1–4 with less dense microsculpture and shinier than
     anterior part of those tergites. Anterior part of tergites 2 and 3 with punctures
     less obvious or missing. White hair fringes of tergites 2–4 narrower and less
     conspicuous. Hairs of face and scape shorter (those of latter much shorter than
     the width of an eye) and often tinged brownish 10

10   Antennal segment 5 viewed from the front much wider than long, about the
     same length as 4 but much shorter than 3 (Fig. 104). Hind margin of tergite 1
     broadly shining (with shallow microsculpture) and strongly convex so as to
     appear thickened (Fig. 93) .... *falsifica*

—   Antennal segment 5 squarish or slightly longer than wide in front view, longer
     than 4 but about the same length as 3 (Fig. 105). Hind margin of tergite 1 at
     most narrowly shining and flatter 11

11   Scutum very dull with punctures barely discernible (Fig. 99). Scutellum as dull
     as adjacent scutum. Apical depressed area of tergite 2 with a similar microsculpture
     to the anterior part of that tergite, with the rim separating the two zones very
     weak in the middle .... *subopaca*

—   Scutum shinier with distinct punctures (Figs 100 & 101). Scutellum shinier than
     scutum. Apical depressed area of tergite 2 clearly shinier than the anterior part
     of that tergite, with the rim separating the two zones more evident 12

12   Punctures of scutum denser, separated by about their own diameter
     (Fig. 100). Tergites 2 and 3 with stronger lateral hair fringes.
     Build broader, especially across the thorax .... *minutula* (summer generation)

—   Punctures of scutum sparse, separated by much more than their
     own diameter and with general surface slightly shinier than previous
     species (Fig. 101). Scutellum strongly shining between punctures.
     Tergites 2 and 3 with relatively weak lateral hair fringes.
     Build relatively narrow, especially across the thorax .... *minutuloides* (summer generation)

MALE THORAXES

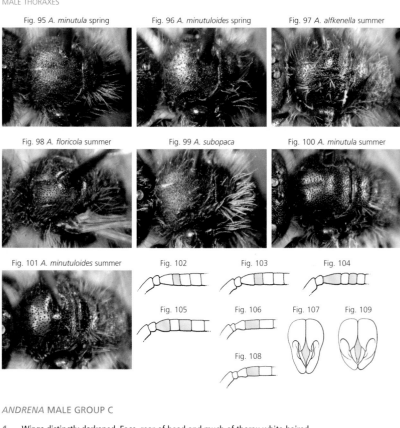

Fig. 95 *A. minutula* spring   Fig. 96 *A. minutuloides* spring   Fig. 97 *A. alfkenella* summer

Fig. 98 *A. floricola* summer   Fig. 99 *A. subopaca*   Fig. 100 *A. minutula* summer

Fig. 101 *A. minutuloides* summer   Fig. 102   Fig. 103   Fig. 104

Fig. 105   Fig. 106   Fig. 107   Fig. 109

Fig. 108

ANDRENA MALE GROUP C

1   Wings distinctly darkened. Face, rear of head and much of thorax white-haired. Abdomen shiny black with rather inconspicuous white hairs at base of tergites 2–5. Large (typical wing length 10–12mm) (Channel Islands) .... *agilissima*

—   Wings clear or slightly darkened. If abdomen black and shiny, the face is black-haired 2

2   Face entirely pale-haired. Tergite 6 with orange-brown hairs. Hind tibiae mostly orange .... *haemorrhoa*

—   Face entirely or largely black- or brown-haired. Hind tibiae dark, at most orange at tip 3

3   Legs and much or all of abdomen black-haired 4

—   Legs and abdomen mostly pale-haired 5

4   Top of thorax, back of head and tergites 1 and 2 grey-haired. Antennal segment 4 longer, at least 1.5 times length of segment 3 (Fig. 106). Genitalia (Fig. 107) .... *nigrospina*

—   Top of thorax, back of head and tergites 1 and 2 brown-haired or entire body black-haired. Antennal segment 4 shorter, up to 1.3 times length of segment 3 (Fig. 108). Genitalia (Fig. 109) .... *pilipes*

5   Hind legs with tarsus and tip of hind tibia orange. Surface of tergites entirely black, including the apical depression .... *tibialis*

—   Hind legs entirely dark. Tergites 1 and 2 often reddish at sides, the apical depressions of the tergites often brownish or reddish .... *bimaculata*

ANDRENA MALE GROUP D

1   Antennal segment 3 viewed from front almost twice as long as segment 4 (Fig. 110). Tergites 1–5 usually entirely buff-haired, with tergites 3–5 relatively densely haired and not contrasting so strongly with the longer hairs on tergite 1 and the base of tergite 2 .... *fulva*

—   Antennal segment 3 viewed from front 1–1.3 times as long as 4 (Fig. 111). Tergites 3–5 and hind margin of 2 with hairs either dark or greyish-white and much shorter than the hairs on tergite 1 and the base of tergite 2 2

2   Sides of propodeum partially blackish-haired 3

—   Sides of propodeum entirely pale-haired 4

3   Projection of sternite 8 squared off at tip without any notch (Fig. 113). Projection at base of mandibles narrower and sharper (Fig. 117). Tergites 3 and 4 mainly black-haired .... *apicata*

—   Projection of sternite 8 notched at tip (Fig. 112). Projection at base of mandibles broader and blunter (Fig. 118). Tergites 3 and 4 mostly pale-haired .... *praecox*

4   Sternites 2–5 with very dense and conspicuous pale hair fringes along the hind margins, these fringes obscuring the underlying integument (Fig. 114). Projection at base of mandible relatively small (Fig. 119) .... *helvola*

—   Sternites without such dense and conspicuous hair fringes 5

5   Projection at base of mandibles larger and longer (Fig. 120). Hind tarsi blackish. Sternites 2–5 with very short hair fringes (Fig. 115) .... *lapponica*

—   Projection at base of mandibles smaller and shorter (Fig. 121). Hind tarsi orange. Sternites 2–5 with long but sparse hair fringes (Fig. 116) .... *fucata*

ANDRENA MALE GROUP E

1   Genae with a long downward-directed spine just before the base of the mandible (Fig. 123) 2

—   Genae without a distinct spine, at most a short projection (Fig. 125) 4

2   Tip of mandibles without a tooth or emargination (Fig. 124). Basal tergites and sternites often partially red, but these not forming a conspicuous red band across the abdomen .... *trimmerana* (spring generation)

—   Tips of mandibles with a distinct tooth or emargination (Fig. 126) 3

Fig. 110    Fig. 111    Fig. 112 *A. praecox* 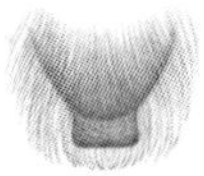   Fig. 113 *A. apicata*

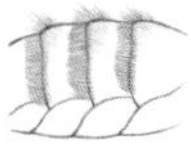

Fig. 114 *A. helveola*    Fig. 115 *A. lapponica*    Fig. 116 *A. fucata*

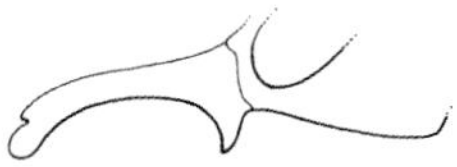

Fig. 117 *A. apicata*    Fig. 118 *A. praecox*    Fig. 119 *A. helvola*    Fig. 120 *A. lapponica*    Fig. 121 *A. fucata*

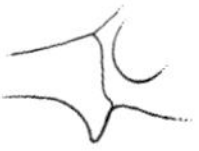

Fig. 122 *A. fulva*    Fig. 123    Fig. 124    Fig. 125    Fig. 126

3   Genal spine well-developed, usually as long as the basal width of a mandible
(Fig. 123). Abdomen usually with a broad red band across tergites 2 and 3
(sometimes reduced). Facial hairs usually black .... *rosae* (spring generation)

—   Genal spine small. Abdomen usually black, any red markings confined to
the apical depressions of the tergites. Facial hairs usually brown ..... *scotica* (form with genal spine)

4   Pile on top of thorax and tergites shorter, that of propodeum about
equal to the greatest width of an eye (view from side). Hairs on top of
tergites 3 and 4 very short and adpressed. At least sides of tergites 1 and
2 usually red, sometimes with a complete red bands across tergites 2
and 3. Hind tibiae dark at tip. Face usually extensively black-haired .... *rosae* (summer generation)

—   Pile on top of thorax and tergites longer, that of propodeum at least
1.5 times the greatest width of an eye. Hairs of tergites 3 and 4 longer
and semi-upright. Hind tibiae usually pale at tip. Face usually entirely brown-haired 5

5   Abdomen entirely dark, at most red along apical depressions of tergites
1–3. Scutum duller, with inconspicuous punctures (usually spring-flying) .... *scotica*

—   Abdomen extensively red on first 2 or 3 tergites, the red markings
extending onto the first 2 or 3 sternites. Scutum shinier, with
punctures more distinct .... *trimmerana* (summer generation)

ANDRENA MALE GROUP F

1   Abdomen, legs, face and underside of thorax entirely black-haired, contrasting with a
conspicuous red-brown pile on top of the thorax. Large (wing length at least 9.5mm) .... *thoracica*

—   Abdomen, legs and underside of thorax at least partially pale-haired 2

2   Hind tibiae and tarsi orange .... *fulvago* (examples with dark-haired clypeus)

—   Hind tibiae and tarsi dark 3

3   Tergites 2–5 with conspicuous bands of whitish hairs occupying the
apical depressions (Fig. 131). Antennal segment 3 in front view
about twice as long as segment 4 (Fig. 127) .... *flavipes* (darker-faced examples)

—   Tergites 2–5 without conspicuous hair bands. Antennal segment 3 at most
1.5 times as long as segment 4 (Figs 128 & 129) 4

4   Frons between ocelli and antennal insertions with numerous fine longitudinal
furrows (Fig. 130). Apical depressions of tergites 2 and 3 with numerous fine
punctures. Top of thorax and tergites 1–4 with an orange-buff pile, legs mostly
orange-haired. Larger (wing length at least 8mm) .... *nigroaenea*

—   Frons between ocelli and antennal insertions without longitudinal furrows. Apical
depressions of tergites 2 and 3 with scarcely any punctures. Top of thorax, tergites
and legs with less conspicuous, paler hairs. Smaller (wing length up to 7mm) 5

5   Antennal segment 3 in front view clearly longer than segment 4 and with short (but not
minute) hairs beneath (Fig. 128). Femora and sides of thorax often extensively black-haired ..... *bicolor*

—   Antennal segment 3 as long as, or slightly shorter than, segment 4 and with only
minute hairs beneath (Fig. 129). Mid and hind femora and sides of thorax never black-haired 6

Fig. 127   Fig. 128 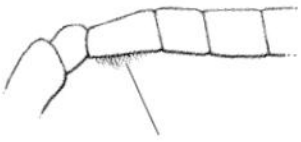   Fig. 129 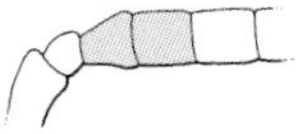   Fig. 130

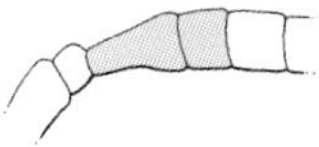

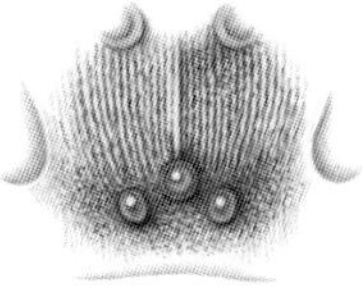

Fig. 131 *A. flavipes*   Fig. 132 *A. congruens*   Fig. 133 *A. lepida*

6   Scutum dull without obvious punctures. Tergites rather sparsely and finely punctate,
the apical depressions of tergites 2–4 smooth, shiny and barely punctate;
hind margins of tergites 2–4 with relatively narrow white hair fringes (Fig. 132) .... *congruens*

—   Scutum semi-shiny with obvious punctures. Tergites densely punctate, including
the apical depressions of tergites 2–4; hind margins of tergites 2–4 with relatively
broad white hair fringes (comprising longer hairs), tergite 2 with a further band
of white hairs across the base (Fig. 133) .... *lepida*

ANDRENA MALE GROUP G

1   Antennal segment 3 viewed from front about twice as long as segment 4 (Fig. 127) 2

—   Antennal segment 3 viewed from front at most 1.5 times as long as segment 4 5

2   Tergites with conspicuous bands of creamy-white hairs occupying the apical depressions (Fig. 131) ... 3

—   Abdomen without conspicuous bands 4

3   Pile on top of thorax shorter and not contrasting strongly with the buffish pile on the
sides and underside of the thorax. Pale hair bands of the tergites denser and
more conspicuous. Face mostly buff-haired .... *flavipes* (paler-faced examples)

—   Pile on top of thorax longer and contrasting strongly with the white pile on the sides
and underside of the thorax. Pale bands of the tergites less dense and consisting of
longer hairs. Face white-haired, with dark hairs narrowly confined to the inner eye margins ... *gravida*

4   Tergites (including apical depressions) dulled by microsculpture. Antennal scapes
extensively black-haired. Facial hairs mostly buff. Hind tibiae and tarsi usually
partially or mostly orange. Larger and furrier (wing length at least 8mm) .... *clarkella*

—   Tergites shinier with weak microsculpture, the apical depressions smooth.
Face and antennal scapes whitish-haired. Hind tibiae and tarsi usually blackish.
Smaller and less furry (wing length 7mm) .... some *angustior*

5   Top of thorax densely grey-haired, and tergites 3–5 mostly black-haired 6

—   Top of thorax brown-haired, or if greyish (older, sun-bleached examples),
not as dense as previous, and tergites without extensive black hairs 7

6   Top of thorax with some black hairs at rear of scutum and front of scutellum. Hind tibiae
black-haired. Abdomen slimmer, in side view with the tip not downcurved (Fig. 134) .... *cineraria*

—   Top of thorax entirely grey-haired. Hind tibiae white-haired. Abdomen broader and
more oval, in side view with the tip distinctly downcurved (Fig. 135) .... *vaga*

7   Hind tibiae and tarsi orange. Scutum shiny with obvious
punctures and only weak microsculpture .... *fulvago* (examples with pale-haired clypeus)

—   Hind tibiae and tarsi dark or at most dusky orange at tips
of tibiae. Scutum very dull with any punctures inconspicuous 8

Fig. 134 Fig. 135 Fig. 136 Fig. 137 Fig. 138 Fig. 139

Fig. 142

Fig. 140 Fig. 141

8   Mandibles very long, over 1.5 times the length of an eye, the hind margins of
the genae viewed from the side strongly angled at hind corner (Fig. 136).
Apical depressions of tergites 2–4 very broad and smooth (like Fig. 68) .... *synadelpha*

—   Mandibles shorter (about as long as the length of an eye). Hind margins of genae
more smoothly rounded. Apical depressions of tergites narrower, with either punctures
or microsculpture 9

9   Scutellum and propodeum with scattered black and sooty hairs. Antennal segment 3
clearly longer than segment 4 .... *ruficrus*

—   Scutellum and propodeum with only white or buff hairs. Antennal segment 3
no longer than segment 4 10

10   Hind tarsi dark (best seen from side). Tergites 2–4 without obvious fringes of white
hairs along the hind margins but with long fringes of white hairs arising from the
base. Facial hairs white. Larger (typical wing length 9mm) .... *nitida*

—   Hind tarsi entirely orange-brown (best seen from side). Tergites 2–4 with sparse
but obvious fringes of white hairs along the hind margins at least at the sides.
Facial hairs buff when fresh. Smaller (typical wing length 6.5–7mm) .... some *dorsata*

ANDRENA MALE GROUP H

1   Hind margins of genae with a flange which can be seen both in side view and as
an outcurved projection behind the eyes in top view (Figs 137 & 138) 2

—   Hind margins of genae without a flange 3

2   Top of thorax with some black hairs. Tergites 2–4 with conspicuous white bands
occupying the apical depressions. Lower edge of each gena with a triangular
projection close to the base of the mandible (Fig. 138) .... *denticulata*

—   Top of thorax entirely brown-haired. Tergites buff-haired without conspicuous white
bands along hind margins. Lower edge of each gena without a triangular projection
close to the base of the mandible .... *tridentata*

3   Antennal segment 4 viewed from front wider than long, and less than half as
long as segment 3 (Fig. 139) 4

—   Antennal segment 4 viewed from front at least as long as wide, and always
more than half as long as segment 3 5

4   Tergites 2–4 distinctly punctate. Base of abdomen with red marking of variable
extent and shape. Larger (wing length at least 7.5mm) .... *florea*

—   Tergites with weak and inconspicuous punctures and completely black. Smaller
(wing length up to 7mm) .... some *angustior*

5   Mandibles without a subapical tooth (Fig. 140) 6

—   Mandibles with a subapical tooth (Fig. 141) 7

6   Hind tibiae largely yellow. Antennal segment 3 clearly shorter than 4. Tergites 1–3
usually extensively reddish. Genal spines often present (Fig. 140) .... *ferox*

—   Hind tibiae only pale at tip. Antennal segment 3 longer than 4 (Fig. 142). Tergites 1–3
usually entirely black (sometimes obscurely reddish on apical depressions). Genal
spines never present .... *bucephala*

7   Mandible very long and curved, much longer than the length of an eye and strongly crossed when folded. In side view gena strongly angled at lower hind corner (Fig. 136). Tergites 2–4 with short hairs above (much shorter than those of tergite 1), those of the apical depressions black .... *varians*

—   Mandibles no longer than the length of an eye. In side view, lower hind corner of gena smoothly rounded. Tergites 2–4 (including the apical depressions) with longer pale buff hairs 8

8   Galeae of mouthparts smooth and shiny (Fig. 66). Apical depressions of tergites 2–4 with dense, pale hair bands that obscure the underlying surface and do not disappear with angle of view. Face with shorter hairs (length about half the greatest width of an eye). Smaller (wing length to 6.5mm) .... *fuscipes*

—   Galeae dulled by microsculpture (Fig. 67). Apical depressions of tergites 2–4 less densely haired, any bands weaker and disappearing when viewed from behind. Face with longer hairs (length equal to the greatest width of an eye). Larger (wing length at least 7mm) 9

9   Antennal segment 3 viewed from above at most slightly longer than segment 4 (Fig. 143). Tarsal segments 2–5 reddish-brown .... *nigriceps*

—   Antennal segment 3 viewed from above distinctly longer than 4 (Fig. 144). Tarsal segments 2–5 yellowish .... *simillima*

ANDRENA MALE GROUP I

1   Antennal segment 3 clearly longer than segment 4 (Fig. 145) 2

—   Antennal segment 3 as long or shorter than segment 4 (Figs 146 & 147) 6

2   Top of thorax shining with distinct punctures. Hind margin of genae with a flange (Fig. 77). Tarsal segments 2–5 of all legs yellow. Small (typical wing length 6mm) .... *nitidiuscula*

—   Top of thorax dulled by microsculpture, with or without distinct punctures. Hind margin of genae without a flange. Tarsi dark, at most the hind tarsi dull orange. Mostly larger 3

3   Hind tarsi and much of tibiae dull orange .... *lathyri*

—   Hind tarsi and tibiae dark 4

4   Scutum with distinct punctures, semi-shining. Tergites densely punctate, the apical depressions translucent brownish. Hind margins of tergite 1 without longitudinal creases. Hairs of tergites, head and femora buff. Large (wing length usually at least 8.5mm) .... *polita*

—   Scutum dull with any punctures very faint. Tergites sparsely punctate, the apical depressions dark. Hind margins of tergite 1 with longitudinal creases (Fig. 38) (angle of lighting critical). Hairs of tergites, head and femora white. Smaller (wing length up to 8mm) 5

5   Tergites 2–5 with dense, relatively broad and conspicuous white hair fringes (Fig. 153), the anterior parts of tergites 2–4 with a pile of tiny, adpressed black hairs (view from side). Smaller (wing length up to 6mm) .... *argentata*

—   Tergites 2–4 with rather inconspicuous dull white hair fringes (Fig. 154), the anterior parts of tergites 2–4 with a pile of longer, semi-upright whitish hairs (view from side), those of tergite 2 about as long as the width of a hind tibia. Larger (wing length at least 6.5mm) .... *barbilabris*

Fig. 143   Fig. 144    Fig. 145    Fig. 146    Fig. 147

Fig. 148 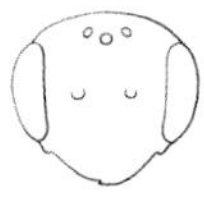   Fig. 149   Fig. 150

6   Head in front view very broad (Fig. 148). Tergite 1 shining with barely any
microsculpture and small, sparse punctures, broadly puncture-free along the hind
margin. Apical depressions of tergites 2–4 shining and almost puncture-free. Entire
propodeum with very coarse rugose reticulation. Scutum with very large but
shallow punctures that resemble abutting moon craters (Fig. 155) .... *proxima*

—   Head in front view less transverse (Fig. 149). Tergite 1 and apical depressions of tergites
2–4 with either obvious microsculpture or dense punctures or both. Propodeum with
only shallow, fine reticulation. Scutum with any punctures smaller and less extremely dense 7

7   Hind tarsi longer, about 1.5 times length of hind tibiae, with segments 2–5 orange
and tarsal segment 5 about 4 times as long as wide (Fig. 151). Top of thorax
extremely dull with barely discernible punctures .... typical *dorsata*

—   Hind tarsi shorter, up to 1.25 times length of hind tibiae, with segments 2–5 orange
or dark and tarsal segment 5 about 3 times as long as wide (Fig. 152). Top of thorax
weakly shining with more obvious punctures 8

8   Tergites 2–4 with whitish hair fringes of hind margins restricted to the extreme sides of the
tergites and very inconspicuous (Fig. 156). Antennal segment 3 viewed from above about
as long as segment 4 (Fig. 146). Hind basitarsi and tips of hind tibiae orange .... *similis*

—   Tergites 2–4 with more obvious whitish hair fringes, that of tergite 4 always
complete. Antennal segment 3 usually shorter than segment 4. Hind basitarsi
and tips of hind tibiae usually darker 9

9   Tergites 3 and 4 with complete hair fringes on hind margins, that of tergite 2 only narrowly
broken in middle (Fig. 157). Antennae relatively short with the flagellar segments less
elongate, segment 3 viewed from above usually slightly shorter than segment 4 (Fig. 150) ..... *ovatula*

—   Only tergite 4 with a complete hair fringe, that on tergite 3 broken in the middle
third, the fringes of tergite 2 widely separated (Fig. 158). Antennae relatively longer
with the flagellar segments more elongate, segment 3 viewed from above usually
distinctly shorter than segment 4 (Fig. 147) .... *wilkella*

Fig. 151   Fig. 152

Fig. 153 *A. argentata*

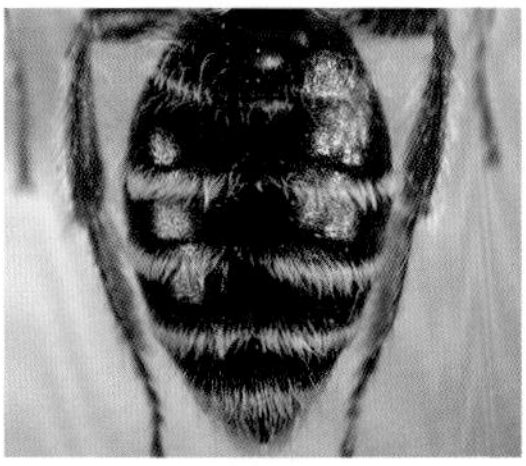

Fig. 154 *A. barbilabris*

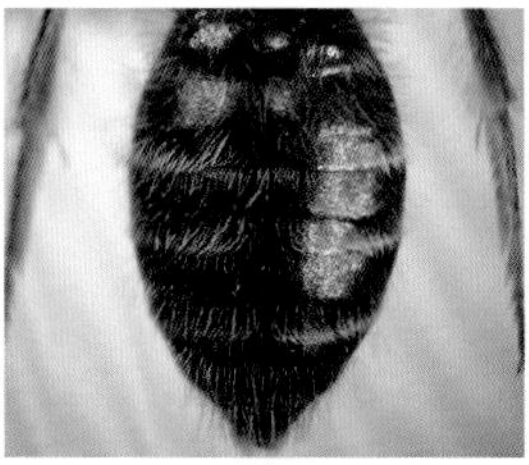

Fig. 155 *A. proxima*

Fig. 156 *A. similis*

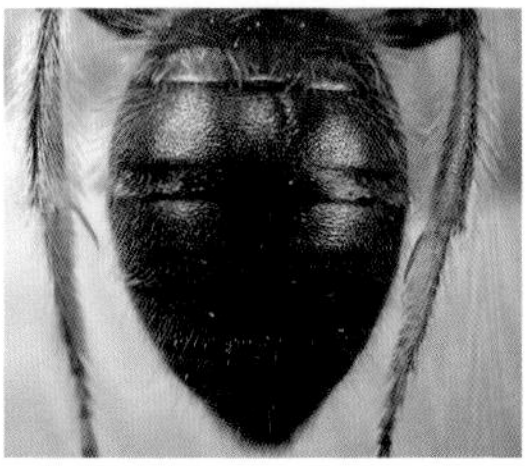

Fig. 157 *A. ovatula*

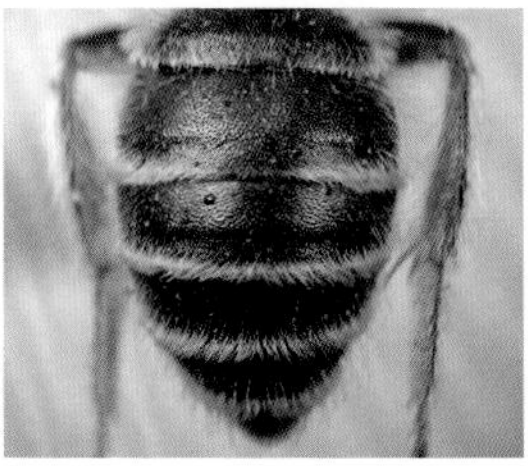

Fig. 158 *A. wilkella*

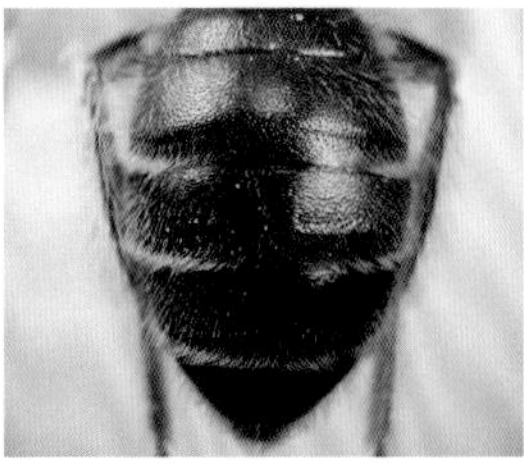

Andrena agilissima (Scopoli, 1770)   **Violet-winged Mining Bee**

Plate 3

Description & similar species FW 10–13mm female, 8.5–12.0mm male. Females are large and striking mining bees with a slim build, darkened wings with blue and violet reflections, and a shiny blue-black abdomen. Conspicuous patches of white hairs occur on the sides of the face, rear of the head, sides of the thorax, sides of tergites 4 and 5 and parts of the legs, including much of the pollen brushes of the hind tibiae. The top of the thorax is coarsely punctate with an inconspicuous grey pile and the top of the propodeum is strongly rugose. *A. cineraria* comes closest to it in appearance but has black-haired legs, a more densely haired thorax (with a black band between the wing bases) and paler wings. The narrowly built males have a white-haired

female

face, a more conspicuous grey pile on top of the thorax and rather faint bands of white hairs across the bases of tergites 2–5. The dark wings and white hairs of the face and rear of the head allow easy separation from males of *A. nigrospina* and *A. cineraria*. **Variation** Little beyond moderate size variation. **Flight season** Univoltine, flying from mid-May to early August. **Habitat** Various flowery habitats, especially where flowering large crucifers are common and soft rock cliffs and other vertical earth faces are present. **Flowers visited** Pollen is gathered exclusively from crucifers, with Sea Radish much used on the Channel Islands. Other flowers such as Hogweed, Thrift and buttercups seem to be nectar sources only. When foraging, the wings are usually held in a splayed fashion. **Nesting habits** Nesting typically occurs in vertical earth faces and sometimes in the mortar of old walls, especially where recesses and crevices are present. South-facing soft rock cliffs support some large nesting aggregations on the Channel Islands. Several females will share a common nest entrance, though there is no evidence of eusocial behaviour. **Status & distribution** Only known from the Channel Islands (Jersey, Guernsey, Sark, Alderney and Chausey), and locally common on

male

the first two. **Parasites & associates** Possibly parasitised by *Nomada subcornuta* on the Channel Islands. On the continent it is parasitised by the non-British *Nomada melathoracica* and '*fulvicornis*' (possibly *subcornuta*).

Andrena angustior (Kirby, 1802)   **Groove-faced Mining Bee**

Plate 4

Description & similar species FW 7.5–8mm female, 6.5–7mm male. A medium-small species. Females closely resemble *A. bicolor* but normally have a whitish-haired face. The legs and sides of the thorax are entirely pale-haired, never with the substantial black hairs of typical spring *A. bicolor*. The most reliable characters are the longitudinal groove on the upper part of the clypeus (revealed under careful lighting) and the broader apical depressions of tergites 2–4 which extend well into the basal half of the tergites in the middle. The rather nondescript males are difficult to confirm in the field but have a white-haired face with a brown pile on top of the thorax, which is very dull and barely punctate. The inconspicuously haired abdomen is shiny with weak microsculpture and sparse, fine punctures. The genae are particularly deep, resulting in a rather squarish head in top view, and antennal segment 3 is about 1.5 times as long as segment 4. **Variation** Females occasionally have the clypeus entirely black-haired, and these are easily overlooked as *A. bicolor*. Males typically have a row of black hairs along the inner eye margins, but these are sometimes absent. **Flight season** Univoltine, flying from mid-April to early July, usually peaking with the Hawthorn blossom. **Habitat** Usually base-poor sites, especially open heathy woodland

female

male

but also heathland and moorland edge, soft rock cliffs, coastal grassland/heathland and occasionally brownfield sites. **Flowers visited** A variety of flowers are used including spring blossoms such as Hawthorn and roses and herbaceous plants such as Wood Spurge, Bluebell, Herb-Robert, Bilberry, speedwells, brambles, dandelions, Daisy, various umbellifers and crucifers. **Nesting habits** Nesting has been observed in loose aggregations, typically along sandy paths and in south-facing slopes and faces. **Status & distribution** Widespread in England and Wales, extending into southern Scotland but localised with a curiously patchy distribution. Records are most numerous in the Weald, New Forest, Dorset heaths, Cornish and Welsh coasts and West Midlands, but the species is rare in places like East Anglia. Widely recorded in southern Ireland but seemingly much declined. Recorded from several of the Channel Islands. **Parasites & associates** The cleptoparasitic bee *Nomada fabriciana*.

Andrena apicata Smith, 1847   **Large Sallow Mining Bee**

Plate 3

Description & similar species FW 10–11mm female, 7–9.5mm male. Females are fairly large (*A. scotica*-sized) and furry-looking with a dull brownish pile on the thorax and tergites 1–4. In the field they can resemble species such as *A. bimaculata* (which has the top of the propodeum rugose, scutum strongly punctate) and *A. trimmerana* or *A. scotica* (with much smaller flocci). Females of *A. praecox*, which often flies alongside *A. apicata*, are in many ways a small version of *apicata*, and size alone is usually a reliable indicator, though *praecox* also has redder thoracic hairs and a more densely furry abdomen which is brown-haired at the tip

female

male

(black-haired in *A. apicata*). The big-headed, long-jawed males have the combination of a large projection at the base of the mandibles and some black hairs arising from the sides of the propodeum. *A. praecox* is the only other species matching this description but has pale hairs on tergites 3 and 4 (black haired in *A. apicata*), a broader and blunter projection on the base of the mandibles, and the projection of sternite

8 notched at its tip (straight-ended in *A. apicata*). **Variation** Females are fairly constant in appearance, though old ones can fade and lose their furry appearance. Males vary substantially in size, and size is not a reliable separator of male *A. apicata* and *A. praecox* in the field (*A. praecox* often produces giant males that match the largest *A. apicata*). **Flight season** Univoltine, flying from early March to early May and peaking with the flowering of the pussy-willow. **Habitat** Various willow-rich locations including open woodland, quarries, sandpits and other brownfield sites. It can use a range of soil types. **Flowers visited** Pollen is gathered primarily from Goat Willow and Grey Willow. Pollen from Gorse, Blackthorn and cherries may also be used to a small extent and nectar may be obtained from dandelions and Colt's-foot. **Nesting habits** Nesting occurs in light soils, usually either singly or in loose aggregations. **Status & distribution** Widespread but rather scarce in England and Wales north to Cumbria. Known from a few sites in southeast Ireland and from Herm in the Channel Islands. Rarely numerous at a site (in contrast to *A. praecox*). **Parasites & associates** The cleptoparasitic bee *Nomada leucophthalma*. Occasionally stylopised.

Andrena argentata Smith, 1844   **Small Sandpit Mining Bee**

Plate 5

Description & similar species FW 6.5–7mm female, 5–6mm male. In the field, females resemble small versions of *A. barbilabris* and share with this species a relatively small head with very pale facial foveae and the presence of longitudinal creases along the hind margin of tergite 1. However, the hind tibiae have much paler pollen brushes, the white hair fringes along the hind margins of tergites 2–4 are much better developed, and the tergites are only microscopically hairy between the fringes (*A. barbilabris* has a sparse pile of fairly long hairs). Males can look very silvery in the field with a long whitish pile on the sides of the thorax and distinct white hair fringes on the abdomen. Like *A. barbilabris*, antennal segment 3 is longer than segment 4 and the hind margin of tergite 1 has longitudinal creases. **Variation** Relatively little, though the white hair fringes of the abdomen are easily abraded. **Flight season** Univoltine, flying from late June to early September. **Habitat** Dry lowland heathland with a liking for loose, soft sand, especially where pits, cuttings and well-used tracks are present.

female

Flowers visited Mostly heathers, with records for plants such as Tormentil, Wild Parsnip and Sea-holly possibly representing nectar sources. **Nesting habits** Nesting usually occurs in aggregations in loose sandy ground, such as well-trodden heathland paths and heathland sandpits. Males can swarm about these areas in large numbers. **Status & distribution** Almost entirely restricted to heathland between Dorset and Surrey with a few outlying records in Suffolk, Norfolk and Worcestershire; also Jersey. Quite common at some sites within its strongholds. Not recorded from Wales, Scotland or Ireland. **Parasites & associates** The cleptoparasitic bee *Nomada baccata*, and possibly *Sphecodes reticulatus*.

Andrena barbilabris (Kirby, 1802)   **Sandpit Mining Bee**
Plate 5

Description & similar species FW 7.5–8.5mm female, 6.5–8.5mm male. The medium-sized females have a very furry thorax with a red-brown pile above contrasting with yellower hairs on the sides and on the head. The abdomen is fairly shiny with weak whitish hair fringes along the hind margins of tergites 2–4 and a short but distinct pile of semi-erect pale hairs between these fringes. The hind margin of tergite 1 has longitudinal creases, a feature also seen in *A. argentata*. The proportionately small head with very pale facial foveae and particularly oval abdomen add to its distinctiveness in the field. Males can appear silvery in the field owing to the long white pile on the sides of the thorax. Like *A. argentata*, antennal segment 3 is longer than segment 4 and the hind margin of tergite 1 has longitudinal creases, though the white hair fringes of the tergites are much less conspicuous in *A. barbilabris* and it is somewhat larger. **Variation** Little other than moderate size variation. **Flight season** Univoltine, flying from March until July (peaking later in the north). Southern records for August may represent a partial second brood. **Habitat** Sandy habitats of various sorts including heathland, heathy woodland, coastal dunes, soft rock cliffs, sandpits and sandy brownfield sites. This species is often associated with particularly loose sands. **Flowers visited** Various, including spring-flowering shrubs such as willows, Hawthorn and Blackthorn; also dandelions and other hawkish composites, umbellifers, crucifers, speedwells and buttercups. **Nesting habits** Nesting occurs in bare or sparsely vegetated sandy ground, especially footpaths, mounds of loose sand and Rabbit-disturbed areas. It can form particularly large and dense nesting aggregations. Males can swarm about these in large numbers. **Status & distribution** Widespread but rather patchily distributed in Britain and Ireland, extending north to the Inverness area. Recorded from Jersey and Guernsey in the Channel Islands. Locally common in heathland and sandy coastal districts. **Parasites & associates** The cleptoparasitic bee *Sphecodes pellucidus*.

female

male

Andrena bicolor Fabricius, 1775   **Gwynne's Mining Bee**
Plate 4

Description & similar species FW 6–8mm female, 6–7.5mm male. The medium-small females have a reddish-brown pile on top of the thorax, an entirely black-haired face and rather indistinct bands of long yellowish hairs across the hind margins of tergites 1–3. The sides of the thorax and femora can be extensively black-haired in the spring brood, but less so in the summer one. The hind tibiae are dark but have conspicuous orange hairs. *A. angustior* is very similar, especially the form with a black-haired face, but has a longitudinal groove on the upper part of the clypeus and never has black hairs on the femora or sides of the thorax like *A. bicolor*. Spring males typically have the head and sides of the thorax almost entirely black-haired, and the femora can be extensively black-haired. The top of the thorax is very dull with scarcely discernible punctures, and the tergites have weak punctures. Summer males often have the face partially brown-haired, and black hairs may be missing from the sides of the thorax. The top of the thorax is shinier and the tergites more distinctly punctate. Males of *A. congruens* resemble *A. bicolor* but have antennal segment 3 shorter than or equal in length to segment 4 (segment 3 is clearly longer in *A. bicolor*). **Variation** Pronounced brood dimorphism as outlined above, especially in males, where it affects surface punctures and microsculpture as well as hair colour. **Flight season** Bivoltine, with a spring generation that flies from March to early June in the south (but peaking later in the north) and a smaller second generation appearing from mid-June and persisting to late August. **Habitat** One of our most versatile mining bees, found in most habitats except high altitudes or the shady interiors of woods. **Flowers visited** Many species used, the spring generation foraging heavily from spring-blossoming shrubs and herbaceous species such as dandelions, Daisy, Colt's-foot, Lesser Celandine, Wood Anemone, Greater Stitchwort, forget-me-nots, speedwells, buttercups, crucifers, daffodils and Bluebell. The summer generation uses White Bryony, bellflowers, Sheep's-bit, brambles, cinquefoils, crane's-bills, mallows, thymes and assorted composites and legumes. **Nesting habits** Nesting occurs singly or in loose aggregations, typically in sparsely vegetated south-facing slopes and banks. **Status & distribution** One of our commonest mining bees, occurring throughout lowland districts of Britain and Ireland. Recorded from most of the larger Channel Islands. **Parasites & associates** The cleptoparasitic bee *Nomada fabriciana*. Occasionally stylopised.

Andrena bimaculata (Kirby, 1802)   **Large Gorse Mining Bee**

Plate 5

Description & similar species FW 9.5–10.5mm female, 8.5–11mm male. The brown-haired females average a little smaller than a Honey Bee and superficially resemble species such as *A. trimmerana*, *A. scotica*, *A. apicata* and dark summer *A. rosae* (alongside any of which it can fly). Many females have patches of red at the sides of tergites 1 and 2 like *A. trimmerana* and dark summer *A. rosae* (both of which have much smaller flocci and darker pollen brushes on the hind tibiae). The best confirmatory features for *A. bimaculata* are the rugose top of the propodeum, punctate scutum and pale pollen brushes on the hind tibiae, characters only otherwise shared with *tibialis*, which has orange hind tibiae (dark in *A. bimaculata*) and a greyer pile on the abdomen. Males have dark-haired faces (black or dark brown) and some have red bands across the apical depressions of tergites 1 and 2. In the field males can resemble those of *A. nigroaenea* (which lack the rugose area on the top of the propodeum) and *A. tibialis* (tip of hind tibiae orange). **Variation** Both sexes can have the abdomen entirely black or with red markings of variable extent on tergites 1 and 2. The extent of black hairs on the face also varies. Spring individuals often have the face entirely black-haired whilst some summer ones have the hairs entirely pale brown. Males of both generation can have the black hairs confined to the lower clypeus. In both sexes, the spring generation has a longer body pile than the summer one. **Flight season** Bivoltine, with a spring generation that flies from late March to late May and a summer one that flies from late June until late August. **Habitat** Sandy sites, including heathland, open heathy woodland, sandpits, soft rock cliffs and moorland edge. Gorse seems to be very important for the spring generation (males can often be found swarming around it). **Flowers visited** The spring generation forages mainly on blossoming shrubs such as Gorse, willows and Blackthorn. The summer one is very keen on brambles, umbellifers and Common Ragwort. **Nesting habits** Nesting typically occurs in sparsely vegetated sandy ground, especially south-facing slopes and the edges of footpaths. It can form loose nesting aggregations. **Status & distribution** Widespread but local in coastal and heathland districts of England north to Shropshire and Norfolk. Rare in Wales. Not recorded from Scotland or Ireland. Recorded from Jersey, Alderney and Sark in the Channel Islands. **Parasites & associates** The cleptoparasitic bee *Nomada fulvicornis*, which attacks both generations. Occasionally stylopised.

female

male

Andrena bucephala Stephens, 1846   **Big-headed Mining Bee**

Plate 3

Description & similar species FW 8.5–10mm female, 7–10mm male. Females average slightly smaller than a Honey Bee and have a denuded appearance except for a buff pile around the sides of the thorax and subtle white hair fringes on the hind margins of tergites 2–4. The facial foveae are pale buff and the dark hind tibiae have a pale yellow-buff pollen brush. The abdomen is dull with a characteristic slim-oval shape (creating a rather waisted appearance) and the wings are noticeably yellowish. The flocci are very poorly formed. Males can develop greatly oversized heads and have a relatively small and slender abdomen. Males of *A. ferox* are very similar in build but have red markings at the base of the abdomen, mostly yellow hind tibiae and often well-formed genal spines. The long mandibles lacking a subapical tooth or emargination are seen only in male *A. bucephala*, *A. ferox* and spring-generation *A. trimmerana*. **Variation** Females are fairly constant in appearance but males vary greatly in size, and large ones are proportionately bigger-headed than small ones. **Flight season** Univoltine, flying from mid-April to mid-June, peaking with the flowering of Hawthorn and Field Maple. **Habitat** A variety of habitats can be used including scrubby hillsides, coastal scrub, old quarries and cuttings, open woodland and occasionally more formal locations such as churchyards and larger gardens. It predominates in chalk and limestone districts. **Flowers visited** Pollen is mainly

female

male

gathered from Hawthorn and Field Maple. Other flower visits are noted for Cherry Laurel, Sycamore, Wild Cherry, Wayfaring-tree, Alder Buckthorn, Holly, dandelions and Wood Spurge. Males can swarm in very large numbers around blossoming shrubs. **Nesting habits** Nesting is communal (but not social), with numerous females sharing a common nest entrance, and sometimes even with females of *A. scotica*. Nesting locations include Rabbit burrows, old rodent holes and cavities in tree stumps, typically in scrubby grassland and south-facing slopes and banks. **Status & distribution** Widespread but scarce in southern England and south Wales, extending north to Staffordshire and Northamptonshire. Not recorded from Scotland, Ireland or the Channel Islands. **Parasites & associates** *A. bucephala* is the special host of the cleptoparasitic bee *Nomada hirtipes*, the nomad often revealing the nesting locations of its host.

Andrena chrysosceles (Kirby, 1802)   Hawthorn Mining Bee

Plate 5

Description & similar species FW 6.5–8.5mm female, 6–7.5mm male. The medium-sized females have a short, dull brown pile on the top of the thorax, orange hind tibiae and an almost bare abdomen except for conspicuous white hair bands along the hind margins of tergites 2–4 and orange hairs at the tip. The tergites are shining with obvious punctures and the facial foveae are very pale, unlike similar species such as *A. wilkella* and *A. ovatula*. The build of *A. chrysosceles* is also slightly slimmer than these species. Males are one of a small group of species with the clypeus surface pale yellow and bearing a pair of black spots. They are easily distinguished from the others by the partly orange hind tibiae and the fringes of dense white hairs across the sternites. A flange is present along the hind margin of the genae. **Variation** Males can have the hind tibiae mostly orange or only orange at the tip and also vary somewhat in size. **Flight season** Univoltine, flying from late March to early July (later in the north) and typically peaking with the blossoming of Hawthorn and Cow Parsley. **Habitat** Found in a variety of habitats including woodland rides and margins, scrubby grassland, heathland edge, quarries and other

female

male

brownfield sites, and sometimes gardens and formal greenspaces. More tolerant of heavy clay soils than most mining bees. **Flowers visited** A variety of spring-blossoming shrubs and trees, plus flowers such as umbellifers and crucifers, dandelions, Oxeye Daisy, buttercups and speedwells. **Nesting habits** Nesting is rarely observed and is presumed to occur singly or in very loose aggregations in locations such as south-facing slopes and hedge banks. **Status & distribution** Locally common throughout most of England, though rare in the southwest. Rather scarce in Wales and rare in Scotland. Not recorded in Ireland or the Channel Islands. **Parasites & associates** Possibly *Nomada fabriciana*. This is one of the most frequently stylopised mining bees, with stylopised intersexes often appearing in early spring before the rest of the population.

Andrena cineraria (Linnaeus, 1758)   **Ashy Mining Bee**
Plate 4

Description & similar species FW 10–11mm female, 9–10mm male. Females are very distinctive with a shiny black abdomen (giving bluish reflections in some lights), a black- and grey-haired thorax, white-haired face and hind legs almost entirely black-haired. *A. vaga* is similar but with an entirely grey-haired thorax and white hairs on the hind femora. Males resemble small, slim females but with much more conspicuous whitish hairs on the sides of the thorax, base of the abdomen and femora. The face is mostly white-haired but black-haired alongside the inner eye margins. Some black hairs are usually present at the front of the scutellum and rear edge of scutum. Males of *A. vaga* look rather similar but are stouter with extensively pale-haired legs, the top of the thorax entirely grey-haired and the tip of the abdomen downcurved. Males of *A. nigrospina* are more elongate, with a black-haired face and rugose area on top of the propodeum. **Variation** Males vary in the amount of grey hairing they have on tergites 1 and 2, with the abdomen mainly black-haired in some examples, like *A. vaga*. **Flight season** Univoltine, flying from late March to June, with records for July and August possibly representing a partial second brood. **Habitat** Surprisingly adaptable, with records for heathland, moorland edge, downland, open woodland, coastal grassland, cliffs, quarries and other brownfield sites. Occasionally found in gardens and urban greenspace. **Flowers visited** A wide variety of spring-blossoming shrubs and flowers, including willows, Gorse, Blackthorn, Hawthorn, fruit trees, umbellifers, composites, buttercups, spurges, larger crucifers, Silverweed and Thrift. An important pollinator of Rape in areas such as the Cotswolds and Wiltshire Downs. **Nesting habits** Capable of forming very dense and extensive nesting aggregations. Typical nesting sites include south-facing slopes (both short-grazed turf and the barer ground created by soil creep or Rabbit activity) and more level footpaths, tracks and occasionally managed lawns. **Status & distribution** Widespread and locally common over much of England and Wales but with a central and western bias; also a few sites in western Scotland. Widespread in Ireland and recorded from many of the Channel Islands. Evidence of a recent increase in southern and central England. **Parasites & associates** The cleptoparasitic bee *Nomada lathburiana*, and

female

male

possibly *N. goodeniana* to a small extent. It is also a major host for the bee-fly *Bombylius discolor* in areas such as the Cotswolds, and nests are much frequented by the anthomyiid fly *Leucophora obtusa*. The conopid fly *Myopa pellucida* (formerly *M. extricata*) is often found in association with *A. cineraria* and is a suspected parasite.

Andrena clarkella (Kirby, 1802) Clarke's Mining Bee

Plate 3

female

Description & similar species
FW 10–11mm female, 8–9.5mm male. Females average a little larger than a Honey Bee and are very furry with a black pile on the abdomen and a dark red one on the top of the thorax. They are not easily confused with any other species, though females of *A. bicolor* can resemble diminutive versions. The much smaller, brown-haired males have the face mostly buff-haired but with strips of black hairs alongside the inner eye margins. The hind tibiae and tarsi are usually dull orange. The tergites are completely dulled by microsculpture with very inconspicuous punctures. **Variation** Females can have tergite 1 either black- or brown-haired and in extreme cases pale hairs can extend onto tergite 3. The male hind tibia and tarsi are variably orange and occasionally black. **Flight season** A univoltine, spring-flying species that peaks with the blossoming of pussy-willow. Males can appear in mid-February in mild winters and females sometimes persist to late May. **Habitat** A variety of willow-rich locations, especially those with sandy soil such as heathland, heathy woodland, sandpits, quarries and sandy brownfield sites. **Flowers visited** Pollen is obtained almost entirely from willows, especially Goat Willow and Grey Willow. It has also been observed visiting Colt's-foot and dandelions, probably for nectar. **Nesting habits** This species can form large and dense nesting aggregations in sandy ground, especially south-facing slopes (e.g. hedge banks), vertical sandpit faces, Rabbit-disturbed ground and well-used footpaths and tracks. **Status & distribution** Widespread and locally common throughout Britain and Ireland, especially in heathland districts of southern and central England. Only recorded from Guernsey in the Channel Islands. **Parasites & associates** The cleptoparasitic bee *Nomada leucophthalma*. It is also a major host for the bee-fly *Bombylius major* and the nests are much frequented by the anthomyiid fly *Leucophora obtusa*.

male

Andrena coitana (Kirby, 1802) Small Flecked Mining Bee

Plate 5

Description & similar species FW 6.5–7mm female, 5.5–6.5mm male. A small, dark-looking species with narrow white hair fringes along the hind margins of tergites 2–4 in both sexes. The pollen brushes of the female hind tibiae are dark-haired above. *A. nitidiuscula* looks similar in the field but has a whitish pollen brush and (in top view) a more transverse head and rearward-projecting propodeum. Small *A. coitana* females could also be confused with the mini-miner group of small *Andrena* bees, but these have pale pollen brushes on the hind legs and much paler facial foveae. Males are one of several *Andrena* species with the surface of the face white or yellow but can be easily distinguished by the extent of the whitish facial markings (which extend onto the lower face outside the boundaries of the clypeus) combined with a shiny thorax and black abdomen. **Variation** One Cornish female seen has considerable microsculpture on the tergites and is much duller than normal but is typical in all other respects. **Flight season** Univoltine, flying from mid-May to late August

female

(peaking later in the north). **Habitat** British habitats include heathland, heathy woodland, moorland edge, fenland and coastal grassland, predominantly on base-poor soils. **Flowers visited** Preferences are unclear but records include Cat's-ear, Tormentil, thistles, Common Knapweed, Hogweed, Harebell, Lesser Spearwort, Lesser Stitchwort and ragworts. **Nesting habits** Nesting has rarely been observed but appears to occur solitarily in light soils. **Status & distribution** Widespread but scarce over Britain and Ireland, predominating in heathland and moorland districts. On the Channel Islands recorded

male

from Guernsey and Alderney. It appears to have shown a substantial decline in central and southern England. **Parasites & associates** The cleptoparasitic bee *Nomada obtusifrons*.

Andrena congruens Schmiedeknecht, 1883   **Long-fringed Mining Bee**
Plate 6

Description & similar species FW 7.5–8mm female, 6.5–7mm male. Females closely resemble *A. dorsata* and *A. lepida* but have much slimmer hind tibiae with a relatively long dorsal hair fringe. The tergites are also somewhat shinier than in *A. dorsata*, the scutum much duller (with punctures barely discernible) and the tarsi darker. Males have black-haired faces and could be overlooked as *A. bicolor* but have antennal segment 3 shorter than segment 4 and the mid and hind femora completely pale-haired. Males of *A. lepida*, which have never been found in Britain, are very similar (see that species). **Variation** The

female

male

spring generation has longer body hairs than the summer one, especially on the thorax.
Flight season Bivoltine, the spring generation flying in April and May, the summer one in July and August. **Habitat** British records include sand and gravel pits, heathland, chalk grassland, coastal scrubby grassland, open woodland and occasionally gardens. **Flowers visited** The spring generation forages heavily from spring-blossoming shrubs such as willows, *Prunus* species and Gorse, also dandelions. The summer generation likes umbellifers and brambles. **Nesting habits** Nesting usually occurs in sparsely vegetated sandy ground, and large aggregations have been noted. **Status & distribution** A scarce species, with records largely confined to southern England within Wiltshire, Hampshire, Sussex and Surrey, with outliers in Herefordshire, Worcestershire and south Wales. Not recorded from Scotland, Ireland or the Channel Islands. **Parasites & associates** None known in Britain.

Andrena denticulata (Kirby, 1802)   Grey-banded Mining Bee

Plate 4

Description & similar species FW 7.5–8.5mm female, 6.5–7.5mm male. The medium-sized females have greyish-white hair bands occupying the apical depressions of tergites 2–4, these being preceded by a short black pile across the base of the tergites. The face is pale-haired and the thorax has a pale pile at the sides but a black one on top. There is a slight resemblance to *A. flavipes*, though *A. denticulata* is somewhat smaller, has darker pollen brushes on the hind tibiae and lacks the brown-haired thorax, appearing much more greyish. Males resemble small, slim females. They have a flange running along the hind margin of the genae which can be seen by viewing the head from the side but also in top view where the top of each ridge forms an outcurved lobe behind the eyes. The abdomen is particularly shiny with narrow whitish hair fringes along the rear margins of tergites 2–4. **Variation** Giant males are occasionally encountered. **Flight season** Univoltine, flying from late June to September. **Habitat** Various composite-rich habitats, including heathland, coastal dunes, chalk downland, acid grassland, brownfield sites and the rides and clearings of woods. **Flowers visited** Pollen is gathered from composites of various sorts including ragworts, thistles, knapweeds and hawkish types. Other flowers may act as nectar sources. **Nesting habits** Nesting occurs in sparsely vegetated, often sandy ground, singly or in loose aggregations. **Status & distribution** Widespread but patchily distributed throughout Britain and Ireland. Not recorded from the Channel Islands. **Parasites & associates** The cleptoparasitic bee *Nomada rufipes*.

female

male

Andrena dorsata (Kirby, 1802)   **Short-fringed Mining Bee**
Plate 6

Description & similar species FW 6.5–8mm female, 5–7mm male. Females are medium-sized with a short reddish-brown pile on top of the thorax which contrasts with the yellowish pile on the sides and on the face. The abdomen is dull and appears hairless except for conspicuous white hair fringes along the hind margins of tergites 2–4 (broken in the middle on tergites 2 and 3). The hind tibiae are dark beneath the pale hairs. Several other species can look similar (notably *A. congruens* and *A. lepida*) but *A. dorsata* can be easily distinguished by the particularly broad hind tibiae, which bear an exceptionally short dorsal fringe (only about one-fifth the greatest width of the tibia). Males resemble species such as *A. ovatula* and *A. wilkella* but have much longer hind tarsi with the second tarsal segment about 4 times as long as broad (about 3 times as long in the others) and a much duller thorax. **Variation** Moderate size variation. Some males have dark hairs alongside the inner eye margins. **Flight season** Bivoltine, with a spring generation that flies from March to May and a summer one from July to September. **Habitat** Rather varied, including heathland, coastal dunes, soft rock cliffs, cliff-top grassland and scrub, brownfield sites of various sorts and occasionally gardens. **Flowers visited** The spring generation forages heavily on spring-flowering shrubs such as willows, *Prunus* species and Gorse, as well as early umbellifers and crucifers, Daisy, dandelions and speedwells. The summer generation is especially keen on brambles, umbellifers and thistles but will also use heathers, ragworts, cinquefoils and melilots. **Nesting habits** Nesting usually occurs in light soils, including sparsely vegetated ground and short turf, often in loose aggregations. **Status & distribution** Widespread and locally common in southern England north to Lincolnshire. Very rare in Wales. Not recorded in Scotland or Ireland. Recorded from several of the Channel Islands. It appears to have increased in both range and frequency over recent decades.

Parasites & associates The cleptoparasitic bee *Nomada zonata* (only currently known from Jersey), and possibly *Sphecodes reticulatus* on the mainland. Rarely stylopised.

Andrena ferox Smith, 1847   **Oak Mining Bee**
Plate 3

Description & similar species FW 9–10.5mm female, 7.5–9mm male. Females average slightly smaller than a Honey Bee and are one of the small group of mining bees with orange hind tibiae. In the field, they most resemble species such as *A. scotica* and *A. trimmerana* but have much paler pollen brushes on the hind legs and larger flocci. Males can develop greatly oversized heads and have a small and slender abdomen that is extensively reddish on the basal segments. The hind tibiae and tarsi are mostly orange. A well-formed genal spine is often present and the long mandibles lack a subapical tooth or emargination. Males of

female

male

A. bucephala are very similar but typically have a dark abdomen and mostly dark hind tibiae, and lack a genal spine. Males of *A. trimmerana* and *rosae* have a genal spine and often similar abdominal markings but average larger, and antennal segment 3 is only about half as long as segment 4 (about two-thirds as long in *A. ferox*). **Variation** Females are fairly constant in appearance but males vary greatly in size and large ones are proportionately more robust and bigger-headed than small ones. There is also variation in the size of the male genal spines (which can be missing at one extreme or almost as large as *A. trimmerana* and *A. rosae* at the other) and the amount of orange on the male tergites. **Flight season** Univoltine, flying from late April to early June, peaking with the flowering of Pedunculate Oak and Hawthorn. **Habitat** Open structured oak woodland on light soils. **Flowers visited** Pollen appears to be gathered almost entirely from oaks, though both males and females visit Hawthorn, Field Maple, Blackthorn and Buckthorn flowers for nectar (the easiest places to find them), and males may also visit Wood Spurge. On the continent, females will also take pollen from pines and Walnut after oaks have finished flowering. **Nesting habits** Nesting is communal (but not social), with numerous females sharing a common nest entrance. British nesting locations include Rabbit burrows, tree stumps and beneath bushes. **Status & distribution** Seemingly very rare, with modern records confined to the New Forest (the modern stronghold) and a few further sites in Surrey, Sussex and Kent. Older records also exist for Cornwall, Berkshire and the Bristol area. The arboreal foraging habits mean it may be under-recorded in places such as the Weald and other large tracts of old oak woodland. **Parasites & associates** The cleptoparasitic bees *Nomada flava* and *N. marshamella* are suspected cuckoos in Britain, and on the continent it is the special host of *N. mutica*. Freshly emerged individuals of the bee-fly *Bombylius major* and conopid fly *Myopa buccata* have also been found close to a nest entrance, and the anthomyiid fly *Leucophora obtusa* has also been observed close to burrows.

Andrena flavipes Panzer, 1799   Yellow-legged Mining Bee

Plate 5

Description & similar species FW 8–9mm female, 7–9mm male. Females average a little smaller than a Honey Bee and have broad buff-white bands occupying the apical depressions of tergites 2–4, bright orange pollen brushes on the hind legs and a brown pile on top of the thorax. The face, sides and undersides of the thorax, femora and flocci are buff-haired. Separation from the much rarer *A. gravida* is discussed under that species. The smaller, browner males are fairly easily recognised in the field by the combination of a banded abdomen and the buff- and black-haired face. **Variation** Females are fairly constant in appearance, though the pale buff bands of the tergites and other hairs can bleach white with age. Males vary considerably in size and giant males are not uncommon. Spring males generally have the lower face extensively black-haired whilst summer ones usually have buff-haired faces with black hairs restricted to the sides of the face and occasionally so reduced in extent that they can resemble *A. gravida* once faded. In old individuals of both sexes the abdominal bands can become completely abraded. **Flight season** Bivoltine, with a spring generation that flies from March to June and a second one from mid-June to September. **Habitat** Capable of exploiting a wide variety of open habitats on the coast and inland, with some of the strongest populations on soft rock cliffs, chalk downland, abandoned quarries and brownfield sites. Colonies can also be found in gardens and formal greenspace. **Flowers visited** Many flowers are exploited, with the spring generation foraging heavily on spring-blossoming shrubs, composites, umbellifers and crucifers, whilst the summer generation likes brambles, composites and legumes. **Nesting habits** Often forming large and dense nesting aggregations, typically along south-facing slopes and faces. It can use bare or sparsely vegetated ground, and short turf (including regularly mown lawns) on a range of soils. **Status & distribution** Widespread and locally common in southern Britain with a recent expansion into the Midlands and north Wales (as far

female

male

north as Shropshire, Lincolnshire and Denbighshire). Not recorded from Scotland or Ireland. Recorded from many of the Channel Islands. **Parasites & associates** The cleptoparasitic bee *Nomada fucata*. Probably the most important host nationally for the bee-fly *Bombylius discolor*, and also much exploited by *Bombylius major* and *Leucophora* flies.

Andrena florea Fabricius, 1793   **Bryony Mining Bee**

Plate 5

Description & similar species FW 9–10mm female, 7.5–9mm male. Females are medium-sized with a brown pile on the top of a dull thorax and an inconspicuously haired abdomen. Tergites 1 and 2 are variably red, often with two complete bands across the base of the abdomen but sometimes with the red confined to the extreme sides of tergites 1 and 2. They can resemble *A. rosae* and *A. trimmerana* but the tergites are shiny and distinctly punctate and the flocci better formed. *A. bimaculata* can also look similar but has the top of the thorax strongly punctate and the top of the propodeum rugose. Males resemble small, slim females and could be mistaken for males of *A. trimmerana* and *A. rosae* but have darker tarsi and much shorter antennae, with segment 3 longer than 4. **Variation** The amount of red on the abdomen, as noted above. **Flight season** Univoltine, flying from late May to mid-August. **Habitat** Sites with plentiful White Bryony, including woodland edge, scrubby grassland and scrubby heathland. It uses both sandy and chalky soils. **Flowers visited** Pollen is gathered exclusively from White Bryony. Other flowers such as brambles and umbellifers seem to act as nectar sources. **Nesting habits** Nesting occurs in light soils such as hard sandy paths, sometimes in large aggregations. **Status & distribution** Modern records are confined to southern England within Surrey, Sussex, Hampshire, Middlesex and the Thames Gateway area of Kent and Essex.

Older records exist for the Isle of Wight and Wiltshire. Despite this restricted occurrence it can be common in some districts. **Parasites & associates** None known.

female

male

Andrena fucata Smith, 1847   **Painted Mining Bee**

Plate 3

Description & similar species FW 8.5–9.5mm female, 7–8mm male. The medium-sized females have a reddish-brown pile on the thorax and a mainly black abdomen with longer pale hairs on tergites 1 and 2. They most resemble *A. lapponica* and the typical form of *A. varians* but have a mostly pale-haired face, pale hair fringes on the sternites and a slimmer build. Males belong to a group of three species with the combination of a ventral projection at the base of very long mandibles, antennal segments 3 and 4 of similar length and only pale hairs on the propodeum. The relatively small mandibular projections, orange-brown hind tarsi and long but sparse hair fringes on the hind margins of the sternites separate it from the other two (*A. helvola* and *A. lapponica*). **Variation** Giant males with a wing length to 9.5mm can occasionally be found. **Flight season** Univoltine, flying from mid-May to July and occasionally into August. **Habitat** Woodland rides and clearings, coastal scrub, heathland and moorland edge (especially where woodland or scrub is present nearby). **Flowers visited** Records include hawthorns, roses, brambles, Raspberry, currants, Bilberry, Wood Spurge, umbellifers and crucifers. **Nesting habits** Nesting can occur singly or in small aggregations but is not often observed. **Status & distribution** Widely recorded in England, Wales, Scotland and Ireland but somewhat local and rarely common. Not known from the Channel Islands. **Parasites & associates** The cleptoparasitic bee *Nomada panzeri*.

female

male

Andrena fulva (Müller, 1766)   **Tawny Mining Bee**
Plate 3

Description & similar species FW 10–11mm female, 6.5–9mm male. The Honey Bee-sized females are amongst our most unmistakable bees, with a densely orange-furred abdomen and reddish pile on top of the thorax. The head and legs are completely black-haired. Males belong to a group of six species with a ventral projection at the base of very long mandibles but are the only species with antennal segment 3 about twice as long as 4. They have a rich brown pile on top of the thorax and at the base of the abdomen, and the lower face is conspicuously white-haired, giving the impression of a white moustache in the field. **Variation** Females are very constant in appearance but males vary considerably in size, and very robust giant males with a wing length to 10.5mm can occasionally be encountered. **Flight season** Univoltine, flying from late March to mid-June (late June in Scotland), peaking with spring-blossoming shrubs. **Habitat** Found in a great variety of habitats without any strong preferences. It is one of the more frequent mining bees of urban environments, often nesting in gardens and municipal parks.

Flowers visited Much foraging is from spring-flowering shrubs such as willows, Blackthorn, hawthorns, fruit trees, maples and currants. It will also visit herbaceous plants such as Rape, umbellifers, buttercups and dandelions. **Nesting habits** Capable of forming large nesting aggregations. Typical nesting sites include footpaths, south-facing grazed hillsides with Rabbit activity or soil creep, arable field margins and the managed lawns and flowerbeds of gardens and formal greenspace. **Status & distribution** Common over much of southern Britain, with records extending north to central Scotland, where it seems to be increasing since having been discovered in 2010. Very rare in Ireland. Recorded from several of the Channel Islands. **Parasites & associates** The cleptoparasitic bees *Nomada signata* and *N. panzeri*. Also attacked by the bee-fly *Bombylius major* and *Leucophora* flies. Occasionally stylopised.

Andrena fulvago (Christ, 1791)   **Hawk's-beard Mining Bee**
Plate 5

Description & similar species FW 7–7.5mm female, 6.5–7.5mm male. Females are medium-sized and rather shiny with the tip of the abdomen conspicuously orange-haired. The hind tibiae and their hairs are bright yellow-orange. *A. humilis* looks rather similar in the field but is usually larger, with scutum and tergites much dulled by microsculpture and hind tibiae dark beneath the orange hairs. Males resemble small, slim females and have orange hind tibiae and tarsi, a feature only otherwise seen in the males of *A. haemorrhoa*, *A. clarkella*, *A. chrysosceles* and *A. ferox*, which are obviously distinct. **Variation** Males can have the clypeus extensively dark brown-haired or paler-haired with dark hairs confined to the extreme edges alongside the inner eye margins. **Flight season** Univoltine, flying from mid-May to early August. **Habitat** Many records are from chalk and limestone grassland but it can also use acid grassland and non-calcareous coastal grasslands, soft rock cliffs and quarries. Occasionally recorded in gardens. **Flowers visited** Pollen is gathered mainly from yellow hawkish composites, especially hawk's-beards,

hawkbits, Mouse-ear-hawkweed, Cat's-ear and dandelions. It has also been observed visiting ragworts. **Nesting habits** Nesting occurs in light soils, and large nesting aggregations are occasionally reported. **Status & distribution** Widespread but generally scarce in England north to Staffordshire with records concentrated in coastal and calcareous districts. Very rare in Wales. Not recorded from Scotland or Ireland. Recorded from several of the Channel Islands. **Parasites & associates** None known.

Andrena fuscipes (Kirby, 1802) — **Heather Mining Bee**

Plate 4

Description & similar species FW 6.5–7mm female, 6–6.5mm male. A medium-small mining bee with a short brown pile on the top of the thorax and distinct bands of buff hairs across the apical depressions of tergites 2–4. One of several species with female hind tibiae that broaden progressively to their tips (side view). Smaller and shorter-haired than *A. simillima* with buff rather than white flocci. Males resemble small, slim females and are most like *A. simillima* and *A. nigriceps* but are smaller, shorter-haired with a more strongly banded abdomen. Both sexes have shiny galeae (dull in *A. simillima* and *A. nigriceps*).

In the field, most likely to be seen flying alongside *Colletes succinctus* but this is less hairy and more strongly banded with slightly larger females. **Variation** Moderate size variation. **Flight season** Univoltine, typically flying from July to September and peaking with the blooming of Heather (Ling) in August. **Habitat** Dry ericaceous heathland, both classic lowland heath and also upland heath and moorland edge in the north and west of its range. **Flowers visited** Heathers, particularly Ling. **Nesting habits** Nesting occurs singly

or in very loose aggregations in sandy ground. **Status & distribution** Fairly common in southern heathland districts of England but much scarcer elsewhere, with scattered locations extending to the north of Scotland and into Wales. Scarce in Ireland. Recorded from Jersey and Alderney in the Channel Islands. **Parasites & associates** The cleptoparasitic bee *Nomada rufipes*.

Andrena gravida Imhoff, 1832   White-bellied Mining Bee
not illustrated

Description & similar species FW 9–10.5mm female, 8.5–9mm male. Females are very similar to *A. flavipes* but are slightly larger, paler and fluffier-looking with a longer, orange-brown pile on top of the thorax which contrasts strongly with the rather long white hairs on the sides and underside of the thorax, face and femora (hairs buff in *A. flavipes*). The pale bands on the tergites are broader and consist of longer, whiter hairs. The most reliable character (though difficult to see) is the lack of a longitudinal groove along the underside of the hind femora separating the hind face from the underside. Males also resemble *A. flavipes* but

female

have a white-haired face with black hairs narrowly confined to the inner eye margins. As in females, there is a much stronger contrast between the brown pile on top of the thorax and the pure white hairs below, with the pale abdominal bands consisting of longer hairs and less sharply defined than in *A. flavipes*. **Variation** Little noted. **Flight season** A univoltine species flying from March to May, with July and August records possibly representing a partial second brood. **Habitat** British records include churchyards, cemeteries, woodland edge and well-hedged, sheltered areas of farmland with spring-blossoming shrubs and trees. **Flowers visited** British records include Apple and Cherry, and it is an important pollinator of orchard trees on the continent. Foreign records include Blackthorn, Goat Willow, Oxeye Daisy, dandelions, Yarrow and Cuckooflower. **Nesting habits** Nesting occurs singly or in small aggregations in sparsely vegetated light soils of various sorts, especially south-facing banks. **Status & distribution** Very rare, with records confined to southeast England, mostly in Kent but also extending into Sussex and Essex. Possibly only surviving at a handful of sites in Kent. **Parasites & associates** None known in Britain, but attacked by the cleptoparasitic bee *Nomada bifasciata* on the continent.

male

Andrena haemorrhoa (Fabricius, 1781)   Orange-tailed Mining Bee
Early Mining Bee

Plate 4

Description & similar species FW 8–10mm female, 7–9.5mm male. One of several species with coarse rugosity on the top of the propodeum. Females average a little smaller than a Honey Bee and are fairly distinctive with a very neat, brick-red pile on the top of the thorax and a dull, slate-black abdomen with bright orange hairs at the tip and very coarsely punctate tergites. The face is whitish-haired with very pale facial foveae, and the hind tibiae are yellow. Males are smaller and much less distinctive but have a buff pile on the face and sides of the thorax, and a brighter brown pile on top of the thorax and the tip of the abdomen. The hind tibiae and tarsi are mostly orange (the tibiae usually have a dark patch beneath halfway along). **Variation** Males vary considerably in size, and large ones are proportionately more robust. Old, worn females with the top of the thorax bare and black can be frequent towards the end of the flight season. **Flight season** Univoltine, with a long flight period that can extend from late March into July, peaking later in the north. **Habitat** Found in a great variety of habitats without any strong preferences. It is one of the more frequent mining bees of urban environments and intensively farmed landscapes and can tolerate quite heavy clays. **Flowers visited** Much foraging is from blossoming shrubs such as willows, *Prunus* species, Gorse, hawthorns, maples and fruit trees. It will also use herbaceous plants such as dandelions, Colt's-foot, Greater Stitchwort, Wood Anemone, Cow Parsley, Rape, buttercups, spurges and mignonettes. **Nesting habits** Nesting occurs singly or in very loose aggregations, often in south-facing grassy slopes and banks. **Status & distribution** Common over much of Britain and Ireland. Recorded from several of the Channel Islands. **Parasites & associates** The cleptoparasitic bee *Nomada ruficornis*.

female

male

Andrena hattorfiana (Fabricius, 1775)   Large Scabious Mining Bee

Plate 6

Description & similar species FW 11–12mm female, 10.5mm male. Females are our largest mining bees in terms of body size (though several smaller species have greater wingspans) with an abdomen that varies from all black to conspicuously red-banded across its base. The top of the thorax has a short, inconspicuous pile. The tergites are shining and appear bare except for narrow white hair fringes on the hind margins of tergites 2–4 and bright orange hairs at the tip of the abdomen. The hind tibiae are dark but bear a yellow pollen brush. The wings are darkened and the facial foveae very pale. Males are by far the largest of those species that have the surface of the clypeus yellow or white. They resemble oversized males of *A. marginata* (alongside which it often flies), but the clypeus does not have outcurving points at

female, black form

female, red form

male

its lower corners and the wings are rather darkened. The male abdomen is typically black but can occasionally have limited red markings. **Variation** The variable amount of red on the abdomen. Size fairly constant. **Flight season** Univoltine, flying from late June to mid-August and peaking with the flowering of Field and Small Scabiouses. **Habitat** Scabious-rich habitats such as chalk downland and the chalk-influenced sandy grasslands of the East Anglian Brecks; also nearby arable margins, road verges and grassy woodland rides. Less commonly found on non-calcareous coastal grasslands, soft rock cliffs, fixed coastal dune and moorland edge (mostly southwest England). **Flowers visited** Pollen is gathered from Field Scabious and to a lesser extent Small Scabious (the hind legs are often thick with the sticky pink pollen grains of these plants). Flowers such as Wild Parsnip, knapweeds, clovers and hawk's-beards appear to represent nectar sources. **Nesting habits** Nesting occurs in bare ground and very short turf, with nests dispersed rather than in aggregations. **Status & distribution** Southern England and the south coast of Wales, extending north to Oxfordshire, Bedfordshire and Norfolk. Not recorded from Scotland, Ireland or the Channel Islands. Very scarce and much declined. **Parasites & associates** The cleptoparasitic bee *Nomada armata*.

Andrena helvola (Linnaeus, 1758)   **Coppice Mining Bee**

Plate 3

Description & similar species FW 9–10mm female, 6.5–8.5mm male. Females are medium-sized with a reddish-brown pile on the top of the thorax and an orange or yellowish pile on tergites 1 and 2 which contrasts with the greyish or pale buff pile on tergites 3 and 4. The hind tibiae have pale yellow-brown hairs dorsally and the face is white-haired. *A. synadelpha* and form *mixta* of *A. varians* look very similar but have dark-haired hind tibiae. Males belong to a group of three species with the combination of a ventral projection at the base of very long mandibles, antennal segments 3 and 4 of similar length and only pale hairs on the propodeum. The very dense and conspicuous fringes of white hairs on the hind margins of the sternites allow easy separation from the other two (*A. fucata* and *A. lapponica*). **Variation** Females are fairly constant in appearance but males can vary substantially in size, and large ones are proportionately much more robust and bigger-headed than small ones. **Flight season** A univoltine bee that flies from late April until late June (peaking in May) and

137

occasionally as late as August (Ireland). **Habitat** Most frequent in open structured woodland but also found associated with blossoming scrub in coastal areas, on downland and in old quarries. **Flowers visited** Spring-blossoming trees and shrubs such as Blackthorn, Cherry, hawthorns, apples, roses, Field Maple and Guelder-rose, also herbaceous species such as Wood Spurge and dandelions. **Nesting habits** Nesting occurs singly or in loose aggregations in locations such as wood banks and the edges of woodland rides that receive plenty of sunshine. **Status & distribution** Fairly frequent in woods of southern and central England but decidedly scarce in East Anglia, southwest England, Wales, northern England and Scotland. Only recorded from Jersey in the Channel Islands. Not recorded from Ireland. **Parasites & associates** The cleptoparasitic bee *Nomada panzeri*. Occasionally stylopised.

female

male

Andrena humilis Imhoff, 1832

Buff-tailed Mining Bee

Plate 5

Description & similar species 8–8.5mm female, 7.5–8mm male. The medium-sized females are rather uniform brown-black with a conspicuous pile of buff hairs at the tip of the abdomen and a buff-coloured pollen brush on the hind legs. They most resemble *A. fulvago* in the field but are duller and have the tibiae dark beneath the buff hairs (tibiae orange in *A. fulvago*). Males belong to a group of species with the surface of the clypeus yellow or white, but can be distinguished by the very dull thorax and the rough, pustulose surface of tergite 1. **Variation** Relatively little. **Flight season** A univoltine species that flies from early May to mid-July. **Habitat** A variety of habitats featuring compacted sandy soils are used, including heathland and acid grassland, soft rock cliffs, coastal grassland, open heathy

female

male

woodland, sandpits and sandy brownfield sites. Occasionally found on chalk downland, usually where there is a capping of sandy clays. **Flowers visited** Pollen is gathered entirely from yellow hawkish composites such as Cat's-ear, Mouse-ear-hawkweed, hawk's-beards, hawkbits and dandelions. **Nesting habits** Nesting is usually in sandy ground, especially footpaths but also slopes and vertical banks. Very large nesting aggregations are occasionally reported. **Status & distribution** Widespread but generally scarce in England and Wales north to Cumbria, with records concentrated in heathland and coastal districts. Not recorded in Scotland. Very rare in Ireland. Only recorded from Sark in the Channel Islands. **Parasites & associates** The cleptoparasitic bee *Nomada integra*.

Andrena labialis (Kirby, 1802)   **Large Meadow Mining Bee**

Plate 6

Description & similar species FW 8–9mm female, 7.5–9mm male. A fairly large and robustly built, dull-looking *Andrena*. Females have a short dull brown pile on top of the densely punctate thorax and pale buff hairs on the face and legs. The tergites are also densely punctate and tergites 2–4 have buffish-white hair fringes along the hind margins (broken in the middle on 2 and 3). Males are one of several *Andrena* species with the surface of the face white or yellow but are easily distinguished by the extent of the yellow facial markings, which extend onto the sides of the face outside the boundaries of the clypeus as high as the level of the antennal insertions. **Variation** Moderate size variation in both sexes. Old males can become very sun-bleached with whitish hairs. **Flight season** Univoltine, flying from late April to mid-July. **Habitat** Legume-rich grasslands of various sorts (even species-poor pasture with clovers); also quarries and other brownfield sites, woodland rides and clearings. **Flowers visited** Pollen seems to be gathered entirely from legumes, including clovers (especially White Clover), vetches, bird's-foot-trefoils and Goat's-rue. **Nesting habits** Nesting is not often observed and seems to occur singly or in loose aggregations, probably favouring short turf or sparsely vegetated banks and slopes. It can tolerate quite heavy clays. **Status & distribution** Widespread but rather localised in southern England and the Midlands (rare in the southwest and East Anglia) with records extending north to Yorkshire. Rare in Wales and the Channel Islands (Sark). Not recorded from Scotland or Ireland. **Parasites & associates** The cleptoparasitic bee *Sphecodes rubicundus*; also the bee-fly *Bombylius major*. Occasionally stylopised.

female

male

Andrena labiata Fabricius, 1781   **Red-girdled Mining Bee**

Plate 6

Description & similar species FW 6–6.5mm (sexes similar). A medium-small *Andrena* with a bright red abdominal band in both sexes that extends from the hind margin of tergite 1 to the base of tergite 4. The tip of the abdomen is deep black and contrasts strongly with the red band. This creates the appearance of a large *Sphecodes*, though the obvious facial foveae of the female and conspicuous white face of the male allow easy separation. **Variation** Relatively little. **Flight season** Univoltine, flying from late March until late June. **Habitat** Unimproved grasslands of various sorts, heathland edge, quarries and brownfield sites, woodland edge, soft rock cliffs and occasionally urban greenspace and gardens. **Flowers visited** Often seen on Germander Speedwell and forget-me-nots but it will visit a variety of other flowers such as buttercups, stitchworts, Common Rock-rose, Hawthorns, roses and various composites, crucifers and legumes. **Nesting habits** Nesting occurs in short or sparse vegetation on a range of soils, sometimes in large aggregations. **Status & distribution** Widespread but generally scarce in the southern half of England. Old records extend north to Northumberland. Rare and mostly coastal in Wales. Not recorded from Scotland or Ireland. Recorded from several of the Channel Islands. **Parasites & associates** The cleptoparasitic bee *Nomada guttulata*.

Andrena lapponica Zetterstedt, 1838   **Bilberry Mining Bee**

Plate 3

Description & similar species FW 8.5–10mm female, 7.5–8mm male. The medium-sized females have a black-haired head, reddish-brown pile on top of the thorax and a mainly black abdomen with longer pale hairs on tergites 1 and 2. They closely resemble the typical form of *A. varians* (see that species for differences). *A. fucata* can also look rather similar in the field but has a mostly pale-haired face, pale hair fringes on the sternites and a much slimmer build. Males belong to a group of three species with a ventral projection at the base of very long mandibles, antennal segments 3 and 4 of similar length and only pale hairs on the propodeum. The very short fringes of white hairs on the hind margins of the sternites and relatively large mandibular projections allow easy separation from the other two (*A. fucata* and *A. helvola*). **Variation** Females are fairly constant in appearance. Males are rather variable in size. **Flight season** Univoltine, flying from early April to June in the south but often persisting until July in the north. It peaks with the flowering of Bilberry. **Habitat** Typically open-structured heathy woodland (both broadleaved and coniferous) where there is plentiful Bilberry, though in upland areas it will use upland heathland and moorland. **Flowers visited** Pollen is gathered primarily from *Vaccinium* species, typically Bilberry in the south but also Cowberry in the north, and occasionally Rhododendron. Foraging on hawthorns, Blackthorn, willows, dandelions, violets and Germander Speedwell has also been noted, possibly for nectar only. **Nesting habits** Nesting can occur singly or in loose aggregations, often along the edges of sandy woodland paths and tracks that get plenty of sunshine. **Status & distribution** Widespread but with a very patchy and localised distribution in England, Wales and Ireland. Fairly common in the Scottish Highlands. Only recorded from Herm in the Channel Islands. **Parasites & associates** The cleptoparasitic bee *Nomada panzeri* (a particularly dark form). The conopid fly *Myopa buccata* probably uses this species as one of its hosts.

Andrena lathyri Alfken, 1899   **Burbage Mining Bee**
not illustrated

Description & similar species FW 9–10mm female, 8.5–10mm male. The largest and rarest of a group also containing *A. ovatula*, *A. similis* and *A. wilkella*. Females of this group feature the combination of orange hind tibiae (except some *ovatula*), brown-haired thorax and white hair fringes on the hind margins of almost hairless and dull tergites 2–4. *A. lathyri* can be separated from the others by the deep, semicircular notch at the tip of the pygidium (which can sometimes be obscured by hairs), larger average size, longer and paler pile on the top of the thorax and very weak punctures on the tergites. Males resemble oversized *A. ovatula* and *A. wilkella* in having distinct hair fringes along the hind margins of tergites 2–4, but have antennal segment 3 clearly longer than segment 4 (segment 3 clearly shorter in the other two)

and less distinct punctures on tergite 1. **Variation** A little size variation. **Flight season** Univoltine, with British records extending from mid-May to early July. **Habitat** Legume-rich calcareous grasslands and woodland rides. The Burbage site is a disused railway. **Flowers visited** Pollen seems to be gathered primarily from legumes of the genera *Vicia* (e.g. Common, Bush and Tufted Vetches) and *Lathyrus* (e.g. Meadow Vetchling and everlasting-peas). Other flowers may be visited for nectar. **Nesting habits** Nesting typically occurs solitarily in light soils. **Status & distribution** Only known from two sites: Moorlinch, Somerset (1950), and Burbage, Wiltshire (1970–1990). Possibly extinct. **Parasites & associates** None known in Britain, but attacked by the non-British cleptoparasitic bee *Nomada villosa* abroad.

Andrena lepida Schenck, 1861 — Aldworth Mining Bee
not illustrated

Description & similar species FW 8mm female. Females superficially resemble *A. dorsata* and *A. congruens* but have the scutum fairly shiny with dense and obvious punctures and little microsculpture. The lateral hair fringes of tergites 2–4 are also larger, occupying almost the full depth of the apical depressions at the sides. The dorsal fringe of the hind tibiae viewed from the side is about one-third the greatest width of the tibia (compared to one-fifth the width in *A. dorsata* or equal to the tibial width in *A. congruens*). No males have been encountered in Britain but the

female

limited foreign material checked has the face dark-haired like *A. congruens* but with densely punctate tergites (including the apical depression) and a semi-shining, distinctly punctured scutum. The white hair bands across the hind margins of the tergites are composed of longer hairs than in *A. congruens*, and a further band of white hairs is present at the base of tergite 2. **Variation** Little noted. **Flight season** Bivoltine. British records are for May, July and August. **Habitat** Chalk grassland. **Flowers visited** The only British record is for Hogweed, but a variety of legumes, crucifers, umbellifers and spring-flowering shrubs are known to be used abroad. **Nesting habits** Little known but probably similar to species such as *A. dorsata*. **Status & distribution** Only three records: Aldworth, Berkshire (1931), Witchampton, Dorset (1951), and nearby Badbury Rings (1952). Possibly extinct. **Parasites & associates** None known.

Andrena marginata Fabricius, 1776 — Small Scabious Mining Bee
Plate 6

Description & similar species FW 7.5mm female, 6mm male. The medium-sized females can have the abdomen varying from entirely dark to entirely dull red from the hind margins of tergite 1 onwards. A full range of intermediates can occur, though the abdomen never has a sharply defined dark apex as in *A. labialis*. The top of the thorax has an obvious brown pile. The pollen brush of the hind tibiae is dark-haired. The scutum and tergites are polished and punctured, and there are only weak white fringes on the hind margins of the tergites. Males are one of a small number of *Andrena* species with the clypeus surface white or yellow-coloured and can be easily distinguished from the others by the outcurved points on the lower corners of the clypeus. A flange is present along the hind margin of the genae. **Variation** Primarily the colour of the female abdomen, as noted above. **Flight season** Univoltine, flying from mid-July to late September, with populations associated with Devil's-bit Scabious generally peaking later than populations using Small Scabious or Field Scabious. **Habitat** Scabious-rich habitats including chalk grassland, acid grassland, heathland, moorland, open

female, red form

female, black form

male

woodland and the stabilised parts of coastal dunes. **Flowers visited** Pollen is obtained almost exclusively from scabiouses, typically Field and Small Scabious in southern calcareous districts and Devil's-bit Scabious at more acidic sites (all of its northern sites plus a few southern ones too). The hind legs can be thick with the sticky pink or white pollen grains of these plants. Plants such as brambles, knapweeds, thistles, Meadowsweet and willowherbs may be nectar sources. **Nesting habits** Nesting occurs in light soils, both short turf/herbage and the bare ground of tracks, and on both flat and sloping areas. Aggregations of several hundred nests have been noted at strong colonies. **Status & distribution** Most records are for southern England north to Oxfordshire, Norfolk and Lincolnshire, plus south Wales. A further cluster of sites occurs in the Scottish Highlands and there also a couple of records from Co. Durham. Scattered records are present in Ireland. Not known from the Channel Islands. A severe decline has occurred almost everywhere. **Parasites & associates** The cleptoparasitic bee *Nomada argentata*.

Andrena nigriceps (Kirby, 1802) **Black-headed Mining Bee**

Plate 4

Description & similar species FW 7.5–9.5mm female, 7–8mm male. The medium-sized females are one of several species with hind tibiae that progressively broaden towards the tip (side view). They have an almost entirely black-haired head and a reddish pile on the top of the thorax which contrasts with an orange-buff pile below. Tergites 1–4 are densely buff-haired but with wedges of black hairs at the anterior corners of tergites 3 and 4 that help to create a banded appearance when the abdomen is extended. Tergite 5 is black-haired. The legs are entirely black- and grey-haired and the pollen brush of the hind legs is sooty-coloured. No other female *Andrena* matches this description, though *A. simillima* resembles an *A. nigriceps* with a pale-haired face and whitish scopae. Males have a white-haired face, reddish-brown pile on top of the thorax and a buff pile on the abdomen that produces weak

female

bands across the apical depressions of the tergites. The galeae are dulled by microsculpture. Males of *A. simillima* are very similar but have antennal segment 3 slightly longer than 4 (segment 3 at most as long as segment 4 in *A. nigriceps*) and tarsal segments 2–5 yellowish (reddish-brown in *A. nigriceps*). **Variation** Moderate size variation. The 'bandedness' of the female abdomen is quite variable, and not obvious in some. **Flight season** Univoltine, flying from late June to late September. **Habitat** Dry grassland, heathland, soft rock cliffs, coastal dunes and brownfield sites. **Flowers visited** Pollen is mainly gathered from composites such as thistles, ragworts, knapweeds and Tansy, though it will also visit Meadowsweet, brambles, Sheep's-bit, stonecrops, thymes, scabiouses, umbellifers and bedstraws probably for nectar only. **Nesting habits** Nesting occurs singly or in sparse aggregations in short turf or bare ground such as footpaths. **Status & distribution** A scarce species but with records scattered widely in England and Wales; also Ayrshire, Scotland. Not recorded from Ireland. Recorded from several of the Channel Islands. **Parasites & associates** The cleptoparasitic bee *Nomada rufipes*.

Andrena nigroaenea (Kirby, 1802)

Buffish Mining Bee

Plate 4

Description & similar species FW 10–10.5mm female, 8–10mm male. The Honey Bee-sized females have a dense brown pile on the top of the thorax and a paler buff pile on tergites 1–4 which contrasts with the black hairs of tergite 5. The hind tibiae are dark but have very dense and neat orange pollen brushes. The head is mostly black-haired. The most similar-looking species in the field is *A. tibialis*, but this has a greyer pile on the abdomen, the hind tibiae orange beneath the hairs and the top of the propodeum rugose. Males of *A. nigroaenea* are mainly brown-haired with black hairs across the clypeus and at the sides of the face. Males of *A. bimaculata* and *A. tibialis* can look similar in the field, but these have the top of the propodeum rugose and *A. tibialis* also has the tip of the hind tibiae orange. **Variation** Females can have the face entirely black-haired or partly brown-haired. Males are somewhat variable in size, and giant males with wing lengths to 11.5mm are occasionally

female

male

encountered. Females from the Channel Islands and Isles of Scilly can be much darker, with tergite 3 onwards mostly black-haired, patches of black hairs on the sides of the thorax and a darker tawny-brown pollen brush on their hind legs. These have been assigned to ssp. *sarnia*, though populations on the Channel Islands are variable and grade into more typical-looking individuals. **Flight season** Typically univoltine, with a long flight period, males appearing from mid-March and females sometimes lingering until late July, though the peak is April and May. There may be a partial second generation in some southern

female, Channel Islands

areas. **Habitat** Found in a great variety of habitats without any strong preferences. It is one of the more frequent mining bees of urban environments and intensively farmed landscapes. **Flowers visited** Much foraging is from blossoming shrubs such as willows, Gorse, Blackthorn, Hawthorn and fruit trees. It will also use herbaceous plants such as dandelions, hawk's-beards, umbellifers, crucifers, mignonettes, buttercups, Thrift and spurges. **Nesting habits** Nesting occurs in bare ground (e.g. footpaths and cliff faces), short-cropped turf and within the soft mortar of walls. It can form large dense nesting aggregations at some sites. It will sometimes nest in garden lawns and flowerbeds. **Status & distribution** One of the commonest mining bees of southern Britain and the Channel Islands but scarce in Scotland. Widespread in eastern Ireland. **Parasites & associates** The cleptoparasitic bees *Nomada goodeniana*, *N. marshamella* and, on the Channel Islands, *N. succincta*.

Andrena nigrospina Thomson, 1872   **Scarce Black Mining Bee**
Plate 5

Description & similar species FW 10.5–11.5mm female, 9.5–11mm male. One of two large *Andrena* species with almost entirely black females (white hairs are confined to the underside of the hind femora and tibiae). Females are scarcely distinguishable from *A. pilipes*, though the white hairs on the outer face of the hind tibiae tend to be more restricted and leave the dorsal fringe black-haired (usually a mix of black and pale hairs in *A. pilipes*). Date, habitat and any associated males and nomad bees can also give a strong indication of identity, and some *A. nigrospina* females can have the wings distinctly darkened.

female

male

Males are more readily distinguished from *A. pilipes* in having the top of the thorax, back of the head and tergites 1 and 2 grey-haired (rather than black- or brown-haired) and a longer antennal segment 4. They could potentially be confused with males of *A. cineraria* and *A. vaga* in the field but have the top of the propodeum rugose. **Variation** Relatively little. **Flight season** Univoltine (in contrast to the bivoltine *A. pilipes*). Males can emerge in late April and females can fly until mid-July, but most records are between late May and mid-July, peaking between the two generations of *A. pilipes*. **Habitat** Strongly association with sandy ground, especially in heathland districts, with the preferred foraging habitat being sandy arable land and other disturbed habitats with plentiful crucifers, though it will nest on heathland. There are also a few records for coastal areas, the normal domain of *A. pilipes*. **Flowers visited** Crucifers seem to be major pollen sources, with Wild Radish much used at some arable sites, and Rape and Hoary Mustard elsewhere. Some British pollen loads can contain a lot of Common Poppy pollen, and it will also take pollen from umbellifers (e.g. Hogweed), Rosaceae species (probably bramble) and Asteraceae (possibly hawk's-beards or Cat's-ear). Males have been observed swarming around Broom on several occasions but were not visiting the flowers. **Nesting habits** Nesting has been observed in sandy soil at the margins of arable fields and at the edges of sandy footpaths, in both flat and sloping ground. It will form loose nesting aggregations. The nest tumuli tend to be large for a mining bee. **Status & distribution** It is likely that most inland records for the *nigrospina–pilipes* complex (which tend to relate to May and June) refer to *A. nigrospina*. These suggest it was formerly widespread in southern England and has shown a catastrophic decline. Modern records are concentrated in the Worcestershire–Staffordshire border and brownfield sites of the Essex Thames Gateway, with a few further ones for Surrey, West Kent, the east Essex coast and Norfolk. Known from several of the Channel Islands but not from Wales, Scotland or Ireland. **Parasites & associates** The cleptoparasitic bee *Nomada subcornuta*.

Andrena nitida (Müller, 1776)   **Grey-patched Mining Bee**

Plate 4

Description & similar species FW 9.5–12.5mm female, 8.5–10mm male. Females average slightly larger than a Honey Bee and have a bright reddish pile on the top of the thorax that contrasts with the black, shiny abdomen. It most resembles *A. thoracica* but has patches of white hairs (which look grey in the field) at the sides of tergites 1–3, white-haired femora, a paler pile on the thorax and a face that is often substantially white-haired. Males have the face white-haired but with black hairs alongside the inner eye margins. The top of the thorax has a bright orange pile and the abdomen is polished black with distinct punctures.

146

Sparse bands of white hairs occur across the bases of tergites 2 and 3. **Variation** Moderate size variation and occasional giant males with wing length to 11mm. The female face varies from entirely black-haired to mainly white-haired. Older faded individuals acquire a dull brown thorax, and the pale hairs of the tergites can become abraded. **Flight season** Univoltine, with a long flight period that extends from late March to mid-July with a peak in April and May. **Habitat** Found in a wide range of situations with spring-blossoming shrubs and fairly dry soils, including fairly intensively farmed countryside and urban locations. **Flowers visited** Much foraging is from spring-blossoming shrubs such as willows, Gorse, Blackthorn, cherries, Hawthorn and maples. It will also visit herbaceous flowers such as umbellifers, dandelions, hawk's-beards, Colt's-foot, dead-nettles, speedwells, Rape and Raspberry. **Nesting habits** Nesting typically occurs in flat or sloping turf, including formal lawns and sheep-grazed hillsides. Nests are scattered rather than in aggregations. **Status & distribution** One of the commonest mining bees of southern Britain, with records extending north to Lancashire and Yorkshire. Not known from Scotland, Ireland or the Channel Islands. Note that this species is widely referred to as *A. pubescens* in recent literature. **Parasites & associates** The cleptoparasitic bee *Nomada goodeniana*. Occasionally stylopised.

Andrena nitidiuscula Schenck, 1853   **Carrot Mining Bee**

Plate 5

Description & similar species FW 6–6.5mm female, 5.5–6mm male. A rather small, dark-looking mining bee with white hair fringes along the hind margins of tergites 2–4. The pollen brushes of the hind tibiae are whitish-haired and the tergites are shiny with distinct punctures. *A. coitana* looks similar in the field but has the pollen brush longer and darker. A small *A. nitidiuscula* could also be confused with a mini-miner, but these mostly have much duller tergites and paler facial foveae, though confusion with the rare *A. nana* is possible (see key for distinctions). Males are not much larger than mini-miners but have

a proportionately slimmer thorax, a flange along the hind margin of each gena and tarsal segments 2–5 orange. The tergites are glossy with fine punctures on tergites 2–5 and white hair fringes on the hind margins of tergites 2–4. Antennal segment 3 is longer than 4. **Variation** Moderate size variation in the males. **Flight season** Univoltine, flying from June to September. **Habitat** Most records are from chalk downland and soft rock cliffs, though it can occur on heathland, coastal grazing marsh, vegetated shingle and in woodland rides and clearings. **Flowers visited** Pollen is obtained from umbellifers, especially Wild Carrot but also Upright Hedge-parsley and Wild Parsnip. Other flowers such as ragworts, brambles and melilots may be nectar sources. **Nesting habits** Nesting can occur solitarily or in small aggregations. **Status & distribution** Very scarce in southern England north to the Bristol area and Surrey. Unrecorded in Wales, Scotland, Ireland and the Channel Islands. **Parasites & associates** The cleptoparasitic bee *Nomada errans* (probably extinct), and possibly *N. rufipes* on Salisbury Plain.

Andrena ovatula (Kirby, 1802)   **Small Gorse Mining Bee**

Plate 6

Description & similar species FW 7–7.5mm female, 5–7mm male. The medium-sized females have a short brown pile on top of the thorax, an abdomen that is largely hairless but with white hair fringes along the hind margins of tergites 2–4, and usually orange or partially orange hind tibiae. They closely resemble small, dusky *A. wilkella*, but the abdomen is proportionately smaller with a brown-haired tip (orange-haired in *A. wilkella*). The top of the thorax has a darker pile and the white hair fringes of tergites 2–4 are better formed, with that of tergite 3 continuous (broken in *A. wilkella*). The hind tibiae and their pollen brushes are usually duller buff-orange and darkened at the base. The males have complete hair fringes on hind margins of both tergites 3 and 4 (only tergite 4 in *A. wilkella*), that of tergite 2 only narrowly broken in the middle (widely broken in *A. wilkella*). The antennae are relatively shorter than in *A. wilkella*, with the individual flagellar segments less elongate. **Variation** The hind tibiae of females vary from virtually all orange to entirely dark. Males vary somewhat in size, and some have the hind tibiae partially pale. **Flight season** Bivoltine, with a spring generation that flies from late March into early June and a second generation that can emerge by mid-June and persist until September. **Habitat** Various, but especially sandy and gravelly habitats with plentiful gorses such as heathland, coastal grassland and soft rock cliffs. Much less frequent in calcareous and clay districts than *A. wilkella*. **Flowers visited** Pollen is gathered mainly from legumes. Common Gorse appears to be especially important for the spring generation. Clovers, bird's-foot-trefoils and summer-flowering gorses are important for the second generation. Other plants such as willows, Blackthorn, heathers and brambles seem to be mainly nectar sources. **Nesting habits** Nesting can occur singly or in aggregations, usually along south-facing slopes. **Status & distribution** Locally common in coastal and heathland districts of southern England and south Wales but scarce in central and northern England with records extending sparingly north to Cumbria. Not recorded from Scotland or Ireland. Recorded from most of the Channel Islands. **Parasites & associates** Not parasitised by any cuckoo bees in Britain (attacked by *Nomada rhenana* on the continent). Occasionally stylopised.

female

male

Andrena pilipes Fabricius, 1781   **Black Mining Bee**
not illustrated

Description & similar species FW 10.5–11.5mm female, 9.5–11mm male. A large *Andrena*, one of two species with almost entirely black females (white hairs are confined to the underside of the hind femora and tibiae). Females are scarcely distinguishable from *A. nigrospina*, though the white hairs on the outer face of the hind tibiae are more extensive and are mixed with black hairs on the dorsal fringe (dorsal fringe largely black-haired in *A. nigrospina*). The wings tend to be paler. Date, habitat and associated males or nomad bees can also give a strong indication of identity. Males are more readily distinguished from *A. nigrospina* in having top of thorax, back of head and tergites 1 and 2 black- or brown-haired (grey-haired in *A. nigrospina*) and a shorter antennal segment 4. **Variation** The pile on top of the male thorax varies from black to brown. Females from Jersey can have pale grey hairs on face, around the shoulders and scutellum. **Flight season** A bivoltine species (in contrast to the univoltine *A. nigrospina*), with the first generation flying mainly in April and May and the second mainly in

July and August. **Habitat** Strongly associated with coastal cliffs (especially soft rock cliffs) and the flowery habitats near to these, though occurring inland on brownfield land and heathland/acid grassland in the Thames Gateway area. Blossoming scrub is crucial for the spring generation. **Flowers visited** The spring generation visits Blackthorn, willows, Thrift, spring umbellifers such as Alexanders and spring crucifers. The summer generation uses brambles and summer umbellifers such as Hogweed. **Nesting habits** Nesting typically occurs in cliff faces and south-facing slopes. Nesting aggregations can be large and sometimes mixed with other *Andrena* species such as *A. flavipes* and *A. thoracica*. **Status & distribution** Many old *pilipes–nigrospina* records have not been assigned but the true *A. pilipes* seems to be almost entirely coastal with a strong southern bias. For the most part it is scarce and localised, though some very strong populations occur in Devon and Cornwall and further hotspots occur in the Thames Gateway. A handful of Irish records exist and it is thought

female

male

to be univoltine here. Recorded from the Channel Islands (Jersey, Sark and Herm). **Parasites & associates** The cleptoparasitic bee *Nomada fulvicornis* and the conopid fly *Myopa buccata*.

Andrena polita Smith, 1847   **Maidstone Mining Bee**
not illustrated

Description & similar species FW 9–10mm female, 9–9.5mm male. Females are about the size of *A. haemorrhoa* and most resemble a large *A. humilis*, sharing with this species the presence of yellow-buff hairs on the pollen brush of the hind tibiae and at the tip of the abdomen, though in *A. polita* the apical depressions of tergites 2–4 are translucent brownish and bear more obvious pale hair fringes. The thorax is also longer-haired and the facial foveae almost white. Males rather resemble oversized *A. haemorrhoa* but have dark hind tibiae, antennal segment 3 much longer than segment 4, and lack a rugose zone at the top of the propodeum. **Variation** Little noted. **Flight season** Univoltine, flying from late May to late August on the

149

female

male

continent. **Habitat** British records include chalk downland and chalk pits. **Flowers visited** Pollen is gathered entirely from composites, including Chicory, oxtongues and various hawkish types. Other flowers may be visited for nectar. **Nesting habits** On the continent, it is recorded nesting in small aggregations on slopes. **Status & distribution** Only ever known in Britain and Ireland from two sites in Kent: Northfleet Chalkpits and Upper Halling. Last recorded in Britain from the latter site in 1934. **Parasites & associates** None known in Britain, but attacked by the non-British cleptoparasitic bee *Nomada pleurosticta* abroad.

Andrena praecox (Scopoli, 1763)   **Small Sallow Mining Bee**

Plate 3

Description & similar species FW 9–9.5mm female, 6.5–8.5mm male. Females are medium-sized, rather furry-looking with a buff-haired abdomen and reddish-brown pile on the thorax. They are relatively easy to distinguish from other spring-flying mining bees in the field. *A. apicata* is most similar but is rather larger and has black hairs on tergite 5 and the apical depression of tergite 4 (brown-haired in *A. praecox*). The big-headed, long-jawed males have the combination of a large projection at the base of the mandibles and black hairs arising from the sides of the propodeum. They can be separated from the very similar males of *A. apicata* by the pale hairs on tergites 3 and 4 (black in *A. apicata*), the blunter projection on the base of the mandibles, and the notched tip to the projection of sternite 8 (straight-ended in *A. apicata*). **Variation** Females are fairly constant in appearance, though they can fade very pale towards the end of their flight season. Males vary greatly in size, and, unlike females, size is not a reliable separator of *A. praecox* from *A. apicata*. Larger males are proportionately much bigger-headed than small ones. **Flight season** Univoltine, with males appearing in late February in some years and females often persisting well into May.

female

male

Populations peak with the blossoming of pussy-willow. **Habitat** Various willow-rich locations, including open woodland, heathland, quarries, sandpits and other brownfield sites. It can use a range of soil types but is often especially abundant on clays. **Flowers visited** Pollen is gathered primarily from short-leaved willows, typically Grey Willow and Goat Willow, though Eared Willow and longer-leaved willows (even Weeping Willow) can also be used at some sites. **Nesting habits** Nesting occurs in light soils, especially on south-facing slopes. It can form loose but extensive nesting aggregations at some sites. **Status & distribution** Widespread but localised in England and Wales north to southern Scotland. It seems to have increased in abundance in areas such as the Midlands. Scattered Irish localities exist, mostly in the southeast. Not recorded from the Channel Islands. **Parasites & associates** The cleptoparasitic bee *Nomada ferruginata*. The early-flying conopid fly *Myopa vicaria* seems to target *A. praecox* at some sites. Rarely stylopised.

Andrena proxima (Kirby, 1802)   **Broad-faced Mining Bee**
Plate 6

Description & similar species FW 7.5–8.5mm female, 6–7.5mm male. The medium-small, rather slim females have an inconspicuous brown pile on top of the coarsely punctate thorax and almost bare, semi-shining tergites with white lateral hair fringes on the hind margins of tergites 2–4. Those of tergites 2 and 3 are most conspicuous, giving the impression of four rectangular spots. The bases of tergites 2 and 3 are dulled by microsculpture with very weak punctures and a slight bloom but the apical depressions are more strongly shining. Tergite 1 is unusual in having a slight apical depression demarcated by a transverse band of punctures. The head is unusually transverse in top view, and the hind tibiae are black with the pollen brush mostly straw-coloured. Males resemble small slim females but have more obvious punctures on the tergites. Tergites 2–4 have white hair fringes on the hind margins. The apical depression of tergite 1 is polished and almost puncture-free. The scutum has densely packed, shallow punctures that resemble moon craters. Both sexes have the propodeum unusually rough throughout, the wings disproportionately long for the size of the bee and the head very broad in front view. **Variation** Two forms appear to be present, with females from chalk and limestone areas of central and southeast England less elongate than those from southwest England, with the scutum much dulled by microsculpture between the punctures and duller apical depressions of tergites 2–4. Males of the two forms are more similar but can also be distinguished by the shininess of the scutum. The taxonomic status of the two forms requires further investigation. **Flight season** Univoltine, flying from May to July. **Habitat** Various umbellifer-rich habitats, including chalk grassland, coastal grassland, soft rock cliffs, quarries and sometimes coastal grazing marsh. **Flowers visited** Pollen seems to be obtained entirely from umbellifers, e.g. Cow Parsley, Hemlock Water-dropwort, Hogweed, Alexanders and Ground-elder. Other species such as Hawthorn and spurges may be nectar sources. **Nesting habits** Nesting seems to occur typically in very short turf or sparsely vegetated areas on south-facing slopes. **Status & distribution** A scarce southern species recorded as far north as Shropshire but with the majority of records in southeast England and along the south coast. It seems to be increasing in southeast England and the Midlands. Only recorded from Jersey in the Channel Islands. Not recorded from Wales, Scotland or Ireland. **Parasites & associates** The cleptoparasitic bee *Nomada conjungens*.

female

Andrena rosae Panzer, 1801   Perkins' Mining Bee

Plate 4

Description & similar species FW 9.5–11mm female, 7.5–9.5mm male. Females are structurally close to *A. scotica* and *A. trimmerana* (small flocci, tergites dulled by microsculpture) but average smaller. They are very variable in appearance; some having the abdomen conspicuously red-banded (especially those of the spring generation) but others are very dark (especially the summer generation). The darkest females resemble *A. trimmerana* in having only the extreme sides of tergites 1 and 2 and the basal sternites red, but they have a shorter pile on the thorax and an extremely short and dark pile on tergites 2–4. Dark individuals can also resemble *A. bimaculata* but have much smaller flocci, lack punctures on the scutum and lack a rugose area at the top of the propodeum. Males are equally variable. Those of the spring generation have a well-developed genal spine, and whilst most of them are conspicuously red-banded, dark ones could be overlooked as *A. trimmerana*, though the mandibles have a distinct tooth at the apex (mandibles simple in *A. trimmerana*). Summer males lack a genal spine and some have a red-banded abdomen, though others are very dark with red restricted to the sides of tergites 1 and 2. These have a shorter body pile than *A. trimmerana* and the hind tibiae are entirely dark (tips usually pale in *A. trimmerana*). **Variation** Highly variable as noted above, with spring individuals of both sexes usually more extensively red-marked. The two generations are still considered separate species (*A. stragulata* and *A. rosae*) by some foreign workers, but the brood dimorphism is equivalent to that seen in the related *A. trimmerana* and the two forms have broadly similar distributions with many sites in common. **Flight season** Bivoltine, the first generation flying from late March to late May, the second from mid-July to early September. **Habitat** Typically exposed coastal scrublands and cliffs, also moorland settings high up on Dartmoor, suggesting it may favour harsher maritime climates. **Flowers visited** The spring generation forages mainly on Blackthorn and willows. The summer generation is thought to obtain pollen only from umbellifers (e.g. Hogweed, Wild Carrot, Wild Angelica and Sea-holly), though it will also visit brambles and thistles for nectar.

female, spring

Nesting habits Little known. **Status & distribution** Very rare, with recent records confined to a few sites in Cornwall, Devon, Kent and Oxfordshire. Older records exist for Hampshire, Surrey, the Bristol area, south Wales and Co. Carlow, Ireland. Not recorded from Scotland or the Channel Islands. **Parasites & associates** Possibly the cleptoparasitic bee *Nomada marshamella*.

female, summer

male, spring

Andrena ruficrus Nylander, 1848   Northern Mining Bee
not illustrated

Description & similar species FW 8mm female, 7mm male. Females are a similar size to *A. bicolor* and *A. angustior* but have the hind tibiae clear orange, the tergites almost bare, and a long, dense thoracic pile which is brownish on top but conspicuously whitish on the sides. There is also conspicuous white hairing on the face, genae and femora. The scutum is very dull with inconspicuous punctures. Males are rather nondescript and dark grey-brown with the face and lower genae densely white-haired. Zones of black hairs occur alongside the inner eye margins and at the tops of the genae. Blackish hairs are present on the scutellum and propodeum, and males could thus be mistaken for *A. praecox*, though the mandibles are much shorter and lack a projection at their base below. The hind tarsi and tips of the hind tibiae are dusky orange. The tergites are entirely dulled by microsculpture and lack any obvious punctures. **Variation** Seemingly little. **Flight season** Univoltine, flying from mid-March to late May and occasionally into June, peaking with the blossoming of willows. **Habitat** Assorted willow-rich habitats, including heathland, moorland edge, open woodland and brownfield sites. **Flowers visited** Pollen is gathered almost entirely from willows of various species. Dandelions seem to be used as a nectar source but may provide a supplementary pollen source at some sites. **Nesting habits** Nesting occurs in bare or sparsely vegetated sandy ground including banks and the bases of tree trunks. It can produce small nesting aggregations. **Status & distribution** A northern-biased species which is widespread but highly localised in Scotland and parts of northern England (Yorkshire and Cumbria). **Parasites & associates** None known in Britain, but on the continent attacked by the cleptoparasitic bee *Nomada obscura*.

female

male

Andrena scotica Perkins, 1916   Chocolate Mining Bee
Plate 3

Description & similar species FW 9.5–10.5mm female, 7.5–9.5mm male. The Honey Bee-sized females resemble several other species, notably *A. trimmerana* and the darkest forms of *A. rosae*, sharing with these two species a dull, weakly punctate abdomen and much reduced flocci. The completely black sides of tergites 1 and 2 distinguish *A. scotica* from these, and the body pile is longer than in *A. rosae*. Fresh females have a brown-haired abdomen and slightly redder-brown thorax and tend to look darker and more chocolate-coloured in the field than *A. trimmerana*, *A. apicata* and *A. bimaculata* (the latter two with large flocci). Males belong to a group of three species with relatively long antennae where antennal segment 4 is about twice as long as segment 3, but they never have red at the sides of tergites

1 and 2 or on the basal sternites (in contrast to *A. trimmerana* and *A. rosae*). They typically also lack the long genal spine that characterises spring males of *A. trimmerana* and *A. rosae*, and they have a subapical tooth on the mandibles (missing in spring *A. trimmerana*). **Variation** Northern females tend to have more extensive black hairs on the abdomen and face. Second-generation females also tend to look darker than spring ones and have a slightly shorter body pile, though they still remain longer-haired than the darkest *A. rosae*. Males can vary substantially in size, and giants with a wing length of 10.5mm are occasionally encountered. Males occasionally have a medium-sized genal spine but can be separated from spring *A. trimmerana* males by the toothed mandibles, and they are darker and longer-haired than spring *A. rosae*. **Flight season** Typically univoltine, flying from mid-March to July (later in the north), peaking with the blossoming of Blackthorn and hawthorns. A partial second generation

can occur in some southern districts, with males appearing as early as mid-June and females persisting into August. **Habitat** Various blossom-rich habitats, including open and wooded, acidic and base-rich, rural and urban. This is one of the more frequent mining bees of gardens and intensively farmed landscapes. **Flowers visited** A wide variety of blossoming shrubs and flowers, notably willows, Blackthorn, hawthorns, fruit trees, maples, umbellifers, dandelions, hawk's-beards and crucifers such as Rape. The second generation likes brambles and umbellifers. **Nesting habits** Nesting can occur singly or in loose aggregations, often amongst vegetation and leaf litter on sunlit banks and slopes, the location sometimes best revealed by the presence of its nomad bees. Several females will sometimes share a common nest entrance. **Status & distribution** One of our commonest mining bees, found throughout Britain and Ireland, the Channel Islands and many of the other larger offshore islands. Note that this species has been known as *A. carantonica* in recent literature and has also been known as *A. jacobi*. In much older literature it was regarded as a variety of *A. trimmerana*, so old records need to be treated with caution. **Parasites & associates** The cleptoparasitic bees *Nomada flava* and *N. marshamella*, also the bee-fly *Bombylius major*. This is one of the most frequently stylopised bees, with infected intersexes common in some populations.

Andrena similis Smith, 1849   **Red-backed Mining Bee**

Plate 6

Description & similar species FW 7.5–8.5mm female, 7.5–8mm male. A medium-sized *Andrena* with females that can resemble oversized *A. dorsata* or *A. congruens* in the field owing to the reddish pile on the top of the thorax (which is especially dense around the scutellum), but the hind tibiae are orange beneath the orange hairs and the tip of the abdomen is orange-haired. *A. wilkella* and *A. ovatula* are also similar but average smaller, with a brownish thoracic pile and the white hair fringes of tergites 2 and 3 less widely separated in the middle. Males also resemble *A. ovatula* and *A. wilkella* but have the whitish hair fringes

female

of tergites 2–4 restricted to the extreme sides of the tergites and very inconspicuous, antennal segment 3 about as long as segment 4 (segment 3 usually shorter than segment 4 in the other two), and the hind basitarsi and tips of the hind tibiae are orange. **Variation** Relatively little. **Flight season** Univoltine, flying from late April to late June. **Habitat** Various legume-rich habitats including calcareous grassland, gorse-clad hillsides, heathland edge, brownfield sites, soft rock cliffs and woodland rides. **Flowers visited** Pollen is gathered mainly from legumes, including Common Gorse, clovers and bird's-foot-trefoils. Other plants such as spring-blossoming shrubs and trees, dandelions, fumitories, speedwells and Ground-ivy seem to act as nectar sources. **Nesting habits** Nesting can occur singly or in large aggregations but has rarely been observed in Britain. **Status & distribution** Scarce but widespread in the southern half of Britain north to Yorkshire. A cluster of further records occurs in the northern Highlands region of Scotland. Not recorded from Ireland or the Channel Islands. Rarely ever numerous at a site and seemingly much declined in southeast England. **Parasites & associates** Occasionally stylopised.

Andrena simillima Smith, 1851   **Buff-banded Mining Bee**

not illustrated

Description & similar species FW 8.5–9.5mm female, 7–7.5mm male. The medium-sized females most resemble *A. nigriceps* but the face, flocci and most other parts of the legs are pale-haired with few if any dark hairs at the anterior corners of the tergites. Compared with *A. fuscipes*, it is a larger, much more densely hairy species with a redder pile on top of the thorax and a duller scutum. *A. tridentata* is also similar but has the tip of the abdomen pale-haired. Males closely resemble *A. nigriceps* but have antennal segment 3 distinctly longer than 4 when viewed from above (segment 3 at most slightly longer than segment 4 in *A. nigriceps*) and tarsal segments 2–5 yellowish (reddish-brown in *A. nigriceps*). Records are best based on females. **Variation** As in *A. nigriceps*, the 'bandedness' of the female abdomen is quite variable and more obvious when the abdomen is distended. **Flight season** Univoltine, flying in July and August. **Habitat** The few British records include soft rock cliffs, cliff-top grassland, heathland and chalk grassland. **Flowers visited** Records include thistles, knapweeds, Common Fleabane, Hemp-agrimony, brambles and Wild Marjoram. **Nesting habits** Rarely observed but thought to nest singly, especially in sparsely vegetated south-facing banks and slopes. **Status & distribution** A very rare species with a few recent records from the Salisbury Plain/north Hampshire area and coasts of Cornwall. Older records exist for the coasts of Devon, Dorset and Kent. Not recorded from Wales, Scotland, Ireland or the Channel Islands. Considered by some to be a form of *A. nigriceps*. **Parasites & associates** The cleptoparasitic bee *Nomada rufipes*.

female

Andrena synadelpha Perkins, 1914   **Broad-margined Mining Bee**

Plate 3

Description & similar species FW 8.5–9.5mm female, 6.5–7.5mm male. Typical females are similar in appearance to *A. helvola* but have the hairs of the hind tibiae dark, and the face is usually partially or entirely dark-haired too (always pale-haired in *A. helvola*). They also closely resemble form *mixta* of *A. varians* but can be separated by checking the apical depressions of tergites 3 and 4, which in *A. synadelpha* almost fill the entire surface of these tergites without the usual defining ridge running across the middle. The long-jawed males superficially resemble species such as *A. helvola*, *A. fucata* and *A. lapponica* but lack a projection at

female, typical

the base of the mandibles. In this regard they resemble *A. varians* but can be distinguished by the presence of black hairs along the inner eye margins and the very large apical depressions of the tergites (as in females). **Variation** The female face varies from black-haired to mainly pale-haired. Males vary in size, and large ones tend to have a more robust build. Channel Island females and occasionally mainland ones can have tergites 3 and 4 mainly black-haired. These resemble *A. varians* but look furrier and can be separated by the much broader apical depressions of tergites 3 and 4. **Flight season** Univoltine, flying from mid-April until late June. **Habitat** Particularly associated with heathland edge and open heathy woods but also found on coastal scrub, downland, well-hedged farmland and sometimes urban habitats.

female, dark

Flowers visited Records include Blackthorn, hawthorns, willows, maples, roses, Gorse, Broom, Holly, Raspberry, various umbellifers, Wood Spurge and dandelions. **Nesting habits** Nesting has rarely been observed but seems to occur singly or in loose aggregations in locations such as sunny south-facing banks. **Status & distribution** Widespread but generally scarce in the southern half of Britain, though rare in Wales and southwest England. Very rare in Scotland. Not recorded from Ireland. Recorded from most of the Channel Islands. **Parasites & associates** The cleptoparasitic bee *Nomada panzeri*. Occasionally stylopised.

Andrena tarsata Nylander, 1848   **Tormentil Mining Bee**

Plate 5

Description & similar species FW 6–7.5mm female, 6–6.5mm male. The smallish females are easily distinguished by the combination of orange hind tibiae and tarsi and a thorax that is partially black-haired above with dense, pale grey hair fringes on either side of the propodeum. The tergites are shiny black with rather weak white hair fringes along the hind margins of tergites 1–4. Females have a three-toothed mandible, a unique feature within the genus. Males are one of several *Andrena* species with the surface of the clypeus white or yellow, but can be distinguished from the others by the presence of black hairs on top of the thorax and the partly orange tarsi. Both the thorax and the abdomen are shiny with fine but distinct punctures. Males of *A. coitana* are somewhat similar but have the whitish facial markings extending outside the clypeus onto the lower face beside the eyes. **Variation** Relatively little. **Flight season** Univoltine, flying from mid-June to late August. **Habitat** Typically heathland, moorland, heathy woodland rides and clearings, plus quarries and brownfield sites with base-poor rocks or soils. It also occurs in gardens in the Scottish Highlands in association with cultivated Shrubby Cinquefoil. **Flowers visited** Pollen is typically gathered from Tormentil though it can use related species such as Shrubby Cinquefoil. It will also visit brambles, Harebell, heathers, Wild Angelica and Yarrow, possibly just for nectar. Foraging is unusually rapid for a mining bee. **Nesting habits** Nesting occurs in light, sparsely vegetated soils, with a preference for south-facing slopes. It can nest singly or in compact aggregations. **Status & distribution** Widely recorded in heathland and moorland districts of England,

Wales, Scotland and Ireland but scarce and much declined in many areas. Not recorded from the Channel Islands. **Parasites & associates** The cleptoparasitic bee *Nomada roberjeotiana* and possibly also *N. obtusifrons* at some Scottish sites. Occasionally stylopised.

Andrena thoracica (Fabricius, 1775)   Cliff Mining Bee

Plate 4

Description & similar species FW 10–12mm female, 9.5–11mm male. Females are slightly larger than a Honey Bee with a deep reddish pile on the top of the thorax, the head and legs completely black-haired, and a shiny black abdomen that appears almost naked. *A. nitida* is the most similar-looking species but has a slightly paler thorax, patches of pale hairs at the sides of tergites 1–3, and the legs partially white-haired. Males resemble small, slim females. **Variation** Older faded individuals of both sexes can acquire a dull brown thorax, and old females can resemble *A. nitida* in the field. **Flight season** Bivoltine, with males of

the spring generation sometimes emerging as early as February and females lingering into May. The summer generation appears in late June and can fly until late August. **Habitat** Strongly associated with coastal habitat (especially soft rock cliffs) and other flowery habitats nearby. It can also occur on heathland, in sandpits and at other sandy sites inland. **Flowers visited** A variety of flowers are visited, including spring-flowering shrubs such as Blackthorn and willows, dandelions and various summer-flowering herbaceous species such as Hogweed, Hemlock Water-dropwort, Common Ragwort and thistles. **Nesting habits** This species can form large dense nesting aggregations, especially in vertical cliff faces but sometimes flatter areas. **Status & distribution** Most records are from coastal districts of southern Britain from north Wales to Norfolk, with an old record for the Yorkshire coast. Inland, it is largely confined to heathland districts of counties such as Surrey, Norfolk and Staffordshire. Not recorded from Scotland or Ireland. Recorded from many of the Channel Islands. **Parasites & associates** The cleptoparasitic bee *Nomada goodeniana*.

Andrena tibialis (Kirby, 1802)   Grey-gastered Mining Bee

Plate 5

Description & similar species FW 10–12mm female, 9.5–10.5mm male. Females are Honey Bee-sized or slightly larger and rather resemble *A. nigroaenea* in the field due to the orange pollen brush on the hind tibiae. However, the underlying tibiae are orange not dark, the abdomen has a grey rather than buff pile (contrasting more strongly with the brown-haired thorax) and the facial hairs are white not brown or black. *A. tibialis* also has the top of the propodeum rugose and the scutum punctate, characters it shares with *A. bimaculata* (a slightly smaller, browner species, with the hind tibiae dark beneath the hairs and often red markings on the sides of tergites 1 and 2). Males of *A. tibialis* have a dark-haired face and also resemble *A. nigroaenea* but have the tips of the hind tibiae orange and the top of the propodeum rugose. Males of *A. bimaculata* are also similar to *A. tibialis* but have the hind tibiae dark at the tip and often have red markings on the basal tergites. **Variation** The orange hind tibiae of some females can be somewhat darkened in the basal half. Males are fairly constant in appearance. **Flight season** Univoltine, flying from mid-March to late May or occasionally early June, peaking in April and May. A few July records suggest that a partial second brood may be attempted. **Habitat** A variety of sites on light soils can be used, including heathland, quarries, sandpits and other brownfield sites, chalk grassland and occasionally gardens. **Flowers visited** Much foraging is from spring-blossoming shrubs such as willows, hawthorns, Gorse and *Prunus* species, though it will use herbaceous

female

species such as dandelions, Colt's-foot and *Brassica* species. **Nesting habits** Rarely observed, but probably sparsely vegetated dry ground such as south-facing slopes and the edges of footpaths. **Status & distribution** Widespread but very localised in England north to Yorkshire and seemingly absent from the southwest. Not recorded from Wales, Scotland, Ireland or the Channel Islands. **Parasites & associates** A univoltine form of the cleptoparasitic bee *Nomada fulvicornis*. Occasionally stylopised.

Andrena tridentata (Kirby, 1802) **Pale-tailed Mining Bee**
not illustrated

Description & similar species FW 7.5mm female, 7mm male. Females most resemble *A. fuscipes* and *A. simillima*, sharing with these the rather broad, triangular hind tibiae that broaden progressively to their tip (in side view). They differ in having tergite 5 entirely buff-haired (dark-haired in the other two), which creates a very uniformly buff appearance, but beware old, faded specimens of the others. Males resemble *A. simillima* and *A. nigriceps* but have a flange along the hind margin of each gena as in *A. denticulata*. **Variation** Little noted. **Flight season** Univoltine, with British records for June and July. **Habitat** Dry heathland and sandy grassland. **Flowers visited** The few records include Smooth Hawk's-beard, Common Ragwort and Purple Loosestrife. **Nesting habits** Not observed, but probably singly in sandy ground. **Status & distribution** Confirmed records are confined to the Dorset heaths and the Suffolk Brecks. It was last seen in 1969 (Durlston Head, Dorset) and may be extinct. **Parasites & associates** None known.

Andrena trimmerana (Kirby, 1802) **Trimmer's Mining Bee**
Plate 4

Description & similar species FW 9.5–11mm female, 8–9.5mm male. Females resemble *A. scotica* (alongside which it usually flies in spring) but have reddish markings at the sides of tergites 1 and 2 and on the basal sternites, paler apical depressions of the tergites (making the abdomen appear slightly banded), and spring females also have a longer, paler body pile. Dark summer females of *A. rosae* can resemble *A. trimmerana* but have a shorter body pile, especially on tergites 2 and 3. Males of *A. trimmerana* are one of three *Andrena* species with antennal segment 3 about half the length of segment 4 (*A. scotica* and *A. rosae* are the others), but the spring brood has the combination of long genal spines coupled with simple, untoothed mandibles. This combination is only otherwise seen in *A. ferox* (which has antennal segment 3 about two-fifths as long as segment 4 and the hind tibiae mostly orange). Spring *A. rosae* also has long genal spines but the mandibles have a subapical tooth and the abdomen usually has a conspicuous red band. Summer *A. trimmerana* males lack the genal spine and have shorter mandibles with a subapical tooth on the mandibles. They tend to have the basal tergites and sternites more extensively red than in spring and are occasionally red-banded like *A. rosae*, though the band is never as bright, the body pile is much longer everywhere, and the hind tibiae have a pale tip (hind tibiae all

male mandibles, spring

male mandibles, summer

female, spring

male, spring

male, summer

dark in *A. rosae*). It is perhaps not surprising that the two generations have been treated as distinct species by some workers until quite recently. **Variation** Considerable seasonal dimorphism as described above, notably in relation to the male mandibles (much longer and untoothed apically in the spring generation), male genal spines (absent in the summer generation) and the extent of red on abdomen of both sexes (usually greater in the summer generation). Both sexes of the spring generation have a longer body pile than the summer one, and spring males tend to have a black-haired face (typically brown-haired in summer males). The spring generation used to be treated as a separate species, *A. spinigera*. **Flight season** Bivoltine, with a spring generation that flies from mid-March to May and occasionally June. The summer generation can appear from late June and persist into September. **Habitat** Many blossom-rich habitats are exploited but it can be especially common in coastal areas (especially in association with coastal scrub and soft rock cliffs) and on chalk downland. It is much less frequent in gardens and other urban habitats than *A. scotica* but can use a variety of brownfield sites. **Flowers visited** The spring generation forages mainly on Blackthorn, willows and Gorse but will also visit dandelions, Alexanders, Lesser Celandine and fruit trees such as plums. The summer generation mostly forages on brambles, umbellifers, thistles and mignonettes. **Nesting habits** Nesting can occur singly or in loose aggregations, typically on south-facing slopes but also alongside paths and tracks. **Status & distribution** Common in some southern coastal districts, but much scarcer elsewhere, with records extending thinly into Wales and north to Cumbria. Very rare in Ireland. Present on several of the Channel Islands. It appears to have increased within the Midlands in recent decades. Old literature records need to be treated with caution, given the nomenclatural confusion between this species, *A. scotica* and *A. rosae*. **Parasites & associates** Probably one of the hosts of the cleptoparasitic bee *Nomada marshamella*. Occasionally stylopised.

Andrena vaga Panzer, 1799   **Grey-backed Mining Bee**

not illustrated

Description & similar species FW 11–12.5mm female, 8.5–11.5mm male. Females rather resemble *A. cineraria* but are somewhat larger, with the thorax entirely grey-haired (with a slight hint of buff) and white-haired flocci and hind femora. The abdomen is shiny black with some white hairs laterally (as in *A. nitida*). Males also resemble *A. cineraria* but have a rather broader abdomen and extensively pale-haired legs, and they lack any black hairs on the top of the thorax. In side view, the tip of the abdomen is more strongly downcurved. Old sun-bleached individuals of *A. nitida* and *A. clarkella* can look similar but will usually have very frayed wing edges. **Variation** Males vary substantially in size, and giant males are frequent. **Flight season** A univoltine, spring-flying species that peaks with the blossoming of the pussy-willow. All British records are for April, though it will fly from mid-March to mid-May on the continent. **Habitat** A variety of willow-rich habitats on light soils are used. **Flowers visited** Pollen is gathered entirely from willows of various species. **Nesting habits** Nesting occurs in both slopes and flat areas, and some huge nesting aggregations have been noted abroad. The nest tumuli are particularly large. **Status & distribution** Until recently known only from three pre-1947 records within Kent and Sussex. Since 2010 it has been found at several new sites in Hampshire and Kent, possibly representing recent recolonisation from the continent. **Parasites & associates** The cleptoparasitic bee *Nomada lathburiana*.

Andrena varians (Kirby, 1802)

Plate 3

Blackthorn Mining Bee

Description & similar species FW 9–10mm female, 6.5–8mm male. Females closely resemble *A. lapponica* but have a much denser, orange-brown pile on tergites 1 and 2, denser punctures on tergite 1, duller apical depressions and a slightly slimmer build. Form *mixta* is a very different-looking form (originally treated as a separate species) with tergites 3 and 4 pale-haired and often a mainly white-haired face (black-haired in the normal form). This form closely resembles *A. synadelpha* but has the apical depressions of tergites 3 and 4 well separated from the base of the tergites. The long-jawed males superficially resemble species such as *A. helvola*, *A. fucata* and *A. lapponica* but lack a projection at the base of the mandibles. In this regard they resemble *A. synadelpha* but can be distinguished by the absence of any black hairs along the inner eye margins and the less extensive apical depressions of the tergites (as in the females). **Variation** The very different form *mixta* is noted above, and it is possible to find a full range of intermediates between this and the typical form. Males vary in size, and large ones tend to have a more robust build. **Flight season** Univoltine, flying from late March until June and occasionally into July. It tends to peak with the Blackthorn blossom. **Habitat** Various habitats where Blackthorn and fruit trees are plentiful, including downland, heathland edge, old quarries, coastal scrub, woodland edge, well-hedged farmland, orchards and occasionally gardens. **Flowers visited** Pollen seems to be gathered primarily from *Prunus* species such as Blackthorn and various sorts of plum (both feral and cultivated). Apples, pears, Hawthorn and naturalised cotoneasters are also visited, whilst herbaceous plants such as dandelions, Colt's-foot and umbellifers are probably just nectar sources. **Nesting habits** Nesting can occur singly or in loose aggregations, in both bare ground and short-cropped turf, with south-facing slopes preferred. **Status & distribution** Widespread but generally scarce in England north to Yorkshire and showing a substantial decline in some areas. Very rare in Wales and southwest England. Modern hotspots include areas such as the Sussex South Downs. Not recorded from Scotland or Ireland. Recorded from Jersey and Guernsey in the Channel islands. **Parasites & associates** The cleptoparasitic bee *Nomada panzeri*. Occasionally stylopised.

Andrena wilkella (Kirby, 1802)   **Wilke's Mining Bee**

Plate 6

Description & similar species FW 7–8mm (sexes similar). A medium-sized *Andrena* with females that closely resemble *A. ovatula* but average slightly larger with the abdomen proportionally bigger. They also have the tip of the abdomen orange- rather than brown-haired, a paler brown pile on top of the thorax and the white hair fringe of tergite 3 broken in the middle. The hind tibiae and their pollen brushes are usually brighter orange. *A. similis* is similar but larger with a redder pile on top of the thorax and the white hair fringes of tergite 3 more widely separated. The males of *A. wilkella* closely resemble *A. ovatula*, but the white hair fringe of tergite 3 is broken in the middle, and that of tergite 2 is much more widely broken than in *A. ovatula*. The antennae are also relatively longer, with the individual flagellar segments more elongate. **Variation** Relatively little in females though males vary somewhat in size and old ones can become very sun-bleached and silvery. **Flight season** Univoltine, flying from late April to early July, peaking in May and June, usually between the two generations of *A. ovatula*. Occasional records for late July and August may represent a partial second brood. **Habitat** Legume-rich grasslands (even quite improved clover leys), heathland/acid grassland, brownfield sites, soft rock cliffs, coastal dunes and occasionally gardens and open woodland. **Flowers visited** Pollen is gathered mainly from legumes, including clovers, bird's-foot-trefoils, vetches, gorses, Broom and melilots. Other plants such as composites, umbellifers and spurges seem to act as nectar sources. **Nesting habits** Nesting can occur singly or in large aggregations. A range of soils can be used, including quite heavy clays. **Status & distribution** Widespread and locally common over much of England but scarcer in Wales, Scotland and Ireland. Recorded from most of the larger Channel Islands. **Parasites & associates** The cleptoparasitic bee *Nomada striata*. Often stylopised.

female

male

MINI-MINERS

A particularly discrete group within *Andrena* (subgenus *Micrandrena*) that is separated out here to allow easier comparison. Most species have a wing length no greater than 5.5mm, and only very rarely does a dwarf of any of the other *Andrena* species come close to this. Mini-miners are the most challenging section of *Andrena* and identification relies heavily on having reliably named comparative material to hand. In the absence of this, microscope images on the author's web feature

A typical mini-miner, *Andrena minutuloides* (right) contrasted with our largest *Andrena*, *A. hattorfiana* (left).

will provide invaluable assistance, because some species can be recognised by checking just one key body part, such as the raised hind margin of tergite 1 of *A. falsifica* or the very well-defined and shiny apical depressions of tergites 2–4 in *A. semilaevis*. A complication to be aware of is the brood dimorphism that affects the males of bivoltine species such as *A. minutula*, *A. minutuloides* and *A. alfkenella*. In these, spring males tend to have extensively black-haired faces and a duller scutum with fainter punctures, and they could easily be interpreted as completely different species to summer-generation males, which have entirely pale-haired faces and more strongly punctured scutums.

Andrena alfkenella Perkins, 1914   **Alfken's Mini-miner**

not illustrated

Description & similar species FW 4.5–5mm female, 4.5mm male. Females resemble a broadly built *A. minutula* but have distinct punctures amongst the microsculpture of tergites 2 and 3, and small pin-prick punctures over much of tergite 1. The apical depressions of tergites 2 and 3 are somewhat duller than in *A. minutula* (more reminiscent of *A. niveata*) and the stigma paler. First-generation males have extensive black hairing on the face like first-generation males of *A. minutula* and *A. minutuloides* but can be separated by shinier and clearly punctate tergites. Summer generation males have white-haired faces and even shinier tergites. The densely punctate tergites with relatively little microsculpture are otherwise seen only in male *A. floricola* and *A. nana* (see key for differences). **Variation** Substantial brood dimorphism in the males, those of the spring generation having extensively black-haired heads, a very dull scutum with weak punctures, and much more microsculpture on the tergites. **Flight season** Bivoltine, with the first generation flying from late April to early June and the second from late June to early September. **Habitat** Some of the best populations are associated with soft rock cliffs and dry coastal grassland, but it also occurs on heathland, chalk grassland, coastal dunes and chalk heath. **Flowers visited** The first generation visits a variety of spring-flowering shrubs and herbs including Blackthorn, Daisy, dandelions, *Brassica* species, Hemlock Water-dropwort and speedwells. The second generation likes umbellifers (e.g. Wild Carrot, Wild Parsnip and Upright Hedge-parsley) but also visits cinquefoils, mayweeds and knapweed. **Nesting habits** Little information, but presumed to be similar to *A. minutula*. **Status & distribution** A scarce southern species with confirmed records extending north to Lincolnshire. Present on the Channel Islands (Jersey and Sark). Not recorded from Wales, Scotland or Ireland. **Parasites & associates** Occasionally stylopised.

Andrena falsifica Perkins, 1915   **Thick-margined Mini-miner**

not illustrated

Description & similar species FW 5mm female, 4.5mm male. Females resemble a broadly built *A. minutula* but the basal areas of tergites 2 and 3 have weak punctures amongst the microsculpture (much less obvious than in *A. alfkenella* but similar to *A. semilaevis*) and the apical depressions of those tergites are somewhat shinier (though not polished or strongly demarked in the manner of *A. semilaevis*). The best character is the hind margin of tergite 1, which is rather shining and strongly convex, appearing inflated in a manner not seen in other mini-miners. Males also have the margin of tergite 1 inflated and broadly shiny but in most other respects resemble *A. subopaca* (the scutum being dull with barely discernible punctures), though antennal segment 5 is clearly shorter than segment 3 and much wider than long in front view (about as long as 3 and more squarish in *A. subopaca*). **Variation** Little noted. **Flight season** Late March to late July. Possibly bivoltine, though regarded as univoltine in some European countries. **Habitat** Recorded from heathland, calcareous grassland and moorland edge, with one Cumbrian record from limestone pavement. **Flowers visited** Records include a cinquefoil, dandelion, Daisy, Wild Strawberry, Germander Speedwell and umbellifers. **Nesting habits** Little information, but presumed to be similar to *A. minutula*. **Status & distribution** A scarce species, with scattered records in England north to Cumbria and Yorkshire; also south Wales. Not recorded from Scotland, Ireland or the Channel Islands. **Parasites & associates** The cleptoparasitic bee *Nomada flavoguttata*. Occasionally stylopised.

Andrena floricola Eversmann, 1852   **Chilterns Mini-miner**

not illustrated

Description & similar species FW 6.5mm female, 5.5–6mm male. Females are one of a pair of mini-miners characterised by dense and conspicuous punctures on tergite 1 and the basal sections of tergites 2 and 3. Other mini-miners either lack punctures here or have the punctures weak and set within obvious and often dense microsculpture. The various differences from *A. nana* are listed in the key, though the very broad apical depressions of tergites 2–4 and rather conspicuous buff hairs of the top of the head and thorax, the abdomen tip and pollen brush of the hind legs, make the single British female (an example from the spring generation) quite distinctive. The apical depressions are also very sharply defined, as in *A. semilaevis*. Males of the spring generation have the face extensively black-haired, whilst those of the summer generation have snow-white hairs here. The densely punctate tergites with relatively little microsculpture is a character otherwise seen only in male *A. nana* and *A. alfkenella* (see key for differences). **Variation** Brood dimorphism resembling that shown by *A. minutula*. Spring females have longer and more conspicuous buff hairs on top of the head and thorax, and a duller scutum with finer punctures and denser microsculpture. Tergites 1–3 are duller with denser punctures. Spring males, as well as having the head substantially black-haired, have the scutum and tergites duller than summer examples, with slightly more pronounced microsculpture between the punctures. **Flight season** Bivoltine, with foreign records indicating that typical flight periods are April and May for the first generation, July and August for the second. **Habitat** Preferences unclear. **Flowers visited** Pollen seems to be obtained largely from crucifers, though sallows, dandelions and speedwells will be used by the first generation, umbellifers and Sheep's-bit by the second, presumably for nectar. **Nesting habits** Abroad, observed ground-nesting in both loamy and sandy soils. **Status & distribution** Known as British on the basis of a single female taken near Princes Risborough in the Chilterns, Buckinghamshire (11 May 1939). **Parasites & associates** None known.

Andrena minutula (Kirby, 1802)   **Common Mini-miner**
Plate 6

Description & similar species FW 4.5–5.5mm female, 4–5mm male. The commonest mini-miner in lowland Britain, so a useful yardstick for the others. Females are one of three species with the tergites almost entirely dulled by microsculpture and no obvious punctures. The rather obvious and dense punctures of the scutum (separated by about their own diameter) help distinguish it from the other two (*A. subopaca* and *A. minutuloides*). The hind margins of tergites 2–3 have obvious lateral hair fringes (very weakly formed in *A. minutuloides*) and the front of the scutellum is less shiny than in *A. minutuloides*. Males of the spring generation usually have the face extensively black-haired and inconspicuous punctures on a very dull scutum. Those of the summer generation look rather different, with a pale-haired face and both the scutum and tergites shinier and more obviously punctured. Spring males of *A. alfkenella* and *A. minutuloides* also have black-haired faces (see accounts for those species), and males of *A. minutuloides*, *A. semilaevis*, *A. falsifica* and *A. subopaca* can all easily mistaken for second-generation *A. minutula* without very careful comparison of key features. **Variation** Seasonal dimorphism of the males as discussed above. Spring males occasionally have the face mostly white-haired with black hairs restricted to the areas around the antennal insertion points. There is also some variation within each generation in the strength of the punctures of the male scutum. Old individuals of both sexes can lose the hair fringes of the tergites and resemble *A. minutuloides*. Females occasionally have the antennal flagella as reddish as *A. nanula* but can be distinguished by the duller scutum and tergite 1, and lack of punctures on the anterior sections of tergites 2 and 3. **Flight season** Bivoltine, the first generation typically flying from mid-March until May, the second from early June until late September. Females found in early June can be impossible to assign to a generation. **Habitat** Found in a wide variety of open and wooded habitats. **Flowers visited** The most polylectic mini-miner. The first generation visits a variety of spring-flowering shrubs and herbaceous species and can be especially noticeable on sallow, dandelions and Colt's-foot in April. The summer generation is especially keen on umbellifers and composites. **Nesting habits** Nesting occurs in dry soil, probably in loose aggregations, though it is not often observed. It is clear that a range of soil types can be used. **Status & distribution** Common over much of southern Britain, extending north to southern Scotland. Widely recorded in Ireland and present on several of the Channel Islands. **Parasites & associates** The cleptoparasitic bee *Nomada flavoguttata*. Occasionally stylopised.

female

male, spring

Andrena minutuloides Perkins, 1914   **Plain Mini-miner**

not illustrated

Description & similar species FW 4.5–5mm female, 4–4.5mm male. Closely resembling *A. minutula*. Females have the scutum shinier with sparser punctures and the scutellum is particularly shiny with little microsculpture between the punctures. The thorax is relatively narrower, especially the propodeum, which is less transverse and more protruding than in *A. minutula*. The abdomen is slimmer and the tergites have an almost uniform, puncture-free microsculpture throughout and are very dull. No distinct lateral hair fringes are present along the hind margins of tergites 2 and 3, even in fresh individuals (unique amongst mini-miners).

female

This creates a very plain and dark appearance in the field. Males resemble a rather slim *A. minutula* with a more sparsely punctured scutum, shinier scutellum and weaker lateral hair fringes along the hind margins of tergites 2 and 3. First-generation males have the face variably black-haired. **Variation** Brood dimorphism of males as described above. Some variation in the density of punctures on the scutum. **Flight season** Bivoltine, the first generation flying from April to early June (appearing later than *A. minutula*), the second from mid-July to September. The second generation is much more abundant than the first. **Habitat** Strongly associated with open chalk grassland (especially downland), but also recorded from chalk heath in the East Anglian Brecks, coastal grasslands, vegetated shingle and heathland. **Flowers visited** The first generation visits a variety of spring-flowering shrubs and herbs including Hawthorn, Cow Parsley, speedwells, Daisy, spurges and *Brassica* species. The summer generation is particularly attracted by umbellifers (notably Wild Carrot, Wild Parsnip, Upright Hedge-parsley and Burnet-saxifrage). **Nesting habits** Little information, but presumed to be similar to *A. minutula*. **Status & distribution** Most records are for the chalk districts of southeast England west to Dorset, with a few modern sites in the East Anglian Brecks; also several old Devon records. It can be quite common where it occurs, especially in late summer. Not recorded from Wales, Scotland or Ireland. An unconfirmed record exists for Guernsey. **Parasites & associates** Considered a host for the cleptoparasitic bee *Nomada flavoguttata*.

Andrena nana (Kirby, 1802)   **Barham Mini-miner**

not illustrated

Description & similar species FW 5.5–6mm female, 5.5mm male. Females are one of a pair of mini-miners characterised by dense and conspicuous punctures on tergite 1 and the basal sections of tergites 2 and 3. Other mini-miners either lack punctures here or have the punctures weak and set within dense, dull microsculpture. The various differences from *A. floricola* and small examples of *A. nitidiuscula* (which can resemble a mini-miner) are listed in the key. Males of the spring generation have the face extensively black-haired, whilst those of the summer generation have snow-white hairs here. The densely punctate tergites (more so than in any other mini-miner) with relatively little microsculpture are characters otherwise seen only in male *A. alfkenella* and *A. floricola* (see key for differences). **Variation** Brood dimorphism resembling that shown by *A. minutula*. Spring females have longer and darker hairs on the top of the head and thorax, a duller scutum with finer punctures and denser microsculpture, and tergites 1–3 are duller with denser punctures. Spring males, as well as having the head substantially black-haired, have the scutum and tergites duller than summer examples with more pronounced microsculpture between the punctures. **Flight season** Bivoltine, with foreign records indicating that typical flight periods are April to June for the first generation and July and August for the second. **Habitat** Preferences unclear. **Flowers visited** Known to visit flowers from a variety of plant families, with a particular liking for umbellifers and crucifers. **Nesting habits** Little information, but presumed to be similar to *A. minutula*. **Status & distribution** Only five confirmed British records: Barham, Suffolk (pre-1802); Luddesdown, Kent (1899); Oxshott, Surrey (1915); Sudbury, Suffolk (1923) and Eynsford, Kent (1930). Possibly extinct. The type specimen is the female from Barham. **Parasites & associates** None known.

Andrena nanula Nylander, 1848   Red-horned Mini-miner
not illustrated

Description & similar species FW 5mm female. Females closely resemble *A. minutula* but have all tergites somewhat shinier and tergite 1 with only weak microsculpture and sparse fine punctures (tergite 1 shinier than in all the other mini-miners except *A. nana* and *A. floricola*). Tergites 2 and 3 have microsculpture on the apical depression and very fine punctures amongst the microsculpture of the basal section, though these punctures are not as obvious as in *A. alfkenella* and *A. falsifica*. The scutum is shinier than in *A. minutula* with sparser punctures and much weaker microsculpture, more like *A. minutuloides*. The antennal flagella are much more extensively reddish than in other mini-miners except the occasional *A. minutula*. Male specimens have not been seen, but these apparently also have the antennal flagella extensively reddish as in the females. **Variation** None known. **Flight season** Univoltine, typically flying in July and August on the continent. **Habitat** Preferences unclear. **Flowers visited** On the continent, known to visit flowers from several plant families, especially umbellifers such as Wild Carrot, Wild Angelica and Burnet-saxifrage. **Nesting habits** Little information, but presumed to be similar to *A. minutula*. **Status & distribution** Known as British on the basis of a single female thought to have been found in Norfolk in the period 1875–77. **Parasites & associates** None known.

Andrena niveata Friese, 1887   Long-fringed Mini-miner
not illustrated

Description & similar species FW 5–5.5mm female, 5mm male. One of the more easily recognised mini-miners, with the white hair fringes at the sides of tergites 2 and 3 and across the posterior parts of tergites 4 and 5 much denser and longer than in the other species. The tergites are particularly dull, with heavy microsculpture throughout and dense punctures on the basal parts of tergites 2–4. The body hairs are much whiter than in other mini-miners and particularly long in males (especially on the face, thorax and legs). The facial foveae of the female are white and grey with little hint of brown. The overall effect is thus of a very silvery, strongly marked mini-miner. **Variation** Very little, though the abdominal hair fringes can become abraded.

female

Flight season Univoltine, flying from mid-May to late June. **Habitat** Strongly associated with crucifer-rich habitats such as arable margins and soft rock cliffs, less frequently found on heathland, vegetated shingle, gardens and allotments. **Flowers visited** Pollen seems to be obtained exclusively from crucifers, with species such as Charlock, Hedge Mustard and Rape important in places such as the South Downs. It will also use cultivated brassicas of various sorts in vegetable plots. Visits to umbellifers, Hawthorn and speedwells are probably for nectar. **Nesting habits** Rarely observed, but probably similar to *A. minutula*. **Status & distribution** A rare species, with modern records seemingly confined to Sussex, Kent and Surrey and older records extending west to Somerset and north to Oxfordshire and Norfolk. An isolated old record also exists for the north coast of Wales within Caernarvonshire. Not recorded from Scotland, Ireland or the Channel Islands. **Parasites & associates** Occasionally stylopised.

Andrena semilaevis Pérez, 1903

Shiny-margined Mini-miner

not illustrated

Description & similar species FW 5–5.5mm female, 4.5–5mm male. In both sexes, this species can be most easily recognised by the strongly defined, shiny apical depressions of tergites 2–4 (especially tergites 3 and 4). The sculpturing of the top of the propodeum is also distinctive, with a rugose basal area that contrasts with a more granular area beyond (top of propodeum more uniformly sculptured in other mini-miners). Females have the top of the thorax and face shinier than *A. minutula*, a paler stigma and more conspicuous orange hairs at the tip of the abdomen. The build is usually slightly slimmer than *A. minutula*. Males have the facial hairs longer and whiter than *A. minutula*, a paler stigma and a dull scutum with sparser punctures amongst the

female

microsculpture. The very similar non-British *A. anthrisci* occurs on the near-continent and should be looked out for now that its possible cuckoo (*Nomada castellana*) is known from the Channel Islands. It has somewhat duller apical depressions on tergites 2 and 3 and the hind margin of tergite 1 is as dull as the preceding areas (clearly shinier in *A. semilaevis*). **Variation** Little noted. **Flight season** Early May to August, possibly as two generations or a single protracted one (males tend to peak once in May or June). It tends to peak between the two generations of *A. minutula*. **Habitat** Found in a wide variety of open and wooded habitats. **Flowers visited** Known to visit flowers from a variety of plant families but with a particular liking for umbellifers and speedwells. **Nesting habits** Little information, but presumed to be similar to *A. minutula*. **Status & distribution** Widespread and locally common in southern Britain and the Channel Islands, extending more sparingly north to the Inverness area. Widely recorded in Ireland. **Parasites & associates** The cleptoparasitic bee *Nomada flavoguttata*. Occasionally stylopised.

Andrena subopaca Nylander, 1848   **Impunctate Mini-miner**

not illustrated

Description & similar species FW 4.5–5.5mm female, 4.5–5mm male.
Females resemble *A. minutula* but have a very dull scutum and scutellum
with the punctures so shallow that they are difficult to discern (no other
female mini-miner has punctures this faint), and the punctures on the
clypeus are sparser. Males have a similar scutum and scutellum and thus
resemble first-generation male *A. minutula* but never have black hairs
on the face. The male abdomen tends to be more ovate and less
elongate than in *A. minutula*, with the apical depressions less well
defined. **Variation** Little noted. **Flight season** Late April to mid-August,
possibly as two generations (the first evidently the strongest). It tends to peak between the two
generations of *A. minutula*. **Habitat** Found in a wide variety of habitats and relatively frequent
in the rides and clearings of woods. It is the mini-miner most likely to be found in upland areas.
Flowers visited Known to visit a variety of flowers, though little indication of the liking for
umbellifers shown by some mini-miners. **Nesting habits** Small nesting aggregations have
been observed along south-facing wood banks and other slopes with short, sparse vegetation.
Status & distribution Widespread and locally frequent over much of Britain and Ireland, though
not known from the Channel Islands. **Parasites & associates** The cleptoparasitic bee *Nomada
flavoguttata*. Occasionally stylopised.

female

male

PANURGUS – SHAGGY BEES

Small to medium-sized, mostly black and sparsely haired bees with well-developed pollen brushes on the hind legs. The head is very broad when viewed from the front and the labrum sits within a deep emargination along the lower edge of the clypeus. The marginal cell of the forewing has a truncate tip. About 50 species have been described, distributed throughout the Palaearctic. Nesting occurs in light soil, often in large aggregations. The nest cells are lined with a wax-like material and filled with round pollen balls. All species seem to gather pollen from hawkish composites, especially the yellow-flowered ones.

♀   ♂

Panurgus
banksianus

Panurgus
calcaratus

Many species provide hosts for cleptoparasitic *Nomada* bees, and both British *Panurgus* species support such parasites on the Channel Islands but not on the mainland.

PANURGUS

| 1 | Females (antennae with 12 segments, hind legs with a dense pollen brush) | 2 |
| — | Males (antennae with 13 segments, hind legs sparsely haired) | 3 |

2   Antennae entirely black. Tergites with erect black hairs that are as long as the width of an eye (view from side). Top of propodeum relatively smooth without longitudinal ridges. Larger (wing length 7–8mm) .... *banksianus*

—   Flagella of antennae partially orange/brown. Tergites with mostly short, pale hairs. Top of propodeum with longitudinal ridges. Smaller (wing length 5–6mm) .... *calcaratus*

3   Hind femora without a ventral projection, the hind tibiae barely curved in dorsal view (Fig. 1). Antennae entirely black. Larger and hairier (wing length 7–8mm) .... *banksianus*

—   Hind femora with a tongue-like projection beneath the hind femora, the hind tibiae distinctly curved in dorsal view (Fig. 2). Flagella of antennae partially orange/brown. Smaller and less hairy (wing length 5–6mm) .... *calcaratus*

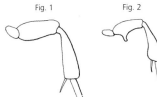

Fig. 1   Fig. 2

Panurgus banksianus (Kirby, 1802)   **Large Shaggy Bee**

Plate 6

Description & similar species FW 7–8mm (sexes similar). A medium-sized, shiny black bee with a sparse body pile and large and conspicuous yellow pollen brushes on the female hind legs. Much the larger of the two *Panurgus* species; even small specimens are considerably larger than *P. calcaratus*. **Variation** Very little. **Flight season** Early June to August, peaking somewhat earlier than *P. calcaratus*. **Habitat** Sandy and dry clay habitats, especially soft rock cliffs, sandy coastal grassland, heathland and dry acid grassland. **Flowers visited** Strongly associated with hawkish composites, perhaps especially Cat's-ear, Mouse-ear-hawkweed, hawkbits and hawk's-beards. Males will shelter in the flowers during dull weather. **Nesting habits** Nesting occurs in bare or sparsely vegetated light soil, both flat areas and slopes.

Footpaths with compacted soil feature in many records. **Status & distribution** Widespread and locally common in southern coastal districts from north Wales to Norfolk. Inland it is largely restricted to southern heathland districts from Dorset to East Anglia, also Dartmoor and sites in Lincolnshire and Yorkshire. Not recorded from Scotland or Ireland. Known from several of the Channel Islands. **Parasites & associates** The cleptoparasitic bee *Nomada similis* attacks it on the Channel Islands.

Panurgus calcaratus (Scopoli, 1763)

Plate 6

Small Shaggy Bee

Description & similar species FW 4.5–6mm (sexes similar). Much smaller than *P. banksianus*, with the antennal flagella partially pale (more pronounced in males) and the male femora with a large projection below near the base. **Variation** Moderate size variation, with pronounced allometry in males – i.e. large males are proportionately bigger-headed and more robust than smaller ones. **Flight season** Late June to August, peaking later than *P. banksianus*. **Habitat** Sandy and gravelly habitats, typically heathland and acid grassland but occurring at far fewer coastal sites than *P. banksianus*. **Flowers visited** Like *P. banksianus*, strongly associated with hawkish composites, including Cat's-ear, Beaked Hawk's-beard and Autumn Hawkbit. Males will also shelter in the flowers during dull weather. **Nesting habits** Similar to *P. banksianus* but perhaps more inclined to form nesting aggregations. **Status & distribution** Mostly found in southern heathland districts between Dorset and the Thames Estuary, with sparse records for southwest England, south Wales and the coastal belt of East Anglia. Not recorded from Scotland or Ireland. Recorded from several of the Channel Islands. **Parasites & associates** The cleptoparasitic bee *Nomada fuscicornis* attacks it on the Channel Islands.

FAMILY HALICTIDAE

HALICTUS – END-BANDED FURROW BEES

Bees that range from small to slightly larger than a Honey Bee. They have short, pointed tongues and in females tergite 5 is densely haired with a bare-looking median 'furrow' (rima) as also seen in *Lasioglossum*. Unlike most *Lasioglossum* species, any pale hair bands on the tergites are along the hind margins and occasionally the bases too (pale hair bands or hair patches are typically only on the bases of the tergites in *Lasioglossum*). The head can be large and box-shaped in some species, notably *H. maculatus*. Species of the subgenus *Seladonia* are metallic bronze, but are always more heavily punctate on the tergites than metallic *Lasioglossum* species and thus appear duller. Pollen is collected on pollen brushes on the hind tibiae, femora and trochanters and occasionally the underside of the abdomen.

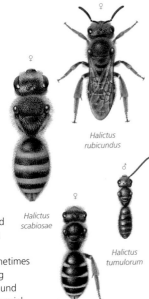

Halictus
rubicundus

Halictus
scabiosae

Halictus
tumulorum

Halictus
eurygnathus

Nesting usually occurs underground or in vertical faces, sometimes including the mortar of walls. Many species form large nesting aggregations, and some species nest communally in underground chambers. The genus contains both solitary and primitively eusocial species. In the latter, a queen will emerge in spring and her first brood will be workers. These usually then rear a brood of males and new virgin queens. Only fertilised queens overwinter. There is little outward difference in appearance between queens and workers, though ovaries are poorly developed in the latter. In solitary species, no females behave as workers, but they can still form dense nesting aggregations and occasionally share a common nest entrance. Most *Halictus* are polylectic but some show family-level flower preferences, especially for composites. *Halictus* species are attacked by various species of cleptoparasitic *Sphecodes* bees plus smaller conopid flies such as *Zodion* species.

Over 300 species have been described worldwide, mostly in the Palaearctic and Nearctic, and the habit of drinking perspiration in some foreign species has resulted in an alternative name of 'sweat bees' (also used for halictids generally). Eight species are recorded from the British Isles, but one (*H. maculatus*) seems to have become extinct and two (*H. scabiosae* and *H. quadricinctus*) are currently known only from the Channel Islands. A number of additional species occur on the near-continent. In using the following key beware of *Lasioglossum sexstrigatum*, which has a narrow fringe of whitish hairs along the hind margins of the tergites – though the almost impunctate and shining tergite 1 provides an immediate distinction from the *Halictus* species below.

HALICTUS FEMALES

1   Larger non-metallic species (wing length at least 7.5mm in the extant species) **2**

—   Smaller metallic bronze, golden or green species (wing length to 5.5mm in the extant species) **6**

2   Tergites 1–4 with broad, continuous, cream-coloured hair bands occupying the entire apical depressions, also less conspicuous greyer bands along the anterior margins of tergites 2–4. A large species (typical wing length 9–10mm) with a rather squarish head in top view (Channel Islands) .... *scabiosae*

—   Tergites 1–4 with much narrower bands that are narrowed or broken in the middle **3**

3   Hind tibiae orange with orange hairs. Hairs of top of thorax reddish-brown in fresh individuals. Medium-sized (typical wing length 8mm) .... *rubicundus*

—   Hind tibiae dark with buffish hairs. Hairs on top of thorax brownish **4**

4   Very large (typical wing length 13–14mm). Tergites dulled by microsculpture but without obvious punctures. Top of thorax sparsely punctate (Channel Islands) .... *quadricinctus*

—   Smaller (maximum wing length 7.5mm). Top of thorax and most tergites densely punctate throughout **5**

5   Head almost squarish in top view (Fig. 1). Hind margins of tergites 1–4 with lateral white bands that are widely separated and occupy no more than a third of the tergite width. Hind margin of tergite 1 impunctate centrally .... *maculatus*

—   Head more transverse in top view (Fig. 2). Hind margins of tergites 3 and 4 with continuous hair bands, the lateral bands on tergite 2 occupying more than a third of the tergite width. Tergite 1 densely punctate throughout .... *eurygnathus*

6   Top of head and thorax with a dense pile of short golden hairs that obscure the underlying integument. Tergites 2–3 with conspicuous pale bands occupying the apical depressions and the extreme bases; tergite 1 with tomentose patches basally. Top of propodeum with a polished, shiny black hind margin. Larger (typical wing length 6mm) .... *subauratus*

—   Top of head and thorax with an inconspicuous pile of yellowish hairs that do not obscure the integument. Tergites 2–4 with whitish hair bands along hind margins only (unless highly distended). Hind margins of propodeum not brightly shining. Smaller (wing length to 5.5mm) **7**

7   Tergites 3 and 4 with narrower apical bands, clearly narrower than the apical depressions in the middle when viewed from behind (Fig. 3) .... *tumulorum*

—   Tergites 3 and 4 with broader apical bands that occupy the full width of the apical depressions when viewed from behind (Fig. 4) .... *confusus*

Fig. 1   Fig. 2 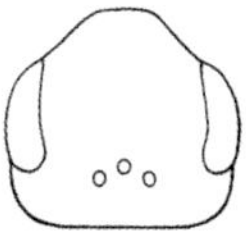   Fig. 3    Fig. 4

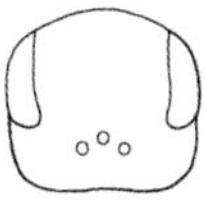

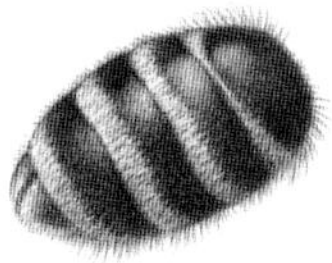

HALICTUS MALES

1   Larger, non-metallic species (wing length at least 7mm in the extant species) **2**

—   Smaller, metallic bronze, golden or green species (wing length not exceeding
5.5mm in the extant species) **6**

2   Tergites 1–6 with broad, continuous cream-coloured hair bands, those of 2–6
occupying the entire apical depressions. Hind tibiae entirely yellow. A large,
very elongate species (typical wing length 9–10mm) (Channel Islands) .... *scabiosae*

—   Tergites with narrower bands that become narrowed or interrupted in the middle.
Hind tibiae with at least a dark smudge posteriorly. Build less elongate **3**

3   Very large (typical wing length 12–13mm) with a club-shaped abdomen (broadest
at tergite 4). Bands on tergites continuous (but tending to become narrower in
the middle). Antennal flagella with long hairs on hind face. Sternite 6 deeply
notched apically with a pair of lateral prominences bearing dense hair brushes
(Fig. 5) (Channel Islands) .... *quadricinctus*

—   Smaller species (wing length no more than 7.5mm). Bands on tergites 1–3
broken in the middle. Abdomen parallel-sided. Antennae without long hairs
on hind face and sternite 6 unremarkable **4**

Fig. 5   Fig. 6   Fig. 7

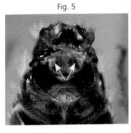

4   Head in side view with a strongly concave lower margin that takes in the lower
half of the eye orbit (Fig. 6). Base of mandibles very broad. Antennal flagella with
underside entirely orange .... *eurygnathus*

—   Head in side view with lower margin straighter, the eye orbits well separated from
the lower margin except at their bottom corners. Base of mandibles not so broad
(Fig. 7). Antennal flagella with at least apical segments 4–5 dark below **5**

5   Antennal flagella entirely dark below. Sternites 4–5 with hind margins concave,
those margins bearing a narrow band of dense, felt-like, brownish hairs. Hind part
of head behind ocelli not especially expanded and without clear punctures. Hind
tibiae with a discrete dark oval spot on outer face. Pile on top of thorax hairs
ginger in fresh individuals .... *rubicundus*

—   Antennal flagella with basal segments orange below. Sternites 4–5 with straight
hind margins that lack bands of dense brown hairs. Head squarish in top view
(Fig. 1), the area behind the ocelli expanded and bearing distinct punctures.
Hind tibiae extensively darkened on outer face. Pile on top of thorax dull brown .... *maculatus*

6   Tergites with conspicuous bands on hind margins. Antennae relatively short,
not capable of stretching back to base of abdomen. Sternite 6 without a
median pit. Hind tibiae with dark oval spots on inner and outer faces .... *subauratus*

—   Tergites lacking conspicuous bands. Antennae long, capable of stretching back
to base of abdomen. Sternite 6 with a median pit. Hind tibiae with inconspicuous
orange marks on inner and outer faces **7**

7   Gonostyli of genitalia with hind margins concave and sinuous when viewed
    dorsally (Fig. 8) .... *tumulorum*

—   Gonostyli of genitalia with hind margins smoothly convex (Fig. 9) .... *confusus*

Fig. 8   Fig. 9

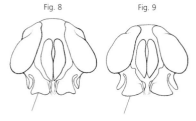

Halictus confusus Smith, 1853   **Southern Bronze Furrow Bee**
not illustrated

Description & similar species FW 4.5–5.5mm female, 4–5.5mm male. A small bronzy *Halictus* that is extremely similar to *H. tumulorum*. In females, the pale bands across tergites 3 and 4 are wider than in *H. tumulorum*, occupying almost the entire apical depression even when viewed from behind, with little narrowing centrally. However, this feature can be lost in older abraded individuals. Males have very long antennae and lack pale tomentose bands on the tergites. They can only be reliably separated from *H. tumulorum* by checking the genitalia, though the mid and hind trochanters of the males tend to be extensively yellow (typically dark in *H.tumulorum* but occasionally mainly yellow).

female

Variation Little noted. **Flight season** Females can fly from April to September, males from July to September. **Habitat** Strongly associated with sandy heathland and other disturbed sandy locations such as sandpits. **Flowers visited** British records include brambles, composites of various sorts, cinquefoils, heathers and speedwells. **Nesting habits** Nesting occurs in light soils of various sorts, apparently often at the base of plants. It appears to be primitively eusocial. **Status & distribution** A scarce and restricted species with most records from the heathlands of Dorset, the New Forest, West Sussex, Surrey and the East Anglian Brecks, with a handful of outliers. Recently discovered on Jersey. **Parasites & associates** None known.

Halictus eurygnathus Blüthgen, 1931   **Downland Furrow Bee**
Plate 7

Description & similar species FW 7.5mm female, 7mm male. This species has a similar size and build to *H. rubicundus*, and both sexes could be overlooked as old, sun-bleached examples of that species in the field. Many differences exist under closer examination. Females have dark hind tibiae beneath the buff hairs, the head is squarer in top view and the abdomen much more densely punctate. The thorax has an inconspicuous brown pile above. Males have a uniquely shaped head capsule (with the underside much hollowed out compared with related species) and mandibles that are unusually broad at the base.

Their antennae are very long like *H. rubicundus* but with the flagella orange on their entire undersides. Males have a very silvery, ringed appearance in the field. Two very similar species occur on the near-continent, *H. langobardicus* and *H. simplex*. **Variation** Very little. **Flight season** Females can appear in mid-May, males in mid-July, and both can fly until late September. **Habitat** A chalk downland specialist, especially south-facing escarpments with plentiful Greater Knapweed. **Flowers visited** There is a strong association with Greater Knapweed, and most pollen gathering seems to occur on this plant from mid-June. Both sexes nectar primarily from scabiouses once the knapweed has gone over. **Nesting habits** Known to form nesting aggregations in light soils and to display a low level of eusocial behaviour. **Status & distribution** Modern records are confined to a few sites within the South Downs of East Sussex between Lewes, Woodingdean and Eastbourne. Much older records exist for Kent, with unconfirmed ones for Dorset and the Isle of Wight. Not recorded from Wales, Scotland, Ireland or the Channel Islands. Still widely known under the name of *H. compressus* in foreign literature. **Parasites & associates** None known.

female

male

Halictus maculatus Smith, 1848   **Box-headed Furrow Bee**

not illustrated

Description & similar species FW 6–7mm female, 5–6mm male. Females most resemble a small *H. eurygnathus*, owing to the dark hind tibiae and inconspicuous brown pile on top of the thorax, but they have a slimmer build and a much larger head that is almost square in top view. The lateral white bands on the hind margins of the tergites are much more widely separated than in *eurygnathus*. Males can be easily separated from *H. eurygnathus* and *H. rubicundus* by the extensively darkened outer face of the hind tibiae, much shorter antennae (with the first eight flagellar segments reddish below) and a more expanded hind section of the head which is distinctly punctured behind the ocelli. The bands on the tergites are widely separated in the middle. **Variation** Larger females are generally queens, smaller ones workers.

Flight season Females can fly from May to September, males from July to September. **Habitat** British records include soft rock cliffs, gravel pits, dry pasture and possibly heathland – with dry, sandy soils seemingly the common feature. **Flowers visited** The only British record is for Smooth Hawk's-beard, but a variety of plant families is known to be used abroad, with composites particularly favoured. **Nesting habits** Large aggregations can be formed in light soils, with spoil spread widely around nest entrances rather than as tumuli. The nest entrances are narrowed and females will often

female

rest with their large heads filling the entrance hole. It appears to be eusocial, with several females helping to create a complex underground nest system served by one entrance. **Status & distribution** Last recorded in 1930 at Chudleigh, Devon, and presumed extinct. Further old records exist for another site in Devon (Gooseham), Isle of Wight (Sandown Bay), Hampshire (Blackwater), Sussex (Hastings), Kent (Upper Halling) and Surrey (Weybridge); also the Channel Islands (Sark). Not recorded from Wales, Scotland or Ireland. **Parasites & associates** The cleptoparasitic bee *Sphecodes gibbus* is known to attack it on the continent; also the non-British *S. rufiventris*.

Halictus quadricinctus (Fabricius, 1776)   **Giant Furrow Bee**

Plate 7

Description & similar species FW 12.5–14mm female, 12–13mm male. Britain's largest *Halictus* (considerably larger than a Honey Bee), with tergite bands much narrower than in our other large *Halictus* (*H. scabiosae*). Females are more likely to be mistaken for a very large *Andrena* in the field, though the box-shaped head (with the area behind the eyes much expanded) and lack of facial foveae along the eye margins allow easy separation. They have pale bands along the hind margins of tergites 1–4 that are narrowed or broken centrally. The tergites are dulled by microsculpture but lack distinct punctures. Males also stand out due to their great size and unusual shape – the abdomen is club-shaped, broadest at tergite 4. They have narrow but continuous white abdominal bands, and the antennal flagella are orange beneath except for the last two segments, the orange sometimes spreading onto the dorsal surface. The hind faces of the flagellar segments bear numerous long hairs. Sternite 6 is strongly notched apically with lateral hair tufts that arise from prominences. **Variation** Little noted. **Flight season** On the continent, females can emerge from April, males from July,

both flying until September or October. **Habitat** Coastal grassland on the Channel Islands but using a variety of open flowery habitats on the continent. **Flowers visited** Spear Thistle noted on the Channel Islands; on the continent known to rely heavily on composites such as thistles, knapweeds, Bristly Oxtongue, Cat's-ear, dandelions, sowthistles and hawkbits. Non-composites used include Viper's-bugloss, Field Scabious, Common Poppy, Common Valerian and Field Bindweed. **Nesting habits** The nesting habits are very distinctive, with several females hollowing out an underground chamber, usually with supportive pillars, within which clusters of 4–20 cells are arranged in a tight, comb-like arrangement against the wall of the cavity. Females seem to have equal reproductive status, which makes it a solitary rather than a eusocial species. **Status & distribution** Known only from the Channel Islands (Guernsey and Sark), where it is considered a recent colonist. **Parasites & associates** The parasitic bee *Sphecodes gibbus* is known to attack it on the continent.

Halictus rubicundus (Christ, 1791) Orange-legged Furrow Bee

Plate 7

Description & similar species FW 7.5–8mm female, 7–7.5mm male. Amongst the medium-sized *Halictus*, the orange hind tibiae and ginger pile on top of the thorax make females fairly easy to recognise. In the field they are most likely to be confused with *Lasioglossum xanthopus*, but that species has the hair patches of tergites 2–5 located on the anterior corners of the tergites, not the hind margins. *Andrena similis* is also somewhat similar but has facial foveae beside the eyes and the white stripes of tergites 2 and 3 much shorter and restricted to the sides. Males have long antennae like *H. eurygnathus* but have a brighter brown thoracic pile, entirely black antennal flagella and a very different-shaped head that lacks the ventral hollowing of *H. eurygnathus* or the broad mandible bases. **Variation** Males from Lundy (form *nesiotis*) have the antennal flagella pale beneath. Small specimens of both sexes are occasionally encountered. Sun-bleached individuals, especially males, can become greyish and resemble *H. eurygnathus*. **Flight season** Females can fly from March to October, males from mid-June to October. **Habitat** A great variety of flowery habitats can be used, on a variety of soils. Sites range from sea level, e.g. saltmarsh edge and vegetated shingle, to upland moors and meadows. **Flowers visited** Flowers from numerous families are visited, though there is a particular liking for composites such as thistles, knapweeds and ragworts as pollen sources and umbellifers such as Hogweed and Wild Parsnip as nectar sources. Newly emerged spring females will also visit blossoming shrubs and trees. **Nesting habits** Nesting occurs in light soils, sometimes in large aggregations. This is a eusocial species in the south but solitary and single-brooded in the north, though it seems to form larger nesting aggregations in the north. Queens and workers are indistinguishable in the field. **Status & distribution** Widespread and locally common over much of Britain and Ireland. Recorded from several of the Channel Islands. **Parasites & associates** The cleptoparasitic bees *Sphecodes gibbus* and *S. monilicornis*; also the conopid fly *Zodion cinereum*, the larvae of which develop inside the adult bees.

female

male

Halictus scabiosae (Rossi, 1790) Great Banded Furrow Bee

Plate 7

Description & similar species FW 8.5–10.5mm female, 7.5–10.5mm male. A large and very distinctive *Halictus* with conspicuous buff abdominal bands that take the form of broad, almost perfect rings from tergite 1 onwards. In females the bands occupy the apical depressions of tergites 1–4 with less conspicuous greyer bands along the anterior margins of tergites 2–4 (most obvious when the abdomen is extended). Males have a very elongate build, completely yellow hind tibiae and abdominal bands that occupy the apical third of tergites 2–6. Paler grey bands

female

occur on the anterior parts of tergites 2 and 3. The male antennal flagella are completely dark. *H. sexcinctus*, which occurs in France close to Jersey, is a similar size and shape but the tergites lack the basal bands of *H. scabiosae* and the male's antennae are longer and mostly reddish. **Variation** Moderate size variation in both sexes, with smaller females probably representing workers. The abdominal bands and thoracic pile can fade whitish in older individuals. **Flight season** Females can fly from mid-April to September, males from July to September. **Habitat** A variety of open flowery habitats are used on the Channel Islands, including coastal soft rock cliffs, grasslands of various sorts, dunes, heathland, flowery waste ground and gardens. **Flowers visited** Pollen is obtained from composites such as thistles, knapweeds, artichokes, Chicory, Common Fleabane, Bristly Oxtongue and Cat's-ear. Nectar sources include various umbellifers (Hogweed, Wild Carrot, Rock Samphire), Hemp-agrimony, heathers, scabiouses and bindweeds. **Nesting habits** Nesting occurs in aggregations in south-facing slopes and cliff faces, and also in flat sandy areas. The species is considered eusocial at

male

some populations with overwintered, fertilised females acting as queens that use their smaller, non-reproducing daughters as workers, though some nests can apparently be communal with more than one reproducing female. **Status & distribution** Known only from the Channel Islands (Jersey, Guernsey, Sark and Herm), where it is locally common. **Parasites & associates** None known within its British range.

Halictus subauratus (Rossi, 1792)   Golden Furrow Bee

not illustrated

Description & similar species FW 5.5–6mm female, 5–5.5mm male. One of three small green or bronze *Halictus* species but obviously distinct from the slightly smaller *H. tumulorum* and *H. confusus*. Females have a thick covering of felt-like golden hairs on the top of the head and thorax which mask the underlying integument and create a very matt-looking bee with conspicuous dark eyes. The head is proportionately larger than in the other two due to the more inflated area behind the eyes. Tergites 1–4 have conspicuous creamy-buff bands occupying the posterior third of tergites 2–4, with narrower greyer bands occupying the anterior of tergites 2 and 3 (most obvious when the abdomen is distended). The top of the propodeum is reticulately sculptured, but the rim beyond this is shiny black. Males have strongly banded tergites and considerably shorter antennae than the other two species. **Variation** Seemingly very little. **Flight season** On the continent, females can fly from April to September, males from June to September. **Habitat** On the continent,

female

this species is found in a variety of open, flowery habitats. **Flowers visited** Flowers from several families are visited, though it shows a strong preference for composites such as thistles, knapweeds, Chicory, Cat's-ear, chamomiles and various chrysanthemum-type species. **Nesting habits** Nesting occurs in dry sandy or clay soils, usually in small aggregations. Nest cells may be located within a system of cavities. A eusocial species. **Status & distribution** Purportedly recorded from Hampshire (near Farnborough) and Guernsey, both pre-1900, but no supporting specimens appear to exist. **Parasites & associates** None known in Britain, but parasitised by the non-British *Sphecodes cristatus* abroad.

Halictus tumulorum (Linnaeus, 1758) Bronze Furrow Bee

Plate 7

Description & similar species FW 4.5–5.5mm female, 4–5.5mm male. The commonest of our three small metallic *Halictus* but extremely difficult to distinguish from *H. confusus*. In females, the pale hair band of tergite 3 is narrowed in the middle, where it occupies only half the width of the apical depression (the band fills the entire depression in *H. confusus*). Angle of view is critical in assessing this, because from some angles the band looks as if it fills the depression (always obtain the angle that shows the band at its narrowest extent, usually from behind). Males have very long antennae and lack obvious hair bands on the tergites. They can only be reliably separated from *H. confusus* by checking the genitalia. **Variation** Very little apart from moderate size variation. **Flight season** Females can be found from mid-March until October. Males can appear from late June. **Habitat** Found in a wide variety of open habitats including grasslands, heathland, brownfield land and various coastal habitats. **Flowers visited** Many sorts of flowers are visited, and blossoming shrubs and trees such as willows and Blackthorn are used by spring females. **Nesting habits** Nesting occurs in light soils of various sorts, usually in aggregations. This is a eusocial species. **Status & distribution** Widespread and common over much of lowland England and Wales, becoming scarcer in the north, with records extending thinly into southern Scotland. Widely recorded in Ireland but seemingly declining here. Recorded from most of the Channel Islands. **Parasites & associates** One of the hosts of the cleptoparasitic bee *Sphecodes ephippius* and possibly *S. geoffrellus*.

female

male

LASIOGLOSSUM – BASE-BANDED FURROW BEES

Bees that range in size from tiny (*L. minutissimum*) to almost the size of a Honey Bee (*L. xanthopus*), with short, pointed tongues and tergite 5 densely hairy with a bare-looking median 'furrow' (the rima) as also seen in *Halictus*. Unlike *Halictus*, any pale hair bands or patches on the tergites are usually located only at the base (typically located on the hind margin, or a combination of hind margin and base, in *Halictus*). *Lasioglossum sexstrigatum* is the only species to defy this rule, but the almost impunctate and shining tergite 1 provides an immediate distinction from *Halictus* species. *Lasioglossum* species also vary from *Halictus* in having the outer cross veins of the forewings narrower and paler than the other typical wing veins.

♀

Lasioglossum xanthopus

♀

♂

Lasioglossum calceatum

♀

Lasioglossum calceatum

♀

Lasioglossum leucozonium

Lasioglossum smeathmanellum

The subgeneric classification has recently been revised and is complex, but the non-metallic females can be divided into 'carinate' species that have the rear face of the propodeum fully enclosed by lateral ridges (carinae) and usually a ridge along the top of the hind face (which results in angulated 'shoulders') versus 'non-carinate' species where the rear face of the propodeum is unenclosed or only partially enclosed and merges more smoothly into the sides (with the shoulders at the top rounded off). This is useful for identification, though species such as *L. pauxillum* and *L. puncticolle* are somewhat intermediate so keyed out twice.

Nesting habits resemble *Halictus*, with most species nesting underground in light soils, often in aggregations and sometimes using underground chambers. Both solitary and eusocial species are present. In the latter, a queen will emerge in spring and her first brood will be workers. These then rear a brood of males and new virgin queens, and in the warmest places additional broods may be produced. Only fertilised queens overwinter. There is little outward difference in appearance between queens and workers. In solitary species, no females behave as workers, though they can still form dense nesting aggregations and occasionally share a common nest entrance. Most species are polylectic but some show family-level flower preferences, especially for composites.

British and Irish *Lasioglossum* species are attacked by cleptoparasitic bees mostly of the genus *Sphecodes* but also *Nomada sheppardana*. Parasitoids seem to include the mutillid wasps *Myrmosa atra* and *Smicromyrme rufipes*, conopid flies of the genera *Thecophora* and *Zodion* and the bee-fly *Bombylius canescens*. Some species are stylopised.

This is the world's largest bee genus, with over 1,700 described species worldwide. Like *Halictus* they are often termed 'sweat bees' owing to the liking of some foreign species for human sweat. Thirty-four species are recorded from the British Isles, but at least one seems to have become extinct (*L. laeve*) and two (*L. limbellum* and *L. mediterraneum*) are currently only known from the Channel Islands. Numerous additional species occur on the near-continent, and the recent discovery of *L. sexstrigatum* in Britain and *L. mediterraneum* in the Channel Islands indicates the need for vigilance. This genus contains some difficult identification challenges and the keys are best used in conjunction with the author's web feature (see p.59), which furnishes the microscopic photos given here, plus others, at much higher resolution.

LASIOGLOSSUM FEMALE GROUPS

HEAD LENGTHS

Fig. 1
Wide

Fig. 2
Round

Fig. 3
Oval

Fig. 4
Long

1   Head, thorax and sometimes abdomen metallic green or turquoise. Small species (wing length to 5mm) .... **female group A**

—   Body non-metallic or if thorax very slightly so (*prasinum*) then wingspan at least 6mm and sides of tergite 1 with grey tomentum **2**

2   Top of propodeum with angulated hind corners (angle of view critical), the hind face 'carinate' i.e. separated from the sides by vertical ridges that reach the angulated hind corners (Figs 5 & 6) .... **female group B**

—   Top of propodeum with smoothly rounded hind corners, the hind propodeal face not usually obviously carinate, any lateral ridges not reaching the top (Fig. 7) **3**

3   At normal distention, tergites 2 and 3 with large white tomentose patches at anterior corners that are clearly visible without magnification (Fig. 8) or with complete grey tomentose bands that extend onto the sides of tergite 1 (Fig. 44) .... **female group C**

—   At normal distention, tergites 2 and 3 with any tomentose patches at anterior corners small, inconspicuous or missing, never extending onto the sides of tergite 1 .... **4**

4   Scutum with sparse and relatively large punctures, the surface between these punctures shining and without microsculpture (Fig. 9) .... **female group D**

—   Scutum with denser, smaller punctures, the surface between these usually dulled to varying extents with microsculpture (Fig. 10) .... **female group E**

Fig. 5   Fig. 6 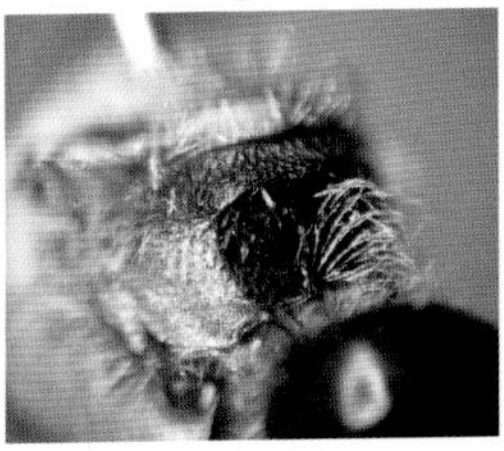   Fig. 7

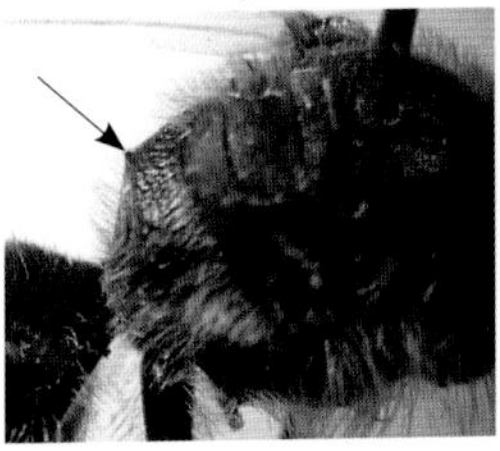

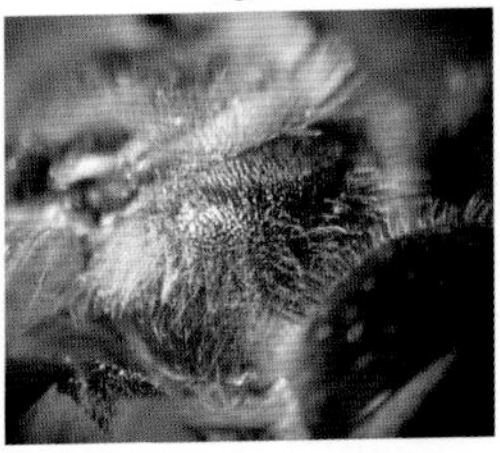

Fig. 8    Fig. 9    Fig. 10

LASIOGLOSSUM FEMALE GROUP A

1   Scutum with dense, even-sized punctures (Figs 12 & 13) 2

—   Scutum with punctures sparser and of variable size (Figs 14 & 16) 3

2   Apical depression of tergites 2 and 3 dulled by minute transverse ridges (angle of
light critical to see these) and scattered fine punctures (Fig. 11). Scutum duller,
with obvious microsculpture between the punctures (Fig. 12). Build more elongate .... *morio*

—   Apical depression of tergite 2 and often 3 smooth and shining without minute ridges.
Scutum shinier with weak microsculpture between the punctures (Fig. 13). Build
squatter, the thorax squarer in top view .... *leucopus*

Fig. 11 *L. morio*

Fig. 12 *L. morio*

Fig. 13 *L. leucopus*

Fig. 14 *L. smeathmanellum*

Fig. 15

Fig. 16 *L. cupromicans*

Fig. 17

3   Top of propodeum dull and rugose throughout (Fig. 18). Tergites metallic green, dulled by dense
punctures and with the hind margins pale and translucent. Tergite 4 extensively tomentose.
Head in front view oval (Fig. 3). Scutum more densely punctured (Figs 14 & 15) .... *smeathmanellum*

—   Top of propodeum smooth and semi-shining with weak longitudinal ridges that
end well before the hind margin (Fig. 19). Tergites shining blackish with
any punctures or minute ridges weak, the hind margins dark brown. Head in
front view long (Fig. 4). Scutum very sparsely punctured (Figs 16 & 17) .... *cupromicans*

Fig. 18   Fig. 19

LASIOGLOSSUM FEMALE GROUP B

1 Hind tibiae with dorsal fringe blackish. Relatively large, robust species with conspicuous white tomentose patches on tergites 2 and 3 (beware, these can get rubbed off in old individuals) 2

— Hind tibiae with dorsal fringe pale brown, buffish or whitish 3

2 Tergite 1 with punctures of uniform density almost throughout (Fig. 20), the surface dulled by light microsculpture. Pile on top of thorax grey-brown, even in fresh individuals. Wing stigmas dark brown .... *leucozonium*

— Tergite 1 with punctures of the apical depression, clearly denser than those of the basal section (Fig. 21), the surface shining and without microsculpture. Pile on top of thorax a brighter brown in fresh individuals. Wing stigmas orange-brown .... *zonulum*

3 Scutum shining with relatively large, sparse punctures (Fig. 22) 4

— Scutum dulled by microsculpture, with punctures small and dense (Fig. 23) 5

4 Tergites 2 and 3 with very large tomentose patches at sides; all tergites strongly shining with exceptionally broad apical depressions (Fig. 24). Thorax with a conspicuous orange-brown pile. Tergite 1 with numerous strong punctures. Wing stigmas orange. Larger (wing length 7mm) .... *laevigatum*

— Tergites without tomentose patches, the apical depressions clearly occupying less than half the surface of tergites 2 and 3. Top of thorax with an inconspicuous greyish pile. Tergite 1 inconspicuously punctate except sides of apical depression. Wing stigmas dark brown. Smaller (wing length 5.5mm) .... some *puncticolle*

5 Viewed from above, the pronotal angles of the thorax strongly produced, (about 90 degrees) and conspicuous (Fig. 25). A densely punctate, rather slim species with a wide face (Fig. 26) .... *malachurum*

— Pronotal angles obtuse and less protruding 6

Fig. 20   Fig. 21 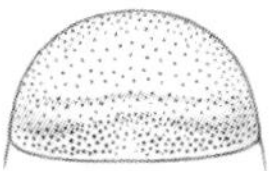   Fig. 22

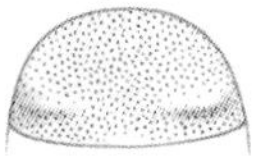

Fig. 23    Fig. 24 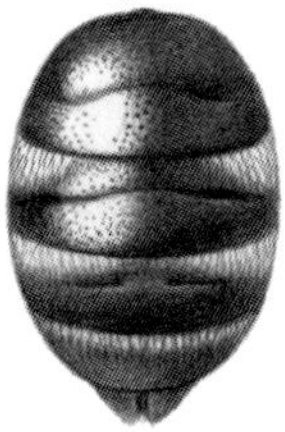   Fig. 25 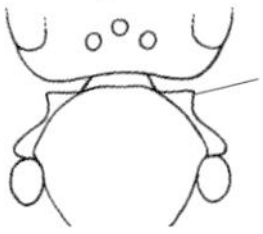   Fig. 26

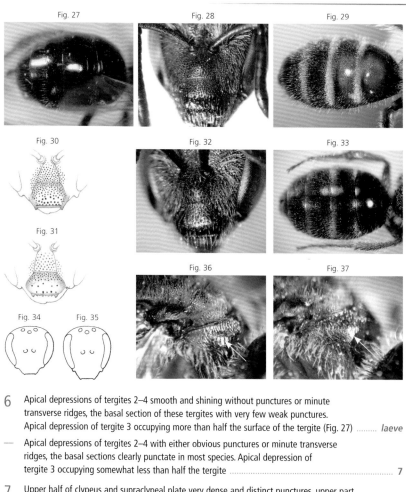

Fig. 27 Fig. 28 Fig. 29 Fig. 30 Fig. 31 Fig. 32 Fig. 33 Fig. 34 Fig. 35 Fig. 36 Fig. 37

6   Apical depressions of tergites 2–4 smooth and shining without punctures or minute transverse ridges, the basal section of these tergites with very few weak punctures. Apical depression of tergite 3 occupying more than half the surface of the tergite (Fig. 27) .... *laeve*

—   Apical depressions of tergites 2–4 with either obvious punctures or minute transverse ridges, the basal sections clearly punctate in most species. Apical depression of tergite 3 occupying somewhat less than half the tergite 7

7   Upper half of clypeus and supraclypeal plate very dense and distinct punctures, upper part of clypeus with at least 50 punctures (Figs 28 & 30). Apical margins of tergites translucent and appearing orange or pale brownish due to the basal tomentum of the following segment visible beneath (Fig. 29). Larger (wing length usually at least 6.5mm) 8

—   Upper part of clypeus and supraclypeal plate less densely or obviously punctate, upper part of clypeus usually with fewer than 30 punctures (Figs 31 & 32). Apical margins of tergites usually darker and more opaque (Fig. 33). Smaller (wing length to 5.5mm) 9

8   Head in front view roundish (Fig. 34). Tergite 1 at most lightly grey-bloomed and with the lateral ridges of the apical depression broadly interrupted centrally (best viewed from front). Upper propodeum to the sides of the semicircular ridged area more strongly ridged (Fig. 36) (angle of lighting critical). Thoracic hairs brighter brown (but fading in older individuals). Averaging larger (typical wing length 7mm) .... *calceatum*

—   Head in front view oval (Fig. 35). Tergite 1 often strongly grey-bloomed (Fig. 29) and with the lateral ridges of the apical depression almost meeting in the middle (best viewed from front). Upper propodeum to the sides of the semicircular ridged area usually smoother with few ridges and a more granular texture (Fig. 37). Thoracic hairs light brown. Averaging smaller (typical wing length 6.5mm) .... *albipes*

9   Inner spur of the hind tibiae with four projections, the final three of which are broad and bluntly rounded lobes (Fig. 38). Tergite 1 with the ridge defining the apical depression fully defined centrally (Fig. 39) (angle of lighting critical) .... **some *pauxillum***

—   Inner spur of the hind tibiae either with four or more sharp projections or with a single basal one (Figs 40 & 41). Tergite 1 with the ridge defining the apical depression broken centrally **10**

10 Tergite 1 densely punctate almost throughout, the punctures of the anterior area in places as dense as those of the apical depression **11**

—   Tergite 1 at most sparsely punctate, the apical depression never densely punctate **12**

11 Inner hind tibial spur usually with a single basal peg-like projection (Fig. 41). Wing stigmas buff. Tergite 1 more finely and sparsely punctate. Head in front view wide (Fig. 7). Hind margins of tergites relatively pale and translucent .... *laticeps*

—   Inner hind tibial spur with four peg-like projections (Fig. 40). Wing stigmas blackish. Tergite 1 slightly more densely and strongly punctate. Head in front view rounder (Fig. 2). Hind margins of tergites darker and opaque (Channel Islands) .... *mediterraneum*

12 Head in front view roundish (Fig. 34). Face including upper clypeus obviously punctate. Basal sections of tergites 2–4 with fine but obvious punctures. Tergites 2 and 3 with small but conspicuous tomentose patches at basal corners .... *fulvicorne*

—   Head in front view oval (Fig. 35). Face including upper clypeus with any punctures sparse and poorly defined. Tergites almost impunctate. Tomentose patches at basal corners of tergites 2 and 3 scarcely evident .... *fratellum*

LASIOGLOSSUM FEMALE GROUP C

1   Hind tibiae and tarsi orange with bright orange hairs throughout. Thorax with a bright orange-brown pile. Large (typical wing length 9mm) .... *xanthopus*

—   Hind tibiae and tarsi blackish without orange hairs. Wing length less than 7mm in all species except *sexnotatum* **2**

2   Top of thorax extremely dull, with dense punctures and microsculpture (Fig. 42). Larger (wing length usually at least 6.5mm) **3**

—   Top of thorax densely punctate but shining, with no microsculpture between punctures (Fig. 43). Smaller (typical wing length 5.5mm) **4**

3   Abdomen with extensive grey tomentum, this occupying the sides of tergite 1, forming dense bands across the base of tergites 2 and 3, and less dense patches across the hind margin of tergite 3 and throughout tergite 4 (Fig. 44). Dorsal fringe of hind tibiae brown-haired. Wings clear with stigmas pale brown. Smaller (wing length to 7mm) .... *prasinum*

—   Abdomen with white tomentose markings confined to the basal corners of tergites 2–4 (Fig. 45). Dorsal fringe of hind tibiae blackish-haired. Wings greyish with stigmas and veins blackish. Larger (typical wing length 8mm) .... *sexnotatum*

4   Tergite 1 moderately and rather evenly punctate throughout, without excessively dense punctures in the apical depression (Fig. 46). Tergite 2 less densely punctate and shinier. Wing stigmas orange-brown or brown .... *lativentre*

—   Tergite 1 with the apical depression very densely punctate and contrasting with the sparser punctures of the basal section (Fig. 47). Tergite 2 more densely punctate and duller. Wing stigmas yellowish .... *quadrinotatum*

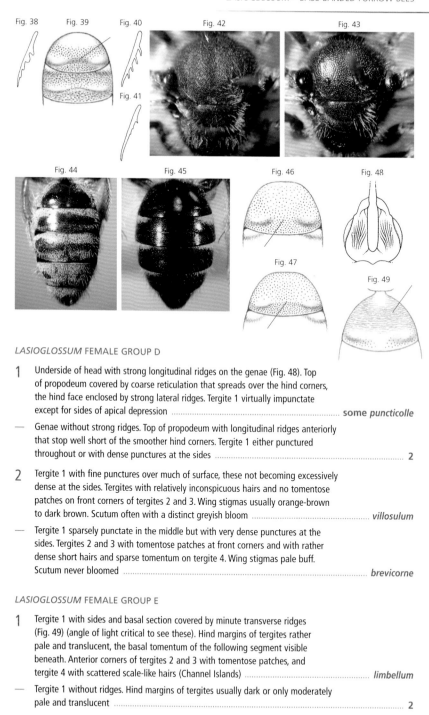

Fig. 38   Fig. 39   Fig. 40

Fig. 41

Fig. 42   Fig. 43

Fig. 44   Fig. 45   Fig. 46   Fig. 48

Fig. 47

Fig. 49

LASIOGLOSSUM FEMALE GROUP D

1   Underside of head with strong longitudinal ridges on the genae (Fig. 48). Top of propodeum covered by coarse reticulation that spreads over the hind corners, the hind face enclosed by strong lateral ridges. Tergite 1 virtually impunctate except for sides of apical depression .... **some *puncticolle***

—   Genae without strong ridges. Top of propodeum with longitudinal ridges anteriorly that stop well short of the smoother hind corners. Tergite 1 either punctured throughout or with dense punctures at the sides **2**

2   Tergite 1 with fine punctures over much of surface, these not becoming excessively dense at the sides. Tergites with relatively inconspicuous hairs and no tomentose patches on front corners of tergites 2 and 3. Wing stigmas usually orange-brown to dark brown. Scutum often with a distinct greyish bloom .... *villosulum*

—   Tergite 1 sparsely punctate in the middle but with very dense punctures at the sides. Tergites 2 and 3 with tomentose patches at front corners and with rather dense short hairs and sparse tomentum on tergite 4. Wing stigmas pale buff. Scutum never bloomed .... *brevicorne*

LASIOGLOSSUM FEMALE GROUP E

1   Tergite 1 with sides and basal section covered by minute transverse ridges (Fig. 49) (angle of light critical to see these). Hind margins of tergites rather pale and translucent, the basal tomentum of the following segment visible beneath. Anterior corners of tergites 2 and 3 with tomentose patches, and tergite 4 with scattered scale-like hairs (Channel Islands) .... *limbellum*

—   Tergite 1 without ridges. Hind margins of tergites usually dark or only moderately pale and translucent **2**

Fig. 50 Fig. 51 Fig. 52 Fig. 53

Fig. 54 Fig. 55 Fig. 56

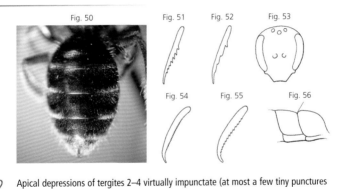

2   Apical depressions of tergites 2–4 virtually impunctate (at most a few tiny punctures
but with minute transverse ridges in *sexstrigatum* and *rufitarse*) **3**

—   Apical depressions of tergites 2–4 with more obvious punctures (rather fine and
sparse in *parvulum*) **5**

3   Hind margins of tergites with pale hair fringes (Fig. 50). Top of propodeum
at sides with numerous oblique ridges .... *sexstrigatum*

—   Hind margins of tergites without pale hair fringes. Top of propodeum at sides
without numerous oblique ridges **4**

4   Top of propodeum rough throughout, including the hind margins. Apical depressions
of tergites 2–4 dulled by minute transverse ridges (angle of light critical to see these).
Inner spur of hind tibiae with 5–6 peg-like projections that are longer than wide
(Fig. 51). Larger (typical wing length 5.5mm) .... *rufitarse*

—   Top of propodeum relatively smooth and only roughened along the front. Apical
depressions of tergites 2–4 smooth without any minute transverse ridges. Inner
spur of hind tibiae with 3–4 short and broad projections (Fig. 52). Very small (typical
wing length 4mm) .... *semilucens*

5   Head in front view long (Fig. 53). Sides of thorax with dense, strong and definite punctures **6**

—   Head in front view round or oval (Figs 2 & 3). Sides of thorax with any punctures relatively weak **7**

6   Outer hind tibial spur less strongly curved apically (Fig. 54) .... *punctatissimum*

—   Outer hind tibial spur strongly curved apically (Fig. 55) .... *angusticeps*

7   Inner spur of hind tibiae with four projections, the final three of which are broad
with bluntly rounded lobes (Fig. 38). Top of propodeum with a sharply angulated
hind margin where it meets the hind face. Tergite 1 with the defining ridge
of the apical depression complete in the middle (Fig. 39) (angle of view and
lighting critical to see this) .... *some pauxillum*

—   Inner spur of hind tibiae with narrower, peg-like projections (Fig. 40). Top of
propodeum merging smoothly into the hind face. Tergite 1 with the defining
ridge of the apical depression broken centrally (except in *L. minutissimum*) **8**

8   A very small, slim species (wing length usually less than 4mm), the thorax
viewed from above about 1.5 times as long as wide. Abdomen viewed from side
with a pronounced transverse depression where tergites 1 and 2 meet (Fig. 56) .... *minutissimum*

—   More broadly built species (wing length usually more than 4mm), the thorax
viewed from above at most 1.25 times as long as wide. Abdomen viewed from
side with a fairly smoothly curved junction of tergites 1 and 2 .... **9**

9   Wing stigmas orange. Top of propodeum with rather widely spaced longitudinal ridges that remain strong to the hind margin, surface between them rather smooth and shining (Fig. 57). Thorax almost square in top view. Face in front view wide (Fig. 1) .... *pauperatum*

—   Wing stigmas brown. Top of propodeum with reticulate rather than longitudinal ridges. Thorax somewhat longer in top view. Face in front view round (Fig. 2) **10**

10   Top of propodeum relatively smooth with weak ridges confined to the base, leaving the hind margin relatively smooth and shiny (Fig. 58). Tergites fairly obviously punctured throughout (including the basal section of tergite 1), the hind margins brown and somewhat translucent, resulting in a paler, duller appearance .... *nitidiusculum*

—   Top of propodeum more evenly rough throughout (Fig. 59). Tergites 2, 3 and the apical depression of tergite 1 with fine, sparse punctures, and the basal section of tergite 1 barely punctate. Hind margins of tergites dark, resulting in a darker, shinier appearance .... *parvulum*

Fig. 57 *L. pauperatum*   Fig. 58 *L. nitidiusculum* 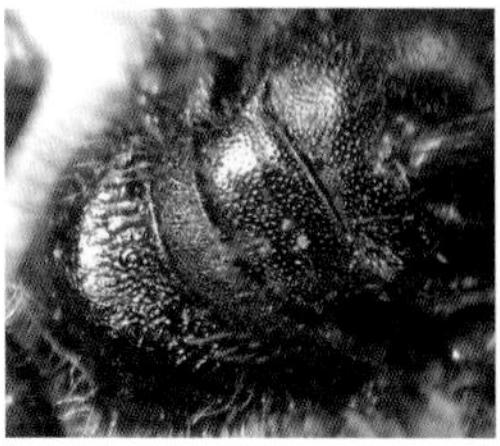   Fig. 59 *L. parvulum*

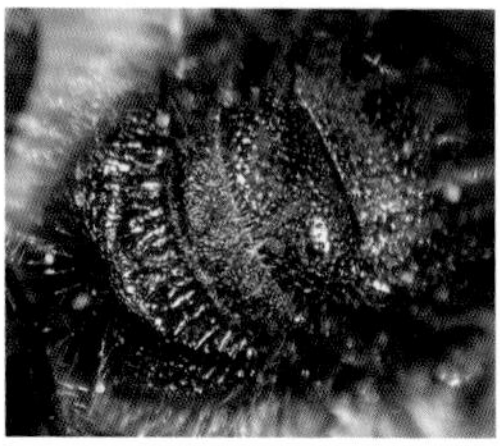

LASIOGLOSSUM MALE GROUPS

1   Head, thorax and sometimes abdomen metallic green or turquoise. Small species (wing length to 5mm) .... **male group A**

—   Body non-metallic **2**

2   Sternite 2 (viewed from side) either virtually hairless or with hairs that are mostly shorter than 0.75 times the width of an ocellus and often inclined (Fig. 61). Antennae always long or very long, at least capable of stretching back to beyond the hind margin of the thorax (Fig. 60). If the hairs on sternite 2 are about as long as the width of an ocellus (*laticeps* and *mediterraneum*), the second segment of the hind tarsi is 3 times as long as wide in side view (Fig. 64) .... **male group B**

—   Sternite 2 with longer, usually denser and more upright hairs that are at least as long as the width of an ocellus (Figs 62 & 63). If the length of the hairs on sternite 2 is about the width of an ocellus (*malachurum* and *prasinum*) the second segment of the hind tarsi is no more than twice as long as wide in side view. Antennae often shorter than previous group **3**

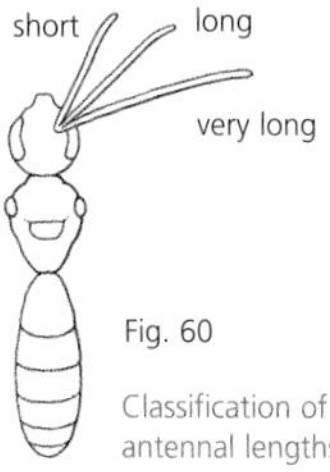

short   long
very long

Fig. 60

Classification of male antennal lengths.

Fig. 61   Fig. 62 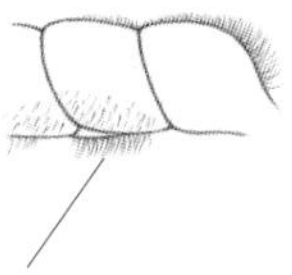   Fig. 63

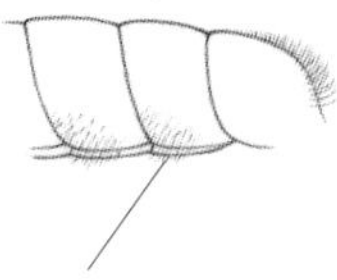

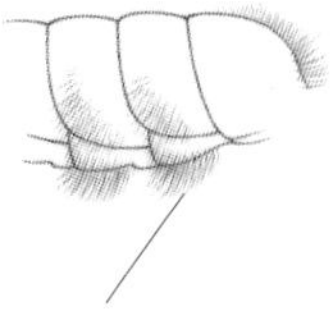

3   Antennae very long, capable of stretching back to well beyond the hind margin
of the thorax (Fig. 60) .... **male group C**

—   Antennae long, only capable of stretching to the hind margin of the thorax (Fig. 60) **4**

4   Hind legs including the tarsi entirely dark (at most knees and tarsi dull brownish) ...... **male group D**

—   Hind legs with at least the basitarsi clear whitish or yellow, often the bases and
tips of the hind tibiae too **5**

5   Antennal flagella obviously orange or reddish beneath, at least on a number of
basal segments .... **male group E**

—   Antennal flagella dark, at most obscurely brownish beneath .... **male group F**

LASIOGLOSSUM MALE GROUP A

1   Mid and hind tarsi pale .... *leucopum*

—   Mid and hind tarsi dark **2**

2   Scutum with dense punctures and much dulled by microsculpture between these (Fig. 12) .... *morio*

—   Scutum with sparser punctures and shiny, with little microsculpture between punctures **3**

3   Top of propodeum almost entirely roughened and dull. Clypeus yellow-marked
apically. Scutum more densely punctate (Figs 14 & 15) .... *smeathmanellum*

—   Top of propodeum smoother and shinier with weak ridges confined to the base.
Clypeus usually entirely dark. Scutum more sparsely punctate (Figs 16 & 17) .... *cupromicans*

LASIOGLOSSUM MALE GROUP B

1   Antennal flagella black beneath **2**

—   Antennal flagella obviously orange or reddish beneath, at least basally **4**

2   Scutellum rugose and dull, without obvious punctures. Hind tibiae only vaguely
pale at base. A small species (wing length typically 5mm) with tergites always
dark .... *fulvicorne* **(form with dark antennae)**

—   Scutellum with clearly defined punctures. Hind tibiae broadly yellow at base.
Larger species (wing length usually at least 5.5mm) with tergites often red-marked **3**

3   Labrum and often the mandibles and pronotal tubercles dark. Tergites 2–4
with larger and denser tomentose patches at front corners. Head in front view
roundish, the eyes more curved (Fig. 34). Hairs on top of thorax browner.
Averaging larger (typical wing length 6.5–7mm) .... *calceatum*

—   Labrum, mandibles and pronotal tubercles yellow. Tergites 2–4 with smaller and
weaker tomentose patches. Head in front view oval, the eyes less curved (Fig. 35).
Hairs on top of thorax greyer. Averaging smaller (typical wing length 5.5–6mm) .... *albipes*

4   Hind tarsi in side view with second segment about 3 times as long as wide and
almost parallel-sided (Fig. 64). Sternite 2 with relatively long hairs (Fig. 62). Head
in front view wide with the lower edge of the clypeus only a little lower than the
bottom of the eyes. Tergites often partially red **5**

—   Hind tarsi in side view with second segment at most twice as long as wide and
more triangular (Figs 65 & 66). Head in front view roundish or oval with the clypeus
more strongly produced below the eyes. Tergites always dark **6**

Fig. 64 *L. laticeps*   Fig. 65 *L. fulvicorne*   Fig. 66 *L. fratellum*

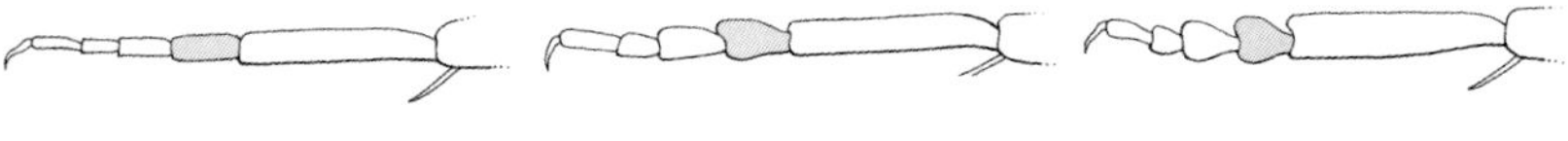

5   Wing stigmas buff .... *laticeps*

—   Wing stigmas blackish (Channel Islands) .... *mediterraneum*

6   Antennae long but only capable of stretching about halfway along tergite 1.
     Sternite 2 with short but not minute hairs. Tergite 1 densely punctate, with the
     transverse ridge defining the apical depression complete in the middle (angle
     of view and lighting critical to see this). Propodeum with upper hind corners
     smoothly rounded and with the hind face unenclosed .... *pauxillum*

—   Antennae very long, capable of stretching to the hind margin of tergite 1.
     Sternite 2 with minute hairs. Tergite 1 sparsely punctate with the ridge
     defining the apical depression broken centrally. Propodeum with upper
     hind corners angled and the hind face enclosed by weak lateral ridges 7

7   Scutellum rugose and without obvious punctures. Hind tarsi in side view slimmer
     and longer, with second segment about 1.5 times as long as wide (Fig. 65).
     Tergites 2–5 in side view with only tiny hairs above (Fig. 67). Tergites 2 and 3
     with obvious tomentose patches at front corners. Head in front view roundish
     (Fig. 34) .... **typical** *fulvicorne*

—   Scutellum with clearly defined punctures. Hind tarsi in side view shorter and
     stouter, with second segment about as long as wide (Fig. 66). Tergites 2–5 in side
     view with a distinct pile of upright hairs above (Fig. 68). Tergites 2 and 3 without
     obvious tomentose patches at front corners. Head in front view oval (Fig. 35) .... *fratellum*

Fig. 67   Fig. 68    Fig. 69 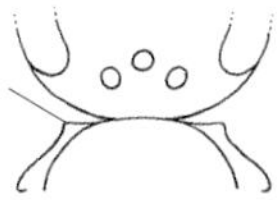   Fig. 70

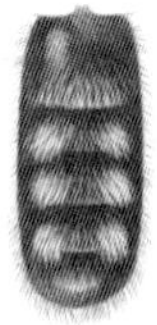

Fig. 71    Fig. 72

LASIOGLOSSUM MALE GROUP C

1   Clypeus, labrum, mandibles and undersides of the antennal flagella black
     (mandible tips can be reddish) .... *laevigatum*

—   At least clypeus yellow-marked apically 2

2   Viewed from above, the pronotal angles of the thorax squarely produced and
     conspicuous (Fig. 69). All tibiae predominantly yellow, with dark patches not
     forming complete rings. Tergites 2 and 3 with tomentose patches at front
     corners. Scutum much dulled by microsculpture. Tergites sometimes reddish .... *malachurum*

—   Pronotal angles inconspicuous. Mid and hind tibiae mostly dark. Tergites 2
     and 3 without tomentose patches. Scutum shinier. Tergites always dark 3

3   Viewed from below, sternites 3–5 with conspicuous lateral hair tufts
     (Fig. 70). Top of propodeum relatively smooth, with ridges confined to base .... *nitidiusculum*

—   Sternites without lateral hair tufts. Top of propodeum more extensively rugose 4

4   Hind tarsi slimmer, in side view with segment 2 about twice as long as wide,
     all segments dark (Fig. 71). Tergite 3 with apical depression finely punctate
     and lacking minute transverse ridges. Head in front view roundish (Fig. 34) .... *parvulum*

—   Hind tarsi stouter, in side view with segment 2 about 1.5 times as long as wide,
     the basal segments often orange (Fig. 72). Tergite 3 with apical depression impunctate with
     minute transverse ridges (angle of light and strong magnification needed). Head
     in front view oval (Fig. 35) .... *rufitarse*

LASIOGLOSSUM MALE GROUP D

1 Large species (wing length usually at least 6mm) with distinct tomentose
   patches on anterior corners of tergites 2 and 3 2

— Small species (wing length to 4.5mm) without tomentose patches on the tergites 3

2 Head with little production of the hind corners behind the eyes (Fig. 73). Scutum
   dull grey with dense punctures and microsculpture. Tergite 1 densely punctate
   throughout. Wing stigmas dark brown. Build slimmer, the thorax clearly longer
   than wide .... *sexnotatum*

— Head in top view larger and more box-shaped, the hind corners much inflated (Fig. 74).
   Scutum shinier with weaker microsculpture. Wing stigmas orange. Build more
   robust and bull-headed, the thorax squarer with well-developed pronotal angles .... *zonulum*

3 Very small (wing length 3–3.5mm) with a pronounced transverse groove across
   the top of the abdomen where tergites 1 and 2 meet (Fig. 75). Hind tarsi slim and
   longer than the hind tibiae .... *minutissimum*

— Larger (wing length 4–4.5mm). Top of abdomen more evenly convex. Hind tarsi
   stouter and shorter (not longer than the hind tibiae) 4

4 Head in front view long (Fig. 4), the clypeus yellow-marked apically. Thorax
   in top view much longer than wide, the scutum densely punctate (Fig. 10) .... *angusticeps*

— Head in front view roundish (Fig. 2), the clypeus usually dark apically. Thorax
   squarer, the scutum smooth and shining with large, sparse punctures (Fig. 9) .... some *villosulum*

Fig. 73   Fig. 74   Fig. 75

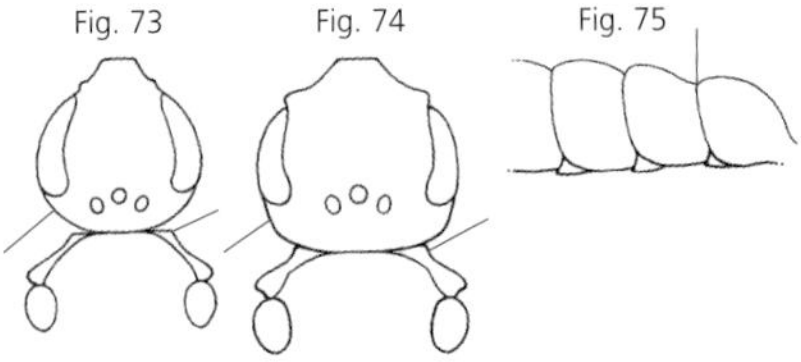

LASIOGLOSSUM MALE GROUP E

1 A very large species (typical wing length 8mm) with hind tibiae and tarsi orange.
   Tergites 2–4 with tomentose patches at anterior corners. Top of thorax with a
   conspicuous brown pile .... *xanthopus*

— Smaller species (wing length to 6mm) with hind tibiae mostly dark and no
   tomentose patches on the tergites 2

2 Apical depressions of tergites 2 and 3 shining and virtually impunctate. Tergite 1
   with only scattered fine punctures 3

— Apical depressions of tergites 2 and 3 and most of tergite 1 with obvious and dense punctures 5

3 Head in side view with lower corner of gena strongly angulated (Fig. 76) .... *sexstrigatum*

— Head in side view with lower corner of gena gently rounded 4

4 Top of propodeum with short longitudinal ridges restricted to the base, the hind margin
   broadly smooth and shining. Basal sections of tergites 2–4 obviously punctate.
   Small (wing length 4mm) .... some *semilucens*

— Top of propodeum coarsely rugose throughout. Basal sections of tergites 2–4
   barely punctate. Larger (wing length 5.5–6mm) .... *laeve*

5   Scutum smooth and shining with large and sparse punctures (Fig. 9).
Clypeus not usually yellow-marked apically .... **some** *villosulum*

—   Scutum more densely punctate. Clypeus yellow-marked apically.................................. **6**

6   Head in front view long (Fig. 4). Scutum dulled by microsculpture between the
punctures, which are relatively small and dense (Fig. 10). Antennal segment
4 clearly longer than wide when viewed from front (Fig. 77) .... *punctatissimum*

—   Head in front view broad or round-oval. Scutum shinier, with somewhat larger
and sparser punctures and barely any microsculpture. Antennal segment 4 squarish
in front view (Fig. 78) **7**

7   Head in front view oval (Fig. 3) with labrum black. Sternite 5 bare along midline with
longer hairs on either side, sternite 6 with a bare depression centrally (Fig. 79).
Wing stigmas straw-coloured .... *brevicorne*

—   Head in front view broad (Fig. 1) with labrum yellow. Sternites 5 and 6 flat and
uniformly haired. Wing stigmas orange-brown .... *pauperatum*

| Fig. 76 | Fig. 77 | Fig. 78 | Fig. 79 | Fig. 80 |

LASIOGLOSSUM MALE GROUP F

1   Mandibles largely yellow. Tergites 2–4 without conspicuous tomentose patches
at anterior corners. Small species (wing length 4–4.5mm) **2**

—   Mandibles black or dark reddish. Tergites 2 and 3 or 2–4 with tomentose patches.
Larger species (wing length usually at least 5.5mm) **4**

2   Hind margins of tergites (at least 1 and 2) translucent brown. Sides of tergite 1 basally
with minute transverse ridges (Fig. 49). Hind tibiae broadly yellow at base and tip.
Top of propodeum relatively smooth (Channel Islands) .... *limbellum*

—   Hind margins of tergites 1 and 2 blackish. Sides of tergite 1 without minute ridges.
Hind tibiae mostly black **3**

3   Top of propodeum coarsely rugose throughout (including the hind corners) and
sharply angled along the rear edge where it meets the hind face. Larger (wing
length 4.5–5mm) .... *puncticolle*

—   Top of propodeum with longitudinal ridges confined to the base, the hind margin
broadly smooth and shining, merging smoothly into the rear face. Smaller (wing
length 4mm) .... **some** *semilucens*

4   Tergite 7 unusually large and red, at least apically, with a flat rear face that is
bare on the apical half. Tip of abdomen downcurved in side view (Fig. 80).
Sternite 5 with a fringe of very long hairs along the hind margin. Tergite 1
with scale-like white hairs at sides (these can get rubbed off) .... *prasinum*

—   Tergite 7 small, dark and with hairs on apical half, the tip of the abdomen
not appearing downcurved in side view. Sternite 5 without a long hair fringe.
Tergite 1 without scale-like hairs **5**

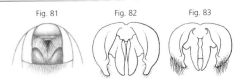

Fig. 81   Fig. 82   Fig. 83

5   Sternite 6 with a pair of divergent ridges that form a V-shaped area enclosing a patch of dense pale hairs (Fig. 81). Propodeum very coarsely rugose on top, sides and rear face. Hind tarsi with segments 2–5 dark and contrasting with the whitish basitarsi. Averaging larger and more broadly built than the following species .... *leucozonium*

—   Sternite 6 with a simple apex. Propodeum less coarsely rugose, the top with smoothly rounded, semi-shining hind margins. Hind tarsi entirely pale 6

6   Wing stigmas yellowish. Gonostyli of the genitalia with only short and sparse hairs, the gonocoxites that precede these bare (Fig. 82) .... *quadrinotatum*

—   Wing stigmas brownish. Gonostyli and the tips of the gonocoxites densely hairy (Fig. 83) .... *lativentre*

Lasioglossum albipes (Fabricius, 1781)   **Bloomed Furrow Bee**

not illustrated

Description & similar species FW 5–6.5mm female, 5–6mm male. Females are one of a pair of similar species characterised by the combination of angled propodeal shoulders (and a carinate hind face), a very densely punctate upper face (upper clypeus and supraclypeal plate) and translucent hind margins to the tergites. Compared to *L. calceatum*, the head in front view is oval as opposed to roundish, the transverse ridges defining the apical depression of tergite 1 extend further towards the midline, and tergites 1 and 2 are often strongly grey-bloomed. There are also subtle differences in the sculpturing of the propodeal shoulders. The average size is smaller than *L. calceatum* and the top of the thorax has a duller grey-brown pile. The abdomen tends to look duller and more strongly banded, with more abundant short hairs. Males of this species and *L. calceatum* have the unusual combination of dark undersides to the antennal flagella and short hairs on sternite 2, though *L. albipes* is typically smaller and slimmer, with the head slightly longer, and the labrum, mandibles and pronotal tubercles are yellow. The abdomen has less conspicuous tomentose patches on tergites 2–4. The tergites can be all black or extensively red, but the former state is scarcer. Small males could be confused in

female

male

the field with red-marked *L. laticeps* and *L. mediterraneum*, but these have rounder heads in front view and pale undersides to the antennal flagella. **Variation** Moderate size variation, overlapping with smaller *L. calceatum* (larger females may be queens). The female head shape in front view varies and can approach *L. calceatum*. Older females tend to lose the bloom on the abdomen. Males can have the abdomen all black or extensively red. **Flight season** Females can appear in March in the south and produce workers by early summer. Males and further females usually appear in July. Both sexes can fly well into September. **Habitat** Found in a wide variety of habitats, without any strong preferences, and quite frequent in urban greenspace. More frequent in exposed coastal districts and uplands than *L. calceatum*. **Flowers visited** Flowers from various families are visited, though females are fond of buttercups. In late summer males can be particularly abundant on umbellifers, scabiouses and composites such as ragworts, thistles, knapweeds and Yarrow. Like *L. calceatum*, males sometimes cluster overnight on flowerheads and other low vegetation. **Nesting habits** Nesting occurs in light soils, sometimes in small aggregations. It is primitively eusocial in some parts of its range but possibly solitary in northern areas. **Status & distribution** Locally common throughout Britain and Ireland, though generally less abundant than *L. calceatum*. Recorded from several of the Channel Islands. **Parasites & associates** The cleptoparasitic bee *Sphecodes monilicornis*.

Lasioglossum angusticeps (Perkins, 1895)   Cliff Furrow Bee
not illustrated

Description & similar species FW 4–4.5mm female, 4mm male. One of two small, non-metallic, non-carinate *Lasioglossum* species with a very long head in front view and densely punctate tergites. Females can be separated from the commoner *L. punctatissimum* by the greater apical curvature of the outer hind tibial spur, but there is much variation of this feature in *L. punctatissimum* so records should ideally be based on males. Males resemble *L. punctatissimum* but have the hind tarsi dark, and there are differences in the genitalia. **Variation** Little noted. **Flight season** Females fly from May until August, males from July to late September. **Habitat** South-facing coastal soft rock cliffs and associated landslips, especially those with clay. **Flowers visited** Females seem to obtain pollen primarily from bird's-foot-trefoils. Males like Wild Carrot and Common Fleabane. **Nesting habits** Nesting aggregations have been observed in clay on the lower sections of cliffs and landslips. **Status & distribution** Restricted to a small number of soft rock cliffs in east Devon, Dorset and the Isle of Wight, though common at some of these. Originally described as new to science from Devon. **Parasites & associates** Occasionally stylopised.

Lasioglossum brevicorne (Schenck, 1870) Short-horned Furrow Bee
not illustrated

Description & similar species FW 4.5mm female, 4mm male. A small non-carinate *Lasioglossum* with very pale wing stigmas, a roundish-oval head in front view and a shiny, sparsely punctate scutum which lacks microsculpture. The top of the propodeum is relatively smooth with semi-shining hind margins. Females have pale, translucent hind margins to the tergites, and tomentose patches are present on the anterior corners of tergites 2 and 3. Tergite 4 is entirely covered by pale hairs which are scale-like basally, and the whole tip of the abdomen appears very pale-pubescent compared with most other small species. Tergite 1 is

female

shiny centrally but very densely punctured at the sides. The antennae are particularly short with the flagella orange beneath. *L. villosulum* and *L. puncticolle* are the only other small species with such a sparsely punctured scutum but are much darker, and *L. puncticolle* has the top of the propodeum strongly rugose and deep furrows on the genae. Males can be confirmed by examination of sternites 5 and 6. The former has a densely hairy hind margin except in the middle which is bare, the latter has a hairless depressed area centrally. The antennae are exceptionally short for a male. The mandibles and lower clypeus are yellow but the labrum is black. **Variation** Some variation in the extent of black markings on the male legs. **Flight season** Females fly from May to August, males in July and August. **Habitat** Sandy habitats including coastal dunes, heathland, acid grassland and sandy-chalky grassland in the East Anglian Brecks. **Flowers visited** Typically yellow hawkish composites such as Cat's-ear and Smooth Hawk's-beard. **Nesting habits** Presumed to nest in sandy ground, but little information available. **Status & distribution** A very localised species, with scattered records as far north as Co. Durham, but mostly within the heathland districts of Dorset, Surrey and the East Anglian Brecks. It appears to have become more common and to have spread north in recent decades. Not recorded from Wales, Scotland or Ireland. Recorded from several of the Channel Islands. **Parasites & associates** Possibly a host of the cleptoparasitic bee *Sphecodes puncticeps* on the continent. Stylopised examples have been found in Jersey.

Lasioglossum calceatum (Scopoli, 1763)   **Common Furrow Bee**

Plate 7

Description & similar species FW 5.5–7mm (sexes similar). A medium-sized carinate species resembling a large *L. albipes* but with the head rounder in front view. Females have a brighter brown pile on top of the thorax and a less bloomed, barer-looking abdomen with the transverse ridges at the sides of tergite 1 more widely separated in the middle. Males can have the abdomen all black or extensively red-marked and have larger, denser tomentose patches on tergites 2–4 than *L. albipes*. The labrum is dark, and usually the mandibles and pronotal tubercles too. **Variation** Moderate size variation (larger females may be queens).

female

male, dark

male, red-banded

The female head shape in front view varies from slightly broader than high to somewhat oval and approaching *L. albipes*. Males can have the abdomen all black or extensively red. **Flight season** Females can appear in March in the south and produce workers by early summer. Males and new females appear in July, and both can fly into October (the last solitary bee to disappear in most districts). **Habitat** Like *L. albipes* (alongside which it often occurs), found in a wide variety of habitats without any strong preferences, and quite frequent in urban greenspace. **Flowers visited** Flowers of many families are visited, including a variety of spring-flowering shrubs. Males can be abundant on thistles, knapweeds and ragworts in late summer. Like *L. albipes*, males will often roost overnight in clusters on flowerheads and other low vegetation. **Nesting habits** Nesting seems to occur solitarily or in small aggregations in light soils. It is a primitively eusocial species in some districts but possibly solitary in the north where the flight period is shorter. **Status & distribution** Found throughout Britain and Ireland and common in most districts except the most exposed uplands. Common on the Channel Islands. **Parasites & associates** The cleptoparasitic bee *Sphecodes monilicornis* and possibly *S. ephippius*. Occasionally stylopised.

Lasioglossum cupromicans (Pérez, 1903) Turquoise Furrow Bee

not illustrated

Description & similar species FW 4mm (sexes similar). One of four small metallic *Lasioglossum* species. Females resemble *L. smeathmanellum* in having a shiny scutum that bears unevenly sized punctures and little obvious microsculpture, but the punctures are much sparser in *L. cupromicans*. The tergites are shiny black and inconspicuously punctured with less extensive tomentum and pale hair than *L. smeathmanellum*. The top of the propodeum is relatively smooth, with shallow ridges confined to the base, and the head is much longer than in the other metallic species. It appears much darker in the field than the other three species. Males also resemble *L. smeathmanellum* in having a shiny scutum but have the top of the propodeum much smoother and the clypeus is usually entirely dark. **Variation** The metallic colouration can vary, with some individuals greener and others bluer. Some males can have a weak yellowish mark at the tip of the clypeus but this is usually much weaker than in *L. smeathmanellum*. The Irish form is sometimes regarded as a separate subspecies. **Flight season** Females can fly from April to October, males from late July to October. **Habitat** Various habitats are used, including sites with calcareous and acid soils. Quarries and brownfield sites are important in areas such as the Midlands, whereas in the west and north it tends to favour higher ground and will occur on moorland.

Flowers visited Various, including hawkish composites, thistles, Rosebay Willowherb, Heather (Ling), Sheep's-bit, Turnip, cinquefoils and stonecrops. **Nesting habits** Nesting has been observed in the mortar of stone walls and rock faces. **Status & distribution** Widely recorded in Britain and Ireland but generally very scarce away from the English Midlands, northern England and north Wales. Particularly rare in southeast England. Not recorded from the Channel Islands. **Parasites & associates** Possibly a host of the cleptoparasitic bee *Sphecodes geoffrellus*.

Lasioglossum fratellum (Pérez, 1903) **Smooth-faced Furrow Bee**

not illustrated

Description & similar species FW 5–5.5mm female, 5mm male. Females are one of a number of small carinate species with a dull and densely punctured scutum, and barely punctate first tergite. They can be separated from the similar *L. fulvicorne* by the longer head (oval in front view) and unusually weak and shallow punctures on the face. The basal parts of tergites 2 and 3 lack distinct tomentose patches on the anterior corners and are scarcely punctate basally (obviously punctured in *L. fulvicorne*). The wing stigmas are orange-brown (pale straw-coloured in *L. fulvicorne*). Males of this species and *L. fulvicorne* are unique in

female

having very long antennal flagella and only minute hairs on sternite 2, but *L. fratellum* males have a more oval head (front view), a more obviously punctured scutellum, no tomentose patches on tergites 2 and 3, shorter and stouter hind tarsi and longer hairs on top of tergites 2–5. **Variation** Little other than minor variation in the extent of dark on the male legs. **Flight season** Females fly from April to October, males from July to October. **Habitat** Particularly characteristic of heathland, moorland, acid woodland and other base-poor places. **Flowers visited** Various, including willows, heathers, Tormentil, Cat's-ear, dandelions, thistles, ragworts, Devil's-bit Scabious, brambles, Bilberry, Sheep's-bit, bellflowers and Rosebay Willowherb. **Nesting**

male

habits Small nesting aggregations have been observed in south-facing banks and slopes. In some districts, females have been shown to nest across two years (iteroparity), possibly an adaptation to harsher environments with limited foraging time. Thought to be primitively eusocial. **Status & distribution** Widely recorded in Britain and Ireland, though generally avoiding calcareous geology. Locally common in some districts, especially in the north and west. On the Channel Islands, known only from Jersey. **Parasites & associates** The cleptoparasitic bee *Sphecodes hyalinatus* and possibly *S. ferruginatus*.

Lasioglossum fulvicorne (Kirby, 1802) **Chalk Furrow Bee**

Plate 7

Description & similar species FW 5–5.5mm female, 5mm male. A small species with females closely resembling *L. fratellum* but with the head rounder in front view and the face distinctly punctured. Small but obvious tomentose patches are present at the anterior corners of tergites 2 and 3, the top of the propodeum is more coarsely roughened and the wing stigmas paler. *L. laticeps* and *L. mediterraneum* are also rather similar but have fine punctures covering most of tergite 1 and broader heads in front view. Males of this species and *L. fratellum* are unique in having very long antennae combined with only minute hairs on sternite

2. The rugose and impunctate scutellum, more coarsely rugose propodeum and longer, slimmer hind tarsi of *L. fulvicorne* are some of the more obvious differences between males of the two. **Variation** In males, the antennal flagella, which are normally orange beneath, can occasionally be almost entirely dark, and the amount of black on the legs can vary somewhat. **Flight season** Females can fly from late March until October, males from June to October. **Habitat** Strongly associated with calcareous habitats, including chalk and limestone grassland, brownfield sites and woodland, but occasionally on more acidic and sandy sites. **Flowers visited** Many sorts of flowers, including spring-blossoming shrubs such as willows. Males can be especially abundant on late-summer umbellifers and composites. Spring females have a particular liking for Ground-ivy. **Nesting habits** Nesting has rarely been observed but is likely to occur in sparsely vegetated or short-cropped light soils. It is not thought to form large nesting aggregations and is regarded as solitary. **Status & distribution** Widespread in England and often abundant in chalk and limestone districts. Scarcer in Wales and the southwest and rare in Scotland. Not recorded from Ireland or the Channel Islands. **Parasites & associates** The cleptoparasitic bees *Sphecodes hyalinatus* and *S. ferruginatus*.

female

male

Lasioglossum laeve (Kirby, 1802)   Shiny-gastered Furrow Bee

not illustrated

Description & similar species FW 6.5mm female, 5.5–6mm male. A carinate species about the size of *L. calceatum* but with unusually shiny and puncture-free tergites with dark hind margins. The head is roundish in front, with the male lower face little produced (as in *L. laticeps* and *L. mediterraneum*). Small tomentose patches are present at the anterior corners of tergites 2 and 3, and the apical depressions of these tergites are very broad, occupying about half of the visible segment. The wing stigmas are brown. The top of the female propodeum has angled hind corners and longitudinal ridges that reach the hind margins, but the male propodeum is more rugose throughout. The male has rather short antennae with the flagella orange beneath and a yellow-marked clypeus; the legs are mostly black but with yellow tarsi. Only *L. semilucens* has such shiny, puncture-free tergite margins, but it is a much smaller non-carinate species with smooth hind margins to the propodeum. **Variation** None noted. **Flight season** On the continent known to fly from April to September, with males appearing in August. **Habitat** Preferences unclear. **Flowers visited** On the continent records include various composites, umbellifers and Devil's-bit Scabious. **Nesting habits** Unknown. **Status & distribution** Only known as British from Barham and Nacton, both in Suffolk (near Ipswich), pre-1802. It was described as new to science on the basis of this material but appears to be long extinct in Britain. **Parasites & associates** None known.

Lasioglossum laevigatum (Kirby, 1802) **Red-backed Furrow Bee**

not illustrated

Description & similar species FW 6.5–7mm female, 5.6mm male. Females are medium-sized, robustly built and carinate (resembling *L. leucozonium* and *L. zonulum* in this respect) with a bright chestnut pile on the thorax (as in the larger *L. xanthopus*). Tergites 2–4 have unusually large tomentose patches (composed of unusually long white hairs) and the legs are golden-haired. The scutum and tergite 1 are shiny with rather large punctures and all tergites have the apical depressions exceptionally broad (occupying most of tergites 2 and 3 and about one-third of tergite 1). The head in front view is round. The propodeum

female

is very coarsely rugose. Males are readily identified from other *Lasioglossum* species by the completely dark clypeus, labrum, mandibles and antennae. They have fairly long antennae capable of stretching to about the midpoint of tergite 1 and have the tergites shiny, moderately punctate, with tomentose patches on the anterior corners of tergites 2–4. The legs are mainly black but with pale yellow tarsi. **Variation** Little noted. **Flight season** Females can fly from April to September, males from July to September. **Habitat** Strongly associated with unimproved chalk and limestone grasslands, less frequently on sandy sites and in woodland rides and clearings. **Flowers visited** Various, including umbellifers, composites, buttercups, Greater Stitchwort, speedwells and brambles, also blossoming shrubs such as willows, plums and Guelder-rose. **Nesting habits** Not known, but presumed to nest in light soils where sparsely vegetated or short-cropped. **Status & distribution** Widespread but localised in chalk and limestone districts of southern England, extending north to Cumbria; also south Wales. Not recorded from Scotland, Ireland or the Channel Islands. It seems to have shown a substantial decline. **Parasites & associates** None known.

Lasioglossum laticeps (Schenck, 1870) **Broad-faced Furrow Bee**

not illustrated

Description & similar species FW 5–5.5mm (sexes similar). Females can be separated from all other British *Lasioglossum* species by the unique form of the inner hind tibial spur, which has a single tooth-like projection at its base. The hind face of the propodeum is carinate and the head in front view is clearly broader than long (as in *L. malachurum*, but slightly wider than in *L. mediterraneum* and *L. fulvicorne*). Males have very long antennae that are orange below and have short sparse hairs on sternite 2. The head in front view is roundish-broad with the clypeus much less produced below the lowest point of the eyes than in other small species except the very similar *L. mediterraneum* (see that species for differences). **Variation** Males can have the abdomen black or extensively red-marked (the latter can superficially resemble small males of *L. albipes* but have the head rounder in front view and the antennal flagella pale below). Females can occasionally have a second tooth on the inner spur of the hind tibiae. There is some variation in the extent of black markings on the male legs and the darkness of the antennae and tegulae. Larger females are probably queens. **Flight season** Hibernated females (queens) appear from mid-April and produce a brood of slightly smaller workers by early summer. Males and new queens are produced in July and fly until September. **Habitat** South-facing coastal soft rock cliffs and associated landslips, seemingly only those with clay. **Flowers visited** Various, including Wild Carrot, dandelions, ragworts, Common Fleabane, Hemp-agrimony and spring-flowering Colt's-foot and willows. **Nesting habits** Nesting occurs in aggregations in exposed clay slopes with nest entrances often located within desiccation cracks, which makes them hard to spot. The entrance leads into a brood chamber containing cells. A eusocial species. **Status & distribution** Confined to a few cliffs on the south coast of England between Seaton (Devon) and Kimmeridge (Dorset). Extremely vulnerable to storm damage and major cliff collapses. **Parasites & associates** Possibly the cleptoparasitic bees *Sphecodes ephippius* and *S. monilicornis*; also the conopid fly *Thecophora atra*.

male

Lasioglossum lativentre   **Furry-claspered Furrow Bee**
(Schenck, 1853) not illustrated

Description & similar species FW 5.5–6mm female, 4.5–5.5mm male. One of a pair of similar medium-small, robustly built, non-carinate *Lasioglossum* species with conspicuous tomentose patches on tergites 2 and 3 and roundish heads in front view. Females can be separated from the other species (*L. quadrinotatum*) by the orange-brown rather than yellowish wing stigmas and more even punctures on tergite 1 (the punctures of the apical depression being not much denser than those of the basal section). Males have rather short antennae, pale yellow tarsi and long hairs on sternite 2. The top of the propodeum has the hind margin rather smooth. Males have a darker stigma than *L. quadrinotatum* and have the gonostyli and gonocoxite tips densely haired. **Variation** Moderate size variation, and some variation in the extent of black on the male tibiae. **Flight season** Females can fly from March to October, males from July to September. **Habitat** Found in a variety of open flowery habitats, including grasslands of various sorts, brownfield sites, open woodland and heathland. **Flowers visited** Various, but especially composites. **Nesting habits** Poorly known, but presumed to nest in light soils and probably solitary. **Status & distribution** Widespread and frequent (though rarely ever common) over much of southern England north to Yorkshire, also south Wales and the Channel Islands (Alderney, Sark, Jersey). Not recorded from Scotland. Scarce and mostly southern in Ireland. **Parasites & associates** The cleptoparasitic bees *Sphecodes ephippius* and *S. puncticeps*.

female

male

Lasioglossum leucopus (Kirby, 1802) White-footed Furrow Bee
not illustrated

Description & similar species FW 4mm female, 3.5mm male. One of four small metallic *Lasioglossum* species. Females resemble *L. morio* in having a densely and evenly punctured scutum but can usually be readily separated by the shinier scutum, the smooth and shining apical depression of tergite 2 (without minute transverse ridges) and the smoother, semi-shining hind margins to the top of the propodeum. The head is roundish rather than oval in front view (but beware, as some *L. morio* can have roundish heads) and the build is squatter, with the thorax squarer in top view. Males are readily separable from all other metallic species by the pale mid and hind tarsi, and they are also less elongate in build and have shorter antennae. Some females are extremely difficult to assign to either *L. leucopus* or *L. morio*. **Variation** Females with tergite 2 (including the apical depression) more punctate than normal are not uncommon. The most extreme examples, which also have the top part of the propodeum more rugose, have been assigned to the form 'aeratum', which is treated as a separate species by some European workers. **Flight season** Females can fly from May to October, males from July to September. **Habitat** Found in a wide variety of habitats (both coastal and inland) on a range of soils and with little obvious preferences. **Flowers visited** Various plant species from numerous families. **Nesting habits** Little known, but probably similar to species such as *L. morio*. **Status & distribution** Widespread and locally common over much of Britain and Ireland. Recorded from several of the Channel Islands. **Parasites & associates** Possibly one of the hosts of the cleptoparasitic bee *Sphecodes geoffrellus*.

female

male

Lasioglossum leucozonium White-zoned Furrow Bee
(Schrank, 1781) Plate 7

Description & similar species FW 5.5–6.5mm female, 5–6mm male. A medium-large, robustly built carinate species. Females closely resemble *L. zonulum*, and this pair have the combination of conspicuous tomentose patches on tergites 2–4 (which form complete basal bands when the abdomen is distended) and blackish hairs on the dorsal face of the hind tibiae (otherwise only seen in the non-carinate *L. sexnotatum*). Females of *L. leucozonium* can be separated from *L. zonulum* by the duller surface and more uniform punctures of tergite 1, darker wing stigmas and duller pile on top of the thorax. Males have the hind basitarsi and bases of the hind tibiae whitish, and are more likely to be confused with larger individuals of *L. lativentre* and *L. quadrinotatum* but have divergent ridges (forming a V-shape) at the tip of sternite 6, the propodeum much more coarsely rugose and segments 2–5 of the hind tarsi dark. **Variation** Moderate size variation in both sexes, and also some variation in the density of punctures on the tergites. **Flight season** Females usually fly from April to October, males from July to October. **Habitat** Assorted habitats are used, especially sandy ones such as coastal dunes, heathland and sandy brownfield sites, though it can turn up on calcareous grasslands. **Flowers visited** A wide variety of plant species from numerous families are used, though it has a strong liking for composites such as Cat's-ear, hawkbits, Common Fleabane and thistles. **Nesting habits** Nesting usually occurs on south-facing slopes or along sandy paths in either bare ground or short-cropped vegetation. It seems to be a solitary species. **Status & distribution** Widespread and locally common in southern Britain including south Wales, with records extending north to Cumbria. Not recorded in Ireland. Recorded from several of the Channel Islands. **Parasites & associates** One of the hosts of the cleptoparasitic bee *Sphecodes ephippius*, and possibly *S. pellucidus*.

female

male

Lasioglossum limbellum   Ridge-gastered Furrow Bee
(Morawitz, 1876) not illustrated

Description & similar species FW 5mm female, 4.5mm male. A smallish, non-carinate *Lasioglossum* with the unique character of minute transverse ridges over the basal section of tergite 1 at the sides. The tergites have translucent orange-brown hind margins, tomentose patches on the anterior corners of tergites 2–4 (but rather inconspicuous in males), and are dulled by dense punctures and microsculpture. The top of the propodeum is relatively smooth with semi-shining hind margins. The wing tegulae are pale brown whilst the stigmas are dark brown. The female head is roundish in front view, the male head more oval. Females have all the knee joints pale brown. In males the tarsi are pale and the tibiae have dark rings which are sometimes incomplete. The male antennae are rather short with the flagella dark beneath. **Variation** The male tibiae can vary in the amount of darkening, and some have complete rings whilst in others the rings are reduced and incomplete. In both sexes the brightness of the hind margins of the tergites can vary. **Flight season** On the continent, females fly from April to October and males from August to October. **Habitat** Coastal soft rock cliffs and coastal grassland. **Flowers visited** Channel Island records include Smooth Sowthistle and Creeping Thistle, and it favours composites on the continent. **Nesting habits** In Jersey it seems to nest in vertical cliff faces alongside other *Lasioglossum* species. **Status & distribution** Only known from the Channel Islands (Jersey and Guernsey). **Parasites & associates** Occasionally stylopised.

female

203

Lasioglossum malachurum   Sharp-collared Furrow Bee
(Kirby, 1802) not illustrated

Description & similar species FW 5.5–6.5mm female, 4.5–6.5mm male. A rather small carinate *Lasioglossum*. Females are readily identified from all others except *L. zonulum* (a much larger species) by the very prominent pronotal angles. The tergites have translucent hind margins and are finely punctate almost throughout. Tomentose patches are present at the front corners of tergites 2 and 3. The head in front view is broader than long. Males do not have quite such pronounced pronotal angles, though they are still more prominent than in all other species except *L. zonulum*. Their antennae are reasonably long with the flagella orange beneath, the scutum and tergites are dulled by dense punctures, and tomentose patches are present on the front corners of tergites 2 and 3. The legs are extensively yellow and the tibiae usually lack complete dark rings. **Variation** Moderate size variation (larger females are probably queens). Males can have the abdomen all black or extensively red, though the latter state is much less frequent than in *L. albipes* and *L. calceatum*. **Flight season** Overwintered females (queens) can emerge from March and produce a brood of workers by early summer. New males and females are produced from July and fly to October. **Habitat** Various, including soft rock cliffs and coastal grasslands, chalk downland, brownfield sites of various sorts and occasionally urban greenspace, gardens and arable land. It prefers clay soils. **Flowers visited** A wide variety of plant species from numerous families are used, including spring-blossoming shrubs such as willows and Blackthorn. **Nesting habits** Capable of forming huge nesting aggregations along well-trodden paths and tracks and south-facing slopes that are sparsely vegetated or short-cropped. A well-studied eusocial species which shows considerable variation in its social strategy. Some nests have more than one queen (polygynous), and alien workers (from other nests) can be present. In warmer conditions, several broods of workers may be produced before the new queens, whilst in cooler places there is usually just one. **Status & distribution** Widespread in southern England (excluding the southwest) and East Anglia, also the Midlands (north to Warwickshire), where it is a recent colonist. Not recorded from southwest England, Wales, Scotland or Ireland. On the Channel Islands, known only from Jersey. Formerly regarded as scarce, it is now one of the most frequent *Lasioglossum* species of southern England. **Parasites & associates** One of the hosts of the cleptoparasitic bee *Sphecodes monilicornis*, and possibly the oil beetle *Meloe proscarabaeus*.

female

male

Lasioglossum mediterraneum   Mediterranean Furrow Bee
(Blüthgen, 1926) not illustrated

Description & similar species FW 5.5–6mm female, 5.5mm male. Extremely similar to *L. laticeps* but with blackish wing stigmas. Females average slightly larger and have tergite 1 more densely punctate. The hind margins of the tergites are darker and more opaque. The most reliable difference relates to the inner hind tibial spurs, which have four oblique peg-like projections rather than a single basal one as in *L. laticeps*. Males have the head slightly rounder in front view than *L. laticeps*, and the tibiae tend to be more extensively darkened. **Variation** As with *L. laticeps*, males can have the abdomen black or extensively red-marked. The latter can superficially resemble small males of *L. albipes* but have rounder heads (front view) and the antennal flagella pale below. Larger females are probably queens. **Flight season** Probably similar to *L. laticeps*. **Habitat** The Jersey sites are south-facing soft rock cliffs with adjacent heathland and grassland. **Flowers visited** Uncertain, though possibly swept from Rock Samphire or yellow composites such as Cat's-ear at its Jersey sites. **Nesting habits** Probably similar to *L. laticeps*. **Status & distribution** Discovered at two Jersey sites in 2014. **Parasites & associates** None known.

Lasioglossum minutissimum (Kirby, 1802)   **Least Furrow Bee**

Plate 7

Description & similar species FW 3.5–4mm female, 3–3.5mm male. Our smallest *Lasioglossum*, with a very slim build. One of the best identification characters is the transverse depression across the top of the abdomen where tergites 1 and 2 meet (best seen from the side). The propodeum is non-carinate, with the top part smooth and semi-shining around the hind margin. The wing stigmas are dark. In females, tergite 1 has punctures mostly confined to the apical depression, whilst tergites 2–4 are all densely punctate. Males have all the tergites densely punctate and are one of a small number of *Lasioglossum* males with entirely dark hind legs. They have a rather squarish head in top view.

female

L. semilucens is almost equally small but lacks the transverse depression of the abdomen, and has the apical depressions of the tergites smooth and virtually impunctate (obviously punctate in *L. minutissimum*). There are further differences in the hind tibial spurs of the female, and males of *L. semilucens* have pale hind tarsi. **Variation** Little noted. **Flight season** Females can fly from March to October, males from July to October. **Habitat** Found in a range of habitats both coastal and inland, with a preference for sandy soils. **Flowers visited** A wide variety of species from various families, including spring-flowering shrubs such as Blackthorn. **Nesting habits** Nesting has been observed in light soils, sometimes in large aggregations. **Status & distribution** Widespread but rather local in southern England and the Midlands, with records extending north to Yorkshire. Scarce in southwest England and Wales. Recorded from several of the larger Channel Islands. Not recorded from Scotland or Ireland. **Parasites & associates** The cleptoparasitic bee *Sphecodes longulus*.

Lasioglossum morio (Fabricius, 1793)   **Green Furrow Bee**

not illustrated

Description & similar species FW 4mm (sexes similar). One of four small metallic *Lasioglossum* species. Females resemble *L. leucopus* in having an evenly punctate scutum, but are slimmer with the scutum much dulled by microsculpture between the punctures, and the apical depression of tergite 2 dulled by minute transverse ridges. Males have entirely black tarsi and can be separated from *L. smeathmanellum* and *L. cupromicans* by the denser punctures and microsculpture of the scutum, and they also have the tip of the clypeus yellow-marked (usually all black in *L. cupromicans*). **Variation** Considerable variation in female head shape (which can vary from round to oval in front view), the sculpturing on top of the propodeum, and the density of punctures on tergite 1 (which can be dense or relatively fine as in most *L. leucopus*). Some individuals can be extremely difficult to separate from *L. leucopus*. **Flight season** Females can fly from March to October, males from June to October. **Habitat** Found in a great variety of open habitats both coastal and inland. One of the most frequent *Lasioglossum* species of gardens. **Flowers visited** Many species, native and cultivated, though most often seen on composites; also spring-flowering shrubs such as willows and Blackthorn. **Nesting habits** Nesting usually occurs in south-facing slopes and faces, including walls, often in large aggregations. It is primitively eusocial, with workers (which are indistinguishable from queens) produced in early summer. **Status & distribution** Widespread and locally abundant over much of southern Britain but scarce in the north, with records extending to southern Scotland. Not recorded from Ireland. Common on the Channel Islands. **Parasites & associates** The cleptoparasitic bee *Sphecodes niger*, and possibly *S. geoffrellus* and *Nomada sheppardana*; also the conopid fly *Thecophora atra*.

female

male

Lasioglossum nitidiusculum (Kirby, 1802) **Tufted Furrow Bee**

not illustrated

Description & similar species FW 5mm female, 4.5mm male. Females are one of several similar small non-carinate *Lasioglossum* species with roundish heads (in front view), densely punctate scutums and no tomentose patches on the tergites. *L. nitidiusculum* can be separated from species such as *L. parvulum*, *L. rufitarse* and *L. semilucens* by the combination of very short and weak longitudinal ridges on the top of the propodeum plus the rather densely punctured tergites (including the basal section of tergite 1 and the apical depressions of tergites 2 and 3). Males have the same combination of very long antennae and long hairs on sternite 2 as *L. parvulum* and *L. rufitarse* but are easily distinguished by the presence of conspicuous lateral hair tufts on sternites 3–5. They have completely pale tarsi, black-ringed hind tibiae and a yellow labrum. **Variation** Little noted. **Flight season** Females can fly from March to October, males from June to September. **Habitat** Found in a range of habitats including soft rock cliffs and coastal grasslands and heathlands, also inland on brownfield sites and other disturbed locations, especially where soils are sandy. **Flowers visited** Various and from assorted families, though most often observed on hawkish composites such as Cat's-ear and Smooth Hawk's-beard. **Nesting habits** Nesting has been observed in south-facing cliff faces and slopes. It can form large nesting aggregations, though it appears to be solitary. **Status & distribution** Recorded widely but rather sparingly in England and Ireland but rare in Wales and Scotland. Recorded from several of the Channel Islands. It has shown a substantial decline and is rarely frequent anywhere today. **Parasites & associates** The cleptoparasitic bees *Sphecodes geoffrellus*, *S. crassus*, *S. miniatus* and *Nomada sheppardana* are all claimed parasites. Occasionally stylopised.

Lasioglossum parvulum   **Smooth-gastered Furrow Bee**
(Schenck, 1853) not illustrated

Description & similar species FW 4–5mm female, 4–4.5mm male. Females resemble *L. nitidiusculum* but have the top of the propodeum roughened throughout, and finer, sparser punctures on the tergites. *L. rufitarse* is also very similar but has tergite 1 and the apical depressions of tergites 2 and 3 virtually puncture-free and with minute transverse ridges. Males of *L. parvulum* have a combination of very long antennae and long hairs on sternite 2, like *L. nitidiusculum* and *L. rufitarse*. They vary from *L. nitidiusculum* in lacking conspicuous lateral hair tufts on sternites 3–5 and in having dark hind tarsi, a dark labrum and the top of the propodeum rugose throughout. They differ from *L. rufitarse* in having punctured hind margins to tergites 2 and 3 and longer, darker hind tarsi with tarsal segment 2 narrower in side view. **Variation** Little noted. **Flight season** Females can fly from March to October, males from July to October. **Habitat** Found in a range of habitats including soft rock cliffs, chalk downland, heathland, moorland, woodland clearings, sandpits and other brownfield sites. **Flowers visited** Plants of various families are used including spring-flowering shrubs such as Blackthorn and maples, though it is most often seen on yellow-flowered composites. **Nesting habits** Nesting typically occurs in sparsely vegetated south-facing slopes and banks, and it will use the earth of exposed tree root plates more frequently than other *Lasioglossum*. **Status & distribution** Widely recorded and locally frequent in southern Britain with records extending north to Cumbria. Not recorded from Scotland or Ireland. Recorded from several of the Channel Islands. **Parasites & associates** The cleptoparasitic bee *Nomada sheppardana*, and possibly several smaller *Sphecodes* species. Occasionally stylopised.

Lasioglossum pauperatum (Brullé, 1832)   **Squat Furrow Bee**
not illustrated

Description & similar species FW 4mm female, 3.5mm male. A small and noticeably squat non-carinate *Lasioglossum* with the wing stigmas pale buff to mid-brown. Females have a wide head (viewed from the front) and larger punctures on the scutum than most other small species except Group D species. The apical depression of tergite 1 is very densely punctate and contrasts strongly with the sparsely punctured basal section, and tergites 2–4 are densely punctate throughout. The top of the propodeum has longitudinal ridges that reach the hind margins and join a weak semicircular ridge. The thorax is squarer and tergite 1 shorter (and therefore more transverse) than in all other small species. Males also have a very wide head in front view and rather short antennae (for a male). The tarsi, lower clypeus and labrum are yellow. The abdomen is rather short (for a male) and the tergites strongly punctate. The top of the propodeum resembles that of the female. **Variation** Some females have relatively

female

little microsculpture on the scutum and are shinier (beware *L. brevicorne*, which has much paler hind margins to the tergites). **Flight season** Females fly from April to October, males from July to October. **Habitat** Coastal grasslands, sea banks and soft rock cliffs, also inland on heathland and in sandpits. **Flowers visited** Preferences unclear, though some records are from yellow-flowered composites. **Nesting habits** Unknown. **Status & distribution** Mostly recorded from coastal and heathland districts of southeast England between Dorset, Kent and Essex, with a few additional records extending north to Norfolk. Scarce and seemingly much declined except in Kent. Recorded from the Channel Islands (Jersey and Guernsey). Not recorded from Wales, Scotland or Ireland. **Parasites & associates** None known.

Lasioglossum pauxillum (Schenck, 1853) Lobe-spurred Furrow Bee
not illustrated

female

Description & similar species FW 4–4.5mm female, 3.5–4.5mm male. A small *Lasioglossum* resembling species such as *L. laticeps* and *L. fulvicorne*. Females have a uniquely armed inner hind tibial spur with four projections of which the final three are broad and bluntly rounded rather than narrow and pointed. They also have a complete transverse ridge defining the apical depression of tergite 1 (ridge broken centrally in other small species) and a band of fine punctures anterior to this. Tergites 2–4 have pale, translucent hind margins and are densely punctate. The head is round in front view and the antennal flagella are usually partially orange beneath. The hind face of the propodeum is carinate and the wing stigmas buffish. Males can be separated from *L. laticeps* and *L. mediterraneum* by the slightly shorter antennae, shorter second segment to the hind tarsi and more strongly produced clypeus. Compared to *L. fulvicorne*, they are on average smaller with slightly shorter antennae. The hairs on sternite 2 are longer, the hind tarsi longer and slimmer and the scutellum shinier with obvious punctures. **Variation** The hind corners of the propodeum are more angulated in some females (termed form *immarginatum*). Larger females are probably queens. The extent of yellow on the male legs is quite variable. **Flight season** Overwintered females (queens) can emerge from April and produce a brood of workers by early summer. New males and females are produced from July and fly to October. **Habitat** Found in a range of open habitats both on the coast and inland, with a particular liking for chalk downland and calcareous brownfield sites. Occasionally found on arable land. **Flowers visited** Plants of various families are used including buttercups, Rape, umbellifers and a variety of composites (especially Common Fleabane in late summer); also spring-flowering shrubs such as Blackthorn. **Nesting habits** Nesting occurs in bare or sparsely vegetated light soils, sometimes in large aggregations. It is a primitively eusocial species. **Status & distribution** Formerly regarded as scarce, it is now one of the most frequent *Lasioglossum* species of southern England. Records extend as far north as Yorkshire. Rare in southwest England and south Wales. Not recorded from Scotland or Ireland. Present on the Channel Islands. **Parasites & associates** The cleptoparasitic bees *Sphecodes crassus* and *S. ferruginatus* are regarded as possible parasites abroad.

Lasioglossum prasinum (Smith, 1848) Grey-tailed Furrow Bee
Plate 7

Description & similar species FW 6–7mm female, 5–6mm male. The medium-sized females have a unique pattern of grey tomentum on the abdomen that forms conspicuous bands across tergites 2 and 3 and also spreads up the sides of tergite 1 and, in a sparser fashion, covers all of tergite 4, creating a grey-tailed appearance. The hind face of the propodeum is non-carinate and the top of the thorax is very densely punctate and dull grey, often with a slight greenish tint. The head is oval in front view. The more narrowly built males are easily distinguished by the unusually large and entirely or partially red tergite 7 which has a

female

flattened hind face that is bare in its apical half. In side view, the tip of the abdomen appears more strongly downcurved than in any other male *Lasioglossum*. The mid and hind legs are mostly dark except for the tarsi. **Variation** Moderate size variation. Tergite 7 of the male can be entirely red or substantially darkened at the base. **Flight season** Females can fly from April to October, males mostly in August and September. **Habitat** Sandy heathland including that on coastal dunes. **Flowers visited** British records include heathers, yellow composites such as Cat's-ear, Spotted Rock-rose (Jersey) and Early Forget-me-not. It will also take pollen from Scots Pine. Males are particularly fond of Common Fleabane in late summer. **Nesting habits** Nesting occurs in firm sandy ground, especially footpaths and south-facing slopes, often in aggregations. Probably solitary. **Status & distribution** Most records are for the dry heathlands of Dorset, Hampshire, West Sussex and Surrey, where it can be common. Further sites occur in the East Anglian Brecks, East Devon, south Wales (Gower) and the Channel Islands (Jersey). Not recorded from Scotland or Ireland. **Parasites & associates** Possibly the cleptoparasitic bee *Sphecodes reticulatus*.

Lasioglossum punctatissimum   Long-faced Furrow Bee
(Schenck, 1853) not illustrated

Description & similar species FW 4–4.5mm female, 3.5–4mm male. The commoner of a pair of small non-carinate species with long heads (viewed from the front) and densely punctate tergites. Females can only be separated from *L. angusticeps* with great difficulty (see that species for differences), and records should ideally be based on male specimens, though females recorded away from the very restricted range of *L. angusticeps* can probably be regarded as *L. punctatissimum*. Males have relatively short antennae (for a male), the labrum and tip of the clypeus yellow and the hind tarsi usually pale. **Variation** Some males can apparently have the hind tarsi dark, and these will be indistinguishable from *L. angusticeps* without checking the genitalia. **Flight season** Females can fly from April to October, males from July to September. **Habitat** Various sandy habitats including soft rock cliffs, saltmarsh edge, heathland, sandpits plus woodland rides and clearings. **Flowers visited** Assorted species from various families but often most obvious on yellow-flowered composites such as Cat's-ear. **Nesting habits** Nesting seems typically to occur in south-facing slopes and vertical faces. **Status & distribution** Widespread and locally common in southern England but scarcer in the Midlands, Wales, northern England and Ireland and only a few Scottish records (Ayrshire). Recorded from several of the Channel Islands. **Parasites & associates** Attacked by the cleptoparasitic bee *Sphecodes crassus* abroad. Occasionally stylopised.

female

Lasioglossum puncticolle   Ridge-cheeked Furrow Bee
(Morawitz, 1872) not illustrated

Description & similar species FW 5.5mm female, 4.5–5mm male. One of three smallish *Lasioglossum* species where females have unusually large but sparse punctures on a shiny scutum that has little obvious microsculpture. Easily overlooked as the common *L. villosulum* but, when the head is viewed from below, the genae will be seen to be very deeply ridged, quite unlike any other *Lasioglossum* species. The top of the propodeum is coarsely rugose throughout (including the hind angles) and the hind face of the propodeum is carinate. Tergite 1 is barely punctate except for the sides of the apical depression. Males have smaller and denser punctures on the scutum than females and the ridges of the genae are much weaker. Their antennal flagella are dark below (except for segment 3). The mandibles, labrum and clypeal apex are yellow (dark in *L. villosulum*). All tarsi and tibial bases are yellow. Sternite 2 has long hairs. **Variation** Little noted. **Flight season** Females can fly from May to October, males in August and September. **Habitat** Various, including soft rock cliffs, sea walls, vegetated shingle and saltmarsh edge on the coast. Also inland chalk downland, heathland, open woodland, old quarries and pits and arable margins. **Flowers visited** Various, including buttercups, composites (e.g. Cat's-ear, mayweeds, Common Fleabane, thistles and oxtongues), umbellifers (Wild Carrot and Hogweed) and Field Scabious. **Nesting habits** Nesting aggregations have been recorded in steep slopes, but nesting is rarely observed. Possibly a eusorial species. **Status & distribution** A scarce and localised species, with most records in southeast England between Dorset and Essex plus a few outliers extending north to Worcestershire and Norfolk. **Parasites & associates** None known.

Lasioglossum quadrinotatum   Four-spotted Furrow Bee
(Kirby, 1802) not illustrated

Description & similar species FW 5.5–6mm female, 4.5–5.5mm male. Closely resembles *L. lativentre* but with yellowish rather than orange-brown wing stigmas. Tergite 1 of the female has the apical depression very densely punctate and contrasting with the more sparsely punctate basal section. Tergite 2 is more densely punctate than *L. lativentre* and less shining. Males are most easily distinguished from *L. lativentre* by the genitalia, which lack the dense hairs of the gonostyli and tips of the gonocoxites seen in *L. lativentre*. **Variation** Little noted. **Flight season** Females can fly from April to September, males from July to September. **Habitat** Mostly recorded from heathland and acid grassland. **Flowers visited** Assorted species including Ling, Lesser Celandine, Germander Speedwell, spurges, Rosebay Willowherb, Tansy and Smooth Sowthistle. **Nesting habits** Poorly known, but presumed to nest in sandy ground. **Status & distribution** A scarce species, with records concentrated within heathland districts of southern England and the Midlands but extending north to Yorkshire and Lancashire; also several of the Channel Islands. Not recorded from Scotland or Ireland, and only unconfirmed records for Wales. **Parasites & associates** A possible host of the cleptoparasitic bees *Sphecodes ephippius* and *S. puncticeps*.

female

Lasioglossum rufitarse
(Zetterstedt, 1838) not illustrated

Rufous-footed Furrow Bee

Description & similar species FW 5–5.5mm female, 4–5mm male. This non-carinate species resembles *L. nitidiusculum* and *L. parvulum* but has the apical depressions of tergites 2–4 virtually impunctate and those of 2–4 (females) or 3–4 (males) with minute transverse ridges (angle of light critical). In females tergite 1 has punctures confined to the sides of the apical depression and the top of the propodeum is almost entirely rugose, including the hind margins. *L. semilucens* also has unpunctured apical depressions but is smaller with a smoother propodeum and untoothed inner hind tibial spurs. The recently discovered *L. sexstrigatum*

female

is also very similar, but fresh females have narrow white hair fringes on the hind margins of tergites 2–4. *L. laeve* (probably extinct) is larger with a carinate propodeum. Males of *L. rufitarse* have the same combination of very long antennae and long hairs on sternite 2 seen in *L. nitidiusculum* and *L. parvulum*, but have the hind tarsi rather short and stout with segment 2 only about 1.5 times as long as wide. The tergites are shiny with very few punctures. **Variation** The male hind tarsi can vary in colour from blackish to almost entirely orange. **Flight season** Females fly from March (and exceptionally February) to October, males in July and August. **Habitat** Open woodland and partially wooded brownfield sites, and heathland, mostly in base-poor areas. The most woodland-loving *Lasioglossum*. **Flowers visited** British records include Grey Willow, brambles, ragworts and hawkish composites such as Cat's-ear. **Nesting habits** Nesting occurs in slopes such as banks and ditch sides, also the exposed root plates of fallen trees. **Status & distribution** Widespread and locally frequent on the British mainland from Wales and the Midlands northwards. Rare in southern England, and only a few recent Irish records. Not recorded from the Channel Islands. **Parasites & associates** A possible host of the cleptoparasitic bee *Sphecodes ferruginatus*.

Lasioglossum semilucens (Alfken, 1914)
not illustrated

Small Shiny Furrow Bee

Description & similar species FW 4mm (sexes similar). A very small, non-carinate species easily overlooked in the field for *L. minutissimum*, but with the tergites strongly shining and the apical depressions wholly or virtually impunctate (as in the larger carinate *L. laeve*). The top of the abdomen also lacks the characteristic transverse depression of *L. minutissimum* where tergites 1 and 2 meet. The inner hind tibial spurs of the female only have 3–4 short and broad projections, rather like the spurs of *L. pauxillum* (4–5 peg-like projections present in *L. minutissimum*). Males have the hind tarsi and hind tibial bases pale (hind legs of male *L. minutissimum* almost entirely dark). **Variation** The inner hind tibial spurs of the female vary in detail, and sometimes only have a single basal lobe. The antennal flagella of the male can be dull orange or dark below. **Flight season** Females fly from April to September, males in August and September. **Habitat** Preferences unclear though several records are from open woodland and on sandy or gravelly soils. **Flowers visited** Preferences unclear but records exist for composites and a cinquefoil. **Nesting habits** Nesting has been observed in low sandy banks and on level ground. It can form nesting aggregations. **Status & distribution** A rare species known from scattered sites in southeast England west to Dorset and north to Oxfordshire. **Parasites & associates** Possibly the cleptoparasitic bee *Sphecodes marginatus* on the continent, though the ranges of the two species do not overlap in Britain.

Lasioglossum sexnotatum (Kirby, 1802)   **Ashy Furrow Bee**

Plate 7

Description & similar species FW 8–8.5mm female, 7mm male. Females are our second largest *Lasioglossum* after *L. xanthopus*, with a densely punctured and very dull grey thorax, rather long, grey-tinted wings with a blackish stigma, an oval face (viewed from the front) and a shiny abdomen with conspicuous tomentose patches on tergites 2–4. The hind face of the propodeum is non-carinate but a weak ridge surrounds the top area. The hind tibiae have a blackish dorsal fringe (like *L. leucozonium* and *L. zonulum*, which have the thorax shinier and the hind face of the propodeum carinate). Females look very dark and ashy in the field. Males are similar but slimmer with antennae capable of stretching back to the hind margin of the thorax. They have the flagella vaguely orange below. Their legs are entirely dark, which can create confusion with male *L. zonulum* (a more robustly built species with a squarer head and thorax, shinier scutum and paler wing stigmas). A number of similar species occur on the near-continent. **Variation** Little noted. **Flight season** Females can fly from April to September, males in August and September. **Habitat** In East Anglia, known from heathland districts, estuarine grasslands and urban greenspace. In Jersey, most frequent in damp and lush habitats (some also suburban), though often close to heathland and other sandy habitats. **Flowers visited** In Jersey, females have been observed foraging on Water Mint, Yellow Iris, Bugloss, Creeping Thistle, brambles and buttercups. Males visit Common Fleabane and possibly Fennel. Mainland records include ragworts, brambles, White Bryony, figworts and dandelions. **Nesting habits** On the continent, nests have been found in sandy–loamy soil close to shrubs or small trees, often in lightly shaded areas. The nest entrances were well hidden between perennial herbs and grasses, and were well scattered. **Status & distribution** Very rare on the British mainland, with modern records from a few sites in Suffolk and Norfolk plus older records from Surrey and some unconfirmed ones for several other counties. On the Channel Islands recorded from Jersey and Sark, and relatively frequent on the former. **Parasites & associates** None known.

Lasioglossum sexstrigatum (Schenck, 1870)   **Fringed Furrow Bee**

not illustrated

Description & similar species FW 5mm (sexes similar). Fresh females of this non-carinate species are readily separable from all other *Lasioglossum* species by the pale hair fringes along the hind margins of tergites 2–4. In other respects they resemble *L. rufitarse*, and like that species they have the apical depressions of the tergites virtually impunctate and bearing minute transverse ridges. However, *L. sexstrigatum* has a broader head (in front view) with the clypeus almost twice as wide as high and with little microsculpture on the upper part (about 1.5 times as wide as high and with extensive microsculpture on the upper part in *L. rufitarse*). In top view, *L. sexstrigatum* has a squarer thorax, with the scutum much dulled by microsculpture between the punctures (scutum mostly shining between the punctures in *L. rufitarse*). The propodeum is shorter and more transverse in top view and the sides of the upper part have oblique ridges with shining interstices (dull and finely granular without obvious oblique ridges in *L. rufitarse*). These characters will allow separation of older females of *L. sexstrigatum* that have lost their hair fringes. Males are easily distinguished from all other *Lasioglossum* species by the strongly angled lower hind corner of the genae (viewed from the side). They lack hair fringes along the hind margins of the tergites. Their antennae are relatively short (for a male), with the flagella orange below. Tergite 1 has sparse,

female

fine punctures whilst the apical depressions of tergites 2–4 are shiny and virtually impunctate. The mandibles, labrum and lower clypeus are yellow. An almost identical species, *L. sabulosum*, occurs on the near-continent. **Variation** The degree of angulation of the male genae can vary. **Flight season** Abroad, females fly from April to October, males from late June possibly to September. **Habitat** British records include heathland and sandpits, and it is known to favour sandy habitats abroad. **Flowers visited** Cat's-ear at some British sites with White Bryony, cinquefoils, willows, plums, pears and apples noted abroad. **Nesting habits** Nesting occurs in sandy soils, sometimes in large aggregations. It may be primitively eusocial. **Status & distribution** Only discovered in Britain in 2006, with records currently for a handful of sites in Kent and Surrey. **Parasites & associates** The cleptoparasitic bees *Nomada sheppardana* and *Sphecodes miniatus*, *S. geoffrellus* and *S. longulus* are said to attack it abroad.

Lasioglossum smeathmanellum Smeathman's Furrow Bee
(Kirby, 1802) Plate 7

Description & similar species FW 4.5mm female, 4–4.5mm male. One of four small metallic *Lasioglossum* species. Females resemble *L. cupromicans* in having a shiny scutum that bears unevenly sized punctures and little obvious microsculpture, but the punctures are denser in *L. smeathmanellum*. The tergites are greenish and conspicuously punctured with obvious tomentose patches at the front corners of tergites 2 and 3 and more sparingly around the base of tergite 4. The apical depression of tergite 2 has minute transverse ridges like *L. morio*. The top of the propodeum is dull and rugose throughout and the head

female

male

is oval in front view. They appear greener in the field than any other metallic species. Males also resemble *L. cupromicans* in having a shiny scutum but have the top of the propodeum much rougher and the clypeus yellow-marked apically. **Variation** The metallic reflections can vary from greenish to turquoise, and the tergites are more obviously metallic in some than others. **Flight season** Females can fly from late March to September, males from July to September. **Habitat** Often abundant on soft rock cliffs but also uses quarries and other brownfield sites inland, and occasionally present in gardens and formal greenspaces. **Flowers visited** A wide variety of flowers from numerous plant families are visited, including spring-flowering shrubs. **Nesting habits** Cliff faces, bare or sparsely vegetated slopes and old walls seem to be the favoured nesting locations, and it will often form large nesting aggregations. **Status & distribution** Widespread and locally common over much of southern Britain, including Wales. Scarcer in northern England, Scotland and Ireland. Recorded from several of the Channel Islands. **Parasites & associates** None known.

Lasioglossum villosulum (Kirby, 1802)   **Shaggy Furrow Bee**

not illustrated

Description & similar species FW 4.5–5.5mm female, 4–4.5mm male. Females are one of three small *Lasioglossum* species with unusually large but sparse punctures on a shiny scutum that has little obvious microsculpture. The head in front view is oval. They most resemble *L. puncticolle*, but the hind face of the propodeum is non-carinate and the genae lack deep ridges. They have shallower punctures on the scutum (which is often distinctly bloomed), smooth margins to the upper part of the propodeum and more extensive fine punctures on tergite 1.

L. brevicorne has pale hind margins to the tergites, paler wing stigmas and a denser pile of pale hairs on tergites 3 and 4. Males have the scutum punctured similarly to the females (the punctures somewhat more widely spaced than in male *L. puncticolle* or *L. brevicorne*). The abdomen and antennae are rather short, and the antennal flagella are orange below. The hind tarsi are unusually short and stout and can be dark or yellowish. The clypeus apex and mandibles lack yellow markings. Sternite 2 has long hairs. **Variation** The wing stigmas can vary from dark brown to pale orange (the latter can be confused with *L. brevicorne*). The male hind tarsi can be dark or pale yellow. Older females can lose the bloom on the scutum. **Flight season** Females can fly from March to October, males from June to October. **Habitat** Many habitats are used, though it can be especially abundant along soft rock cliffs, on chalk downland and on brownfield sites. **Flowers visited** Flowers from various families are used but especially hawkish composites such as Cat's-ear and hawk's-beards, also buttercups and umbellifers. Blossoming shrubs such as hawthorns and plums can also be important in spring. **Nesting habits** Very large nesting aggregations can form in cliff faces and bare or sparsely vegetated slopes. **Status & distribution** Widespread and locally abundant over much of England (often the commonest *Lasioglossum* of soft rock cliffs and brownfield sites), but scarcer and mostly coastal in Wales and Scotland. Widespread but local in Ireland. Locally common on the Channel Islands. **Parasites & associates** The cleptoparasitic bee *Sphecodes puncticeps* seems to attack this species, and

female

male

S. geoffrellus may parasitise it in Ireland. It may also be a host for *S. marginatus* on the Channel Islands. The conopid fly *Thecophora atra* can be frequent around nesting colonies.

Lasioglossum xanthopus (Kirby, 1802)   Orange-footed Furrow Bee

Plate 7

Description & similar species FW 8–9.5mm (sexes similar). The largest *Lasioglossum* and the only one with orange hind tibiae and tarsi. Females have a conspicuous reddish pile on top of the thorax and conspicuous white tomentose patches on the front corners of tergites 2–4 (which form complete bands when the abdomen is distended). They are most likely to be confused with *Halictus rubicundus*, but this has white tomentose patches on the hind margins of tergites 1–4. Males of *L. xanthopus* can be very large and have a characteristic club-shaped abdomen and a rather dense brown pile on the thorax.

female

Variation Moderate size variation in both sexes. Males can occasionally have the underside of the antennae only obscurely reddish and would probably fall out in Group F of the key, but are easily distinguished by their much greater size. **Flight season** Females can fly from April to August, males from August to October, usually peaking in late September when females have apparently finished flying. **Habitat** Most records come from soft rock cliffs, chalk downland and calcareous brownfield sites (especially quarries and cuttings). **Flowers visited** Various plants from assorted families, including knapweeds, thistles, ragworts, brambles, Wild Strawberry, speedwells, Ground-ivy, Kidney Vetch, clovers, scabiouses and Sea Campion. Males particularly favour scabiouses and late Perennial Sowthistle. **Nesting habits** Nesting occurs in south-facing vertical faces and sparsely vegetated or short-cropped slopes, sometimes in extensive aggregations. It is thought to be solitary. **Status & distribution** Widespread in southern England north to Staffordshire and Lincolnshire but scarce in most areas and seemingly much declined. Very rare in Wales (Glamorganshire). Not recorded from Scotland or Ireland. On the Channel Islands, recorded only from Guernsey. **Parasites & associates** The cleptoparasitic bee *Sphecodes spinulosus*, and possibly also attacked by *S. monilicornis*. Occasionally stylopised.

Lasioglossum zonulum (Smith, 1848)   Bull-headed Furrow Bee

not illustrated

Description & similar species FW 6–7mm female, 5.5–7mm male. A medium-sized, robustly built *Lasioglossum* with a carinate propodeum. Females closely resemble *L. leucozonium* but have tergite 1 shinier with sparser punctures (except for the densely punctured apical depression), brighter brown hairs on top of the thorax and paler wing stigmas. In top view, the pronotal angles and the hind corners of the head are more produced, creating a more bull-headed appearance. Males have entirely black hind legs and rather short antennae. They are most likely to be confused with *L. sexnotatum* but are more robustly built with the head

and thorax squarer in top view, paler
wing stigmas and a shinier scutum. They
are also more bull-headed than any
L. leucozonium and have the pronotal
angles produced and angulated to an
extent only matched by *L. malachurum*.
Variation Moderate size variation, with
large males tending to be more bull-
headed. **Flight season** Females can fly
from April to October, males from June
to September. **Habitat** Various, including
coastal dunes (especially where damp
slacks are present), coastal grazing
marsh, heathland (especially where
mire is present), brownfield sites with
damp areas, woodland rides with lush
vegetation, and occasionally chalk
downland. As with *L. sexnotatum*,
there may be a liking for damp, lushly
vegetated habitats for foraging. **Flowers
visited** Females forage on many sorts of
flowers from numerous families. Males
have a particular liking for Common
Fleabane and Devil's-bit Scabious in late
summer. **Nesting habits** Nesting occurs
in dry soils, but preferences are unclear.
Probably a solitary species. Females can

female

male

apparently live for two years with a nest cycle in each year. **Status & distribution** Widespread
and locally frequent in southern England between Bristol and south Essex, also coastal districts
of south Wales. A few further sites occur north to Gloucestershire and Suffolk. Recorded from
the Channel Islands (Guernsey and Sark). Not recorded from Scotland or Ireland. **Parasites &
associates** The cleptoparasitic bee *Sphecodes scabricollis*.

SPHECODES – BLOOD BEES

Very small to medium-sized, inconspicuously haired bees, usually with a red and black abdomen. They are cleptoparasites of various ground-nesting bees, with British species attacking members of the genera *Lasioglossum*, *Halictus* and *Andrena*. Females are usually most evident around host nesting areas. They will enter a host nest (often forcibly), open up a cell, destroy the egg or grub and replace it with their own egg before resealing it. Some *Sphecodes* (e.g. *S. spinulosus*) have very specific hosts, whilst others (e.g. *S. ephippius* and *S. monilicornis*) use several species, though our understanding of parasite–host relationships is rather poor and speculative for some species, and some claimed hosts are questionable. Males are more likely to be found on flowers, especially composites and umbellifers, and usually appear considerably later than females, peaking in late summer. The exceptions are *S. rubicundus* and *S. spinulosus*, where hibernated males and females appear together in spring.

♀

Sphecodes monilicornis

This is a near-cosmopolitan genus with several hundred described species. Seventeen are recorded from the British Isles, though *S. marginatus* is known only from the Channel Islands. An online account of the central European species (Bogusch & Straka, 2012) provides coverage of a number of additional species on the near-continent that could conceivably be found in Britain.

Sphecodes identification can be very challenging and is much easier with comparative material to hand or the resources on the author's web feature (p.59) which furnishes the microscope photos used here at higher resolution. It is important to ensure that pinned specimens have the wings splayed to allow easier examination of the tergite punctures; also to set females with their mandibles open (to help separate out species such as *S. puncticeps* and *S. longulus*). Male identification is sometimes only possible using genitalia, so remember to pull these out when pinning material. Another useful feature of males that can help direct you to a smaller selection of species options is the extent of pubescence on the anterior face of the antennal flagellar segments. Lighting and angle of view are critical for seeing this feature properly. For very difficult species, such as female *S. miniatus* and *S. marginatus*, specimens will need expert verification.

SPHECODES FEMALE GROUPS

1   Top of head between rear ocelli and hind margin with numerous punctures (Fig. 1) .... **female group A**

—   Top of head between rear ocelli and hind margin rough (often ridged), without distinct punctures **2**

2   Anterior sloping part of tergite 1 with only short, sparse hairs, these being no more than about half as long as those arising from the adjacent hind face of the propodeum (Fig. 2) .... **female group B**

—   At least lower part of anterior sloping section of tergite 1 with hairs as long as those arising from the adjacent hind face of the propodeum, and often as dense (Fig. 3) **3**

3   Mandibles simple and sickle-shaped without an apical tooth or emargination (Fig. 4) .... **female group C**

—   Mandibles with an apical tooth or emargination (Fig. 5) .... **female group D**

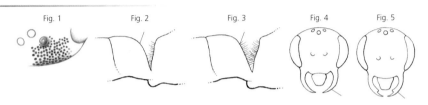

Fig. 1   Fig. 2   Fig. 3   Fig. 4   Fig. 5

SPHECODES FEMALE GROUP A

1   Head in strict dorsal view (with the axis of the eyes vertical) rather box-shaped (Fig. 6) with expanded hind corners and a broad punctured zone behind the ocelli. Pygidium relatively broad. Hind tibiae dorsally with reddish bristles surrounded by whitish hairs. A slimmer species in top view, with the dorsal propodeal area more expanded rearwards (Fig. 6) .... *monilicornis*

—   Head in strict dorsal view more transverse, with the hind corners acutely curved inwards (Fig. 7) and the punctured zone behind the ocelli narrower. Pygidium relatively narrow. Hind tibiae dorsally with blackish bristles surrounded by blackish hairs. More broadly built species, with the dorsal propodeal area less expanded (Fig. 7) 2

2   Zone of punctures behind the ocelli deeper, occupying a distance about 2.5 times the width of an ocellus, with the punctures in this zone sparser and arranged in 5–6 irregular rows (Fig. 8). Base of tergite 4 with sparse punctures. Wings darkened. Usually larger (wing length to 8mm) .... *gibbus*

—   Zone of punctures behind ocelli narrower, occupying a zone about 1.5 times the width of an ocellus, with the punctures in this zone more crowded and in 2–3 irregular rows (Fig. 9). Base of tergite 4 with a band of dense punctures. Wings paler. Averaging smaller (wing length to 6.5mm) .... *reticulatus*

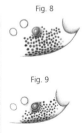

Fig. 6 *S. monilicornis*   Fig. 7 *S. gibbus*   Fig. 8

Fig. 9

SPHECODES FEMALE GROUP B

1   Tergite 2 with a continuous band of dense punctures across the basal third (Fig. 10). Tergite 4 extensively red, only becoming darker along hind margin. Hind tibiae dorsally with blackish bristles surrounded by blackish hairs. Head and scutum more densely punctate. Averaging larger (typical wing length 6.5–7mm) .... *rubicundus*

—   Tergite 2 with only sparse punctures across the basal third and virtually none in centre (Fig. 11). Tergite 4 entirely black. Hind tibiae dorsally with reddish bristles surrounded by whitish hairs. Head and scutum less densely punctate. Smaller (typical wing length 5–6mm) .... *ephippius*

Fig. 10 *S. rubicundus*

Fig. 11 *S. ephippius*

Fig. 12 *S. puncticeps*

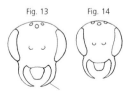

Fig. 13   Fig. 14

SPHECODES FEMALE GROUP C

1   Front of scutum with a distinct median groove (Fig. 12). Head in front view much wider than high (Fig. 13). Legs usually mainly dark, especially hind tibiae and tarsi. Larger and more robust (typical wing length 4.5mm) .... *puncticeps*

—   Front of scutum without a distinct median groove. Head in front view rounder (Fig. 14). Legs usually extensively pale, including hind tibiae and tarsi. Smaller and slimmer (typical wing length 3.5–4mm) .... *longulus*

SPHECODES FEMALE GROUP D

1   Apical antennal segments as long or slightly longer than wide (Fig. 15). Base of sternite 2, viewed from side, with a pronounced transverse step which rises at 45 degrees to meet the main surface of the tergite (Fig. 16). Extreme hind margin of head at top with a sharp upcurved flange (Fig. 19) (can be obscured by front of the thorax if the head is reflexed upwards). Large (wing length usually over 7mm) with densely punctate scutum (Fig. 17) .... *spinulosus*

—   Apical antennal segments wider than long (Fig. 18). No obvious groove across base of sternite 2. No flange along hind margin of head at top. Smaller (wing length to 7mm) 2

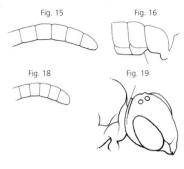

Fig. 15   Fig. 16   Fig. 17

Fig. 18   Fig. 19

2   Scutum and scutellum with extremely dense and large punctures which are almost touching in the front part of the scutum and on the scutellum to create a rugose rather than punctate surface (Fig. 20). Viewed from side, extreme hind margins of genae defined by a flange (Fig. 24) .... *scabricollis*

—   Scutum and scutellum with well-defined punctures separated by obvious shining surface. No flange along hind margins of genae **3**

3   Pygidium 1.5 times the greatest width of a hind basitarsus in top view (Fig. 25). Sides of thorax immediately behind head above front coxae with a sharply angled plate (Fig. 26) (may require removal of one front leg to see clearly). Medium-sized (wing length to 7mm) with densely punctate scutum (Fig. 21) .... *pellucidus*

—   Pygidium in top view no wider than the greatest width of a hind basitarsus (Fig. 27). Sides of thorax immediately behind head above front coxae with an obtusely angled or rounded-off plate. Smaller species (wing length to 6mm) usually with fewer, sparser punctures on the scutum **4**

4   Sides of thorax just below wing bases with a discrete, brightly shining smooth patch (Fig. 22). Top of propodeum with a few weak longitudinal ridges that end well short of the brow. Tergite 3 extensively darkened. A very small species (typical wing length 3.5mm) .... *niger*

—   Sides of thorax just below wing bases entirely dulled by surface sculpture. Top of propodeum with stronger ridges, often arranged as a reticulation, and usually extending rearwards to the brow. Tergite 3 usually entirely red (the underlying tergite 4 can make it look darker). Larger species (wing length usually at least 4mm) **5**

5   Bases of hind femora, viewed from beneath, swollen in a bulbous fashion so that the dorsal edge is concave midway along and humped at the base (Fig. 28). Scutum relatively sparsely punctate (Fig. 23). Labrum almost as long as wide (Fig. 29). A small species (typical wing length 5mm) .... *crassus*

—   Bases of hind femora less swollen with the dorsal edge either straight or slightly convex (Fig. 30). With the exception of *ferruginatus*, labrum shorter (Fig. 31) **6**

Fig. 20 *S. scabricollis*

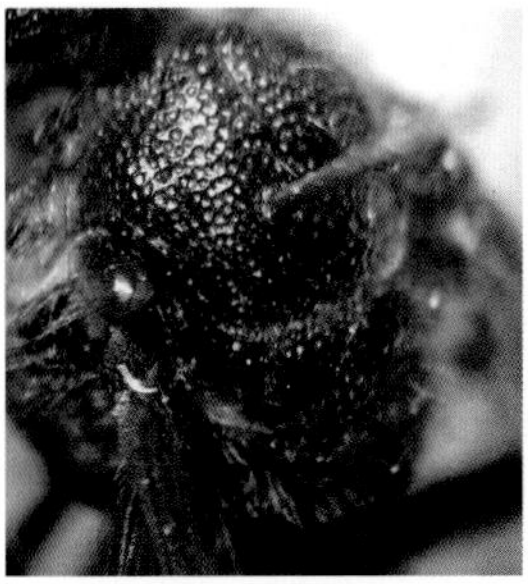

Fig. 21 *S. pellucidus*

Fig. 22 *S. niger*

Fig. 23 *S. crassus*

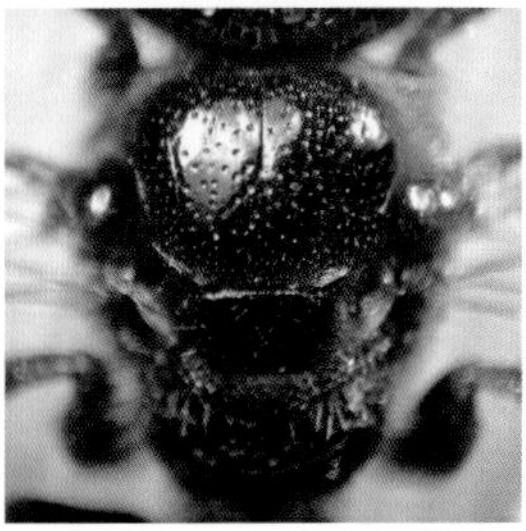

Fig. 24

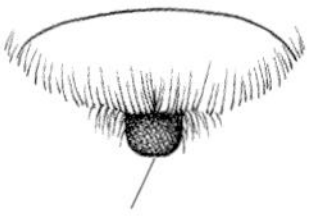

Fig. 25

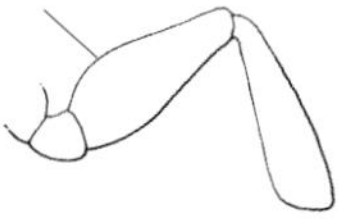

Fig. 28

Fig. 26

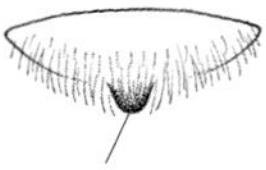

Fig. 27

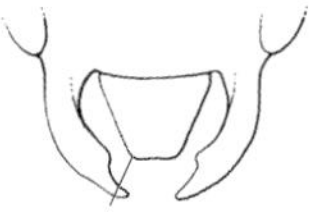

Fig. 29

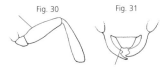

Fig. 30   Fig. 31

6   Clypeus, supraclypeal plate and frons very densely punctate and slightly dulled by
    microsculpture between these punctures (Fig. 32). Labrum almost as long
    as wide (Fig. 29). A rather robust species (thorax squarer in top view) averaging a
    little larger than the following species (typical wing length 5.5–6mm) and with
    a more densely punctate scutum (Fig. 33) .... *ferruginatus*

—   Clypeus, supraclypeal plate and frons with sparser punctures and shining
    between these punctures (Fig. 34). Labrum much shorter than wide (Fig. 31).
    Slimmer species, with scutum less densely punctate (Figs 38 & 40) 7

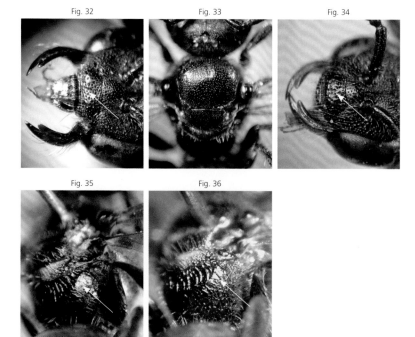

Fig. 32   Fig. 33   Fig. 34

Fig. 35   Fig. 36

7   Upper sides of propodeum relatively smooth (Fig. 35) and shining, the sides of
    the thorax also relatively smooth. Base of second and third tergites barely punctate.
    Underside of thorax between front and mid legs with a denser pile of short hairs
    underlying the longer hairs (best seen in side view, less obvious if the specimen
    has been subjected to damp) .... *hyalinatus*

—   Upper sides of propodeum and sides of thorax more obviously ridged or rugose (Fig. 36).
    Base of second and third tergites with obvious punctures, even if rather fine and
    sparse. Underside of thorax between front and mid legs without such a dense short
    pile underlying the longer hairs (some females of the following three species are
    very difficult to assign) 8

8   Top of propodeum with a semicircular zone containing rather simple longitudinal ridges (Fig. 37), the area immediately outside of this zone and the sides of the propodeum relatively smooth (but not as smooth and shiny as in *hyalinatus*). Scutum with sparse, fine punctures (Fig. 38). Hind tarsi usually orange-brown. Typically smaller and slimmer .... *geoffrellus*

—   Top of propodeum with a semicircular zone containing a reticulate pattern of ridges, the area immediately outside of this zone similarly textured (Fig. 39). Scutum with larger and usually slightly denser, deeper punctures (Fig. 40). Hind tarsi usually dark. Typically slightly larger and more robust 9

9   Base of tergites 2 and 3 with a band of rather fine and sparse punctures, the punctures of tergite 2 petering out well before the ridge demarking the apical depression (Fig. 41) .... *miniatus*

—   Base of tergites 2 and 3 with a broad band of rather dense and coarse punctures that almost extend as far as the ridge demarking the apical depression (Fig. 42) (Channel Islands) .... *marginatus*

Fig. 37   Fig. 38   Fig. 39

Fig. 40   Fig. 41

Fig. 42

SPHECODES MALE GROUPS

1   Scutum and scutellum rugose with extremely dense and coarse punctures with few shining interstices (Fig. 43). Extreme hind margins of genae defined by a flange (Fig. 24). Genitalia (Fig. 56) .... *scabricollis*

—   Scutum and especially scutellum always with obvious shining interstices between the punctures. No flange along the hind margin of the genae **2**

2   Antennal flagellar segments longer, with a sharply defined shining zone (with fine punctures) on the front face, contrasting markedly with the dull, greyer rear face, this rear face somewhat compressed and flattened on top (Fig. 44) .... **male group A**

—   Antennal flagellar segments somewhat shorter and rounder in cross section, covered in rather coarse punctures behind; the front face with extensive zones of pubescence in some species (Figs 45 & 46) **3**

3   Three options (angle of view and lighting critical):

(a)   Anterior face of most antennal flagellar segments with a very broad zone of pubescence covering three-quarters to four-fifths of the segment (Fig. 45) .... **male group B**

(b)   Anterior face of apical 4–5 antennal segments with a narrower zone of pubescence that occupies about half the length of the segment (Fig. 46) .... **male group C**

(c)   Anterior face of apical 4–5 antennal segments with a very narrow zone of pubescence that occupies at most one-third the length of the segment, sometimes less (Fig. 47) .... **male group D**

Fig. 43   Fig. 44

Fig. 45    Fig. 46    Fig. 47

SPHECODES MALE GROUP A

1   Hind tibiae with about 10 dark spines along dorsal edge amongst the paler hairs. Base of sternite 2, viewed from side, with a pronounced transverse step, which rises at 45 degrees to meet the main posterior section of the tergite (Fig. 16). Extreme hind margin of head at top defined by a sharp upcurved flange (Fig. 19) (can be obscured by front of the thorax if the head is reflexed upwards). Genitalia (Fig. 57). Usually large (typical wing length 8mm) .... *spinulosus*

—   Hind tibiae without dorsal spines. Sternite 2 without an obvious basal groove. No flange along rear margin of head at top. Smaller (wing length rarely exceeding 7mm) **2**

2   Top of head between rear ocelli and hind margin well developed, with a broad zone of distinct punctures in 5–6 irregular rows (Fig. 1). Scutum with strong but sparse punctures. Genitalia (Fig. 58) .... *gibbus*

—   Top of head between rear ocelli and hind margin much narrower, entirely rugose or with just a few punctures. Scutum more densely punctate **3**

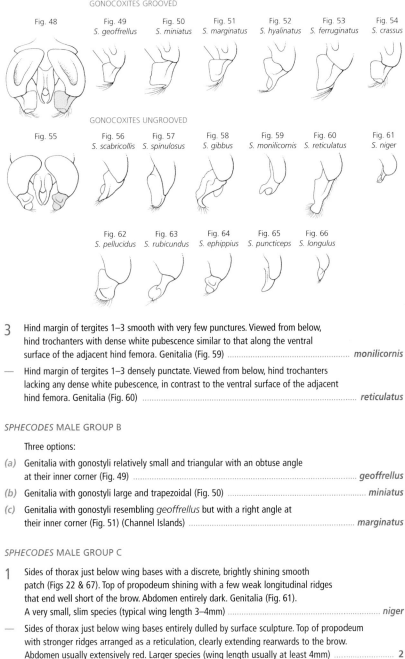

GONOCOXITES GROOVED

Fig. 48

Fig. 49
S. geoffrellus

Fig. 50
S. miniatus

Fig. 51
S. marginatus

Fig. 52
S. hyalinatus

Fig. 53
S. ferruginatus

Fig. 54
S. crassus

GONOCOXITES UNGROOVED

Fig. 55

Fig. 56
S. scabricollis

Fig. 57
S. spinulosus

Fig. 58
S. gibbus

Fig. 59
S. monilicornis

Fig. 60
S. reticulatus

Fig. 61
S. niger

Fig. 62
S. pellucidus

Fig. 63
S. rubicundus

Fig. 64
S. ephippius

Fig. 65
S. puncticeps

Fig. 66
S. longulus

3   Hind margin of tergites 1–3 smooth with very few punctures. Viewed from below, hind trochanters with dense white pubescence similar to that along the ventral surface of the adjacent hind femora. Genitalia (Fig. 59) .... *monilicornis*

—   Hind margin of tergites 1–3 densely punctate. Viewed from below, hind trochanters lacking any dense white pubescence, in contrast to the ventral surface of the adjacent hind femora. Genitalia (Fig. 60) .... *reticulatus*

SPHECODES MALE GROUP B

Three options:

(a) Genitalia with gonostyli relatively small and triangular with an obtuse angle at their inner corner (Fig. 49) .... *geoffrellus*

(b) Genitalia with gonostyli large and trapezoidal (Fig. 50) .... *miniatus*

(c) Genitalia with gonostyli resembling *geoffrellus* but with a right angle at their inner corner (Fig. 51) (Channel Islands) .... *marginatus*

SPHECODES MALE GROUP C

1   Sides of thorax just below wing bases with a discrete, brightly shining smooth patch (Figs 22 & 67). Top of propodeum shining with a few weak longitudinal ridges that end well short of the brow. Abdomen entirely dark. Genitalia (Fig. 61). A very small, slim species (typical wing length 3–4mm) .... *niger*

—   Sides of thorax just below wing bases entirely dulled by surface sculpture. Top of propodeum with stronger ridges arranged as a reticulation, clearly extending rearwards to the brow. Abdomen usually extensively red. Larger species (wing length usually at least 4mm) 2

Fig. 67

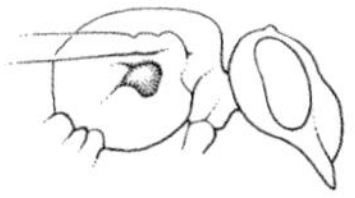

2   Ventral surface of mid femora with numerous hairs as long as the greatest width of the femora. Surface of clypeus obscured by dense whitish hairs. Bases of tergites 2–4 with bands of obvious punctures. Legs blackish. A more robust, hairier species with coarser punctures on the scutum. Genitalia (Fig. 62) .... *pellucidus*

—   Ventral surface of mid femora with most hairs no longer than half the width of the femora. Surface of clypeus with sparser hairs that do not obscure the underlying surface. Bases of tergites 2–4 with bands of fine, inconspicuous punctures. Legs extensively brownish. A slimmer, less hairy species with finer punctures on the scutum. Genitalia (Fig. 52) .... *hyalinatus*

SPHECODES MALE GROUP D

1   Tergites 2 and 3 bearing dense, deep punctures throughout except hind margins, tergite 1 with dense punctures along hind margin. Tergites 1–3 usually clear red, with red extending onto the sides of tergite 4. Hind tibiae with rather stout, bristly hairs dorsally. Typically large (wing length 6–7.5mm) with a very densely punctured scutum. Genitalia (Fig. 63) .... *rubicundus*

—   Tergites less conspicuously punctate and with hind margin of tergite 1 impunctate. Tergites 1–3 often partially darkened, tergite 4 always entirely black. Smaller species (wing length up to 6mm) 2

2   Gonocoxites of genitalia with a dorsal groove (Fig. 48) 3

—   Gonocoxites of genitalia without a dorsal groove (Fig. 55) 4

3   Genitalia (Fig. 53). A larger, broader species (typical wing length 5–6mm) with a more densely punctate scutum. Tergites 1–3 usually entirely reddish .... *ferruginatus*

—   Genitalia (Fig. 54). A smaller, slimmer species (typical wing length 4–5mm) with a more sparsely punctate scutum. Tergites 1–3 usually partially darkened .... *crassus*

4   3 options:

(a)   Genitalia (Fig. 64). Scutum relatively densely punctate. Top of propodeum not defined by an obvious semicircular ridge. Tibiae blackish .... *ephippius*

(b)   Genitalia (Fig. 65). Scutum less densely punctured than previous species but punctures deep. Top of propodeum defined by a fairly obvious semicircular ridge. Tibiae blackish .... *puncticeps*

(c)   Genitalia (Fig. 66). A very small, slim species with relatively shallow punctures on the scutum. Top of propodeum not defined by an obvious semicircular ridge. Tibiae usually extensively brown .... *longulus*

Sphecodes crassus Thomson, 1870   **Swollen-thighed Blood Bee**

not illustrated

Description & similar species FW 4–5mm (sexes similar). One of our smallest *Sphecodes*, with females most likely to be confused with *S. geoffrellus* owing to the sparsely punctate scutum. However, the bases of the hind femora of *S. crassus* are much more swollen (more swollen than in any other small *Sphecodes*), the labrum much longer and the hind tarsi dark (typically pale in *S. geoffrellus*). Males are one of the small species with narrow zones of pubescence on the antennal segments and dorsal grooves on the gonocoxites. They should always be confirmed using genitalia. **Variation** Some size and colour variation, with occasional dwarfs (wing length as little as 3mm). Small females tend to have the hind femora less swollen, but the long labrum remains a distinction from *S. geoffrellus*. Small males and females tend to be darker and can occasionally have all-black abdomens. There is some variation in the sculpturing of the top of the propodeum, though it usually remains more reticulate than in *S. geoffrellus*. A large form has been found on the Isle of Man. **Flight season** Females fly from late April to mid-September, males mostly in July and August. **Habitat** Found in a wide variety of open habitats. **Flowers visited** Various, but especially hawkish and mayweed-type composites, thistles and umbellifers. **Status & distribution** Widespread and locally common in southern England and the Midlands, scarcer in Wales and very rare in Scotland (a location near Edinburgh). Unknown in Ireland, but recorded from several of the Channel Islands. It was once regarded as scarce but appears to have become more frequent in recent decades. **Host(s)** *Lasioglossum nitidiusculum* and *L. parvulum* are both cited as British hosts but are often scarce at *S. crassus* strongholds (e.g. South Downs), suggesting other hosts must be involved, possibly *L. punctatissimum* and *L. pauxillum*, which are known hosts abroad and more often encountered in abundance alongside *S. crassus*.

Sphecodes ephippius (Linnaeus, 1767)   **Bare-saddled Blood Bee**

not illustrated

Description & similar species FW 4.5–6.5mm female, 4.5–5.5mm male. A medium-small species with the thoracic dorsum rather densely punctate. Females are readily separable from all other *Sphecodes* except *S. rubicundus* by the very short, sparse hairs on the sloping anterior face of tergite 1 (long, denser hairs present in fresh individuals of all other species). Readily separable from *S. rubicundus* by the smaller size, paler hairs of the hind tibiae, lack of a dense puncture band around the base of tergite 2, and the black tergite 4. Males are one of three smaller species with narrow zones of pubescence on the anterior faces of the

female

antennal segments and no dorsal grooves on the gonocoxites. They should always be confirmed using genitalia but have denser punctures on the scutum than the other two (*S. puncticeps* and *S. longulus*). **Variation** Considerable size and colour variation in both sexes (larger specimens may be associated with *Lasioglossum leucozonium*), with dwarfs featuring wing lengths as short as 3.5mm occasionally encountered. Smaller individuals can be considerably darkened and occasionally have all-black abdomens. **Flight season** Females fly from mid-April to late September, and are amongst the first *Sphecodes* to appear in spring. Males fly from July to October.

Habitat Found in a wide variety of open habitats and often common on brownfield sites.
Flowers visited Various, but females can be especially numerous on dandelions in spring. Status
& distribution Widespread and locally common in southern Britain, with records extending
north to Cumbria. Widespread in Ireland and recorded from several of the Channel Islands. Not
recorded from Scotland. Host(s) *Halictus tumulorum*, *Lasioglossum leucozonium* and *L. lativentre*
are thought to be the main hosts, and it may also parasitise *L. laticeps* and *L. quadrinotatum*.
Various further British *Lasioglossum* and *Halictus* species, plus several *Andrena* species, are
claimed hosts on the continent.

Sphecodes ferruginatus Hagens, 1882   Dull-headed Blood Bee
not illustrated

Description & similar species FW 5–6mm (sexes similar). One of our
smaller *Sphecodes*. Females can be most easily distinguished from other
small species by the densely punctate face and frons, both of which
have the punctures only narrowly separated and the surface between
the punctures dulled by microsculpture. This renders the whole head
relatively dull, especially the frons. Compared with other small species,
the thorax is more densely punctate, the size typically a little larger and
the build a little more broad and robust. Other features that should be
present include well-formed rugosity on the sides of the thorax, the
upper sides of the propodeum fairly smooth and shining (as in *S. hyalinatus*), a long labrum (as
in *S. crassus*), and bands of small punctures across the bases of tergites 2 and 3. Males are one
of the smaller species with narrow zones of pubescence on the antennal segments and dorsal
grooves on the gonocoxites. They have a broader build than most small male *Sphecodes*, with
tergites 1–3 often entirely red, which tends to render them fairly distinctive, though they should
always be confirmed using genitalia (some *S. hyalinatus* males can look similar). Variation Some
variation in size, colour and build, with individuals with wing lengths as short as 4.5mm (usually
semi-melanic) occasionally encountered. Flight season Females fly from mid-May to September,
males from mid-July to September. Habitat Prefers chalk and limestone districts, using habitats
such as chalk and limestone grassland, open woodland and limestone quarries (reflecting the
needs of its main host). Flowers visited Composites (especially hawkish types), umbellifers and
cinquefoils. Status & distribution Widespread but scarce in England and Wales, with scattered
records north to Cumbria. Rare in Ireland. Not recorded from Scotland or the Channel Islands.
Host(s) *Lasioglossum fulvicorne* (shared with *S. hyalinatus*), with species such as *L. fratellum*,
L. laticeps, *L. pauxillum* and *L. rufitarse* possibly acting as minor hosts.

Sphecodes geoffrellus (Kirby, 1802)   Geoffroy's Blood Bee
not illustrated

Description & similar species FW 4–5mm female, 3–4.5mm male. One
of our smallest *Sphecodes*, the females having only fine and sparse
punctures on the scutum and simple longitudinal ridges on the top
of the propodeum. *S. hyalinatus*, *S. miniatus* and *S. marginatus* are
similar but have the scutum more densely punctate. *S. miniatus* and
S. marginatus also have a reticulate pattern of ridges on the top of
the propodeum and darker hind tarsi (hind tarsi usually pale brown
in *S. geoffrellus*). *S. crassus* has more swollen hind femora and a much
longer labrum. Males are one of three small species with the anterior
face of the antennal flagellar segments largely covered by pubescence but can be separated
from *S. miniatus* and *S. marginatus* using genitalia. Variation Some variation in size, colour
and build. Smaller individuals of both sexes are usually semi-melanic and occasionally have an
all-black abdomen. The female hind tarsi can occasionally be as dark as in *S. miniatus* and
S. marginatus. The sculpturing of the top of the female propodeum varies somewhat and
can become more reticulate in some individuals. Flight season Females fly from late April to

mid-September, males from July into September. **Habitat** Found in a wide variety of open habitats. **Flowers visited** Various, but especially composites and umbellifers. **Status & distribution** Widespread and locally common throughout much of the British Isles, including Scotland and Ireland; also most of the Channel Islands. **Host(s)** *Lasioglossum morio, L. leucopus, L. nitidiusculum, L. pauxillum* and *L. parvulum* are all considered hosts here.

Sphecodes gibbus (Linnaeus, 1758)   **Dark-winged Blood Bee**

not illustrated

Description & similar species FW 6–8mm female, 5.5–7.5mm male. Big females are amongst our largest *Sphecodes*, and with their dark-tinted wings and broad head (distinctly wider than the thorax) can be fairly distinctive in the field. Females are one of three *Sphecodes* with distinct punctures on the top of the head behind the ocelli. They lack the box-shaped head of *S. monilicornis* but have a broader zone of punctures behind the ocelli than *S. reticulatus*, involving 5–6 irregular transverse rows of punctures as opposed to 2–3 rows in *S. reticulatus*. The scutum of *S. gibbus* also has sparser punctures than those other two species. Males belong to a group of larger species with somewhat compressed and shiny antennal flagellar segments, though only *S. gibbus* features numerous, well-defined punctures on the top of the head behind the ocelli. The scutum is also more sparsely punctured than in the others, and the male genitalia are very distinctive. **Variation** Both sexes vary considerably in size, colour and build, with smaller individuals often much darkened and featuring allometry (larger individuals tend to have a proportionally larger head). There is also variation in the strength of sculpturing on the top and sides of the propodeum. Female wings vary in darkness but are usually noticeably darker than those of other *Sphecodes*. **Flight season** Females fly from April until September, males from July to September. **Habitat** Found in a wide variety of open habitats and occasionally in woodland rides and clearings. **Flowers visited** Various, but especially composites (e.g. mayweeds and thistles) and umbellifers. **Status & distribution** Widespread and locally common in England and Wales. Rare in Scotland (recorded as far north as Ayrshire) and Ireland. Recorded from several of the Channel Islands. **Host(s)** *Halictus rubicundus* is the main British host, and it is also known to parasitise *H. quadricinctus* on the continent.

female

male

Sphecodes hyalinatus Hagens, 1882   **Furry-bellied Blood Bee**
not illustrated

Description & similar species FW 4–5mm (sexes similar). One of our smaller *Sphecodes*. Females can be most easily distinguished from other small species by the lack of conspicuous puncture bands around the bases of tergites 2 and 3 (bands of fine punctures present in all other small species), the particularly smooth sides of the propodeum and the unusually shallow sculpturing on the sides of the thorax. The scutum is less densely punctate than in *S. ferruginatus* but somewhat more so than in *S. geoffrellus*, and it is slightly more broadly built. In fresh and well-preserved specimens, the underside of the thorax has a particularly dense pile of short, pale hairs between the fore and mid coxae. The size is typically intermediate between *S. ferruginatus* and species such as *S. miniatus*, *S. marginatus* and *S. geoffrellus*. Males are one of three small species with zones of pubescence occupying about half the length of the apical antennal segments on their anterior face. They should be confirmed using genitalia. **Variation** Some variation in size and build, with individuals featuring wing lengths as short as 3.5mm (usually semi-melanic) occasionally encountered. **Flight season** Females fly from mid-May to October, males from mid-July to October. **Habitat** Prefers chalk and limestone districts over much of its range (often alongside *S. ferruginatus*), using habitats such as chalk and limestone grassland, cuttings and quarries (reflecting the preferences of *Lasioglossum fulvicorne*); also occurs in heathland, coniferous woodland and moorland districts in the north and west of its range, seemingly in association with *L. fratellum*. **Flowers visited** Various, but especially umbellifers and hawkish composites. **Status & distribution** Widespread and locally common in chalk and limestone districts of England, with records extending thinly into Wales and to the north of Scotland. Recorded widely in Ireland but apparently declining. Not recorded from the Channel Islands. **Host(s)** *Lasioglossum fulvicorne* and *L. fratellum*, sharing the former with *S. ferruginatus*.

Sphecodes longulus Hagens, 1882   **Little Sickle-jawed Blood Bee**
not illustrated

Description & similar species FW 3.5–4mm (sexes similar). This species and *S. niger* compete for being our smallest *Sphecodes*, and indeed are amongst our smallest bees. *S. longulus* is one of two *Sphecodes* with females that have simple mandibles lacking an apical tooth or emargination. It can be separated from the other (*S. puncticeps*) by its smaller size and slimmer build, rounder head (in front view), paler legs and lack of a median groove at the front of the scutum. Males are one of three small species with narrow zones of pubescence on the anterior faces of the antennal segments and no dorsal grooves on the gonocoxites. They should always be confirmed using genitalia but average smaller than the other two (*S. ephippius* and *S. puncticeps*), with paler legs and shallower punctures on the scutum. **Variation** A little variation in size and colour, with some individuals darkened and males occasionally having a completely black abdomen and darker legs. **Flight season** Females fly from late April to September, males from July to September. **Habitat** Found in a wide variety of open sandy habitats, including heathland, acid grassland, soft rock cliffs and sandpits. **Flowers visited** Various, but especially composites and umbellifers. **Status & distribution** A rather scarce and localised species, with records mostly within southeast England between Dorset and Norfolk, with outliers in south Wales. Not recorded from Scotland or Ireland. An old records exists for Jersey. **Host(s)** *Lasioglossum morio* and *L. minutissimum* are thought to be the typical hosts, though *L. leucopus*, *L. punctatissimum* and *L. semilucens* may occasionally be used.

Sphecodes marginatus Hagens, 1882   **Margined Blood Bee**
not illustrated

Description & similar species FW 4–5mm female, 3–4.5mm male. One of our smaller *Sphecodes*, and difficult to separate from *S. geoffrellus* and *S. miniatus*. In females, the top of the propodeum has a reticulate pattern of ridges, as in *S. miniatus* (but without the more simple longitudinal ridges of typical *S. geoffrellus*), and the scutum punctures are similar, being somewhat larger and denser than in *S. geoffrellus*. It differs most clearly from both *S. geoffrellus* and *S. miniatus* in the rather broad and dense bands of punctures around the base of tergites 2 and 3, which extend almost as far as the ridge demarking the apical depression (these puncture bands being less extensive and sparser in the other two). Males also resemble *S. geoffrellus* and *S. miniatus* in having the anterior face of the antennal flagellar segments largely covered by pubescence, but they can be confirmed using genitalia. **Variation** Moderate size variation, and much variation on the colour of the male abdomen, which can be extensively red or almost entirely black. **Flight season** Available records are from May to August. **Habitat** Mainly coastal on the Channel Islands, using soft rock cliffs, dunes, coastal heathland, flowery grassland and waste ground. **Flowers visited** Jersey records include umbellifers such as Rock Samphire and Fennel, also thistles, knapweeds and heathers. **Status & distribution** Known only from the Channel Islands, where it can be locally common. **Host(s)** Several *Lasioglossum* species are thought to be hosts on the continent, with *L. punctatissimum* being the most likely of these to be used on the Channel Islands.

Sphecodes miniatus Hagens, 1882   **False Margined Blood Bee**
not illustrated

Description & similar species FW 4–5mm female, 3.5–4.5mm male. One of our smaller *Sphecodes*, and amongst the most difficult to identify. Females are somewhat intermediate between *S. geoffrellus* and *S. ferruginatus*, with the punctures of the scutum larger and denser than in the former but sparser than in the latter, and without the dull, microsculptured head and dense clypeal punctures of *S. ferruginatus*. The top of the propodeum has a reticulate pattern of ridges, very different from the arrangement of longitudinal ridges seen in typical *S. geoffrellus*. The sides of the propodeum are also much more coarsely sculptured than in *S. geoffrellus*. *S. marginatus* is very similar but has denser and more extensive bands of punctures around the bases of tergites 2 and 3. Males are one of three small species with the anterior face of the antennal flagellar segments largely covered by pubescence, but they can be separated from *S. geoffrellus* and *S. marginatus* using genitalia. **Variation** Little known. **Flight season** Females fly from late April to early September, males from late July to mid-September. **Habitat** Most records relate to heathland, acid grassland and other sandy habitats, but it is also present at some chalk grassland sites. **Flowers visited** Typically composites and umbellifers. **Status & distribution** Scarce, with most records confined to southeast England within West Sussex, Surrey, north Kent and Norfolk, with outliers in Hampshire, Devon and Suffolk. Not recorded from Wales, Scotland or Ireland. Recorded from several of the Channel Islands (though some records may result from confusion with *S. marginatus*). **Host(s)** *Lasioglossum nitidiusculum* is cited as a host, but is often absent at *S. miniatus* sites and *L. morio* may be more typical. *L. smeathmanellum* is also a suspected host.

Sphecodes monilicornis (Kirby, 1802)   **Box-headed Blood Bee**
Plate 8

Description & similar species FW 6.5–7.5mm female, 5–6.5mm male. Females are one of three medium to large *Sphecodes* with distinct punctures on the top of the head behind the ocelli. They are easily distinguished from the other two (*S. gibbus* and *S. reticulatus*) by the box-shaped head (in top view), narrower build and paler hairs of the hind tibiae. Males belong to the group of larger species with somewhat compressed and shiny antennal flagellar segments. Of these, it is most likely to be confused with *S. reticulatus* but can be distinguished by the presence of dense white pubescence on the hind trochanters and the

female

distinct genitalia. **Variation** Moderate size variation accompanied by allometry, with larger individuals tending to be more robustly built and bigger-headed than smaller ones. **Flight season** Females fly from late March to mid-September and are amongst the first *Sphecodes* to appear in spring. Males fly from July into September.

Habitat Found in a wide variety of open habitats. **Flowers visited** Various, but especially composites and umbellifers. **Status & distribution** Widespread and locally common in the southern half of Britain, including Wales; also most of the larger Channel Islands. Scarcer in Scotland and Ireland. **Host(s)** Primarily *Halictus rubicundus* and members of the *Lasioglossum calceatum* group, including *L. calceatum*, *L. albipes* and *L. malachurum*.

Sphecodes niger Hagens, 1874   **Dark Blood Bee**
Plate 8

Description & similar species FW 3–4mm (sexes similar). This species and *S. longulus* are our two smallest *Sphecodes*, and indeed are amongst our smallest bees. Both sexes of *S. niger* can be readily identified from all other *Sphecodes* by the smooth shiny patch on the upper sides of the thorax just below the wing bases. Females look distinctive, as tergite 3 is predominantly dark (mostly or entirely red in other female *Sphecodes* except for the occasional semi-melanic individual). The top of the propodeum has very short longitudinal ridges that stop well short of the brow. Males are one of three small species with zones of pubescence

female

male

occupying about half the length of the apical antennal segments on their anterior face. They always have a black abdomen and are often mistaken for a *Lasioglossum*, though the distinctive male genitalia (with very small gonostyli) allow easy separation. **Variation** Moderate size variation. In females, the extent of red on the sides of tergite 3 varies somewhat. **Flight season** Females fly from early April to September (occasionally October). Males fly from July to late September. **Habitat** Found in a wide variety of open habitats, including chalk grassland, heathland, soft rock cliffs, brownfield sites and sunny woodland rides. **Flowers visited** Various, but especially composites and umbellifers. **Status & distribution** Widespread and locally common in southeast England, becoming scarcer in southwest England, with records extending as far north as Shropshire and Lincolnshire. Not recorded in Wales, Scotland or Ireland. Recorded from several of the Channel Islands. It has increased substantially in recent decades, especially within the Midlands. **Host(s)** Probably *Lasioglossum morio*.

Sphecodes pellucidus Smith, 1845   **Sandpit Blood Bee**
not illustrated

Description & similar species FW 5–7mm female, 4.5–6mm male. A medium-sized, robustly built *Sphecodes* with a particularly broad and transverse head when viewed from above, a densely punctate scutum and rather long whitish hairs on the head and thorax. Females have a broad and dull pygidium. The best character for separating females from similar species such as *S. ephippius* can be a little difficult to see but is located on the sides of the thorax just above the fore coxae: it is a chitin flange that acts as a protective collar to the neck. In *S. pellucidus* this bears a sharp angle, whereas in most other *Sphecodes* (except *S. gibbus*, *S. reticulatus* and *S. scabricollis*) it is rounded. Males are one of three small species with zones of pubescence occupying about half the length of the apical antennal segments on their anterior face. They are best confirmed using genitalia. **Variation** Moderate size and colour variation, with smaller individuals tending to be darker. Some females can have rather sooty hairs on the hind tibiae. **Flight season** Females fly from April to September, males from July to September. **Habitat** Strongly associated with very sandy habitats such as heathland, coastal dunes, soft rock cliffs, sandpits and sandy footpaths of wider woodland rides (reflecting the preferences of its main host). **Flowers visited** Various, but especially composites, and often common on dandelions and Cat's-ear in spring and early summer; also mayweeds, thistles and Heather (Ling) in later summer. **Status & distribution** Widespread and locally common in heathland and sandy coastal districts throughout lowland England and Wales, with records extending north to southern Scotland. Only a single 1973 Irish record. Recorded from Jersey and Guernsey in the Channel

female

male

Islands. **Host(s)** Primarily *Andrena barbilabris*, though sometimes occurring at sites where *A. barbilabris* seems absent and flying much later, suggesting it may be bivoltine and using other hosts at some sites.

Sphecodes puncticeps Thomson, 1870   **Sickle-jawed Blood Bee**
not illustrated

Description & similar species FW 4.5–5mm female, 4–5mm male. One of our smaller *Sphecodes*, with a rather robust build, strongly punctate scutum and very broad head (in front view). It is one of two *Sphecodes* with females that have simple mandibles lacking an apical tooth or emargination, and it can be separated from the other (*S. longulus*) by its larger size, broader build, broader head (in front view), darker legs and the presence of a distinct median groove at the front of the thoracic dorsum. Males are one of three smaller species with narrow zones of pubescence on the anterior faces of the antennal segments and no dorsal grooves on the gonocoxites. They should always be confirmed using genitalia but have denser punctures on the scutum and darker legs than *S. longulus,* and the scutum less densely punctate than *S. ephippius*. **Variation** Dwarfs of both sexes with a wing length as short as 3.5mm can occasionally be encountered, and these can have black abdomens. **Flight season** Females fly from April to October, males from July to October. **Habitat** Found in a wide variety of open and lightly wooded habitats including coastal habitats such as soft rock cliffs. **Flowers visited** Various, but especially composites and umbellifers. **Status & distribution** Widespread and locally common in southern England and the Midlands, with records extending north to Cumbria and into south Wales. Not recorded from Scotland or Ireland. Recorded from several of the Channel Islands. **Host(s)** *Lasioglossum lativentre* and *L. quadrinotatum* are thought to be the typical hosts, though *L. villosulum* and *L. brevicorne* may be used occasionally.

Sphecodes reticulatus Thomson, 1870   **Reticulate Blood Bee**
not illustrated

Description & similar species FW 5–7mm (sexes similar). One of our larger *Sphecodes*. Females are one of three medium to large *Sphecodes* with distinct punctures on the top of the head behind the ocelli. Female *S. reticulatus* lacks the squarish head of *S. monilicornis* and has a narrower zone of punctures behind the ocelli than *S. gibbus* (2–3 irregular transverse rows of punctures as opposed to 5–6 rows in *S. gibbus*). A particularly dense band of punctures occurs around the base of tergite 4. Males belong to a group of larger species with somewhat compressed and shiny antennal flagellar segments and no punctures behind the ocelli. Of these, it is most likely to be confused with *S. monilicornis* but can be distinguished by the lack of dense white pubescence on the hind trochanters and the distinct genitalia. **Variation** Moderate size variation, with smaller individuals tending to be darker. **Flight season** Females fly from late May until mid-September, males mainly in August and September. **Habitat** Strongly associated with sandy habitats such as heathland, acid grassland, soft rock cliffs and sandpits, often alongside *S. pellucidus*. **Flowers visited** Various, but especially composites, umbellifers and heathers. **Status & distribution** Widespread but localised in southern heathland districts between Dorset and Norfolk, with scattered populations north to Yorkshire. Some indication of a recent expansion in the Midlands. Rare in Wales. Not recorded from Scotland or Ireland. Recorded from several of the Channel Islands. **Host(s)** *Andrena barbilabris*, and possibly *A. dorsata*, *A. argentata* and *Lasioglossum prasinum*.

Sphecodes rubicundus von Hagens, 1875   Red-tailed Blood Bee

not illustrated

Description & similar species FW 6.5–7mm female, 5.5–7.5mm male. One of our larger *Sphecodes*. Females are readily separable from all other species except *S. ephippius* by the very short, sparse hairs on the sloping anterior face of tergite 1. Readily separable from *S. ephippius* by the larger size, darker hairs of the hind tibiae, the dense and continuous puncture band around the base of tergite 2 and the red tergite 4 (which renders it superficially similar in the field to some *S. gibbus*). Males average the largest of the group of species with non-compressed, coarsely punctured antennal segments, and have red basal corners to

tergite 4. The genitalia are distinctive. **Variation** Some size variation, with smaller individuals usually darker but generally retaining some red on tergite 4. **Flight season** Females fly from May to July, males in May and June. **Habitat** Found in a variety of open habitats including chalk downland, heathland, soft rock cliffs, brownfield site (especially old claypits) and open areas in woods. The main host is heavily dependent on legume-rich habitats. **Flowers visited** British records include thistles, Wood Spurge and various umbellifers. **Status & distribution** Scarce and localised, with most records for southeast England but extending north to Staffordshire and Norfolk, and also recorded from several sites in south Wales. On the Channel Islands, known only from Guernsey. Not recorded from Scotland or Ireland. **Host(s)** Typically *Andrena labialis*, though *A. flavipes* may be an occasional host.

Sphecodes scabricollis Wesmael, 1835   Rough-backed Blood Bee

not illustrated

Description & similar species FW 7mm female, 6mm male. A medium-sized *Sphecodes*. Both sexes can be distinguished by the extremely densely punctured scutum and scutellum, much more so than any other *Sphecodes* species. In males, the punctures are so close that they create a rugose texture with barely any shining interstices. In females, the

punctures are less tightly packed but still unusually large and separated by much less than their diameter over much of the scutum and scutellum. Another unique feature is the presence of a ridge along the extreme hind margin of each gena. The male genitalia are distinctive. **Variation** Little noted. **Flight season** Females fly from April to September, males from July to September. **Habitat** The relatively few British records involve heathland, coastal dunes, brownfield sites and the rides and clearings of clay woodland. **Flowers visited** Usually composites (thistles, oxtongues, Yarrow, Common Fleabane) and umbellifers. **Status & distribution** A rare southern species, with most records from southeast England and a few outliers in Devon, Dorset, Somerset and south Wales. **Host(s)** *Lasioglossum zonulum*.

Sphecodes spinulosus Hagens, 1875   **Spined Blood Bee**
Plate 8

Description & similar species FW 7–8mm female, 6.5–8mm male. Averaging as our largest *Sphecodes* and easily separable from other species by the transverse step across the base of sternite 2 and the upcurved flange along the extreme hind margin of the head at the top (which can be difficult to see if the head is reflexed upwards). Females have relatively longer antennae than other species, with the flagellar segments distinctly longer than wide. Males have the unique feature of about 10 dark spines along the dorsal edge of each hind tibia, and have distinctive genitalia. **Variation** Moderate size variation. **Flight season** Both sexes fly from May to late June. **Habitat** Chalk and limestone grassland, quarries, cuttings and coastal landslips, reflecting the habitats of its host. **Flowers visited** British records include a spurge, buttercups, brambles and umbellifers such as Wild Carrot. **Status & distribution** A rare species of southern England north to Northamptonshire, with a couple of records for the south coast of Wales and an old record for Guernsey. Relatively few modern records, and indications of a significant decline. Not recorded in Scotland or Ireland. **Host(s)** *Lasioglossum xanthopus*.

ROPHITES – BRISTLE-HEADED BEES

Mostly medium-sized halictid bees with only two submarginal cells and a very short face (the clypeus barely longer than the labrum), as in *Dufourea* species. Much larger and more densely punctate than *Dufourea* bees, with a strongly banded abdomen and densely furry thorax. Easily separable from *Halictus* species by the short face, fewer submarginal cells and lack of a rima (furrow) on tergite 6 of the female. Pollen is collected from labiates, and females have specialised bristle-like hairs on the top of the head (between the ocelli and the antennae) to help achieve this (Fig. 1). This is a Palaearctic genus with about a dozen European species. Represented in Britain by one species that is probably extinct here. Abroad, they are attacked by cleptoparasitic bees of the genus *Biastes*.

Fig. 1

Rophites quinquespinosus Spinola, 1808   **Five-spined Rophites**
not illustrated

Description & similar species FW 6mm (sexes similar). Females are about the size of *Halictus rubicundus* but with only two submarginal cells and very short antennae which are orange beneath. The top of the thorax is very dull with a dense but short pile of straw-coloured hairs. The tergites are densely punctate with entire pale hair bands along the hind margins of tergites 2–4 and the sides of tergite 1. Males are more broadly built than *Halictus* males, and have pale hair bands along the hind margins of tergites 1–5 and a rather box-shaped head (in top view). The medium-length antennae are entirely orange underneath. The legs are black with rather short, yellow tarsi. Sternite 6 has a densely hairy ridge along the midline and a pair of lateral spines. **Variation** Little noted. **Flight season** June to late August in central Europe. **Habitat** Abroad, assorted habitats with suitable forage plants. **Flowers visited** Pollen is obtained from labiates such as Black Horehound, woundworts and Wild Basil. Males also visit *Campanula* flowers. **Nesting habits** Abroad, nesting aggregations of various sizes have been observed in light soils. **Status & distribution** Known as British on the basis of two females captured at Guestling, near Hastings, Sussex, in 1877 and 1878. **Parasites & associates** On the continent, attacked by the non-British *Biastes emarginatus*.

female

male

DUFOUREA – SHORT-FACED BEES

About 150 described species of small, mainly blackish halictid bees that closely resemble small dark *Lasioglossum* species but have two rather than three submarginal cells on the wings (like the larger and more strongly banded *Rophites*). Also, like *Rophites*, the face is unusually short with the clypeus barely longer than the labrum, and no furrow (rima) is present on tergite 5 of the female (in contrast to *Lasioglossum* and *Halictus*). Represented in Britain by two species that are probably extinct here. Several further species occur on the near-continent. Nesting occurs in light soils, usually in aggregations. In contrast to most halictids, males appear before females. Abroad, they are attacked by cleptoparasitic bees of the genus *Biastes*.

♀

Dufourea halictula

DUFOUREA

— Smaller (wing length 3.5mm) with a densely punctate scutum (punctures separated by less than their own diameter). Male with longer antennae (segments 5–7 longer than wide viewed from front), segments 6–13 without zones of pubescence at front .... *halictula*

— Larger (wing length at least 4mm) with a very sparsely punctate scutum (punctures separated by several times their diameter). Male with shorter antennae (segments 5–7 about as long as wide viewed from front), segments 6–13 with zones of dense pubescence on the anterior face (Fig. 1) .... *minuta*

Fig. 1

Dufourea halictula (Nylander, 1852)   **Sheep's-bit Dufourea**

Plate 8

Description & similar species FW 3.5mm (sexes similar). A small shining black bee superficially resembling a small *Lasioglossum* (e.g. *L. minutissimum*) or tiny *Andrena* of the *minutula* group, but with two rather than three submarginal cells and no tomentose spots or hair fringes on the tergites. Smaller and more densely punctate than *D. minuta*, the males lacking zones of pubescence on the flagellar segments. The female antennae are very short, with the underside of the flagella orange. **Variation** Little noted. **Flight season** Late June to mid-August, with males appearing first. **Habitat** In Britain associated with sandy heathland and acid grassland supporting plentiful Sheep's-bit. **Flowers visited** Pollen is seemingly obtained exclusively from Sheep's-bit,

female

male

though it has been observed visiting bellflowers and a knapweed abroad, probably for nectar. **Nesting habits** British nests have been observed along a hard sandy footpath between stones and to a lesser extent on an adjacent moss-covered sandy bank. **Status & distribution** Known as British from Woking Heath (Horsell Common), Surrey (about 1910), Byfleet, Surrey (various dates between 1913 and 1920), Ferndown, Dorset (1948), and Parley, Dorset (1953). Possibly extinct. **Parasites & associates** Abroad it is attacked by the non-British cleptoparasitic bee *Biastes truncatus*.

Dufourea minuta Lepeletier, 1841   **Shiny Dufourea**

not illustrated

Description & similar species FW 4–4.5mm (sexes similar). Somewhat larger and shinier than *D. halictula*, rather resembling a dark-looking *Lasioglossum* or small male *Panurgus calcaratus* in the field. Males have zones of dense pubescence on the anterior face of most antennal segments, much like some *Sphecodes*, and could be mistaken for the black males of *S. niger*. **Variation** Little noted. **Flight season** British records are late June to mid-August. **Habitat** British

female

records include heathland, dry acid grassland and soft rock cliffs. Sandy ground may be essential. **Flowers visited** Pollen seems to be obtained entirely from Asteraceae such as ragworts, mayweeds, dandelions, hawkbits and hawkweeds. The bee apparently has a characteristic wriggling flight as it approaches a flower. **Nesting habits** Nesting occurs in aggregations in sandy soils. **Status & distribution** The only British records are from Holt, Dorset (1956), Chewton on the Dorset–Hampshire border (1879), Woking, Surrey (1881), and Chobham, Surrey (1891). Possibly extinct. This is the *D. vulgaris* of older literature. **Parasites & associates** None known.

PLATE 1

COLLETES – PLASTERER BEES

Heather Colletes (p.79)
Colletes succinctus

Ivy Bee (p.76)
Colletes hederae

Davies' Colletes (p.73)
Colletes daviesanus

Early Colletes (p.73)
Colletes cunicularius

HYLAEUS – YELLOW-FACE BEES

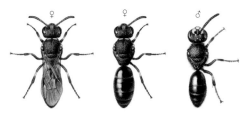

Common Yellow-face Bee (p.85)
Hylaeus communis

×2.5 actual size

PLATE 2

HYLAEUS – YELLOW-FACE BEES *continued*

Shingle Yellow-face Bee (p.84)
Hylaeus annularis

Chalk Yellow-face Bee
(p.87)
Hylaeus dilatatus

Common Yellow-face Bee
(p.85)
Hylaeus communis

Reed Yellow-face Bee
(p.89)
Hylaeus pectoralis

Short-horned Yellow-face Bee
(p.84)
Hylaeus brevicornis

Little Yellow-face Bee
(p.90)
Hylaeus pictipes

White-jawed Yellow-face Bee
(p.86)
Hylaeus confusus

White-lipped Yellow-face Bee
(p.88)
Hylaeus incongruus

Hairy Yellow-face Bee
(p.88)
Hylaeus hyalinatus

Large Yellow-face Bee
(p.91)
Hylaeus signatus

Onion Yellow-face Bee
(p.90)
Hylaeus punctulatissimus

Spined Hylaeus
(p.86)
Hylaeus cornutus

PLATE 3

ANDRENA – MINING BEES

Large Sallow Mining Bee (p.119) *Andrena apicata*

Small Sallow Mining Bee (p.150) *Andrena praecox*

Clarke's Mining Bee (p.126) *Andrena clarkella*

Tawny Mining Bee (p.133) *Andrena fulva*

Painted Mining Bee (p.132) *Andrena fucata*

Bilberry Mining Bee (p.140) *Andrena lapponica*

♀ f. *mixta*

Blackthorn Mining Bee (p.161) *Andrena varians*

Broad-margined Mining Bee (p.156) *Andrena synadelpha*

Coppice Mining Bee (p.137) *Andrena helvola*

Violet-winged Mining Bee (p.118) *Andrena agilissima*

Big-headed Mining Bee (p.123) *Andrena bucephala*

Oak Mining Bee (p.129) *Andrena ferox*

Chocolate Mining Bee (p.153) *Andrena scotica*

×2.5 actual size

PLATE 4

ANDRENA – MINING BEES *continued*

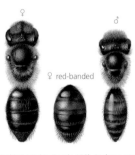

Perkins' Mining Bee (p.152) *Andrena rosae*

♀ red-banded

Trimmer's Mining Bee (p.159)
Andrena trimmerana

Gwynne's Mining Bee (p.121)
Andrena bicolor

Groove-faced Mining Bee
(p.118) *Andrena angustior*

Ashy Mining Bee (p.125)
Andrena cineraria

Buffish Mining Bee (p.144)
Andrena nigroaenea

Grey-patched Mining Bee (p.146)
Andrena nitida

Cliff Mining Bee (p.157)
Andrena thoracica

Grey-banded Mining Bee
(p.128) *Andrena denticulata*

Heather Mining Bee (p.134)
Andrena fuscipes

Black-headed Mining Bee (p.143)
Andrena nigriceps

Orange-tailed Mining Bee (p.136)
Andrena haemorrhoa

×2.5 actual size

PLATE 5

ANDRENA – MINING BEES *continued*

Large Gorse Mining Bee (p.122)
Andrena bimaculata

Grey-gastered Mining Bee (p.158)
Andrena tibialis

Scarce Black Mining Bee (p.145)
Andrena nigrospina

Yellow-legged Mining Bee (p.130)
Andrena flavipes

Bryony Mining Bee (p.131)
Andrena florea

Tormentil Mining Bee (p.156)
Andrena tarsata

Small Flecked Mining Bee
(p.126) *Andrena coitana*

Sandpit Mining Bee (p.121)
Andrena barbilabris

Small Sandpit Mining Bee
(p.120) *Andrena argentata*

Hawthorn Mining Bee
(p.124)
Andrena chrysosceles

Carrot Mining
Bee (p.147)
Andrena nitidiuscula

Hawk's-beard Mining
Bee (p.133)
Andrena fulvago

Buff-tailed Mining Bee (p.138)
Andrena humilis

×2.5 actual size

PLATE 6

ANDRENA – MINING BEES *continued*

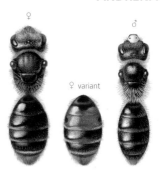

♀ variant

♀ variant ♀ variant

Large Scabious Mining Bee (p.136)
Andrena hattorfiana

Small Scabious Mining Bee (p.142)
Andrena marginata

Red-girdled Mining Bee
(p.140) *Andrena labiata*

Large Meadow Mining Bee
(p.139) *Andrena labialis*

Long-fringed Mining Bee
(p.127) *Andrena congruens*

Short-fringed Mining Bee
(p.129) *Andrena dorsata*

Red-backed Mining Bee
(p.154) *Andrena similis*

Wilke's Mining Bee (p.162)
Andrena wilkella

Small Gorse Mining Bee
(p.148) *Andrena ovatula*

Broad-faced Mining Bee
(p.151) *Andrena proxima*

Common Mini-miner
(p.165) *Andrena minutula*

PANURGUS – SHAGGY BEES

Large Shaggy Bee (p.170) *Panurgus banksianus*

Small Shaggy Bee (p.171) *Panurgus calcaratus*

×2.5 actual size

PLATE 7

HALICTUS – END-BANDED FURROW BEES

Downland Furrow Bee (p.175)
Halictus eurygnathus

Giant Furrow Bee (p.177)
Halictus quadricinctus

Great Banded Furrow Bee (p.178)
Halictus scabiosae

Orange-legged Furrow Bee (p.178) *Halictus rubicundus*

Bronze Furrow Bee (p.180) *Halictus tumulorum*

LASIOGLOSSUM – BASE-BANDED FURROW BEES

hind leg

White-zoned Furrow Bee (p.202)
Lasioglossum leucozonium

Grey-tailed Furrow Bee
(p.208)
Lasioglossum prasinum

Ashy Furrow Bee
(p.212)
Lasioglossum sexnotatum

Orange-footed Furrow Bee
(p.215)
Lasioglossum xanthopus

variant

Common Furrow Bee (p.196)
Lasioglossum calceatum

Chalk Furrow Bee (p.198)
Lasioglossum fulvicorne

Least Furrow
Bee (p.205)
*Lasioglossum
minutissimum*

Smeathman's Furrow
Bee (p.213)
*Lasioglossum
smeathmanellum*

×2.5 actual size

PLATE 8

SPHECODES – BLOOD BEES

Box-headed Blood Bee (p.231)
Sphecodes monilicornis

Dark Blood Bee (p.231)
Sphecodes niger

Spined Blood Bee (p.235)
Sphecodes spinulosus

DUFOUREA – SHORT-FACED BEES

Sheep's-bit Dufourea (p.237) *Dufourea halictula*

MELITTA – BLUNTHORN BEES

Sainfoin Bee (p.260)
Melitta dimidiata

Red Bartsia Bee (p.262) *Melitta tricincta*

Clover Melitta (p.261)
Melitta leporina

Gold-tailed Melitta (p.261)
Melitta haemorrhoidalis

Red Bartsia Bee (p.262) *Melitta tricincta*

×2.5 actual size

PLATE 9

MACROPIS – OIL-COLLECTING BEES

Yellow Loosestrife Bee (p.264) *Macropis europaea*

DASYPODA – PANTALOON BEES

Pantaloon Bee (p.265) *Dasypoda hirtipes*

ANTHIDIUM – WOOL CARDERS

♀ variant

Wool Carder Bee (p.266) *Anthidium manicatum*

STELIS – DARK BEES

Little Dark Bee (p.268) *Stelis breviuscula*

Spotted Dark Bee (p.269) *Stelis ornatula*

Plain Dark Bee (p.269) *Stelis phaeoptera*

Banded Dark Bee (p.270) *Stelis punctulatissima*

×2.5 actual size

PLATE 10

HERIADES – RESIN BEES

Large-headed Resin Bee (p.272) *Heriades truncorum*

CHELOSTOMA – SCISSOR BEES

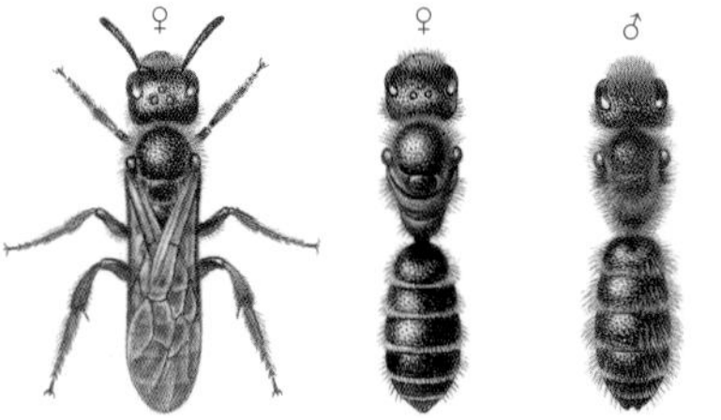

Large Scissor Bee (p.274) *Chelostoma florisomne*

Small Scissor Bee (p.273)
Chelostoma campanularum

OSMIA – MASON BEES

Red Mason Bee (p.282) *Osmia bicornis*

Mountain Mason Bee (p.284)
Osmia inermis

Fringe-horned Mason Bee (p.287)
Osmia pilicornis

Cliff Mason Bee (p.289)
Osmia xanthomelana

×2.5 actual size

Gold-fringed Mason Bee (p.280)
Osmia aurulenta

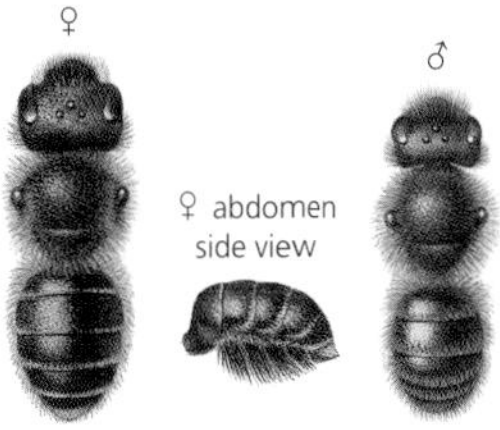

♀ abdomen
side view

Blue Mason Bee (p.283)
Osmia caerulescens

PLATE 11

OSMIA – MASON BEES *continued*

Orange-vented Mason Bee (p.285) *Osmia leaiana*

Red-tailed Mason Bee (p.281) *Osmia bicolor*

Spined Mason Bee (p.288) *Osmia spinulosa*

HOPLITIS – LESSER MASONS

Welted Mason Bee (p.291) *Hoplitis claviventris*

MEGACHILE – LEAFCUTTER AND MUD BEES

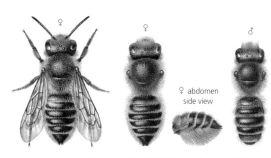

Patchwork Leafcutter Bee (p.297) *Megachile centuncularis*

Wood-carving Leafcutter Bee (p.301) *Megachile ligniseca*

Brown-footed Leafcutter Bee (p.303) *Megachile versicolor*

Silvery Leafcutter Bee (p.300) *Megachile leachella*

×2.5 actual size

PLATE 12

MEGACHILE – LEAFCUTTER AND MUD BEES *continued*

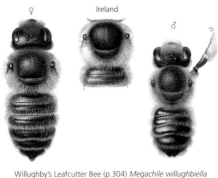

Willughby's Leafcutter Bee (p.304) *Megachile willughbiella*

Black-headed Leafcutter Bee (p.298) *Megachile circumcincta*

COELIOXYS – SHARP-TAIL BEES

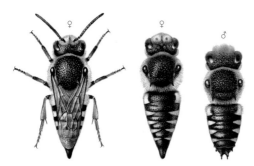

Large Sharp-tail Bee (p.310) *Coelioxys conoidea*

Dull-vented Sharp-tail Bee (p.311) *Coelioxys elongata*

♀ mandibles

Shiny-vented Sharp-tail Bee (p.312) *Coelioxys inermis*

Square-jawed Sharp-tail Bee (p.312) *Coelioxys mandibularis*

Grooved Sharp-tail Bee (p.313) *Coelioxys quadridentata*

tip of ♀ abdomen

tip of ♀ abdomen

Rufescent Sharp-tail Bee (p.313) *Coelioxys rufescens*

Short Sharp-tail Bee (p.309) *Coelioxys afra*

Red-legged Sharp-tail Bee (p.310) *Coelioxys brevis*

×2.5 actual size

PLATE 13

NOMADA – NOMAD BEES

Gooden's Nomad Bee (p.337)
Nomada goodeniana

Yellow-legged Nomad Bee
(p.350)
Nomada succincta

Marsham's Nomad Bee
(p.341)
Nomada marshamella

Six-banded Nomad Bee
(p.346)
Nomada sexfasciata

Blunthorn Nomad Bee
(p.333)
Nomada flavopicta

Orange-horned Nomad Bee
(p.335)
Nomada fulvicornis

Kirby's Nomad Bee
(p.350)
Nomada subcornuta

Early Nomad Bee
(p.341)
Nomada leucophthalma

Lathbury's Nomad Bee
(p.340)
Nomada lathburiana

Painted Nomad Bee
(p.334)
Nomada fucata

Flavous Nomad Bee
(p.331)
Nomada flava

Panzer's Nomad Bee
(p.343)
Nomada panzeri

Fork-jawed Nomad Bee
(p.344)
Nomada ruficornis

Bear-clawed Nomad Bee
(p.328)
Nomada baccata

Long-horned Nomad Bee
(p.338)
Nomada hirtipes

×2.5 actual size

PLATE 14

NOMADA – NOMAD BEES *continued*

Broad-banded Nomad Bee
(p.347)
Nomada signata

Black-horned Nomad Bee
(p.345)
Nomada rufipes

Purbeck Nomad Bee
(p.329)
Nomada errans

Armed Nomad Bee
(p.327)
Nomada armata

Fringeless Nomad Bee
(p.329)
Nomada conjungens

Fabricius' Nomad Bee
(p.330)
Nomada fabriciana

Yellow-shouldered Nomad Bee
(p.331)
Nomada ferruginata

Little Nomad Bee
(p.332)
Nomada flavoguttata

Blunt-jawed Nomad Bee
(p.349)
Nomada striata

Short-spined Nomad Bee
(p.338)
Nomada guttulata

Flat-ridged Nomad Bee
(p.342)
Nomada obtusifrons

Tormentil Nomad Bee
(p.344)
Nomada roberjeotiana

Cat's-ear Nomad Bee
(p.339)
Nomada integra

Silver-sided Nomad Bee
(p.326)
Nomada argentata

Guernsey Nomad Bee
(p.348)
Nomada similis

Sheppard's Nomad Bee
(p.347)
Nomada sheppardana

×2.5 actual size

PLATE 15

EPEOLUS – VARIEGATED CUCKOO BEES

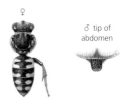

Red-thighed Epeolus (p.353)
Epeolus cruciger

Black-thighed Epeolus (p.354)
Epeolus variegatus

EUCERA – LONG-HORNED BEES

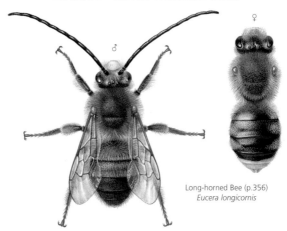

Long-horned Bee (p.356)
Eucera longicornis

ANTHOPHORA – FLOWER BEES

Hairy-footed Flower Bee (p.360) *Anthophora plumipes*

×2.5 actual size

PLATE 16

ANTHOPHORA – FLOWER BEES *continued*

Potter Flower Bee (p.362) *Anthophora retusa*
(female resembles black form of *A. plumipes*)

Fork-tailed Flower Bee (p.359) *Anthophora furcata*

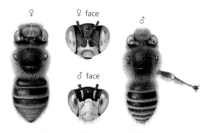

Four-banded Flower Bee (p.361)
Anthophora quadrimaculata

Green-eyed Flower Bee (p.358)
Anthophora bimaculata

MELECTA – MOURNING BEES

Common Mourning Bee (p.363)
Melecta albifrons

CERATINA – SMALL CARPENTER BEES

Little Blue Carpenter Bee (p.365)
Ceratina cyanea

×2.5 actual size

PLATE 17

XYLOCOPA – LARGE CARPENTER BEES

Violet Carpenter Bee (p.366)
Xylocopa violacea

BOMBUS – BUMBLEBEES

queen ♂ queen

White-tailed Bumblebee (p.390) *Bombus lucorum*

queen

queen queen

Northern White-tailed Bumblebee
(p.392) *Bombus magnus*

Cryptic Bumblebee (p.382)
Bombus cryptarum

Buff-tailed Bumblebee (p.406)
Bombus terrestris

queen dark queen worker (♀) ♂

Buff-tailed Bumblebee (p.406) *Bombus terrestris*

×1.5 actual size

PLATE 18

BOMBUS – **BUMBLEBEES** *continued*

queen

♂

queen

♂

♂

Broken-belted Bumblebee (p.402)
Bombus soroeensis

Garden Bumblebee (p.384) *Bombus hortorum*

queen

queen *perniger*

♂

♂

queen

Large Garden Bumblebee (p.400) *Bombus ruderatus*

Red-tailed Bumblebee (p.389) *Bombus lapidarius*

queen

dark queen

♂ variants

queen

♂

Tree Bumblebee (p.387) *Bombus hypnorum*

Bilberry Bumblebee (p.393) *Bombus monticola*

queen

♂

♂

queen

worker
(♀)

♂

Heath Bumblebee (p.388) *Bombus jonellus*

Early Bumblebee (p.398) *Bombus pratorum*

×1.5 actual size

PLATE 19

BOMBUS – BUMBLEBEES *continued*

queen

Great Yellow Bumblebee
(p.383)
Bombus distinguendus

queen ♂

Short-haired Bumblebee
(p.404)
Bombus subterraneus

queen queen *agricolae* queen *allenellus*

Moss Carder Bee (p.394) *Bombus muscorum*

queen

Brown-banded Carder Bee
(p.386) *Bombus humilis*

queen queen ♂ variants

Common Carder Bee (p.395) *Bombus pascuorum*

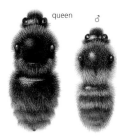

queen ♂

Apple Bumblebee (p.397)
Bombus pomorum

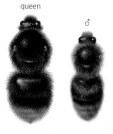

queen ♂

Red-shanked Carder Bee (p.399)
Bombus ruderarius

queen ♂

Shrill Carder Bee (p.405)
Bombus sylvarum

BOMBUS – CUCKOO BUMBLEBEES

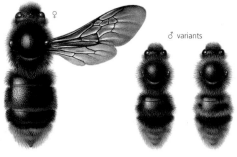

♀ ♂ variants

Red-tailed Cuckoo Bee (p.411) *Bombus rupestris*

×1.5 actual size

PLATE 20

BOMBUS – CUCKOO BUMBLEBEES *continued*

Vestal Cuckoo Bee (p.414) *Bombus vestalis*

Gypsy Cuckoo Bee (p.409) *Bombus bohemicus*

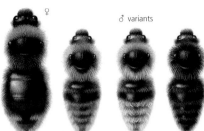

♂ variants

Field Cuckoo Bee (p.410) *Bombus campestris*

Barbut's Cuckoo Bee (p.408) *Bombus barbutellus*

♂ variants

Forest Cuckoo Bee (p.413) *Bombus sylvestris*

APIS – HONEY BEES

queen

worker
(♀)

drone
(♂)

Western Honey Bee (p.415) *Apis mellifera*

×1.5 actual size

FAMILY MELITTIDAE

MELITTA – BLUNTHORN BEES

Medium-sized bees with banded abdomens that superficially resemble certain *Andrena* species (e.g. *A. flavipes*). They are easily distinguished by the blunt tip to the antennae, the much larger final segment of the tarsi and the lack of facial foveae and they also have rather different mouthparts. Pollen is collected on the hind tibiae and basitarsi but never on the hind femora or sides of the propodeum as seen in *Andrena*. *Melitta* species have rather narrow foraging preferences. Two of our species gather pollen exclusively from single plant species, and another mostly uses *Campanula* species. Nesting occurs in light soils, sometimes in loose aggregations. Nest cells are filled with a firm pollen ball.

The most efficient way of finding *Melitta* species is to observe known forage plants in fine weather (e.g. Red Bartsia for *M. tricincta*). Males will often be seen flying at high speed around these plants in search of females, rarely stopping for nectar. Adults fly from mid- to late summer. Overwintering is as a larva enclosed in a cocoon. Most British species are attacked by the cleptoparasitic bee *Nomada flavopicta*. Over 40 species have been described globally, and four of these occur in Britain, though none have been recorded in Ireland.

Melitta tricincta

Melitta haemorrhoidalis

Melitta haemorrhoidalis

Melitta dimidiata

MELITTA FEMALES

1   Tergite 5 and hair pad at tip of hind femora orange-haired. Pale hair bands of tergites narrow and inconspicuous. Top of thorax mainly black-haired .... *haemorrhoidalis*

—   Tergite 5 and hair pad at tip of hind femora blackish-haired. Hair bands of tergites more conspicuous. Top of thorax with mixed black and pale hairs 2

2   Scutum and front of scutellum with shining areas devoid of microsculpture between punctures. Honey Bee-sized (wing length 8.5–9mm) .... *dimidiata*

—   Scutum and front of scutellum dulled by microsculpture between punctures. Smaller (wing length up to 7.5mm) 3

3   Antennal scapes mostly pale-haired. Hair bands of tergites white and relatively narrow (one-third the length of the tergites). Pygidium with an obvious median ridge that usually runs to the tip (angle of lighting critical). Last segment of the fore and mid tarsi brownish .... *tricincta*

—   Antennal scapes mostly black-haired. Hair bands of tergites wider (half the length of the tergites) and pale buff in fresh individuals. Pygidium relatively flat (a very faint median ridge can be present). Last segment of the fore and mid tarsi yellowish-brown .... *leporina*

MELITTA MALES

1   Abdomen with dense, conspicuous bands of pale hairs 2

—   Abdomen lacking obvious bands (though weak bands may appear if the light strikes from certain angles) 3

2   Pale hair band along posterior margin of tergite 2 preceded by a narrow band of black hairs. Hair bands of tergites dense, white, adpressed and narrower (one-third the length of the tergites) .... *tricincta*

—   Pale band along posterior margin of tergite 2 not preceded by black hairs. Hair bands of tergites creamy-yellowish in fresh individuals, wider than in previous species (half the length of the tergites), with hairs less dense and more upright .... *leporina*

3   Larger (wing length 8.5–9mm) with black hairs on tergites 4–6 contrasting strongly with the pale hairs of tergites 1–3 .... *dimidiata*

—   Smaller (wing length 7.5–8mm) with tergite 6 orange-haired and tergites 4 and 5 with a mix of black and pale hairs .... *haemorrhoidalis*

Melitta dimidiata Morawitz, 1876   **Sainfoin Bee**

Plate 8

Description & similar species FW 8.5–9mm (sexes similar). Britain's largest *Melitta*, about the size of a Honey Bee. Females have rather narrow bands on the tergites like *M. tricincta* but have a shinier thorax with the hairs a richer red-brown. Males are much fluffier than females, with the body hairs mostly grey-buff except for the black-haired tip to the abdomen. The strong association with Sainfoin can support identification. **Variation** Very little. Old specimens fade greyish, and the abdominal bands of the females can become abraded. **Flight season** Late June to early August. **Habitat** Chalk grassland and open scrub with plentiful Sainfoin. **Flowers visited** Pollen and nectar are seemingly obtained entirely from Sainfoin in Britain. In dull weather, males can also be found sheltering in the flowers of plants such as mallows, scabiouses, knapweeds, bellflowers and Viper's-bugloss. **Nesting habits** Nesting never observed but presumed to occur in light soil. **Status & distribution** Only ever known in Britain from the Salisbury Plain area, Wiltshire. It is still present at several sites, though some colonies have been lost. **Parasites & associates** None noted.

female

male

Melitta haemorrhoidalis Morawitz, 1876   **Gold-tailed Melitta**
Plate 8

Description & similar species FW 8–8.5mm female, 7.5–8mm male. The orange-haired tip to the abdomen is diagnostic for both sexes. Females are darker-looking than other *Melitta*, having barely discernible abdominal bands and the top of the thorax mostly black-haired. They also have orange 'kneecaps' on the hind femora (dark in the other species). Males lack the strong abdominal bands of *M. leporina* and *M. tricincta*. The strong association with Harebell and other bellflowers can support identification. **Variation** Very little. Fresh males are rather golden-brown but quickly fade to buff-grey. **Flight season** Early July to early September. **Habitat** Heathland, acid grassland, chalk downland and sometimes woodland rides and clearings. It occasionally occurs in gardens, and a population was even discovered in the grounds of Birmingham University close to the city centre. **Flowers visited** Pollen is typically obtained from bellflowers, especially Harebell, but also Clustered Bellflower on chalk grassland, Nettle-leaved Bellflower in more wooded locations and occasionally cultivated *Campanula* species. Round-headed Rampion is also a pollen source at some downland sites. Other flowers such as mallows and crane's-bills appear to be nectar sources. In dull weather, both sexes will shelter in the flowers of bellflowers, and males also use mallows. **Nesting habits** Small aggregations of nests have been observed in light soils. **Status & distribution** Widespread but local south of the Chilterns, with scattered records extending as far north as East Lothian. Not recorded from southwest England, Wales, Ireland or the Channel Islands. **Parasites & associates** The cleptoparasitic bee *Nomada flavopicta* may attack *M. haemorrhoidalis*, though this is not confirmed.

female   male

Melitta leporina (Panzer, 1799)   **Clover Melitta**
Plate 8

Description & similar species FW 6.5–7.5mm (sexes similar). Resembles *M. tricincta*, but females have broader abdominal bands which are pale buff in fresh individuals (white in *M. tricincta*), a richer brown-coloured pile on the thorax and mostly black-haired antennal scapes. Females can also be overlooked as an *Andrena* in the field, especially species such as *A. flavipes*. Fresh males also have a rich brown thorax and bright buff abdominal bands (*M. tricincta* males are never this bright). Both sexes have a yellowish-brown final segment of the fore and mid tarsi. The strong association with legumes such as clovers can provide a good field clue. **Variation** Very little, though ageing can cause considerable fading, and abrasion of the abdominal bands. **Flight season** Late June to late August. **Habitat** Quite varied, including grassland of various sorts (even quite improved), heathland, coastal dunes, brownfield sites and occasionally gardens. **Flowers visited** Pollen seems to be obtained mainly from legumes such as clovers, vetches, Lucerne and melilots; indeed some of its strongest populations are on fairly improved clover-rich grasslands. Other plants may be visited for nectar, and males are often seen on ragworts. They will also roost in clusters on Yarrow flowers. **Nesting habits** Nesting aggregations of various sizes have been observed in light soils. **Status & distribution** Widespread but rather local in southern England south of the Thames, with records extending thinly north to Yorkshire. Scarce in southwest England, the Midlands and Wales. Recorded from the Channel Islands (Jersey and Alderney). Not recorded from Scotland or Ireland. **Parasites & associates** The cleptoparasitic bee *Nomada flavopicta*.

female

male

Melitta tricincta Kirby, 1802   Red Bartsia Bee

Plate 8

Description & similar species FW 7–7.5mm female, 6.5–7mm male. Females resemble a slim *M. leporina* but have narrower, whiter abdominal bands, a duller brown pile on the thorax and mostly pale-haired antennal scapes. Males have much whiter abdominal bands than *M. leporina*, and that of tergite 2 is preceded by a band of black hairs. Both sexes have mid-brown final segments of the fore and mid tarsi. The strong association with Red Bartsia provides a good field clue. **Variation** Very little, though ageing can cause considerable fading and the abdominal bands can become abraded. **Flight season** Late July to early

female

male

September. **Habitat** Associated with Red Bartsia on calcareous grasslands, coastal grazing marsh, calcareous brownfield sites, the rides and clearings of calcareous woods and occasionally sandy or more neutral sites. **Flowers visited** Pollen is obtained exclusively from Red Bartsia in Britain, and adults are nearly always observed around this plant, though nectar is occasionally taken from other plants. **Nesting habits** Nesting has rarely been observed but is presumed to occur in light soils. **Status & distribution** Locally common on the North Downs, South Downs, Salisbury Plain area, chalk areas of Dorset and the Thames Gateway plus a few outlying records in the Chilterns, southwest England and Norfolk. Recorded from Alderney in the Channel Islands. Not recorded from Wales, Scotland or Ireland. Possibly increasing in some areas, e.g. Dorset. **Parasites & associates** The cleptoparasitic bee *Nomada flavopicta*.

MACROPIS – OIL-COLLECTING BEES

Macropis is a genus of medium-sized, blackish bees characterised by having two submarginal cells, a well-developed pygidium in both sexes, much expanded female hind legs and yellow-faced males. There is a special relationship with *Lysimachia* loosestrifes in both the Old and New World species. These plants provide both pollen and floral oils, the latter being essential for waterproofing the nests. This gives some *Macropis* species a special ability to ground-nest in wetlands with damp peaty soils and occasional flooding. The oil is collected using specialised hairs on the fore and mid tarsi, then transferred to the pollen brush to be mixed with pollen. Only a single species occurs in Britain, though *M. fulvipes* occurs on the near-continent and should be looked out for.

Macropis europaea Warncke, 1973   Yellow Loosestrife Bee

Plate 9

Description & similar species FW 7–8mm (sexes similar). A medium-sized, mainly black bee that is not easily confused because of the distinctive form of the hind legs of both sexes. Those of the female have a large pollen brush that is white-haired on the tibiae and black-haired on the basitarsi. Males lack the pollen brush but have the hind femora and tibiae swollen and also have a bright yellow face. Both sexes have narrow white hair bands along the hind margins of tergites 3 and 4 at the sides. The strong association with Yellow Loosestrife in wet places can support identification. *M. fulvipes*, which occurs on the near-continent, is similar but has bright buff hairs on the female hind legs. **Variation** Very little. **Flight season** Late June to early September. **Habitat** Wetlands and watersides with plentiful Yellow Loosestrife, including fens, reedbeds, streams, rivers, ditches and canals. Occasionally recorded in gardens. **Flowers visited** Pollen and floral oils are obtained primarily from Yellow Loosestrife, though it will occasionally visit cultivated Dotted Loosestrife. Nectar (which is not produced by Yellow Loosestrife) is obtained from a variety of flowers including thistles, brambles, willowherbs, Water Mint, bird's-foot-trefoils, umbellifers and Alder Buckthorn. **Nesting habits** Nesting occurs in the ground using elevated banks, slopes and paths where available, often coping with soils too damp for other ground-nesting bees. Nesting can occur singly or in small aggregations. The nesting sites are often at risk of flooding and are waterproofed using oils from the main forage plant. **Status & distribution** Mostly recorded in southeast England from Dorset to Norfolk, with records most frequent in Dorset, Hampshire, Sussex, Surrey, the Norfolk Broads and the Cambridgeshire Fens. Further isolated sites occur in Somerset, Avon and Oxfordshire. Not recorded from Wales, Scotland, Ireland or the Channel Islands. **Parasites & associates** None noted in Britain.

female

male

DASYPODA – PANTALOON BEES

Medium to large, hairy bees with two submarginal cells and oversized, pantaloon-like pollen brushes on the female hind legs. Foraging is often restricted to a single family of plants, e.g. Asteraceae for the single British species, and scabiouses for continental species such as *D. argentata*. Nesting occurs in sandy ground, and the nest cells are not lined with a waterproof substance but the pollen ball is instead sculpted to minimise contact with the cell walls. About 30 species are described, all from the Old World, and a few extend towards the near-continent, e.g. *D. argentata*.

Dasypoda hirtipes (Fabricius, 1793)   **Pantaloon Bee**

Plate 9

Description & similar species FW 9–11mm (sexes similar). Females are easily recognised by the large, orange 'pantaloons' on the hind legs. Males lack these but still have unusually long hairs on the hind legs. Females of *Panurgus* have similar pantaloons but are much smaller, shiny black bees. **Variation** The extent of black hairs on the top of the female thorax varies, and in some, most of the hairs are black. Fresh males have a rich golden colour but eventually fade greyish, and the rich brown thorax hairs of fresh females also fade markedly over time. Unusually small specimens can occasionally be encountered. **Flight season** Mid-June to late August.

Habitat Sandy habitats including coastal dunes, heathland, acid grassland, soft rock cliffs, saltmarsh edge and sandy brownfield sites. **Flowers visited** Strongly associated with yellow composites including Cat's-ear, hawk's-beards, hawkbits, oxtongues, ragworts, Common Fleabane and less frequently non-yellow species such as knapweeds, thistles and Chicory. Flowers in other families may

be visited for nectar. In hot weather, foraging tends to be concentrated in the mornings, as the inflorescences of many composites close up in the afternoon. **Nesting habits** Nesting occurs in sandy ground, especially south-facing slopes and along footpaths and tracks. Nests can often be distinguished from other ground-nesting aculeates (e.g. *Colletes* bees and digger wasps) by the large fan of sandy spoil to one side of the hole. Huge nesting aggregations comprising several thousand nests are occasionally encountered. **Status & distribution** Mainly found in heathland and sandy coastal districts of southeast England from Dorset to Norfolk, and common at many sites. Almost exclusively coastal in SW England and Wales and the dunes of Morfa Harlech represent its most northerly British site. Also known from a few sites in the Midlands. Unrecorded from Ireland but present on several of the Channel Islands. **Parasites & associates** Parasitic sarcophagid flies of the genus *Miltogramma*.

female

male

FAMILY MEGACHILIDAE

ANTHIDIUM – WOOL CARDERS

Medium-sized to large, robustly built bees usually with a pattern of yellow spots or bars on the tergites and sometimes the thorax. Females gather pollen using a pollen brush beneath the abdomen. Nesting habits are varied. The females of many species gather fibres from the leaves and stems of furry or woolly plants for creating nest cells (the true 'wool carders'), but a few

American species use resin from sources such as pines, mixed with earth. This is one of the few bee genera where males can average larger than females. The males of many species are aggressively territorial and have spines at the end of the abdomen that can be engaged to crush an intruder in an aerial wrestling match. Both sexes are capable of highly controlled hovering.

This is a large, cosmopolitan genus with several hundred described species, but only one in Britain. A number of further species occur on the near-continent and should be looked out for.

Anthidium manicatum (Linnaeus, 1758)   **Wool Carder Bee**

Plate 9

Description & similar species FW 8–10mm female, 9.5–12mm male. A robust bee, with males averaging larger than females and often attaining an impressive size. The yellow abdominal spots of both sexes, and the spines at the tip of the male abdomen, make for a very easily recognised species. **Variation** Size variation is marked, and it is possible to encounter dwarfs of both sexes with wing lengths shorter than cited above. The extent of yellow on the tergites and legs also varies, and some individuals on the mainland can have the yellow abdominal spots enlarged into bars on tergites 3–5 (approaching the usual appearance on

female

male

female, ssp. *manicatum*

male, ssp. *manicatum*

the continent), though the thorax usually remains fully black. Mainland British populations are typically assigned to ssp. *nigrithorax*. Channel Island populations are typically assigned to the continental ssp. *manicatum* and females are particularly striking with large yellow bars on tergites 1–5, and often yellow marks on the scutellum, axillae and sides of the scutum. The legs and face are also much more extensively yellow than mainland females and they closely resemble non-British species such as *A. florentinum* and *A. oblongatum*. **Flight season** Late May to late August. **Habitat** Particularly frequent in gardens, especially where cultivated labiates such as Lamb's-ear are present, but also found on heathland, chalk downland, woodland rides and clearings, river banks, wetlands, soft rock cliffs, vegetated shingle and a variety of brownfield sites. **Flowers visited** Strongly associated with labiates, particularly woundworts (including garden Lamb's-ear) and Black Horehound. Individual males will form a territory around a patch of these flowers and defend this from other males and even other large insects such as bumblebees and hoverflies using aerial hovering, head-butts and even wrestling. The abdominal spines can be used to crush an intruder into submission or even kill it. Mating can often be observed on foliage of the forage plants. Females also visit legumes (e.g. bird's-foot-trefoils, Kidney Vetch, *Vicia* vetches and restharrows) and Purple Toadflax. **Nesting habits** Nests are made in pre-existing cavities in walls, dead wood, hollow stems and various man-made objects. The cell walls and closing plug are constructed from compressed hairs gathered by the female from plants with furry leaf surfaces, notably Lamb's-ear, Great Mullein and Yarrow. The female can sometimes be seen flying back to the nest with a large silvery ball of such fibres gripped in her mandibles. **Status & distribution** Fairly frequent within southern England, becoming scarcer north of the Midlands, but with records extending as far north as southern Scotland. Scarce in Wales away from the south coast. Discovered at several sites in Ireland (County Wexford) in 2015. Recorded from several of the Channel Islands. **Parasites & associates** The cleptoparasitic bee *Stelis punctulatissima*.

STELIS – DARK BEES

Small to medium-sized, strongly punctate but inconspicuously haired megachilids. The British species are mainly black, though the tergites can have spots (*S. ornatula*) or narrow bands (*S. punctulatissima*). Males and females look similar. Some foreign species are metallic or strikingly patterned (resembling *Anthidium* species or even wasps). *Stelis* species are cleptoparasites of other megachilid bees, including species of *Anthidium*, *Osmia*, *Chelostoma*, *Hoplitis* and *Heriades*. Females

Stelis
punctulatissima

Stelis
ornatula

Stelis
breviuscula

will repeatedly return to a host nest and may lay an egg in each cell of a nest before it is sealed.

    Stelis bees are surprisingly elusive and mostly seem to occur at low population levels. One of the best ways to find them is to look for females flying, resting or visiting flowers close to host nesting areas. They can also be reared from host nests, and bee hotels are a good source of potentially parasitised nests, especially for *S. breviuscula* and *S. phaeoptera*.

    Four species are recorded from Britain, with one of these (*S. breviuscula*) possibly a recent colonist. Several further species capable of exploiting British hosts occur on the near-continent (e.g. *S. minima*, which parasitises *Chelostoma campanularum*, and *S. odontopyga*, which parasitises *Osmia spinulosa*).

STELIS

1   First 3–4 tergites with lateral whitish spots. Medium-small (wing length typically 5mm) .... **ornatula**

—   Tergites lacking lateral spots **2**

2   Hind margins of tergites 2–4 with translucent hind margins usually overlying conspicuous pale bands around the base of the next segment. Large (wing length typically 7–8mm) .... **punctulatissima**

—   Hind margins of tergites dark **3**

3   Larger and more elongate (wing length typically 7mm). Hind margins of tergites with weak white hair fringes. Punctures of tergites 2 and 3 sparser (mostly separated by more than their own diameter). Segments 4–6 of female antennae (viewed from front) about as wide as long .... **phaeoptera**

—   Very small and dumpy (wing length up to 4.5mm). Tergites 1–4 with more conspicuous white hair fringes which become dense at the sides. Punctures of tergites 2 and 3 denser (mostly separated by less than their own diameter). Segments 4–6 of female antennae (viewed from front) clearly wider than long .... **breviuscula**

Stelis breviuscula (Nylander, 1848)

Little Dark Bee

Plate 9

Description & similar species FW 4–4.5mm (sexes similar). The smallest *Stelis*, easily distinguished from the slightly larger *S. ornatula* by the lack of abdominal spots and the better-formed white hair fringes along the hind margins of the tergites. It could be mistaken for males of its host *Heriades truncorum* in the field but is typically smaller, has a relatively smaller head and lacks the ridge across tergite 1. Very small individuals of *S. phaeoptera* have sparse punctures on the tergites and lack the dense hair fringes on the hind margins of the tergites. **Variation** Very little. **Flight season** July and August. **Habitat** Ragwort-rich habitats, as for its host. Sometimes found in gardens. **Flowers visited** Typically yellow composites such as ragworts, hawkweeds and Common Fleabane, often alongside the host. **Status & distribution** Discovered in Britain in 1984 (West Sussex), since when it has shown a substantial increase within southeast England, spreading west to Hampshire and north to Middlesex, especially within counties such as Surrey (now the commonest *Stelis* there). The once-rare host has also shown a major increase during this period. Not recorded from Wales, Scotland or Ireland. **Host(s)** *Heriades truncorum*. Rearing bees from bee hotels can sometimes produce records of this species.

female

Stelis ornatula (Klug, 1807) — Spotted Dark Bee
Plate 9

Description & similar species FW 5mm (sexes similar). Easily distinguished from other *Stelis* species by the lateral whitish spots on the first 3–4 tergites. **Variation** The tergite spots can vary in size; those on tergites 1 and 4 can be small or missing. **Flight season** Late May to late August. **Habitat** Open habitats with plentiful bird's-foot-trefoils, with the strongest populations usually on chalk downland and coastal dunes. **Flowers visited** Usually yellow composites such as ragworts, hawkweeds and hawk's-beards, also cinquefoils and bird's-foot-trefoils. **Status & distribution** A rare species, with scattered records mostly in southern England and on the Welsh coast with outliers extending north to Shropshire and Lancashire. Not recorded from Scotland or Ireland. **Host(s)** *Hoplitis claviventris*. Rearing bees from nests in twigs and hollow stems can sometimes produce records of this species.

female

Stelis phaeoptera (Kirby, 1802) — Plain Dark Bee
Plate 9

Description & similar species FW 6–7.5mm (sexes similar). A moderately large *Stelis* (between the size of *S. punctulatissima* and *S. ornatula*), which can be distinguished by the lack of lateral spots, pigment bands or distinct hair fringes on the tergites. The body has large punctures throughout, though these are not as dense as in *S. punctulatissima* or *S. breviuscula*. **Variation** Dwarfs with wing lengths as short as 4.5mm are occasionally encountered and could potentially be mistaken for *S. breviuscula* (see key for differences). **Flight season** Late May to mid-August. **Habitat** Much the same as its main host, *Osmia leaiana*, which uses various habitats that have a combination of plentiful composites such as thistles and knapweeds, combined with dead wood (e.g. old fence posts) or old walls. A number of records are from gardens. **Flowers visited** Records include bird's-foot-trefoils, Field Scabious, thistles, hawkweeds and speedwells; also exotic garden flowers like *Cistus*. **Status & distribution** A rare

and much declined species, with old records scattered widely across southern Britain north to mid-Wales and Norfolk. Recent records are very few but include a cluster of sites in Shropshire and Denbighshire, where it may be increasing within gardens. Not recorded from Scotland or Ireland. **Host(s)** The main host is *Osmia leaiana*, and it will also use *O. niveata* and *Anthidium manicatum* abroad. *O. bicornis* is also a claimed host.

Stelis punctulatissima (Kirby, 1802)   **Banded Dark Bee**
Plate 9

Description & similar species FW 7–8mm female, 7mm male. The largest *Stelis*, with translucent hind margins on tergites 2–4 which overlie a pale pigment band on the base of the next segment. The head is relatively small in top view compared with other *Stelis* species and peculiarly shaped with a very sharp-angled hind margin and right-angled hind corners. The whole body is very densely and strongly punctate. **Variation** The bands across tergites 2–4 can vary from creamy-white to brownish, and are less conspicuous when the latter. **Flight season** Mid-June to late August. **Habitat** Much the same as its main host *Anthidium manicatum*, with a high frequency of records in gardens. **Flowers visited** Usually composites of various sorts (e.g. thistles, ragworts, Common Fleabane and various

chrysanthemum-type garden species); also scabiouses, mallows, brambles, bird's-foot-trefoils, speedwells, Black Horehound and Marjoram. **Status & distribution** Widespread but very scarce, with records concentrated within southeast England (especially Surrey) plus a thin scattering of records across Wales, the Midlands, northern England and as far north as Dumfries & Galloway in Scotland. Not recorded from Ireland. The only *Stelis* recorded from the Channel Islands (Jersey and Sark). **Host(s)** The main host is *Anthidium manicatum*, though *Osmia leaiana* and *O. aurulenta* may also be parasitised to a much smaller extent, and several *Osmia* species are reported to be attacked on the continent.

HERIADES – RESIN BEES

Mostly small, blackish, inconspicuously haired bees with a pollen brush beneath the female abdomen. The appearance falls between *Chelostoma* and *Osmia*, but *Heriades* species have a characteristic curved ridge across the top of tergite 1 which separates the vertical anterior face from the top and sides. The body is very coarsely punctate and the axillae project beyond the hind margin of the scutellum. The male abdomen is strongly clavate so that only two sternites are clearly visible when viewed from below. Most species nest in dead wood and hollow plant stems using resin from trees such as conifers to construct cells. Composites are the main pollen sources. This is a near-cosmopolitan genus with over 100 described species. Only one is resident in Britain; *H. rubicola* has been recorded but is regarded as an accidental introduction. Others, such as *H. crenulatus*, occur on the near-continent.

*Heriades
truncorum*

HERIADES

1   Females (antennae with 12 segments, abdomen not clavate) **2**

—   Males (antennae with 13 segments, abdomen strongly clavate) **3**

2   Head in top view larger and box-shaped (Fig. 1), in side view with the gena as wide as an eye (Fig. 2). Lower margin of clypeus with a prominence bearing two points (Fig. 3). Larger (wing length 5–5.5mm) .... ***truncorum***

—   Head in top view smaller and more transverse (Fig. 4), in side view with the gena narrower than an eye (Fig. 5). Lower margin of clypeus slightly concave with five small projections (Fig. 6). Smaller (wing length 4–4.5mm) .... ***rubicola***

3   Head in top view larger and squarer, about 1.5 times as wide as long, in side view with the gena as wide as an eye (Fig. 2). Sternites 1 and 2 with long, dense hairs, those of sternite 1 extending well beyond the hind margin of that sternite. Larger (wing length 5–5.5mm) .... ***truncorum***

—   Head in top view smaller and more transverse, about 2 times as wide as long, in side view with the gena narrower than an eye (Fig. 5). Sternites 1 and 2 with only short hairs, those of sternite 1 not extending beyond the hind margin of that sternite. Smaller (wing length 4–4.5mm) .... ***rubicola***

| Fig. 1 | Fig. 2 | Fig. 3 | Fig. 4 | Fig. 5 | Fig. 6 |

Heriades rubicola Pérez, 1890   Small-headed Resin Bee

not illustrated

Description & similar species FW 4–4.5mm (sexes similar). Resembling a small *H. truncorum* but with a smaller head. Other differences are given in the key. **Variation** Very little. **Flight season** June to September on the continent. **Habitat** Probably similar to *H. truncorum*. **Flowers visited** Strongly associated with composites including ragworts. **Nesting habits** Similar to *H. truncorum*. **Status & distribution** Only known in Britain from a female found in a garden at Briantspuddle, near Dorchester, Dorset (2006), but regarded as an accidental introduction or vagrant rather than a resident. **Parasites & associates** None known.

Heriades truncorum (Linnaeus, 1758)   Large-headed Resin Bee

Plate 10

Description & similar species FW 5–5.5mm (sexes similar). A rather small, dark-looking bee that resembles a narrowly built, big-headed *Osmia* or a robustly built *Chelostoma florisomne*. Under the microscope it is abundantly distinct, with a pronounced ridge separating the vertical front face of tergite 1 from its dorsal surface, plus a particularly coarsely punctate body. The female has a bright orange pollen brush beneath the abdomen and narrow white hair bands across the hind margins of the tergites. Males have a club-shaped abdomen with the tip curved under and facing downwards rather than backwards (view from the side).

Variation Very little. **Flight season** June to September. **Habitat** Heathland, grassland, open woodland, gardens and brownfield sites, usually where Common Ragwort occurs in abundance alongside dead wood such as old fence posts. **Flowers visited** Strongly associated with yellow composites, especially ragworts, but also Common Fleabane, Tansy, sowthistles, Cat's-ear and other hawkweed-types, plus garden species such as heleniums. Males can be found 'sleeping' in such flowers in a similar manner to *Chelostoma*. **Nesting habits** Nests are made in pre-existing cavities in dead wood, walls and hollow stems, e.g. brambles, and there are a number of reports of it using bee hotels in gardens. Cell partitions are made from resin, which seems to be obtained mostly from pines. The terminal plug of the finished nest has tiny bits of grit or fragments of wood and plant material mixed in with the resin. **Status & distribution** Formerly regarded as a great rarity, it has become increasingly frequent in southeast England between the Solent and the Thames Gateway (especially Surrey). A few recent records exist north of this in Oxfordshire and East Anglia, and a record from Shrewsbury suggests it may be expanding within the Midlands. Possibly a Victorian introduction (in imported wood). Not recorded from Ireland or the Channel Islands. **Parasites & associates** The special host of the cleptoparasitic bee *Stelis breviuscula*; also parasitised by *Gasteruption* wasps.

female

male

CHELOSTOMA – SCISSOR BEES

Small to medium-sized, slender megachilid bees with about 60 species worldwide. Nesting occurs in pre-existing cavities in wood, walls and hollow stems, especially beetle holes in wood. Nest cells are arranged linearly, with partitions and plugs created of mud mixed with salivary secretions and small particles such as sand grains. Most species are oligolectic, restricting pollen gathering to plants of a single genus, with species of the bellflower family Campanulaceae and the waterleaf family (Hydrophyllaceae) important for many species. Pollen is collected in a pollen brush under the abdomen. Only two species are recorded in Britain but several further bellflower-exploiting species occur on the near-continent, e.g. *C. distinctum* (which closely resembles *C. campanularum*) and the larger *C. rapunculi*.

Chelostoma florisomne

CHELOSTOMA

1   Females (antennae with 12 segments, tip of abdomen without paired projections) **2**

—   Males (antennae with 13 segments, tip of abdomen with a pair of projections) **3**

2   Larger (wing length at least 6mm). Mandibles and labrum very long and extending far beyond lower edge of face (Fig. 1). Abdomen densely haired below; tergites with white hair bands along hind margins .... *florisomne*

—   Smaller (wing length up to 4.5mm). Mandibles and labrum less elongate (Fig. 2). Abdomen sparser-haired below; no hair bands on the tergites .... *campanularum*

3   Larger (wing length at least 6mm). Tergite 7 with a pair of broad, square-ended lobes (Fig. 3). Sternite 2 with a large wedge-shaped projection; sternite 4 with a dense and conspicuous pale hair band. Antennal flagella with most segments bearing ventral bumps (Fig. 4) .... *florisomne*

—   Smaller (wing length up to 4.5mm). Tergite 7 with a pair of slim lobes with rounded tips (Fig. 5). Sternite 2 with a relatively small rounded welt; no hair band on sternite 4. Antennae simple .... *campanularum*

| Fig. 1 | Fig. 2 | Fig. 3 | Fig. 4 | Fig. 5 |

Chelostoma campanularum (Kirby, 1802)   Small Scissor Bee

Plate 10

Description & similar species FW 4–4.5mm (sexes similar). One of Britain's smallest bees, easily overlooked as a small *Lasioglossum* in the field but with only two submarginal cells and a rather different body shape. The strong association with Harebell and other bellflowers can support identification. **Variation** Very little. **Flight season** June to August. **Habitat** In the wider countryside usually found in association with Harebell in less improved grasslands (both calcareous and acidic) and open woodland. It is also fairly frequent in gardens, especially where Peach-leaved Bellflower is present. **Flowers visited** Pollen is obtained from a variety of wild and cultivated *Campanula* species, with Harebell, Clustered Bellflower and Nettle-leaved Bellflower the main species used in semi-natural situations. Peach-leaved Bellflower is the main one used in gardens. Males can be found sheltering in the flowers during dull weather. It will also visit Sheep's-bit, rampions and the rare Red Helleborine. **Nesting habits** Nesting occurs in pre-existing holes (e.g. woodworm and small nail holes) in dead wood, including dead trees, old building timbers and fence posts. Cells are arranged linearly, with nest partitions made of mud mixed with nectar. Small particles, including sand grains and pebbles, are added to the nest plug. Very large nesting aggregations can sometimes be encountered. **Status & distribution** Widespread though rather localised in southern England including East Anglia and the Midlands north to Lincolnshire, but rare in southwest England and Wales. Unrecorded from Scotland, Ireland and the Channel Islands. **Parasites & associates** None noted in Britain, though parasitised by the non-British *Stelis minima* species abroad.

Chelostoma florisomne (Linnaeus, 1758)

Plate 10

Large Scissor Bee
Sleepy Carpenter Bee

Description & similar species FW 6–8mm (sexes similar). A slim, cylindrical bee considerably larger than *C. campanularum* and with a more strongly banded abdomen. The box-shaped female head and her very elongate and projecting labrum and mandibles are especially distinctive, though the male's head is unremarkable. *Heriades truncorum* is probably the closest in appearance but is less elongate, much more heavily punctate, with much shorter mandibles and a strong ridge across tergite 1. **Variation** Moderate size variation. **Flight season** May to July. **Habitat** This bee requires a combination of buttercups and suitable

nesting sites, so is usually found in meadows close to woods or hedges, or within sunny woodland rides and clearings. **Flowers visited** Pollen is obtained from buttercups. On dull days, males will often be found resting within the flowers, hence the '*florisomne*' of the name. Nectar is taken from other plants such as Common Valerian, speedwells and roses. **Nesting habits** Nesting occurs in pre-existing holes in dead wood, building timbers, roofing thatch, hollow stems and artificial bee hotels. Nests are constructed in a similar manner to *C. campanularum*. Massive nesting aggregations can sometimes form in thatched roofs. **Status & distribution** Widespread though rather localised over much of England, extending north to Cumbria and Co. Durham. Scarce in Wales and unrecorded in Scotland, Ireland and the Channel Islands. **Parasites & associates** The slim, black and yellow sapygid wasp *Monosapyga clavicornis*, which is often evident around *C. florisomne* nesting areas.

The sapygid wasp *Monosapyga clavicornis*.

OSMIA – MASON BEES

A large genus (over 300 species worldwide) of medium-sized to large bees, often with colourful body hairs and sometimes with metallic integument. Females have a pollen brush beneath the abdomen and some have large, box-shaped head capsules and powerful jaws for chewing up leaves to create mastic. Nesting is mostly within pre-existing cavities in wood, hollow stems, walls, cliff faces, empty snail shells and even plant galls. Nest partitions and plugs can be created from leaf mastic, mud (sometimes with embedded pebbles), whole petals, pith or a combination of materials. Nest cells are arranged linearly when tubular holes or snail shells are being used or in clusters when larger cavities are being used (e.g. *O. inermis*). One group of species, which includes our *O. bicornis*, have horns on the female face used to manipulate wet mud during nest construction.

*Osmia
bicornis*

*Osmia
bicolor*

*Osmia
inermis*

*Osmia
caerulescens*

Many *Osmia* species are polylectic, obtaining pollen from several plant families, but a few are more specific and may rely heavily on a single family (e.g. composites or legumes) or a habitat-dictated flower species or genus (e.g. bird's-foot-trefoils in upland areas). Some species, including *O. pilicornis* and *O. caerulescens*, have specialised bristles on the female proboscis or clypeus to assist in pollen collecting. Several species are reared for crop pollination, including the non-British *O. lignaria* (Blue Orchard Mason Bee) which is used for orchard pollination in North America. Most species overwinter as non-emerged adults in their nest cells. Males emerge before females.

Twelve *Osmia* species are currently known here, with several further species present on the near-continent. *Osmia spinulosa* was included in *Hoplitis* until recently (due to the long parapsidal lines on the scutum) and is sometimes placed in a separate genus *Hoplosmia*. Our *Osmia* species are variously exploited by the sapygid wasp *Sapyga quinquepunctata*, chrysidid wasps of the genus *Chrysura*, gasteruptiid wasps (*Gasteruption*), the bee *Stelis phaeoptera*, the drosophilid fly *Cacoxenus indagator* and the spider beetle *Ptinus sexpunctatus*. Various species of mite can live in the nests and are often seen on the adult bees.

OSMIA FEMALES

1   Face with a pair of conspicuous, inwardly curved 'horns' (Fig. 1) .... *bicornis*

—   Face without such horns 2

2   Head and thorax black-haired, contrasting with an abdomen that is
red-haired above and below .... *bicolor*

—   Coloured otherwise 3

Fig. 1   Fig. 2   Fig. 3   Fig. 4

3   Pollen brush beneath abdomen orange-haired **4**

—   Pollen brush blackish-haired **7**

4   Spurs of hind tibiae orange **5**

—   Spurs of hind tibiae dark **6**

5   Thorax and abdomen entirely golden-haired. Axillae not projecting beyond
the scutellum. Larger (typical wing length 7.5mm) .... *aurulenta*

—   Top of thorax with a dull brown pile, the tergites almost bare except for white
hair fringes along the hind margins. Axillae projecting beyond the hind margin
of the scutellum (Fig. 2). Smaller (typical wing length 5.5mm) .... *spinulosa*

6   Lower margin of clypeus shallowly concave with a pair of median projections (Fig. 3) .... *leaiana*

—   Lower margin of clypeus more deeply concave with a single large median
projection (Fig. 4) .... *niveata*

7   Body sparsely haired and with blue reflections, the thorax with dull grey-brown
hairs. Head particularly large and squarish in top view, about as long as the
thorax (Fig. 5). Abdomen never with black hairs .... *caerulescens*

—   Thorax with a denser, longer pile of orange hairs. Head not so large and square
in top view (Fig. 6). Apical tergites entirely or substantially black-haired **8**

Fig. 5	Fig. 6	Fig. 7	Fig. 8	Fig. 9	Fig. 10

8   Clypeus entirely black-haired **9**

—   Clypeus with a mix of black and pale hairs **10**

9   Propodeum mostly smooth shiny black. Mandibles large and as long as the length
of an eye (Fig. 7). Galeae of mouthparts without numerous hooked bristles.
Averaging larger (wing length to 11mm) .... *xanthomelana*

—   Propodeum entirely dull. Mandibles shorter than the length of an eye. Galeae
of mouthparts with numerous hooked bristles (Fig. 8). Averaging smaller
(wing length to 8mm) .... *pilicornis*

10   Hind margin of tergite 1 largely shining, without punctures and much smoother
than the rest of the tergite surface. Hind tibiae slim, with only fine brownish hairs
dorsally, no black bristly hairs. Build slimmer, the abdomen longer than wide when
viewed from above (Fig. 9) .... *parietina*

—   Hind margin of tergite 1 with punctures and microsculpture, like the rest of the
tergite surface. Hind tibiae with at least some black bristly hairs dorsally. More broadly
built, the abdomen usually as wide as long when viewed from above (Fig. 10) **11**

11 Clypeus with a dense pile of mostly pale hairs which obscure the underlying surface from some angles, in front view longer and descending well below the eyes, the lower edge more obviously concave and more strongly angulated at the sides of the concavity. Mandibles with a longer and broader flattened cutting edge between the second and third teeth (Fig. 11) .... *inermis*

— Clypeus with a sparser pile of black and pale hairs that do not obscure the underlying surface from any angle, in front view broader and barely descending below the level of the eyes, the lower edge only shallowly concave and barely angulated. Mandibles with shorter and narrower flattened cutting edge between the second and third teeth (Fig. 12) .... *uncinata*

Fig. 11   Fig. 12

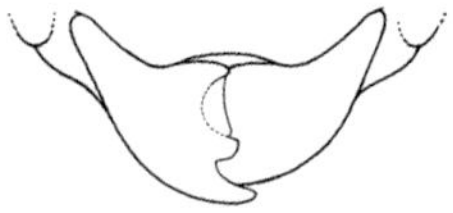

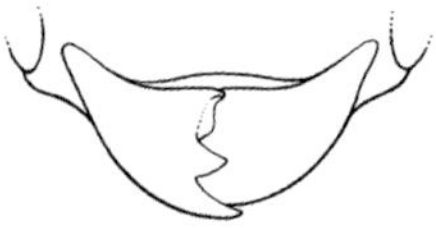

OSMIA MALES

1 Spurs at tip of hind tibiae pale 2
— Spurs at tip of hind tibiae dark 5

2 Sternite 1 with a slim spine positioned between the hind trochanters (Fig. 13). Axillae on either side of the scutellum projecting beyond the hind margin of the scutellum (Fig. 2). Hind margin of tergite 6 with a series of 10–12 small spines. Small (wing length 5mm) .... *spinulosa*
— Sternite 1 without a spine. Axillae inconspicuous 3

3 Antennae very long, capable of reaching back beyond the scutellum. Body surface slightly metallic blue .... *bicornis*
— Antennae shorter, body not metallic 4

4 Hind margin of tergite 6 smoothly rounded (Fig. 14). Head in top view relatively smaller and less box-shaped. Apical tergites with hairs at most with dull orange when fresh .... *bicolor*
— Hind margin of tergite 6 strongly notched at sides (Fig. 15). Head in top view relatively large and box-shaped. Apical tergites with bright orange hairs when fresh .... *aurulenta*

5 Antennae very long, capable of reaching back beyond the scutellum, the flagella fringed with long hairs behind (Fig. 16) .... *pilicornis*
— Antennae shorter and not fringed with long hairs behind 6

6 Tergites 2–5 black-haired .... *inermis*
— Tergites with pale brown or golden hairs 7

Fig. 13   Fig. 14    Fig. 15    Fig. 16

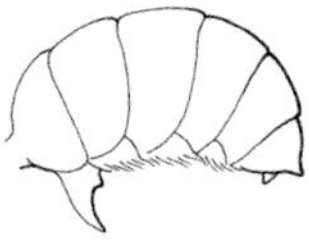

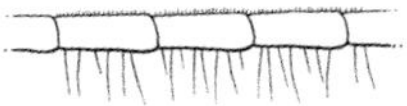

7   Mandibles longer (about three-quarters the length of an eye) with a very asymmetric pointed tip, the tips strongly crossed when folded (Fig. 17). Tergites with a dense orange pile (more or less as bright as the thoracic pile). Large (typically wing length 8–9mm) .... *xanthomelana*

—   Mandibles shorter (no longer than about half the length of an eye), the tips bifid or less extremely pointed (Fig. 18). Tergites with a sparser pile, the abdomen appearing much darker than the thorax. Smaller (wing length usually less than 7mm) **8**

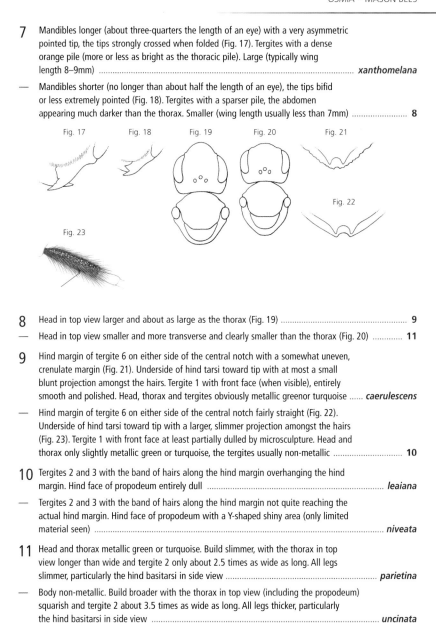

Fig. 17   Fig. 18   Fig. 19   Fig. 20   Fig. 21

Fig. 22

Fig. 23

8   Head in top view larger and about as large as the thorax (Fig. 19) **9**

—   Head in top view smaller and more transverse and clearly smaller than the thorax (Fig. 20) **11**

9   Hind margin of tergite 6 on either side of the central notch with a somewhat uneven, crenulate margin (Fig. 21). Underside of hind tarsi toward tip with at most a small blunt projection amongst the hairs. Tergite 1 with front face (when visible), entirely smooth and polished. Head, thorax and tergites obviously metallic greenor turquoise ...... *caerulescens*

—   Hind margin of tergite 6 on either side of the central notch fairly straight (Fig. 22). Underside of hind tarsi toward tip with a larger, slimmer projection amongst the hairs (Fig. 23). Tergite 1 with front face at least partially dulled by microsculpture. Head and thorax only slightly metallic green or turquoise, the tergites usually non-metallic **10**

10   Tergites 2 and 3 with the band of hairs along the hind margin overhanging the hind margin. Hind face of propodeum entirely dull .... *leaiana*

—   Tergites 2 and 3 with the band of hairs along the hind margin not quite reaching the actual hind margin. Hind face of propodeum with a Y-shaped shiny area (only limited material seen) .... *niveata*

11   Head and thorax metallic green or turquoise. Build slimmer, with the thorax in top view longer than wide and tergite 2 only about 2.5 times as wide as long. All legs slimmer, particularly the hind basitarsi in side view .... *parietina*

—   Body non-metallic. Build broader with the thorax in top view (including the propodeum) squarish and tergite 2 about 3.5 times as wide as long. All legs thicker, particularly the hind basitarsi in side view .... *uncinata*

Osmia aurulenta (Panzer, 1799)   Gold-fringed Mason Bee

Plate 10

Description & similar species FW 7–8mm female, 6–7mm male. Females have the body almost entirely covered in dense orange-tawny hairs, these forming distinct fringes along the hind margins of the tergites and forming the pollen brush beneath the abdomen. Female *Andrena fulva* is the only other common solitary bee that approaches it in appearance, but *A. fulva* has a brighter orange pile on the abdomen and entirely black-haired legs and head. Males of the very rare *O. xanthomelana* also look similar but have a densely whitish-haired face. Males of *O. aurulenta* are slimmer and less obviously orange-haired than females. The abdomen of fresh individuals has orange-red hair bands on tergites 3–5 but these fade quite quickly and they soon come to resemble males of *O. bicolor* in the field, though *O. aurulenta* has a broader build and a larger, squarer head in top view. The two can be easily separated under magnification by checking the hind margin of tergite 6, which is deeply notched at the side in *O. aurulenta* but smoothly rounded in *O. bicolor*. **Variation** Old females lose the rich golden hue and can become dull brownish, whilst sun-bleached males turn silvery, but usually retain some hint of golden hairs on the abdomen. **Flight season** April to July and occasionally early August. Males appear a couple of weeks before females and defend small territories containing empty snail shells. **Habitat** Coastal dunes, vegetated shingle and soft rock cliffs (especially calcareous ones). Inland, it occurs sparingly on chalk downland and limestone quarries and is evidently calcicolous. **Flowers visited** Particularly keen on legumes such as bird's-foot-trefoils (seemingly the main pollen source at many sites), Kidney Vetch and Horseshoe Vetch, also violets, Ground-ivy, Thrift, Wild Strawberry, Horned Poppy, Creeping Willow, dandelions and brambles. **Nesting habits** Nesting occurs in empty snail shells, especially *Cornu* and *Cepaea* species and *Helicella itala*, but occasionally marine species such as whelks. Several nest cells are created in each shell with leaf mastic partitions and plug. The shells are not camouflaged with debris as in *O. bicolor*, though leaf mastic is pasted onto the outside of the shell. **Status & distribution** Predominantly a coastal species, with records extending to southwest Scotland in the west but no further north than Kent in the east. Inland records are concentrated within the South Downs, North Downs, Salisbury Plain and limestone districts of the southern Midlands. In Ireland, mainly found along the east coast. Recorded from several of the Channel Islands. **Parasites & associates** The parasitic wasp *Sapyga quinquepunctata*, which can be particularly numerous at *O. aurulenta* colonies. Also a claimed host of the cleptoparasitic bee *Stelis punctulatissima* and the bee-fly *Villa modesta*.

female

male

Osmia bicolor (Schrank, 1781)

Red-tailed Mason Bee

Plate 11

Description & similar species FW 6.5–8mm female, 6.5–7.5mm male. Females are very distinctive, with a black-haired head and thorax and bright red-haired abdomen (including the pollen brush below). The slimmer males are mostly buff- and brown-haired, the pile being paler and particularly long on the sides of the thorax. In the field they can resemble males of *O. aurulenta* (alongside which they sometimes fly), but they never have the bright golden hairs at the tip of the abdomen featured in fresh *O. aurulenta*, though dull orange hairs are present here in fresh individuals, which rapidly fade. The two can be easily separated under magnification by checking the head shape (more box-shaped in *O. aurulenta*) and the smoothly rounded hind margin of tergite 6 (notched at sides in *O. aurulenta*). **Variation** Both sexes can produce dwarfs. In older females the red abdominal hairs can fade yellowish; old males can turn silvery. Females occasionally have the face red-haired. **Flight season** Males are amongst the first bees to appear in spring (early March in some years), and they peak in April. They often rest on dead foliage and defend small territories containing empty snail shells. Females appear about two weeks later, peaking in late spring and early summer and sometimes persisting into early July. **Habitat** Strongly calcicolous with a liking for chalk and limestone grassland (especially south-facing slopes), the rides and clearings of calcareous woods, chalk and limestone quarries and calcareous brownfield sites. Very occasionally found at brownfield sites and quarries that are not obviously calcareous. **Flowers visited** Various spring-blossoming shrubs such as sallows, Blackthorn, Hawthorn and Gorse; also a good variety of flowers, with a strong liking for bird's-foot-trefoils, Kidney Vetch, Horseshoe Vetch, Ground-ivy, Bugle, Wood Spurge, dandelions, Daisy, violets and dead-nettles. An important pollinator of the scarce Pasqueflower. **Nesting habits** Nesting occurs in empty snail shells, especially *Cepaea* species. There is usually one nest cell per shell but occasionally several. Cell partitions are constructed of leaf mastic, and the plug consists of densely packed particles of earth, chalk or fragments of snail shell between two mastic partitions. Mastic is also pasted onto the outside of the shell. The shell is then camouflaged with items such as stalks of grass, pine needles, bits of dead leaf and old bud scales which are flown in by the females. **Status & distribution** Records are concentrated within southern chalk and limestone districts north to Warwickshire and Northamptonshire, and it can be common at some sites. Outlying records occur in south Wales, Staffordshire and Shropshire. There is some evidence of a recent northward expansion within the Midlands. Not recorded in Scotland, Ireland or the Channel Islands. **Parasites & associates** The spider beetle *Ptinus sexpunctatus* has been observed attacking the nests.

female

male

Osmia bicornis (Linnaeus, 1758) — Red Mason Bee

Plate 10

Description & similar species FW 8–10mm female, 6–8mm male. A fairly easily recognised species. The furry females have a black-haired head, brown-haired thorax and orange-haired abdomen. The face bears a pair of long, incurved 'horns' (not present in any other British *Osmia*). Males are slimmer, with much longer antennae and whitish-haired faces. When fresh, the abdominal pile can be very bright orange. **Variation** Both sexes exhibit significant size variation. The hairs on the top of the thorax can vary from very dark to whitish. Fading and wear can substantially affect the appearance – denuded, blackish individuals of both sexes are frequent towards the end of the flight season. Populations on the Channel Islands (often assigned to ssp. *cornigera* or ssp. *globosa*) have the tip of the abdomen black-haired and the rest of the abdomen often buff- rather than red-haired (the typical appearance over much of the continent). **Flight season** March to July, with males appearing a couple of weeks earlier than females and females persisting long after males have gone. **Habitat** Found in many habitats but particularly attached to the built environment and one of the commonest solitary bees of gardens, churchyards and urban greenspace during spring. **Flowers visited** Many species visited, including a wide variety of cultivated garden plants; also spring-blossoming shrubs such as

female

male

female, Channel Islands

male, Channel Islands

sallows, *Prunus* species, apples and pears. It has economic significance as a pollinator of fruit trees and Oil-seed Rape. It is one of several bee species that can be purchased commercially in Britain to help pollinate crops. **Nesting habits** Nesting occurs in a variety of pre-existing holes and cavities, especially within the soft mortar of walls, in old timbers, cracks around window frames, thatched roofs (where reed stems are used), large beetle holes in dead wood, vertical earth faces (using old nests of other solitary bees), hollow plant stems (e.g. brambles), empty snail shells, even key holes and plug holes. It is usually one of the first species to exploit garden bee hotels. Nest cells are constructed from wet mud, which is collected from damp spots such as puddles and carried back in the mandibles. The facial horns are then used to manipulate the mud into cells. **Status & distribution** Our commonest mason bee, found over much of lowland England and Wales and more sparingly north to mid-Scotland; also most of the Channel Islands. A recent arrival in Ireland. This species has been known as *Osmia rufa* until recently. **Parasites & associates** The parasitic wasp *Sapyga quinquepunctata*, and possibly a subsidiary host of the cleptoparasitic bee *Stelis phaeoptera*. A more regular associate is the drosophilid fly *Cacoxenus indagator*, which is a cleptoparasite, and the spider beetle *Ptinus sexpunctatus* is a frequent inquiline.

Osmia caerulescens (Linnaeus, 1758)   Blue Mason Bee
Plate 10

Description & similar species FW 7–8.5mm female, 5–6mm male. Females are easily recognised by the combination of the very large box-shaped head, black pollen brush and slight bluish reflections. The body pile is less conspicuous than in other *Osmia* species, though the tergites have narrow white hair fringes on the hind margins at the sides. Males are furrier than females, with an orange-brown pile over a metallic green or turquoise body. They are extremely similar to males of *O. leaiana* and *O. niveata* but average smaller and have the tergites more obviously metallic. Under magnification, the underside of the hind basitarsi will be seen to lack a pointed projection (a very small, blunt one can be present) and the hind margin of tergite 6 is usually crenulate on either side of the central notch (margin smoothly curved in *O. leaiana* and *O. niveata*). **Variation** Not much, beyond some size variation. Old individuals can become denuded and blackish. **Flight season** Typically late April to late July, with males appearing first. A second generation, peaking in August, occurs in some southern districts. **Habitat** Various habitats can be exploited but it is often most frequent in urban settings (especially in gardens) and at flowery brownfield sites. **Flowers visited** Pollen is obtained largely from legumes (bird's-foot-trefoils, White Clover, Sainfoin), labiates (Ground-ivy, Black

female

male

Horehound, woundworts, catmints, garden lavenders) and snapdragon types. Knapweeds, hawk's-beards and speedwells are probably nectar sources. Males also like Garlic Mustard. **Nesting habits** Nesting occurs in a variety of holes and cavities, usually above ground. This includes the soft mortar of walls, old timbers and fence posts, also the hollow stems of plants such as brambles. Cells are arranged linearly, with nest partitions and plugs made of leaf mastic and occasionally chewed-up petals. *O. caerulescens* is a fairly frequent user of garden bee hotels in southern Britain, the green nest entrances helping to distinguish them from the mud plugs of *O. bicornis* (but not those of *O. leaiana*). **Status & distribution** Widespread in southern Britain but rather localised and rarely common anywhere. Records extend north to Perthshire in Scotland. Not recorded in Ireland. On the Channel Islands recorded only from Sark. **Parasites & associates** The parasitic wasp *Sapyga quinquepunctata*, which can often be found resting on walls and fence posts near to *O. caerulescens* nests. On the continent, listed as a host of the chrysidid wasp *Chrysura radians*.

Osmia inermis (Zettestedt, 1838)   **Mountain Mason Bee**

Plate 10

Description & similar species FW 6–8mm female, 5.5–6mm male. One of three similar, medium-sized mason bees that occur in northern or upland areas. Females have an orange-brown pile on the thorax and base of the abdomen which contrasts with a black pile on the remaining tergites. The face is partially pale-haired. The pollen brush beneath the abdomen is black, and the hind tibiae have some black bristly hairs dorsally amongst the finer brown hairs. *O. uncinata* is very similar but *O. inermis* has a more densely haired face (the hairs obscuring the underlying surface from some angles) and the clypeus descends further below the eyes and has the lower margin more deeply concave. The mandibles have a much larger flattened cutting edge between the second and third teeth, and the hind legs are not quite as black-haired as those of *O. uncinata*. *O. parietina* can be distinguished by its slimmer, less furry appearance, entirely pale-haired hind tibiae and smooth, shiny hind margin of tergite 1. Males are easily distinguished from other male *Osmia* species by the extensively black-haired abdomen, and they have a stocky build like males of *O. uncinata*. **Variation** The precise shape of the clypeal lower margin of females can vary and is rarely ever symmetrical. **Flight season** Late May to late July. **Habitat** The limited British data include both upland grassland on base-rich soils at altitudes of 260–550 metres, plus large expanses of partially vegetated upland river shingles at somewhat lower altitudes. In both situations it requires Common Bird's-foot-trefoil plus plentiful loose boulders. In the latter habitat, there is potential for it to fly alongside *O. uncinata*. **Flowers visited** Common Bird's-foot-trefoil is clearly important for Scottish populations, though *Vaccinium* species and montane willows are known to be used abroad. **Nesting habits** Nest cells are constructed in clusters under rocks and loose stones which overlie shallow depressions. Many nests can be present under some rocks, probably representing the work of several females sharing a rock but also old nests alongside new ones. Nest cells are made from leaf mastic and are green when new but darken with age to resemble rabbit droppings. It is thought that the life cycle lasts 2–4 years and involves parsivoltinism (staggered emergence) where a proportion of the nest cells take a year or two longer to hatch than others, probably as an insurance against poor summers. **Status & distribution** The Scottish Highlands, with relatively recent records from the Blair Atholl area of Perthshire and the Mar Lodge area of the Cairngorms. Older records exist for Glen Almond and Loch Rannoch, Perthshire, and the Kincraig area of the Cairngorms. **Parasites & associates** The parasitic chrysidid wasp *Chrysura hirsuta*.

Osmia leaiana (Kirby, 1802)   **Orange-vented Mason Bee**
Plate 11

Description & similar species FW 7–8mm female, 6–7mm male. Females of this medium-sized mason bee and the virtually identical *O. niveata* (check clypeus to distinguish the two) have particularly large, box-shaped heads, a sparse, brownish pile on top of the thorax and a relatively inconspicuous pile on the black tergites which emphasises the bright orange pollen brush on the underside of the abdomen. The wings are rather darkened. In the field, *O. leaiana* can be mistaken for a leafcutter (especially *Megachile centuncularis*) but is much bigger-headed with a narrower, more cylindrical abdomen. Males have a rather conspicuous golden pile on the head and thorax and golden hair bands across the hind margins of the shiny black tergites. The head and thorax are slightly metallic green or turquoise. Males of *O. caerulescens* can look very similar but average smaller and more strongly metallic (especially the tergites). Males of the rare *O. niveata* can only be separated with difficulty (see that species). The hind basitarsi of *O. leaiana* and *O. niveata* have a pointed projection on the underside just beyond the middle which is absent or very small and blunt in *O. caerulescens*, but this can be obscured by dense hairs and hard to see. **Variation** The lower margin of the female clypeus is somewhat variable. The paired clypeal projections are more prominent in some individuals than others, and a third projection can sometimes occur between them. The projections can also start to coalesce into a single large prominence. Old individuals of both sexes can become extensively denuded and blackish. **Flight season** Early May to late August. **Habitat** Various habitats can be exploited, but it is most frequent in scrubby grassland or woodland rides and clearings with plentiful thistles and knapweeds. It can also occur in gardens. **Flowers visited** Pollen is obtained from composites, especially thistles, knapweeds and hawk's-beards; also a variety of garden species such as chrysanthemums (but not the double varieties). Plants from other families (e.g. crane's-bills, brambles and Green Alkanet) probably represent nectar sources. **Nesting habits** Nesting occurs in a variety of holes and cavities, especially those in dead wood and old fence posts, walls and sometimes vertical cliff faces. Cells are arranged linearly. A fairly frequent user of garden bee hotels, the nest entrances being plugged with leaf mastic like *O. caerulescens* but preferring larger-diameter tubes. **Status & distribution** Widespread in southern Britain, with records extending north to Cumbria. Not recorded in Ireland or Scotland. On the Channel Islands recorded only from Jersey. **Parasites & associates** The cleptoparasitic bee *Stelis phaeoptera* and possibly *S. punctulatissima*; also the parasitic chrysidid wasp *Chrysura radians*.

female

male

Osmia niveata (Fabricius, 1804)

Jersey Mason Bee

not illustrated

Description & similar species. FW 7–8mm female, 6–7mm male. Almost identical to *O. leaiana* in the field. Separation requires microscopic examination of the female clypeus (lower edge rather deeply concave with a large central projection) and male propodeum and abdomen. **Variation** Moderate size variation noted in continental specimens. **Flight season** Seemingly similar to *O. leaiana*, with the two Leicestershire records from early June. **Habitat** Probably associated with thistle-rich habitats that also support suitable nesting sites such as dead wood, much as *O. leaiana*. Both Leicestershire records are from garden

female

trap nests. **Flowers visited** Pollen is obtained from composites, especially Spear Thistle. Other flowers, including legumes, crucifers and labiates are thought to be nectar sources only. **Nesting habits** Similar to *O. leaiana*. **Status & distribution** Long known from Jersey, and with mainland records from East Kent (pre-1850 but only recently identified as *niveata*) and Leicestershire (2004 and 2008). **Parasites & associates** Abroad, attacked by the cleptoparasitic bee *Stelis phaeoptera* and the parasitic chrysidid wasp *Chrysura radians*.

Osmia parietina Curtis, 1828

Wall Mason Bee

not illustrated

Description & similar species FW 6.5mm female, 5–5.5mm male. The brown- and black-haired females resemble *O. inermis* and *O. uncinata* in the field but are smaller, slimmer and less furry-looking with a shinier abdomen. Under magnification, the hind margin of tergite 1 will be seen to be polished and much smoother than the rest of the tergite. The body also tends to have slight metallic blue or greenish reflections. The hind tibiae are slimmer than in *O. inermis* and *O. uncinata* and have fine brown hairs but no black bristly hairs. Males have the integument of the head and thorax weakly greenish-metallic, rather like those of

O. bicornis (which is usually much larger with much longer antennae) and *O. caerulescens* (which has a much larger head). **Flight season** Early May to late July. **Habitat** Some sites relate to limestone pavement with scattered scrub and patches of floristically rich grassland, others represent unimproved upland pasture with drystone walls and also brownfield land associated with old quarries, ironworks etc. **Flowers visited** Common Bird's-foot-trefoil is the main pollen source, though further British flower records include Common Vetch, Western Gorse, various hawkish composites, Bugle, brambles and Ramsons, with foreign records for stonecrops, strawberries and speedwells. **Nesting habits** British nests have been observed in cavities of

female

male

drystone walls, but it is presumed that natural fissures are used in limestone pavement areas. Abroad, it is also known to nest in dead wood and the old nests of other aculeates. **Status & distribution** Most records are from north Wales, the southern Lake District and adjacent parts of north Lancashire. There are also a few widely scattered Scottish records (though old ones often refer to *O. inermis* and *O. uncinata*). Not recorded from Ireland or the Channel Islands. **Parasites & associates** Possibly the parasitic sapygid wasp *Sapyga quinquepunctata*; the parasitic chrysidid wasp *Chrysura hirsuta* is known to attack it abroad.

Osmia pilicornis Smith, 1846   **Fringe-horned Mason Bee**
Plate 10

Description & similar species FW 6.5–8mm female, 7–7.5mm male. Females have a reddish-brown pile on the thorax and the base of the abdomen, contrasting with the black pile on the remaining tergites. The face is entirely black-haired. They look very similar to smaller individuals of *O. xanthomelana*, though *O. pilicornis* has a matt propodeum, smaller mandibles and a sparser pile on the face and abdomen. *O. inermis*, *O. parietina* and *O. uncinata* are on average smaller with the face partially pale-haired and occur well north of the range of *O. pilicornis*. The best structural feature for confirming female *O. pilicornis* (when visible) are the galeae, which are fringed with numerous black hooked bristles. Males are greyish-looking in the field and can resemble older, faded males of *O. bicolor* (alongside which it sometimes flies), but on closer examination will be seen to have longer antennae with many long hairs on the hind face of the flagella.

Variation Very little, though older, faded males gain a very silvery appearance in the field.
Flight season Late March into June but sometimes lingering to July, males emerging first and females persisting long after these have gone. **Habitat** Typically old coppice woodland with flowery rides and clearings, both calcareous (e.g. on the South Downs) and more acidic (in the Weald). Occasionally rides in coniferised woods. **Flowers visited** Pollen seems to be obtained primarily from Bugle. The numerous hooked, black spiny hairs of the female galeae are designed to obtain pollen from anthers hidden within the tubular corollas. Other flowers visited include Ground-ivy, violets, Selfheal, comfreys and sallows. Lungworts are important abroad. Males fly between flowers at great speed in search of females. **Nesting habits** Nests are made in pre-existing cavities within fallen dead wood, stumps and coppice stools, probably in sheltered, sunny locations. **Status & distribution** Mostly recorded from southern England between Dorset, Somerset and Kent, with old outliers in south Wales, East Anglia and the Midlands. Much declined, with just a few modern colonies, mainly within Kent and Sussex. Not recorded from Scotland or Ireland. **Parasites & associates** None known.

female

male

Osmia spinulosa (Kirby, 1802)   **Spined Mason Bee**
Plate 11

Description & similar species FW 5–6mm (sexes similar). The smallest British *Osmia* and a rather aberrant one, as the axillae on either side of the scutellum are well developed with their tips protruding beyond the edge of the scutellum, and the parapsidal lines on the scutum are as long as in *Hoplitis* species. Females have a bright orange pollen brush beneath the abdomen (forming an orange halo around the abdomen when viewed from above) and fairly well-developed white hair bands along the hind margins of the tergites at the sides. Males resemble *Hoplitis claviventris* in the field but are easily distinguished by the presence of a slim, downward-pointing spine on sternite 1 between the hind trochanters (as opposed to a larger, blunter projection on sternite 2) and the more pointed axillae. **Variation** Very little, though worn females can become denuded and blackish. **Flight season** Mid-May to late September, a very long flight period but thought to represent a single generation. **Habitat** Rather strongly calcicolous, with a liking for sparsely vegetated chalk and limestone grassland, calcareous coastal dunes (usually mid and hind dunes), vegetated shingle, chalk and limestone quarries and other calcareous brownfield sites. **Flowers visited** Pollen is obtained from composites, including hawkbits, hawk's-beards, Oxeye Daisy, Common Fleabane, ragworts, knapweeds and thistles. Males will sometimes gather on other flowers, e.g. scabiouses, and have been found with orchid pollinia attached to their abdomens. **Nesting habits** Nesting occurs in medium-sized, empty snail shells, e.g. *Cepaea*, *Cernuella* and *Helicella* species. Between one and three cells are created in each shell, using leaf mastic to create cell partitions and the plug. **Status & distribution** Widespread and locally common in chalk and limestone districts of England south of the Severn–Wash line and along the coast of south Wales, though largely absent from southwest England. Isolated records in Cumbria and Yorkshire; also Jersey. Not recorded from Scotland or Ireland. **Parasites & associates** None apart from a chalcidoid wasp.

Osmia uncinata Gerstäcker, 1869   **Pinewood Mason Bee**
not illustrated

Description & similar species FW 7mm female, 6mm male. Females closely resemble *O. inermis* but have a more sparsely haired face with hairs that do not obscure the underlying surface from any angle. The clypeus is relatively shorter and broader and does not extend so far beneath the eyes. Its lower edge is straighter than in *O. inermis* with a shallower concavity and less angulated edges to the concavity. The mandibles have a much smaller flattened cutting edge between the second and third teeth. The hind tibiae are almost entirely black-haired. Males are more easily distinguished from *O. inermis*, as the hairs on tergites 2–6 are whitish (mostly black in *O. inermis*). Males of *O. parietina* have a much narrower build and a distinctly metallic head and thorax. **Variation** Little noted. **Flight season** Late April to early July. **Habitat** Mature pine woodland, both native Caledonian forest and older plantations. Within these it favours sheltered, sunny edges, rides and clearings where dead wood and flowers such as bird's-foot-trefoils occur together. **Flowers visited** Bird's-foot-trefoils, Bilberry and Broom. **Nesting habits** Nesting occurs in old beetle holes and other cavities in the trunks, stumps and other detached dead wood of pines. Nest partitions and plugs are made of leaf mastic. **Status & distribution** The Scottish Highlands, with most records from the Cairngorms and Moray Firth area. **Parasites & associates** The parasitic chrysidid wasp *Chrysura hirsuta*.

female

male

Osmia xanthomelana (Kirby, 1802)

Plate 10

Cliff Mason Bee
Large Mason Bee

Description & similar species FW 8–11 female, 8–9mm male. One of our largest and most striking mason bees (large females almost matching the size of large *O. bicornis* females). Females have a dense reddish pile on the thorax and an orange pile on tergites 1–3, contrasting with a black pile on the remaining tergites. The facial hairs are black as in *O. pilicornis*, and small *O. xanthomelana* individuals look very like that species. The most obvious differences are the shiny propodeum, larger mandibles and denser body pile of *O. xanthomelana*. The slimmer males have the tergites almost entirely orange-haired, a densely white-haired face and relatively long, crossed mandibles. They can look similar to female *O. aurulenta* in the field (the densely white-haired face is the most obvious difference). **Variation** Considerable size variation, with some females as small as typical *O. pilicornis*. **Flight season** Males usually appear in mid-April, females a little later. The peak is late May and early June, but females can persist into July. **Habitat** Most records relate to south-facing soft rock cliffs with extensive slumping and plenty of seepages, though it is also recorded from chalk cliffs in counties such as Sussex. **Flowers visited** Most British observations relate to bird's-foot-trefoils and Horseshoe Vetch. **Nesting habits** Pot-like nest cells are constructed of mud and grit, usually with their bases sunk below the soil surface and often located amongst grass roots. Cells may be arranged singly or in clusters of a dozen or more. Occasionally they are sunken fully below the soil surface and resemble burrows. Females are reliant upon cliff seepages and associated wet mud as a source of nest-building material, and this species seems to have been badly impacted by cliff stabilisation schemes. **Status & distribution** One of our most severely declined bees. Formerly known from scattered coastal locations across the south of England, north Wales,

Lancashire and Cumbria; also some doubtful inland records. It now appears to be confined to a few sites in north Wales. Not recorded from Scotland, Ireland or the Channel Islands. **Parasites & associates** The parasitic sapygid wasp *Sapyga quinquepunctata*.

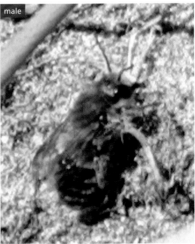

HOPLITIS – LESSER MASONS

One of the largest megachilid genera, with over 350 described species found within most continents except South America and Australasia. In their general appearance and range of nesting and foraging habits these bees are very much like *Osmia*, and the main structural difference is the longer longitudinal groove (parapsidal line) on each side of the scutum above the wing bases, though *Osmia spinulosa* (until recently placed in *Hoplitis*) also has a long groove. Only two species are recorded from Britain, though one of these is considered long extinct if ever native. Several further *Hoplitis* species occur on the near-continent.

Hoplitis claviventris

HOPLITIS

1   Females (antennae with 12 segments, underside of abdomen with a dense pollen brush) **2**

—   Males (antennae with 13 segments, underside of abdomen without a dense pollen brush) **3**

2   Antennal segment 3 viewed from front about twice as long as wide and about as long as the combined length of segments 4 and 5 (Fig. 1). Hind tibial spurs pale orange-brown. Build robust, the thorax squarish in top view and tergite 1 about twice as wide as long .... *claviventris*

—   Antennal segment 3 viewed from front barely longer than wide and shorter than the combined length of segments 4 and 5 (Fig. 2). Hind tibial spurs dark brown. Build slimmer, the thorax clearly longer than wide in top view, tergite 1 no more than 1.5 times as wide as long .... *leucomelana*

3   Final antennal segment normal (Fig. 3). Sternite 2 with a large projection (Fig. 4) .... *claviventris*

—   Final antennal segment strongly bent and claw-like (Fig. 5). Sternite 2 without a large projection .... *leucomelana*

Fig. 1   Fig. 2   Fig. 3   Fig. 4   Fig. 5

Hoplitis claviventris (Thomson, 1872)   **Welted Mason Bee**
Plate 11

Description & similar species FW 5–6mm female, 4.5–6mm male. A small mason bee that resembles *Osmia spinulosa* in size. Females have an inconspicuous dull brown pile on the top of the thorax and a blue-black shining abdomen with conspicuous white hair patches on the hind margins of tergites 1–4. The pollen brush beneath the abdomen is creamy-white (no *Osmia* has a pollen brush this colour). Males superficially resemble *O. spinulosa* or small individuals of *O. bicolor*, but are easily distinguished under magnification by the large semicircular projection on sternite 2 (not to be confused with the sharp spine on sternite 1 of *O. spinulosa*). **Variation** A little size variation, with small males not uncommon. Worn individuals can become grey-haired and denuded, and females can lose the white patches on the tergites and come to resemble small *O. caerulescens* (which has a much bigger head capsule, duller tergites and a black pollen brush). **Flight season** May to September, peaking in June and July, with males appearing before females. **Habitat** A variety of habitats are used, especially flowery, sparsely vegetated parts of coastal dunes, vegetated shingle, heathland, quarries and other brownfield sites; also chalk downland, acid grassland, woodland clearings and limestone pavement. Most sites are characterised by an abundance of bird's-foot-trefoils. **Flowers visited** Typically bird's-foot-trefoils but also Horseshoe Vetch, Purple Toadflax, hawk's-beards, buttercups and scabiouses. **Nesting habits** Nesting usually occurs in hollow twigs (e.g. roses and brambles) and stems (e.g. ragwort), less often in the ground or using holes in dead wood or root plates. The cell partitions and plug are made of leaf mastic, and the cell closest to the plug is sometimes filled with pebbles and grass spikes. **Status & distribution** Widespread in southern Britain north to Cumbria, with most records in southeast England and a curiously patchy distribution elsewhere. Decidedly local in many areas. Unrecorded in Scotland and Ireland. On the Channel Islands recorded only from Jersey. **Parasites & associates** The cleptoparasitic bee *Stelis ornatula*.

female

male

Hoplitis leucomelana (Kirby, 1802)   **Kirby's Mason Bee**

not illustrated

Description & similar species FW 5.5mm females, 5mm male. Females are smaller and much slimmer than *H. claviventris* and more likely to be mistaken in the field for a *Chelostoma*, *Heriades* or smaller *Stelis* species. They also have darker hind tibial spurs and a shorter third antennal segment. Males have the final antennal segment strongly bent and claw-like, and lack a large projection on sternite 2. **Variation** Little noted. **Flight season** May to August seem to be typical abroad. **Habitat** The Suffolk specimen apparently came from a pinetum, though it is probable that a variety of open, flowery habitats can be used. **Nesting habits** Nesting

occurs in hollow stems and twigs, also the old 'cigar galls' created by the chloropid fly *Lipara lucens* at the growth tips of Common Reed. **Flowers visited** Pollen is mostly obtained from legumes, though plants from several families are used for nectar, and the British female was apparently visiting a hawkbit. **Status & distribution** Recorded from Coddenham, Suffolk, prior to 1802 (a female that is the type specimen), and also reared from an imported rose stem in Scotland in 1920. No evidence that it is a resident species today. It should be noted that *H. claviventris* was called *H. leucomelana* until 1970. **Parasites & associates** The cleptoparasitic bee *Stelis ornatula*.

female

MEGACHILE – LEAFCUTTER AND MUD BEES

One of the largest and most cosmopolitan bee genera, with almost 1,500 species worldwide. Most species are medium-sized, but the Indonesian *M. pluto* is the world's largest bee. Females have a pollen brush beneath the abdomen. Males of the subgenus *Xanthosarus* have expanded front tarsi which are used to cover the female's eyes when mating. The term 'leafcutter' is derived from the nesting behaviour of many species, where the females

Megachile centuncularis

Megachile leachella

Megachile willughbiella

cut out sections of leaf (and sometimes petal) and carry these back to the nest in their jaws. The leaf sections are then used to create linearly arranged nest cells and a terminal plug. This behaviour is not universal, and members of the subgenus *Chalicodoma* (often treated as a separate genus) construct their nests from earth or sand mixed with a waterproofing secretion from the labial gland. Nest cells are filled with a semi-liquid mix of pollen and nectar. Many species forage on a variety of plants, but some restrict pollen collecting to certain families such as legumes or composites and some species are important crop pollinators. The European *M. rotundata* (the Alfalfa Leafcutter) is managed on a large scale to pollinate Lucerne (Alfalfa) in North America.

Megachile versicolor carrying a leaf section.

There are seven extant species in the British Isles, with three more known from very old records (one only in Jersey) and possibly never resident. Our fauna includes aerial nesters that use cavities in dead wood, walls and plant stems and also several ground-nesters associated with sandy habitats. A number of further species occur on the near-continent, some of which closely resemble British ones and should be watched out for (e.g. *M. pilidens*, which is very like *M. leachella*). Most of the British and Irish species are hosts for cleptoparasitic bees of the genus *Coelioxys*. When checking the colour of the pollen brush hairs in the key below, be careful not to confuse with pollen colour.

MEGACHILE FEMALES

1   Body entirely jet black-haired except for some orange hairs within the pollen brush beneath the abdomen and on the tarsi. Wings darkened. Large (typical wing length 14mm) (questionably British) .... *parietina*

—   Body usually substantially brown-haired. Wings clear. Smaller (wing length to 12mm but usually less than 10mm) 2

2   Tergite 6 in side view with virtually all the hairs of the dorsal surface short and adpressed, at most with a few short semi-erect ones at the base (Fig. 1) 3

—   Tergite 6 in side view with long erect or semi-erect hairs over much of the dorsal surface, especially in the basal half (Fig. 2) 7

3   Tergites 2–5 with complete and distinct hair bands across the hind margins. Pollen brush beneath the abdomen either white- or buff-haired, never orange-haired, and never black-haired apically **4**

—   Tergites either with any hair bands weak and confined to the sides, or, if complete on tergites 4 and 5, then the pollen brush is orange-haired or has black hairs apically **5**

4   Tergite 6 with two patches of adpressed white hairs (Fig. 5). Pollen brush entirely silvery-haired. Mandibles with a bevelled cutting edge (Fig. 3). A small, greyish species (typical wing length 6mm) .... *leachella*

—   Tergite 6 without such patches of white hairs. Pollen brush buff-haired. Mandibles without a bevelled cutting edge (Fig. 4). A larger, browner species (typical wing length 10mm) .... *ericetorum*

Fig. 1   Fig. 2 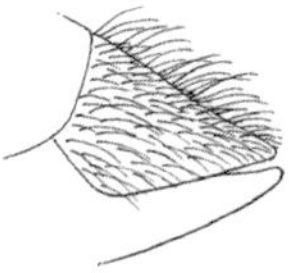   Fig. 3    Fig. 4

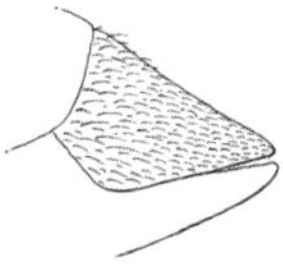

Fig. 5 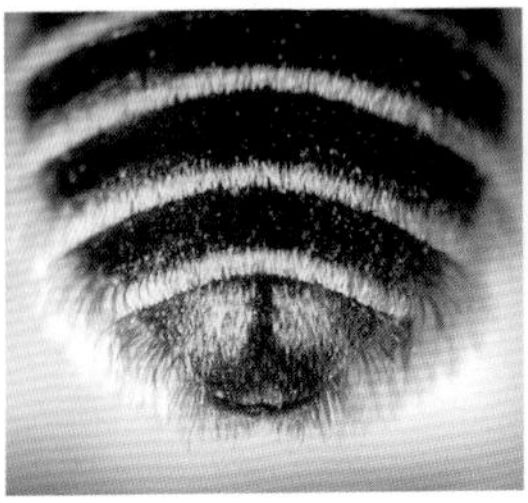   Fig. 6    Fig. 7

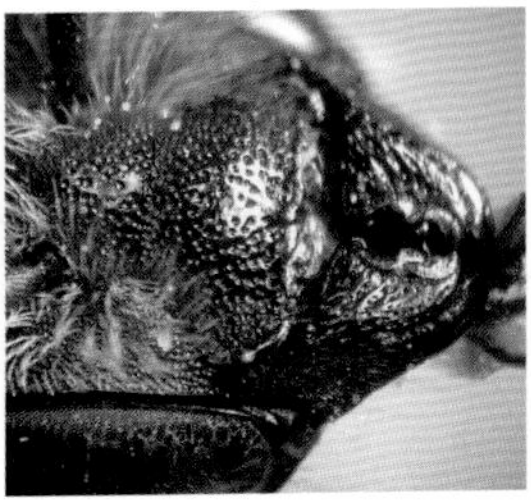

5   Clypeus with dense punctures throughout, these almost touching to create a dull surface (Fig. 6). Hind margins of tergites 2–5 with pure white hair bands, usually complete and conspicuous on tergites 4 and 5 but broken on tergites 2 and 3 (pollen brush orange-haired with black hairs apically) .... *lapponica*

—   Clypeus more sparsely punctate (Fig. 7), especially centrally where the punctures are separated by more than their own width by shining integument. Tergites with inconspicuous buff hair bands or lateral fringes **6**

6   Apex of tergite 6 broadly rounded (Fig. 8). Pollen brush mostly buff-haired (beware orange pollen) with a black-haired tip. Usually larger (typical wing length 10mm) .... *ligniseca*

—   Apex of tergite 6 more pointed (Fig. 9). Pollen brush orange-haired except for a black-haired tip (orange-haired tip in Irish populations). Smaller (wing length to 8.5mm) .... *versicolor*

7   Pollen brush orange-haired to tip (Fig. 10), with orange hairs extending to sides of tergites and conspicuous in dorsal view. Relatively small (wing length typically 8mm) with rather conspicuous lateral whitish hair fringes along the hind margins of tergites 2–4 .... *centuncularis*

—   Pollen brush black-haired apically (Fig. 11), or, if not (Irish *willughbiella*), orange hairs of pollen brush not conspicuous in dorsal view and tergites 2–4 lacking white hair fringes at sides of hind margins **8**

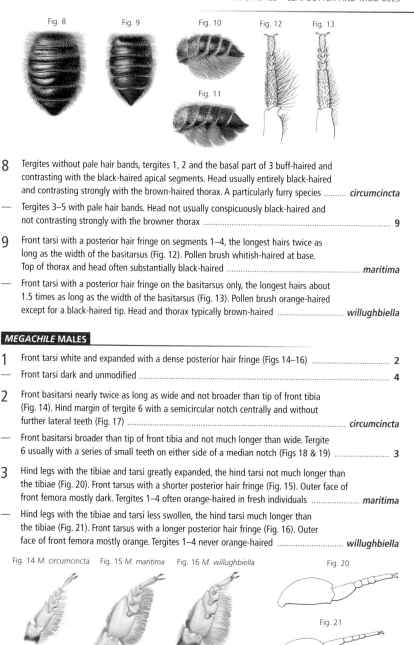

Fig. 8   Fig. 9   Fig. 10   Fig. 12   Fig. 13

Fig. 11

8 Tergites without pale hair bands, tergites 1, 2 and the basal part of 3 buff-haired and contrasting with the black-haired apical segments. Head usually entirely black-haired and contrasting strongly with the brown-haired thorax. A particularly furry species .... *circumcincta*

— Tergites 3–5 with pale hair bands. Head not usually conspicuously black-haired and not contrasting strongly with the browner thorax **9**

9 Front tarsi with a posterior hair fringe on segments 1–4, the longest hairs twice as long as the width of the basitarsus (Fig. 12). Pollen brush whitish-haired at base. Top of thorax and head often substantially black-haired .... *maritima*

— Front tarsi with a posterior hair fringe on the basitarsus only, the longest hairs about 1.5 times as long as the width of the basitarsus (Fig. 13). Pollen brush orange-haired except for a black-haired tip. Head and thorax typically brown-haired .... *willughbiella*

MEGACHILE MALES

1 Front tarsi white and expanded with a dense posterior hair fringe (Figs 14–16) **2**

— Front tarsi dark and unmodified **4**

2 Front basitarsi nearly twice as long as wide and not broader than tip of front tibia (Fig. 14). Hind margin of tergite 6 with a semicircular notch centrally and without further lateral teeth (Fig. 17) .... *circumcincta*

— Front basitarsi broader than tip of front tibia and not much longer than wide. Tergite 6 usually with a series of small teeth on either side of a median notch (Figs 18 & 19) **3**

3 Hind legs with the tibiae and tarsi greatly expanded, the hind tarsi not much longer than the tibiae (Fig. 20). Front tarsus with a shorter posterior hair fringe (Fig. 15). Outer face of front femora mostly dark. Tergites 1–4 often orange-haired in fresh individuals .... *maritima*

— Hind legs with the tibiae and tarsi less swollen, the hind tarsi much longer than the tibiae (Fig. 21). Front tarsus with a longer posterior hair fringe (Fig. 16). Outer face of front femora mostly orange. Tergites 1–4 never orange-haired .... *willughbiella*

Fig. 14 *M. circumcincta*   Fig. 15 *M. maritima*   Fig. 16 *M. willughbiella*   Fig. 20

Fig. 21

Fig. 17 *M. circumcincta*   Fig. 18 *M. maritima*   Fig. 19 *M. willughbiella*

Fig. 22   Fig. 23   Fig. 24

Fig. 25

Fig. 26

4   Viewed from below, front coxae each with a projecting spine (Fig. 22). Tergites 2–4 with complete bands of pale hairs along hind margin **5**

—   Front coxae without a spine. Abdomen not strongly banded, at most lateral fringes **6**

5   Tergite 6 covered with dense white hairs that obscure the underlying surface (Fig. 23). Small (typical wing length 6mm), with bright green eyes in life .... *leachella*

—   Tergite 6 with black hairs that do not obscure the punctured surface. Large (typical wing length 9mm), with dark eyes in life .... *ericetorum*

6   Body covered in a dense buff pile except for tergites 4–6 which have a dense black pile. Large (wing length 10–12mm) (questionably British) .... *parietina*

—   Body with a sparser, less conspicuous pile without a contrasting black-haired abdomen tip. Smaller (except for the largest *ligniseca*) **7**

7   Hind margin of tergite 6 with a deep V-shaped notch (Fig. 24). Sternites 1–3 with very long straggly hairs (longer than the greatest width of the hind femora) which do not form bands. Typically large (wing length up to 10mm) .... *ligniseca*

—   Hind margin of tergite 6 without such a deep notch (Figs 25 & 26). Sternites 1–3 with shorter hairs (shorter than the greatest width of the hind femora) forming bands along the hind margins. Smaller (wing length up to 8.5mm) **8**

8   Tergite 6 with a distinct depression centrally above the upturned apical flange based on the little material seen (Fig. 27, angle of lighting critical to see this) .... *lapponica*

—   Tergite 6 flat or slightly convex above the upturned apical flange **9**

Fig. 27

Fig. 28   Fig. 29   Fig. 30   Fig. 31

9   Depressed hind margin of sternite 4 strongly shining, devoid of tiny hairs and transparent like clear cellophane (Figs 28 & 29). Sternites 2 and 3 with longer hairs that do not form dense fringes along the hind margins. Apical tarsal segments usually reddish and much paler than basitarsi .... *versicolor*

—   Depressed hind margin of sternite 4 dulled by tiny hairs and microsculpture and more opaque (Figs 30 & 31). Sternites 2 and 3 with shorter hairs that form dense hair fringes along the hind margins. Apical tarsal segments usually darker .... *centuncularis*

Megachile centuncularis (Linnaeus, 1758) **Patchwork Leafcutter Bee**
Plate 11

Description & similar species FW 7–8.5mm female, 7–8mm male. A medium-sized, brownish leafcutter, females of which have the pollen brush orange all the way to the tip and extending up the sides of the tergites to produce an orange halo around the abdomen in dorsal view. Tergites 2–4 have narrow fringes of white hairs along the hind margins (widely broken centrally on tergites 2 and 3). *M. versicolor* can look similar in the field but has the pollen brush black-haired at the tip, a much weaker orange halo and scarcely any hair bands on the tergites. *M. centuncularis* also has long, semi-upright hairs on tergite 6 when viewed from the side (hairs adpressed in *M. versicolor*), as in *M. circumcincta*, *M. maritima* and *M. willughbiella*, which all average larger and have the pollen brush black-haired apically (except Irish *M. willughbiella*).

Males of *M. centuncularis* have unmodified front legs and closely resemble *M. versicolor*, requiring microscopic checking of the hind margin of sternite 4 (dull in *M. centuncularis*, shining in *M. versicolor*) to provide a reliable determination. However, the darker apical tarsal segments of *M. centuncularis* and more pronounced fringes of white hairs across the hind margins of sternites 2 and 3 can provide an initial clue. Small males of *M. ligniseca* can also look similar but

female

have a much deeper apical notch on tergite 6 and much longer hairs on the sternites. **Variation** Small individuals can occur in both sexes. Older females can lose their abdominal hair bands, and males can become sun-bleached and greyish. **Flight season** Mid-June to early September. **Habitat** A variety of habitats are used both inland and on the coast. It is one of the most frequent leafcutters of gardens. **Flowers visited** Various flowers, especially composites (e.g. thistles, knapweeds, burdocks, Common Fleabane and Cat's-ear) and legumes (e.g. bird's-foot-trefoils), also St John's-worts and brambles. **Nesting habits** Nesting occurs in dead wood, cavities in walls and other man-made objects (including bee hotels), and occasionally in the soil or in hollow twigs of plants such as brambles. Leaves used for nest building include roses, Lilac, birches, Horse Chestnut, Ash, Amelanchier, willowherbs and honeysuckles. **Status & distribution** Widespread and frequent in the southern half of Britain, with records extending to north Scotland. Scarce in Ireland. Recorded from several of the Channel Islands. **Parasites & associates** One of the hosts of the cleptoparasitic bee *Coelioxys inermis*.

Megachile circumcincta (Kirby, 1802) **Black-headed Leafcutter Bee**
Plate 12

Description & similar species FW 7.5–9.5mm female, 7.5–9mm male. A medium-large leafcutter. Females are very distinctive, with the head and tergites 4–6 black-haired and contrasting with the rich tawny-haired thorax and buff-haired tergites 1–3. There are no obvious pale hair bands on the abdomen and the body pile is longer than in any other *Megachile*, creating a rather *Osmia*-like appearance. The pollen brush beneath the abdomen is tawny at the base and black at the tip. Males have expanded, whitish front tarsi as in *M. willughbiella* and *M. maritima* but the tarsi are much slimmer than in those species. **Variation** Older individuals can become sun-bleached and lose their distinctiveness. **Flight season** Late May to early August. **Habitat** Coastal dunes, sandy coastal brownfield sites and heathland. **Flowers visited** Assorted legumes (including bird's-foot-trefoils, Broom and restharrows), thistles and brambles. **Nesting habits** Nesting occurs in sandy ground, especially south-facing banks and slopes, often in loose aggregations. Nesting in wood and under stones has also been reported. Leaves used for nest building include roses and birches. **Status & distribution** Never a common species but historically known from a mix of coastal and inland locations. Modern records are mainly from coastal sites in Wales, northern England, Scotland and the Channel Islands. A severe decline has seen a loss from nearly all of its inland and southern coastal sites. Not recorded in Ireland. **Parasites & associates** Apparently attacked by several cleptoparasitic bees of the genus *Coelioxys*, including *C. elongata*, *C. quadridentata*, *C. mandibularis* and *C. rufescens*.

female

male

Megachile ericetorum (Lepeletier, 1841)   Banded Mud Bee

not illustrated

female

Description & similar species FW 10mm female, 9mm male. Size and shape resembling *M. ligniseca* but with a strongly banded abdomen as in the much smaller *M. leachella*. Females differ from all other British leafcutters except *M. parietina* in lacking a bevelled cutting edge to the mandibles (a reflection of the fact that they do not cut leaves). Males resemble slim females and have coxal spines like *M. leachella* but lack a dense covering of adpressed white hairs on tergite 6. The front tarsi have a posterior fringe of long white hairs and the hind margin of tergite 6 is very uneven and crenulate with a central notch. **Variation** The female can have the top of the thorax entirely brown-haired or extensively black-haired. **Flight season** April to August on the continent. **Habitat** Various habitats are used abroad. **Flowers visited** Pollen is obtained from legumes such as bird's-foot-trefoils, *Lathyrus* peas and restharrows. Males also visit woundworts. **Nesting habits** Nesting occurs in banks, walls, dead wood, hollow stems and abandoned burrows of other bees in the ground. The cell partitions are constructed of clay or sand coated with resin on the inside. It is not a leafcutter. **Status & distribution** Regarded as British on the basis of a female and male taken at Weybridge, Surrey, in 1844. Other old British records are doubtful, though it seems to be a species prone to artificial introduction, having been discovered in Canada in 2003. **Parasites & associates** Parasitised by non-British *Coelioxys* species on the continent.

Megachile lapponica Thomson, 1872   Willowherb Leafcutter Bee

not illustrated

Description & similar species FW 8–8.5mm female, 7.5–8mm male. Females resemble a rather slimly built *M. centuncularis* in the field, owing to their size and the narrow hair bands across the hind margins of tergites 4 and 5, but they have short, adpressed hairs on the dorsal surface of tergite 6 (as in *M. versicolor* and *M. ligniseca*) and black hairs at the tip of the orange pollen

female

brush (as in *M. versicolor*). The hairs of the tergite bands are also snow-white (buff-white in *M. centuncularis*). The very densely punctate clypeus distinguishes it from all these species, and the hairs of the face, sides of the thorax and sides of the propodeum tend to be whiter than in most other leafcutters, contrasting with the brown hairs on the top of the thorax. Males closely resemble *M. centuncularis* and *M. versicolor* but in the limited number of specimens seen there is a distinct depression in the centre of tergite 6. The semi-translucent hind margin of sternite 4 is not as shiny as in *M. versicolor* but not as dull as in *M. centuncularis*. Seek expert verification if you think you have found this species. **Variation** Little known. **Flight season** May to August on the continent. **Habitat** Assorted willowherb-rich habitats. **Flowers visited** Pollen seems to be obtained entirely from willowherbs (particularly Rosebay Willowherb), though flowers such as composites, legumes and brambles are visited for nectar. **Nesting habits** Nesting typically occurs in holes in dead wood and hollow stems, with Rosebay Willowherb leaf sections apparently favoured as a nesting material. **Status & distribution** Regarded as British on the basis of a single freshly emerged female taken at Weybridge, Surrey, in 1847 (when Rosebay Willowherb was a scarce, mostly northern species). It is always worth checking any leafcutters you find foraging on willowherbs just in case. **Parasites & associates** The cleptoparasitic bee *Coelioxys inermis*.

Megachile leachella Curtis, 1828 — Silvery Leafcutter Bee
Plate 11

Description & similar species FW 5–7mm female, 5.5–7mm male. Our smallest leafcutter, and very distinctive owing to its strongly banded tergites and silvery-brown appearance (note that very fresh individuals have a strong golden hue which is rapidly lost). The female has a silvery pollen brush beneath the abdomen and two white hair patches on tergite 6. Males have tergite 6 covered in dense white hairs and very green eyes in life. *Anthophora bimaculata* males also have green eyes and a banded abdomen, but the ground colour of the face is yellow and they have three rather than two submarginal cells. The non-British *M. pilidens*, which is recorded from the near-continent, has denser punctures on tergite 4 of the female, whilst males have tarsal segments 2–4 of the front legs yellowish and rather expanded. **Variation** Dwarfs are not unusual. In older sun-bleached individuals, the brown thoracic hairs turn greyish and the buff tergite bands turn white and can become abraded. **Flight season** Late May to early September. **Habitat** Sandy habitats, especially coastal dunes but also vegetated shingle, sandpits, soft rock cliffs and coastal brownfield sites. Occasionally reported well inland, usually from sandpits. **Flowers visited** A variety of flowers are used, especially legumes (e.g. bird's-foot-trefoils, clovers and restharrows), Wild Thyme, Viper's-bugloss, Sheep's-bit, stonecrops, Thrift, Common Sea-lavender, ragworts and brambles. Males will shelter in the flowers of Sea Bindweed. **Nesting habits** Nesting occurs in very sandy ground (preferring non-compacted sand with fine plant roots), and nesting aggregation can be large and noisy. Leaves of various plants are used for nest building, and it also regularly uses the petals of bird's-foot-trefoils. **Status & distribution** Widespread and locally common around the coastline of southern Britain north to Morfa Harlech in Wales and Gibraltar Point in Lincolnshire. Very occasionally found inland. Not recorded in Ireland or Scotland. Present on the Channel Islands (Guernsey and Jersey). **Parasites & associates** The cleptoparasitic bee *Coelioxys brevis* attacks it on the Channel Islands, and a small form of *C. mandibularis* may attack it in Kent.

female

male

Megachile ligniseca (Kirby, 1802) **Wood-carving Leafcutter Bee**

Plate 11

Description & similar species FW 10–12mm female, 8.5–11mm male. Typically a large, brownish leafcutter with a slightly more elongate and 'bigger-headed' build than other large species such as *M. maritima* and *M. willughbiella*. Females lack upright hairs on the top of tergite 6, in contrast to those other two large species but like the much smaller *M. leachella* and *M. versicolor*. Small females can be separated from *M. versicolor* by the more rounded tergite 6 and the much paler pollen brush beneath the abdomen (but beware orange pollen). Males have unmodified front legs, and can be separated from species such as *M. versicolor* and *M. centuncularis* by the deep notch in the hind margin of tergite 6. **Variation** Dwarfs of both sexes are not unusual, overlapping in size with species such as *M. versicolor* and *M. centuncularis*. **Flight season** Early June to early September. **Habitat** A great variety of habitats are used and it can be

female

frequent in gardens and on brownfield sites. It seems to prefer structurally diverse habitat where a combination of Spear Thistle, brambles and shrubs is present. **Flowers visited** Most frequently observed on Spear Thistle gathering the whitish pollen, but it will also visit other thistles, burdocks, knapweeds, Chicory, brambles, everlasting-peas and Indian Balsam.

Nesting habits Nesting typically occurs in dead wood, especially old fence posts, tree stumps and log piles, though it will use artificial cavities

male

such as iron pipes and bee hotels where larger-diameter tubes are provided. The powerful jaws are used to actively fashion nesting holes to a greater extent than by other wood-nesting leafcutters, and it will often leave sawdust beneath a nest. **Status & distribution** Widespread and locally frequent in the southern half of England with records extending north to Cumbria and Yorkshire. Very few records for Devon and Cornwall, and most Welsh records are from the south coast. Not recorded in Scotland or the Channel Islands. Only one unconfirmed Irish record from 1979. **Parasites & associates** Possibly attacked by cleptoparasitic bees of the genus *Coelioxys*, but this is not confirmed.

Megachile maritima (Kirby, 1802) **Coast Leafcutter Bee**
not illustrated

Description & similar species FW 9–10.5mm female, 9–10mm male. A large brownish or blackish leafcutter. The biggest females have a bulk that can match the biggest *M. ligniseca* but are broader and less elongate in build (much as in *M. willughbiella*) and have upright hairs on the top of tergite 6 (hairs adpressed in *M. ligniseca*). Females closely resemble *M. willughbiella* but have much longer hairs on the outer sides of the front tarsi, a paler pollen brush beneath the abdomen, and usually extensive dark hairs on top of the thorax. Males have greatly expanded whitish front tarsi, much as in *M. willughbiella*, but are easily distinguished by the massively swollen and curved hind tibiae and shorter hind tarsi with a very broad basitarsus. The mandibles also have just three teeth (*M. willughbiella* has four). Large males can be very impressive, exceeding male *M. ligniseca* in size and with ginger-coloured body hairs when fresh. **Variation** Females vary greatly in the extent of black hairs on the head and thorax. Some can be almost as pale as *M. willughbiella* whilst others are almost black. Fresh males are ginger-haired but this rapidly fades, and sun-bleached individuals are greyish. The margin of the male's tergite 6 varies somewhat but usually features a series of lateral teeth on either side of a central notch. **Flight season** Early June to mid-August. **Habitat** Sandy habitats, especially coastal dunes, soft rock cliffs, vegetated shingle and sandy coastal brownfield sites; also inland on the sandiest heaths and within sandpits. **Flowers visited** A variety of flowers are visited, especially legumes (e.g. bird's-foot-trefoils, vetches, restharrows, everlasting-peas, Broom) and composites (thistles, knapweeds, ragworts), also Viper's-bugloss, Black Horehound, brambles, heathers, Sea-holly and mignonettes. **Nesting habits** Nesting typically occurs in sandy ground, sometimes in small aggregations, but nesting has also been observed in a wall. Leaves used for nest building include birches, willows and Hound's-tongue. **Status & distribution** Widespread and locally frequent in coastal areas of southern Britain, with records extending to southwest Scotland; also present inland within heathland districts, notably those of southern England and the East Anglian Brecks. In Ireland, restricted to a few sites on the southeast coast. Recorded from several of the Channel Islands. **Parasites & associates** The cleptoparasitic bee *Coelioxys conoidea*, and possibly also *C. mandibularis* at a few sites.

female

male

Megachile parietina (Geoffroy, 1875) **Black Mud Bee**
not illustrated

Description & similar species FW 14mm female, 10–12mm male. A large *Megachile* with females that are almost entirely jet black-haired with darkened wings (resembling a small *Xylocopa*). The pollen brush often appears orange or yellow due to pollen. As in *M. ericetorum*, the mandibles lack a bevelled cutting edge (a reflection of the fact that they do not cut leaves). The furry males have the top of the thorax and tergites 1–3 buff-haired, with tergites 4–6 black-haired. The head is comparatively small for a *Megachile*. In the field it is more likely to be mistaken for *Anthophora plumipes* than other *Megachile* species. **Variation** Little noted. **Flight season** April to June on the continent. **Habitat** Various dry, open habitats are used abroad. **Flowers visited** Mainly legumes such as Kidney Vetch, bird's-foot-trefoils, Sainfoin, clovers and Lucerne; also Viper's-bugloss and some labiates. Like *Eucera* bees, males are sexually attracted to the flowers of certain orchids. **Nesting habits** Females build a nest of mud and pebbles attached to rocks and walls. This is a globular structure usually containing 5–10 cells. It is not a leafcutter. **Status & distribution** Reported from Jersey in the mid-nineteenth century (as *Chalicodoma muraria*), but not seen since. There is always the possibility that it was confused with *Andrena pilipes*, *A. nigrospina* or *Anthophora plumipes*. **Parasites & associates** Parasitised by non-British *Stelis* and *Dioxys* species abroad.

female

male

Megachile versicolor Smith, 1844   **Brown-footed Leafcutter Bee**
Plate 11

Description & similar species FW 7–9mm female, 6–8.5mm male. A medium-sized, brownish leafcutter superficially resembling *M. centuncularis*. Females lack the upright hairs on tergite 6 of *M. centuncularis* and have the mainly orange pollen brush black-haired on sternites 5 and 6 (except in Ireland). The whitish hair bands on the hind margins of the tergites are less conspicuous than in *M. centuncularis*. Smaller individuals of *M. ligniseca* can resemble *M. versicolor* but have a paler pollen brush and a more rounded tip to tergite 6. Males have unmodified front legs and closely resemble *M. centuncularis*, requiring microscopic checking of sternite 4 to provide a reliable determination, though the redder apical tarsal segments of *M. versicolor* can provide an initial clue. Small males of *M. ligniseca* have a much deeper apical notch on tergite 6. **Variation** The size is variable and very small individuals are not unusual. Irish and Isle of Man females can have the pollen brush orange to the tip of the abdomen (like *M. centuncularis*) and the hairs of the head and top of the thorax mainly black and contrasting strongly with paler hairs on the sides of the thorax and base of the abdomen. Females from southwest Scotland can also have the hairs on top of the thorax black. **Flight season** Late May to early September. **Habitat** A variety of habitats are used both inland and on the coast, including gardens and brownfield sites. It is more frequent than *M. centuncularis* in open, expansive habitats such as downland and heathland. **Flowers visited** Particularly keen on composites such as thistles, knapweeds and Cat's-ear, though it will also use bird's-foot-trefoils, everlasting-peas, brambles and Wild Angelica. **Nesting habits** Nesting typically

female

female, SW Scotland

male

occurs in dead wood and old hollow thistle stalks and bramble twigs, also sometimes in the ground. Leaves used for nest building include rose. **Status & distribution** Widespread and frequent in southern England and the Midlands, but scarcer in southwest England, Wales and northern England, with records extending thinly to southwest Scotland. Widespread in Ireland. An unconfirmed record exists for Guernsey in the Channel Islands. **Parasites & associates** One of the hosts of the cleptoparasitic bee *Coelioxys inermis*.

Megachile willughbiella (Kirby, 1802) Willughby's Leafcutter Bee
Plate 12

Description & similar species FW 8.5–10.5mm female, 7.5–9mm male. The commonest of the large leafcutters. Females have a broad build like *M. maritima* but average slightly smaller with a paler appearance and a longer body pile. Females have a mostly orange pollen brush beneath the abdomen but with black hairs on sternites 5 and 6 (except in Ireland). The posterior hair fringe on the fore tarsi is much shorter than in *M. maritima*. The hind margins of the tergites have rather ill-defined bands of buff hairs which are less dense than those of *M. maritima*. Males have greatly expanded whitish front tarsi, much as in *M. maritima*,

female

male

but without the massively swollen and curved hind tibiae and with slimmer hind basitarsi. The outer faces of the front femora are mostly orange (mostly black in *M. maritima*). The hind margin of the male tergite 6 varies somewhat but usually features a series of small lateral teeth on either side of a central notch. **Variation** Irish females tend to have the pollen brush with less black at the tip, and in some it is virtually entirely orange-haired. Irish females can also have extensive black hairs on the head and top of thorax, contrasting with whitish hairs on the face below the antennal insertions, propodeum, sides and underside of thorax and base of abdomen, and the abdomen tends to be less banded than in British populations. Irish males also tend to have very white hairs on the thorax and base of the abdomen. In all parts of its range old sun-bleached males can gain a greyish appearance, and females can lose their body pile on the tergites and appear dark and unbanded. **Flight season** Late May to late August. **Habitat** A great variety of habitats are used, and it is one of the commonest leafcutters of gardens, brownfield sites and agricultural settings. **Flowers visited** Various, including legumes (e.g. bird's-foot-trefoils, everlasting-peas, vetches), composites (thistles, knapweeds, assorted garden species), brambles, willowherbs and bellflowers. **Nesting habits** A particularly versatile nester, capable of using dead wood and all manner of artificial cavities including gaps around window frames, holes in walls, earth-filled plant pots, rubber hoses, even folded garden parasols. It will also sometimes nest in the ground. It is one of the main leafcutters to use garden bee hotels. Leaf sections are obtained from a variety of herbaceous plants, shrubs and trees. **Status & distribution** Widespread and locally common over much of southern Britain, with records extending more thinly to the north of Scotland. Widely recorded in Ireland but apparently declining. Recorded from several of the Channel Islands. **Parasites & associates** Cleptoparasitic bees of the genus *Coelioxys*, including *C. quadridentata*, *C. rufescens* and *C. elongata*.

COELIOXYS – SHARP-TAIL BEES

♀

Medium-sized, densely punctate megachilid bees, with a projecting axilla on each side of the scutellum and conspicuous patches of dense adpressed white hairs on tergites and sternites. They are unusual in having hairy eyes (*Apis* is the only other British bee genus with hairy eyes). The abdomen narrows progressively towards the tip, and that of the female is characteristically pointed with a terminal prolongation of tergite 6 and sternite 6. The male abdomen is blunter and bears several spines on tergite 6 and sometimes on each side of tergite 5. Tergite 2 (and to a lesser extent tergite 3) has a deep groove (gradulus) running across the middle, the precise details of which can be of use in identification.

Coelioxys
conoidea

    Coelioxys species are cleptoparasites of *Megachile* and *Anthophora* bees. The pointed female abdomen is used to cut a slit in the partition of the host's cell so that an egg can be placed inside. The first-instar *Coelioxys* larva has very long curved jaws which are used to kill the host egg or grub. *Coelioxys* bees are surprisingly elusive and mostly seem to occur at low population levels. One of the best ways to find them is to look for females flying or resting close to host nesting areas. They can also be reared from host nests, and bee hotels are an easy source of potentially parasitised nests as they are used by several species of *Megachile*.

    This is a large genus with several hundred species globally. Seven species are recorded from the British Isles (*C. brevis* only from the Channel Islands). Several species with suitable hosts in Britain occur on the near-continent and should be looked out for. Identification can be difficult for some species without comparative material. Refer to the author's web feature (p.59) for further resources.

COELIOXYS FEMALES

1   Sides of thorax and outer face of the legs with dense, scale-like white hairs that obscure the underlying surface, such hairs also present above the wing bases and at the front of the scutum and scutellum. Tip of the abdomen and much of the mandibles reddish. Small (wing length to 6mm) with a black and white pattern **2**

—   Sides of thorax with longer hairs, the legs and scutum without scale-like hairs (except sparingly on the legs in *conoidea*). Mandibles, legs and tip of abdomen entirely dark beneath any hairs. Larger (wing length usually over 6.5mm) and often brownish or buff-tinged **3**

2   Tergite 6 long and reddish on at least the apical half and with a median ridge; sternite 6 long and pointed, protruding well beyond tergite 6 (Figs 1 & 2). Tibiae reddish (Channel Islands) .... ***brevis***

—   Tergite 6 shorter, only reddish at extreme tip and lacking a median ridge; sternite 6 short and rounded, only protruding a little way beyond tergite 6 (Figs 3 & 4). Tibiae dark .... ***afra***

Fig. 1 *C. brevis*	Fig. 2 *C. brevis*	Fig. 3 *C. afra*	Fig. 4 *C. afra*	Fig. 5 *C. rufescens*

Fig. 6 *C. mandibularis*	Fig. 7 *C. inermis*	Fig. 8 *C. elongata*	Fig. 9 *C. conoidea*	Fig. 10 *C. quadridentata*

3   Sternite 6 with a triangular tip bearing 'shoulders' but no acute lateral teeth and sternite 5 pointed at tip (Fig. 5). Face with rather long, semi-adpressed hairs of uniform length (Fig. 11) .... *rufescens*

—   Apical section of sternite 6 either with small acute lateral teeth before tip (e.g. Fig. 8) or with a blunt tip (Fig. 9). Face either with numerous bristle-like hairs projecting through the semi-adpressed hairs (Fig. 12) or with a zone of very dense short grey hairs of uniform length on the clypeus. Sternite 5 with an indented tip in some species (e.g. Fig. 6) 4

4   Apical section of sternite 6 with small acute lateral teeth before tip (Figs 6–8) 5

—   Apical section of sternite 6 without such lateral teeth (Figs 9 & 10) 7

5   Mandibles in front view with a right-angled outer edge and bearing a dense fringe of white hairs at the base underneath (Fig. 13). Sternite 5 with a deep 'V-shaped' incision at the tip (Fig. 6). Tergites 2–4 with white hair fringes widely separated .... *mandibularis*

—   Mandibles in front view with a gently curved outer edge and bearing a fringe of golden hairs at the base underneath. Sternite 5 with at most a shallow notch at the apex. Tergites 2–4 with white hair fringes either complete or only narrowly broken in the middle 6

6   Sternites 1–4 shining with relatively large and sparse punctures that only get a little smaller and denser towards sternite 5 (Fig. 14). Sternite 5 semi-shining, pointed or bluntly rounded at the tip (Fig. 7) .... *inermis*

—   Sternites 1–4 dulled to varying extents by microsculpture, the punctures getting progressively smaller and denser towards sternite 5 and sometimes replaced by microsculpture at the sides of 4 (Fig. 15). Sternite 5 dull with a shallow notch at the tip (Fig. 8) .... *elongata*

Fig. 11   Fig. 12    Fig. 13

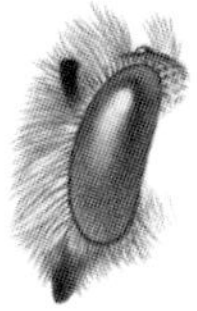

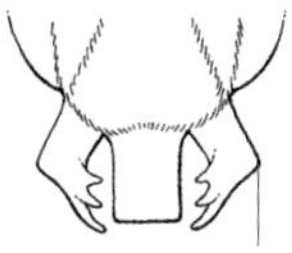

Fig. 14 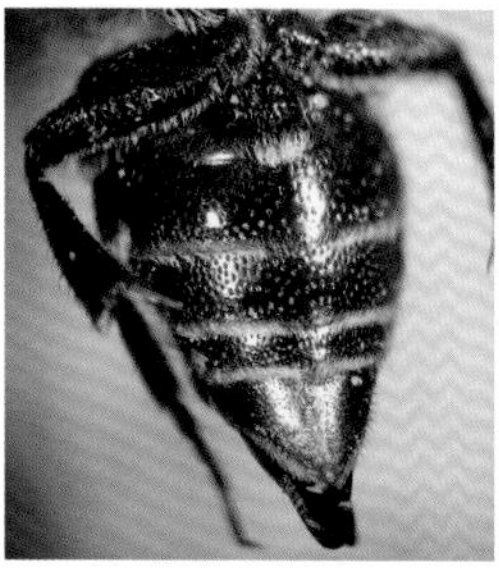   Fig. 15    Fig. 16

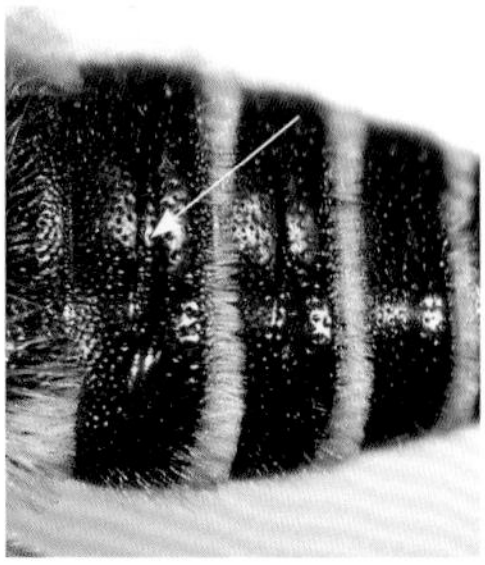

7   Tip of sternite 6 broader and blunter at apex (Fig. 9). Gradulus across tergites 2 and 3 interrupted in middle. Clypeus with very short dense hairs of uniform length. Tergites 2–4 with lateral white hair patches. Tibial bases with white scale-hairs .... *conoidea*

—   Tip of sternite 6 with a narrow apical section. Gradulus across tergites 2 and 3 deep and continuous across the middle (Fig. 16). Clypeus with numerous, bristle-like hairs projecting through the adpressed pile (Fig. 12). Tergites 2–4 with continuous white hair fringes. Bases of tibiae without white scale-hairs .... *quadridentata*

COELIOXYS MALES

1 Sides of thorax and outer face of the legs with dense snow-white, scale-like hairs that obscure the underlying surface, such hairs also present above the wing bases and at the front of the scutum and scutellum. Tip of mandibles reddish, the legs often too. Always black- and white-patterned and small (wing length to 6mm) **2**

— Sides of thorax with longer hairs, the legs and scutum without scale-like hairs (except sparingly on the legs in *conoidea*). Mandibles, legs and tip of abdomen entirely dark beneath any hairs. Larger (wing length usually over 6.5mm) and often brownish or buff-tinged **3**

2 Antennal flagella completely black. Tergites 3 and 4 with white hair bands broken in middle .... *afra*

— Antennal flagella extensively reddish. Tergites 3 and 4 with white hair bands complete in fresh specimens (Channel Islands) .... *brevis*

3 Tergites 2–4 with white lateral hair patches occupying no more than a quarter of the tergite's width. Hair patches on tergite 1 rectangular and not spreading along the hind margin. Outer face of hind tibiae with a patch of white hairs basally. Hind margin of sternite 4 with a semicircular or triangular indentation bounded by a pair of longitudinal ridges (Fig. 18). Large and pied (wing length typically 8.5–9mm) .... *conoidea*

— Tergites 2–4 with white hair patches either forming a continuous band along the hind margins or occupying at least a third of the tergite's width. Hair patches on tergite 1 triangular and spreading to varying extents along hind margin. Outer face of hind tibiae without a patch of white hairs basally. If hind margin of sternite 4 has a semicircular indentation this is unbounded by ridges. Usually smaller and browner **4**

4 Tergite 5 viewed from above with no blunt tooth at extreme sides of hind margin (Figs 19 & 20). Hind margin of sternite 4 with a semicircular indentation. White hair bands of tergites 2–4 continuous **5**

— Tergite 5 viewed from above with a short blunt tooth at extreme sides of hind margin (Fig. 21). Hind margin of sternite 4 unmodified. White hair bands of tergites 2–4 narrowed or broken centrally **6**

5 Top of tergite 1 with long, upright hairs covering entire surface between the white lateral hair patches (length of hairs equal to greatest width of the hind tibia). Gradulus across tergites 2 and 3 deep and continuous across the middle (Fig. 16). White hair bands of tergites 2–4 broad throughout .... *quadridentata*

— Tergite 1 with shorter, less conspicuous hairs between the white lateral hair patches. Gradulus of tergites 2–4 clearly broken or weakened centrally .... *rufescens*

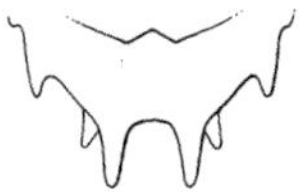

Fig. 17 *C. afra* 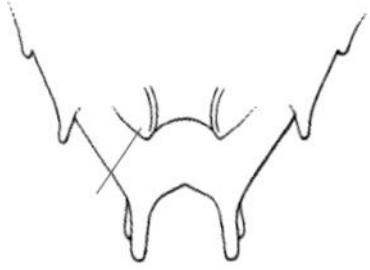   Fig. 18 *C. conoidea* 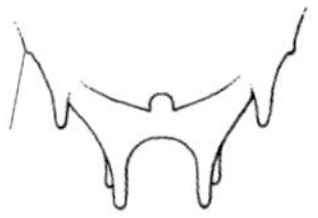   Fig. 19 *C. quadridentata* 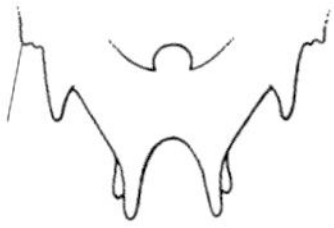   Fig. 20 *C. rufescens*

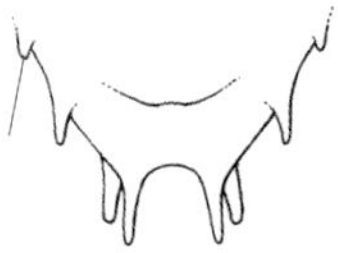

Fig. 21 *C. elongata* 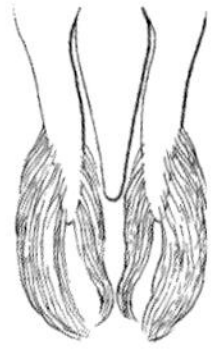   Fig. 22 *C. elongata* 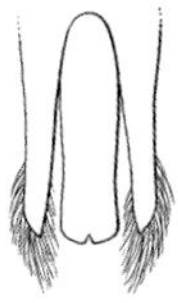   Fig. 23 *C. inermis*

6   Gradulus grooves of tergite 2 with short, adpressed, greyish hairs that completely obscure the underlying surface, these hairs extending in a sparser state right across the middle of the tergite between the grooves (Fig. 24). Facial hairs and abdominal bands whiter .... *mandibularis*

—   Gradulus grooves of tergite 2 with sparser hairs that do not extend across the middle of the tergite, which is virtually hairless between the grooves (Figs 25 & 26). In fresh specimens, facial hairs golden and bands of tergites buffish **7**

7   Gonostyli of genitalia apically with long, dense hairs that mask the apical shape of the gonostylus (Fig. 22). Tergites usually dulled by microsculpture, especially at base (Fig. 25) .... *elongata*

—   Gonostyli of genitalia apically with shorter, sparser hairs (Fig. 23). Tergites usually shinier (Fig. 26) .... *inermis*

Fig. 24 *C. mandibularis*	Fig. 25 *C. elongata*	Fig. 26 *C. inermis*

Coelioxys afra Lepeletier, 1841   **Short Sharp-tail Bee**

Plate 12

Description & similar species FW 5–6mm (sexes similar). One of two small sharp-tails with white scale-like hairs covering the sides and underneath of the thorax, genae, base of mandibles, outer face of the legs and sides of the abdomen. Females have the tip of the abdomen reddish with tergite 6 and sternite 6 shorter than in any other *Coelioxys* and bluntly rounded, the latter barely extending beyond the former. Males have entirely black antennae (reddish in *C. brevis*) and the white hair bands of tergites 2 and 3 interrupted in the middle. **Variation** The legs vary in colour from black to reddish. The white scale hairs of the abdomen, legs and thorax can become rubbed off in older individuals. **Flight season** On the continent, it flies from June until August. **Habitat** Sandy habitats such as coastal dunes. **Flowers visited** Various reported abroad, including bird's-foot-trefoils, melilots, thymes, Marjoram, Viper's-bugloss and knapweeds. **Status & distribution** Records exist for Guernsey (the last one seems to be 1956) whilst on the British mainland there is an old and rather dubious record for the New Forest (1892). **Host(s)** Primarily *Megachile leachella*, though some other *Megachile* species are used abroad.

female

Coelioxys brevis Eversmann, 1852   **Red-legged Sharp-tail Bee**
Plate 12

Description & similar species FW 5–6mm (sexes similar). Closely resembling *C. afra* but females have a long pointed sternite 6 that projects far beyond tergite 6. Tergite 6 is more extensively red at the tip and has a ridge running down the midline. The tibiae and tarsi have a reddish ground colour. Males have reddish antennal flagella and complete white bands across tergites 2 and 3. **Variation** Little noted, though the white scale hairs of the abdomen, legs and thorax can become rubbed

female

off in older individuals. **Flight season** July to early October. **Habitat** Sandy habitats such as coastal dunes, usually around host nesting colonies. **Flowers visited** Records include Viper's-bugloss, thymes and stonecrops. **Status & distribution** Only recorded from the Channel Islands (Jersey and Guernsey). **Host(s)** *Megachile leachella* on the Channel Islands, though some other *Megachile* species are used abroad.

Coelioxys conoidea (Illiger, 1806)   **Large Sharp-tail Bee**
Plate 12

Description & similar species FW 7–9.5mm female, 7–9mm male. This is typically our largest sharp-tail and is distinctive owing to the widely separated, pure white lateral spots on the tergites, a strong pattern of paired white patches (rather than complete bands) on sternites 2–4, and the particularly white-haired sides of the thorax and head behind the eyes. These combine to create a pied appearance. The presence of white scale-like hairs at the bases of the tibiae is unique to this species. Females have a broad, blunt sternite 6 and a very short even pile on the clypeus, quite unlike any other species. Males have a triangular or semicircular incision along the hind margin of sternite 4 rather like *C. rufescens* and *C. quadridentata* but bound by longitudinal ridges. *C. mandibularis*, which can fly with *C. conoidea* on some dunes, also has a rather pied appearance, but is smaller, lacks white hairs

female

male

at the tibial bases, has angled female mandibles and has a simple hind margin on sternite 4 of the male. **Variation** Moderate size variation, with smaller individuals overlapping in size with other sharp-tails. **Flight season** Mid-June to late August. **Habitat** Coastal dunes, soft rock cliffs, vegetated shingle, sandy heathland and sandy brownfield sites, as per its host. **Flowers visited** Knapweeds, ragworts, mallows, brambles, Sea Rocket, Sea-holly, thymes, Sea Bindweed and sea-lavenders. **Status & distribution** Mostly recorded from southern coastal and heathland districts with records extending north to Cumbria and Yorkshire and a sparse presence in heathland districts of the Midlands. Not recorded from Scotland or Ireland. Recorded from Alderney, Herm and Jersey in the Channel Islands. It can be quite numerous at some sites. **Host(s)** *Megachile maritima*.

Coelioxys elongata Lepeletier, 1841   **Dull-vented Sharp-tail Bee**

Plate 12

Description & similar species FW 6–8.5mm (sexes similar). A medium-sized, brownish sharp-tail best considered as part of a trio with *C. inermis* and *C. mandibularis*. Females of this trio have a similar-shaped sternite 6 bearing small, acute lateral teeth, and (together with *C. quadridentata*) an inclined hair pile on the face through which protrude erect bristly hairs. Females of *C. mandibularis* are easily separable by the shape of the mandibles. Separation from *C. inermis* requires examination of the sternites. In *C. elongata* these are dulled to a varying extent by microsculpture, and the punctures of sternites 2–4 get progressively smaller and denser towards sternite 5 and may be absent at the sides of tergite 4 (sternites shiny with the punctures of more uniform size in *C. inermis*). Sternite 5 is very dull and has a shallow notch at the tip (bluntly pointed in *C. inermis*). Males of the trio are very challenging, and *C. elongata* and *C. inermis* can only be reliably separated by checking the gonostyli of the genitalia. Separation of this pair from *C. mandibularis* is described under that species. **Variation** Moderate size variation. Some variation in size and extent of punctures and microsculpture on the sternites, also the size and the shape of the hair bands on tergites 2–4 (which can become abraded in older specimens). **Flight season** June to August. **Habitat** Quite varied, including coastal dunes, heathland, brownfield sites, gardens and the rides and clearings of woodland. **Flowers visited** British records include Greater Bird's-foot-trefoil and Common Fleabane, but uses a wide variety of flowers abroad. **Status & distribution** A widespread species, with records extending to the north of Scotland, but scarce and infrequent in most districts despite the abundance of the main host. Rare in Ireland, with a scattering of mostly old records. The only Channel Islands records are from Jersey. **Host(s)** The main host is *Megachile willughbiella*, but it clearly parasitises *M. circumcincta* at some northern coastal sites.

female

male

Coelioxys inermis (Kirby, 1802) — Shiny-vented Sharp-tail Bee
Plate 12

Description & similar species FW 6–9mm (females average larger). Closely resembling *C. elongata*. Females can be readily separated by checking the sternites (see *C. elongata* for details). Males resemble *C. elongata* and *C. mandibularis* and can only be reliably separated from the former by examination of the genitalia. **Variation** Moderate size variation. Some variation in size and the shape of the hair bands on tergites 2–4 (which can become abraded in older specimens). **Flight season** June to August. **Habitat** Quite varied, including heathland, chalk downland, woodland and gardens. **Flowers visited** British records include brambles, Cross-leaved Heath and bird's-foot-trefoils, but a wider variety of flowers are used abroad. **Status & distribution** Most frequent in southern England, though rarely numerous here. Records extend sparingly into Wales and as far north as Cumbria and Yorkshire. Rare in Ireland. Not recorded from Scotland. The only Channel Islands records are from Jersey. **Host(s)** *Megachile centuncularis*, *M. versicolor* and possibly *M. ligniseca*.

female

Coelioxys mandibularis Nylander, 1848 — Square-jawed Sharp-tail Bee
Plate 12

Description & similar species FW 7–8mm (sexes similar). Resembling *C. elongata* and *C. inermis*, but with whiter abdominal markings and whiter hairs on the face and sides of thorax (rather like *C. conoidea*). Females can be easily distinguished from all other sharp-tails by the 'elbowed' mandibles. The bands on tergites 2–4 are well separated in the middle (bands continuous in fresh *C. elongata* and *C. inermis*) and sternite 5 has a deep V-shaped notch at the tip. Males resemble *C. elongata* and *C. inermis* but have denser hairs within the gradulus grooves of tergite 2, these hairs extending thinly across the middle of the tergite between the two grooves (this area is hairless in the other two). The hind tibial spurs are usually darker (dark red rather than orange). **Variation** A consistently small form thought to be associated with *Megachile leachella* is known from Kent. Some size variation also occurs in Welsh populations. There is some variation in the size and shape of the hair bands on tergites 2–4. Worn males can become very silvery-looking. **Flight season** Early June to late August. **Habitat** Coastal dunes. **Flowers visited** British preferences unclear, but a wide variety of flowers is used abroad. **Status & distribution** A very restricted species, with most records from the larger dunes of south Wales where it can be common. Further records exist in Gwynedd, Lancashire (the dune systems near Liverpool), Sussex (West Wittering) and Kent (Deal and Sandwich). Not recorded from Scotland, Ireland or the Channel Islands. **Host(s)** Seemingly *Megachile maritima* at most sites, but probably *M. leachella* in Kent.

female

Coelioxys quadridentata (Linnaeus, 1758)   **Grooved Sharp-tail Bee**
Plate 12

Description & similar species FW 6.5–8.5mm (sexes similar). Both sexes have the pale bands of tergites 2–4 continuous, with barely any narrowing in the middle (narrowed or broken centrally in most other sharp-tails). The gradulus grooves of tergites 2 and 3 are deep and continuous without any weakening centrally (weak or broken centrally in all other sharp-tails). Females have a uniquely shaped sternite 6. Males have a long, upright pile across tergite 1 (short and adpressed in other species), and a semicircular incision on the hind margin of sternite 4 centrally (like *C. conoidea* and *C. rufescens*). **Variation** Some size variation. **Flight season** Mid-June to early August. **Habitat** Many records relate to sandy heathland and coastal dunes, but it also occurs on calcareous grassland and in suburban situations. **Flowers visited** British records include bird's-foot-trefoils and White Bryony, though a much wider variety of species is used abroad. **Status & distribution** Severely declined, with few recent records. Historically it was found locally in southern England (especially Dorset, Surrey and Kent) with records extending north to Yorkshire; also south Wales (Glamorganshire). Not recorded from Scotland or Ireland. An old record exists for Jersey. **Host(s)** British hosts include *Megachile circumcincta*, *Anthophora furcata* and *A. quadrimaculata*, though the pattern of decline and choice of sites suggests a strong dependence on the first species.

Coelioxys rufescens Lepeletier & Serville, 1825   **Rufescent Sharp-tail Bee**
Plate 12

Description & similar species FW 6.5–8mm female, 5.5–8mm male. Females are readily distinguished by the apical shape of sternite 6, and also the long, semi-inclined pile of the face, which lacks the erect bristle-like hairs of *C. elongata*, *C. inermis*, *C. mandibularis* and *C. quadridentata*. Like *C. quadridentata*, males have a semicircular incision along the hind margin of sternite 4 (sometimes obscured by hairs) and no hint of lateral teeth along the hind margin of tergite 5, but the pale hair bands of tergites 2–4 are distinctly narrowed in the middle, the gradulus grooves of tergites 2 and 3 are weakened or broken in the middle, and tergite 1 has much shorter hairs between the lateral pale spots. **Variation** Individuals associated with *Anthophora bimaculata* tend to average smaller than those using other larger

female

hosts; also variation in the apical shape of sternite 6 and the punctures and markings of the tergites. **Flight season** Late May to mid-August. **Habitat** Populations exploiting *Anthophora bimaculata* are associated with sandy habitats such as soft rock cliffs, heathland and sandpits, but it can also occur in wetlands, claylands, chalk districts and non-sandy brownfield sites where other hosts are involved. **Flowers visited** British records include brambles and thistles, but a wide variety of flowers is used abroad. **Status & distribution** Widespread and fairly frequent in coastal and heathland districts of southern England, with records extending thinly into Wales and north to Lancashire and Yorkshire. Not recorded from Scotland or Ireland. On the Channel Islands recorded from Alderney, Sark and Jersey. **Host(s)** *Anthophora bimaculata*, *A. furcata*, and possibly *Megachile willughbiella* and *M. circumcincta*. Preferred hosts elsewhere are unclear but seem to include *Anthophora furcata*, *Megachile willughbiella* and *M. circumcincta*.

FAMILY APIDAE

NOMADA – NOMAD BEES

Small to moderately large, relatively hairless bees, often with bold wasp-like markings. Males have a conspicuous pygidium at the tip of the abdomen, and the face is usually more extensively yellow than in the females, whilst the thorax is often darker and hairier. In females, the pygidium is largely overhung by the densely hairy hind margin

♂

♀

♀

Nomada goodeniana

Nomada hirtipes

Nomada sexfasciata

of tergite 5 and is less obvious. All species are cleptoparasites, primarily on *Andrena* species, but to a lesser extent *Melitta*, *Lasioglossum*, *Panurgus*, *Eucera* plus some non-British genera. Females enter the host's nesting burrow and lay an egg in the wall of an unsealed nest cell. The first-instar *Nomada* grub then destroys the host egg or grub with its large sickle-shaped mandibles and proceeds to feed on the food store.

♀

♀

Females can be quite easy to spot around host nesting areas (they can be very useful at revealing the precise location of host nests) and also visit flowers nearby, especially spring-flowering shrubs, composites, umbellifers and heathers. Some species (e.g. *N. armata* or

Nomada fucata

Nomada sheppardana

N. roberjeotiana) have very specific hosts, whilst others (e.g. *N. panzeri* and *N. flavopicta*) use several closely related species, though may achieve this using genetically distinct host races. Most species are univoltine, but those using bivoltine hosts are generally also bivoltine (e.g. *N. fucata* and *N. fabriciana*). Spring is the best time to see a good variety of species (up to ten species can be recorded at one site on a good day) but several late-summer-peaking species exist, notably *N. armata* and *N. argentata*, which use hosts that forage on scabiouses.

Nomada is a near-cosmopolitan genus with about 850 described species, making it the largest genus of cleptoparasitic bees. Thirty-four species are currently known from the British Isles, though there is potential for several further species found on the near-continent to colonise southern England or the Channel Islands, and *N. zonata* was only discovered on Jersey in 2011. There is also potential for discovery of new species arising from DNA analysis of host 'races'. Recent analysis of British '*fulvicornis*' revealed that the bivoltine form parasitising species such as *A. bimaculata* and *A. pilipes* is not conspecific with the univoltine form parasitising *Andrena nigrospina*, and the latter is treated as a separate species (*N. subcornuta*) here for the first time.

Nomada identification can be quite challenging, especially without comparative material. Always remember to ensure the mandibles are open when pinning material. The arrangement of small spines at the tip of the hind tibiae dorsally (the comb spines: Fig. 1) also provides a useful character in many species. The author's web feature (p.59) provides extensive additional resources.

Fig. 1

NOMADA FEMALE GROUPS

1	Abdomen red, brown or blackish without any yellow or whitish markings	**female group A**
—	Abdomen with yellow or whitish markings, at least as small lateral spots on tergite 2	**2**
2	Tergites black and yellow without any red markings (faint reddish halos may occur where black and yellow meet)	**female group B**
—	Tergites with obvious red markings, i.e. either red with yellow spots or black and yellow with some additional obvious red markings	**3**

3 Labrum entirely or predominantly dark .... **female group C**

— Labrum entirely or predominantly red, orange or yellow (any dark markings
occupy less than half the surface area) **4**

4 Scutum entirely black .... **female group D**

— Scutum with red marks, at least at the sides above the wing bases .... **female group E**

NOMADA FEMALE GROUP A

1 Scutellum entirely black **2**

— Scutellum with red markings **4**

2 Mandibles bifid at tip (Fig. 2). Scutum dull with punctures virtually touching.
Antennal flagella usually bright orange in basal section and at tip, with a broad
black subapical band (occasionally much darker) .... **some *fabriciana***

— Mandibles bluntly pointed at tip (Fig. 3). Scutum clearly shining between the
punctures. Antennal flagella at most obscurely reddish at base (Channel Islands) **3**

3 Scutellum clearly depressed in the middle with bumps on either side (Fig. 4).
Antennae relatively long, with segment 3 in top view about 2.5 times as long as
wide (Fig. 5), the flagella dark at base. Hind femora extensively red, the mid
and hind tibiae mostly or entirely red. Larger and slimmer (wing length 6.5–7mm) .... ***similis***

— Scutellum fairly evenly convex. Antennae relatively short, with segment 3 in top
view about twice as long as wide (Fig. 6), the flagella slightly reddish basally.
Hind femora mostly black, the mid and hind tibiae extensively darkened. Smaller
and stockier (wing length 5.5–6mm) .... ***fuscicornis***

Fig. 2   Fig. 3    Fig. 4    Fig. 5

Fig. 6

4 Labrum orange-red. Tiny (typical wing length 4mm). Rear face of propodeum
towards bottom with a discrete patch of dense silvery hairs on each side that
mask the underlying surface (like Fig. 13) .... ***sheppardana***

— Labrum black. Wing length usually at least 5mm **5**

5 Head with orange markings that broadly occupy the lower part of the clypeus
and often surround much of the eyes. Rear face of propodeum towards bottom
with a discrete patch of dense silvery hairs on each side that mask the underlying
surface (Fig. 13) .... **some *flavoguttata***

— Clypeus at most orange-red along extreme lower edge. Eyes mostly surrounded
by black integument. Rear face of propodeum with a more general covering of
long silvery hairs **6**

6   Antennal flagella clear reddish below, much paler than upper surface. Hind femora extensively red, the underside smooth and shining apically but dulled by dense punctures in basal half. Scutum dull with small, dense punctures. Sides of thorax entirely black .... *integra*

—   Antennal flagella dusky red below, barely paler than the upper surface. Hind femora black, at most narrowly red above, the underside shining throughout with only sparse punctures basally. Scutum shinier, with sparser punctures. Sides of thorax with a large red patch .... *argentata*

NOMADA FEMALE GROUP B

1   Scutellum with a single yellow or cream-coloured mark. Tergite 1 always black. Smaller (wing length to 7mm) 2

—   Scutellum with a pair of yellow or orange spots. Tergite 1 usually yellow-marked (except some *marshamella*). Larger (wing length usually at least 7.5mm) 3

2   Antennal flagella black. Tergites yellow-marked, tergite 4 with a complete yellow band or lateral streaks. Sides of thorax below wing bases with a yellow spot. Underside of abdomen yellow-marked. Hind face of propodeum densely punctate at sides and bottom. Tergites 2 and 3 closely punctured .... **some *rufipes***

—   Antennal flagella orange. Tergites creamy-white-marked, tergite 4 with at most small lateral whitish spots. Underside of abdomen black, sides of thorax entirely black. Hind face of propodeum smooth and shining at sides and bottom, barely punctate. Tergites 2 and 3 shinier, with punctures finer and sparser .... *errans*

3   Tergites 2–4 and often tergite 1 with complete yellow bands 4

—   At least tergite 2 with lateral yellow spots or a distinctly broken yellow band 5

4   Tibiae orange, at most with limited yellow markings, the hind pair not black-marked posteriorly. Hind femora orange on dorsal and anterior surfaces. Face orange along lower edge of clypeus and narrowly yellow alongside the eyes (Fig. 7). Labrum and antennal scapes usually entirely or mainly orange .... *goodeniana*

—   Tibiae yellow, the hind pair with a dark mark posteriorly. Hind femora mainly black except for yellow tip. Face with large yellow patches at the side of the face and often a third on the clypeus (Fig. 8). Labrum mostly dark. Antennal scapes entirely black behind, contrasting with an orange or yellow front (Channel Islands) .... *succincta*

Fig. 7   Fig. 8

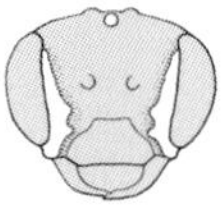

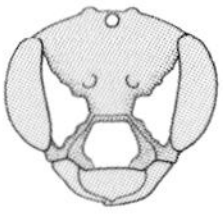

5   Antennal flagella mostly black. Thorax (including the ventral surface) with hairs for the most part minute and inconspicuous. Front coxae (viewed from below) triangular with a pointed tip .... *flavopicta*

—   Antennal flagella orange, at most darkened dorsally towards tip. Thorax hairier, at least ventrally, usually with the hairs on the top and on the propodeum as long as the width of an antennal flagellum. Front coxae with bluntly rounded tips 6

6   Malar gap wide, about 0.75 times the width of an antennal flagellum; clypeus in front view projecting well below the lowest point of the eyes, in side view distinctly inflated (Fig. 9). Labrum almost round. Hind femora usually only dark on the underside basally .... *sexfasciata*

—   Malar gap narrow, about 0.3 times the width of an antennal flagellum; clypeus in front view barely projecting below the lowest point of the eyes, in side view not much inflated (Fig. 10). Labrum clearly wider than long. Hind femora usually substantially darkened **7**

7   Sternites usually black and yellow (sometimes all black) with any red very limited in extent. Labrum with a small, triangular central projection (Fig. 11). Yellow markings of tergites 1 and 2 without red halos, those of tergite 1 always well separated and sometimes tiny or missing. Pronotal collar often without yellow markings. Scutellar spots often orange. Sides of thorax below wing bases usually unmarked .... *marshamella*

—   Sternites usually predominantly red or yellow, with any black markings limited in extent. Labrum with a large, triangular central projection (Fig. 12). Yellow markings of tergites 1 and 2 with red halos (sometimes hard to see with the naked eye), those of tergite 1 usually large and meeting or nearly meeting on the midline. Pronotal collar usually all yellow. Scutellar spots yellow. Sides of thorax below wing bases often with large yellow or orange markings .... **some** *fulvicornis*

Fig. 9   Fig. 10 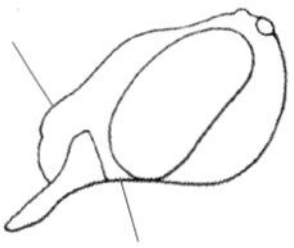   Fig. 11    Fig. 12

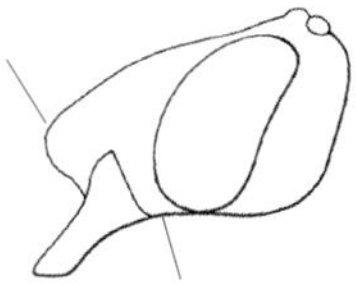

NOMADA FEMALE GROUP C

1   Scutum with longitudinal red stripes, at least at sides above wing bases, often a pair centrally too. Eyes usually completely surrounded by orange markings **2**

—   Scutum entirely black. Eyes mostly surrounded by black integument **3**

2   Hind face of propodeum with a discrete patch of dense silvery hairs on each side (Fig. 13). Sides of thorax below wing bases usually with one large but irregularly shaped patch of red. Smaller and stockier (typical wing length 5mm) .... **typical** *flavoguttata*

—   Hind face of propodeum without discrete patches of dense silvery hairs on each side (Fig. 14). Sides of thorax below wing bases usually with two discrete red patches. Larger and slimmer (typical wing length 6.5mm) .... *conjungens*

Fig. 13 *N. flavoguttata*   Fig. 14 *N. conjungens*

3   Antennal flagella with dorsal surface entirely dark. Tergite 5 mostly whitish.
Ridge between antennal bases broad and flat on top (Fig. 15). Small (typical
wing length 5mm) .... *obtusifrons*

—   Antennal flagella bright orange in basal section and at tip, with a broad black
subapical band. Tergite 5 at most with a yellow patch. Area between antennal
bases with a sharp median crest. Larger (wing length usually at least 6mm) **4**

4   Mandibles bifid (Fig. 2). Labrum with at most a small central projection.
Scutellum black. Hind face of propodeum and outer face of hind coxae with
less conspicuous silver hairs. Tergites 4 and 5 without yellow marks. Smaller
(wing length to 7.5mm) .... **typical** *fabriciana*

—   Mandibles bluntly pointed. Labrum with a large, triangular projection close to
the lower edge centrally (Fig. 16). Scutellum with a pair of red spots. Hind face
of propodeum at sides and outer face of hind coxae with conspicuous silver hairs.
Tergites 4 and 5 with yellow marks. Larger (typical wing length 9mm) .... *armata*

Fig. 15   Fig. 16

NOMADA FEMALE GROUP D

1   Scutellum with a single yellow or red mark **2**

—   Scutellum with a pair of yellow, orange or red spots **4**

2   Scutellar spot, pronotal collar, pronotal tubercles and tegulae orange or red. Abdomen
with whitish spots on the sides of tergites 2 and 3 and the greater part of tergite 5,
tergite 4 mostly black. Small (wing length 5.5mm) with very short body hairs .... *roberjeotiana*

—   Scutellar spot, pronotal collar, pronotal tubercles and tegulae yellow. Tergites with any
markings yellow, tergite 4 with a complete band. Larger (wing length usually 6–8mm) **3**

3   Antennal flagella entirely orange. Tergite 2 with yellow band either complete or
narrowly broken in the middle, tergite 3 with a complete band. Thorax with an
obvious pile. Front coxae apically blunt .... *fucata*

—   Antennal flagella mostly black. Tergites 2 and 3 with well-separated yellow spots.
Thorax with short, inconspicuous hairs. Front coxae with an apical projection .... **some** *rufipes*

4   Antennal scapes entirely or partially blackish in front **5**

—   Antennal scapes entirely reddish or orange in front **6**

5   Pronotal tubercles reddish. Tergites 2–4 with large yellow markings. Thorax with a
longer pile, the hairs on top about as long as the width of an antennal flagellum ...... *leucophthalma*

—   Pronotal tubercles yellow. Tergites mostly red, with small yellow spots on the
sides of tergite 2 only. Thorax with a shorter, less conspicuous pile .... *ferruginata*

6   Thorax with a rather long reddish pile (when fresh). Tergites 2 and 3 with complete
yellow or yellow and red bands. Scutellar spots yellow with reddish edges. Inner eye
margins entirely red. Propodeum never with red or yellow marks .... *lathburiana*

—   Thorax with a shorter, paler pile. Tergites 2 and 3 usually with yellow bands
divided by black (except some *zonata*, which tend to have red or yellow
propodeal marks and the antennal flagella dark above on segments 6–11) **7**

7   Hind tibiae black-marked on their inner face. Tergites 2 and 3 with substantial patches of red centrally between the yellow spots. Scutellar spots often red or orange (occasionally fused). Antennal segments 7–11 darkened above, with the final segment conspicuously paler. Smaller and dumpier (typical wing length 7mm) (Channel Islands) .... ***zonata***

—   Hind tibiae without blackish markings. Tergites 2 and 3 with any red narrowly surrounding the yellow spots. Scutellar spots always paired and yellow. Antennal segments either entirely orange or with progressive darkening of the final segments above without a conspicuously paler final segment. Larger (wing length usually at least 8mm) **8**

8   Tergite 1 with a pair of yellow spots (often fused) surrounded by red. Tergite 2 with yellow spots narrowly separated. Sternites often extensively yellow. Labrum with a larger central projection (Fig. 17). Typically smaller (typical wing length 8.5mm) .... **typical *fulvicornis***

—   Tergite 1 red-marked (either one large patch or two narrowly separated spots) without any yellow. Tergite 2 with yellow spots usually more widely separated. Sternites always predominantly red. Labrum with a smaller central projection (Fig. 18). Typically larger (typical wing length 9.5mm) .... *subcornuta*

Fig. 17   Fig. 18    Fig. 19    Fig. 20

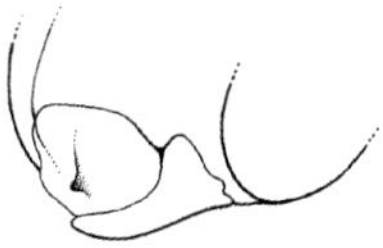

                                                        Fig. 21 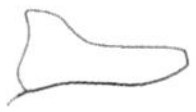   Fig. 22

NOMADA FEMALE GROUP E

1   Mandibles bifid at tip (Fig. 19) .... *ruficornis*

—   Mandibles with pointed or squared-off tips (Figs 20–22) **2**

2   Tergite 2 with a complete yellow band, or large yellow spots that are separated by less than their own width **3**

—   Tergite 2 with smaller yellow spots that are separated by more than their own width. If in doubt (some *baccata*), a small species with tergite markings cream-coloured rather than yellow and head and rear face of propodeum extensively reddish **5**

3   Tergites 2 and 3 with very broad, continuous and almost straight-sided bands. Hind face of propodeum with a pair of conspicuous yellow marks. Sternites 2–4 extensively yellow .... *signata*

—   Tergites 2 and 3 either with narrowly separated yellow spots or, if a continuous yellow band is present, this narrows in the middle. Hind face of propodeum with any marks reddish. Sternites 2–4 mainly red **4**

4   Lower part of propodeum, sides of thorax and hind coxae with yellow-tinted hairs. Hind face of propodeum at most with small reddish marks. Clypeus and labrum with the long, erect hairs yellowish. Antennal flagella as pale above as below. Wing margins usually paler. Averaging larger (typical wing length 9.5mm) and paler-looking .... *flava*

—   Lower part of propodeum, sides of thorax and hind coxae with silvery hairs. Hind face of propodeum often extensively red-marked. Clypeus and labrum with the long, erect hairs blackish. Antennal flagella usually slightly darker above. Wing margins usually darker. Averaging smaller (typical wing length 8.5mm) and darker-looking .... **paler** *panzeri*

5   Extreme tip of hind tibiae dorsally with 3–4 very short blunt black comb spines
     that are touching and give the impression of a single black appendage (Fig. 23).
     Antennal scapes blackish at front, at most a small reddish mark apically. Small
     (typical wing length 6mm) with very blunt mandibles (Fig. 26) .... *guttulata*

—   Extreme tip of hind tibiae dorsally with 4–5 longer and more widely spaced comb spines
     (Figs 24 & 25). Antennal scapes usually reddish or orange at front (occasionally darkened in
     striata). Larger (except *castellana*) and with sharply pointed mandibles (except *striata*) **6**

6   Tip of hind tibia with 4–5 long black and curved comb spines that look like bear
     claws (Fig. 25). Propodeum extensively orange at sides with a black median stripe
     and extensive patches of long silvery hairs (longer than the width of an antennal
     flagellum) at the sides. Head extensively orange, the orange broadly surrounding
     the eyes and often crossing the head in front of the ocelli. Tergite markings
     cream-coloured. Small (typical wing length 5.5mm) .... *baccata*

—   Tibial comb spines shorter and straight (Fig. 24). Propodeum with any markings
     red and small, any silvery hairs short and less extensive. Head with less extensive
     markings which are red and never cross the top of the head in front of the ocelli.
     Tergite markings yellow (except *striata*). Larger (wing length usually 7mm or more) **7**

7   Mandibles squared off or very bluntly rounded at their tips (Fig. 27). Tergite 2 with
     lateral yellow spots small and roundish, never triangular. Typical wing length 7mm .... *striata*

—   Mandibles pointed at their tip (Fig. 20), or, if rather blunt (*castellana*; Fig. 3), wing
     length no more than 5.5mm **8**

8   Small (wing length up to 5.5mm) with very small, ill-defined yellow spots on the sides
     of tergite 2, and tergite 5 reddish. Antennal flagella brown or blackish on top (Channel
     Islands) .... *castellana*

—   Larger (wing length usually at least 7mm) with larger, sharply defined yellow spots
     on the sides of tergite 2, and tergite 5 mainly yellow. Antennal flagella reddish above **9**

9   Antennae shorter, segment 3 in dorsal view about 1.5 times as long as wide (Fig. 30).
     Legs relatively short, stout and longer-haired, the second segment of the hind
     tarsi only about 2.5 times as long as wide in top view (Fig. 28). Antennal flagella
     with only minute adpressed hairs on hind face. Tergite 2 with lateral yellow
     markings usually triangular with pointed inner margins, wider than high .... darker *panzeri*

—   Antennae longer, segment 3 in dorsal view about twice as long as wide (Fig. 31).
     Legs relatively long, slim and shorter-haired, the second segment of the hind
     tarsi about 4 times as long as wide in top view (Fig. 29). Antennal flagella with
     some longer, semi-erect hairs on hind face. Tergite 2 with lateral yellow markings
     rounder, higher than wide .... *hirtipes*

| Fig. 23 |  Fig. 24 |  Fig. 25 |  Fig. 26 |  Fig. 28 |  Fig. 29 |

Fig. 27

Fig. 30    Fig. 31

NOMADA MALE GROUPS

1   At least tergites 1–3 with bold black and yellow markings without any obvious red or brown .... **male group A**

—   At least tergite 1 with some red or brown, abdomen often substantially red or a mix of red and yellow **2**

2   Labrum entirely or extensively darkened .... **male group B**

—   Labrum entirely yellow **3**

3   Antennal scapes entirely or partially black in front .... **male group C**

—   Antennal scapes entirely yellow or orange in front **4**

4   Pronotal collar almost entirely yellow (only black at extreme sides) .... **male group D**

—   Pronotal collar dark, or obscurely yellow, or with any red or yellow marks smaller and stopping well short of the sides .... **male group E**

NOMADA MALE GROUP A

1   Scutellum with a single large yellow or cream-coloured mark **2**

—   Scutellum with either two spots or completely black **3**

2   Sternites 3–6 with yellow bands. Tergite 4 usually with a complete yellow band. Hind face of propodeum densely punctate at sides and bottom .... **some *rufipes***

—   All sternites black. Tergite 4 with well-separated lateral streaks. Pale body markings whitish rather than yellow. Hind face of propodeum smooth and shining at sides and bottom, barely punctate .... ***errans***

3   Hind face of propodeum virtually bare. Thorax and head short-haired (hairs on top of thorax shorter than the width of an antennal flagellum). Underside of hind femora shining throughout with only short, sparse hairs (Fig. 32). Outer face of hind coxae with a dense covering of adpressed silvery hairs .... ***flavopicta***

—   Hind face of propodeum with long hairs almost throughout. Thorax and head longer-haired (hairs on top of thorax at least as long as the width of an antennal flagellum). Underside of femora either with dense hairs and extensive punctures (Fig. 33) or, if shiny, then with a patch of dense, adpressed yellow or whitish hairs at base (Fig. 34). Outer face of hind coxae with silvery hairs longer and semi-erect **4**

Fig. 32	Fig. 33	Fig. 34

4   Underside of hind femora extensively shining and devoid of hairs but with a patch of excessively dense, adpressed yellow or whitish hairs in the basal quarter, the adjacent trochanters also densely hairy (Fig. 34). Tergite 2 with a complete yellow band **5**

—   Underside of hind femora only shining and hairless at tip, for the most part densely punctate and densely haired (Fig. 33) **6**

5   Hind tibiae orange, sometimes partially yellow but without a dark marking on the posterior face. Hind femora mostly or entirely orange on dorsal and anterior faces .... *goodeniana*

—   Hind tibiae entirely yellow except for a dark marking on the posterior face. Hind femora mostly black on dorsal and anterior faces (Channel Islands) .... *succincta*

6   Head viewed from side with malar gap as broad as the width of an antennal flagellum and with the lower face much inflated (Fig. 9). Antennae viewed from the front with segment 3 about as long as 4 (Fig. 35). Hind tibiae without obvious apical comb spines. Thorax furrier, the hairs of the top and sides mostly twice as long as the width of an antennal flagellum .... *sexfasciata*

—   Malar gap only about half the width of an antennal flagellum, the lower face less inflated (Fig. 10). Antennae viewed from the front with segment 3 clearly shorter than 4 (Figs 36–38). Hind tibiae with several obvious apical comb spines above. Hairs on top and sides of thorax mostly 1.5 times as long as the width of an antennal flagellum 7

Fig. 35   Fig. 36 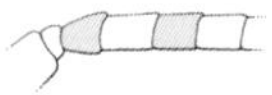   Fig. 37    Fig. 38

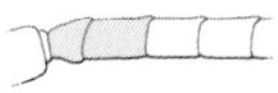

Fig. 39 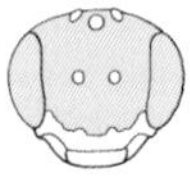   Fig. 40

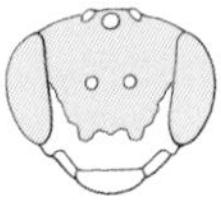

7   All tibiae bearing conspicuous black markings, those of hind tibiae occupying most of the posterior face. Antennal segment 3 viewed from below usually less than half as long as segment 4 (Fig. 37). Smaller (wing length up to 6.5mm) with yellow markings of the lower face usually extending up the eye margins as far as the antennal insertions (Fig. 40) (Channel Islands) ....*zonata*

—   Tibiae usually without conspicuous black markings, but if present (the occasional *marshamella*), antennal segment 3 viewed from below is more than half as long as segment 4 (Fig. 36) and the yellow markings of lower face do not extend above the lower third of the inner eye margin (Fig. 39). Averaging larger (wing length usually more than 7 mm) 8

8   Antennal segment 3 viewed from below more than half as long as segment 4 (Fig. 36). Yellow markings of lower face not usually extending above the lower third of the inner eye margin (Fig. 39). Tegulae usually partially or mainly brown. Tergite 1 usually with yellow spots small and well separated, or absent .... *marshamella*

—   Antennal segment 3 viewed from below at most half as long as segment 4 (Fig. 38). Yellow markings of the lower face usually extending halfway up the inner eye margin and attaining the level of the antennal insertions (Fig. 40). Tegulae, aside from the black basal part, entirely yellow with a transparent margin. Tergite 1 usually with the yellow spots large and almost fused .... *fulvicornis*

NOMADA MALE GROUP B

1   Labrum with a large, triangular projection close to the lower edge centrally (Fig. 16). Antennal flagella almost entirely orange. Front femora dilated at base. Large (wing length usually over 8.5mm) .... *armata*

—   Labrum without a large central projection. Antennal flagella dark above. Front femora not dilated at base. Smaller (wing length to 7mm) 2

2   Mandibles bifid at tip (Fig. 2) .... *fabriciana*

—   Mandibles pointed or bluntly rounded at tip (Figs 20–22) 3

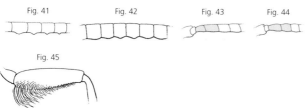

Fig. 41 Fig. 42 Fig. 43 Fig. 44

Fig. 45

3   Tergite 2 reddish or dark with no hint of lateral yellow or whitish spots. Antennae with underside of mid flagellar segments either strongly bulbous or with small, sharp projections (Figs 41 & 42) **4**

—   Tergite 2 with lateral yellow or whitish spots; if rather faint or small (*fuscicornis* and *similis*), underside of mid flagellar segments not especially bulbous and lacking small, sharp projections **5**

4   Dorsal surface of hind femora reddish, at least in apical half. Underside of antennal segments 6–10 with small, sharp projection (Fig. 41). Abdomen predominantly red. Larger (wing length usually at least 6mm) .... *integra*

—   Dorsal surface of hind femora dark except at tip. Underside of antennal segments 5–9 bluntly swollen (Fig. 42). Abdomen darker, at most with a red band across tergite 2. Smaller (wing length no more than 5.5mm) .... *argentata*

5   Antennal segment 3 viewed from the front no more than half the length of segment 4 (Fig. 43) .... typical *flavoguttata*

—   Antennal segment 3 at least as long as segment 4, often longer (Fig. 44) **6**

6   Underside of hind femora with short sparse hairs that do not get longer or denser towards the base. Area between antennal bases with a broad, flat-topped ridge (Fig. 15). Lower edge of clypeus yellow-marked .... *obtusifrons*

—   Underside of hind femora with longer, denser hairs at the base (Fig. 45). Area between antennal bases with a sharp median crest. Lower edge of clypeus dark **7**

7   Posterior face of propodeum with a discrete patch of dense silvery hairs on each side (like Fig. 13). Front tibiae mostly black with yellow markings. Sides of labrum yellow. Abdomen black with conspicuous lateral yellow spots on tergite 2 .... *sheppardana*

—   Posterior face of propodeum without discrete patches of silvery hairs. Front tibiae reddish, at most with a dark posterior mark. Labrum entirely dark. Abdomen mostly reddish with weakly formed lateral yellow spots on tergite 2 (Channel Islands) **8**

8   Scutellum fairly evenly convex. Mid and hind tibiae black dorsally. Smaller (typical wing length 5mm) .... *fuscicornis*

—   Scutellum clearly depressed in the middle with bumps on either side (Fig. 4). Mid and hind tibiae orange dorsally. Larger (typical wing length 6.5mm) .... *similis*

NOMADA MALE GROUP C

1   Pronotal tubercles partially yellow. Abdomen usually extensively red with conspicuous yellow spots or bands on tergites 1–6, tergite 2 typically with narrowly separated yellow spots .... *ferruginata*

—   Pronotal tubercles reddish, brownish or black without any yellow. Abdomen either red with small lateral spots on tergite 2 or, if with extensive yellow marks (*leucophthalma*), the yellow lower face markings barely extend up the inner eye margin **2**

2   Scutellum with red spots or a single red mark. Mandibles with a squared-off or very bluntly
    rounded tip (Figs 21 & 22) **3**

—   Scutellum entirely black. Mandibles more obviously pointed at tip (Fig. 20) **4**

3   Antennal segment 3 clearly shorter than 4 in top view (Fig. 46). Yellow markings
    of lower face extending up the inner eye margin to the midpoint of the eye (Fig. 40).
    Hind femora usually reddish along the entire length of the top; the underside with
    a large shiny hair- and puncture-free zone occupying the apical half. Antennal
    scapes usually partially red in front .... **some *striata***

—   Antennal segment 3 about as long as 4 in top view (Fig. 47). Yellow markings
    of lower face only extending up the lower third of an eye (Fig. 39). Hind femora
    with the top usually only reddish apically; the underside with the shiny hair- and
    puncture-free zone only occupying the apical third. Antennal scapes usually
    entirely black in front .... ***guttulata***

4   Tergites 2–6 with conspicuous yellow bands or narrowly separated spots. Middle
    femora with a long fringe below (Fig. 48). Hind face of propodeum with long
    hairs throughout. Large (typical wing length 8.5mm) .... ***leucophthalma***

—   Abdomen darker, usually with small yellow spots on the sides of tergites 2 and 3.
    Middle femora with a short fringe below (Fig. 49). Hind face of propodeum
    largely bare except for side margins. Small (typical wing length 5mm) .... **some *flavoguttata***

Fig. 46	Fig. 47	Fig. 48	Fig. 49

NOMADA MALE GROUP D

1   Scutellum with a single large yellow mark **2**
—   Scutellum with a pair of yellow or red spots **3**

2   Antennal flagella black above. Tergite 2 with well-separated spots. Surface of
    scutum shining between the punctures. Front coxae with an apical projection .... **some *rufipes***

—   Antennal flagella entirely or mostly yellow above. Tergite 2 with a complete
    yellow band (at most narrowly broken in middle). Surface of scutum very
    dull and roughened. Front coxae blunt apically .... ***fucata* (summer generation)**

3   Scutum shining between the punctures. Underside of hind femora shining
    with just a few punctures and tiny hairs (Fig. 50). Hind face of propodeum
    without long, erect hairs. Clypeus entirely yellow. Small and dumpy (wing
    length 6mm) .... ***roberjeotiana***

—   Scutum dull, the punctures virtually touching. Underside of hind femora with dense short
    hairs and dense punctures. Hind face of propodeum with long erect hairs. Clypeus
    black-marked at top. Slimmer and usually larger (wing length to 10mm) **4**

Fig. 50

4   Tergites 1–3 black with paired yellow spots, any red markings limited to halos around the yellow markings. Scutellum with a pair of conspicuous yellow spots. Tibiae orange and yellow-marked .... *subcornuta*

—   Tergite 1 with a red band and usually without yellow spots. Tergites 2 and 3 with yellow bands or spots and variable amounts of red integument along hind margin and along midline. Scutellum black or with a pair of red markings. Tibiae red and black-marked .... **some *flava* and some *panzeri* (see group E)**

NOMADA MALE GROUP E

1   Tergite 2 with a complete yellow band, or large yellow spots that are separated by less than a quarter of their width **2**

—   Tergite 2 with yellow spots separated by at least half their width **7**

2   Antennae with segment 4–13 bearing pointed tubercles on their hind faces (Fig. 41), with segment 3 in front view about as long as 4 (Fig. 51) .... *lathburiana*

—   Antennae without such tubercles, with segment 3 in front view clearly shorter than 4 (Fig. 52) **3**

3   Scutellum with a single yellow mark. Antennal flagella orange with a discrete black mark on dorsal face usually taking in segments 6–8. Tibiae and tarsi extensively yellow, the tibiae without black markings .... *fucata* **(spring generation)**

—   Scutellum black or with a pair of red spots. Antennal flagella reddish with any darkening of the dorsal face extending from the base towards the tip. Tibiae and tarsi reddish, with black markings sometimes present on the fore and mid tibiae **4**

4   Mandibles bifid at tip (Fig. 19) .... *ruficornis*

—   Mandibles pointed at tip (Fig. 20) **5**

5   Yellow markings of lower face only extending up the lower third of the inner eye margin (Fig. 39). Tergites 2–6 always with broad, continuous yellow bands, at most slightly incised in the middle. Middle femora with hair fringe below about as long as the greatest width of the femora (Fig. 48) .... *signata*

—   Yellow markings of lower face extending halfway up the inner eye margin (Fig. 40). Tergites 2–6 with yellow bands often narrower and more interrupted in the middle or clearly broken **6**

6   Underside of middle femora with the hair fringe about half as long as the greatest width of the femora (Fig. 53). Pile on top of the thorax orange-brown in fresh specimens, other hairs of the thorax and legs buffish. Often large and robust with extensive yellow on the tergites (wing length to 10mm) .... *flava*

—   Underside of middle femora with the hair fringe about as long as the greatest width of the femora (Fig. 48). Body hairs paler, often silvery on the legs. Typically smaller, slimmer and darker-looking (typical wing length 7mm) .... **typical** *panzeri*

7   Pygidium with apical margin rounded or straight, not or barely notched (Fig. 54) **8**

—   Pygidium distinctly notched apically (Fig.55) **9**

Fig. 51   Fig. 52 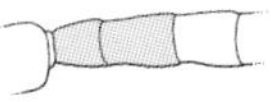   Fig. 53    Fig. 54 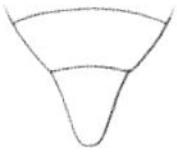   Fig. 55

8   Flagellar segments of antennae without tubercles below. Lower face (including entire clypeus), front of antennal scapes and markings of the tergites creamy-white. Tibiae without any dark markings .... *baccata*

—   Antennal segments 4–12 with distinct subapical tubercles below (Fig. 56). Lower face (including the lower part of the clypeus) and markings of the tergites yellow. All tibiae with dark markings (Channel Islands) .... *castellana*

9   Underside of middle femora with tiny hairs, their length only about a quarter the width of an ocellus (Fig. 57) .... *conjungens*

—   Underside of middle femora with a distinct hair fringe (Figs 48 & 58) **10**

Fig. 56   Fig. 57   Fig. 58

10   Mandibles squared off or very bluntly rounded at their tips (Fig. 22). Scutellum frequently with a single large red mark. Build relatively stocky, the legs rather short with stouter femora .... **some** *striata*

—   Mandibles pointed at their tip (Fig. 20). Scutellum either black or with a pair of red spots. Build slimmer and longer-legged **11**

11   Underside of middle femora with the hair fringe about half as long as the greatest width of the femora (Fig. 58). All legs longer and slimmer, the second segment of the hind tarsi in top view about 3–4 times as long as wide (Fig. 29). Antennae longer, the final segment about twice as long as wide .... *hirtipes*

—   Underside of middle femora with the hair fringe almost or fully as long as the greatest width of the femora (Fig. 48). All legs shorter and stouter, the second segment of the hind tarsi about 2.5 times as long as wide (Fig. 28). Antennae shorter, the final segment about 1.5 times as long as wide .... **darker** *panzeri*

Nomada argentata Herrich-Schäffer, 1839   **Silver-sided Nomad Bee**

Plate 14

Description & similar species FW 6–6.5mm female, 6mm male. A rather small, dark nomad, one of the few lacking any yellow or whitish markings on the tergites. Females have a broad dark red band across the middle of the abdomen, red spots on the scutellum and sides of the thorax, also red tegulae, pronotal collar, mandibles and extreme lower face. The legs are red and black. The sides of the abdomen have dense patches of silvery hairs. Confusion is most likely with females of *N. integra* but the legs and antennae of *N. argentata* are darker and a large red patch is present on each side of the thorax. Males are similar to females but usually darker, and have the face and labrum almost entirely black, in contrast to most male nomads. The antennae are very short for a male nomad and the middle segments of the flagella have sharp projections on their hind face (a character only otherwise seen in the very different-looking *N. lathburiana*). **Variation** Males can have an abdomen that ranges from almost completely black to broadly red-banded like the females, and some have red scutellar spots. The

female

amount of black on the male legs also varies considerably, though the hind femora are usually entirely black except for the extreme apex. **Flight season** Univoltine, flying from mid-July to mid-September, peaking later where the host forages on Devil's-bit Scabious. **Habitat** Typically dry chalk grassland, but also coastal grassland, heathland/acid grassland, moorland edge, coastal dunes and woodland rides. Plentiful scabiouses (Field, Small or Devil's-bit) are a requirement of the host. **Flowers visited** Typically scabiouses, though they will visit thistles before scabiouses are in flower. **Status & distribution** A rare species, mostly recorded from southern England north to Oxfordshire and the East Anglian Brecks. Greatly declined (especially in southwest England), with most modern locations within Dorset, Salisbury Plain, Surrey and the Brecks. Very rare in Ireland. Not recorded from Wales, Scotland or the Channel Islands. **Host(s)** *Andrena marginata*.

Nomada armata Herrich-Schäffer, 1839   **Armed Nomad Bee**
Plate 14

Description & similar species FW 8.5–9.5mm (sexes similar). The largest of our reddish nomads (*N. flava*-sized), easily distinguished from all others by the large triangular projection of the labrum. Females have small yellow lateral spots on tergites 2–4 and a vaguer orange patch on 5. The scutellum has a pair of red spots and the antennal flagella are orange with a broad dark subterminal band and orange tip, reminiscent of *N. fabriciana*. Dense patches of silvery hairs occur along the sides of the propodeum and along the sides of the thorax. Males are similar but slimmer with a furrier thorax, entirely orange antennal flagella and no

red spots on the scutellum. The front femora are strangely flattened and broadened. **Variation** Little noted. **Flight season** Univoltine, flying from late June to early August. **Habitat** Mostly chalk grassland (all modern sites), but previously also found off chalk on coastal grassland, moorland edge and soft rock cliffs. Plentiful Field Scabious is a requirement of the host. **Flowers visited** Mostly Field Scabious and Small Scabious. **Status & distribution** Rare and declining, with modern records confined to Salisbury Plain, with outliers in Dorset and Oxfordshire. Older records are scattered across southern England from Cornwall to Kent north to Norfolk, also south Wales (Glamorganshire). Not recorded from Scotland, Ireland or the Channel Islands. It has always been much rarer and more geographically restricted than its host. **Host(s)** *Andrena hattorfiana*.

Nomada baccata Smith, 1844   Bear-clawed Nomad Bee
Plate 13

Description & similar species FW 4.5–5mm female, 5mm male. A smallish nomad with very distinctive females that have extensively orange-red bodies with rather limited black markings on the head and thorax (the red longitudinal stripes of the scutum being much broader than the black ones). The propodeum is mostly reddish with a black median stripe. The antennae are completely orange.

The tergites have creamy-white rather than yellow markings. Several particularly long black comb spines are present at the tips of the hind tibiae (resembling the claws of a bear paw). Females often appear pinkish-orange in the field. Males have the thorax and top of the head black, and the antennae extensively darkened above. The lower face and front of the antennal scapes are creamy-white. The orange pygidium lacks a notch at its tip. **Variation** Minor variation in markings. **Flight season** Univoltine, flying from mid-July to early September. **Habitat** Dry, sandy heathland, especially where pits and cuttings are present. The host has a liking for soft sand. **Flowers visited** British records include heathers, bramble, Common Ragwort, Creeping Thistle and thymes. **Status & distribution** Almost entirely confined to the southern heaths of Dorset, Hampshire, Surrey and Sussex, with a small outlying population in the Suffolk Sandlings. Often abundant where found. Also recorded from the Channel Islands (Jersey). **Host(s)** *Andrena argentata*.

Nomada castellana Dusmet, 1913   Castell's Nomad Bee
not illustrated

Description & similar species FW 4.5–5.5mm (sexes similar). Extremely similar to *N. flavoguttata*, though both sexes have a yellow rather than dark labrum. Foreign literature cites differences in the hind tibial comb spines of the females of these two species, but this appears to be overstated, and this character varies greatly in *N. flavoguttata*. In the few female specimens seen, the lateral patches of silvery hairs on the hind face of the propodeum are less conspicuous than in *N. flavoguttata*. Males have distinct subapical tubercles on the undersides of antennal segments 4–12 (such tubercles barely if at all present in *N. flavoguttata*), and the pygidium has a rounded tip with at most a slight apical notch (tip distinctly notched in *N. flavoguttata*). In the limited male material seen, small red markings are present on the sides of the thorax beneath the wings and the front of the scape is entirely yellow (usually dark in *N. flavoguttata*). Beware the occasional male of *N. flavoguttata* with a pale labrum. **Variation** Moderate variation in the extent of red and yellow markings in both sexes. Some males (including the Jersey specimen) have a pair of yellow spots on the scutellum; in others red spots are present. **Flight season** Regarded as univoltine on the continent, flying from late April to mid-July. **Habitat** Preferences unclear. **Flowers visited** Unknown. **Status & distribution** The only British record is for a male found on Jersey in June 1991. **Host(s)** Unclear, but possibly some of the univoltine 'mini-miner' *Andrena* species, with *A. anthrisci* (a non-British species which occurs in Normandy not far from Jersey) and *A. alfkenella* cited in literature.

Nomada conjungens Herrich-Schäffer, 1839   **Fringeless Nomad Bee**
Plate 14

Description & similar species FW 6.5–7mm female, 6.5mm male. A medium-sized reddish nomad. Females have a dark labrum and resemble a large, slim, long-legged *N. flavoguttata* but lack patches of silvery hairs on the sides of the propodeum and have two discrete patches of red on each side of the thorax as opposed to one large one. The tips of the hind tibiae have several comb spines but one of these is much longer than the others. Tergites 2, 3 and sometimes 4 have small lateral yellow spots. The scutum has two longitudinal red stripes down the middle, and red markings from the lower face extend completely around the eyes. The rather long antennae can be almost completely orange except for some darkening of the back of the scape. Males have the thorax and base of tergite 1 completely black, and darker antennae than females. The labrum

female

is yellow, and they are more likely to be confused with species such as *N. hirtipes* rather than *N. flavoguttata* but can be easily separated by the presence of only tiny hairs on the underside of the mid femora as opposed to an obvious hair fringe. **Variation** Minor variation in the shape of the body markings. **Flight season** Univoltine, flying in May and June. **Habitat** British records include chalk downland, soft rock cliffs, coastal grasslands and heathland. The host requires plentiful umbellifers (e.g. Hemlock Water-dropwort). **Flowers visited** British records include various umbellifers and a spurge. **Status & distribution** A rare species, with relatively few records scattered across southern England north to Herefordshire. Also recorded from the Channel Islands (Guernsey). **Host(s)** *Andrena proxima* (both forms).

Nomada errans Lepeletier, 1841   **Purbeck Nomad Bee**
Plate 14

Description & similar species FW 5mm female, 4.5mm male. Both sexes resemble small examples of the black and yellow form of *N. rufipes* but can be distinguished by the shiny, puncture-free lower propodeum, the black sternites and more extensively black tergite 4 (with pale marks restricted to the sides). Body markings are creamy-white rather than yellow. Females have reddish antennae (mostly black in *N. rufipes*). **Variation** Little noted. **Flight season** Univoltine, flying in July and August. **Habitat** Cliff-top limestone grassland and clay-rich soft rock cliffs. The host requires plentiful umbellifers, especially Wild Carrot. **Flowers visited** Wild Carrot, Common Ragwort and Yarrow. **Status & distribution** Only ever known in Britain from Durlston Head, Dorset. The last British record appears to be 1982, and it may be extinct. **Host(s)** *Andrena nitidiuscula*.

Nomada fabriciana (Linnaeus, 1767)   **Fabricius' Nomad Bee**

Plate 14

Description & similar species FW 5.5–8mm female, 5–7mm male. A small to medium-sized reddish nomad usually with small yellow spots on the sides of tergites 2 and 3 and an almost entirely black face and thorax. Easily distinguished from all other nomads by the unique combination of a black labrum and bifid mandibles. Females usually have antennal segments 4–7 and 12 orange and the rest dark. Of the other reddish nomads only *N. armata* shows this character. Males resemble females but have the antennae and tegulae entirely dark and longer hairs on the head and thorax. **Variation** Substantial size variation that can result in a superficial resemblance to *N. flavoguttata* in small examples but an appearance approaching *N. armata* in the largest females (possibly individuals that have developed in the nests of larger host species such as *Andrena nigroaenea*). Females occasionally lack any yellow spots on the tergites, and both sexes can have black bands of variable intensity across the tergites. The mid and hind tibiae vary from mostly reddish to mostly blackish. Very dark females can have the antennae and legs almost entirely black. **Flight season** Mostly bivoltine, flying from March to June and June to August. Possibly univoltine in some places, e.g. in Ireland and where

female

species such as *Andrena nigroaenea* are being used. **Habitat** Like the main host, uses a wide variety of habitats, both open and wooded, coastal and inland. **Flowers visited** Assorted flowers, including spring-blossoming shrubs, dandelions, buttercups, Garlic Mustard and Primrose in spring; ragworts, thistles and scabiouses in summer. **Status & distribution** Locally common in southern Britain but scarcer in the north, with a few records for Scotland. Widespread but local in Ireland. Recorded from several of the Channel Islands. **Host(s)** Primarily *Andrena bicolor* but possibly also *A. angustior*, *A. nigroaenea*, *A. flavipes*, *A. varians* and *A. chrysosceles*.

female, dark example

male

Nomada ferruginata

Yellow-shouldered Nomad Bee

(Linnaeus, 1767) Plate 14

Description & similar species FW 6–8mm female, 6–7.5mm male. A medium-sized reddish nomad with females that superficially resemble *N. fabriciana* but have bright yellow pronotal tubercles, unbanded antennae, a pale labrum and a pair of yellow or orange scutellar spots. The lower face is orange and the labrum often has a pair of dark spots. The antennae are orange below but brownish above. Tergite 2 has small, round yellow spots at the sides. Tergite 5 can be mainly yellow. Males have considerably more yellow on the tergites than females. The combination of partially yellow pronotal tubercles and entirely black antennal scapes will separate them from other nomads with red and yellow tergites. **Variation** In females, the scutellar spots can be yellow or reddish, and the yellow mark on tergite 5 can be weak or absent. The orange or yellow markings of the lower face can extend completely around the eyes in some individuals or not at all in others. The dark spots on the labrum can be missing. The pronotal collar can be dark or have small yellow spots. Some males have black bands across tergites 1–5, whilst in others these bands may be restricted to tergites 4 and 5. **Flight**

female

season Univoltine, flying from late March to mid-May, peaking with the pussy-willow blossom. **Habitat** A variety of willow-rich habitats, including old quarries, woodland rides and heathland. **Flowers visited** Grey and Goat Willow, dandelions, Lesser Celandine and Blackcurrant. **Status & distribution** A rare species, with records scattered across southern Britain (including Wales) north to Warwickshire and Norfolk. It has always been much scarcer than the host. Not recorded from Scotland, Ireland or the Channel Islands. **Host(s)** *Andrena praecox*.

Nomada flava Panzer, 1798

Flavous Nomad Bee

Plate 13

Description & similar species FW 7.5–10mm (sexes similar). Usually the commonest of the large tricoloured nomads with a red-marked thorax, so a useful yardstick for comparing others. In females, the tergites are extensively yellow, usually with the yellow spots of tergite 2 narrowly separated by red. Tergite 1 has a broad red band but usually lacks any yellow. The scutum is red-striped, the scutellum entirely red, and the sides of the thorax have a red patch that is sometimes divided into two. The propodeum can be all black or have small red markings. The hairs on the propodeum, hind coxae and sides of the thorax have a yellowish tint and are never silvery. The lower face is extensively red, with markings extending completely around the eyes. The antennal flagella are completely orange, usually without any darkening above. The erect hairs of the clypeus and labrum are yellowish. Males average smaller than females, with an almost completely black thorax (a pair of red scutellar spots can be present) that bears longer hairs. Males are often stated to be indistinguishable from *N. panzeri* but large, robust *flava/panzeri* males with a short hair fringe beneath the hind femora, brownish thoracic hairs and all flagellar segments darkened above will almost certainly be *N. flava*. Some males can also closely resemble *N. signata* but have the yellow markings of the lower face extending much further up the inner eye margins. It is worth noting that *N. flava* does not occur in Scotland or

Ireland, making the identification of *N. panzeri* more straightforward here. **Variation** Some variation in the extent of yellow on the tergites of both sexes and of red on the female thorax and head. Females with dark scutums and much reduced yellow markings on the tergites can occasionally be encountered. Males vary considerably in size. They can have the scutellum entirely black or with red spots, and the pronotal collar can be red- or yellow-marked (though rarely conspicuously so). Some males cannot be confidently assigned to either *N. flava* or *N. panzeri*. **Flight season** Univoltine, flying from late March to June, peaking in late spring. **Habitat** Varied, including open and wooded habitats, coastal and inland. It is one of the commoner nomads of farmland, urban settings and woods. **Flowers visited** A variety of spring-blossoming shrubs and smaller flowers such as dandelions, Greater Stitchwort, Garlic Mustard, Wood Spurge, Rape, Bluebell and Cow Parsley. **Status & distribution** One of the commonest large nomads over much of southern Britain, but few records north of Yorkshire. Recorded from several of the Channel Islands. Not recorded from Scotland or Ireland. **Host(s)** Primarily *Andrena scotica*, but possibly also *A. nigroaenea*, *A. nitida* and *A. ferox*.

female

male

Nomada flavoguttata (Kirby, 1802) **Little Nomad Bee**
Plate 14

Description & similar species FW 4–6.5mm (sexes similar). A small reddish nomad typically with a dark labrum. Females have the abdomen extensively red, usually with small yellow spots at the sides of tergites 2 and 3. The scutellum has two red spots and the sides of the thorax have a large red patch (sometimes divided into two). The scutum has red side margins and often a pair of longitudinal stripes down the middle. The tegulae, pronotal collar and pronotal tubercles are reddish. The propodeum is black with a conspicuous patch of silvery hairs on each side. The lower face is reddish, with the markings sometimes extending completely around the eyes. The antennae are orange below but brownish above. Females of *N. conjungens* are similar but larger and slimmer, without patches of silver hairs on the propodeum. *N. castellana* is barely distinguishable but apparently never has a dark labrum (see that species for more details). Males of *N. flavoguttata* usually have the thorax entirely dark, the lower face yellow, the tops of the antennal flagella blackish and tergites 1–3 often black- and red-banded. The legs are more extensively black than in females. Antennal segment 3 is very short, and less than half as long as 4 when viewed from below. **Variation** The yellow spots at the sides of tergites 2 and 3 are occasionally missing. The extent of red on the female head and thorax is variable, with red markings completely surrounding the eyes in some individuals but barely in others. A pair of well-formed longitudinal stripes can run down the middle of the scutum but are often absent, though a red stripe remains above each wing base. Both sexes have variable amounts of black on the tergites, and at one extreme well-formed black bands are present on the intermediate tergites, whilst at the other extreme the abdomen is almost entirely red except for the yellow spots. Males sometimes have the labrum yellow and could be mistaken for *N. castellana*, but lack tubercles on the antennal segments, have a more deeply notched pygidium, and the scape is usually dark. They occasionally have a pair of small red scutellar spots. Size variation in both sexes is substantial, with the smallest examples matching (and resembling) *N. sheppardana* and the largest ones almost matching typical *N. fabriciana*. **Flight season** Bivoltine in most areas (like the main host *Andrena minutula*) with a spring generation flying from late March to June and a summer one from late June to September. Almost certainly univoltine in northern and upland areas where *A. subopaca* is being used. **Habitat** Highly varied, reflecting the various hosts being used, but extending to higher altitudes than many nomads when using *A. subopaca*. **Flowers visited** Assorted species, including spring-flowering shrubs, composites such as dandelions, also umbellifers, crucifers, Sheep's-bit and Tormentil. **Status & distribution** Common over much of southern England but scarcer in Wales, Scotland and Ireland. Only known on the Channel Islands from an old Jersey record. **Host(s)** Mini-miners, including *Andrena minutula*, *A. subopaca*, and possibly *A. semilaevis* and *A. falsifica*.

female

male

Nomada flavopicta (Kirby, 1802)   **Blunthorn Nomad Bee**
Plate 13

Description & similar species FW 6.5–7.5mm female, 7–8mm male. A medium-sized, boldly black- and yellow-marked nomad with almost completely black antennae and two yellow spots on the scutellum. The tegulae, pronotal collar and pronotal tubercles are also bright yellow. The yellow spots on tergites 2 and 3 are widely separated, but those on tergite 1 almost touch or narrowly fuse. The hind tibiae lack any comb spines. Females have an almost hairless thorax (even the underside), orange legs and an orange lower face. The front coxae are unusually triangular with pointed tips. Males are very similar to females (more so than most nomads) but with yellow lower faces, partially black femora and longer hairs on the thorax. The black and yellow form of *N. rufipes* is the only other black and yellow species with black antennae but is smaller, with a single yellow spot on the scutellum and an entirely black tergite 1. **Variation** Minor variation in the extent of pale markings. **Flight season** Univoltine, flying from late June to mid-September. **Habitat** Varied, reflecting the preferences of its hosts, though often using *Melitta tricincta* on chalk downland, *M. leporina* on more neutral grasslands and *M. haemorrhoidalis* on heathland. **Flowers visited** British records include ragworts, thistles, knapweeds, brambles, heathers, scabiouses, Common Fleabane and umbellifers such as Upright Hedge-parsley. **Status & distribution** Widespread but very local in England north to Yorkshire, though hotspots of abundance occur in places such as the North and South Downs. Rare in Wales. Not recorded from Scotland or Ireland. Recorded from Jersey, Guernsey and Alderney in the Channel Islands. **Host(s)** The blunthorn bees *Melitta leporina*, *M. tricincta* and *M. haemorrhoidalis*.

Nomada fucata Panzer, 1798

Painted Nomad Bee

Plate 13

Description & similar species FW 6.5–8.5mm female, 6.5–9mm male. A medium-sized, tricoloured species with a black- and red-banded tergite 1 and usually more or less complete yellow bands on tergites 2–5. The scutellum has a single yellow spot and the scutum and propodeum are black. The tegulae, pronotal tubercles and often the pronotal collar are yellow. Females have the lower face, antennae and most parts of the legs orange. In males the lower face is yellow, the femora more extensively black, and the tibiae and tarsi extensively yellow. They can also have a small yellow patch on the sides of the thorax at the front and

their antennal flagella usually have a black patch halfway along the dorsal face. The only other tricoloured nomad with a single spot on the scutellum is the red-marked form of *N. rufipes*, but this has widely separated yellow spots on tergite 2 and mostly dark antennae. **Variation** Both sexes can have variable amounts of red on tergite 1, and the yellow band of tergite 2 can be interrupted by red in the middle, creating an appearance approaching *N. rufipes*. The summer generation is much shorter-haired than the spring one and generally brighter with more extensive yellow markings. Most spring males have a black pronotal collar and the sides of the thorax entirely black. Summer males often have a yellow mark on

male

the side of the thorax, and occasionally have some yellow on tergite 1 and the antennal scapes entirely orange. **Flight season** Bivoltine as per the host, with a spring generation that flies from April to June and a summer one that flies in July and August. **Habitat** Various, as for the host, but most frequent on soft rock cliffs, chalk downland and brownfield sites such as quarries and sandpits. **Flowers visited** Records include spring-blossoming shrubs, composites of various sorts, buttercups and cinquefoils. **Status & distribution** Widespread and locally common in southern England with a recent expansion into the Midlands (north to Shropshire) following a similar expansion of the host. Most records in Wales are for the south coast, but it was recently discovered in Denbighshire. Not recorded in Scotland and Ireland. Recorded from several of the Channel Islands. It was considered a rarity in Victorian times even in the south and is one of our most rapidly increasing bees. **Host(s)** *Andrena flavipes*.

Nomada fulvicornis Fabricius, 1793   Orange-horned Nomad Bee
Plate 13

Description & similar species FW 7.5–9.5mm female, 7–9mm male. Females of the darker spring generation rather resemble *N. marshamella* in the field, whilst the brighter second generation often resembles oversized *N. flavopicta*. They can usually be easily separated from these by the reddish edges to the yellow markings of tergites 1, 2 and sometimes 3 and the extensively reddish sternites. They vary from the closely related *N. subcornuta* by the presence of yellow markings on tergite 1 plus various other features (see *N. subcornuta*). Males tend to lack any obvious red on the tergites and closely resemble *N. subcornuta*, but the yellow spots on tergite 2 tend to be more narrowly separated or even fused. They can also be overlooked as *N. marshamella*, but the yellow markings of tergite 1 and the inner eye margins are more extensive in *N. fulvicornis*, the tegulae are yellow without any brown markings, and the antennae have a shorter third segment. **Variation** Considerable, particularly within females. Those of the spring generation generally have less extensive yellow markings, with the propodeum and sides of the thorax usually completely black. The tibiae and tarsi are entirely orange, and the tegulae often have brown markings. Second-generation females often have a pair of yellow marks on the propodeum, yellow and orange patches on the sides of the thorax, larger scutellar and tergite spots, yellow tegulae and partially yellow tibiae and tarsi. The sternites are usually more extensively yellow-marked. Some subtle variation also exists between populations parasitising *Andrena bimaculata* versus those parasitising *A. pilipes*. Females occasionally have the tops of the antennae considerably darkened, and some can lack any red markings on the tergites or have these restricted to tergite 1. In males, the extent of yellow on the tergites, pronotal collar and scutellum can all vary (scutellar spots can be present or absent) and a yellow spot is occasionally present on the sides of the thorax. In both sexes, the spring generation has much longer hairs on the head and thorax. **Flight season** Bivoltine in most parts of its range, with a spring generation that flies from March to May and a second one that usually appears in July and flies until late August. Populations in Yorkshire (presumably parasitising *A. tibialis*) appear to be univoltine, flying in spring (but peaking much earlier than *N. subcornuta*). **Habitat** Heathland and sandy brownfield sites (especially populations associated with *A. bimaculata*), also soft rock cliffs (especially populations associated with *A. pilipes*). Occasionally on chalk grassland and at saltmarsh edge. **Flowers visited** The spring generation will visit willows, Wild Cherry, spurges, brassicas and daisy. The summer one uses brambles, thistles, Rosebay Willowherb, Common Ragwort and Goldenrod. **Status & distribution** Widespread but very localised in England north to Yorkshire and with a few records for south Wales. Not recorded from Scotland or Ireland. Present on the Channel Islands, though records need to be checked for *N. subcornuta* (early spring and late summer records are likely to represent *N. fulvicornis*). **Host(s)** *Andrena bimaculata*, *A. pilipes* and *A. tibialis*.

female

male

Nomada fuscicornis Nylander, 1848   **Small Guernsey Nomad Bee**
not illustrated

Description & similar species FW 5.5–6mm female, 5–5.5mm male. Females, which are about the size of *N. flavoguttata*, are one of three reddish species lacking pale markings on the tergites

female

and without any red or yellow spots on the scutellum. They can be separated from the form of *N. fabriciana* without yellow spots on the tergites by the mostly yellow mandibles, which have bluntly-pointed rather than bifid tips. *N. similis* is a larger, redder species with the scutellum clearly depressed in the middle, longer antennae, redder legs and a discrete patch of silvery hairs on the sides of the thorax. Males resemble females but have ill-defined yellow spots on the sides of tergite 2 and a tuft of long white hairs on the underside of the hind femora at the base. **Variation** Not noted. **Flight season** Univoltine, flying from July to September. **Habitat** On the Channel Islands, coastal heathland, dunes and dry, sandy grassland with plentiful hawkish composites for the host. **Flowers visited** Foreign records include Yellow-flowered hawkish composites, thistles, Common Ragwort, Yarrow and Sheep's-bit. **Status & distribution** Recorded only from the Channel Islands (Jersey and Sark), but possibly extinct on Jersey. **Host(s)** *Panurgus calcaratus*.

Nomada goodeniana (Kirby, 1802)   Gooden's Nomad Bee
Plate 13

Description & similar species FW 7.5–10mm female, 7.5–8.5mm male. A large, boldly marked, black and yellow nomad with complete yellow bands on tergites 2–5 and often also 1. In females, the scutellum has a pair of yellow spots and the tegulae, pronotal collar and pronotal tubercles are yellow. A pair of yellow spots can also be present on the propodeum. The lower edge of the clypeus is orange, with narrow yellow markings alongside the inner eye margins. The antennae (including the scapes) are usually completely orange. The legs are orange with the femora variably black at the base. Males have the lower face and inner eye margins more broadly yellow than females and the hind face of antennal segments 1–7 blackish. A small yellow mark is usually present at the side of the thorax near the front coxae. There are patches of dense adpressed hairs on the underside of the hind femora and on the adjacent trochanters. Over much of Britain, confusion in the field is most likely with *N. marshamella*, which has well-separated spots on tergite 2, the spots on tergite 1 small or absent and, in the females, orange tegulae. On the Channel Islands great care is required to distinguish *N. goodeniana* from the very similar *N. succincta* (see that species for distinctions). **Variation** Moderate variation in the extent of yellow markings on the tergites, thorax and face. Tergite 1 can have narrowly separated spots or complete bands. The yellow propodeal spots can be quite large, especially in the second generation (both male and female), but are typically small or absent in the spring generation and males sometimes lack scutellar spots. The antennal scape of the female is occasionally black behind, as in *N. succincta*. The labrum can be all orange or partially darkened. **Flight season** Typically univoltine, flying from April to June, but regularly bivoltine in some coastal districts, probably mostly where it uses *Andrena thoracica*. **Habitat** Assorted habitats, both open and wooded, coastal and inland. One of the more frequent nomads of urban settings. **Flowers visited** Records include various spring-flowering blossoms, yellow composites such as dandelions, also Cow Parsley, Rape, forget-me-nots, buttercups and Greater Stitchwort. **Status & distribution** Common throughout much of southern Britain but more localised in Scotland and Ireland. Recorded from most of the Channel Islands. **Host(s)** *Andrena nigroaenea*, *A. nitida* and *A. thoracica*; possibly also *A. scotica* to a small extent.

female

male

Nomada guttulata Schenck, 1861   **Short-spined Nomad Bee**

Plate 14

Description & similar species FW 5.5–6mm (sexes similar). Females are rather small and reddish with small lateral yellow spots on the tergites, a red-striped scutum and red markings on the lower face that extend around the eyes. The mandibles have blunt, rounded-off or even somewhat squared-off tips like *N. striata*. Indeed, they are very easily overlooked as small *N. striata*, but the 3–4 comb spines at the end of the hind tibiae take the form of tiny black blunt projections arranged in such a tight row that they look almost like a single black appendage. There are also two patches of rather conspicuous silvery hairs on the hind face of the propodeum (propodeum almost bare in *N. striata*). Males closely resemble small individuals of *N. striata* but have the antennal scapes completely black, a longer third antennal segment and the yellow markings of the lower face barely extending up the eye margins. The hind femora are usually more extensively black, and the shiny apical zone on the underside is much more limited in extent. As in *N. striata*, the scutellum is red-marked and the pronotal collar orange, unusual features for male nomads. **Variation** Minor variation in the extent of yellow and red body markings. **Flight season** Univoltine, flying in May and June. **Habitat** Quite varied as per the host, including open woodland, unimproved grassland, vegetated shingle and occasionally gardens. **Flowers visited** Germander Speedwell, buttercups and Silverweed. **Status & distribution** A very scarce species, with scattered records across southern England north to Shropshire, though relatively few modern ones. Like the host, it seems to exist at very low population levels and can be hard to detect. Not recorded from Wales, Scotland or Ireland. **Host(s)** *Andrena labiata*.

female

male

Nomada hirtipes Pérez, 1884   **Long-horned Nomad Bee**

Plate 13

Description & similar species FW 6.5–8mm (sexes similar). Females are one of several medium-sized reddish nomads with a red-marked thorax, red markings on the lower face that extend around the eyes and well-separated yellow spots on the sides of tergite 2. Those spots are especially round and higher than broad. The build is also relatively slim and long-legged, and the antennae are unusually long. Under a microscope, the antennal flagella will be seen to have tiny but outstanding hairs on the hind surface. Darker *N. panzeri* can look similar but have different body proportions, the lateral spots of tergite 2 wider and more triangular, and no outstanding hairs on the antennae; *N. striata* females have squared-off mandible tips and a stockier, shorter-legged build. Males of *N. hirtipes* have a dark, rather furry thorax, more extensive yellow markings on the tergites than females, a yellow lower face and darker antennae. The antennal scapes are yellow in front and the flagella unusually long. The hair fringe beneath the hind femora is shorter than in *N. panzeri* but much longer than in *N. conjungens*. Males of *N. ferruginata* can look very similar but have partially yellow pronotal tubercles, entirely black antennal scapes and a longer hair fringe below the mid femora. **Variation** Minor variation in the extent of red and yellow markings in both sexes. **Flight season** Univoltine, flying from late April to mid-June. **Habitat** Quite varied, like the host, but including south-facing scrubby grassland slopes, old cuttings and quarries, even churchyards. The host forages heavily on Hawthorn. **Flowers visited** Cow Parsley, dandelions, Wild Strawberry, Cypress Spurge and Cuckooflower. **Status & distribution** Very scarce with scattered records across southern England from Devon to Kent and north to Shropshire; also south Wales (Glamorganshire). Not recorded from Scotland, Ireland or the Channel Islands. **Host(s)** *Andrena bucephala*.

Nomada integra Brullé, 1832   Cat's-ear Nomad Bee

Plate 14

Description & similar species FW 6–7mm (sexes similar). One of a small number of nomads with a complete lack of yellow or white markings on the tergites. Females have the tergites extensively red with black patches at the sides of tergites 2 and 3 and a black band around the base of 4 which tends to show through the translucent apical margin of 3. The thorax is black apart from a pair of red spots on the scutellum and reddish tegulae, pronotal collar and pronotal tubercles. The face is black except for the mandibles and lower edge of the clypeus, and the antennal flagella are reddish with some darkening above. The mandibles are very bluntly rounded. They can be separated from *N. argentata* by the lack of a red patch on the sides of the thorax, more extensively red antennae, legs and abdomen (the latter without such conspicuous patches of silvery hairs at the sides), duller scutum and dense punctures on the underside of the hind femora basally. Females of the two Channel Island species *N. fuscicornis* and *N. similis* have the scutellum entirely black. Males resemble females (more so than most nomads) but have projections beneath antennal segments 5–9 and a hairier thorax. The hind femora have the

undersides densely white-haired. **Variation** Both sexes show variation in the amount of black on the tergites, legs and antennal scapes, and also in the size of the scutellar spots, which can be missing in some males. **Flight season** Univoltine, flying from May to July. **Habitat** Typically heathland, moorland edge, acid grassland and coastal cliff-top grassland. The host requires plentiful yellow-flowered composites such as Cat's-ear. **Flowers visited** Yellow-flowered composites such as Cat's-ear and dandelions, also buttercups and mouse-ears. **Status & distribution** Widespread but localised in England north to Yorkshire. Rare in Wales and not recorded from Scotland and Ireland. On the Channel Islands recorded only from Sark. **Host(s)** *Andrena humilis*.

Nomada lathburiana (Kirby, 1802)   **Lathbury's Nomad Bee**
Plate 13

Description & similar species FW 7–9mm female, 7.5–9mm male. A *N. flava*-sized tricoloured nomad. Fresh females are readily recognised by the reddish pile on top of the thorax (this can fade in old individuals) and the red-bordered yellow spots on the scutellum. The scutum is black, and the red markings of the lower face do not extend around the eyes. Tergite 1 has a broad red band. Tergites 2 and 3 have continuous yellow bands which can be variably infiltrated by red in the middle. Males have small scutellar spots, yellow face markings and darker antennae. They are easily distinguished from similar nomads by the presence of a sharp projection on the hind face of antennal segments 4–13. **Variation** Both sexes show variation in the extent of the scutellar and head markings. Females can have variable amounts of red on tergites 2 and 3, and dwarf females with wing lengths as short as 6.5mm are occasionally encountered. Males show additional variation in the extent of yellow on the tibiae, and the tegulae can be yellow or orange. **Flight season** Univoltine, flying from April to July (occasionally into August), peaking in late spring. **Habitat** Usually associated with large host colonies on gorse-clad hillsides, sandy heathland paths and the vertical faces of sandpits. **Flowers visited** Various spring-blossoming shrubs, dandelions and Germander Speedwell. **Status & distribution** Widespread but patchily distributed in Britain north to Co. Durham and locally common in some districts, e.g. the Cotswolds and West Midlands, with recent increases in some areas. It was regarded as a great rarity in Victorian times. Not recorded from Scotland or Ireland. Recorded from several of the Channel Islands. **Host(s)** *Andrena cineraria* and *A. vaga*.

female

male

Nomada leucophthalma (Kirby, 1802)   **Early Nomad Bee**

Plate 13

Description & similar species FW 7–9mm female, 6.5–8.5mm male. A tricoloured nomad resembling a dark *N. flava* or *N. panzeri* with a completely black scutum and propodeum. Females have a red band across tergite 1, yellow spots on the sides of tergites 2 and 3 (separated by less than their own width), yellow bands across tergites 4 and 5, and black bands across the bases of tergites 2–5 which show through the translucent hind margins of the previous segment. The scutellum has a pair of reddish spots (often fused), and the tegulae, pronotal tubercles, extreme lower face and sometimes the pronotal collar are also reddish.

female

The antennal flagella are dark above but not black, the scapes mainly black usually with limited red markings in front. The thorax has a rather dense pile of brownish hairs. Confusion is most likely with *N. lathburiana*, but this has the scutellar spots yellow with red edges, continuous yellow bands across tergites 2 and 3 and more extensive red markings on the face. Males of *N. leucophthalma* have more extensive yellow on the tergites than females (often complete bands on tergites 2 and 3), with brown and yellow marks on tergite 1 and brownish-black bands across the hind margins. The thorax has a rather dense greyish pile and the antennae are blackish above. **Variation** Some variation in the extent of yellow, black and red/brown markings on the tergites; also in the extent of black on the antennal scape of the female. **Flight season** Early March to mid-May, peaking later in the north. The first nomad to appear in many districts. **Habitat** Various, including open woodland, brownfield sites of various sorts, heathland and moorland edge. The host bees require plentiful sallows. **Flowers visited** Sallows and other willows, dandelions, Colt's-foot, forget-me-nots, Bilberry and Barren Strawberry. **Status & distribution** Widespread but rather localised throughout Britain and Ireland. Recorded only from Jersey in the Channel Islands. **Host(s)** *Andrena clarkella* and *A. apicata*.

Nomada marshamella (Kirby, 1802)   **Marsham's Nomad Bee**

Plate 13

Description & similar species FW 7–9.5 (sexes similar). A large black and yellow species with the spots on tergite 2 clearly but narrowly separated with rather squared-off inner edges. Females usually have a pair of yellow spots on the scutellum, orange tegulae, a yellow pronotal collar and yellow pronotal tubercles. The lower face is reddish but the inner eye margins are black. The antennae are completely orange, and the legs are mostly orange with partially black femora. Tergite 1 usually has a pair of small yellow spots. Males are similar but have a yellow lower face, partially yellow tegulae, partially black antennal scapes and the basal segments of the antennal flagella black on top. They often lack scutellar spots. Both sexes could be confused with *N. goodeniana* in the field, though this has a complete yellow band on tergite 2, larger yellow markings on tergite 1 and, in females, yellow tegulae. Males of *N. fulvicornis* are also similar but have the yellow markings of tergite 1 and the inner eye margins more extensive, the tegulae yellow without any brown markings, and antennae with a shorter third segment.

Variation The extent of yellow on the tergites varies. Tergite 3 can have a complete yellow band or two separated spots, and the spots on tergite 1 are often tiny or missing. Some females have orange scutellar spots. In bivoltine populations, the second generation has much shorter hairs on the thorax than the first. **Flight season** Univoltine in most areas, flying from April to June (peaking later in the north), but with a second generation in some southern areas that flies in July and August. This seems mostly to coincide with sites where the bivoltine *Andrena trimmerana* is present. **Habitat** Assorted habitats, both open and wooded, coastal and inland. One of the more frequent nomads of urban settings and woods. **Flowers visited** A wide variety of spring and early summer-flowering shrubs and herbs. **Status & distribution** Widespread and common over much of Britain, extending north to Ross and Cromarty and the Inner Hebrides. Probably the commonest nomad in Ireland. Not recorded from the Channel Islands. **Host(s)** *Andrena scotica*, probably *A. trimmerana*, and possibly *A. rosae* and *A. ferox*.

female

male

Nomada obtusifrons Nylander, 1848   **Flat-ridged Nomad Bee**

Plate 14

Description & similar species FW 5.5mm (sexes similar). A small, dumpy species easily recognised in both sexes by the large, flat-topped ridge between the antennae. Females have the head and thorax almost entirely black, and brownish antennae. The scutum is rather shiny between the punctures. The abdomen is predominantly red with a black subterminal band and a cream-coloured tergite 5. Small lateral cream spots are present on tergites 2–4. Males are generally much darker, with wedge-shaped cream markings on the sides of tergites 2 and 3 and usually cream-coloured pronotal collar and pronotal tubercles. The labrum is dark, and they could be overlooked as *N. flavoguttata* but have a shinier scutum and rather shorter antennae.

female

Variation Females are fairly constant but males have very variable amounts of red on the tergites and can resemble females at one extreme or be almost entirely black with cream spots at the other. The darkest ones tend to have a black pronotal collar. **Flight season** Univoltine, flying from late June to late August and occasionally September. **Habitat** Usually open woodland, scrubby grassland and heathland edge in base-poor districts. **Flowers visited** Tormentil, brambles, thistles, Sheep's-bit, assorted yellow composites and Wild Angelica. **Status & distribution** A scarce species with scattered records across England, Wales, Scotland and Ireland, though relatively few of these are modern, suggesting a serious decline. Where it is found at a site it seems to occur at very low population levels. Not recorded from the Channel Islands. **Host(s)** Typically *Andrena coitana*, but possibly *A. tarsata* at some Scottish sites.

Nomada panzeri Lepeletier, 1841   **Panzer's Nomad Bee**
Plate 13

Description & similar species FW 6.5–9mm female, 6–8mm male. Separating this species from *N. flava* is one of the biggest challenges in British bee identification, and it is not helped by the considerable variation within each species. Females typically resemble a small, dark *N. flava* but usually with less extensive yellow markings on the tergites and darker wing margins. The hairs on propodeum, hind coxae and sides of the thorax are silvery without a hint of yellow. The antennae are slightly shorter and have the apical segments slightly darkened above (entirely orange in *N. flava*). The long, erect hairs of the clypeus and labrum are black rather than yellow. The propodeum can have extensive red markings in many (never extensive in *N. flava*). In the field, they tend to look more purple than *N. flava*. Males are often stated to be indistinguishable from *N. flava*, but small, slim *flava/panzeri* males with a long hair fringe beneath the hind femora and the final six antennal segments orange above will almost certainly be *N. panzeri*. Some males, however, are impossible to confidently assign. *N. ruficornis* can look superficially similar in the field, but its bifid mandibles allow easy separation. Very dark female *N. panzeri* can also resemble *N. hirtipes* (see that species). Fortunately, *N. flava* is not present in Scotland or Ireland, making identification of *N. panzeri* more straightforward here. **Variation** Considerable variation in the extent of the yellow markings on the tergites, also the amount of red on the female thorax, scutum and head. The propodeum can be completely black in some females. The darkest females tend to be associated with *Andrena lapponica*, whilst relatively large (*N. flava*-sized) ones seem to be associated with *A. fulva*. Males can have the scutellum black or red-marked, and the pronotal collar can have red or yellow marks (though rarely conspicuously so). **Flight season** Univoltine, flying from late March into June and occasionally July, peaking later in the north. **Habitat** Various habitats are exploited, but it is much more frequent in woods than

female

female, dark form

N. flava and often thriving in coppice woodland (using *Andrena helvola*) and woods, heathland or moorland edge with Bilberry (using *A. lapponica*). **Flowers visited** Various, including spring-blossoming shrubs, Greater Stitchwort, dandelions, Wood Spurge and Cow Parsley. **Status & distribution** Found throughout Britain and Ireland and recorded from several of the Channel Islands. Locally common in the north and west and more heavily wooded districts of the south, e.g. the Weald, but scarce in some districts. **Host(s)** Various spring-flying mining bees of the subgenus *Andrena*, namely *A. fucata*, *A. fulva*, *A. helvola*, *A. lapponica*, *A. synadelpha* and *A. varians*.

Nomada roberjeotiana Panzer, 1799   Tormentil Nomad Bee
Plate 14

Description & similar species FW 5.5–6 (sexes similar). A small, dumpy species with a unique pattern of black, red and cream markings. In females, the scutellum, tegulae, pronotal collar, pronotal tubercles, lower face and antennae are orange. An orange band crosses the base of the abdomen, and cream spots are present on the sides of tergites 2 and 3 and much of 5. The scutum and propodeum are entirely black and the body hairs mostly minute. Males have the tegulae, pronotal collar, tubercles, greater part of the face and front of the antennal scapes cream-coloured. Tergites 2–5 have cream-coloured lateral streaks.

Variation Little noted. **Flight season** Univoltine, flying from late June to late August. **Habitat** Various Tormentil-rich habitats. **Flowers visited** Tormentil and occasionally ragworts. **Status & distribution** Old records are scattered thinly across moorland and heathland districts of England, Wales and southwest Scotland, but modern records are very few and mostly from Cornwall. Not recorded from Ireland or the Channel Islands. **Host(s)** *Andrena tarsata*.

female

male

Nomada ruficornis (Linnaeus, 1758)   Fork-jawed Nomad Bee
Plate 13

Description & similar species FW 7–8mm female, 6.5–8mm male. A medium-sized, tricoloured nomad that is not easily distinguishable from *N. panzeri* or *N. flava* in the field but can be easily separated under magnification by the bifid tips to the mandibles (a feature only otherwise seen in the much darker *N. fabriciana*). The details of the female body markings are much as for *N. panzeri* (with the yellow tergite markings usually less extensive than for *N. flava*), though females of *N. ruficornis* have longer hairs on the thorax, especially the sides of the propodeum. Males resemble *N. flava* and *N. panzeri* but are noticeably hairier, especially on the sides of the thorax. **Variation** Some variation in the extent of yellow markings on the tergites, which are sometimes missing from tergite 3 of the female, also the extent of red markings on the head and thorax of the female. Males sometimes have yellow markings on tergite 1 and can have a complete or interrupted yellow band on tergite 2. **Flight season** Univoltine, flying from April to June and occasionally July. **Habitat** Like its host, it uses a variety of habitats, including open woodland, heathland, scrubby grasslands, brownfield sites and occasionally gardens. **Flowers visited** A variety of spring-blossoming shrubs, plus flowers such as dandelions, Greater Stitchwort and forget-me-nots. **Status & distribution** Common throughout much of southern Britain. Widespread but scarcer in Scotland and Ireland. Recorded from Jersey and Sark in the Channel Islands. **Host(s)** *Andrena haemorrhoa.*

female

male

Nomada rufipes Fabricius, 1793   **Black-horned Nomad Bee**
Plate 14

Description & similar species FW 5–7mm (sexes similar). A medium-small nomad, the only one with a single yellow spot on the scutellum combined with almost entirely black antennal flagella. It can have a bold black and yellow pattern or a tricoloured pattern with much of the black of the tergites replaced by red. Tergites 2 and 3 have well-separated, rather triangular yellow spots. The tegulae, pronotal collar and pronotal tubercles are yellow, and a yellow spot is present on the sides of the thorax. The front coxae have an apical projection. Females usually have the lower face and first three antennal segments orange. The legs are mostly orange with partially black femora. Males have the lower face yellow, more yellow on the legs and the underside of the hind femora shiny with only sparse hairs. *N. errans* closely resembles a small example of the black and yellow form of *N. rufipes* but has paler antennae, tergite 4 mostly black, and cream-coloured body markings. Some examples of *N. fucata* can also approach *N. rufipes* in appearance but have orange antennae. **Variation** The main variation is the replacement of black markings on the tergites by red (especially in females), and this shows a gradation that at its extreme results in a mostly red and yellow abdomen. Further variation can affect the markings of the face (some females can have an almost entirely black face) and the amount of black or yellow on the legs. Dwarfs with wing lengths as short as 4mm are occasionally encountered. **Flight season** Univoltine, flying from July to September, with heathland populations peaking with the blossoming of Heather (Ling). **Habitat** Most frequent on heathland in association with *Andrena fuscipes*, though it can occur on other habitats such as chalk downland and brownfield sites in association with *A. denticulata* and *A. nigriceps*. **Flowers visited** Ragworts, heathers, thistles and thymes. **Status & distribution** Frequent in southern heathland districts of England and Wales, becoming scarcer in the north, with only a few Scottish records. Widespread but scarce in Ireland. Recorded from several of the Channel Islands. **Host(s)** *Andrena fuscipes*, *A. denticulata*, *A. nigriceps* and possibly also *A. nitidiuscula*.

female, reddish example

male

Nomada sexfasciata Panzer, 1799 — **Six-banded Nomad Bee**

Plate 13

Description & similar species FW 9–9.5mm (sexes similar). A large and robust black and yellow nomad with paired spots on tergites 1–3 and yellow scutellar spots. The scutum, propodeum and pronotal collar are always black. The most unusual feature of this species is the greatly inflated and protruding lower face and relatively wide malar gap between the bottom of the eyes and mandible bases. Females have the antennal flagella mostly orange, but males have black markings on the dorsal face of segments 3–8. Males resemble females and can match their size. They have an unusually furry thorax for a nomad. The hind tibiae of the male lack any obvious comb spines at the tip; in the female a dense brush of yellowish hairs replaces the comb spines. **Variation** Minor variation in the extent of the yellow markings; also size, with large females qualifying as our largest nomad, though many are no larger than typical *N. goodeniana* or *N. marshamella*. **Flight season** Univoltine, flying from late May to July and occasionally early August. **Habitat** Historical records include heathland and woodland rides, though today it is confined to soft rock cliffs. Legume-rich habitats are vital for the host. **Flowers visited** Bloody Crane's-bill,

female

sowthistles and Kidney Vetch. **Status & distribution** Always a rarity, but with old records scattered across southern England and south Wales north to Somerset and Norfolk. Today it is seemingly confined to a short stretch of South Devon coastline. Not recorded from Scotland, Ireland or the Channel Islands. **Host(s)** *Eucera longicornis*, and on the continent *E. nigrescens*.

Nomada sheppardana (Kirby, 1802)   Sheppard's Nomad Bee

Plate 14

Description & similar species FW 4–4.5mm (sexes similar). Britain's smallest nomad bee (only the smallest *N. flavoguttata* can match it). Females are one of a small number of species lacking any pale spots on the tergites. They have a pair of red spots on the scutellum, large red patches on the sides of the thorax, red tegulae, pronotal collar and pronotal tubercles. The lower face (including the labrum) is red, with markings usually extending fully up the inner eye margins. The antennae are largely brownish with a pale final segment. The scutum and propodeum are black but the latter has conspicuous patches of silvery

female

hairs on either side, as do the sides of the thorax. The abdomen is blackish with ill-defined reddish bands across tergites 1 and 2. Males are generally very blackish with small yellow spots on the sides of tergite 2, yellow dashes on the subsequent segments, and often weak reddish bands across tergites 1 and 2. The labrum is usually yellow or orange at the sides and black down the middle. The undersides of the hind femora have a patch of very dense whitish hairs in the basal third. In both sexes, to be certain you have not got a dwarf *N. flavoguttata*, check that antennal segments 3 and 4 are about the same length (segment 3 much shorter than 4 in *N. flavoguttata*). **Variation** Very dark males are almost entirely black except for small yellow markings on the tergites. **Flight season** Univoltine, flying between late April and late July. **Habitat** Often the edge of woodland and scrub in the vicinity of host nesting areas along banks and footpaths. **Flowers visited** British records include Cat's-ear and Daisy. **Status & distribution** Recorded widely in the southern half of Britain, including Wales, as far north as Shropshire and Lincolnshire, but rarely seen in any numbers and seemingly much declined. Only one old Irish record. Not recorded from Scotland. Old records from the Channel Islands. **Host(s)** *Lasioglossum* species, possibly including *L. morio*, *L. parvulum*, *L. nitidiusculum* and *L. villosulum*.

Nomada signata Jurine, 1807   Broad-banded Nomad Bee

Plate 14

Description & similar species FW 8–9.5mm female, 7.5–9.5mm male. The *N. flava*-sized females have exceptionally broad and straight-sided yellow bands on tergites 2–4 and a pair of yellow patches on the propodeum, a unique combination within the large tricoloured nomads with red-striped scutums. The scutellum is usually entirely red, a pair of red markings are present on the sides of the thorax and tergite 1 has a pair of yellow spots. The red markings of the lower face usually extend around the eyes. The antennae are completely orange. Males also have straight-sided yellow bands on tergites 2–4 but the thorax is black except for two reddish scutellar spots, and the antennae are darkened on top. The yellow markings of the lower face barely extend upwards along the inner eye margins. The antennal

347

scapes are red in front. Some males of *N. leucophthalma* can look very similar but have the antennal scapes completely black. Similar-looking *N. flava* males have the yellow markings of the lower face extending alongside the inner eye margins to the midpoint of the eye. **Variation** In females, the yellow marks of the propodeum and red markings of the head and thorax can vary considerably in extent. Males can have tergite 1 entirely dark brown or with yellow and reddish markings and a pair of black spots. **Flight season** Univoltine, flying from early April to late May. **Habitat** Assorted open habitats as per the host. **Flowers visited** Dandelions, willows and Wood Spurge. **Status & distribution** A scarce bee, with records scattered widely across southern Britain (including Wales) north to Shropshire. Not recorded from Scotland or Ireland. Old records from the Channel Islands. Much declined in some areas but showing a local recovery and expansion in others. It has always been much rarer than its host. **Host(s)** *Andrena fulva*.

female

male

Nomada similis Morawitz, 1872   **Guernsey Nomad Bee**
Plate 14

Description & similar species FW 6.5–7mm female, 6–6.5mm male. Females, which are about the size of *N. fabriciana*, are one of three reddish species lacking pale markings on the tergites and without any red or yellow spots on the scutellum. They can be separated from the form of

female

N. fabriciana without yellow spots on the tergites by the paler mandibles with bluntly pointed rather than bifid tips. *N. fuscicornis* is a smaller, darker species with the scutellum evenly convex (depressed centrally in *N. similis*), shorter antennae, darker legs and sparser punctures on the top of the thorax. *N. similis* also has a discrete patch of silvery hairs on the sides of the thorax. Males resemble females but have ill-defined yellow spots on the sides of tergite 2 and a tuft of long white hairs on the underside of the hind femora at the base. **Variation** Not noted. **Flight season** Univoltine, flying from late June to September. **Habitat** On the Channel

Islands on coastal heathland, dunes and dry sandy grassland with plentiful hawkish composites for the host. **Flowers visited** Foreign records include yellow-flowered hawkish composites, thistles, Tormentil and Sheep's-bit. **Status & distribution** Recorded only from Jersey, Guernsey and Sark in the Channel Islands, but possibly extinct on the first of these. **Host(s)** *Panurgus banksianus*.

Nomada striata Fabricius, 1793   Blunt-jawed Nomad Bee
Plate 14

Description & similar species FW 6–7.5mm female, 5.5–7.5mm male. Females are one of several medium-sized, reddish nomads with a red-marked thorax, red markings on the lower face that extend around the eyes, and well-separated yellow spots on the sides of tergite 2. The mandibles have squared-off tips, which allows separation from all species except *N. guttulata*, but the comb spines at the tip of the hind tibiae are longer and more widely spaced in *N. striata*. Males also have the unusual mandible shape, and can be separated from *N. guttulata* by the shorter third antennal segment, more extensive yellow markings along the inner eye margins, partially red antennal scapes and a much larger apical shiny zone on the underside of the hind femora. **Variation** Both sexes show variation in the precise extent of the red or yellow markings on the head and thorax and the extent of black and yellow on the tergites. The extent of red on the antennal scapes is variable, and occasionally they are entirely black at the front (as in *N. guttulata*) or entirely red at the front (as in species such as *N. panzeri* and *N. hirtipes*). The male scutellum usually has one large red marking but sometimes has two red spots. **Flight season** Univoltine, flying from mid-May to July (occasionally August), peaking in June. **Habitat** Legume-rich grasslands, heathland and open woodland. The host likes sites with plentiful bird's-foot-trefoils and clovers. **Flowers visited** Buttercups, various yellow composites, heathers, White Bryony, Wood Spurge, Germander Speedwell, Bogbean, Raspberry, Wood Avens and bird's-foot-trefoils. **Status & distribution** Widespread but local throughout England, scarcer in Wales, Scotland and Ireland. Recorded only from Sark in the Channel Islands. **Host(s)** *Andrena wilkella*.

Nomada subcornuta (Kirby, 1802)   **Kirby's Nomad Bee**

Plate 13

Description & similar species FW 9–10mm female, 8.5–9.5mm male. Closely related to *N. fulvicornis*, and regarded as just a variant of it until recently. However, females of *N. subcornuta* are typically larger, with a pair of red patches (often fused) but no yellow on tergite 1, and the yellow spots of tergites 2 and 3 are more widely separated. The central projection of the labrum is usually smaller, and the sternites are mostly red and usually lack any yellow. Males are also typically larger than *N. fulvicornis*, with the yellow spots on tergite 1 surrounded by red, and the spots on tergites 2 and 3 are more widely separated. DNA analysis has confirmed

that they are distinct species. **Variation** The female propodeum usually has a pair of red spots, but these can be missing in some or replaced by larger yellow spots in others. Females from Jersey show the latter state and also have the yellow spots of tergite 2 less widely separated than the mainland form. Males show minor variation in the size of the spots on tergites 1–4 and the scutellum. **Flight season** Univoltine, flying from early May (males) until mid-July (females), peaking between the two generations of *N. fulvicornis*, which is typically a bivoltine species. **Habitat** Sandy habitats such as heathland, sandy arable margins and brownfield sites; also soft rock cliffs in Jersey but rarely at coastal sites on the mainland. **Flowers visited** Bramble is the only species noted. **Status & distribution** Scattered records in southern England north to Staffordshire, and an old record for Gwynedd, Wales; also Jersey and Guernsey in the Channel Islands. Much declined, with modern records confined to a few sites in Worcestershire, Staffordshire, Essex and Jersey. Not recorded from Scotland or Ireland. **Host(s)** *Andrena nigrospina* on mainland Britain but possibly *A. agilissima* (a purported host for '*N. fulvicornis*' on the continent) on Jersey.

Nomada succincta Panzer, 1798   **Yellow-legged Nomad Bee**

Plate 13

Description & similar species FW 8–10mm female, 8–9mm male. Closely resembles *N. goodeniana*, but females have two or three large yellow patches on the face (depending on whether the clypeus is yellow-marked), the femora mostly black, and the tibiae yellow (legs mostly orange in *N. goodeniana*). The antennal scape is black behind (entirely or mainly orange in most *N. goodeniana*). The yellow bands on the tergites are broader, making for a paler-looking nomad in the field. Large yellow spots can be present on the propodeum. Males are even more similar to *N. goodeniana* but have the tibiae and tarsi almost completely yellow, a dark mark on the posterior face of the hind tibiae, and the hind

femora mainly black on the dorsal and anterior surfaces. **Variation** Moderate variation in the extent of yellow markings on the tergites, thorax and face. **Flight season** Univoltine, flying from April to June. **Habitat** In Jersey found on a soft rock cliff. **Flowers visited** Continental records include dandelions and willows. **Status & distribution** Only recorded from the Channel Islands (Jersey and Guernsey). **Host(s)** Probably *Andrena nigroaenea* on the Channel Islands, though *A. nitida* is apparently also attacked on the continent.

Nomada zonata Panzer, 1798   **Variable Nomad Bee**
not illustrated

Description & similar species FW 7mm female, 5.5–6.5mm male. A medium-small nomad (about the same size as *N. rufipes*) with tricoloured females that have a black scutum, two reddish or yellow spots on the scutellum (and sometimes the propodeum too), brown or orange tegulae and yellow or reddish pronotal tubercles. Tergite 1 has a red band and black hind margins, often also with yellow markings. Tergites 2–4 are black with lateral yellow spots, those on 2 usually with red patches at their inner ends which may be divided by black in the middle. The yellow spots on tergite 3 are more widely separated than those on 2 and 4 and again have red patches at their inner end. The lower face and inner eye margins are broadly red, and red or orange markings can completely surround the eyes. The tops of antennae are typically reddish on segments 2–6, and dark on 7–11 with 12 conspicuously yellowish, rather reminiscent of *N. fabriciana* or *N. armata*. The legs are dark red with partially black femora. Males have yellow lower faces, tegulae and pronotal tubercles and yellow, red and black legs. Antennal segment 3 is clearly shorter than 5 in front view. The scutellum and pronotal collar are usually black. They usually lack any red on the tergites and can resemble male *N. rufipes* (which has a bright yellow scutellar spot and pronotal collar) or a very small *N. marshamella* (which has antennal segment 3 about as long as 5 in front view). **Variation** A notoriously variable species, even within northwest Europe. Females can have one or two scutellar spots, and these can be yellow or orange. A pair of red or yellow spots can be present on the propodeum. The pronotal tubercles vary from yellow to orange, and the antennal flagella are variably darkened. There is

also considerable variation in the extent of yellow and red markings on the tergites and head, and males can have tergite 1 yellow spotted or entirely black. **Flight season** Bivoltine on the continent, the first generation flying from April to June and the second from July to September. **Habitat** In Jersey, recorded on scrubby cliff-top grassland. **Flowers visited** Observed on bramble and Common Ragwort in Jersey, though a variety of flowers is used abroad. **Status & distribution** Discovered on Jersey in 2011. **Host(s)** *Andrena dorsata*.

female, darker form

female, paler form

male

EPEOLUS – VARIEGATED CUCKOO BEES

Medium-sized, inconspicuously haired but brightly patterned and stockily built bees. Some foreign species are banded and called 'zebra bees'. Males are easily distinguished from females by the protruding pygidium at the tip of the abdomen, and in the British species by the black scutellum and axillae (typically red, or partially red in females). All species are cleptoparasites of *Colletes* bees. Females enter the host's nesting burrow and lay an egg in the wall of an unsealed nest cell. The first-instar *Epeolus* grub then destroys the host's egg or grub with its large sickle-shaped mandibles and proceeds to feed on the food store.

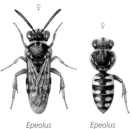

Epeolus cruciger   *Epeolus variegatus*

This is a near-cosmopolitan genus with about 100 species described globally. Only two are currently known in Britain, though DNA analysis is required to ascertain the taxonomic status of some of the host-specific races. Several further species occur on the near-continent, and two species to look out for are *E. tarsalis*, which specialises on *Colletes halophilus*, and *E. fallax*, which specialises on *C. hederae*. The latter is a rather striking pied species with black and white legs and is expanding its European range in the shadow of its much spread host. *Epeolus* species can be quite easy to spot around host nesting areas and also visit flowers nearby, especially composites and heathers.

It is strongly recommended that, if taking voucher material, the male genitalia are pulled out to allow more confident separation of the two species.

EPEOLUS

1 Females (antennae with 12 segments, pygidium not protruding, scutellum usually reddish) **2**

— Males (antennae with 13 segments, pygidium protruding, scutellum and axillae dark) **3**

2 Tip of abdomen blunter (Fig. 1), sternite 5 seen from below wider than long (Fig. 2), usually reddish, the lower edge straight in side view. Sternite 2 more finely punctate. Coxae, trochanters, femora, axillae and sternites usually reddish. Labrum usually entirely reddish with a pair of tubercles about three-quarters of the way to the apex .... *cruciger*

— Tip of abdomen more protruding (Fig. 3), sternite 5 seen from below about as long as wide (Fig. 4), blackish, the lower edge concave in side view. Sternite 2 more coarsely punctate. Coxae, trochanters, femora, axillae and sternites usually extensively darkened. Labrum usually darkened basally with a pair of tubercles in the middle just beyond halfway .... *variegatus*

Fig. 1   Fig. 2    Fig. 3 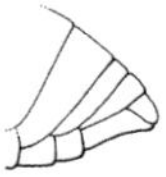   Fig. 4    Fig. 7 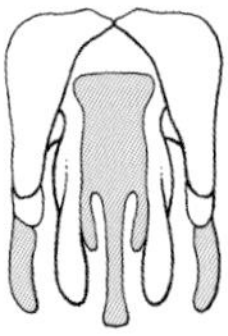   Fig. 8

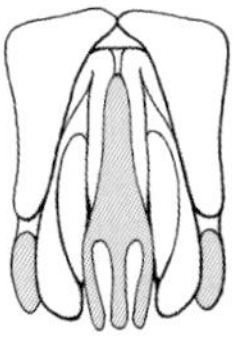

Fig. 5 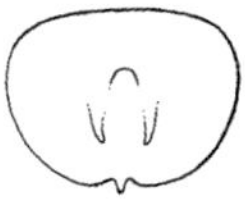   Fig. 6

3 Labrum rounder, the surface roughened in a more even manner, the lower margin barely indented and with any central tooth usually projecting beyond the lower margin (Fig. 5). Pygidium usually partially red. Genitalia (Fig. 7) .... *cruciger*

— Labrum more transverse, the whole surface very unevenly rough, the lower margin usually deeply indented in the middle with a small tooth centrally that does not protrude beyond the edges of the indentation (Fig. 6). Pygidium usually black. Genitalia (Fig. 8) .... *variegatus*

Epeolus cruciger (Panzer, 1799)   **Red-thighed Epeolus**
Plate 15

Description & similar species FW 4–7mm female, 4.5–6.5mm male. A medium-small, cream and black patterned bee with inconspicuous body hairs. Females closely resemble *E. variegatus* but have a much less produced tip to the abdomen, and reddish femora, sternites and axillae. Sternite 2 is more finely punctate. Males have mainly blackish femora (like *E. variegatus*) and checking the genitalia is the most reliable method for separating the two species, though *E. cruciger* typically has a red pygidium and the labrum is usually slightly rounder in shape, with a more evenly roughened surface and with the lower margin less indented in the middle than *E. variegatus*. Some males cannot be assigned to either species on the basis of external morphology. **Variation** Populations associated with *Colletes marginatus* average significantly smaller than those associated with *C. succinctus*. The amount of black versus red on the legs can vary, so it is important to use structural features to provide a reliable determination. Females occasionally have the scutellum and axillae black. **Flight season** Late June to late September, with populations associated with *C. marginatus* appearing first and peaking in July, whilst populations associated with *C. succinctus* peak in August and linger longer. **Habitat** As per its hosts, i.e. heathland for the more widespread form that parasitises *C. succinctus* and coastal dunes and sandy Breck grassland for populations associated with *C. marginatus*. **Flowers visited** Most often seen on heathers (especially Ling) and Common Ragwort. **Status & distribution** The form that parasitises *C. succinctus* is widespread and frequent in heathland districts, extending as far north as Ayrshire. The *C. marginatus*-parasitising form is much rarer, with most records from western dune systems and the East Anglian Brecks. Not recorded from Ireland. On the Channel Islands recorded only from Jersey. **Host(s)** A cleptoparasite of *Colletes succinctus* and *C. marginatus*.

female

male

Epeolus variegatus (Linnaeus, 1758)

Plate 15

Black-thighed Epeolus

Description & similar species FW 5–6.5mm (sexes similar). A female *Epeolus* with dark femora is most likely to be *E. variegatus*, but it is important to confirm it by checking for the more produced tip of the abdomen, which has a concave lower margin when viewed from the side. Many other parts of the body are typically darker than in *E. cruciger* – the sternites, labrum and axillae. Males are best confirmed using genitalia but usually have a dark pygidium and a more transverse labrum. **Variation** The amount of black versus red on the legs can vary, so it is important to use structural features to provide a reliable determination. **Flight season** Typically late June to early September, but populations associated with *Colletes halophilus* will persist to mid-October. **Habitat** Quite varied, reflecting the various hosts used, though typical habitats include heathland, sandpits, coastal dunes, soft rock cliffs and coastal shingle. Populations using *C. halophilus* are usually associated with saltmarsh edge. This is the *Epeolus* most likely to be seen on brownfield land and within arable settings. **Flowers visited** Most often seen on Common Ragwort and Common Fleabane, but also Sea Aster at *C. halophilus* sites. **Status & distribution** Widespread and often common in southern heathland and coastal districts, with records extending into southwest Scotland. Not recorded from Ireland. Recorded from several of the Channel Islands. **Host(s)** A cleptoparasite of various *Colletes* including *C. daviesanus*, *C. fodiens*, and *C. halophilus*.

female

male

EUCERA – LONG-HORNED BEES

Medium-large solitary bees with outlandishly long male antennae. Females are less distinctive and can resemble *Anthophora* species but have two rather than three submarginal cells. Males have yellow faces. This is mainly a Palaearctic and Nearctic genus with several hundred described species (about 80 in Europe). Only two are known from Britain, and one of these may be extinct. Nesting occurs in light soils, often in aggregations. Pollen is obtained from larger-flowered legumes of varying sorts and is moistened with nectar during the foraging process. Some foreign species are important pollinators of fodder crops such as Alfalfa. Nest cells are filled with a semi-liquid pollen and nectar mix. Males can be important pollinators of *Ophrys* orchids, to which they are sexually attracted. *Eucera* species are parasitised by certain *Nomada* species (*N. sexfasciata* in Britain).

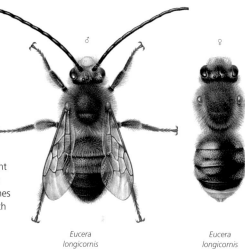

Eucera longicornis

Eucera longicornis

EUCERA

1 Females (antennae about half as long as the forewings and with 12 segments) **2**

— Males (antennae longer than the forewings and with 13 segments) **3**

2 Fore basitarsi with a well-developed ventral projection at the tip (Fig. 1). Scutum densely punctured, the punctures almost touching. Clypeus with small, dense punctures and relatively dull .... ***longicornis***

— Fore basitarsi without a ventral projection at the tip (Fig. 2). Scutum with shallow punctures that are separated by about their own width. Clypeus with larger, sparser punctures and relatively shining .... ***nigrescens***

3 Hind basitarsi in side view becoming progressively broader towards the tip, where they are distinctly downcurved (Fig. 3) .... ***longicornis***

— Hind basitarsi in side view parallel-sided and not downcurved at the tip (Fig. 4) .... ***nigrescens***

Fig. 1   Fig. 2    Fig. 3

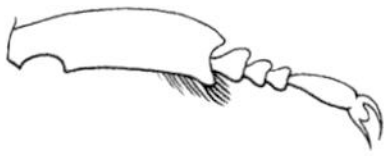

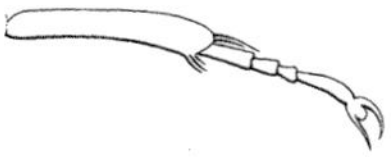

Fig. 4

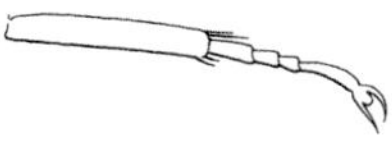

Eucera longicornis (Linnaeus, 1758)   **Long-horned Bee**
Plate 15

Description & similar species FW 9–10.5mm (sexes similar). Males are instantly recognisable, owing to their extraordinarily long antennae. The larger, stockier females have short antennae and rather resemble *Anthophora* species but they have two rather than three submarginal wing cells. Separating the two British species is best done under the microscope. **Variation** Little noted, though the brown hairs of the male thorax can fade to silver in very old ones. Very old males can become denuded and look slim and black. **Flight season** Males typically appear in mid-May, females a week or two later. Females can persist into August.

Habitat A number of rather different habitats are exploited, including soft rock cliffs, dry and relatively unimproved meadows, coastal grazing marsh, flowery heathland edge, the rides and clearings of clay woodland, and occasionally brownfield sites such as quarries and claypits. **Flowers visited** Strongly associated with legumes. On soft rock cliffs, Kidney Vetch and everlasting-peas are often the main flowers used; in old meadows and grazing marsh, Meadow Vetchling, clovers and *Vicia* vetches are important, whilst on brownfield sites bird's-foot-trefoils, everlasting-peas and Lucerne may be critical.

Nectar is gathered from a variety of other plants, and males like labiates such as Ground-ivy and Bugle. **Nesting habits** Nesting typically occurs in aggregations in bare or sparsely vegetated light soils on south-facing slopes or cliff faces. Loose swarms of males will often fly over nesting areas at great speed. **Status & distribution** A much declined bee, formerly found in most of the English counties south of Worcestershire and Oxfordshire and along the coast of south Wales. There is also an old record for Yorkshire. Recent mainland records are confined to a few dozen sites, mostly along the south coast of England and Wales with a scattering of inland sites north to Shropshire. Not recorded from Ireland. On the Channel Islands recorded from Alderney, Jersey and Guernsey. **Parasites & associates** The cleptoparasitic bee *Nomada sexfasciata*.

Eucera nigrescens Pérez, 1879   **Scarce Long-horned Bee**
not illustrated

Description & similar species Similar to *E. longicornis*, and not easily distinguishable in the field. The best distinctions are the shape of the female front basitarsi (lacking the apical ventral projection of *E. longicornis*) and the male hind basitarsi (parallel-sided without the downcurved tip of *E. longicornis*). Further differences are given in the key, and female *E. nigrescens* also has a longer face (viewed from the front) with a wider malar gap. **Variation** Little noted. **Flight season** Mid-May to late June, apparently peaking a little earlier than *E. longicornis*. **Habitat** The few known British sites include legume-rich grasslands, soft rock cliffs and open woodland. **Flowers visited** Legumes such as clovers, *Vicia* vetches and *Medicago* species for pollen, plus various other plants for nectar. Like *E. longicornis*, males are known to pollinate *Ophrys* orchids. **Nesting habits** Probably similar to *E. longicornis*. **Status & distribution** Only ever known with certainty from a small number of sites in southern England (mainly Kent and East Sussex). Not seen in Britain since 1970 (Maplesden, Kent) and possibly extinct. **Parasites & associates** Abroad, the cleptoparasitic bee *Nomada sexfasciata*, though it is unclear if the *Nomada* ever parasitised *E. nigrescens* in Britain.

ANTHOPHORA – FLOWER BEES

A large and near-cosmopolitan genus of medium to large, robustly built bees, sometimes with strong sexual dimorphism. Males usually have faces partly yellow or white; some also have legs modified by hairs and armature. Most species nest in the ground or use cliffs and walls, sometimes in large and noisy aggregations. Despite this, they are all technically solitary, with no evidence of worker behaviour. Some species prefer to nest in wood or hollow stems. Nest cells are lined with a waterproof substance, and entrance turrets/chimneys are constructed by some foreign species.

    Anthophora species are mostly polylectic, though labiates, legumes and plants of the Boraginaceae tend to feature highly in the European species. Foraging can involve much highly controlled hovering. *Anthophora* species are attacked by cleptoparasitic bees of various genera including *Melecta*, *Coelioxys* and the non-British *Ammobates* and *Thyreus*. There are over 450 described species globally, but only five occur in Britain, and none in Ireland. Several further species occur on the near-continent.

♀

Anthophora plumipes

♀

Anthophora furcata

♀

Anthophora bimaculata

ANTHROPHORA FEMALES

1   Body entirely or mainly black-haired. Large species (wing length 10–11mm) **2**

—   Body extensively pale-haired **3**

2   Spurs at tip of hind tibiae blackish. Surface of scutum and scutellum very dull (Channel Island females have a grey-haired abdomen) .... **typical *plumipes***

—   Spurs at tip of hind tibiae orange. Surface of scutum and scutellum relatively shiny .... ***retusa***

3   Tergites with conspicuous pale hair bands **4**

—   Tergites without conspicuous bands **5**

4   Lower clypeus and labrum yellow (Fig. 3). Tergites 2 and 3 with white bands consisting of dense adpressed hairs .... ***bimaculata***

—   Face and labrum entirely dark. Abdominal hair bands less dense, consisting of sparser, more outstanding hairs .... ***quadrimaculata***

5   Large and robust (wing length 10–11mm). Body hairs mainly pale buff with tip of abdomen dark-haired. Antennal segment 3 longer than scape .... **pale *plumipes***

—   Smaller and slimmer (wing length 8–8.5mm). Body largely brown-haired, tip of abdomen orange-haired. Antennal segment 3 shorter than scape .... ***furcata***

ANTHROPHORA MALES

1   Mid-basitarsi broad and with fringes of long black hairs. Larger species (wing length
9.5–11mm) 2

—   Mid-basitarsi not broadened and with any hair fringes pale. Smaller species (wing
length not more than 8.5mm) 3

2   Mid-tarsi with very long hairs (twice the length of a basitarsus) arising from all five
tarsal segments and forming a loose fringe (Fig. 1). Body hairs mostly buff with
tergites 3–5 black-haired. Larger (wing length typically 10–11mm) .... *plumipes*

—   Mid-tarsi with long hairs confined to the basitarsi, shorter than the length of a
basitarsus and forming a dense brush (Fig. 2). Body hairs darker brown, with
tergites 2–5 black-haired. Smaller (wing length typically 9.5mm) .... *retusa*

Fig. 1   Fig. 3 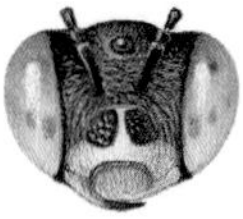   Fig. 5 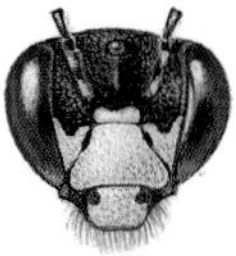   Fig. 7

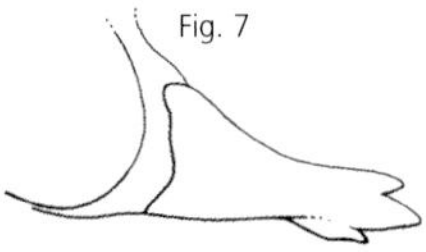

Fig. 2    Fig. 4 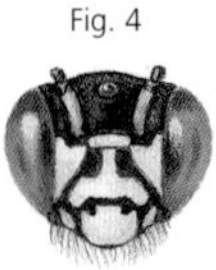   Fig. 6

3   Face yellow with a pair of large black marks below the antennal insertions (Fig. 4)
(tergites with rather weak hair bands across hind margins) .... *quadrimaculata*

—   Face yellow without large black marks beneath the antennae (Figs 5 & 6) 4

4   Abdomen lacking pale hair bands. Mandibles with three apical teeth (Fig. 7).
Hind tibiae and basitarsi relatively slender. Eyes in life dark. A medium-sized,
rather elongate species (wing length 8.5mm). Face (Fig. 5) .... *furcata*

—   Conspicuous pale bands across the hind margins of the tergites. Mandibles with
two apical teeth. Hind tibiae and basitarsi thickened. Eyes in life bright green.
A small, squat species (wing length 6.5mm). Face (Fig. 6) .... *bimaculata*

Anthophora bimaculata (Panzer, 1798)   Green-eyed Flower Bee
Plate 16

Description & similar species FW 6–7mm (sexes similar). Our smallest
Anthophora, with a strongly banded abdomen and partially yellow-faced
female (female face entirely dark in all other species). *A. quadrimaculata*
looks similar but is usually larger and has less intense abdominal bands.
Males of *A. bimaculata* lack the pair of black spots on the yellow face
below the antennae found in *A. quadrimaculata* and have more swollen
hind legs. Live males have particularly bright green eyes; those of the
female are greyish-green. **Variation** In females, the hairs of the thoracic
dorsum can vary from mainly brown to mainly black, and these can fade
greyish in old individuals. Fresh males have rich golden-brown thoracic hairs that also fade grey
over time. The abdominal bands can become fully abraded in very old individuals of both sexes.
Flight season May to late September. **Habitat** Strongly associated with sandy habitats including
heathland, sandpits, soft rock cliffs, coastal dunes, the sandy parts of vegetated shingle and sandy
brownfield sites. **Flowers visited** Various, especially composites (e.g. Cat's-ear, ragworts, thistles,

burdocks and Golden-samphire), labiates (e.g. Black Horehound, Thyme, Wood Sage and garden catmints) and Viper's-bugloss; also brambles, heathers, Sheep's-bit, Sea-lavender, Sea Bindweed and willowherbs. The bees will often forage at high densities around patches of flowers, emitting a high-pitched buzz as they dart and hover rapidly between flowers. **Nesting habits** Nesting occurs in sandy ground, especially south-facing slopes and faces, also commonly on the very edges of cliff tops where Rabbits and desiccation maintain bare ground. It frequently forms large, dense and noisy nesting aggregations. **Status & distribution** Largely confined to southern England, especially coastal areas and southern heathland districts. Scarce in East Anglia and the Midlands. Not recorded from Wales, Scotland and Ireland. Recorded from several of the Channel Islands. **Parasites & associates** The cleptoparasitic bee *Coelioxys rufescens* can be much in evidence around *A. bimaculata* nesting colonies; *C. elongata* may also parasitise it. *A. bimaculata* seems to be one of the main hosts for the sarcophagid fly *Miltogramma germari*, the larvae of which are probably parasitoids of the *Anthophora* grubs.

female

male

Anthophora furcata (Panzer, 1798)   Fork-tailed Flower Bee
Plate 16

Description & similar species FW 8–8.5mm female, 7–8mm male. A medium-sized, brownish *Anthophora* with a furry, unbanded abdomen and a weak dark band on the top of the thorax between the wing bases. The male has unmodified mid-legs and a yellow face. Females have the tip of the abdomen orange-haired; in males it is black-haired. This is the only *Anthophora* with three teeth at the tip of its mandibles. **Variation** Very little, though old, denuded individuals can look very different from fresh ones. **Flight season** Late May to late August. **Habitat** A variety of labiate-rich settings, including hedge margins,

female

male

woodland rides and clearings, wetlands, river banks, disused railway cuttings, brownfield sites and gardens. **Flowers visited** Strongly associated with labiates, particularly woundworts and Black Horehound, also Wood Sage on sandy soils and various exotic labiates in gardens. It will also visit plants from other families such as brambles, Purple Toadflax, thistles, knapweeds and nightshades, presumably for nectar. **Nesting habits** The only *Anthophora* to habitually nest in dead wood, typically rotting tree stumps. **Status & distribution** Fairly frequent across the southern half of Britain, though rarely common. Rare in Scotland but extending north to Culbin Sands. Not recorded from Ireland or the Channel Islands. **Parasites & associates** The cleptoparasitic bees *Coelioxys quadridentata* and *C. rufescens*.

Anthophora plumipes (Pallas, 1772)   Hairy-footed Flower Bee

Plate 15

Description & similar species FW 10–11mm (sexes similar). The largest *Anthophora*. Typical females are black with an orange pollen brush on the hind legs. They are difficult to separate from the rare *A. retusa* in the field, though it should be possible to check the colour of the hind tibial spurs of a captured specimen in a tube with a hand lens (blackish in *A. plumipes*, orange in *A. retusa*). Males are mostly buff-haired, with the apical tergites of the abdomen black-haired. They have a fringe of very long hairs arising from all segments of the mid-tarsi, and a mainly yellow face. They are easy to recognise in the field through size, early flight period and rapid flight action. Males of *A. retusa* are smaller and darker with very different mid-tarsi. **Variation** A very small proportion of mainland females are buff-coloured (see p.13) and resemble robust, dark-faced males (the presence of a pollen load is usually the first clue that they aren't males). Channel Island females have a brown-black pile on the thorax and a paler grey pile on the abdomen and can appear silvery in some lights. Channel Island males tend to have more abundant black hairs on top of the thorax. Dwarf males with wing lengths as short as 8.5mm are occasionally encountered.

female

female, Channel Islands

male

Males fade greyish by late spring. **Flight season** Males are amongst the first bees to appear in spring (late February in some years) and fly into May. Females appear 2–3 weeks after the males and can persist into June and rarely early July. **Habitat** Very frequent in parks, gardens, churchyards and other urban locations, also quarries, Rabbit-grazed hillsides, woodlands and soft rock cliffs. **Flowers visited** A very wide variety of flowers and blossoms are visited; favourites include dead-nettles, Ground-ivy, comfreys, Green Alkanet, lungworts, primroses, Wallflower, Blackthorn, cherries, willows and gorses. Foraging involves rapid darting flight with much hovering, and males seem to hold small territories around patches of flowers. **Nesting habits** Nesting frequently occurs in walls and chimney stacks, also the vertical faces of quarries, cliffs and rabbit burrows. Females will sometimes appear indoors when using

Sitaris muralis parasite.

chimneys. **Status & distribution** Common in most parts of southern England but in Wales mainly confined to the south coast and eastern parts. Discovered in Scotland (Ayrshire) in 2013. Not recorded from Ireland. Present on several of the Channel Islands. **Parasites & associates** The cleptoparasitic bee *Melecta albifrons*, which is fairly frequent in the vicinity of good nesting colonies of *plumipes*. The very rare meloid beetle *Sitaris muralis* is clearly associated with *A. plumipes*.

Anthophora quadrimaculata   Four-banded Flower Bee
(Panzer, 1798) Plate 16

Description & similar species FW 7.5–8.5mm female, 7–8.5mm male. One of two *Anthophora* species with a banded abdomen, though the bands are less intense than in *A. bimaculata* and it is somewhat larger. Males have a pair of black spots on the yellow face below the antennae (missing in *bimaculata*) and less swollen hind legs. Females have a dark face (partially yellow in *A. bimaculata*). Live bees have bluish-grey eyes, but never the bright green ones of male *A. bimaculata*. **Variation** Very little, though older individuals fade greyish and the abdominal bands can become abraded. **Flight season** Early June to mid-August. **Habitat** Gardens, urban parks, soft rock cliffs, chalk downland, flowery heathland edge and brownfield sites. It is not as strongly attached to sandy habitats as *A. bimaculata*. **Flowers visited** Pollen is

female

male

mainly obtained from labiates, especially Black Horehound and dead-nettles in semi-natural habitats, and cultivated catmints and lavenders in gardens. Like *A. bimaculata*, the bees will often forage at high densities, emitting a high-pitched buzz as they hover and dart rapidly between flowers. **Nesting habits** Small aggregations have been observed in sandy ground, especially south-facing slopes and faces, sometimes amongst *bimaculata* nests; also in walls. **Status & distribution** Confined to southern England north to Gloucestershire, Cambridgeshire and Norfolk. Within this range, scarce away from Greater London and the Thames Gateway. Not recorded from Ireland. Recorded from most of the Channel Islands. **Parasites & associates** None noted.

Anthophora retusa (Linnaeus, 1758)　　　Potter Flower Bee
Plate 16

Description & similar species FW 9–10mm female, 8.5–9mm male. The black females resemble the typical form of *A. plumipes* in the field but are a little smaller, slimmer and shinier. The orange hind tibial spurs, which are the best feature, should be detectable with a hand lens if you can tube a specimen. Males are darker and noticeably smaller than *A. plumipes* males (with which they often fly) with the form of the mid-tarsi very different. **Variation** Channel Island females are very different-looking with a grey and black banded thorax and white bands across tergites 2–4. **Flight season** Males appear in April and can persist into June. Females can appear by late April and persist until late June/early July, the whole flight period being 2–3 weeks later than in *A. plumipes*. **Habitat** In the past quite varied, including soft rock cliffs, coastal dunes and inland on heathland and occasionally in gardens. Most modern sites are coastal and involve chalk downland and soft rock cliffs. **Flowers visited** Various, including Ground-ivy, Common Bird's-foot-trefoil, Kidney Vetch, clovers, *Vicia* vetches, Viper's-bugloss, Hound's-tongue, Thrift, Hemlock Water-dropwort, various crucifers and trees such as maples (seemingly an important pollen source in Sussex). **Nesting habits** Nesting aggregations can occur in sandy cliff faces and Rabbit-disturbed slopes. **Status & distribution** One of Britain's most declined bees. Formerly widespread but localised across southern England north to Avon, Oxfordshire and Norfolk. Modern records are confined to a few sites in Dorset, north Hampshire, Isle of Wight and East Sussex. Not recorded from Wales, Scotland or Ireland. Recorded from several of the Channel Islands. **Parasites & associates** The cleptoparasitic bee *Melecta luctuosa*, which has not been seen in Britain since 1912.

female

male

MELECTA – MOURNING BEES

Medium-sized, robust bees, mostly with black bodies marked with grey or white hair bands or spots, plus a somewhat pointed abdomen. The lower face is rather inflated and the marginal cell of the forewings is unusually small. The scutellum has a pair of blunt spines along the hind margin. They are cleptoparasites of *Anthophora* bees (and some related genera), especially those that nest in aggregations. The female *Melecta* creates a hole in a closed *Anthophora* nest cell and then oviposits an egg on the wall inside before sealing the hole. The first-instar larva then destroys the host egg or grub with its long, sickle-shaped mandibles and proceeds to eat the food store. Females fly around host nesting areas with a particularly slow and steady flight and never hover like the host. Both

♀

Melecta albifrons

sexes can also be found visiting flowers nearby. About 60 species are present within Palaearctic and Nearctic regions. Two species are recorded from Britain, though one is presumed extinct.

MELECTA

— Third submarginal cell longer and more pointed (Fig. 1). Apex of hind basitarsi with a pronounced dorsal projection (Fig. 2). White lateral spots of tergites 2–4 small and rounded, sometimes absent. Male antennal flagellar segments with circular sensoria above (Fig. 3). Male mid femora usually with the posterior hair fringe entirely black-haired .... *albifrons*

— Third submarginal cell shorter and blunter (Fig. 4). Apex of hind basitarsi lacking a pronounced dorsal projection. White lateral spots of tergites 2–4 large and rectangular. Male antennal flagellar segments lacking sensoria above. Male mid femora with the posterior hair fringe conspicuously whitish at tip .... *luctuosa*

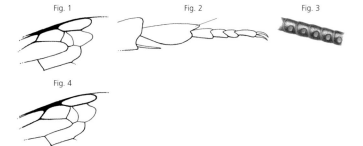

Fig. 1   Fig. 2   Fig. 3

Fig. 4

Melecta albifrons (Forster, 1771)   **Common Mourning Bee**

Plate 16

Description & similar species FW 10–11.5mm (sexes similar). A fairly large bee that, in its normal form, is very distinctive with a broad grey collar and white lateral abdominal spots which are usually roundish. This is one of the few British bees where sexes are not easily distinguishable in the field. *M. luctuosa* (considered long extinct) is a more strongly marked bee with rectangular rather than circular spots on the abdomen, plus structural differences given in the key. **Variation** Some size variation; also variation in the extent and paleness of the thoracic collar, the colour of the facial hairs (which can vary from mostly white to entirely black)

363

female

female, dark form

male

and the size and number of white spots on the tergites (the spots are frequently missing from tergites 3 and 4). Fully black individuals are not uncommon and are sometimes mistaken for female *Anthophora plumipes*, although the body shape is very different. **Flight season** Mid-March to early June. **Habitat** Any of the habitats where its host forms good colonies, and perhaps especially frequent in urban locations, churchyards and soft rock cliffs. **Flowers visited** Spring-blossoming shrubs such as cherries, apples, gorses and flowers such as Ground-ivy, dandelions, Wallflower, Honesty and Kidney Vetch. **Status & distribution** Widespread over much of southern England, where it can be frequent though rarely ever numerous. Extending north to Yorkshire but rare in southwest England and Wales. Unrecorded in Scotland and Ireland. Present on several of the Channel Islands. **Host(s)** The cleptoparasite of *Anthophora plumipes*.

Melecta luctuosa (Scopoli, 1770) **Square-spotted Mourning Bee**
not illustrated

Description & similar species Resembling *M. albifrons* in size but with larger, rectangular spots on most tergites and usually a paler thoracic collar. Confirmation needs to be based on the structural features given in the key. **Variation** Some variation in the size of the abdominal spots and the extent of pale hairs on the thorax. **Flight season** Late April to July. **Habitat** As per its host, with

male

heathland and soft rock cliffs featuring most within its British records. **Flowers visited** Recorded visiting Hound's-tongue in Britain, with plants such as Ground-ivy, Cat-mint and further Boraginaceae noted abroad. **Status & distribution** Historically recorded from Dorset, Hampshire, Surrey, Middlesex, Kent, Essex and Avon. The last British record was from the New Forest in 1912. This demise mirrors the massive decline of its host, and it is presumed long-extinct. **Host(s)** The cleptoparasite of *Anthophora retusa*.

CERATINA – SMALL CARPENTER BEES

A large cosmopolitan genus of small to medium-sized bees related to the much larger carpenter bees of the genus *Xylocopa*. Most have a rather slim build and usually weakly metallic, inconspicuously haired bodies. Males usually have partially yellow or whitish faces. They can be separated from some superficially similar halictid bees by the long tongue, the tiny jugal lobe of the hindwing and rather club-shaped abdomen. Nesting typically occurs in dead wood and hollow stems.

Most species are solitary but a few are eusocial. Parthenogenesis is known in several species. *Ceratina* species are polylectic and carry pollen on a rather weakly formed pollen brush on the hind leg. Numerous further species occur in Europe, though few extend to the near-continent.

Ceratina cyanea (Kirby, 1802)   Little Blue Carpenter Bee
Plate 16

Description & similar species FW 4.5–5mm (sexes similar). A small metallic blue bee rather resembling one of the small metallic *Lasioglossum* species in the field but with a rather different body shape, including a club-shaped abdomen that is widest towards its apex. Males have a cream-coloured lower clypeus and labrum. **Variation** Very little. **Flight season** May to mid-September. **Habitat** Various dry, warm habitats, with a liking for scattered bramble patches or roses in sunny locations, including south-facing chalk downland, heathland edge, brownfield sites and open woodland. **Flowers visited** A great variety of flowers are visited including Yellow-rattle, cinquefoils, Fairy Flax, Cornflower, buttercups, Germander Speedwell, Common Bird's-foot-trefoil, Red Campion, Chickweed, Bugle, Sheep's-bit, Wood Spurge, ragworts, goldenrods, scabiouses, forget-me-nots and dandelions. It moves between flowers with a slow and distinctive flight that is very different from that of *Lasioglossum* or *Halictus* bees. **Nesting habits** Nests are formed in hollow twigs and stems, typically those of brambles and roses close to the ground. New adults overwinter in these twigs and can thus be recorded outside of the flight period. **Status & distribution** Formerly considered a rarity but now known to be widespread in southeast England, mainly between the Solent and Essex but extending north to the Bristol area and Suffolk. It can be locally common on the North and South Downs. Not recorded from Wales, Scotland, Ireland or the Channel Islands. Rearing from stems may be a more efficient method of recording it than looking for the rather elusive adults. **Parasites & associates** An unconfirmed ichneumon wasp.

female

male

XYLOCOPA – LARGE CARPENTER BEES

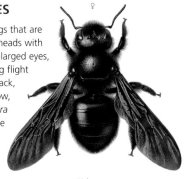

♀

Large to very large, robustly built bees with long wings that are often dark and iridescent. Females have box-shaped heads with powerful jaws. Males have weaker jaws and often enlarged eyes, and those of some foreign species engage in hovering flight when seeking out females. Many species are shiny black, some yellow and black, others entirely brown or yellow, and a few are banded and look rather like *Anthophora* species. Some species have a special pouch at the base of tergite 1 in which they transport symbiotic mites.

Nesting occurs in dead wood, structural timbers, hollow stems and other cavities, with the powerful female jaws helping to tunnel into wood or pith where there is no pre-existing cavity. Cell partitions are made of wood fragments, and in some species

Xylocopa violacea

food is initially stored separately from the brood, as in bumblebees and honey bees. Most species are solitary, but a few exhibit primitive eusocial behaviour. *Xylocopa* species seem to lack any bee cleptoparasites, but some species are attacked by sapygid wasps and bombyliid flies.

These bees can be important pollinators, and some plants seem to have evolved an obligate requirement for pollination by them. The North American *X. virginica* is an economically important pollinator of fruit trees and other crops. Like bumblebees, certain species will cut a hole at the base of tubular flowers to access nectar that is too difficult to reach by normal means.

This is a very large, near-cosmopolitan genus (over 730 described species). No species is yet established in Britain, though the most widespread European species (*X. violacea*) is increasingly turning up as a vagrant or introduction. As well as the two species covered below, two further European species (*X. valga* and *X. iris*) could potentially turn up in Britain.

Xylocopa violacea (Linnaeus, 1758)   Violet Carpenter Bee

Plate 17

Description & similar species FW 20–22mm (sexes similar). One of the largest European bees, a truly impressive shiny black species with long dark wings that have blue and violet reflections. Individuals of *Bombus rupestris* which have lost the red hairs on the tail are occasionally reported as *X. violacea* but have a very different body shape. The south European *X. valga* closely resembles *X. violacea* but males have antennal segments 11 and 12 black (reddish in *X. violacea*); females can only be separated by checking the teeth of the hind tibiae under a microscope. A further European species, *X. iris*, is considerably smaller than the other two. **Variation** Very little. **Flight season** On the continent, hibernated females can emerge in late winter and persist until June. They have been recorded as early as late February in a Leicestershire garden. **Habitat** Quite varied abroad, including coastal scrub and grasslands, orchards, vineyards and gardens. **Flowers visited** British records include Wisteria, Sweet Pea, Runner Bean and Lavender. Abroad it visits a variety of spring-blossoming shrubs and flowers, especially legumes and labiates. **Nesting habits** Nests are excavated in wood and hollow stems, especially the canes of giant *Arundo* grasses in southern Europe but also trees. The female jaws can create tunnels in sound as well as rotten wood. A liking for wooden transport pallets and crates predisposes it to accidental introduction from the continent. After larval development, new adults overwinter in their nesting burrows. **Status & distribution** Relatively few scattered records, mostly in southeast England and the Midlands, but extending as far north as Yorkshire and west to Cardiganshire. Recorded from Sark and Jersey in the Channel Islands. Considered a vagrant or human-assisted introduction, with little evidence of any truly permanent population here, though it has successfully nested and overwintered on several occasions. British records seem to be increasing, and it has been expanding northwards within Europe, possibly in response to climate change. However, it should also be noted that many *Xylocopa* records can only be provisionally assigned to *X. violacea*, as the possibility of imported *X. valga* cannot be ruled out. **Parasites & associates** None known.

Xylocopa virginica (Linnaeus, 1771)   **Eastern Carpenter Bee**
not illustrated

Description & similar species FW 18.5mm (the Warwickshire female). Averaging slightly smaller than *X. violacea*, with the thoracic dorsum and first tergite covered in yellow hairs. Quite unmistakable in a British context, though many other *Xylocopa* species, and also some American bumblebees, look very similar. **Variation** Seemingly little. **Flight season** Spring and early summer. **Habitat** Various habitats are exploited in the USA. **Flowers visited** Many flower species are visited in the USA. **Nesting habits** Nests are excavated in wood, and artificial nest sites are put out in some orchard areas of America to encourage fruit-tree pollination by this bee. **Status & distribution** The commonest *Xylocopa* of eastern North America, occasionally imported into Britain. A free-flying female was recorded feeding on mignonettes near Edge Hill, Warwickshire, in 1996 (a Ministry of Defence site that receives imported items from the USA). **Parasites & associates** None known.

367

BOMBUS – BUMBLEBEES

Large (especially queens), furry bees that are often black with a pattern of yellow or grey bands and a 'tail' that ranges from white to deep red. Some species have a chestnut pile on top of the thorax and lack a coloured tail. Over 250 species are described worldwide, most occurring in cooler parts of the northern hemisphere.

queen

Bombus terrestris

queen

Bombus muscorum

queen

Bombus ruderarius

The genus contains both social and cleptoparasitic species, the latter called 'cuckoo bumblebees' (mostly within subgenus *Psithyrus*). The social species have well-formed pollen baskets (corbiculae) on the hind tibiae, resembling those found in worker honey bees. *Psithyrus* cuckoo bumblebees have no such modifications and typically have a sparser body pile that allows the underlying integument to shine through, and a more armoured build with a squarer head. A few foreign cleptoparasitic species not within *Psithyrus* retain a pollen basket, albeit reduced.

queen

queen

♂

Bombus monticola

Bombus hypnorum

Bombus vestalis

The social species form nesting colonies that range from a few dozen to several hundred individuals, most of these being workers. Nesting typically occurs in old rodent nests, either underground or amongst dense vegetation at the surface. A few species will use nest boxes and holes in trees (these must contain old nesting material), notably *B. hypnorum*, which nearly always nests well above the ground. Nests are typically initiated by a fertilised, overwintered queen that emerges in spring. She will forage heavily from spring-flowering shrubs and flowers such as dandelions and dead-nettles, initiate a nest and raise a brood of workers, which are substantially smaller than her. The first workers of species such as *B. terrestris* are often evident by late April, and males and new queens of the bivoltine *B. pratorum* and *B. jonellus* often appear by May. Most of the early-emerging species will attempt a second nesting cycle, and winter-active *B. terrestris* can be trivoltine (meaning workers can be seen in all months of the year in a few areas).

Cuckoo bumblebees either parasitise a single host species (e.g. *B. rupestris* and *B. vestalis*) or a group of related ones (e.g. *B. sylvestris*). The queen-like females usually emerge a couple of weeks after queens of the host species and can often be observed patrolling banks and grass tussocks in search of host nests with a characteristic low-pitched buzz. Once a nest has been found and selected, the cuckoo bumblebee will kill or subdue the true queen and use the brood cells, food stores and bumblebee workers to bring up her own offspring, consisting of new queen-like females plus males, but no workers.

The long tongue and ability to forage in cool, cloudy, even wet weather makes bumblebees highly effective pollinators. All species use a range of flowers but with biases. The long-faced, long-tongued *B. hortorum* can access nectar from deep flowers such as Foxglove, Honeysuckle, comfreys and sages. Shorter-tongued species such as *B. terrestris*, *B. lucorum* and *B. pratorum* can be numerous on bramble flowers or allotment Raspberry patches. But they will also 'nectar-rob' deeper flowers such as comfreys by biting a hole at the base of the corolla.

Bumblebee nests are untidy affairs compared to those of honey bees, but the cells are constructed of wax in the same way. The larvae are fed in one of two ways. Pocket makers create wax pockets alongside the larvae and keep placing pollen–nectar mix into these. In pollen storers, pollen is stored in wax pots away from the larvae and is carried to the larvae within the crops of the workers. Nests are inhabited by a variety of parasites and inquilines, including the larvae of the Bee Moth *Aphomia sociella*, hoverfly *Volucella bombylans*, sarcophagid fly *Brachicoma devia*, fannid flies, velvet ant *Mutilla europaea* and assorted mites. Adult bumblebees are parasitised by conopid flies such as *Physocephala* and *Sicus*. Smaller internal parasites include the mite *Locustacarus buchneri*, the nematode *Sphaerulea bombi* and the microsporidian *Nosema bombi*.

Twenty-seven bumblebee species are currently on the British list, though *B. cullumanus* and *B. pomorum* are considered extinct, and *B. subterraneus* is the subject of reintroduction following extinction. Several species have shown substantial declines and range contractions, notably *B. distinguendus*, *B. muscorum*, *B. sylvarum* and *B. soroeensis*. By contrast, *B. hypnorum* is a recent colonist (first recorded 2001). Despite their size, identifying bumblebees is challenging. Some species show considerable variation, both within a single population (e.g. mainland *B. pascuorum* and *B. ruderatus*) or depending on geographic location (e.g. *B. muscorum*). Reliable separation of males, workers and many queens of the '*lucorum* complex' (*B. cryptarum*, *B. lucorum* and *B. magnus*) can only be done using DNA. Ageing and fading can also affect their appearance. Field determination gets easier with practice, but even experts will sometimes need to take voucher specimens to confirm identification under a microscope. The male genitalia can be especially useful and should be pulled out of fresh specimens prior to pinning.

Note that FW lengths given below relate to typical-sized specimens, and there is pronounced size variation found in most bumblebee castes. For queens and males, FW lengths significantly greater than those quoted will be unusual, but 'giant' workers approaching the sizes of small queens can be common in some species, e.g. *B. terrestris* and *B. ruderarius*, and it can be tricky to distinguish giant workers from small queens (although queens tend to retain a more robust build than workers). All castes can exhibit dwarfism.

ASSOCIATED SPECIES

Hoverfly *Volucella bombylans* (right), velvet ant *Mutilla europaea* (far right), and conopid flies *Physocephala rufipes* (below left) and *Sicus ferrugineus* (below right).

BOMBUS FEMALE GROUPS

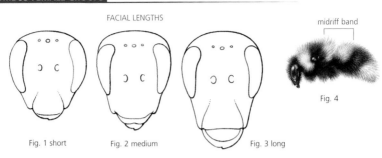

FACIAL LENGTHS

midriff band

Fig. 4

Fig. 1 short   Fig. 2 medium   Fig. 3 long

1   Hind tibia unmodified and densely covered with hairs on its outer face, which
    is convex (Fig. 5). Mandibles triangular-ended (Fig. 6) (cuckoo bumblebees) .... **female group A**

—   Hind tibia with outer face bare, flat and shiny, fringed with long hairs (Fig. 7).
    Mandibles square-ended (Fig. 8) (social bumblebees) **2**

2   Pile on top of thorax ginger or darker brown, unbanded though sometimes
    substantially darkened centrally .... **female group B**

—   Pile on top of thorax black with a pale collar, or with a black band between
    the wings, or entirely black **3**

3   Thorax black-haired (a vague collar or scutellum fringe may be present) .... **female group C**

—   Top of thorax with a distinct collar (yellow, brownish or greyish) **4**

4   Scutellum entirely black-haired, no midriff band present .... **female group D**

—   Scutellum partially or totally pale-haired. Well-formed midriff band present
    in some species (Fig. 4) .... **female group E**

Fig. 5   Fig. 6   Fig. 7   Fig. 8

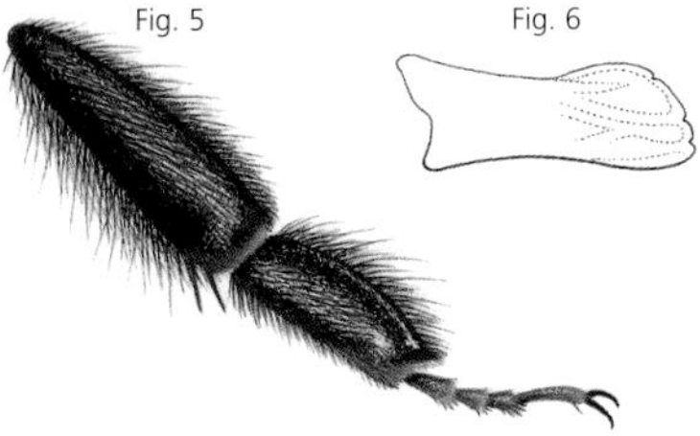

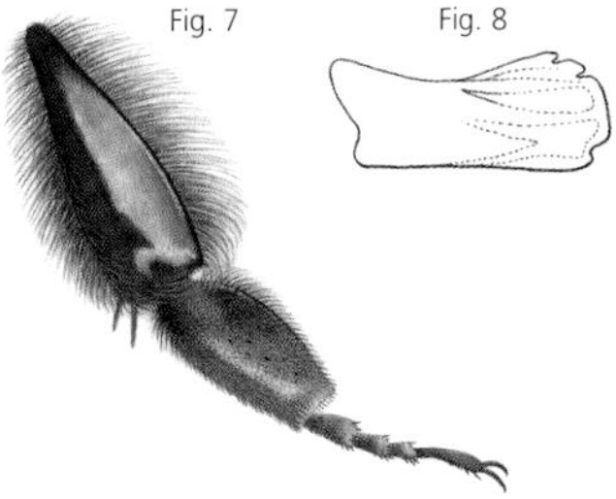

BOMBUS FEMALE GROUP A (CUCKOO BUMBLEBEES)

1   Body entirely black except for a red tail (a weak yellow collar is occasionally
    present). Wings strongly darkened. Head large and box-shaped. Sternite 6 with
    sharply angled lateral ridges (Fig. 9) .... *rupestris*

—   Tail never red-haired. A yellow collar is usually present. Wings not much darkened.
    Head smaller **2**

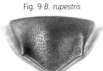

Fig. 9 *B. rupestris*   Fig. 10 *B. campestris*

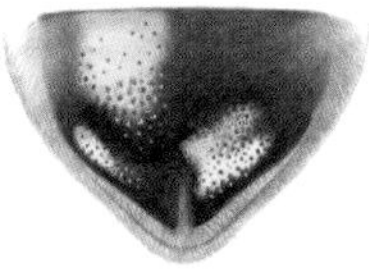

2   Tergites 4 and 5 with buff-coloured hairs at sides but with very sparse black
    hairs centrally. Sternite 6 with large lateral ridges which converge at the tip
    (Fig. 10). Scutellum typically extensively buff-haired and tip of abdomen
    strongly downcurved (darkened or melanic specimens occasional) .... *campestris*

—   Tip of abdomen extensively white-haired **3**

3   Sternite 6 with two large convergent ridges (Fig. 11). Malar gap only about 0.75
    times the basal width of a mandible (Fig. 12). White tail preceded by two lateral
    patches of yellow hairs separated by a patch of black hairs (the yellow patches
    can be very pale in some individuals but the intervening black zone remains) **4**

—   Sternite 6 otherwise. Malar gap about equal to the basal width of a mandible
    (Fig. 13). White tail not preceded by yellow hairs and with a straighter junction
    with the black hairs that precede it **5**

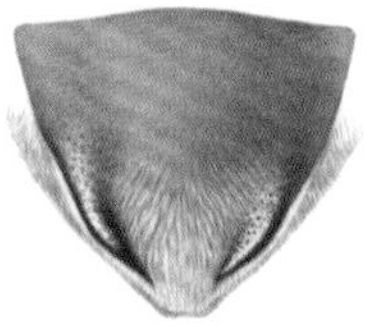

Fig. 11 *B. vestalis*   Fig. 12   Fig. 14 *B. barbutellus* 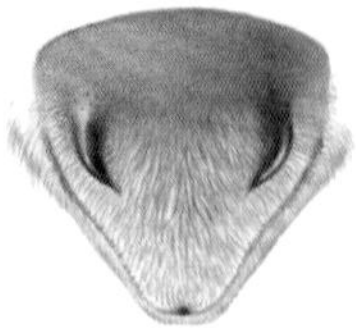   Fig. 15 *B. sylvestris*
(*B. bohemicus* similar)

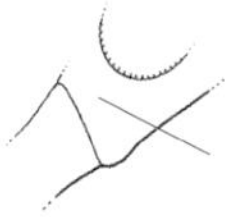

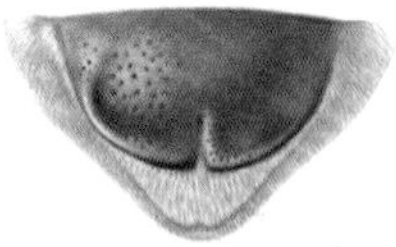

Fig. 13

4   Tergite 6 punctate and dull over most of its surface. Collar yellow-brown. Scutellum
    entirely black-haired. Yellow side patches of the tail usually bright sulphur-yellow.
    Larger (typical wing length 18mm) .... *vestalis*

—   Tergite 6 scarcely punctate and strongly shining over much of its surface except the
    sides. Collar paler yellow. Scutellum usually with a narrow fringe of yellow hairs.
    Yellow side patches of the tail pale yellow. Smaller (typical wing length 16mm) .... *bohemicus*

5   Sternite 6 with a pair of strong semicircular ridges only narrowly interrupted in
    the middle (Fig. 14). Tergite 6 with a narrow ridge running along the midline.
    Scutellum substantially yellow-haired. Abdomen longer in top view, less
    downcurved at the tip (view from side) .... *barbutellus*

—   Sternite 6 with a pair of small, well-separated small ridges, its shining tip protruding
    beyond tergite 6 (Fig. 15). Scutellum black-haired. Abdomen shorter in top view
    and more downcurved at the tip (view from side) .... *sylvestris*

For melanic female cuckoo bumblebees, check the shape of the ridges on sternite 6.

BOMBUS FEMALE GROUP B

1   Abdomen black with a pure white tail. Hind basitarsi with upper corner not formed
    into a projecting point (Fig. 16) .... *hypnorum*

—   Abdomen entirely or extensively pale haired, or, if extensively black-haired, the tail
    is buff or orange. Hind basitarsi with upper corner formed into a projecting point (Fig. 17) **2**

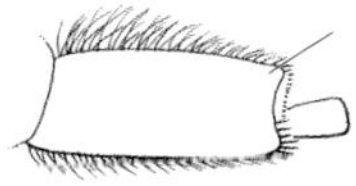

Fig. 16 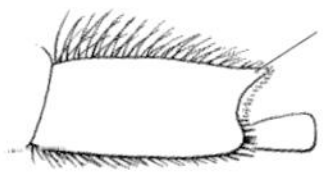   Fig. 17

<table>
<tr><td>2</td><td>Legs and underside of body mainly or entirely black-haired ....</td><td>3</td></tr>
<tr><td>—</td><td>Underside of body pale-haired, the femora entirely or mainly so ....</td><td>4</td></tr>
</table>

2   Legs and underside of body mainly or entirely black-haired **3**

—   Underside of body pale-haired, the femora entirely or mainly so **4**

3   Upperside of abdomen entirely buff or whitish-haired
(various offshore islands of the Atlantic coast) .... *muscorum* ssp. *agricolae/scyllonius*

—   Basal tergites black-haired (Aran Islands) .... *muscorum* ssp. *allenellus*

4   Tergites 2–5 with complete bands of black hairs (tergites 2 and 3
sometimes entirely black-haired), though black hairs sometimes only
visible under magnification. Tail sometimes orange. Pile on top of thorax
often darkened centrally. Body hairs relatively long and uneven. Queen
wing length up to 13mm .... typical *pascuorum*

—   Black hairs usually confined to tergite 6 (occasionally a few at sides of tergites
4 and 5), tail never orange. Pile on top of thorax never darkened centrally, even
if some black hairs are present (extremely difficult trio, especially when faded) **5**

5   Tergite 2 (and occasionally the base of 3) with a chestnut hair band as dark as
the hairs on top of the thorax (view from side). Chestnut pile on top of thorax
usually with scattered black hairs above the wing bases and sometimes more
extensively, the chestnut pile usually strongly demarked from the whitish pile
at the sides of the thorax. Hind margins of tergites 3 and 4 at sides with the
punctures very dense and somewhat elongate. Body hairs relatively long
and uneven. Queen wing length up to 13mm .... *humilis*

—   Tergite 2 at most with a very pale band across tergite 2. Chestnut pile on top of thorax
usually without scattered black hairs above the wing bases, and not usually contrasting
so strongly with the paler pile on the sides of the thorax. Punctures on sides of tergite 3
not elongate **6**

6   Punctures at sides of tergite 4 very dense with their margins raised on one side, the
surface between them dulled by microsculpture. Queens slightly larger (typical wing
length 14mm) with a neat, even body pile. Chestnut pile on top of thorax usually
grading into paler buff hairs behind the head and on the hind part of the
scutellum. Hairs on top of head behind ocelli usually entirely pale .... typical *muscorum*

—   Punctures at sides of tergite 4 less dense and without raised margins, the surface
between them shining. Queens averaging smaller (wing length up to 13mm) with
a longer and less even body pile. Chestnut pile on top of thorax not grading into
paler buff hairs behind the head and on the hind part of the scutellum, and
sometimes with scattered black hairs. Hairs on top of head behind ocelli
partly or entirely black .... *pascorum* (lightest forms)

BOMBUS FEMALE GROUP C

1   Body entirely black with at most a vague tail **2**

—   Body with an obvious white, orange, buff or red tail **3**

2   Face very long, the malar gap about half as long as the length of
an eye (Fig. 18). Sternite 6 never with a median keel .... *ruderatus* (form perniger)

—   Face shorter, the malar gap about one-third the length of an eye
(Fig. 19). Median keel present on sternite 6 (Fig. 20) .... *subterraneus* (dark form)

3   Tergite 2 with a yellowish-brown band. Queens large and
robust with a buff tail (typical wing length 18mm) .... *terrestris* (form without a collar)

—   Tergite 2 without a yellowish-brown band **4**

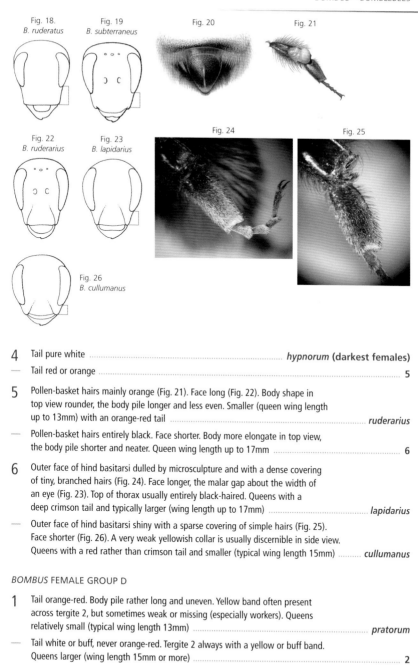

Fig. 18.
B. ruderatus

Fig. 19
B. subterraneus

Fig. 20

Fig. 21

Fig. 22
B. ruderarius

Fig. 23
B. lapidarius

Fig. 24

Fig. 25

Fig. 26
B. cullumanus

4 Tail pure white .... *hypnorum* **(darkest females)**

— Tail red or orange **5**

5 Pollen-basket hairs mainly orange (Fig. 21). Face long (Fig. 22). Body shape in top view rounder, the body pile longer and less even. Smaller (queen wing length up to 13mm) with an orange-red tail .... *ruderarius*

— Pollen-basket hairs entirely black. Face shorter. Body more elongate in top view, the body pile shorter and neater. Queen wing length up to 17mm **6**

6 Outer face of hind basitarsi dulled by microsculpture and with a dense covering of tiny, branched hairs (Fig. 24). Face longer, the malar gap about the width of an eye (Fig. 23). Top of thorax usually entirely black-haired. Queens with a deep crimson tail and typically larger (wing length up to 17mm) .... *lapidarius*

— Outer face of hind basitarsi shiny with a sparse covering of simple hairs (Fig. 25). Face shorter (Fig. 26). A very weak yellowish collar is usually discernible in side view. Queens with a red rather than crimson tail and smaller (typical wing length 15mm) .... *cullumanus*

BOMBUS FEMALE GROUP D

1 Tail orange-red. Body pile rather long and uneven. Yellow band often present across tergite 2, but sometimes weak or missing (especially workers). Queens relatively small (typical wing length 13mm) .... *pratorum*

— Tail white or buff, never orange-red. Tergite 2 always with a yellow or buff band. Queens larger (wing length 15mm or more) **2**

2　Face longer, the malar gap equal to the basal width of the mandibles (Fig. 27). Yellow band across tergite 2 narrowed in the middle and often extending onto the sides of tergite 1. Antennal segment 4 barely longer than wide (Fig. 28). Mandibles without a distinct apical notch towards their outer corner (Fig. 29). Tail white but often with a distinct buffish or orange zone where it meets the black hairs that precede it. Queen wing length to 15mm .... *soroeensis*

—　Face shorter, the malar gap about 0.75 times the basal width of the mandibles (Fig. 30). Yellow or buff band of tergite 2 continuous (unless worn) and not expanding onto tergite 1. Antennal segment 4 somewhat longer than wide (Fig. 31). Mandibles with a distinct apical notch towards their outer corner (Fig. 32). Queen wing length usually 16mm or more 3

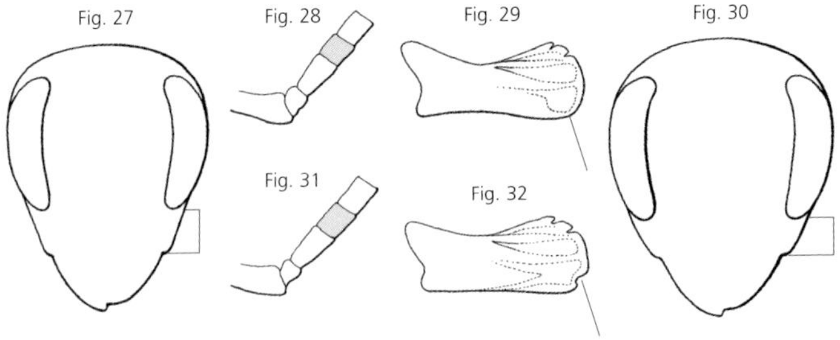

Fig. 27　　Fig. 28　　Fig. 29　　Fig. 30

Fig. 31　　Fig. 32

3　Queens (wing length 16mm or more) 4
—　Workers (wing length rarely exceeding 13mm) 8

4　Tail buff. Collar buff-brown, often much reduced. Large (typical wing length 18mm) .... *terrestris* ssp. *audax*
—　Tail pure white, collar yellow or yellow-buff 5

5　Yellow collar broad and extending down the sides of the thorax usually for a distance twice its width. Band on tergite 2 relatively broad and pale. Typically large, *terrestris*-sized .... *magnus*
—　Yellow collar not extending so far down the side of the thorax 6

6　Ends of collar interrupted by an incursion of black hairs just in front of the wing bases (only DNA can give a definite determination) .... **possible** *cryptarum*
—　Ends of collar blunt and uninterrupted 7

7　Collar and band across tergite 2 paler and yellower. Smaller (wing length to 16mm) (only DNA can give a definite determination) .... **probable** *lucorum*
—　Collar and band across tergite 2 darker buffish-yellow. Larger (wing length to 18mm) (Channel Islands) .... *terrestris* ssp. *terrestris*

8　Collar and band on tergite 2 yellow-buff. Tail white with a buff interface where it meets the black hairs that precede it .... *terrestris* ssp. *audax*
—　Collar and band on tergite 2 yellow. Tail white with a grey interface where it meets the black hairs that precede it .... *cryptarum/lucorum/magnus/terrestris* ssp. *terrestris* **(workers currently indistinguishable)**

BOMBUS FEMALE GROUP E

1　Abdomen red-haired from tergite 2 onwards 2
—　Abdomen never this extensively red-haired 3

2   Face relatively short (Fig. 1). Hind basitarsi without an acutely produced upper apical corner (Fig. 16). Body markings bold and bright, the abdomen bright red-haired in all but the most faded individuals .... *monticola*

—   Face longer (Fig. 2). Hind basitarsi with an acutely produced upper apical corner (Fig. 17). Collar and scutellum with a dull greyish pile containing many black hairs, the abdomen almost entirely orange-red-haired .... *pomorum*

3   Abdomen entirely yellow-haired .... **distinguendus**

—   Abdomen partly black-haired with a white or coloured tail **4**

4   Abdomen yellow-grey-haired with a narrow black band across tergite 3 and a dull orange tail. Pile of thorax greyish with an ill-defined dark band between the wings, the pale collar with scattered black hairs .... *sylvarum*

—   Abdomen mainly black with a well-defined white or buff tail. Thorax with a well-defined yellow collar and scutellum **5**

5   Face relatively short, the malar gap between the bottom of the eyes and base of the mandibles much less than half the height of an eye (Figs 1 & 2) (if in doubt, sternite 6 has a median keel: Fig. 20) **6**

—   Face very long, the malar gap 0.5–0.6 times the length of an eye (Figs 33 & 34). Sternite 6 never with a keel along the midline **7**

6   Face shorter, the malar gap about 0.25 times the length of an eye (Fig. 1). Sternite 6 lacking a median keel. Body pile longer and fluffier. Tail typically white and sharply defined but orange-buff in some Scottish populations. Midriff band usually well formed (Fig. 4). Queens smaller, typical wing length 12–13mm .... *jonellus*

—   Face longer, the malar gap about 0.4 times the length of an eye (Fig. 2). Body pile short and neat, especially in queens. Sternite 6 with a median keel (Fig. 20). Tergite 1 either black-haired or with a weak scattering of yellow hairs resulting in a less well-formed midriff band. Tergite 2 usually with a fringe of pale hairs along its hind margin. Tail white or greyish. Queens larger, typical wing length 17mm (semi-melanic individuals common) .... *subterraneus*

7   Queens (wing length usually at least 15mm) **8**

—   Workers (wing length rarely exceeding 12mm) **9**

8   Tergite 1 usually entirely yellow-haired, combining with the scutellum hairs to create a broad midriff band, this band and the collar both bright yellow. Tergite 6 less roughened with some smooth, shiny surface. Face slightly longer (Fig. 33). Smaller (typical wing length 15mm) .... *hortorum*

—   Tergite 1 either black-haired or with a weak scattering of yellow hairs resulting in a less well-formed midriff band. Pale hairs of collar and scutellum darker yellow-brown and often more restricted in extent than in *hortorum*. Tergite 6 very roughened with no smooth, shiny surface. Face slightly shorter (Fig. 34). Very large (typical wing length 17mm) .... **typical *ruderatus***

Fig. 33 *B. hortorum*   Fig. 34 *B. ruderatus*

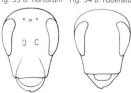

9   Collar and midriff bands broad and bright yellow. Body pile longer, less even.
Face slightly longer .... *hortorum*

—   Collar and midriff bands narrower and darker yellow-brown, the collar usually
taking the form of a narrow crescent and often very weak. Body pile shorter
and neater. Face slightly shorter .... **typical** *ruderatus*

BOMBUS MALE GROUPS

1   Pile on top of thorax ginger or darker brown, unbanded though sometimes
substantially darkened centrally .... **male group A**

—   Pile on top of thorax black with a pale collar, or with a black band between
the wings, or entirely black **2**

2   Tail not differentiated or barely so .... **male group B**

—   A distinct white, buff, orange or red tail present **3**

3   Tail red or orange .... **male group C**

—   Tail white or pale buff **4**

4   Outer face of hind tibiae extensively bare or only sparsely haired, often flattened.
If somewhat denser-haired (*subterraneus*), then antennal segment 3 about
twice as long as wide and face partially yellow-haired .... **male group D**

—   Outer face of hind tibiae densely haired throughout. Antennal segment 3 never
more than 1.5 times as long as wide. Face always black-haired .... **male group E**

BOMBUS MALE GROUP A

1   Abdomen with a pure white tail, tergites 1–3 or 2 and 3 completely black-haired.
Tip of mid-basitarsi viewed from above with apex squared off on outer corner
(Fig. 35). Genitalia (Fig. 39) .... *hypnorum*

—   Abdomen never with a pure white tail, usually substantially buff-haired but
sometimes entirely black-haired or with a buff or orange tail. Tip of mid-basitarsi
viewed from above with apex acutely angled on outer corner (Fig. 36) (genitalia
provide the safest way of separating the following species) **2**

2   Abdomen partially black-haired above, either extensively so or with more discrete
bands amongst the pale hairs (sometimes difficult to see with the naked eye) **3**

—   Abdomen appearing entirely pale-haired above, though a band of brown hairs
may be present across tergite 2 .... **4**

3   Antennal segments 5–9 strongly bulbous beneath, the swellings asymmetrical
(Fig. 37). Pile on top of thorax often partially black-haired centrally. Abdomen
highly variable, often with bands of black hairs on each tergite, sometimes
entirely black-haired, sometimes with an orange tail. Genitalia (Fig. 40) .... *pascuorum*

—   Antennal segment 5–9 less bulbous beneath, the swellings more symmetrical
(Fig. 38). Pile on top of thorax entirely bright chestnut, the top of the abdomen
usually black-haired on tergites 1 and 2, usually buff-haired from tergite 3
onwards. Genitalia (Fig. 41). (Aran Islands) .... *muscorum* **ssp.** *allenellus*

4   Legs and underside of body entirely or mostly black-haired. Genitalia (Fig. 41).
(Various offshore islands of the Atlantic coast) .... *muscorum* **ssp.** *agricolae/scyllonius*

—   Underside of body and femora pale-haired, hind tibiae partially pale-haired **5**

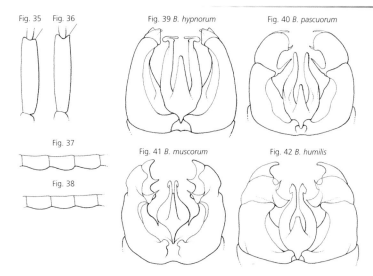

Fig. 35   Fig. 36

Fig. 39 *B. hypnorum*

Fig. 40 *B. pascuorum*

Fig. 37

Fig. 41 *B. muscorum*

Fig. 42 *B. humilis*

Fig. 38

5   Antennal segments 5–9 strongly bulbous beneath (Fig. 37). Genitalia
(Fig. 40). At least a few black hairs at the sides of tergites 5 and 6 when
viewed under magnification .... *pascuorum* (**palest forms**)

—   Antennal segments 5–9 less bulbous beneath (Fig. 38). Genitalia different. Tergites 1–6
without any black hairs, though a band of brown hairs may be present on tergite 2 .... **6**

6   Tergite 2 (and occasionally 3) with a brown band that is as dark as the top of the
thorax and does not disappear with angle of view (best viewed from side, band
can fade in old individuals). Scattered black hairs nearly always present around
the wing bases. Chestnut hairs of thorax typically extending fully to the head
and rear of the scutellum. Genitalia (Fig. 42) .... *humilis*

—   Tergite 2 with at most a yellowish-buff band that is much paler than the chestnut hairs
of the thorax (beware 'false bands' created by the direction of the light). No black
hairs around the wing bases. Chestnut hairs of thorax often grading into paler hairs
behind the head and at the rear of the scutellum. Genitalia (Fig. 41) .... **typical** *muscorum*

BOMBUS MALE GROUP B

1   Body yellow except for a black band across the thorax. Genitalia (Fig. 43) .... *distinguendus*

—   Body entirely or almost entirely black-haired **2**

2   Face short, head squarer in top view. Outer face of hind tibiae
duller with a dense covering of hairs (refer to genitalia) .... **melanic cuckoo bumblebees**

—   Face very long (Figs 47 & 48). Outer face of hind tibiae shining and extensively bare.
Genitalia (Fig. 44) **3**

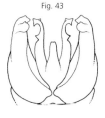

Fig. 43

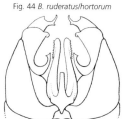

Fig. 44 *B. ruderatus/hortorum*

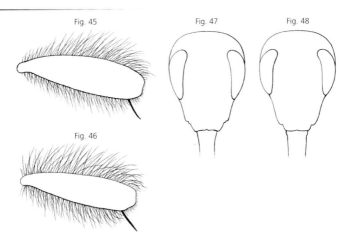

Fig. 45

Fig. 47 Fig. 48

Fig. 46

3 Mandibles with golden hairs. Body pile short, neat and deep black. Dorsal fringe of hind tibiae about equal to the greatest width of a tibia, the fringe much shorter at its base than at its tip (Fig. 45). No hint of a pale tail in most melanic individuals. Face shorter (Fig. 47) .... *ruderatus* (form *perniger*)

— Mandibles with black hairs. Body pile longer and more uneven. Dorsal fringe of hind tibiae longer than the greatest width of a tibia, the fringe as long at its base as at its tip (Fig. 46). Usually some pale hairs remaining at the tip of the abdomen. Face longer (Fig. 48) .... *hortorum* (melanic examples)

BOMBUS MALE GROUP C

1 Face entirely or predominantly black-haired 2

— Face entirely or predominantly pale-haired 5

2 Hind tibiae in side view with a very short dorsal fringe, the longest hairs no more than half the greatest width of the tibia (Fig. 49). Abdomen usually orange-haired from the base of tergite 2 onwards and with tergite 1 buff or grey-haired .... *pomorum*

— Hind tibiae in side view with a longer dorsal fringe, the longest at least equal to the greatest width of the tibia. Abdomen usually partially black-haired (except the occasional *B. rupestris*) 3

3 Hind basitarsi in side view with the base very narrow, only half the greatest width of the basitarsus; the hind tibiae also very slim in side view and barely wider than the basitarsus, the outer face shiny with few punctures (Fig. 61). Thorax with a conspicuous yellow collar and tergites 1 and 2 with a yellow band. Genitalia (Fig. 62) .... *soroeensis* (orange-tailed form)

— Hind basitarsi in side view only slightly narrowed at base. Thorax with at most a dull greyish collar, the abdomen at most with greyish or brownish bands. Hind tibia wider in side view, the outer face with fairly dense hairs and punctures 4

4 Hind basitarsi in side view about 4 times as long as wide and with a relatively long dorsal fringe (Fig. 50). Head in top view more box-shaped, with the distance between the two eyes nearly 3 times the width of an eye (Fig. 51). Genitalia (Fig. 52) .... *rupestris*

— Hind basitarsi in side view about 3 times as long as wide and with a very short dorsal fringe (Fig. 54). Head in top view less box-shaped with the distance between the two eyes only about 2.5 times the width of an eye (Fig. 55). Genitalia (Fig. 53) .... *ruderarius*

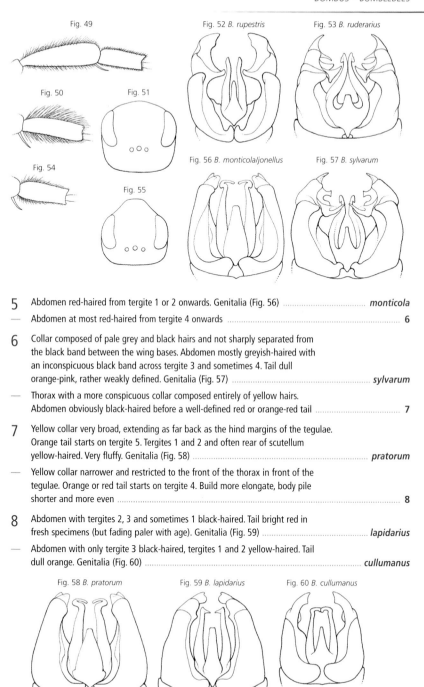

Fig. 49

Fig. 50

Fig. 51

Fig. 54

Fig. 55

Fig. 52 *B. rupestris*

Fig. 53 *B. ruderarius*

Fig. 56 *B. monticola/jonellus*

Fig. 57 *B. sylvarum*

5   Abdomen red-haired from tergite 1 or 2 onwards. Genitalia (Fig. 56) .... *monticola*

—   Abdomen at most red-haired from tergite 4 onwards **6**

6   Collar composed of pale grey and black hairs and not sharply separated from
the black band between the wing bases. Abdomen mostly greyish-haired with
an inconspicuous black band across tergite 3 and sometimes 4. Tail dull
orange-pink, rather weakly defined. Genitalia (Fig. 57) .... *sylvarum*

—   Thorax with a more conspicuous collar composed entirely of yellow hairs.
Abdomen obviously black-haired before a well-defined red or orange-red tail **7**

7   Yellow collar very broad, extending as far back as the hind margins of the tegulae.
Orange tail starts on tergite 5. Tergites 1 and 2 and often rear of scutellum
yellow-haired. Very fluffy. Genitalia (Fig. 58) .... *pratorum*

—   Yellow collar narrower and restricted to the front of the thorax in front of the
tegulae. Orange or red tail starts on tergite 4. Build more elongate, body pile
shorter and more even **8**

8   Abdomen with tergites 2, 3 and sometimes 1 black-haired. Tail bright red in
fresh specimens (but fading paler with age). Genitalia (Fig. 59) .... *lapidarius*

—   Abdomen with only tergite 3 black-haired, tergites 1 and 2 yellow-haired. Tail
dull orange. Genitalia (Fig. 60) .... *cullumanus*

Fig. 58 *B. pratorum*

Fig. 59 *B. lapidarius*

Fig. 60 *B. cullumanus*

379

BOMBUS MALE GROUP D

1   Tergite 2 entirely or predominantly yellow- or buff-haired (usually as a conspicuous band) **2**

—   Tergite 2 entirely or predominantly black-haired (anterior margin can be yellow-haired in some *jonellus*). A well-defined midriff band present, consisting of the extensively yellow-haired scutellum and tergite 1 (Fig. 4) **5**

2   Antennal segment 3 squarish, slightly shorter than 4, both much shorter than 5. Hind legs slender in side view, the basitarsi with a very narrow base (Fig. 61). Abdomen with a more upright, sparser pile, the yellow band on tergite 2 less intense, and the underlying integument shining through. Hairs on face mainly black. Genitalia (Fig. 62) .... *soroeensis*

—   Antennal segment 3 much longer than wide and longer than 5. Hind legs broader, base of the hind basitarsi broader. Abdomen with a denser, more inclined pile that obscures the underlying integument. Hairs on face yellow in some. Genitalia (Fig. 63) **3**

3   Face and top of head with conspicuous yellow hairs. Collar and band across tergite 2 bright yellow, the latter often spreading onto tergite 1 and the scutellum. Tail pure white .... *lucorum* and *magnus*

—   Head entirely black-haired **4**

4   Collar and band on tergite 2 yellow-buff. Tail usually a dull white, with a buffish zone where it meets the black hairs that precede it, but usually pure white on the Channel Islands .... *terrestris*

—   Collar and band on tergite 2 brighter yellow, tail pure white .... possible *cryptarum*

5   Face very long (Figs 47 & 48), the gap between the bottom of the eyes and base of the mandibles at least as long as half the height of an eye, always black-haired. Genitalia (Fig. 44) **6**

—   Face shorter (Figs 1 & 2), usually yellow-haired. Genitalia otherwise **7**

6   Body pile comparatively long and uneven. Hair tufts arising from the mandibles black. Dorsal fringe of hind tibiae longer than the greatest width of a tibia, the fringe as long at its base as at its tip (Fig. 46). Yellow collar and midriff band paler yellow and less sharply defined from adjacent black hairs. Face longer (Fig. 48) .... *hortorum*

—   Body pile shorter and neater. Hair tufts arising from the mandibles golden. Dorsal fringe of hind tibiae about equal to the greatest width of a tibia, the fringe much shorter at its base than at its tip (Fig. 45). Yellow collar and midriff band deeper yellow and more sharply defined from adjacent black hairs. Face slightly shorter (Fig. 47) .... *ruderatus* **(banded form)**

Fig. 61

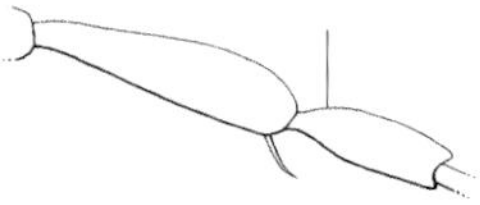

Fig. 62 *B. soroeensis*

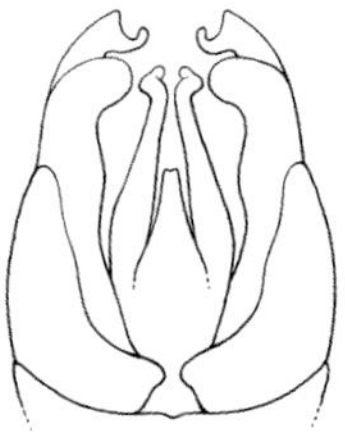

Fig. 63 *B. cryptarum/lucorum/magnus/ terrestris*

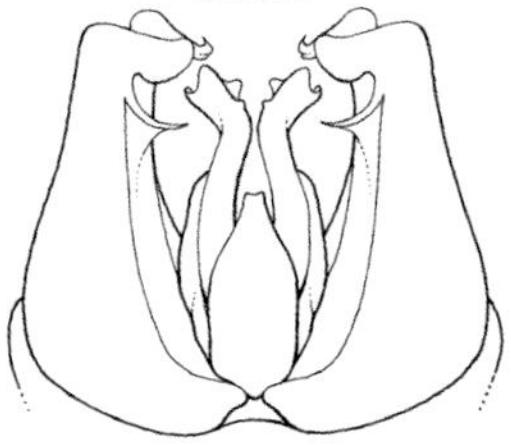

Fig. 64

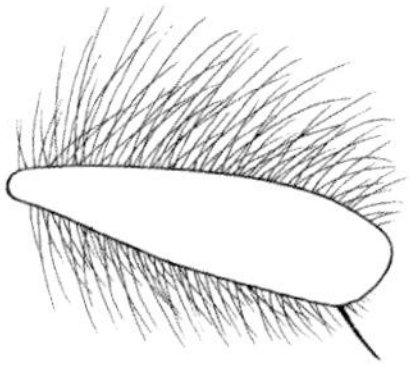

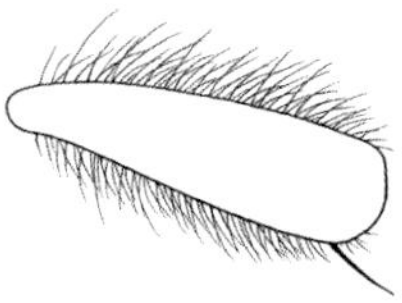

Fig. 65

7 Dorsal fringe of hind tibiae much longer than the greatest width of a tibia (Fig. 64).
   Tibiae and tarsi orange-haired. Face short (Fig. 1). Body pile long and uneven (a very
   fluffy-looking species), body rounder and shorter. Tergites 2 and 3 entirely
   black-haired, the tail white and well-defined. Genitalia (Fig. 56) .... *jonellus*

— Dorsal fringe of hind tibiae much shorter than the greatest width of a tibia (Fig. 65).
   Tibiae and tarsi black-haired. Face longer (Fig. 2). Body pile short and even. Tergites 2 and 3
   black with fringes of buff hairs along their hind margins, the tail pale buff-haired
   and less well defined basally. Genitalia (Fig. 43) .... *subterraneus*

BOMBUS MALE GROUP E (CUCKOO BUMBLEBEES EXCEPT *B. RUPESTRIS*)

1 Sternite 6 with a pair of long and dense hair tufts on either side of the middle (Fig. 66).
   Colour highly variable. Genitalia (Fig. 67) .... *campestris*

— Sternite 6 without such hair tufts **2**

2 Dorsal fringe of hind tibiae long, about 1.5 times the greatest width of a tibia.
   Tip of abdomen typically with tergite 5 black-haired and tergite 6 orange-haired.
   Genitalia with narrow claspers (Fig. 68) (scutellum typically black-haired, tail white
   or yellow) (melanic individuals frequent) .... *sylvestris*

— Dorsal fringe of hind tibiae at most a little longer than the greatest width of a
   hind tibia, often rather shorter. Tergite 6 never orange. Genital claspers broader **3**

3 Sternite 6 with a pair of welts towards tip (Fig. 70). White tail starting abruptly
   on tergite 4, with no yellow hairs on the sides of tergite 3. Genital claspers bluntly
   rounded at tip (Fig. 69). Basal antennal segments as for *vestalis* (Fig. 71) .... *barbutellus*

— Sternite 6 without such protuberances. Tergite 3 with a band of yellow hairs
   (usually interrupted by some black hairs in the middle) preceding the white tail.
   Genital claspers triangular **4**

Fig. 66

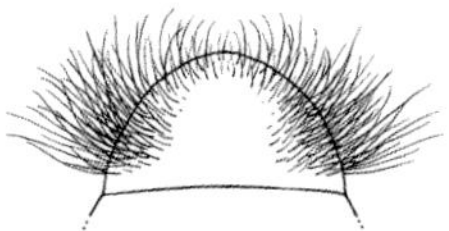

Fig. 67 *B. campestris*

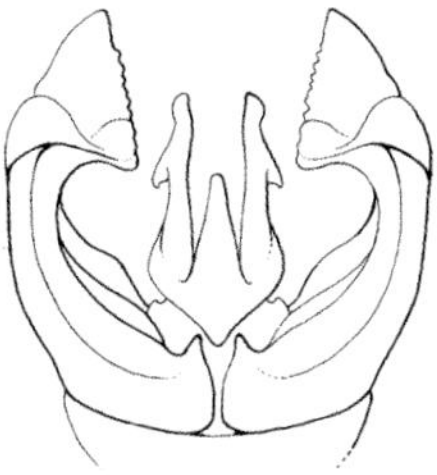

Fig. 68 *B. sylvestris*

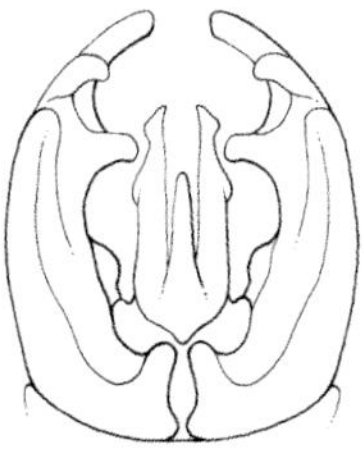

Fig. 69 *B. barbutellus*

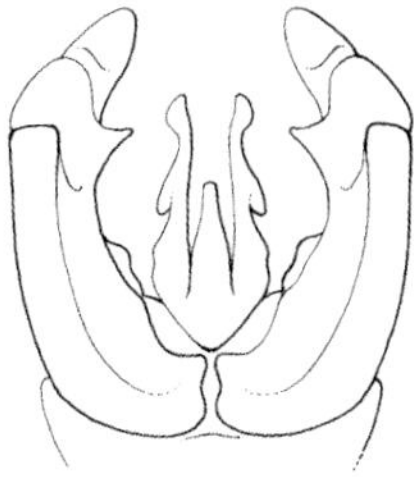

Fig. 70

4   Antennal segment 3 much shorter than 5 (Fig. 71). Body pile relatively short and
    neat. Hair patches at sides of tergite 3 bright sulphur-yellow in fresh specimens
    (but fading with age) and collar darker orange-yellow. Midriff band usually
    weak and confined to tergite 1. Genitalia (Fig. 72) .... *vestalis*

—   Antennal segment 3 about as long as 5 (Fig. 73). Body pile long and uneven
    (a fluffier-looking bee). Yellow hair patches of segment 3 pale yellow
    (fading whitish with age). Hairs of tergite 1 and hind part of scutellum yellow
    and forming a more conspicuous midriff band. Collar paler yellow. Genitalia (Fig. 74) .... *bohemicus*

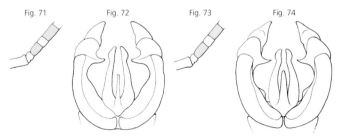

Fig. 71   Fig. 72   Fig. 73   Fig. 74

Bombus cryptarum (Fabricius, 1775)   **Cryptic Bumblebee**
Plate 17

Description & similar species FW 16mm queen, males and workers probably similar to *B. lucorum*. Only recently treated as a valid species, based on DNA studies. Separation based on external appearance is very tentative. Current thinking is that '*lucorum*' queens with a collar that does not extend far down the side of the thorax, contains scattered black hairs and has distinct intrusions of dark hairs where it passes in front of the wing bases, are probably *B. cryptarum* – though this is known to be incompletely reliable. Very little information is available for workers and males, though black-headed '*lucorum*' males that are sometimes encountered in western and upland areas, looking like bright-banded, white-tailed *B. terrestris* males, may represent *B. cryptarum* (this is how they are depicted in some foreign literature), though this is far from proven. **Variation** Poorly understood, though the collar feature is variable and grades into the state shown by *B. lucorum*. **Flight season** Queens can appear from April (later in the north) and the bee can fly into September. **Habitat** It seems to prefer upland areas and can be found alongside *B. magnus* in a variety of habitats at altitudes to over 1,000 metres. Also reported from lowland habitats in counties such as Norfolk and Hampshire. **Flowers visited** Spring and early summer queens visit various blossoming shrubs and flowers, including sallows, *Prunus* species, Bilberry and bird's-foot-trefoils. New summer

queen

queens like heathers, thistles and Devil's-bit Scabious. **Nesting habits** Likely to resemble *B. lucorum*. **Status & distribution** Available data suggests it is widespread in upland areas of the north and west of Britain, and the more upland parts of Ireland. It is also reported from lower-lying parts of east Scotland and a growing number of southern English counties. However, many of these records are unconfirmed by DNA. **Parasites & associates** A likely host of the cuckoo bumblebee *Bombus bohemicus*, with the two often found together.

Bombus cullumanus (Kirby, 1802)   **Cullum's Bumblebee**

not illustrated

Description & similar species FW typically 15mm queen, 10mm worker, 11mm male. Queens and workers of the northwest European race (ssp. *cullumanus*) are typically black with a red tail that starts on tergite 4 and black-haired hind tibiae. They look extremely similar to *B. lapidarius* but have a shorter face (the shortest of any British social bumblebee), and the outer face of the hind basitarsi are shinier with a sparse covering of simple hairs (*B. lapidarius* has a dense covering of tiny branched hairs). A very weak and ill-defined yellowish collar is usually present at the front of the thorax, most obvious from the side. Workers are about the same size as *B. lapidarius* but queens average smaller and have the tail red rather than crimson. The very different-looking males are orange-tailed with a dull (yet obvious) yellow collar and midriff band, the latter occupying the posterior part of the scutellum and all of tergites 1 and 2, leaving only tergite 3 black-haired. The legs are mostly pale-haired. The genitalia are very distinctive. **Variation** The limited British material exhibits little variation, but some very different-looking forms occur on the continent. **Flight season** British males were found from late July to early September. Queens are said to be late-emerging (May). **Habitat** Most British records come from chalk downland and chalk-influenced coastal grassland, and it seems to have required large expanses of such habitat (e.g. the 'sheepwalks' of the past). **Flowers visited** British males were reported visiting Wild Marjoram, Musk Thistle, Dwarf Thistle, Common Knapweed and White Clover. Legumes are reported as being important for females abroad. **Nesting habits** Nesting occurs underground. **Status & distribution** Possibly extinct. Always a rarity in Britain, with most records from the chalk downs of Berkshire, Buckinghamshire, Bedfordshire, Sussex and Kent, and further records from Dorset and Suffolk. The last British record is from Blewbury, Berkshire (1941). However, queens and workers are so similar to those of *B. lapidarius* that it could be overlooked somewhere. This species was described as new to science on the basis of a Suffolk specimen. **Parasites & associates** None reported in Britain.

Bombus distinguendus Morawitz, 1869   **Great Yellow Bumblebee**

Plate 19

Description & similar species FW typically 18mm queen, 12mm worker, 14mm male. A very distinctive bumblebee – almost entirely yellow-haired except for a black band between the wing bases and black hair patches beneath the wing bases. Queens are large with a short, neat and dense pile. Workers and males have a longer, sparser pile. The face is moderately long, much like a carder bee. Some very pale males of the extinct British form of *B. subterraneus* approach *B. distinguendus* in appearance but retain a dark band across tergite 2 and are shorter-haired. The male genitalia of the two species seem to be

383

indistinguishable. **Variation** The width of the band between the wing bases varies somewhat, and the patch of black hairs beneath the wing bases can be very broad (especially females) or minimal (many males). Older specimens can have the yellow hairs bleached whitish. **Flight season** At its modern, northern sites queens typically appear from late May or early June, workers from late June or early July, males and new queens from August. It can persist to mid-October. Historically, queens could appear in April in southern Britain. **Habitat** A variety of habitats were utilised historically but today it tends to be associated with floristically rich coastal grasslands (such as machair), coastal dunes and cliffs. Most of these sites are very low altitude but highly exposed and tend to feature another exposure-tolerant species, *B. muscorum*. **Flowers visited** Queens visit bird's-foot-trefoils, clovers, *Vicia* vetches, Kidney Vetch, Common Knapweed, thistles, woundworts, Phacelia, Yellow-rattle, and garden crane's-bills. Workers visit the same species (Red Clover, Common Knapweed, bird's-foot-trefoils and woundworts seem especially important) and also Hogweed, Wild Carrot, Harebell, Cat's-ear, Devil's-bit Scabious, hemp-nettles and Fodder Radish. Males like clovers, Common Knapweed, thistles and woundworts. **Nesting habits** Nesting can occur underground in old rodent burrows or within vole runs in dense, tussocky grass. The grassy sides of ditches can be an important source of these in places like Orkney. Nest colonies are generally small – those on Orkney rarely contain more than a dozen workers, though larger colonies seemed to occur in the south. This is a pocket-making species. **Status & distribution** One of our most severely declined bees. Formerly widespread (though rarely ever common) throughout much of Britain and Ireland, even along the south coast. It is now almost entirely confined to the Outer Hebrides, the north coast of Caithness, Sutherland, Orkney, Coll and Tiree plus a few sites in western Ireland, but has a patchy presence even in these areas. **Parasites & associates** None known.

Bombus hortorum (Linnaeus, 1761)   **Garden Bumblebee**

Plate 18

Description & similar species FW typically 16mm queen, 13mm worker, 14mm male. The longest-faced bumblebee (with a malar gap at least half the length of an eye), with a bright yellow collar and midriff band plus a conspicuous white tail. The midriff band typically involves the entire scutellum and entire first tergite in all castes. Queens are medium-large (*B. lucorum*-sized). Males have particularly long antennae. *B. jonellus* has an almost identical pattern but has a considerably shorter face and tongue, smaller queens, and males that are rounder, fluffier and with a yellow-haired face (*B. hortorum* males always have a black-haired face). A greater challenge is separating *B. hortorum* from banded males and workers of *B. ruderatus*, or separating semi-melanic *B. hortorum* from *B. ruderatus* (see *B. ruderatus* for discussion). The genitalia of *B. hortorum* and *B. ruderatus* are very similar but distinct from other species. **Variation** All castes can produce semi-melanic individuals, and fully melanic males are occasionally encountered. The male head is typically entirely black-haired but some have yellow hairs on top. In Ireland, the yellow collar and midriff band are often wider than elsewhere and this form is sometimes treated as ssp. *ivernicus*. **Flight season** Queens often appear by late March in the south, workers by late April and males by May. New queens can then appear from June, and it is suspected that a regular second generation occurs in many southern areas, resulting in queens and males lingering into September. **Habitat** Found in a wide variety of habitats including wooded and open habitats, rural and urban ones. It can be especially common in gardens, brownfield land and woodland. **Flowers visited** With its exceptionally long head and tongue, there is a strong association with deeper flowers, particularly by workers. Newly emerged queens visit spring-blossoming shrubs such as sallows, Blackthorn, cherries and gorses alongside the queens of various other bumblebee species but also make good use of any Ground-ivy, dead-nettles, Bluebell, comfreys and dandelions. New summer queens like Spear and Musk Thistles, Teasel, Red Clover, Devil's-bit Scabious and Buddleia. Workers visit a tremendous variety of flowers, but perhaps especially labiates (e.g. woundworts, Wood Sage and Selfheal), legumes (especially Red Clover and vetches), Foxglove, Honeysuckle, thistles and Teasel. Males visit many of the same flowers, and will congregate in large numbers on thistles and burdocks. **Nesting habits** Nesting can occur both underground and amongst dense vegetation on the surface, more rarely at elevation such as in an old bird's nest. Nest colonies are generally quite small, often producing fewer than 100 workers. This is a pocket-making species. **Status & distribution** Widespread and generally common throughout Britain and Ireland, including the Channel Islands. **Parasites & associates** The main host of the cuckoo bumblebee *Bombus barbutellus*. Also known to be attacked by conopid flies such as *Physocephala rufipes*.

Bombus humilis Illiger, 1806

Plate 19

Brown-banded Carder Bee

Description & similar species FW typically 13mm queen, 10mm worker, 11mm male. Closely resembling *B. muscorum* and paler forms of *B. pascuorum*. The pile on top of the thorax is ginger or chestnut, very bright in fresh individuals and contrasting strongly with the pale sides of the thorax. There is no gradation to paler hairs at the front of the thorax or on the scutellum as shown in many *B. muscorum*. Scattered black hairs are nearly always present amongst the ginger/chestnut hairs around the wing bases. The tergites are buff-haired but with a ginger band across tergite 2 and sometimes tergite 3. Those bands are as dark as the

queen

hairs on top of the thorax and much darker than the weak yellowish or buffish bands that may be present in *B. muscorum*. Queens average a little smaller and fluffier than *B. muscorum*. Very pale individuals of *B. pascuorum* never have a brown band across tergite 2 and generally have a less intensely coloured thorax. The male genitalia are very useful for separating these three carder bees. **Variation** A second brown band may be present on tergite 3. Scattered black hairs around the wing bases are occasionally absent, though in rare instances (usually workers) may be quite numerous over the entire top of the thorax and scutellum (but not producing the central zone of darkening found in many *B. pascuorum*). Sun-bleached specimens can lose the intensely coloured thorax and

worker

abdominal band(s). **Flight season** Queens usually appear in May. Workers and males can appear by late May or early June and can still be flying into late September, suggesting that there may be two generations in some areas. **Habitat** Many habitats can be used, though it prefers drier, warmer sites than *B. muscorum* and more open sites than *B. pascuorum*. Especially strong populations can be found on chalk grassland, coastal dunes, vegetated shingle, coastal heathland, coastal flood defences and flowery brownfield sites. **Flowers visited** Queens like legumes (especially Kidney Vetch, clovers, bird's-foot-trefoils, everlasting-

male

peas and *Vicia* vetches), labiates (Black Horehound and dead-nettles), Honeysuckle, roses, thistles and Teasel. Workers and males visit many of the same species but are also known to like Red Bartsia, Wild Basil, knapweeds, scabiouses, sowthistles, Bristly Oxtongue, hawk's-beards, Cat's-ear and Viper's-bugloss. **Nesting habits** Nesting typically occurs on the surface amongst tall grasses but can occasionally be underground. Colonies are

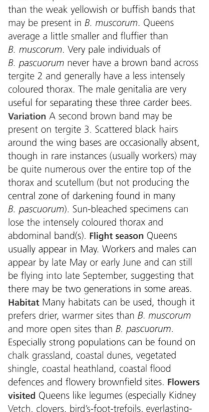

small, usually just 40–50 workers. This is a pocket-making species. **Status & distribution** Historically known from many parts of Britain north to Northumberland, though records are strangely absent from most of East Anglia. Not recorded from Scotland, Ireland or the Channel Islands. A serious decline took place in the twentieth century, leaving modern strongholds in the Thames Gateway, Salisbury Plain, Christchurch Harbour, and the coasts of southwest England, south Wales and southeast England. It seems to have completely disappeared from northern England, though there are signs of a recovery in areas such as the Midlands. **Parasites & associates** The cuckoo bumblebee *Bombus campestris* is known to parasitise this species abroad.

Bombus hypnorum (Linnaeus, 1758)   **Tree Bumblebee**
Plate 18

Description & similar species FW typically 15mm queen, 11mm worker, 13mm male. Typical specimens are very distinctive with the unique combination of a ginger or brownish thorax, black-based abdomen and pure white tail. Other species with a brown thorax lack a pure white tail, though care should be taken as some *B. pascuorum* males have a ginger thorax and completely black abdomen and resemble *B. hypnorum* from some angles. Males can be readily distinguished from workers by the brown hairs on the head. **Variation** Considerable, mainly in relation to the darkening of the thorax in females. This becomes darker from the centre, and the thorax is almost entirely black-haired in some individuals, resulting in a black bee with a pure white tail. These darker forms can superficially resemble *B. ruderatus* but are fluffier with a much shorter face. Males generally have tergite 1 ginger-haired, but tergite 1 can be black-haired or ginger hairs can occupy both tergites 1 and 2. **Flight season** Queens typically

queen

queen, dark form

worker

male

appear in March, workers and males by May. It seems to attempt two generations per year in some districts, with males lingering into September and queens sometimes recorded into early winter. **Habitat** Found in a wide variety of habitats but especially in and around woodland, gardens and other urban habitats such as allotments; also scrubby grasslands, particularly where brambles and cotoneasters are well represented. It is usually absent from open, expansive habitats. **Flowers visited** Spring queens will visit sallows, *Prunus* species, rhododendrons, garden cotoneasters, *Pyracantha* and White Dead-nettle. New summer queens can be found on thistles, brambles and Teasel. The relatively short-tongued workers are especially keen on brambles, Raspberry, roses, cotoneasters, comfreys and Oil-seed Rape. They will also take nectar from umbellifers. Males visit many of the same flowers. **Nesting habits** Nesting typically occurs in aerial situations, especially abandoned bird boxes and under the eaves of houses; also holes in trees and walls. Underground small mammal burrows are very occasionally used. Nests can be quite large, with 150 or more workers. On certain days, males will swarm around the nests in large numbers. This is a pollen-storing species. **Status & distribution** Added to the British list in 2001 from a site in Wiltshire following a well-documented expansion in Europe. It has shown a remarkable rate of spread since then, appearing in almost every county of England and Wales and becoming fairly common in many suburban areas. It was discovered in Scotland in 2013 and had reached Mull by 2014. The spread is being monitored by BWARS and the latest distribution can be seen on their website. Not currently known from Ireland or the Channel Islands. **Parasites & associates** None yet reported in Britain but parasitised by the non-British cuckoo bumblebee *Bombus norvegicus* abroad.

Bombus jonellus (Kirby, 1802)   **Heath Bumblebee**

Plate 18

Description & similar species FW typically 13mm queen, 10mm worker, 11mm male. A short-faced bumblebee (the malar space about a quarter the length of an eye) with a body pattern very similar to *B. hortorum* though all castes are relatively smaller and have a longer body pile and buff rather than yellow bands. Males have substantially yellow-haired heads and a rounder body shape than *B. hortorum*. The male genitalia resemble those of *B. pratorum* and *B. monticola* but with minor differences. **Variation** The width of the collar and midriff band can vary, and queens in particular are prone to becoming semi-melanic and resembling small *B. ruderatus* queens. Forms with yellowish or buff tails and black-haired hind tibiae (sometimes assigned subspecific status such as ssp. *vogtii* and ssp. *hebridensis*) are found on Scottish offshore islands. **Flight season** In the south, queens typically appear in March,

queen

queen, buff-tailed

workers and males in April, and new queens in May. Two generations are typical here. In the far north, queens may not appear until May and only a single generation is attempted. There is often a pronounced peak with the flowering of Heather (Ling), and it will persist into September. **Habitat** Most abundant on heathland and moorland, using sites from near sea level to altitudes of over 900 metres. It will also use chalk grassland, coastal dunes, coastal grazing marsh and saltmarsh edge in southern Britain, and machair grassland in western Scotland. **Flowers visited** Spring queens visit a variety of spring-flowering shrubs and flowers, but especially sallows and upland willows. New summer ones like clovers, heathers, scabiouses and thistles. The short-tongued workers will forage predominantly on heathers and *Vaccinium* species in heathland and moorland but will switch to thymes on chalk grassland and coastal dunes, though many other flowers can be used. Males are especially keen on umbellifers, brambles, thistles, ragworts and scabiouses. **Nesting habits** Nesting can occur both underground and amongst dense vegetation on the surface, more rarely at height such as in old bird nests or roof spaces. Nest colonies are generally small, often producing only about 50 workers. This is a pollen-storing species. **Status & distribution** Widespread and locally common in the north and west of Britain plus Ireland, but with relatively few records in southern Scotland, the Midlands and East Anglia. Evidence of a decline in many parts of lowland England. Old records for Jersey. **Parasites & associates** One of the hosts of the cuckoo bumblebee *Bombus sylvestris*.

Bombus lapidarius (Linnaeus, 1758)   **Red-tailed Bumblebee**

Plate 18

Description & similar species FW typically 17mm queen, 12mm worker, 12mm male. The large, rectangular queens are fairly distinctive, with a neat, jet-black body pile, deep crimson tail that starts on tergite 4 and black-haired hind tibiae. Queens of *B. ruderarius* are similar but smaller, rounder and fluffier with an orange-red tail and long orange-red hairs on the hind tibiae. Females of the cuckoo bumblebee *B. rupestris* have much darker wings, a shinier body, larger head capsule and unmodified hind legs. *B. lapidarius* workers resemble small queens and can be hard to separate from *B. ruderarius* workers in the field but have a shorter, more even pile, black-haired hind tibiae and average smaller (in spite of the larger queens). Females of *B. cullumanus*, which is presumed to be extinct, are also black with a red tail (see account for that species). Males look very different from females, with extensively yellow-haired heads, a yellow collar, weak midriff band, orange-red rather than crimson tail and orange-haired hind tibiae. Males of *B. ruderarius* and *B. rupestris* have black-haired faces. **Variation** Queens with yellow-grey collars are occasionally reported. Workers vary a little in size. Males show some variation in the width and intensity of the collar and midriff band. Males and workers are both prone to becoming sun-bleached and can eventually fade to brown with a whitish tail, which

queen

worker

male

regularly results in misidentifications. **Flight season**. Queens can appear by March, workers by May and males and new queens by June. Colonies decline during August but new queens can persist well into October. **Habitat** Found in a wide variety of habitats including wooded and open habitats, rural and urban ones. It can be especially common in legume-rich grasslands (including lawns with White Clover) and brownfield sites, also frequent in gardens. **Flowers visited** Spring queens visit blossoms and flowers of many sorts, but particularly sallows, *Prunus* species, gorses, dandelions and Oil-seed Rape. New summer ones are most likely to be seen on thistles, Teasel and Buddleia. Workers are particularly keen on clovers, bird's-foot-trefoils, melilots, St John's-worts, and various crucifers and composites. Males like knapweeds, thistles, ragworts and brambles. **Nesting habits** Nesting usually occurs underground, and colonies can be large with up to 300 workers. This is a pollen-storing species. **Status & distribution** Widespread and generally common throughout much of Britain and Ireland, including the Channel Islands, though scarcer in the far north. **Parasites & associates** The host of the cuckoo bumblebee *Bombus rupestris*.

Bombus lucorum (Linnaeus, 1761)   White-tailed Bumblebee

Plate 17

Description & similar species FW 16mm queen, 12mm worker, 14mm male. Queens are medium-large with a bright orange-yellow collar, a broad yellow band across tergite 2 and a pure white tail. Separation from *B. cryptarum* and *B. magnus* is extremely challenging and not always possible (see those species for more detail). As a consequence, the three are sometimes recorded as a single unit 'Bombus lucorum agg.', though it is best to denote queens that most perfectly display either *lucorum*, *cryptarum* or *magnus* characteristics. Queens of *B. terrestris* are more readily separable by their larger size, darker (buff or brown) bands and buffish tail. The exception to this is the form of *B. terrestris* on the Channel Islands, which has a pure white tail and rather bright yellow-buff bands, though *B. lucorum* seems to be absent from the Islands (any Channel Island records are now treated as

queen

worker

male

misidentification of *B. terrestris* ssp. *terrestris*). Queens of *B. soroeensis* also look very similar in the field but average a little smaller, with a longer face, and the yellow band across tergite 2 tends to weaken in the middle and spread onto the side of tergite 1, being less of a strictly transverse solid band.

Workers resemble small queens, and distinguishing these with certainty from *B. magnus* and *B. cryptarum* is not currently possible. Workers of *B. terrestris* (which have a much whiter tail than queens) tend to have a buffish interface where the white hairs of the tail meet the black hairs that precede them (interface grey in *B. lucorum*), and the yellow body bands have a buff tone. Workers of *B. soroeensis* can be distinguished by the longer face and different shape of the yellow abdominal band.

Males of *B. lucorum* are very different-looking from females as they have extensively yellow-haired heads, a broader yellow collar that extends down the sides of the thorax, and a tendency for the yellow band on tergite 2 to spread onto tergite 1 and the hind margin of the scutellum. The tail is always pure white. Males of *B. magnus* and *B. cryptarum* cannot yet be distinguished from *B. lucorum* with certainty, though black-headed '*lucorum*' males that are sometimes encountered in upland areas (looking like bright-banded, white-tailed *B. terrestris* males) may represent *B. cryptarum*. Males of *B. terrestris* have a black-haired head, browner bands, and a buffish-white tail. Males of *B. soroeensis* have a much more upright, sparser-looking pile on the abdomen, and the tail is often buff-tinged or orange around the base. The genitalia of *B. lucorum*, *B. terrestris*, *B. magnus* and *B. cryptarum*, whilst different from other bumblebees, appear to be indistinguishable from each other. **Variation** Queens and workers are fairly constant in appearance, but males show substantial variation in the extent of yellow hairs on the thorax and abdomen. The palest examples are predominantly yellow-haired throughout except for a white tail, an ill-defined black area between the wing bases and weak black bands across tergites 3 and 4. **Flight season** Queens can appear from March and workers from April. Males and new queens can appear from late May. Nests usually die off in August, but males and queens can linger into October. **Habitat** This species can turn up in most habitats, but tends to be replaced by *B. magnus* and *B. cryptarum* in upland areas and along exposed western coastlines. **Flowers visited** Spring queens visit various spring-blossoming shrubs and flowers, with sallows and *Prunus* species often attracting large numbers. Summer queens like thistles, knapweeds, brambles, Teasel and Buddleia. Workers can be especially numerous on brambles, heathers, Viper's-bugloss, knapweeds and umbellifers. They will also nectar-rob comfreys, honeysuckles and certain legumes. Males like thistles, ragworts, umbellifers, scabiouses and brambles. **Nesting habits** Nesting typically occurs underground in old rodent burrows. Colonies can be large, with over 200 workers, and it may be bivoltine in some areas. *B. lucorum* and its close relatives are pollen-storing species. **Status & distribution** One of the commonest bumblebees over much of lowland Britain and Ireland. Its status in upland areas is less certain because of confusion with *B. magnus* and *B. cryptarum*. Its status on the Channel Islands is doubtful, with records likely to refer to the white-tailed form of *B. terrestris*. **Parasites & associates** A host of the cuckoo bumblebee *B. bohemicus*, though the cuckoo is missing from many southern areas where *B. lucorum* abounds, and may prefer to use *B. magnus* and *B. cryptarum*.

Bombus magnus Vogt, 1911   Northern White-tailed Bumblebee
Plate 17

Description & similar species FW 17mm queen, males and workers probably similar to *B. lucorum*. Queens resemble *B. lucorum* and *B. cryptarum* but average larger (almost *terrestris*-sized) with a broader and paler yellow collar that typically extends down the sides of the thorax below the level of the wing bases for a distance about twice its own width. The band across tergite 2 is rather broad and pale – the overall appearance in the field being that of a large, pale *B. lucorum*. Workers and males are not currently distinguishable from *B. lucorum* with certainty, though probable *B. magnus* workers have broader, longer collars than typical *B. lucorum*. **Variation** The collar of the queens can vary somewhat, and some individuals cannot be readily separated from *B. lucorum* and *B. cryptarum*. **Flight season** Queens can appear from April (later in the north) and the bee can fly into September. **Habitat** Strongly associated with the moorland, heathland, meadows and woodland of upland areas, also the grassland and heathland of exposed western coasts. In the New Forest it uses dry heathland, valley mire and open woodland. Gardens and urban greenspace are readily used in the Scottish Highlands, and it will forage in montane habitat at over 600 metres. **Flowers visited** Spring and early summer queens visit various spring-blossoming shrubs and flowers, with sallows (especially Eared Willow), *Prunus* species and Bilberry often attracting large numbers. Kidney Vetch is also used in southwest England. Summer queens like heathers, thistles and Devil's-bit Scabious. Probable workers seem to forage heavily on heathers. **Nesting habits** Likely to resemble *B. lucorum*. **Status & distribution** Widespread and locally common in the Scottish Highlands and Western Scotland, with a more localised presence in the Pennines, Wales, the northern Midlands, southwest England, the New Forest and Ireland. Scarcely recorded in central or eastern England. **Parasites & associates** Seemingly an important host of the cuckoo bumblebee *B. bohemicus*, with the two often found together.

queen

Bombus monticola Smith, 1849
Plate 18

Bilberry Bumblebee
Blaeberry Bumblebee

Description & similar species FW typically 15mm queen, 10mm worker, 10mm male. A very distinctive small, short-faced bumblebee with the abdomen red-haired from tergite 2 onwards, a conspicuous pale yellow collar and a yellow-grey fringe to the scutellum. Queens have a particularly broad build. Queens of the extinct *B. pomorum* have a similar amount of red on the abdomen but are larger, shorter-haired and with a much longer face. Males have the top of the head and face yellow-haired and the body has the same round and fluffy form as males of *B. jonellus* and *B. pratorum*. Males of *B. rupestris* occasionally have a similar amount of red on the abdomen but have larger, black-haired heads and a very different body shape. The male genitalia of *B. monticola* closely resemble *B. pratorum*. **Variation** The extent of yellow hairs on the collar, scutellum and male head can vary somewhat, and the collar can be very weakly formed in some individuals. The red tail can become yellowish or whitish at its tip. **Flight season** Queens typically appear in April (May in the far north or at altitude), workers from late May, and males and new queens from mid-July. It can persist well into September and occasionally into October. **Habitat** Strongly associated with upland heathland and moorland areas (occurring at over 1,000 metres in the Scottish Highlands) but clearly preferring a varied landscape that supports heather-rich areas, species-rich grassland, and open structured woodland with spring-flowering shrubs and Bilberry. It is very rare to find this bee away from areas supporting some Bilberry. **Flowers visited** Spring queens like sallows and other upland willows, *Vaccinium* species (especially Bilberry) and Gorse. New summer ones like heathers, clovers and Devil's-bit Scabious. Workers will forage heavily on Bilberry and then move on to clovers, bird's-foot-trefoils, thistles, brambles, Raspberry, Common Figwort, heathers and Devil's-bit Scabious. Males visit many of the same late-summer flowers but are particularly keen on heathers and scabiouses. Workers also take honeydew from trees and shrubs. **Nesting habits** Nesting usually occurs underground in old rodent burrows. Colonies are generally small, often producing fewer than 50 workers. This is a pollen-storing species. **Status & distribution** Widespread in upland areas of the north and west of Britain (often alongside *B. jonellus*,

worker

queen

male

B. magnus and *B. soroeensis*) but occurring close to sea level in a few areas. The modern strongholds are the Scottish Highlands, Pennines, Welsh uplands, Dartmoor and Exmoor. Scarcely recorded in southern and eastern England, though it occurred historically in the Surrey Weald and some males (possibly vagrants from Scandinavia) were recorded on Scolt Head Island, Norfolk, in 2007. It seems to be declining in many areas, though it was only discovered in Ireland in 1974 and is currently expanding there. **Parasites & associates** Probably one of the hosts of the cuckoo bumblebee *Bombus sylvestris*.

Bombus muscorum (Linnaeus, 1758)   Moss Carder Bee

Plate 19

Description & similar species FW typically 14mm queen, 10mm worker, 12mm male. Queens are our largest carder bees and have a shorter, neater and denser body pile than the others. Those of the typical form have a deep ginger-coloured pile on the top of the thorax which becomes paler on the scutellum and immediately behind the head (a useful field clue). There are never any scattered black hairs within this ginger pile. The abdomen has a pale buff pile, often with a marked yellow wash in very fresh individuals and sometimes a yellowish band across tergite 2 (which can result in misidentification as *B. humilis*). Black hairs on the abdomen are usually confined to tergite 6, and there are never any brownish hair bands across tergite 2 as in *B. humilis* (but beware false bands produced by the angle of the light). Very pale *B. pascuorum* queens on the British mainland are smaller and fluffier with the top of the thorax usually less intensely coloured and they nearly always have some black hairs at

the sides of tergites 2–5, though Channel Islands *B. pascuorum* can be extremely similar looking (see *B. pascuorum* account). Workers and males are coloured much like queens but have a longer body pile. The very distinct western island forms of *B. muscorum* are described below. Fortunately, the male genitalia allow easy separation from *B. humilis* and *B. pascuorum*.

Variation Relatively little within mainland British and typical Irish populations, though northern populations tend to be slightly longer-haired and can have the thorax ginger-haired throughout without paler hairs on the scutellum and immediately behind the head. Queens, workers and often males on the Outer Hebrides, Coll, Tiree, Shetland, the Aran Islands (western Ireland), the Isles of Scilly and some of the Channel Islands have the legs, head and undersides largely or entirely black-haired. The pile on top of the thorax is often a deeper brick-red and the wings are darker than usual. The top of the abdomen can be almost whitish-haired in some populations. The population on the Aran Islands additionally has the basal tergites black-haired, creating an appearance rather like a buff-tailed *B. hypnorum* or some forms of *B. pascuorum*. These various populations are sometimes given subspecific status, e.g. ssp. *agricolae* (Scottish Islands), ssp. *allenellus* (Aran Islands) and ssp. *scyllonius* (Scilly and Channel Islands), though it is possible to find some Scottish populations that are intermediate with the mainland form. **Flight season** In the south, queens usually appear by May, workers by June and males by July. Colonies seem to decline more rapidly than those of *B. pascuorum* and *B. humilis*, but with some individuals persisting into September. In the extreme north, it may not appear until June. **Habitat** There seems to be a distinct preference for damp and exposed locations over much of Britain. In the south this includes western coastal dunes, vegetated shingle, saltmarsh edge and large expanses of coastal grazing marsh. It also uses chalk grassland on Salisbury Plain, but avoids the South Downs (in contrast to *B. humilis*). In the north and in Ireland, moorland, bog and coastal grasslands (e.g. machair and Burren grasslands) are favoured habitats, though it needs at least some patches of flowery habitat, e.g. road verges and meadows in moorland landscapes. It can also exploit urban habitats in Ireland. **Flowers visited** Hibernated queens like legumes, especially clovers, *Lathyrus* peas and *Vicia* vetches. New summer queens will also visit thistles and Teasel. Workers also visit these species plus bird's-foot-trefoils, brambles, Common Knapweed, heathers, wall-rockets, Viper's-bugloss, Sea Aster, sowthistles, Bristly Oxtongue and Devil's-bit Scabious. Males are especially keen on thistles, yellow-flowered composites such as sowthistles and Bristly Oxtongue, also Great Willowherb. This species can forage in surprisingly inclement weather. **Nesting habits** Nesting typically occurs on the surface amongst vegetation, and ditches may provide important nesting habitat in grazing marsh. Colonies typically contain 40–120 workers. This is a pocket-making species. It is said to be especially aggressive in defence of its nest. **Status & distribution** Formerly widespread but a substantial decline took place in the twentieth century which in the southern part of its range has left it largely confined to coastal areas, notably within Cornwall, south Wales, Sussex, Kent and the East Anglian coast. Still fairly frequent in the Scottish Highlands, Scottish offshore islands and the Pennines. Widespread but much declined in Ireland. Recorded reliably from Guernsey and Alderney in the Channel Islands, but with most other records probably misidentification for the local form of *B. pascuorum*. **Parasites & associates** The cuckoo bumblebee *Bombus campestris* may attack this species abroad.

Bombus pascuorum (Scopoli, 1763)   Common Carder Bee

Plate 19

Description & similar species FW typically 13mm queen, 10mm worker, 11mm male. The commonest of our 'brownish' carder bumblebees, with relatively small, fluffy queens. Highly variable in appearance in all castes, with the top of the thorax ginger or brownish and often extensively darkened centrally. The abdomen typically has a mix of cream and black hairs, but can be extensively or even entirely black-haired, or have an orange or cream-coloured tail, or be almost entirely pale-haired to create a close resemblance to *B. muscorum* and *B. humilis*. Those other species (when fresh) tend to have the top of the thorax a deeper ginger or

queen

queen, ssp. *flavidus*

chestnut and any black abdominal hairs restricted to tergite 6. Even in the palest-looking
B. pascuorum, microscopic examination will usually reveal black hairs on the sides of at least
tergite 5. Pale *B. pascuorum* males should be confirmed using genitalia, though the antennal
flagella have the mid-segments very bulbous beneath compared with *B. humilis* and *B. muscorum*.
Variation The most variable of the carder bees. All castes can vary somewhat in size and some
workers can be tiny (wing length as short as 7mm). Sun-bleached individuals can gain a greyish
appearance. Some of the geographical variants have been assigned subspecific status, though

worker

most populations produce a fair degree of
variation. The Channel Islands population,
which is represented by a continental form
or subspecies '*flavidus*', shows a remarkable
resemblance to *B. muscorum* and *B. humilis*,
with a much brighter thorax than on the
mainland and a very pale abdomen, though
black hairs are usually detectable on at
least the sides of tergite 5, and it often has
scattered black hairs amongst the ginger pile
of the thorax like *B. humilis*. **Flight season** In
the south, queens typically appear from late
March, workers from late April and males and
new queens from late May. Two generations

darker male

paler male

seem typical here and it usually persists well into October. In the far north, queens may not appear until May and only a single generation is attempted. **Habitat** Many habitats can be used, without strong preferences. It can be common in gardens and urban greenspace and is often the commonest bumblebee of arable settings. **Flowers visited** Spring queens visit a variety of spring-flowering shrubs and flowers, but especially sallows, *Prunus* species, gorses, dandelions, Colt's-foot, dead-nettles and comfreys. Summer queens like brambles, thistles, labiates of various sorts (especially Black Horehound and Selfheal), assorted legumes, Foxglove, Buddleia and Indian Balsam. Ivy, Devil's-bit Scabious, Michaelmas-daisies and Iceplant are used in autumn. Workers visit a great variety of flowers but especially legumes, labiates, thistles, knapweeds and scabiouses. Males tend to visit the same flowers. **Nesting habits** Nesting typically occurs on the surface amongst dense vegetation such as tussocky grass and under shrubs or hedges; also occasionally above ground in nest boxes or holes in trees. Colony size is variable but typically involves 60–150 workers. This is a pocket-making species. **Status & distribution** The commonest and most widespread bumblebee of the British mainland, only absent from a few offshore Scottish Islands but currently spreading within the Western Isles. Widespread in Ireland. Abundant on the Channel Islands (ssp. *flavidus*). **Parasites & associates** The main host of the cuckoo bumblebee *Bombus campestris*.

Bombus pomorum (Panzer, 1805)   **Apple Bumblebee**

Plate 19

Description & similar species FW typically 15mm queen, 10mm worker, 12mm male. The British queen at Oxford University Museum has a broad but dusky-grey collar (composed of both grey and black hairs) and similar coloured hairs on the scutellum. The abdomen is entirely dull orange-haired except for tergite 1 and the base of tergite 2, which are black-haired. The face is long and the hind basitarsi have an acutely produced upper apical corner as in the carder bumblebees (the group to which it is now considered to belong). Only *B. monticola* has a pattern resembling this, but queens are smaller, rounder and fluffier with much brighter markings, a short face and without an acutely produced upper apical corner on the hind basitarsi. The British males are patterned rather like the queen but have tergite 1 grey- or buff-haired, and the collar can be very indistinct. They could easily be mistaken for a *Bombus rupestris* because of their elongate build and the fact that their hind tibiae are unusually short-haired and densely haired on the outer face. They look very different to the rounded and fluffy males of *B. monticola*. **Variation** The British specimens have a collar, albeit rather dull, but some continental populations have queens that are entirely black-haired except for an orange-red tail that starts gradually on tergite 3. **Flight season** The British queen was captured in June. **Habitat** The British locality was coastal dunes. Abroad it is reported to use coastal

queen

male

dunes, wood edge, open fields and marshes. **Flowers visited** A wide variety of flowers are used abroad, though queens are said to be partial to Red Clover, whilst males like Field Scabious. **Nesting habits** Nesting apparently occurs underground. **Status & distribution** Recorded from the Deal Sandhills and adjacent Kingsdown area of Kent (three males probably in 1857 and a queen in 1864) and considered long extinct in Britain. Much declined abroad. **Parasites & associates** None known.

Bombus pratorum (Linnaeus, 1761) — **Early Bumblebee**

Plate 18

Description & similar species FW typically 13mm queen, 10mm worker, 10mm male. A small, short-faced bumblebee with a fluffy body pile in all castes. Queens have a bright yellow collar, usually a bright yellow band across tergite 2 and a reddish-orange tail that starts on tergite 4. The head and scutellum are entirely black-haired. Workers resemble small queens but tend to have the band on tergite 2 weak or missing, and the red tail usually starts on tergite 5. These castes are not easily confused with any other species. The particularly fluffy, dumpy males have the head mainly yellow-haired, the collar extending back to the wing bases and down the sides of the thorax, and the yellow abdominal band of tergite 2 often extending onto tergite 1 and the hind margin of the scutellum. The genitalia resemble those of *B. monticola*. Males of *B. lapidarius* and *B. cullumanus* are much longer-bodied with narrower collars and very different genitalia. Worn males of *B. pratorum* could be confused with buffer-

queen

tailed males of *B. soroeensis*, but these never have such a yellow-haired head and are also more elongate. **Variation** In all castes the width of the collar and brightness of the abdominal band can vary, and the latter can be missing. The palest males are mainly yellow-haired except for an ill-defined black patch between the wings, two weak black bands across tergites 3 and 4 and an orange tail. **Flight season** In the south, queens typically appear from March, workers and males from April, and new queens from May, and it is clear that two generations are typical here. In the far north, queens appear later and only a single generation is attempted. All castes can persist into September and

worker

male

occasionally October. Very rarely winter-active. **Habitat** Many habitats can be used though it tends to be most abundant in wooded settings, gardens, brownfield sites and scrubby habitats with plentiful brambles. **Flowers visited** Spring queens visit a variety of spring-flowering shrubs and flowers, but especially sallows, *Prunus* species, currants, rhododendrons, dandelions, Colt's-foot and dead-nettles. Summer queens like brambles, Raspberry and clovers; autumn ones Devil's-bit Scabious. Workers visit a tremendous variety of flowers but are particularly keen on brambles, Raspberry, cotoneasters, comfreys and garden crane's-bills. They will nectar-rob flowers such as comfreys. Males tend to visit the same flowers and have a very frenetic foraging behaviour. **Nesting habits** Nesting can occur underground in old rodent burrows, also on the surface amongst vegetation or at height in bird nests, nest boxes, roof spaces and holes in trees. Nest colonies are rather small, usually producing no more than 100 workers. This is a pollen-storing species. **Status & distribution** One of our commonest and most widespread bumblebees, only absent from a few offshore Scottish Islands. It was first recorded in Ireland in 1947 and has become widespread and abundant since. Recorded from most of the Channel Islands. **Parasites & associates** One of the hosts of the cuckoo bumblebee *Bombus sylvestris*.

Bombus ruderarius (Müller, 1776)   Red-shanked Carder Bee

Plate 19

Description & similar species FW typically 13mm queen, 11mm worker, 10mm male. Queens and workers have a black body and red tail and are most likely to be confused with females of *B. lapidarius*. The most obvious difference is the orange-haired hind tibiae (black-haired in female *B. lapidarius*). The body hairs are also longer and less even, the body shape more rounded and the tail orange-red rather than crimson-red. *B. ruderarius* queens average smaller than *B. lapidarius*, but the workers average larger. Males typically have a weak greyish or olive collar and abdominal band, and a black-haired face. They can be very hard to distinguish from males of *B. rupestris* in the field, though the head capsule is smaller with relatively larger and less widely separated eyes and the hind basitarsi are broader in side view. The genitalia are reasonably distinct. **Variation** Queens and workers are fairly constant in appearance, though the tail of old workers can fade whitish. Males are much more variable: the darkest can be entirely black except for a red tail; the palest can have a distinct greyish or olive collar and a dull band that occupies tergites 1 and 2 and the hind margin of the scutellum. **Flight season** Queens usually appear from April, workers from May and males and new queens from June. Colonies decline from late July, and it has usually disappeared by the end of August. **Habitat** A variety of habitats can be used including species-rich calcareous and neutral grasslands, acid grassland, chalk heath, brownfield land, coastal grazing marsh (especially the flood defence banks), road verges and occasionally gardens and woodland rides. **Flowers visited** Spring queens are particularly keen on White Dead-nettle and Ground-ivy but will also visit sallow blossom. New summer queens like Kidney Vetch, Red Clover, bird's-foot-trefoils, Black Horehound and scabiouses. Workers forage on a wide variety of plants especially legumes, labiates, brambles and stork's-bills. Males visit thistles, knapweeds, Viper's-bugloss and Teasel. **Nesting habits** Nesting usually occurs on the surface amongst dense vegetation, occasionally underground using old rodent burrows. Colonies are generally small, with up to 100 workers, but often many fewer. This is a pocket-

queen

making species. **Status & distribution** Formerly found in many parts of England and Wales as far north as Northumberland, also the west coast of Scotland and much of Ireland. It has shown a substantial decline in most areas, largely disappearing from southwest England and areas north of the Midlands, though it survives in the Hebrides (Coll and Tiree). Present on the Channel Islands. **Parasites & associates** The cuckoo bumblebee *Bombus campestris* is known to parasitise it abroad.

Bombus ruderatus (Fabricius, 1775)
Plate 18

Large Garden Bumblebee
Ruderal Bumblebee

Description & similar species FW typically 18mm queen, 13mm worker, 14mm male. This species varies from yellow-banded with a white tail to completely black (form *perniger*, formerly known as form *harrisellus*) and is consequently one of the most challenging to distinguish in the field, notably from *B. hortorum* and *B. subterraneus*. Queens generally stand out by their sheer size, which rivals *B. terrestris* but with a more elongate build. Compared with *B. hortorum*, the body pile is shorter and neater. Banded queens have a yellow-brown collar and scutellum (bright yellow in *B. hortorum*) with tergite 1 either black-haired or obscurely yellow-haired (bright yellow-haired throughout in typical *B. hortorum*), resulting in a less conspicuous midriff band. The tail is often greyish-white. Under magnification, tergite 6 is more roughened than in *B. hortorum* and the face, whilst very long, is slightly shorter than that of *B. hortorum*. Queens of *B. subterraneus* can look very similar but are even shorter-haired and tend to have pale hair fringes along the hind margin of tergite 2. Under magnification *B. subterraneus* queens will be seen to have a much shorter face and a strongly developed keel along the midline of sternite 6. Black *perniger* queens are stunning velvety-black bees.

Fully banded workers closely resemble *B. hortorum* but have a shorter, neater body pile and shorter face. The collar and midriff band is usually narrower and duller than in *B. hortorum*, the scutellum often with just the hind margins pale. Banded workers of *B. subterraneus* have shorter faces and usually pale fringes along the hind margin of tergite 2, and sternite 6 has the same diagnostic keel as in the queen. Black *perniger* workers are fairly distinctive, and are often the first field clue that you have found a *ruderatus* population, as they can account for a significant proportion of the workers at a site.

Banded males have a pattern almost identical to *B. hortorum* and are much brighter than queens and workers. The body pile is again shorter and neater than *B. hortorum*. The yellow collar and midriff band are a deeper yellow and are more sharply defined than in the fluffier *hortorum*, making for a slightly smarter-looking bee in the field. The tail often has a yellow tint, and the white hairs often extend up the sides of the abdomen. A very useful character is the hair tufts of the mandibles, which are golden in *B. ruderatus* but black in *B. hortorum*. Another is the length of the dorsal fringe of the hind tibiae, which is rather shorter than in *B. hortorum*. Black males have the same velvety texture as queens and look rather different from the fluffy black males occasionally produced by *B. hortorum*. The genitalia of *B. ruderatus* and *B. hortorum* are very similar but distinct from other species. **Variation** Considerable, with queens and workers exhibiting a full range of variation between fully banded and fully black individuals, often within a single population. Males are essentially dimorphic with either fully black or fully banded individuals; very occasionally a slight tail will be present in an otherwise black one. Banded males occasionally have the white tail more extensive than usual, even extending to the hind margin of tergite 2. These closely resemble some males of *B. subterraneus* but the face is longer and genitalia different. The form in France (ssp. *eurynotus*) resembles a short-haired *B. hortorum*, the females having a broader midriff band than the typical British form of *B. ruderatus*. **Flight season** Queens appear somewhat later than *B. hortorum*, typically

worker, banded

worker, form *perniger*

male, banded

male, form *perniger*

in early May. Workers can be seen from late May and males and new queens from mid-June. Activity peaks in July and there is usually a rapid tailing-off in August, resulting in a shorter flight period than *B. hortorum* and is probably always univoltine. **Habitat** Particularly associated with open habitats supporting plentiful Red Clover (even quite floristically poor grassland), flowery arable margins, flood banks, ditch margins and brownfield sites. It occasionally turns up in woodland and urban settings, but much less frequently than *B. hortorum*. Surprisingly, some of the best populations are in the intensively farmed Cambridgeshire Fens and south Warwickshire Feldon, both areas characterised by low coverage of semi-natural habitat and little species-rich grassland. **Flowers visited** There is a strong reliance on Red Clover at many sites, and it is possible to find all castes foraging on it simultaneously. Kidney Vetch and everlasting-peas are also very much used where available. Newly emerged queens also like White Dead-nettle and comfreys, and workers will visit bird's-foot-trefoils, woundworts, knapweeds, thistles, Borage and Viper's-bugloss. New summer queens and males will often congregate on Spear Thistle, Musk Thistle and Teasel. Males have a particularly frenetic foraging behaviour (resembling workers). **Nesting habits** Nesting typically occurs underground in old mammal burrows. A single nest can contain both banded and black individuals, and up to 150 workers can be present. This is a pocket-making species. **Status & distribution** Formerly widespread and locally common in England as far north as Northumberland and extending to west Cornwall and Wales. A serious decline took place in the twentieth century, and today it has a sparse presence from Wiltshire to Kent and north to Shropshire and Lincolnshire. A local recovery is being shown in some parts of the Midlands and southeast England. Not recorded in Scotland and Ireland. Queens of the European race *eurynotus* have been recorded on Guernsey. **Parasites & associates** The cuckoo bumblebee *Bombus barbutellus* almost certainly parasitises *B. ruderatus*.

Bombus soroeensis (Fabricius, 1777)   Broken-belted Bumblebee

Plate 18

Description & similar species FW typically 15mm queen, 10mm worker, 12mm male. Queens and workers most resemble *B. lucorum*, though queens of *B. soroeensis* average a little smaller. The best field characters are the substantially longer face and the shape of the yellow band on the abdomen. This band is usually very much weakened in the middle (but beware worn *B. lucorum* workers) and typically spreads onto the sides of tergite 1, often producing a pair of crescent-shaped bands (band confined to tergite 2, solid and transverse, in *B. lucorum*). Queens have a white tail, often with a narrow buff interface where it meets the black hairs that precede it, but workers can have a more obvious orange interface. A number of useful structural features exist – the apical margin of the mandibles lacks a notch towards the outer corner, and antennal segment 4 is scarcely longer than broad (clearly longer than broad in *B. lucorum*).

The black-faced males are much fluffier than those of *B. terrestris*, with the hairs of the tergites more upright, resulting in a less intense yellow band across tergites 1 and 2. The tail can be white or orange-buff, and the buff-tailed form could be confused with sun-bleached males of *B. pratorum*, though the face of *B. soroeensis* is black-haired and the build more elongate. The male hind legs are unusually slender in side view, especially the base of the hind basitarsi, and the male genitalia are reasonably distinct. **Variation** This is mainly related to the colour of the tail in workers and males, which can vary from pure white (especially in Scottish workers) to orange-buff, or white with a broad orange-buff zone at the base. The width of the collar and abdominal band can vary in all castes, and darker queens and workers can have tergite 1 entirely black-haired. **Flight season** This is a late peaking species, with queens that appear in late May in the south and June in the north. Workers appear in July but are most numerous in August and September. Males and new queens peak in September, all castes can persist into October. **Habitat** A variety of late-flowering habitats are used, with abundant scabiouses being a feature of most. Examples include chalk grassland on Salisbury Plain, coastal heathland and grassland in southwest England and south Wales and moorland edge, upland meadows and open-structured woodland in Scotland. It can occur at altitudes exceeding 700 metres in the Scottish Highlands. **Flowers visited** In early summer, hibernated queens will visit White Dead-nettle, clovers, bird's-foot-trefoils, brambles, Raspberry, comfreys and Bell Heather. New autumn queens like Devil's-bit Scabious. Workers also like scabiouses but will visit a variety of legumes, bellflowers, heathers, knapweeds and Rosebay Willowherb. Males are most often seen on scabiouses. This species can

queen

worker

worker, orange-tailed

apparently forage at temperatures close to freezing. **Nesting habits** Nesting occurs underground, usually in old rodent burrows. Colonies are average-sized, with 80–150 workers. This is a pollen-storing species. **Status & distribution** Formerly widespread though very localised. It declined substantially in England and Wales during the twentieth century and few modern records exist away from Salisbury Plain and the coast of south Wales. It remains widespread and fairly frequent in the Scottish Highlands. Not recorded from Ireland or the Channel Islands. **Parasites & associates** None reported in Britain but parasitised by the non-British cuckoo bumblebee *Bombus quadricolor* abroad (a species rather resembling our *B. sylvestris*).

male

Bombus subterraneus (Linnaeus, 1758)   **Short-haired Bumblebee**
Plate 19

Description & similar species FW typically 17mm queen, 11mm worker, 12mm male. Queens and workers most resemble *B. ruderatus* though the body pile of queen *B. subterraneus* is shorter (the shortest of any British bumblebee), the face is shorter, and a strong keel is present along the midline of sternite 6. Individuals of the extinct British form typically have a broad yellow collar and a narrower yellow fringe to the scutellum. Tergite 2 has an obvious pale hair fringe whilst that of tergite 3 merges with the whitish tail, which thus lacks the abrupt delimitation found in *B. ruderatus*. The tail is a dirty rather than clean white. Females of the cuckoo bumblebee *B. barbutellus* can also look superficially similar but have a larger, squarer head capsule, sparser body pile and unmodified hind tibiae. Workers resemble small queens and can be difficult to distinguish from *B. ruderatus* in the field but have a shorter body pile and a shorter face (the malar gap about two-fifths rather than half the length of an eye).

   Males are usually similar but have a longer body pile. Paler males of *B. campestris* can have similar markings but have the larger head capsule, sparser body pile and hairier hind tibiae characteristic of cuckoo bumblebees, plus very different genitalia. Exceptionally pale males of *B. ruderatus* with the tail extending to tergite 2 resemble *B. subterraneus* but have longer faces and different genitalia. Recently introduced Swedish stock is prone to melanism in all castes (see below). The male genitalia of *B. subterraneus* and *B. distinguendus* seem to be indistinguishable but are different from all other species. **Variation** Males of the extinct British form can be exceptionally pale and approach *B. distinguendus* in appearance, but they retain some black hairs on tergite 2 and have a shorter body pile. Females of the recently introduced Swedish stock are quite variable and often semi-melanic but typically have a narrow collar that is prone to being broken in the middle and a very narrow pale fringe around the hind margin of the scutellum. **Flight season** British queens usually appeared in May and could linger into September. **Habitat** This was seemingly a species of extensive legume-rich grasslands, including coastal grazing marsh, vegetated shingle, chalk downland, coastal dunes and unimproved grasslands inland. **Flowers visited** White Dead-nettle seems to be especially important for spring queens whilst Red Clover is much used by workers. It will also visit Honeysuckle, Teasel, brambles, comfreys, Viper's-bugloss and various labiates. **Nesting habits** Nesting typically occurs underground in old mammal burrows, and nests can have 75–100 workers. This is a pocket-making species. **Status & distribution** The original British population went extinct in the late 1980s following a dramatic national decline that probably started in the nineteenth century. Whilst it was rarely common anywhere, it once occurred over much of southern England north

queen, Swedish type

queen, old English type

to Yorkshire, with a strong southeast bias. There were also a number of Welsh sites, but it has never been recorded from Scotland, Ireland or the Channel Islands. Reintroduction into southeast England started in 2012, using Swedish stock. **Parasites & associates** None known, though the closely related *B. distinguendus* has been alleged to usurp *B. subterraneus* nests (when the ranges of the two species overlapped).

worker, dark form

worker, paler form

male

male, pale form

Bombus sylvarum (Linnaeus, 1761)   **Shrill Carder Bee**

Plate 19

Description & similar species FW typically 13mm queen, 9mm worker, 11mm male. A very distinct small bumblebee that looks similar in all castes. The body is substantially grey-haired with a rather ill-defined black zone between the wing bases that usually leaves a weak collar (comprising a mix of whitish and black hairs), also an ill-defined black band across tergite 3 and a pale orange-pink tail (brighter in males). Workers average very small and look much slimmer than other bumblebee workers in the field. **Variation** Not substantial, though the collar varies in intensity and an extra band of black hairs may be present on tergite 4. The tail can be bright orange or much dulled by the whitish hairs. Very rarely a form that is black with a red tail, much resembling *B. ruderarius*, is reported (the normal appearance in parts of Europe). **Flight season** Queens usually appear in May, workers in late June and males and new queens in August. This is a late-peaking species, usually August and early September in the south. **Habitat** A variety of habitats can be used, including species-rich grassland, coastal grazing marsh (especially flood defence banks), coastal dunes, vegetated shingle and brownfield sites. **Flowers visited** Hibernated queens are particularly keen on White Dead-nettle, everlasting-peas, clovers and *Vicia* vetches. Workers visit a wide variety of flowers, especially composites, legumes, labiates, Red Bartsia, brambles, Teasel and scabiouses. On coastal flood defences (critically important now) they forage particularly heavily on Red Clover, Red Bartsia, Creeping Thistle and Bristly Oxtongue. Males like thistles, ragworts, Bristly Oxtongue and Black Horehound. Workers have a peculiar slow hovering flight between flowers,

accompanied by a characteristic high-pitched (shrill) buzz. **Nesting habits** Nesting usually occurs on the surface amongst dense vegetation, more occasionally underground using old rodent burrows. Colonies are generally small, with fewer than 50 workers. This is a pocket-making species. **Status & distribution** Formerly present in many parts of England and Wales as far north as southern Scotland and also various parts of Ireland. It underwent a severe decline in the twentieth century, leaving modern populations largely restricted to the Thames Gateway, Somerset Levels, Salisbury Plain, the coast of south Wales and the Burren area of western Ireland. **Parasites & associates** None known.

Bombus terrestris (Linnaeus, 1758) — Buff-tailed Bumblebee
Plate 17

Description & similar species FW typically 18mm queen, 13mm worker, 14mm male. Queens of the British race (ssp. *audax*) are reasonably distinct through their large size, rather narrow brown collar, orange-brown band across tergite 2 and buff tail. Queens of the *lucorum* complex have pure white tails and brighter yellow bands, and *B. lucorum* s.s. is distinctly smaller. Workers of *B. terrestris* have much whiter tails and yellower bands than queens and can be very difficult to separate from those of the *lucorum* complex, though the tail usually has a narrow buff interface where it meets the black hairs that precede it and the bands have a buffer tint, especially the collar.

Males are patterned like workers, though the collar tends to extend further down the sides of the thorax and the tail is often substantially buffish. The head is entirely black-haired, in contrast to typical *B. lucorum* males. *B. soroeensis* queens and workers can have a partially buff tail but the face is longer and the yellow bands are much brighter, that on tergite 2 having a characteristic shape (see that species). Males of *B. soroeensis* have a sparse and upright pile on the abdomen which creates a very different appearance to *B. terrestris*. **Variation** Queens frequently have the collar reduced or even missing to produce a completely black-haired thorax, and the abdominal bands can be darker, especially when the collar is missing. The tail varies from deep buff throughout to whitish-buff. Workers and males vary in respect of the tint of the bands and tail, with larger workers tending to have stronger queen characteristics such as browner bands and a buffer tail. Semi-melanic or fully melanic males are occasionally encountered. On the Channel Islands, queens, workers and males all have pure white tails (ssp. *terrestris*), though queens average much larger than those of *B. lucorum* and have buffer body bands. This race and the similar ssp. *dalmatinus* are used for greenhouse pollination on the British mainland, and even though they are supposed to be kept under secure conditions, escapees are likely. **Flight season** In the south, queens typically emerge from late February, workers from April and males and new queens from late May. Two generations seem to be regularly attempted here, with queens from the second brood often observed in September and

queen, ssp. *audax*

queen, ssp. *terrestris*

worker

male

October. In some areas (especially southern cities) these queens give rise to a third, winter-active generation that takes advantage of winter-flowering shrubs. **Habitat** Found in most habitats except montane, and often very common in urban areas. **Flowers visited** Spring queens visit various spring-blossoming shrubs and flowers, with sallows, *Prunus* species and gorses often attracting large numbers. It is the bumblebee most likely to be seen visiting spring-flowering bulbs such as daffodils, crocuses and Bluebell. Summer queens like thistles, knapweeds, brambles, Teasel and Buddleia; autumn ones Ivy, Devil's-bit Scabious, Snowberry, Michaelmas-daisies and Iceplant. Workers visit a tremendous variety of summer flowers without the strong preferences exhibited by many bumblebees and can still be foraging on Ivy in October. They regularly nectar-rob. Winter-active ones rely heavily on Oregon-grape and winter-flowering honeysuckles. Males also visit a good variety of flowers but can be especially numerous on thistles and garden lavenders. **Nesting habits** Nesting typically occurs underground in old rodent burrows. Colonies can be very large, with over 500 individuals. *B. terrestris* is a pollen-storing species. **Status & distribution** One of the commonest bumblebees over much of lowland Britain. Scarcer in upland areas and on offshore islands, though it has increased its Scottish range in recent decades, reaching Shetland by 2012. Widespread in Ireland. Common on the Channel Islands (ssp. *terrestris*). **Parasites & associates** The cuckoo bumblebee *Bombus vestalis*.

CUCKOO BUMBLEBEES

Females are readily separated from social bumblebees by the lack of pollen baskets (corbiculae) on the hind tibiae, and they tend to look shinier and more sparsely hairy than social bumblebees. They also fly with a deeper hum. Separating the males from true bumblebees is more difficult, though most social bumblebees have the outer face of the hind tibiae shiny and only sparsely haired, whereas the outer face is densely hairy in cuckoo bumblebees. In cuckoo bumblebees, the head in top view is also more box-shaped.

Bombus barbutellus (Kirby, 1802)   Barbut's Cuckoo Bee
Plate 20

Description & similar species FW typically 16mm female, 13mm male. Females are medium-large cuckoo bumblebees with a well-defined yellow-buff collar and scutellum, plus a conspicuous white tail. The large U-shaped pair of ridges on sternite 6 and the ridge along the midline of tergite 6 allow easy separation from all other species under magnification. Females of *B. sylvestris* look rather similar in the field but average smaller and have the scutellum black-haired, resulting in a much weaker midriff band; the abdomen of *B. sylvestris* is also shorter and more downcurved.

Males have a strong midriff band and can resemble *B. hortorum* in the field but have the larger head and sparser body hairs that characterise cuckoo bumblebees. Males of *B. bohemicus* can also look similar, but the collar and midriff band is brighter yellow (when fresh) and they also have yellow hairs across tergite 3 (black-haired in *B. barbutellus*). The pair of protuberances on sternite 6 and the shape of the genitalia (when visible) allow easy confirmation of *B. barbutellus* under magnification. **Variation** In both sexes the width of the collar can vary, also the extent of yellow hairs on the top of the head, the scutellum and tergite 1. In the darkest specimens tergite 1 can be mainly black-haired, leaving the midriff band confined to the scutellum. Highly sun-bleached males with greyish collars and midriff bands are common in late summer. **Flight season** Females usually appear in late April. Males peak in late June and July. New females can be evident until early September. **Habitat** Found in the full range of habitats used by *B. hortorum* and *B. ruderatus*. **Flowers visited** Spring females like Ground-ivy, dead-nettles, Hawthorn and umbellifers; new summer ones thistles, clovers, vetches and shrubs such as Buddleia. Males can be especially numerous on thistles and knapweeds. **Status & distribution** Widespread and locally frequent in parts of southern and central England, much scarcer in Wales. Rare in Scotland and Ireland. Not recorded from the Channel Islands. Indications of a significant decline in many areas. **Host(s)** A social parasite of *Bombus hortorum* and *B. ruderatus*.

Bombus bohemicus (Seidl, 1837)

Gypsy Cuckoo Bee
Bohemian Cuckoo Bee

Plate 20

Description & similar species FW typically 16mm female, 14mm male. A cuckoo bumblebee with females that closely resemble *B. vestalis* but average slightly smaller, with a paler, broader collar and paler yellow hairs arising from the sides of tergite 3. There is often a very weak midriff band involving the anterior corners of tergite 1 and the hind fringe of the scutellum. In the field, females never look quite as black as *B. vestalis*. Under the microscope, the shiny, scarcely punctate central area of tergite 6 (duller and densely punctate in *B. vestalis*) will also help separate the two.

Males are much longer-haired than *B. vestalis* with a well-formed midriff band that extends onto the scutellum, and the collar is paler yellow. *B. barbutellus* has a more conspicuous midriff band than *B. bohemicus* and lacks yellow hairs on tergite 3, though worn specimens of both species can look similar. A useful structural feature for separating *B. bohemicus* males from *B. vestalis* and *B. barbutellus* is the ratio of the antennal segments. In *B. bohemicus*, segments 3 and 5 are about the same length, whilst in the other two species segment 3 is clearly shorter

than 5. The genitalia of *B. bohemicus* and *B. vestalis* are very similar but distinct from other species. **Variation** A little variation in the width of the collar and brightness of the midriff band. In older individuals of both sexes, the yellow hair patches on tergite 3 can become whitish and merge with the white tail. Males with the tail entirely yellowish have been noted. **Flight season** Females usually appear in April in the south and May in the north. Males and new females appear in June and can persist until September. **Habitat** Rather strongly associated with base-poor or upland habitats such as heathland, moorland edge, upland meadows and open structured birch or pine woodland. **Flowers visited** Spring females visit various flowering shrubs and flowers such as dandelions and Bilberry. Males and summer females like thistles, brambles, heathers and Devil's-bit Scabious. **Status & distribution** Widespread and frequent in upland areas of northern and western Britain, and the commonest cuckoo bumblebee of the Scottish Highlands. Scarce and declining in southern England, with most records from heathland districts. Widespread but local in Ireland. **Host(s)** A social parasite of bumblebees of the *Bombus lucorum* complex. Little data seem to be available on which of the three species in the complex are used, though the distribution of *B. bohemicus* and its habitat preferences indicate that *B. magnus* and *B. cryptarum* may be preferred hosts, and it is much rarer than the true *B. lucorum* in the south.

Bombus campestris (Panzer, 1801)   **Field Cuckoo Bee**
Plate 20

Description & similar species FW typically 15mm female, 13mm male. Typical females have a broad buff collar and conspicuous buff scutellum. The abdomen is much more sparsely haired than the thorax, shiny and strongly downcurved. The 'tail' comprises two lateral patches of buff hairs separated by a broad zone of very short black hairs, a distinctive field character. Under the microscope, sternite 6 will be seen to have a particularly well-developed pair of ridges that extend to the tip of the sternite. Males are extremely variable but the palest ones are relatively easily recognised, as no other cuckoo bumblebee has such extensive pale hairs, though some males of *B. subterraneus* can look similar. Males can be confirmed under magnification by the pair of large hair tufts on sternite 6 and the particularly broad genital claspers. **Variation** Males are extremely variable even within single populations. The palest individuals are almost entirely pale-haired except for a black band across the top of the thorax and across tergite 2. Semi-melanic and fully melanic males are frequent, and where a tail is present it can be buff or white. Females are less variable, but fully melanic individuals are not

female

rare. A variety of female with the top of the thorax almost entirely buff-haired (form *swynnertoni*) has been recorded in Scotland. **Flight season** Females usually appear in April and males by June. Both sexes can persist until September, and it is suspected that it may be bivoltine in some areas. **Habitat** Found in a wide variety of habitats including wooded and open habitats, rural and urban ones. **Flowers visited** Spring females like Ground-ivy, dandelions, clovers and shrubs such as Hawthorn. Summer females and males like

male, black form

male, intermediate form

male, pale form

thistles, knapweeds, brambles and Devil's-bit Scabious. **Status & distribution** Widespread and fairly frequent in England and Wales but rare in Scotland and Ireland. Some indication of a significant decline in southwest and southeast England. Recorded from most of the Channel Islands but apparently declining here. **Host(s)** A social parasite of carder bumblebees, primarily *B. pascuorum*. It is said to attack other carders but does not seem to turn up with any frequency at the strongholds of those other species, e.g. *B. humilis* and *B. muscorum* sites in coastal southeast England.

Bombus rupestris (Fabricius, 1793)
Plate 19

Red-tailed Cuckoo Bee
Hill Cuckoo Bee

Description & similar species FW typically 19mm female, 14mm male. Females are very impressive, with the largest average wingspan of any bumblebee. They have a shiny black body with rather sparse body hairs, a bright red tail and dark grey-brown wings (much darker than any other bumblebee). The head is very large and box-shaped, more so than in any other bumblebee. Only queens of *B. lapidarius* and *B. ruderarius* approach it in appearance, but they have a much denser body pile, clearer wings, a smaller head capsule and pollen baskets on the hind tibiae (hind tibiae simple and densely hairy in *rupestris*). Males are very variable but are the only cuckoo bumblebees with an extensively red-haired tail. The black-haired head and rather greyish bands render them most similar to males of *B. ruderarius*. Indeed it can be quite challenging to separate the two in the field, though *B. rupestris* males have larger box-shaped heads with smaller, more widely separated eyes and slimmer hind basitarsi. Under magnification, the female sternite 6 and the male genitalia are both very distinctive. **Variation** Males are extremely variable, and this variation pervades most populations. The palest individuals have a greyish collar and scutellum and two greyish bands on the abdomen before the red tail. Other individuals are entirely black-haired except for the red tail and some individuals with the red tail starting on tergite 2 are occasionally misidentified as *B. monticola* (but more closely resemble males of the extinct *B. pomorum*). Fully melanic males have also been recorded, and these can be reliably separated from melanics of other cuckoo bumblebees only by checking the genitalia. Females are usually very constant in appearance, though they occasionally have a dull yellow collar, and fully melanic ones have been reported. Dwarf females

female

male

male, very pale

with a wing length as short as 13mm have also been encountered. **Flight season** Females usually appear in May or June, somewhat later than other cuckoo bumblebees. Males and new queens appear in July and both can persist into September. Males will form lekking swarms on grassy hillsides, possibly the basis for its older name of Hill Cuckoo Bee. **Habitat** Found in a wide variety of habitats including wooded and open locations, rural and urban ones. Males have even been recorded visiting cultivated flowerbeds close to Birmingham city centre. **Flowers visited** Spring females like dandelions, comfreys, Oil-seed Rape, Oxeye Daisy and Kidney Vetch. Males and new queens visit thistles, Teasel, ragworts, brambles, Devil's-bit Scabious and a variety of garden plants (especially Lavender, Iceplant and exotic composites). **Status & distribution** Formerly considered a scarce, mostly southern species, but with old records extending north to Northumberland. In the late twentieth century it started a massive increase, to the extent that males are now often the most numerous cuckoo bees at sites from the Midlands southwards, though it remains scarce in southwest England, East Anglia, Wales and northern England. It is unrecorded in Scotland. It is rare in Ireland but has been found on most of the larger Channel Islands. **Host(s)** The special social parasite of *Bombus lapidarius*, but only present in the southern part of the host's range (which extends to north Scotland).

Bombus sylvestris (Lepeletier, 1832)

Forest Cuckoo Bee
Four-coloured Cuckoo Bee

Plate 20

Description & similar species FW typically 15mm female, 13mm male. Females are relatively small, fluffy cuckoo bumblebees with a strongly downcurved abdomen. The midriff band is weak and usually confined to tergite 1. Under magnification, the very small ridges on sternite 6 and triangular projection towards the tip of tergite 6 allow easy separation from all other species. Males are highly variable, though the normal pale form tends to have the unique feature of a white tail, followed by black hairs from tergite 5 then orange hairs from tergites 6 and 7. The male genitalia allow easy confirmation. Lekking males produce quite a strong and unique scent that can be detected with experience (usually in woodland situations).

Variation In females, a little variation can occur in the width of the collar and brightness of the midriff band, which can be absent. Males are considerably more variable: the tail can be white- or yellow-haired and very rarely with a yellow ring before the white hairs (giving a resemblance to *B. bohemicus*). Tergites 6 and 7 can be orange- or black-haired, and semi-melanic or fully melanic males are fairly frequent. **Flight season** In the south, females usually appear from late March and males are often evident by April. It seems to attempt two generations per year in southern areas (related to the bivoltine strategy of the main host) and new females can be seen throughout the summer until September. In the north, it may not appear until May and is probably univoltine. **Habitat** More strongly attached to wooded habitats than other cuckoo

female

bumblebees, but found in a variety of other habitats too. **Flowers visited** Spring females visit various spring-flowering shrubs and flowers such as dandelions, dead-nettles and Bilberry. Males and summer females like thistles, brambles and Devil's-bit Scabious. **Status & distribution** A widespread and common species over much of Britain, but scarcer in Ireland, and on the Channel Islands recorded only from Sark and Jersey. **Host(s)** A social parasite of *Bombus pratorum* and possibly *B. jonellus* and *B. monticola*.

male

male, yellow-tailed

413

Bombus vestalis (Geoffroy, 1785)

Plate 20

Vestal Cuckoo Bee
Southern Cuckoo Bee

Description & similar species FW typically 18mm female, 14mm male. Females closely resemble *B. bohemicus* but average slightly larger, and when fresh have a ginger rather than yellow collar and the yellow side patches at the base of the white tail bright sulphur-yellow. There is never any hint of a midriff band. Under magnification, the rather dull and densely punctate tergite 6 will easily identify *B. vestalis* (shiny and scarcely punctate centrally in *B. bohemicus*). Males have the shortest, neatest body pile of any cuckoo bumblebee, and in fresh individuals the sulphur-yellow band at the base of the white tail is diagnostic (the band is never this bright in *B. bohemicus*). A weak midriff band can be present but is mostly on tergite 1 rather than the scutellum. The best structural feature for separating males of *B. vestalis* from *B. bohemicus* is the proportion of the antennal segments – *B. vestalis* has antennal segment 3 shorter than 5, whilst in *B. bohemicus* the segments are about the same length. The genitalia of *B. bohemicus* and *B. vestalis* are very similar but distinct from other species.

Variation In males, the midriff band varies in intensity. Females are prone to darkening – they sometimes lack a collar and occasionally lose most of the tail too. Old sun-bleached individuals

female

of both sexes can resemble *B. bohemicus* in the field and require checking under a microscope. **Flight season** Females can appear from late March, males from late May. Males and females usually persist until September. **Habitat** Found in the full range of habitats used by *B. terrestris*, so frequent in both wooded and open habitats, rural and urban ones. In the south it is usually the commonest cuckoo bumblebee of gardens and urban greenspace. **Flowers visited** Newly emerged females visit spring-blossoming shrubs such as sallows, Blackthorn and Cherry alongside the queens of social bumblebees. They are also keen on dandelions, Ground-ivy and dead-nettles. Workers and new summer queens like thistles, burdocks, Teasel, brambles and a wide variety of garden plants (especially Lavender, Iceplant and exotic composites). **Status & distribution** The commonest cuckoo bee in most parts of England, but scarcer in Wales. Known from a few sites in southern Scotland, having been discovered there in 2009. Rediscovered in Ireland in 2014 after a gap of 88 years. Recorded from most of the larger Channel Islands. **Host(s)** The social parasite of *Bombus terrestris* and possibly the most successful of the cuckoo bumblebees in the south of England in terms of host–parasite abundance ratios and the number of host populations exploited.

male

APIS – HONEY BEES

worker (♀)

Apis mellifera

A small genus of seven species centred on south and southeast Asia. All species show highly developed eusocial behaviour with workers well differentiated from queens both morphologically and behaviourally. Two species have been domesticated, the Eastern Honey Bee *A. cerana* from Asia and our Western Honey Bee *A. mellifera*, which appears to have an African origin. These are kept in artificial hives to facilitate harvesting of their large honey stores and wax combs, both of which have commercial value. The use of hives also allows bee colonies to be transported to areas requiring bee pollination, especially orchards and other flowering crops.

Pollen is collected in pollen baskets (corbiculae) on the worker's hind tibiae, which resemble those seen in bumblebees, but are very different from the furry pollen brushes of most other pollen-gathering bee genera. Nectar is collected in the crop. The nest consists of wax combs comprising hexagonal cells which are used both for the development of brood and the storage of honey. Queens and males (drones) develop in larger cells. A colony is controlled by a single queen largely through the use of pheromones. Her fertilised eggs produce both workers and new queens, the latter when a developing grub has been fed exclusively on royal jelly. Drones develop from unfertilised eggs that can be laid either by the queen or by workers. Workers perform various roles, including foraging, comb construction, nest maintenance and ventilation, honey production, care of the grubs, care of the queen and defence of the nest. As well as using pheromones, they can exhibit simple non-chemical communication, including the 'waggle dance' used to indicate the direction and distance of foraging areas.

Honey Bees can be very aggressive in defence of their nests and are amongst the few bees that could be considered dangerous (mass stinging could result in serious illness, but is very rare). Workers of *Apis* species have barbed stings and sting sacs that are adapted to become detached following stinging, especially where mammalian flesh is involved. This allows more venom to be pumped into an enemy but results in the death of the worker that has stung. Alarm pheromones alert and attract other workers to a source of danger to facilitate multiple stinging. In 'Africanised' bees (also known as 'killer bees') it is the hypersensitivity of the bees to their own alarm pheromone that results in a much higher frequency of mass stinging events – but fortunately these aggressive strains are not used in Britain or Ireland.

Apis mellifera Linnaeus, 1758   Western Honey Bee

Plate 20

Description & similar species FW 10–11mm queen, 9–10mm worker, 12–13.5mm male. Workers are medium-sized bees with inconspicuously haired abdomens that can be entirely blackish, almost entirely orange, or variably black- and orange-banded. Hair bands are present around the bases of tergites 3–5. They can resemble some *Andrena* species or *Colletes hederae* in the field, but the abdomen is more cylindrical and the hind legs have well-formed corbiculae on the hind tibiae (like bumblebees). This pair of legs tends to dangle down during foraging, unlike mining bees. Queens resemble workers but are larger and more robust in all respects and develop much longer abdomens due to large ovaries, though the abdomen will shrink prior to a queen initiating a swarm. They do not have fully developed corbiculae or the long mouthparts of workers, and the head in front view is rounder. Males are much more broadly built than queens or workers, with proportionately longer wings, a shorter and broader abdomen and large eyes that meet on the top. They lack corbiculae, and the mouthparts are much reduced. Males have 12 antennal segments, unlike other male bees.

Variation Mainly the colour of the abdomen, as noted above. Size is surprisingly constant within the castes. **Flight season** Adults are present throughout the year. Foraging is most active between March and October, starting with spring-blossoming shrubs and tailing off after the flowering of Ivy. Workers will often make short flights on mild winter days. Swarming can occur any time between spring and autumn. Drones do not overwinter. **Habitat** Honey bees can be found in most habitats but generally avoid the interiors of dense woodland and become much scarcer in montane and other very exposed environments. Habitat exploitation is largely dictated by the positioning of hives. **Flowers visited** A very wide variety of flowering trees, herbs, shrubs and herbaceous species are visited by workers as a source of either pollen or nectar. This generally starts with spring-blossoming shrubs such as willows and *Prunus* species. Honey Bees are economically important for the pollination of various crops, including orchard trees, Oil-seed Rape, beans, Raspberry and assorted leguminous fodder crops. Queens and drones do not visit flowers. **Nesting habits** Nesting of British and Irish Honey Bees is mostly within artificial hives under the care of beekeepers. However, feral colonies are not rare and are usually located in hollow trees (especially rot holes and old woodpecker nests) and occasionally in roof spaces. These can sometimes persist for several years. Nests are composed of several sheets of wax comb consisting of hexagonal cells. Cells in the middle are used for developing brood, whilst peripheral ones are used for storing honey and pollen. Swarming occurs when a colony gets too large and the original queen leaves with several thousand workers to establish a new nest. The original nest then comes under the control of a new queen, usually the first queen to emerge from one of the large queen cells. She attempts to kill off all the other newly emerged or developing queens. Once this is achieved, she mates and starts to produce new workers. **Status & distribution** Generally considered an ancient introduction from the continent, but now common in most parts of Britain and Ireland with a limited ability to establish itself in a feral state. Some black varieties are termed 'native', and they often have distinct genetics and are better adapted to cooler northern latitudes. They have been the subject of some conservation concern, and are now protected on two Hebridean Islands (Colonsay and Oronsay) by banning the importation of any other Honey Bee strains to the islands. There have been some recent declines in the national Honey Bee stock through colony collapse disorder. This appears to result from multiple factors including disease, parasites, weather and the use of certain pesticides. **Parasites & associates** Mites associated with the Honey Bee include *Varroa destructor*, an ectoparasite that can transmit serious viruses, and *Acarapis woodi*, which lives in the respiratory tubes. The single-celled microsporidian *Nosema apis* lives in the gut and can produce bee dysentery. Inquilines in the hives include the Lesser Wax Moth *Achroia grisella*, the Greater Wax Moth or Honeycomb Moth *Galleria mellonella* and sometimes the Bee Moth *Aphomia sociella*. The Hornet *Vespa crabro* and bee-wolf wasp *Philanthus triangulum* will often prey upon Honey Bees in preference to other prey species, and there is great concern over the progressive spread of the Asian Hornet *Vespa velutina* across Europe following a recent accidental introduction from China, as it can result in significant losses of workers.

worker, dark form

worker, paler form

CHECKLIST OF THE BEES ─
OF BRITAIN AND IRELAND

This is arranged taxonomically with the genera sequence following Michener (2007) and using the same scientific names as BWARS; species are arranged alphabetically within genera. Alternative English names are shown in parentheses.

KEY

A   Considered non-resident (either an importation or vagrant)
CI   Channel Islands only
Ext   Presumed extinct in Britain, Ireland and the Channel Islands
*****   Doubtfully British

COLLETIDAE
Colletes Latreille, 1802

cunicularius (Linnaeus, 1761)	Early Colletes ☐
daviesanus Smith,1846	Davies' Colletes ☐
floralis Eversmann, 1852	Northern Colletes ☐
fodiens (Geoffroy, 1785)	Hairy-saddled Colletes ☐
halophilus Verhoeff, 1944	Sea Aster Bee ☐
hederae Schmidt & Westrich, 1993	Ivy Bee ☐
marginatus Smith, 1846	Margined Colletes ☐
similis Schenck, 1853	Bare-saddled Colletes ☐
succinctus (Linnaeus, 1758)	Heather Colletes (Girdled Colletes) ☐

Hylaeus Fabricius, 1793

annularis (Kirby, 1802)	Shingle Yellow-face Bee ☐
(= *spilotus* Förster, 1871 of recent literature)	
brevicornis Nylander, 1852	Short-horned Yellow-face Bee ☐
communis Nylander, 1852	Common Yellow-face Bee ☐
confusus Nylander, 1852	White-jawed Yellow-face Bee ☐
cornutus Curtis, 1831	Spined Hylaeus ☐
dilatatus (Kirby, 1802)	Chalk Yellow-face Bee ☐
(= *annularis* Kirby, 1802 of recent literature)	
hyalinatus Smith, 1842	Hairy Yellow-face Bee ☐
incongruus Förster, 1871	White-lipped Yellow-face Bee ☐
(= *gibbus* Saunders, 1850 of recent literature)	
pectoralis Förster, 1871	Reed Yellow-face Bee ☐
pictipes Nylander, 1852	Little Yellow-face Bee ☐
Ext *punctulatissimus* Smith, 1842	Onion Yellow-face Bee ☐
signatus (Panzer, 1798)	Large Yellow-face Bee ☐

ANDRENIDAE
Andrena Fabricius, 1775

CI *agilissima* (Scopoli, 1770)	Violet-winged Mining Bee ☐
alfkenella Perkins, 1914	Alfken's Mini-miner ☐
angustior (Kirby, 1802)	Groove-faced Mining Bee ☐
apicata Smith, 1847	Large Sallow Mining Bee ☐
argentata Smith, 1844	Small Sandpit Mining Bee ☐
barbilabris (Kirby, 1802)	Sandpit Mining Bee ☐
bicolor Fabricius, 1775	Gwynne's Mining Bee ☐
bimaculata (Kirby, 1802)	Large Gorse Mining Bee ☐
bucephala Stephens, 1846	Big-headed Mining Bee ☐

chrysosceles (Kirby, 1802) — Hawthorn Mining Bee ☐
cineraria (Linnaeus, 1758) — Ashy Mining Bee ☐
clarkella (Kirby, 1802) — Clarke's Mining Bee ☐
coitana (Kirby, 1802) — Small Flecked Mining Bee ☐
congruens Schmiedeknecht, 1883 — Long-fringed Mining Bee ☐
denticulata (Kirby, 1802) — Grey-banded Mining Bee ☐
dorsata (Kirby, 1802) — Short-fringed Mining Bee ☐
falsifica Perkins, 1915 — Thick-margined Mini-miner ☐
ferox Smith, 1847 — Oak Mining Bee ☐
flavipes Panzer, 1799 — Yellow-legged Mining Bee ☐
florea Fabricius, 1793 — Bryony Mining Bee ☐
Ext *floricola* Eversmann, 1852 — Chilterns Mini-miner ☐
fucata Smith, 1847 — Painted Mining Bee ☐
fulva (Müller, 1766) — Tawny Mining Bee ☐
fulvago (Christ, 1791) — Hawk's-beard Mining Bee ☐
fuscipes (Kirby, 1802) — Heather Mining Bee ☐
gravida Imhoff, 1832 — White-bellied Mining Bee ☐
haemorrhoa (Fabricius, 1781) — Orange-tailed Mining Bee (Early Mining Bee) ☐
hattorfiana (Fabricius, 1775) — Large Scabious Mining Bee ☐
helvola (Linnaeus, 1758) — Coppice Mining Bee ☐
humilis Imhoff, 1832 — Buff-tailed Mining Bee ☐
labialis (Kirby, 1802) — Large Meadow Mining Bee ☐
labiata Fabricius, 1781 — Red-girdled Mining Bee ☐
lapponica Zetterstedt, 1838 — Bilberry Mining Bee ☐
Ext *lathyri* Alfken, 1899 — Burbage Mining Bee ☐
Ext *lepida* Schenck, 1861 — Aldworth Mining Bee ☐
marginata Fabricius, 1776 — Small Scabious Mining Bee ☐
minutula (Kirby, 1802) — Common Mini-miner ☐
minutuloides Perkins, 1914 — Plain Mini-miner ☐
Ext *nana* (Kirby, 1802) — Barham Mini-miner ☐
***Ext** *nanula* Nylander, 1848 — Red-horned Mini-miner ☐
nigriceps (Kirby, 1802) — Black-headed Mining Bee ☐
nigroaenea (Kirby, 1802) — Buffish Mining Bee ☐
nigrospina Thomson, 1872 — Scarce Black Mining Bee ☐
nitida (Müller, 1776) — Grey-patched Mining Bee ☐
    (= *pubescens* Olivier, 1789 of recent literature)
nitidiuscula Schenck, 1853 — Carrot Mining Bee ☐
niveata Friese, 1887 — Long-fringed Mini-miner ☐
ovatula (Kirby, 1802) — Small Gorse Mining Bee ☐
pilipes Fabricius, 1781 — Black Mining Bee ☐
Ext *polita* Smith, 1847 — Maidstone Mining Bee ☐
praecox (Scopoli, 1763) — Small Sallow Mining Bee ☐
proxima (Kirby, 1802) — Broad-faced Mining Bee ☐
rosae Panzer, 1801 — Perkins' Mining Bee ☐
    (= *stragulata* Illiger, 1806 of recent literature)
ruficrus Nylander, 1848 — Northern Mining Bee ☐
scotica Perkins, 1916 — Chocolate Mining Bee ☐
    (= *carantonica* Pérez, 1902 of recent literature)
semilaevis Pérez, 1903 — Shiny-margined Mini-miner ☐
similis Smith, 1849 — Red-backed Mining Bee ☐
simillima Smith, 1851 — Buff-banded Mining Bee ☐
subopaca Nylander, 1848 — Impunctate Mini-miner ☐
synadelpha Perkins, 1914 — Broad-margined Mining Bee ☐

tarsata Nylander, 1848	Tormentil Mining Bee ☐
thoracica (Fabricius, 1775)	Cliff Mining Bee ☐
tibialis (Kirby, 1802)	Grey-gastered Mining Bee ☐
Ext *tridentata* (Kirby, 1802)	Pale-tailed Mining Bee ☐
trimmerana (Kirby, 1802)	Trimmer's Mining Bee ☐
vaga Panzer, 1799	Grey-backed Mining Bee ☐
varians (Kirby, 1802)	Blackthorn Mining Bee ☐
wilkella (Kirby, 1802)	Wilke's Mining Bee ☐
Panurgus Panzer, 1806	
banksianus (Kirby, 1802)	Large Shaggy Bee ☐
calcaratus (Scopoli, 1763)	Small Shaggy Bee ☐

HALICTIDAE

Halictus Latreille, 1804	
confusus Smith, 1853	Southern Bronze Furrow Bee ☐
eurygnathus Blüthgen, 1931	Downland Furrow Bee ☐
Ext *maculatus* Smith, 1848	Box-headed Furrow Bee ☐
CI *quadricinctus* (Fabricius, 1776)	Giant Furrow Bee ☐
rubicundus (Christ, 1791)	Orange-legged Furrow Bee ☐
CI *scabiosae* (Rossi, 1790)	Great Banded Furrow Bee ☐
Ext *subauratus* (Rossi, 1792)	Golden Furrow Bee ☐
tumulorum (Linnaeus, 1758)	Bronze Furrow Bee ☐
Lasioglossum Curtis, 1833	
albipes (Fabricius, 1781)	Bloomed Furrow Bee ☐
angusticeps (Perkins, 1895)	Cliff Furrow Bee ☐
brevicorne (Schenck, 1870)	Short-horned Furrow Bee ☐
calceatum (Scopoli, 1763)	Common Furrow Bee ☐
cupromicans (Pérez, 1903)	Turquoise Furrow Bee ☐
fratellum (Pérez, 1903)	Smooth-faced Furrow Bee ☐
fulvicorne (Kirby, 1802)	Chalk Furrow Bee ☐
Ext *laeve* (Kirby, 1802)	Shiny-gastered Furrow Bee ☐
laevigatum (Kirby, 1802)	Red-backed Furrow Bee ☐
laticeps (Schenck, 1870)	Broad-faced Furrow Bee ☐
lativentre (Schenck, 1853)	Furry-claspered Furrow Bee ☐
leucopus (Kirby, 1802)	White-footed Furrow Bee ☐
leucozonium (Schrank, 1781)	White-zoned Furrow Bee ☐
CI *limbellum* (Morawitz, 1876)	Ridge-gastered Furrow Bee ☐
malachurum (Kirby, 1802)	Sharp-collared Furrow Bee ☐
CI *mediterraneum* (Blüthgen, 1926)	Mediterranean Furrow Bee ☐
minutissimum (Kirby, 1802)	Least Furrow Bee ☐
morio (Fabricius, 1793)	Green Furrow Bee ☐
nitidiusculum (Kirby, 1802)	Tufted Furrow Bee ☐
parvulum (Schenck, 1853)	Smooth-gastered Furrow Bee ☐
pauperatum (Brullé, 1832)	Squat Furrow Bee ☐
pauxillum (Schenck, 1853)	Lobe-spurred Furrow Bee ☐
prasinum (Smith, 1848)	Grey-tailed Furrow Bee ☐
punctatissimum (Schenck, 1853)	Long-faced Furrow Bee ☐
puncticolle (Morawitz, 1872)	Ridge-cheeked Furrow Bee ☐
quadrinotatum (Kirby, 1802)	Four-spotted Furrow Bee ☐
rufitarse (Zetterstedt, 1838)	Rufous-footed Furrow Bee ☐
semilucens (Alfken, 1914)	Small Shiny Furrow Bee ☐

sexnotatum (Kirby, 1802)	Ashy Furrow Bee ☐
sexstrigatum (Schenck, 1870)	Fringed Furrow Bee ☐
smeathmanellum (Kirby, 1802)	Smeathman's Furrow Bee ☐
villosulum (Kirby, 1802)	Shaggy Furrow Bee ☐
xanthopus (Kirby, 1802)	Orange-footed Furrow Bee ☐
zonulum (Smith, 1848)	Bull-headed Furrow Bee ☐

Sphecodes Latreille, 1804

crassus Thomson, 1870	Swollen-thighed Blood Bee ☐
ephippius (Linnaeus, 1767)	Bare-saddled Blood Bee ☐
ferruginatus Hagens, 1882	Dull-headed Blood Bee ☐
geoffrellus (Kirby, 1802)	Geoffroy's Blood Bee ☐
gibbus (Linnaeus, 1758)	Dark-winged Blood Bee ☐
hyalinatus Hagens, 1882	Furry-bellied Blood Bee ☐
longulus Hagens, 1882	Little Sickle-jawed Blood Bee ☐
Cl *marginatus* Hagens, 1882	Margined Blood Bee ☐
miniatus Hagens, 1882	False Margined Blood Bee ☐
monilicornis (Kirby, 1802)	Box-headed Blood Bee ☐
niger Hagens, 1874	Dark Blood Bee ☐
pellucidus Smith, 1845	Sandpit Blood Bee ☐
puncticeps Thomson, 1870	Sickle-jawed Blood Bee ☐
reticulatus Thomson, 1870	Reticulate Blood Bee ☐
rubicundus von Hagens, 1875	Red-tailed Blood Bee ☐
scabricollis Wesmael, 1835	Rough-backed Blood Bee ☐
spinulosus Hagens, 1875	Spined Blood Bee ☐

Rophites Spinola, 1808

Ext *quinquespinosus* Spinola, 1808	Five-spined Rophites ☐

Dufourea Lepeletier, 1841

Ext *halictula* (Nylander, 1852)	Sheep's-bit Dufourea ☐
Ext *minuta* Lepeletier, 1841	Shiny Dufourea ☐

MELITTIDAE
Melitta Kirby, 1802

dimidiata Morawitz, 1876	Sainfoin Bee ☐
haemorrhoidalis (Fabricius, 1775)	Gold-tailed Melitta ☐
leporina (Panzer, 1799)	Clover Melitta ☐
tricincta Kirby, 1802	Red Bartsia Bee ☐

Macropis Panzer, 1809

europaea Warncke, 1973	Yellow Loosestrife Bee ☐

Dasypoda Latreille, 1802

hirtipes (Fabricius, 1793)	Pantaloon Bee ☐

MEGACHILIDAE
Anthidium Fabricius, 1804

manicatum (Linnaeus, 1758)	Wool Carder Bee ☐

Stelis Panzer, 1806

breviuscula (Nylander, 1848)	Little Dark Bee ☐
ornatula (Klug, 1807)	Spotted Dark Bee ☐

phaeoptera (Kirby, 1802)	Plain Dark Bee ☐
punctulatissima (Kirby, 1802)	Banded Dark Bee ☐

Heriades Spinola, 1808
A *rubicola* Pérez, 1890	Small-headed Resin Bee ☐
truncorum (Linnaeus, 1758)	Large-headed Resin Bee ☐

Chelostoma Latreille, 1809
campanularum (Kirby, 1802)	Small Scissor Bee ☐
florisomne (Linnaeus, 1758)	Large Scissor Bee (Sleepy Carpenter Bee) ☐

Osmia Panzer, 1806
aurulenta (Panzer, 1799)	Gold-fringed Mason Bee ☐
bicolor (Schrank, 1781)	Red-tailed Mason Bee ☐
bicornis (Linnaeus, 1758)	Red Mason Bee ☐
(= *rufa* Panzer, 1806)	
caerulescens (Linnaeus, 1758)	Blue Mason Bee ☐
inermis (Zetterstedt, 1838)	Mountain Mason Bee ☐
leaiana (Kirby, 1802)	Orange-vented Mason Bee ☐
niveata (Fabricius, 1804)	Jersey Mason Bee ☐
parietina Curtis, 1828	Wall Mason Bee ☐
pilicornis Smith, 1846	Fringe-horned Mason Bee ☐
spinulosa (Kirby, 1802)	Spined Mason Bee ☐
uncinata Gerstäcker, 1869	Pinewood Mason Bee ☐
xanthomelana (Kirby, 1802)	Cliff Mason Bee (Large Mason Bee) ☐

Hoplitis Klug, 1807
claviventris (Thomson, 1872)	Welted Mason Bee ☐
Ext *leucomelana* (Kirby, 1802)	Kirby's Mason Bee ☐

Megachile Latreille, 1802
centuncularis (Linnaeus, 1758)	Patchwork Leafcutter Bee ☐
circumcincta (Kirby, 1802)	Black-headed Leafcutter Bee ☐
Ext, * *ericetorum* (Lepeletier, 1841)	Banded Mud Bee ☐
Ext * *lapponica* Thomson, 1872	Willowherb Leafcutter Bee ☐
leachella Curtis, 1828	Silvery Leafcutter Bee ☐
(= *dorsalis* Pérez, 1879)	
ligniseca (Kirby, 1802)	Wood-carving Leafcutter Bee ☐
maritima (Kirby, 1802)	Coast Leafcutter Bee ☐
CI, Ext, * *parietina* (Geoffroy, 1875)	Black Mud Bee ☐
versicolor Smith, 1844	Brown-footed Leafcutter Bee ☐
willughbiella (Kirby, 1802)	Willughby's Leafcutter Bee ☐

Coelioxys Latreille, 1809
Ext *afra* Lepeletier, 1841	Short Sharp-tail Bee ☐
CI *brevis* Eversmann, 1852	Red-legged Sharp-tail Bee ☐
conoidea (Illiger, 1806)	Large Sharp-tail Bee ☐
elongata Lepeletier, 1841	Dull-vented Sharp-tail Bee ☐
inermis (Kirby, 1802)	Shiny-vented Sharp-tail Bee ☐
mandibularis Nylander, 1848	Square-jawed Sharp-tail Bee ☐
quadridentata (Linnaeus, 1758)	Grooved Sharp-tail Bee ☐
rufescens Lepeletier & Serville, 1825	Rufescent Sharp-tail Bee ☐

APIDAE
Nomada Scopoli, 1763
argentata Herrich-Schäffer, 1839 — Silver-sided Nomad Bee ☐
armata Herrich-Schäffer, 1839 — Armed Nomad Bee ☐
baccata Smith, 1844 — Bear-clawed Nomad Bee ☐
CI *castellana* Dusmet, 1913 — Castell's Nomad Bee ☐
conjungens Herrich-Schäffer, 1839 — Fringeless Nomad Bee ☐
Ext *errans* Lepeletier, 1841 — Purbeck Nomad Bee ☐
fabriciana (Linnaeus, 1767) — Fabricius' Nomad Bee ☐
ferruginata (Linnaeus, 1767) — Yellow-shouldered Nomad Bee ☐
flava Panzer, 1798 — Flavous Nomad Bee ☐
flavoguttata (Kirby, 1802) — Little Nomad Bee ☐
flavopicta (Kirby, 1802) — Blunthorn Nomad Bee ☐
fucata Panzer, 1798 — Painted Nomad Bee ☐
fulvicornis Fabricius, 1793 — Orange-horned Nomad Bee ☐
CI *fuscicornis* Nylander, 1848 — Small Guernsey Nomad Bee ☐
goodeniana (Kirby, 1802) — Gooden's Nomad Bee ☐
guttulata Schenck, 1861 — Short-spined Nomad Bee ☐
hirtipes Pérez, 1884 — Long-horned Nomad Bee ☐
integra Brullé, 1832 — Cat's-ear Nomad Bee ☐
lathburiana (Kirby, 1802) — Lathbury's Nomad Bee ☐
leucophthalma (Kirby, 1802) — Early Nomad Bee ☐
marshamella (Kirby, 1802) — Marsham's Nomad Bee ☐
obtusifrons Nylander, 1848 — Flat-ridged Nomad Bee ☐
panzeri Lepeletier, 1841 — Panzer's Nomad Bee ☐
roberjeotiana Panzer, 1799 — Tormentil Nomad Bee ☐
ruficornis (Linnaeus, 1758) — Fork-jawed Nomad Bee ☐
rufipes Fabricius, 1793 — Black-horned Nomad Bee ☐
sexfasciata Panzer, 1799 — Six-banded Nomad Bee ☐
sheppardana (Kirby, 1802) — Sheppard's Nomad Bee ☐
signata Jurine, 1807 — Broad-banded Nomad Bee ☐
CI *similis* Morawitz, 1872 — Guernsey Nomad Bee ☐
striata Fabricius, 1793 — Blunt-jawed Nomad Bee ☐
subcornuta (Kirby, 1802) — Kirby's Nomad Bee ☐
CI *succincta* Panzer, 1798 — Yellow-legged Nomad Bee ☐
CI *zonata* Panzer, 1798 — Variable Nomad Bee ☐

Epeolus Latreille, 1802
cruciger (Panzer, 1799) — Red-thighed Epeolus ☐
variegatus (Linnaeus, 1758) — Black-thighed Epeolus ☐

Eucera Scopoli, 1770
longicornis (Linnaeus, 1758) — Long-horned Bee ☐
Ext *nigrescens* Pérez, 1879 — Scarce Long-horned Bee ☐

Anthophora Latreille, 1803
bimaculata (Panzer, 1798) — Green-eyed Flower Bee ☐
furcata (Panzer, 1798) — Fork-tailed Flower Bee ☐
plumipes (Pallas, 1772) — Hairy-footed Flower Bee ☐
quadrimaculata (Panzer, 1798) — Four-banded Flower Bee ☐
retusa (Linnaeus, 1758) — Potter Flower Bee ☐

Melecta Latreille, 1802
albifrons (Forster, 1771) — Common Mourning Bee ☐
Ext *luctuosa* (Scopoli, 1770) — Square-spotted Mourning Bee ☐

Ceratina Latreille, 1802
cyanea (Kirby, 1802) — Little Blue Carpenter Bee ☐

Xylocopa Latreille, 1809
A *violacea* (Linnaeus, 1758) — Violet Carpenter Bee ☐
A *virginica* (Linnaeus, 1771) — Eastern Carpenter Bee ☐

Bombus Latreille, 1802
barbutellus (Kirby, 1802) — Barbut's Cuckoo Bee ☐
bohemicus (Seidl, 1837) — Gypsy Cuckoo Bee (Bohemian Cuckoo Bee) ☐
campestris (Panzer, 1801) — Field Cuckoo Bee ☐
cryptarum (Fabricius, 1775) — Cryptic Bumblebee ☐
Ext *cullumanus* (Kirby, 1802) — Cullum's Bumblebee ☐
distinguendus Morawitz, 1869 — Great Yellow Bumblebee ☐
hortorum (Linnaeus, 1761) — Garden Bumblebee ☐
humilis Illiger, 1806 — Brown-banded Carder Bee ☐
hypnorum (Linnaeus, 1758) — Tree Bumblebee ☐
jonellus (Kirby, 1802) — Heath Bumblebee ☐
lapidarius (Linnaeus, 1758) — Red-tailed Bumblebee ☐
lucorum (Linnaeus, 1761) — White-tailed Bumblebee ☐
magnus Vogt, 1911 — Northern White-tailed Bumblebee ☐
monticola Smith, 1849 — Bilberry Bumblebee (Blaeberry Bumblebee) ☐
muscorum (Linnaeus, 1758) — Moss Carder Bee ☐
pascuorum (Scopoli, 1763) — Common Carder Bee ☐
Ext *pomorum* (Panzer, 1805) — Apple Bumblebee ☐
pratorum (Linnaeus, 1761) — Early Bumblebee ☐
ruderarius (Müller, 1776) — Red-shanked Carder Bee ☐
ruderatus (Fabricius, 1775) — Large Garden Bumblebee (Ruderal Bumblebee) ☐
rupestris (Fabricius, 1793) — Red-tailed Cuckoo Bee (Hill Cuckoo Bee) ☐
soroeensis (Fabricius, 1777) — Broken-belted Bumblebee ☐
(Ext) *subterraneus* (Linnaeus, 1758) — Short-haired Bumblebee ☐
sylvarum (Linnaeus, 1761) — Shrill Carder Bee ☐
sylvestris (Lepeletier, 1832) — Forest Cuckoo Bee (Four-coloured Cuckoo Bee) ☐
terrestris (Linnaeus, 1758) — Buff-tailed Bumblebee ☐
vestalis (Geoffroy, 1785) — Vestal Cuckoo Bee (Southern Cuckoo Bee) ☐

Apis Linnaeus, 1758
mellifera Linnaeus, 1758 — Western Honey Bee ☐

INDEX

Textual references to species are shown in normal type; **bold** type indicates a species' main text entry, which usually includes photographs. Photographs in the introduction are shown by *italic* page numbers and illustrations in the plate section are referenced by plate number.

SCIENTIFIC NAMES

PHOTOGRAPHIC CREDITS

All photographs by the author with the exception of:

Tristan Bantock
Hylaeus hyalinatus male

Ian Beavis
Andrena gravida female

Chris Bentley
Bombus muscorum queen

Paul Brock
Andrena nigriceps female
Andrena simillima female
Anthophora quadrimaculata female
Colletes hederae mating ball
Colletes marginatus female
Hylaeus confusus female
Megachile leachella female
Nomada baccata female
Osmia pilicornis female
Philanthus triangulum with Honey Bee prey
Xylocopa violacea female and male

Claire Carvell/CEH
Pan traps

Phill Clayton
Osmia bicolor female on snail

Carl Clee
Osmia xanthomelana female and male

Jeremy Early
Andrena argentata female
Andrena fulvago female
Andrena labialis female
Andrena labiata female
Cacoxenus indigator fly
Ceratina cyanea male
Chrysura radians wasp
Colletes fodiens female
Heriades truncorum female
Hylaeus brevicornis female
Hylaeus communis female and male
Hylaeus cornutus male
Hylaeus incongruus female and male
Hylaeus pictipes female and male
Lasioglossum fulvicorne male
Lasioglossum prasinum female
Megachile ligniseca nest
Megachile versicolor female carrying a leaf section
Nomada guttulata male
Nomada sheppardana female
Panurgus calcaratus male
Stelis breviuscula female

Louis Falk
Author (dad) looking down a microscope

Nikki Gammans
Bombus subterraneus queens

Henrik Gyurkovics
Coelioxys afra female

Louise Hislop
Andrena tarsata female
Lasioglossum leucopus male
Osmia bicornis with mites

Bernhard Jacobi
Andrena gravida male
Andrena lathyri female and male
Andrena polita female and male
Andrena tibialis female
Andrena vaga female and male
Anthophora quadrimaculata male
Colletes similis female
Halictus maculatus female
Halictus quadricinctus female and male
Halictus subauratus female
Hoplitis leucomelana female
Lasioglossum laevigatum female
Lasioglossum sexnotatum male
Lasioglossum xanthopus female
Megachile ericetorum female
Megachile lapponica female
Megachile parietina female
Nomada leucophthalma female
Panurgus banksianus female

Nigel Jones
Coelioxys inermis

Kevin McGee
Andrena barbilabris female
Andrena bicolor male
Andrena flavipes male
Andrena scotica male
Coelioxys rufescens female
Dasypoda hirtipes male
Epeolus variegatus male
Hylaeus hyalinatus female
Lasioglossum cupromicans male
Lasioglossum lativentre male
Lasioglossum morio male
Lasioglossum punctatissimum male
Megachile leachella male
Physocephala rufipes fly
Sphecodes monilicornis female

Penny Metal
Andrena dorsata male
Anthophora plumipes male (Introduction)

Anthophora plumipes female (species account)

John Oates
Bombus distinguendus male

Nick Owens
Andrena varians female
Bombus distinguendus queen
Bombus jonellus queen (buff-tailed form)
Bombus muscorum agricolae queen
Bombus soroeensis male
Coelioxys mandibularis female

Ash Perkins
Osmia parietina male

Ed Phillips
Gasteruption wasp
Sphecodes niger female and male
Stylopised *Andrena* abdomen

Sandy Rae
Andrena ruficrus female and male
Nomada obtusifrons female
Xylocopa virginica female

Tim Ransom
Andrena agilissima female and male
Andrena proxima female
Andrena synadelpha female (dark form)
Anthidium manicatum male ssp. *manicatum*
Coelioxys brevis female
Halictus confusus female
Halictus scabiosae female
Lasioglossum sexnotatum female
Nomada fabriciana dark female
Osmia bicornis male (Channel Islands form)
Stelis punctulatissima female

Neil A. Robinson
Osmia parietina female

Bo Söderström
Bombus subterraneus workers and males

Ian Tew
Andrena congruens female and male
Lasioglossum rufitarse female

Robin Williams
Andrena coitana female and male